M000290694

Pro Tools® 9

IGNITE!

Andrew Hagerman

COURSE TECHNOLOGY
CENGAGE Learning™

Australia • Brazil • Japan • Korea • Mexico • Singapore • Spain • United Kingdom • United States

COURSE TECHNOLOGY
CENGAGE Learning

Pro Tools® 9 Ignite!
Andrew Hagerman

Publisher and General Manager, Course Technology PTR:
Stacy L. Hiquet

Associate Director of Marketing:
Sarah Panella

Manager of Editorial Services:
Heather Talbot

Marketing Manager: Mark Hughes

Executive Editor: Mark Garvey

Project Editor: Kate Shoup

Technical Reviewer: Brian Smithers

Copy Editor: Kate Shoup

Interior Layout: Jill Flores

Cover Designer: Mike Tanamachi

CD-ROM Producer: Brandon Penticuff

Indexer: Kelly Talbot Editing Services

Proofreader: Kelly Talbot Editing Services

Library of Congress Control Number: 2011923934

ISBN-13: 978-1-4354-5933-5

ISBN-10: 1-4354-5933-4

Course Technology, a part of Cengage Learning
20 Channel Center Street
Boston, MA 02210
USA

Cengage Learning is a leading provider of customized learning solutions with office locations around the globe, including Singapore, the United Kingdom, Australia, Mexico, Brazil, and Japan. Locate your local office at: **international.cengage.com/region.**

Cengage Learning products are represented in Canada by Nelson Education, Ltd. For your lifelong learning solutions, visit **courseptr.com.**

Visit our corporate Web site at **cengage.com.**

Printed in the United States of America
1 2 3 4 5 6 7 13 12 11

On the day this book was completed, a magnitude 8.9 earthquake struck Japan, where I make my home. Certainly, this will be looked back on as one of the worst natural catastrophes in this country's long history. This book is dedicated to the good people of Japan, and especially to Junko and Sachiko Hagerman.

がんばろう、日本。

Acknowledgments

There's an ancient African quote that goes something like, "It takes a village to raise a child." Well, if that's true (and I believe that it is), it must also be said that, "It takes a team to write a book!" Luckily for me, I've had a great one working with me on the title you're holding right now.

First and foremost, my thanks go to the team at Cengage Learning, who have consistently been the strong backbone of any of my writing projects. Special appreciation goes to Mark Garvey (whose job title is executive editor, but seems to do just about *everything*!) and editor Kate Shoup (whose superb editing makes me sound a lot smarter than I am, trust me). Brian Smithers did the tech editing for this book, and not only is he a dear friend, but his sharp mind kept me honest on all the technical bits.

Behind the success of Pro Tools is the dedicated team of professionals at Avid Technology. Their passion for the work they do, and their commitment to the success of their customers, is a constant inspiration. My thanks go to Andy and Claudia Cook, Tim Mynett, and the entire training team at Avid (led by Kathy-Anne McManus and Patty Montesion) for their friendship and excellent work. Special gratitude also goes to John Rechsteiner, Tim Carroll, Tsukasa Tokiwano, and Bobbi Lombardi for their support and mentorship.

Last, but absolutely not least, my thanks and my love go to my family and friends. Their faith in me gave me the confidence to begin writing in the first place, and their support spurs me to continue. My wife Junko and our daughter Sachiko are the best writing partners a guy could ask for, supplying caffeine and humor just when it's needed.

About the Author

Andrew Hagerman has been a professional musician and teacher for the majority of his 40+ years. He began his musical life at the early age of eight as an aspiring tubist, and continued his studies at the prestigious Northwestern University in Chicago. During his time there, MIDI and computer music were in their infancy, and Andy recognized the usefulness of music technology in aiding the creative process. Hagerman had the opportunity to learn these new technological tools of the trade as they were being invented and refined, and his quest for the best in audio and music technology ultimately brought him to use and teach Avid's Pro Tools.

As a performer and arranger, Hagerman has worked with numerous ensembles of all types, including many years of playing at Disneyland, Walt Disney World, and Tokyo Disneyland. As a composer, he's active in the creation of planetarium and science center productions, and his work can be heard worldwide. With a passion for teaching, Hagerman has also worked as the Associate Course Director of Advanced Audio Workstations at Full Sail Real World University in Winter Park, Florida, and has authored seven books on the topics of audio production and Pro Tools. Hagerman currently works with Avid's Asia-Pacific Training Partner Program, working with excellent educational institutions throughout the region to offer the highest level of audio and video training to the next generation of creative professionals.

Contents

Introduction

First of all, congratulations on becoming a Pro Tools user, and welcome (or welcome *back*, if you're an existing Pro Tools user)! When Digidesign says its powerful digital audio workstation (DAW) is the industry standard, you can believe it. Indeed, you'll find Pro Tools, from the modest Mbox all the way up to high-end HD systems, hard at work in every facet of audio and musical production. It's a serious, professional product, and your decision to buy it (and learn it) is a step in the right direction.

The Chinese philosopher Lao-Tsu once said, "A journey of a thousand miles begins with a single step." That's where this book comes in—it's that first step. Gaining a solid fundamental understanding of the basics of Pro Tools will help you ensure that your journey starts off without a hitch and pointed in the right direction. In this book, you'll learn the basic techniques of creating, recording, editing, and mixing digital audio and MIDI (Musical Instrument Digital Interface). You'll learn how to harness the power of Pro Tools' impressive array of features, from software effects, to virtual instruments, to mixes that are automated and edited with some of the best tools in the business.

This is my sixth book about Pro Tools, the first covering version 6 of the software, followed with titles on Pro Tools 7, 7.4, and 8. The book you're holding stands on the shoulders of those previous books and includes some of the same material as those earlier titles. It also covers the exciting *new* features of Pro Tools 9. Even though Pro Tools has been a world leader for many years, I think you'll find that the radical improvements in Pro Tools 9 are especially exciting and represent a new level of flexibility and power. These new features, combined with the solid design of Pro Tools in general, open the door to inspiring possibilities indeed.

If your aim is to create and produce audio, Pro Tools is an excellent choice. *Pro Tools 9 Ignite!* will be your companion during those critical first steps on the road of discovery!

Who Should Read This Book?

Essentially, this book is geared toward beginners with little or no experience working with a DAW. You'll find that this book's highly visual and plainly worded style makes it easy to follow. Nearly every step in the processes discussed is accompanied by clear illustrations, so you won't have to spend your time hunting around the screen for tools and menus. (What fun is *that*?) Once you're finished with the chapters and exercises, this book will be a valuable reference later on as well.

Don't worry if you're not a formally trained musician or if you haven't really dealt with digital audio before. The beauty of Pro Tools—and computer music in general—is that even untrained (but creative) musicians can enjoy great success in this kind of environment. Of course, any general music or audio knowledge you bring to the table is an added advantage, but it is certainly not a requirement for this book.

With that being said, there's no denying that Pro Tools is a *deep* program. Even those of us who have been using it for years are still finding new tidbits now and then. For that reason, I can't dedicate the limited space I have in this book to covering basic computer operations. That means it's up to you to understand the most basic ins and outs of your particular platform (either a Mac running OS X or a PC running Windows 7). Don't worry too much, though—the general computer knowledge required to use Pro Tools is pretty basic. If you can locate, launch, and close programs already, you're probably in fine shape.

How to Use This Book

Music is fundamentally a progressive process. From creation to performance, it's the result of many small steps taken in order. A solid mastery of Pro Tools works much the same way. This book is laid out to mirror the creative process, from setup, through the recording process, editing, mixing, and putting on the final touches. The first sections of the book also include a bit of information about the nature of DAWs in general so you understand the basic building blocks of digital audio and can work most efficiently. If you're just beginning with DAWs, you'll find this information valuable in the long run.

Because this book is arranged sequentially according to the production process, you'll be able to follow along from the very start of a project through its completion. However, if you're interested in some areas more than others (which is pretty common with more experienced users), feel free to take the book out of order and just concentrate on those sections first; this book will work that way as well.

You'll find that most of this book is laid out in a tutorial-style format, with practice files on the included disc that you can use side by side with the book's examples. Of course, you can also employ this book as a targeted training source, using the clear, illustrated style of this format to your advantage as you locate information on specific functions.

Last but not least, you'll note that peppered throughout this book are a number of notes, tips, and sidebars. Take a look at these to find additional ways to increase your efficiency, additional information on key functions, and even warnings that point out common pitfalls and how to avoid them.

SPEAKING OF NOTES...

Speaking of notes, there's no time like the present to start! If you've already got some experience with previous versions of Pro Tools, you might be particularly interested in checking out what's new in Pro Tools 9. You'll find sections dedicated to features introduced in Pro Tools 9, with titles that call attention to these features.

Finally, a Little Background...

For more than 20 years, Digidesign has been a leader in digital audio workstation technology, and the professional community has chosen Pro Tools as the clear industry standard. Historically, these Pro Tools systems have been broken down into two families:

- **HD:** Short for "high definition," these Pro Tools systems rely on dedicated computer cards and interfaces specifically designed to work with Pro Tools (this is a setup that is referred to as "hardware based"). This means two things: First, Pro Tools|HD is a reliable, scalable, and powerful system—an obvious choice for professional facilities. Second, it costs more (and it can be a *lot* more).

- **LE:** These limited-edition Pro Tools systems are host based, meaning the computer's CPU is used for all Pro Tools-related processing. Pro Tools LE systems required a Digidesign/Avid audio interface in order to run. (In other words, if you didn't have a Pro Tools–compatible interface attached to your computer, Pro Tools LE would not launch.)

The idea behind these two different product lines was to give high-end users the fidelity and performance that professional facilities demand, and to also give lower-level users a powerful limited-edition version to work with. Over time, both these flavors of Pro Tools have established themselves as leaders in their markets, and their compatibility with each other was a key factor in Pro Tools' overall prominence.

Pro Tools 9 marks an important evolution in this structure. In particular, it brings far more power to users of host-based systems. Here are the three new strata of Pro Tools systems:

- **Pro Tools|HD:** Pro Tools|HD has changed least of all in this new organization. Still hardware-based, these systems require powerful DSP computer cards and high-end audio interfaces. For uncompromising power and performance, Pro Tools|HD is the way to go.
- **Pro Tools|HD Native:** This is a new mid-range product that brings powerful aspects of both a hardware-based and host-based system together. With a single hardware card, paired with HD interfaces, users take advantage of their computer's CPU while at the same time getting the high fidelity of Avid's top-of-the-line interfaces.
- **Pro Tools:** Although it's easiest to think of Pro Tools 9 as an upgrade to Pro Tools LE 8, that tells only part of the story. Yes, Pro Tools 9 is a host-based version (meaning that it relies on your computer's CPU to do its work). But in terms of features, it resembles Pro Tools HD more than the previous LE version. Also—and this is perhaps the most striking change—no longer are Avid interfaces required for Pro Tools to run, and the new Avid interfaces themselves are more compatible with other software DAWs. Of course, the recommended combination is an Avid interface paired with Pro Tools 9, but it is no longer the only choice available to users.

That's right—there's no more Pro Tools LE! Not only does the growing community of host-based DAW users have a more flexible version of Pro Tools to use, but a much more powerful one as well.

The good news—and it's great news, really—is that the software environments for these three flavors of Pro Tools are nearly identical. That means you can take advantage of one of the most powerful and well-developed user interfaces on the market without breaking the bank. What's more, when it comes time for you to step up to a Pro Tools|HD system, you'll already know the software.

If a lot of this sounds like Greek right now, don't worry—we'll cover it in the chapters to come. Ready? Let's go!

CD-ROM Downloads

If you purchased an ebook version of this book, and the book had a companion CD-ROM, you may download the contents from www.courseptr.com/downloads.

If your book has a CD-ROM, please check our website for any updates or errata files. You may download files from www.courseptr.com/downloads.

1 Welcome to Pro Tools 9

Congratulations, and welcome to the world of Pro Tools! Throughout Digidesign's and Avid's 20+ year history, Pro Tools has established itself at the forefront of the digital audio workstation (DAW) community. Version 9 represents a major new release, particularly in terms of flexibility and compatibility. Pro Tools 9 will be found in virtually every facet of the audio industry, from music production for CDs to surround sound for movie soundtracks. Now, armed with Pro Tools' powerful array of functions and features, *you'll* be able to tap into this world of digital audio for yourself to realize your own creative vision. Welcome to the party!

The first step in the process is to set up your system and master the essential functions of Pro Tools. This chapter discusses the structure and most basic operations of Pro Tools 9. You'll learn how to do the following:

- Identify the hardware and software components of your Pro Tools system and configure your audio engine.
- Organize sessions and data in Pro Tools.
- Use Pro Tools' most basic functions.
- Create, open, play, and close a session.

What Makes Up a Pro Tools System?

Pro Tools 9 systems fall into one of three families:

- **Pro Tools 9.** Pro Tools 9 is a *host-based* DAW, which simply means the power of your Pro Tools system is based entirely on the processing power of your computer. Your computer's CPU (the *host*) handles all the important operations, including mixing and effects processing, in addition to all other tasks required by your computer.
- **Pro Tools 9|HD.** This version of Pro Tools includes dedicated PCI or PCIe hardware cards, which are added to your computer. These cards not only allow connectivity to Avid's higher-quality audio interfaces (a concept we'll discuss later in this chapter), but the cards take care of essential Pro Tools–related tasks, such as mixing and effects processing. This is known as a *hardware-based* system. HD systems, because of their added processing horsepower, feature more tracks, greater flexibility, and connectivity to Avid's top-level HD audio interfaces.
- **Pro Tools 9|HD Native.** A relative newcomer to the Pro Tools family, Pro Tools 9|HD Native can be thought of as something of a hybrid system. Like the regular Pro Tools 9|HD, there is a PCI or PCIe card added to your computer that allows for connection to Avid's HD interfaces (although it's worth noting that an HD|Native card is different from a regular HD card). In this case, however, the card has very limited processing power. In terms of mixing and processing, this would be classified as a *host-based* DAW, but one that compares to Pro Tools HD systems in terms of audio quality due to connectivity to HD interfaces. This is a welcome addition to the Pro Tools line, giving users a compromise between the lower-cost Pro Tools 9 and the flagship Pro Tools 9|HD.

For the purposes of this book, we'll limit our discussions to basic Pro Tools 9 systems, but the skills you learn here can be applied to any level of Pro Tools system.

The Heart of Your DAW: The Computer

Your computer is the cornerstone of your Pro Tools system. The computer, particularly its central processing unit (CPU), will be called upon to do everything from mixing and automation to effects processing. That mean the more power your CPU has, the more powerful your Pro Tools software will be as a result. The host computer can be either a PC (running Windows 7 Home Premium, Professional, or Ultimate) or a Mac (running OS X 10.6.2, 10.6.3, or 10.6.4).

THINK BEFORE UPDATING!

Updating your computer's operating system might seem to be a no-brainer, but before making any change to your computer's OS, it's best to check with Avid's compatibility documents and the Avid Knowledgebase. We'll cover those two valuable resources later in this chapter.

In addition to CPU speed, your computer's random access memory (RAM) plays an important role in how your digital audio workstation will perform. It probably comes as no surprise to learn that the more RAM your computer has, the better. More RAM will enable your Pro Tools session to run more real-time effects and will make for an overall more powerful DAW. Avid stipulates a minimum of 2 GB of RAM to run Pro Tools, with 4 GB or more recommended.

Ideally, your DAW computer should be dedicated solely to music- and audio-related tasks. Other applications running (or even installed) on your system can steal from your computer's overall efficiency when running Pro Tools. Recording and playing back digital audio can be demanding on your computer's CPU, and other programs interrupting the steady stream of data to and from your hard drive can cause major problems. Of course, having such a dedicated computer can be impractical for many users; if you're not able to devote your computer exclusively to Pro Tools, you should avoid running other programs during your Pro Tools sessions.

Audio Interface

All DAWs, regardless of brand, require some sort of audio interface to record and play back audio (also referred to as *input/output*, or *I/O* for short). Interfaces can vary, from professional quality devices used at large professional facilities (these facilities often use multiple interfaces together), down to using the built-in microphone and headphone outputs of a laptop computer. Along this spectrum, different manufacturers have created a wide range of products featuring different numbers of channels and audio quality.

Your audio interface is the doorway for audio going to and coming from your computer. Generally speaking, your computer will connect directly to the audio interface, and your various audio devices (mixing boards, keyboards, and microphones) will connect to the interface's available audio inputs. To listen to your session, you should connect the main audio outputs of your interface to an amplifier, and from there to monitor speakers. If you're using powered monitors (those that have built-in amplifiers), you should connect the outputs of your interface directly to the inputs of the speakers.

In past versions of Pro Tools, the Pro Tools software has been unbreakably linked to Avid audio interfaces. For example, to run Pro Tools 8 LE, you needed to have a connected Avid interface (such as an Mbox), or the Pro Tools software would not launch. Possibly the most significant change in Pro Tools 9 has been the breaking of this dependence on Avid hardware. Pro Tools 9 is compatible with any interface with ASIO (Windows) or Core Audio (Mac) drivers. That means that you can use Avid interfaces, a third party's, or even the built-in I/O of your computer.

> **WHERE CAN I LEARN MORE?**
>
> Given the wide and varied range of audio interfaces, it's impossible to give a comprehensive rundown of all your options in this book. When considering the right interface for your system, a good place to start is the Avid Web site (http://www.avid.com/US/categories/Audio-MIDI-Interfaces).

Hard Drive(s)

Just as traditional tape-based recording studios rely on magnetic tape as a storage medium, Pro Tools relies on hard drives for the recording and playback of its digital audio. The drives can be IDE/ATA, SATA, eSATA, USB 2.0 (Windows only), or even FireWire based (Mac only).

It is important to remember two factors when choosing a hard drive for Pro Tools: size and speed. First, a larger-capacity drive will enable you to store more audio data. This will translate into more minutes of audio that you can store, higher-resolution digital audio, or both. A fast drive will allow for more efficient transfer of data (also called *throughput*) when you are recording and/or playing back audio. This can translate into higher track counts and more reliability when working with complex sessions.

Using a Second Hard Drive

Adding a second drive dedicated to the storage of your Pro Tools sessions will greatly increase your Pro Tools system's performance, whether your system is used solely for Pro Tools or is more of a general-purpose machine. You' ll still want to install the Pro Tools application on your computer' s system drive, but when you create your sessions (something we' ll get into later in this chapter), put them on your second, "audio" drive. That way, you' ll have one hard drive occupied with the nominal tasks of your computer and another separate drive (with its own read/write head and throughput) dealing only with your Pro Tools session and audio.

Partitioning Your Hard Drive

If you're wondering whether partitioning your drive will do the trick, the short answer is no. Partitioning a single hard drive may give the outward appearance of creating a second drive, but in reality, there is still only one physical hardware device. Although partitioning can be a convenient way of organizing your data, it doesn't add another physical drive with its own read/write head, so it won't give Pro Tools the same benefit with real-time tasks as a second physical drive would.

Great Resources: Avid's Compatibility Documents and Knowledgebase

You might have noticed that although I've talked about desirable qualities in a DAW system, I haven't mentioned many specific details about what kind of hardware you should be using (things such as minimum CPU speed and chipset types). I apologize if I seem evasive on the subject, but the truth of the matter is that the landscape of computer-based products transforms and grows so rapidly that any specs I quote here might well be out of date by the time you read this. Don't despair, though! Avid has provided the help you need to build the Pro Tools system you want in the form of an up-to-date list of compatible hardware. You can find this list on Avid's Web site, at the following URL: http://www.avid.com/compatibility.

To view more technical information and alerts, you can also take a look at the Avid Knowledgebase. On the top of the Avid home page (http://www.avid.com), click the Support and Services link. Then, on the Support and Services page, click the Knowledgebase link along the right margin under the heading "Pro Tools Support." Once you're in the Knowledgebase, you can search in a number of ways, including by product or keyword. Whether you're designing a Pro Tools system or trouble-shooting one, the Knowledgebase is a trove of technical tidbits!

A Word About Installation

When it comes to installation, Pro Tools 9 has made great gains over earlier versions. The installation process is basically broken down into two easy steps:

1. Install the Pro Tools software.
2. Install the appropriate drivers (ASIO or Core Audio) for the interface(s) that you will use with your system. Drivers for Avid interfaces are included on your Pro Tools 9 installation disk.

The documentation you received with your Pro Tools software and hardware is the first place to look for information on installation. In the ever-changing world of computers, though, that documentation could be slightly out of date! Once again, the Avid Web site is an invaluable resource. Just go to the Pro Tools product page (http://www.avid.com/US/products/family/Pro-Tools) and click the Pro Tools CS Updates at the bottom of the page.

The documentation that came with your Pro Tools product, combined with a little Net surfing (if needed), should enable you to successfully install and configure your Pro Tools system. Once that's finished, you're ready to move on.

Checking for Software Updates

Wouldn't it be great if there were a way for Pro Tools to help you out with software updates? Good news: Pro Tools 9 includes exactly that functionality. It can search for any updates, bug fixes, and so on that are relevant to your system. Better yet, Pro Tools 9 can also check to see whether there are any updates needed or available for your installed plug-ins. How cool is that? Pro Tools 9 will even differentiate between paid and non-paid updates, so you can choose to make the larger version leaps at your discretion.

Using this new feature is very easy—so easy, in fact, that there's virtually nothing you need to do. By default, Pro Tools will quickly check for updates when you launch the program. All you need to do is make sure your computer is connected to the Internet, and this will happen automatically. (Don't worry. This check is very quick and doesn't add too much time to the Pro Tools launch.)

If you want to do an update check manually, you can do that as well. It's also a simple process:

1 Once Pro Tools is launched (something we'll go into later in this chapter), **click** on **Help**. The Help menu will appear.

2 **Choose Check for Updates.** The Software Update progress window will appear.

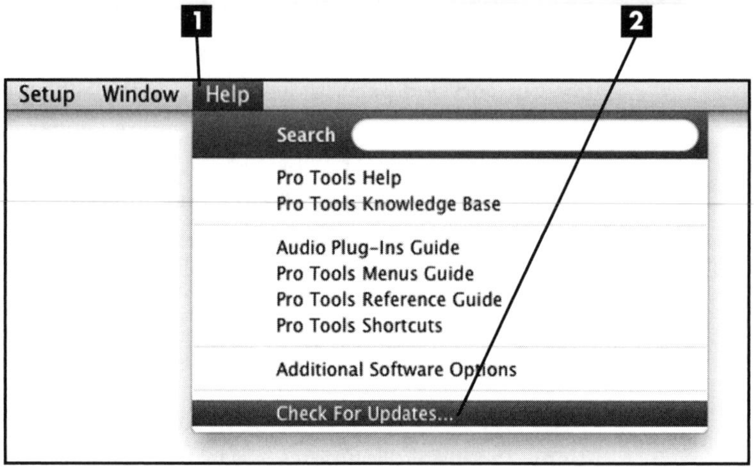

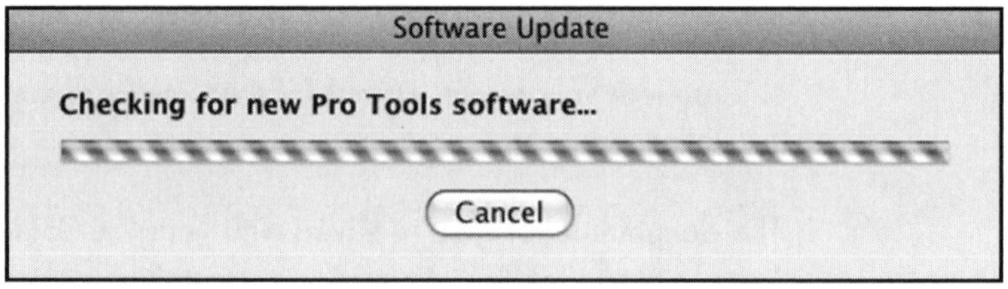

3 If there are updates to be installed, you will be directed to a Web site with links for the appropriate download(s). If you are up to date, you'll see the dialog box shown here. **Click** on **OK** to finish the process.

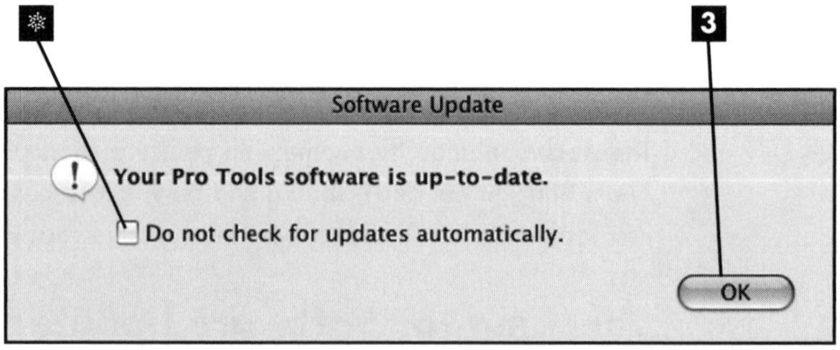

If you don't wish for Pro Tools to perform automatic update searches upon startup in the future, just click the Do Not Check for Updates Automatically checkbox.

New in Pro Tools 9: iLok Protection

Long-time users of Pro Tools may be familiar with the iLok method of copyright protection. It's been widely used for plug-in authorizations by many manufacturers (including Avid). For those who are new to the term iLok, think of it as a key that unlocks your software and enables it to run. Now with Pro Tools 9, all versions of Pro Tools will include this same level of protection.

An iLok is a small USB device—the new "2nd Generation" iLok hardware is the size of a small USB flash drive. It can hold a large number of software licenses; in fact, the new iLok can store more than 500 licenses. When you purchase Pro Tools 9, an iLok is included in the box. This iLok comes pre-loaded with the Pro Tools 9 license, so all you need to do is plug it into an available USB port or a USB hub attached to your computer, and you're ready to launch Pro Tools.

Your iLok hardware can be used for more than just your Pro Tools licenses, though. If you go to http://www.ilok.com, you can create an account into which you can deposit additional software licenses. With the convenience of the iLok copy-protection system, you can even have Pro Tools installed on multiple computers (though of course, you'll only be able to run Pro Tools when the iLok is physically attached)!

New in Pro Tools 9: Choosing an Audio Engine

As we've discussed already, the new, more open design of Pro Tools 9 enables users to use a wide variety of devices for audio I/O—in fact, any audio interface that includes an ASIO or Core Audio driver. To make the most of this new feature, though, you'll need to know how to choose the audio engine that works best in any given situation. To get this fundamental control over Pro Tools, you'll make use of Pro Tools' Playback Engine dialog box.

1. **Click** on **Setup**. The Setup menu opens.
2. **Choose Playback Engine.** The Playback Engine dialog box will appear.

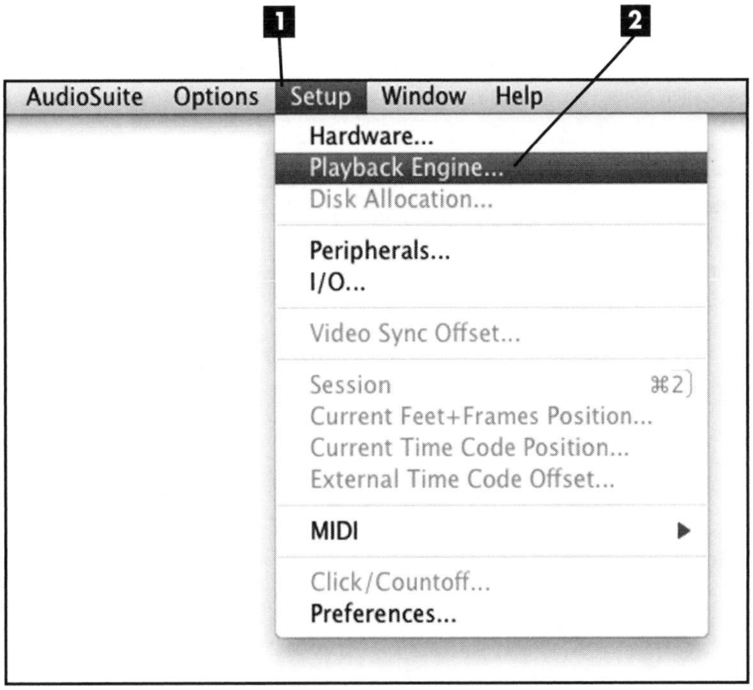

3 **Click** on the **Current Engine** arrow. A menu of available hardware options opens.

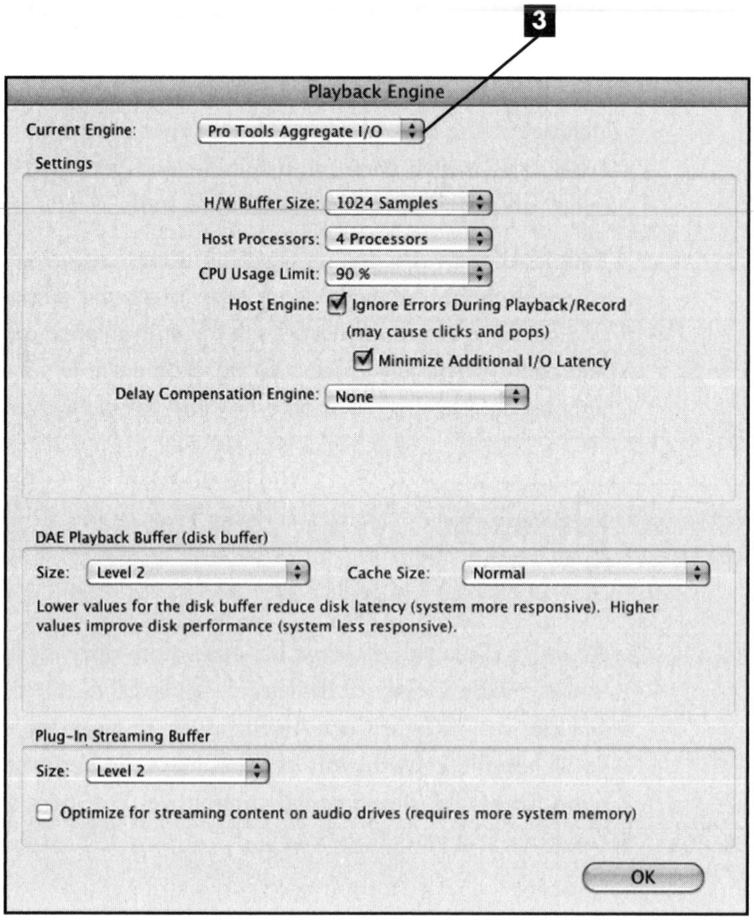

4 **Choose** the **interface** that you want Pro Tools to use for recording and playback of audio. In this case, I'll choose my trusty Mbox2.

5 **Click OK.**

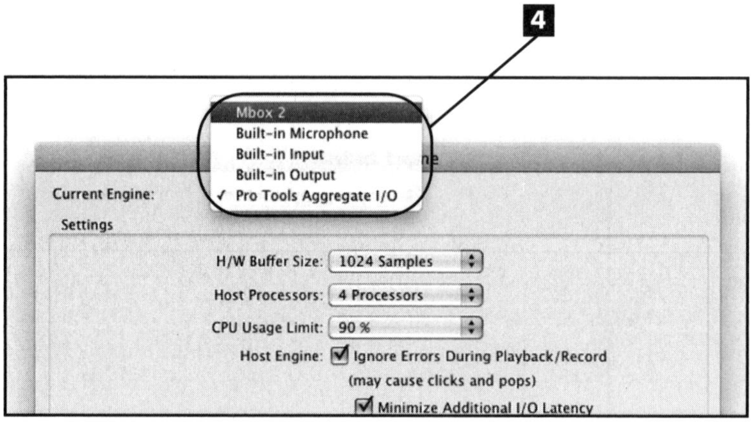

Tips on Choosing an Audio Engine

If there's a downside to this new flexibility, it's that it's sometimes hard to make a choice! Of course, convenience is a factor. Here are some other things to keep in mind:

- When it comes to audio quality, one of the biggest factors in terms of clarity and stereo-imagery width is low jitter. Jitter specs for audio gear is often printed on product documentation, and is readily available for professional interfaces on the Internet. Look for the interface with the lowest jitter, and choose that one for your audio interface in the Playback Engine dialog box. If your audio interface's documentation doesn't include specific information about jitter, it's a safe bet that an external interface will have lower jitter than your computer's built-in I/O.
- If your computer has built-in sound capabilities (most do), you'll see some degree of built-in Input or Output options listed in the Current Engine menu. Take care—they mean what they say! For example, if you choose Built-In Output, you'll have no input capabilities in your Pro Tools system. If you choose Built-In Input, you'll have no output! If you want to use your computer's built-in audio hardware, choose Pro Tools Aggregate I/O. (We'll talk more about that a little later in this chapter.)
- If you have a Pro Tools session open, and you change your audio engine, Pro Tools will automatically save and close your session. Click the OK button to relaunch the session with the new audio engine. If you don't want to overwrite your session file, choose the Save As option before making your audio engine changes. We'll talk about the Save As option at the end of this chapter.

Setting Up Your Hardware

After you've chosen an audio engine, you might want to tweak it a bit, configuring the various options that are included with your audio interface. That's where the Hardware Setup dialog box comes in. It's the second stage in the process of getting your audio hardware properly configured for use with Pro Tools.

1. **Click** on **Setup**. The Setup menu will appear.
2. **Choose Hardware.** The Hardware Setup dialog box will appear.

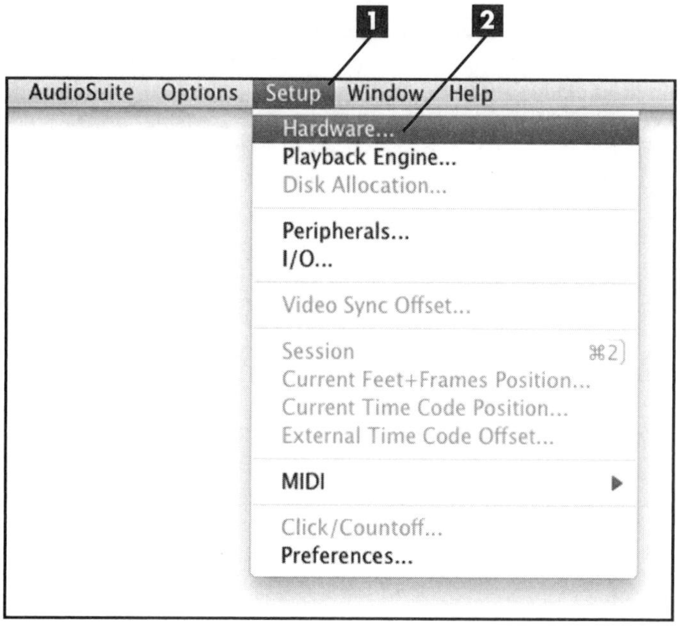

The Hardware Setup dialog box displays information related to the audio engine that you chose in the Playback Engine dialog box. If you change audio engines, the information displayed in the Hardware Setup dialog box will change accordingly. There are a few aspects that are commonly seen in this dialog box (this example shows the Hardware Setup dialog box that you would see with the Mbox Pro):

- On the lower-left side, you can choose a sample rate and clock source.
- Depending on the device, you'll see different options in the center of the Hardware Setup dialog box. In this case, you have the ability to configure the Mbox Pro's Multi-Button.

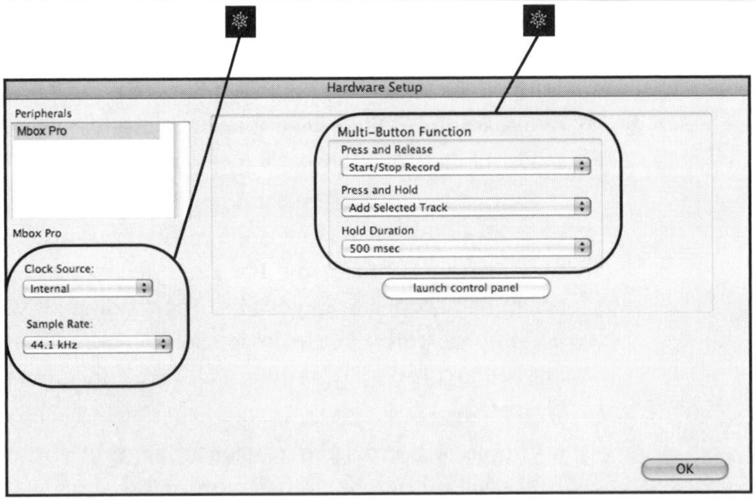

- Many interfaces allow further customization through a dedicated Control Panel. In this case, if you click on the Launch Control Panel button, you'll see the device's dedicated mixer:

Although the appearance of the Control Panel will vary from device to device (shown here is the Mbox Pro Control Panel), it is here that you'll gain a deeper level of control over your audio interface.

The Pro Tools Aggregate I/O

For the most part, Pro Tools is identical whether you're using a PC or Mac. However, there is an interesting feature that is currently available only on Mac computers: the Pro Tools Aggregate I/O. Using the Aggregate I/O, you can simultaneously use multiple interfaces. For example, you can use a professional audio interface, plus your computer's built-in inputs and outputs. Let's take a look:

1. **Click** on **Setup**. The Setup menu will appear.
2. **Choose Playback Engine.** The Playback Engine dialog box will appear.
3. **Click** on **Current Engine.** A menu of available hardware options will appear.
4. Choose **Pro Tools Aggregate I/O**.
5. **Click** the **OK** button to close the Playback Engine dialog box.

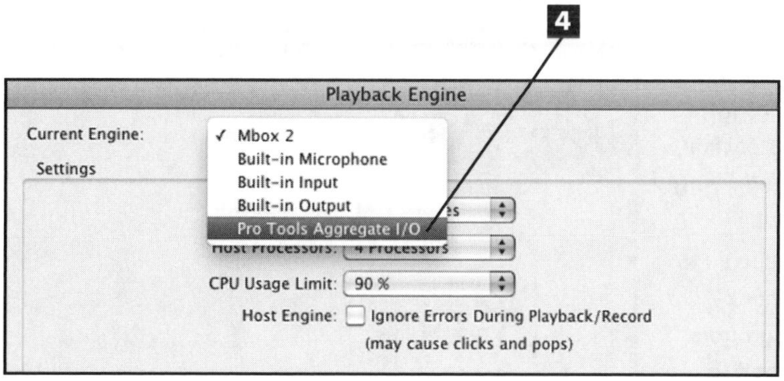

Next, let's go back to the Hardware setup dialog box:

1. **Click** on **Setup**. The Setup menu will appear.
2. **Choose Hardware.** The Hardware Setup dialog box will appear.
3. **Click** the **Launch Setup App** button. The Audio Devices dialog box of the Mac Audio MIDI setup dialog box will appear.

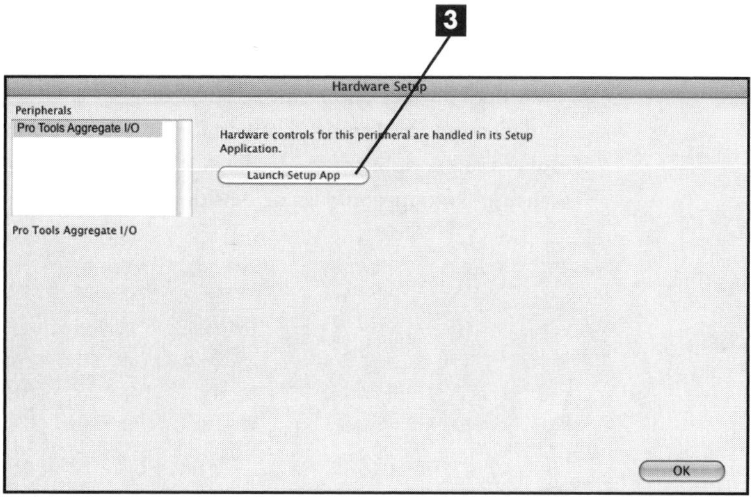

The Audio Devices dialog box lists not only individual audio devices that are attached (or built-in) to your computer, but also a collection (or *aggregate*) of devices that can be used collectively. There are a few essential elements of this dialog box that will help you get the most out of your system:

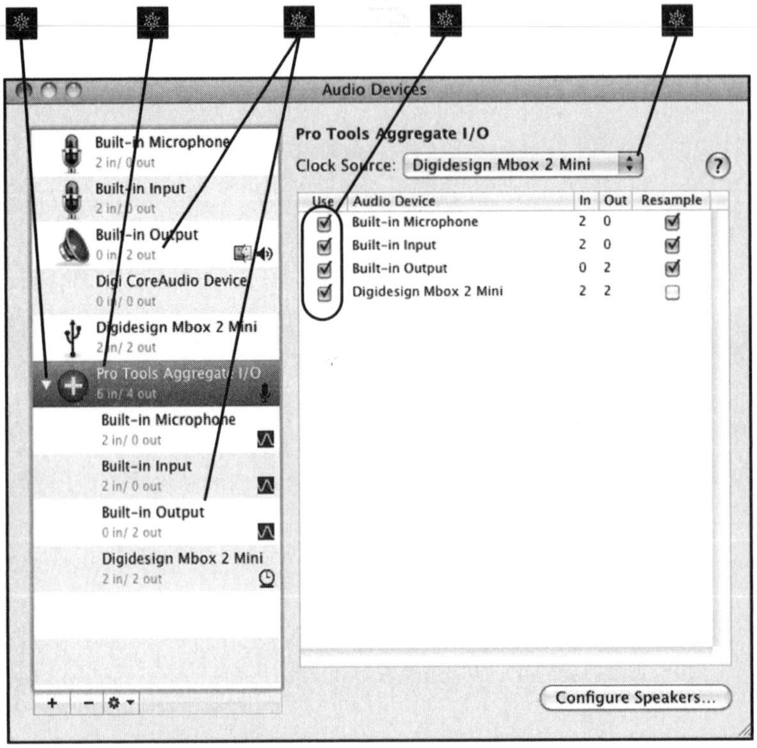

- To reveal a list of all the devices included in the Pro Tools Aggregate I/O, click the triangle icon to the left of the Aggregate icon.
- Click the Pro Tools Aggregate I/O menu item to manage the aggregate devices (in the right section of the Audio Devices dialog box, as shown here).
- The first thing you'll want to do is to choose a clock source for your aggregate devices. Because the Pro Tools Aggregate is intended for use with your Mac's built-in I/O, Avid recommends using the default clock settings.
- You can add or remove devices from your aggregate by clicking the checkboxes in the Use column. As you might expect, checked boxes indicate that the device is an active part of the aggregate (once again, please remember that the Pro Tools Aggregate I/O was designed with only your built-in I/O in mind).
- Individual devices often include some level of configurability—things like volume control, audio source, and so on. Click on the device you want to tweak, and you'll see the setup options in the right section of the Audio Devices dialog box. (You can select a device either in the aggregate list or outside the aggregate.)

MAXIMUM I/O

When dealing with multiple interfaces, you can really start adding up channels of I/O. But is there any limitation? Actually, yes. With Pro Tools 9 (the basic standalone software version), you'll have up to 32 channels of inputs and outputs. That's often just fine for smaller facilities, but if you need more, consider Pro Tools|HD Native, which supports up to 64 channels of I/O, or Pro Tools|HD, which maxes out at a whopping 160 channels of I/O!

Understanding Sessions and Files

Now you've gotten Pro Tools installed, and your system is set up (at least from a hardware perspective). Before you get any deeper into the world of Pro Tools, you should take a moment to understand the general principles behind this powerful digital audio workstation. An understanding of Pro Tools' overall architecture and how different elements work together is important fundamental knowledge as you continue to grow as a Pro Tools user.

Pro Tools Is a Pointer-Based Application

It's common to refer to a cursor as a *pointer*. But when you're discussing a *pointer-based* application like Pro Tools, you're referring to the way the program deals with digital audio data. In Pro Tools' case, this pointer-based structure can be broken down into three basic interdependent elements: session files, folders, and audio files. In this situation, the term *pointer* refers to the way your Pro Tools session file will access (or *point* to) other files on your hard drive as your session plays.

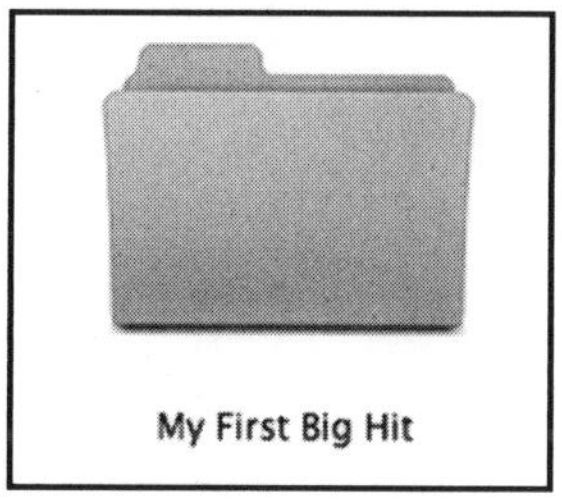

A session folder is created when you create a new session. It contains the following items (as needed):

- **Session file.** The session file is at the top of the Pro Tools hierarchy. This is the file created by Pro Tools when you create a new session, and it's the file you open to return to a session you've already created. Although this file is relatively small, it is the master of all your session elements. Session files have a .ptf extension and contain the following session elements:

- The names, types, and arrangement of all tracks in your session
- All MIDI data
- Essential settings, such as inputs and outputs
- All edits and automation data

SESSIONS AND AUDIO

It might sound as if the only thing you need is a session file, but that's usually not the case. Although session files contain all the important aspects of a project, they don't actually contain any audio. Instead, a session file refers (or *points*) to audio files located in dedicated folders within your session folder.

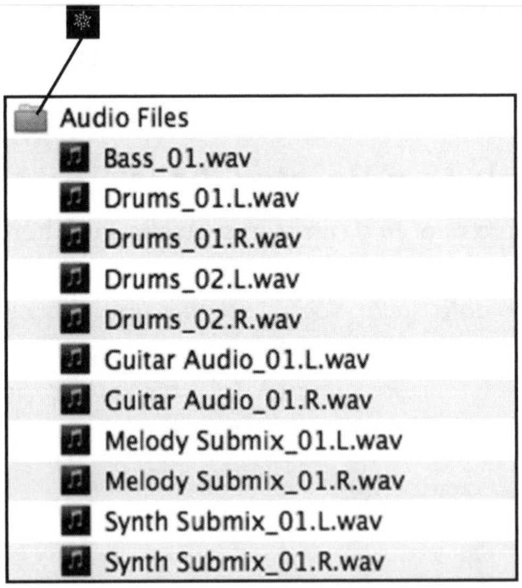

- **Audio Files folder.** As soon as audio is recorded, it's stored in an Audio Files folder within the session folder. Different takes are stored in this folder as individual audio files. When you play a session, Pro Tools accesses, or points to, the audio files in this folder.

HOW DO AUDIO FILES GET THEIR NAMES?

When you record audio in Pro Tools, the name of the file you create follows the name of the track on which it was recorded. For example, if you record onto a mono (one-channel) Audio track named Bass, the files created by Pro Tools in the Audio Files folder will be named Bass_01, Bass_02, and so on as you record takes on this track. In the case of stereo Audio tracks, two mono files (one for the left side and one for the right) are created. If you record onto a stereo Audio track named Drums, two files named Drums_01.L and Drums_01.R will be created.

There are additional folders that can be created by Pro Tools as needed:

- **Fade Files folder.** When you start creating fades (including fade-ins, fade-outs, and crossfades), Pro Tools renders the created fades to files on your hard drive. Audio files are again created, but they're not stored in the Audio Files folder this time. Instead, they're stored in a folder named Fade Files. It's important to keep in mind that even though fades are audio files, they are significantly different in function from the audio files you record or import into your session (in ways that you'll learn about later); thus, they are stored separately.
- **Region groups folder.** Pro Tools enables you to select multiple regions and link them together in a single *region group*. Digital audio, MIDI, and video regions can be grouped together, making editing much faster and easier. You'll learn more about region groups later; for now, just know that groups you create are stored in this folder. (If you don't create any region groups in a given session, a folder won't be created.)
- **Rendered files folder.** Pro Tools 7.4 introduced a great feature called *Elastic Audio*. This is a very cool new addition indeed, and one you'll learn about in Chapter 10, "Moving to the Next Level: Tips and Tricks." For now, all you need to know is that when you're working with Elastic Audio, you have the option of rendering your elasticized audio to an audio file—and when you do, it will be stored in this folder.

- **Session file backups folder.** Depending on your preference settings, Pro Tools can automatically create backups of your sessions and store them in this folder. By default, a new session backup is created every five minutes, and the folder keeps the last 10 backup files. This is highly recommended, particularly for new Pro Tools users; it can help you recover quickly if you encounter technical trouble.
- **Plug-In Settings folder.** In Pro Tools, you have the option of using plug-ins, which are programs designed to work within the Pro Tools environment and function as virtual effects. (You'll learn more about plug-ins in Chapter 8, "Basic Mixing.") When you create specific plug-in presets, you have the option of saving them in this session subfolder.
- **Video Files folder.** When your session calls for a video track, you can save it in this session subfolder.

> **WHAT ABOUT THE WAVECACHE?**
>
> There's one more file you'll often find in your session folder that we haven't talked about yet. It's a small file named WaveCache, and it stores all the waveform overviews for any audio in your session. *Waveform overview* is a fancy way of describing the visual representation of audio waves that you might see on an Audio track. This small file is automatically created and updated, so there's nothing you need to worry about with it!

Regions Versus Files

Given the fact that Pro Tools records audio to individual files on your hard drive, how do you later access these files? Simply put, when audio is recorded to an Audio track (or even MIDI data to a MIDI track), Pro Tools creates an object called a region in the Edit window. In the case of Audio tracks, these regions refer (or *point*) to files on your hard drive, triggering them to sound as your session plays.

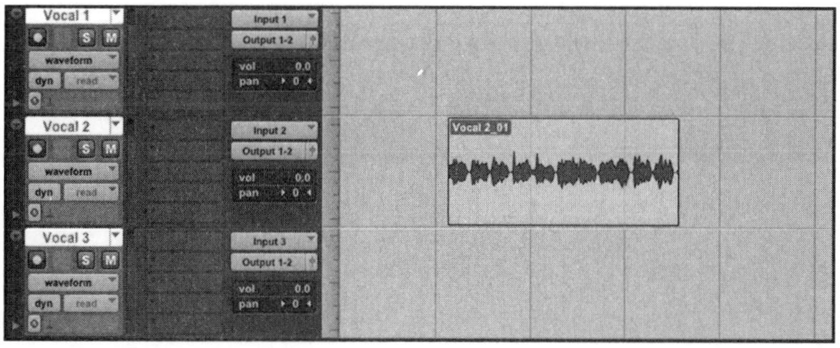

Here's a close-up of Pro Tools' Edit window. There are three Audio tracks in this session (Vocal 1, Vocal 2, and Vocal 3), and a single region on the Vocal 2 track.

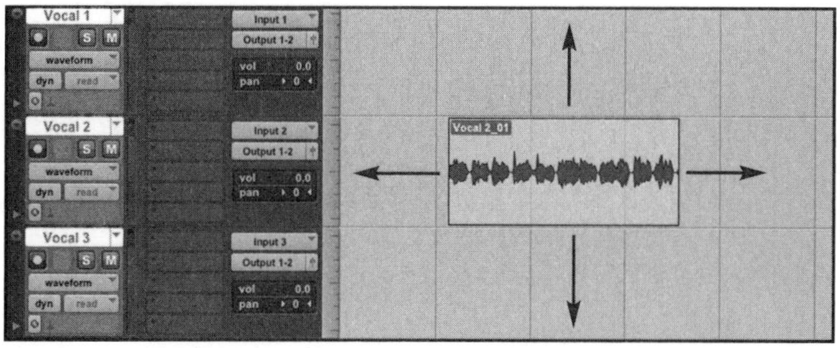

Working with regions has many advantages. One of the first you'll discover is that you have the ability to move them earlier or later on the session's timeline, enabling you to position the regions precisely in time. An environment like this, in which you have the ability to manipulate elements independently on the timeline, is commonly known as *nonlinear*. In addition to moving regions earlier or later in time, you have the option of moving them to other similar tracks. (In other words, you can move a region on a mono Audio track to another mono Audio track, and so on.)

Nondestructive Editing

Another great advantage pointer-based editing is that you can *nondestructively* trim or split the region —meaning that no audio data is being lost, so you can always undo what you've done. This can be a tricky concept, so let's take a look.

In this example, let's assume that the region named Vocal Comp is playing an audio file of the same name in the Audio Files subfolder. What if you don't want to use the whole region in your session? No problem! You can just adjust the start or end points of that region, effectively taking the unwanted bits of audio out of your session.

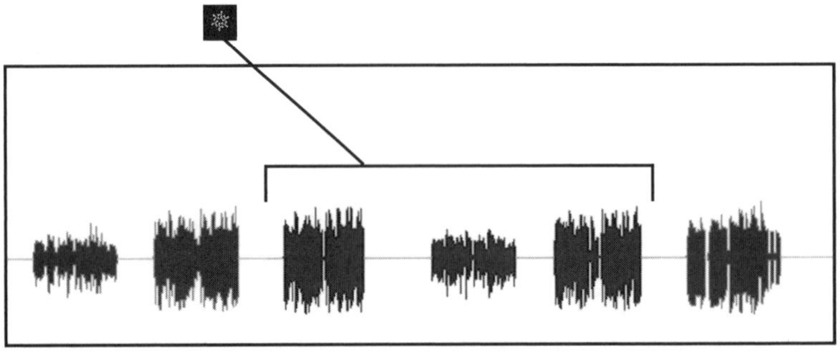

Section of audio used by this trimmed region

Does this mean that you've changed the file on your hard drive? No! You've only changed the *region* that is pointing to that file, so only a portion of that file will be heard in the session. Don't worry; because you haven't changed the audio file (only the region that is pointing to it), you can always drag the region boundaries back out if you change your mind later!

In addition to being able to trim data, there are other situations in which nondestructive editing can aid you in your production work, and you'll discover them as this book proceeds. The bottom line is that a nonlinear pointer-based environment coupled with nondestructive recording and editing gives an educated Pro Tools user a huge amount of flexibility and power, and the ability to undo changes and operations when needed.

Basic Pro Tools Operation

The end of the beginning: You've set up your system efficiently, taken some time to understand the way Pro Tools works, and now, based on that understanding, you're ready to start working. The last step before you dive deeper into Pro Tools is to open a pre-existing session.

THE CHAPTER 1 TUTORIAL SESSION

At this stage, you might not have a pre-existing Pro Tools session to work with. No problem. Just insert the disc included with this book and copy the Chapter 1 Session folder to your hard drive. When you open your session, you may see a few message boxes—this is normal when opening sessions created on a computer other than the one currently being used. For more information on these messages, though, please take a look at the "Setting Up Your Session" PDF document, also included on this book's disc.

The Quick Start Dialog Box

The Quick Start dialog box will appear when you launch Pro Tools and will give you a number of useful options for creating or opening a session. Let's run through them one by one.

To create a session by choosing a template, follow these steps:

1. **Launch** the **Pro Tools** application by clicking the program icon.
2. **Click** the **Create Session from Template** option button in the Quick Start dialog box. A list of template categories and template files will appear to the right of the option button cluster.
3. **Click** on the **template category menu** to reveal a list of categories, as shown here. (Note that you can organize your template list into different categories. You'll learn how later in this chapter.)

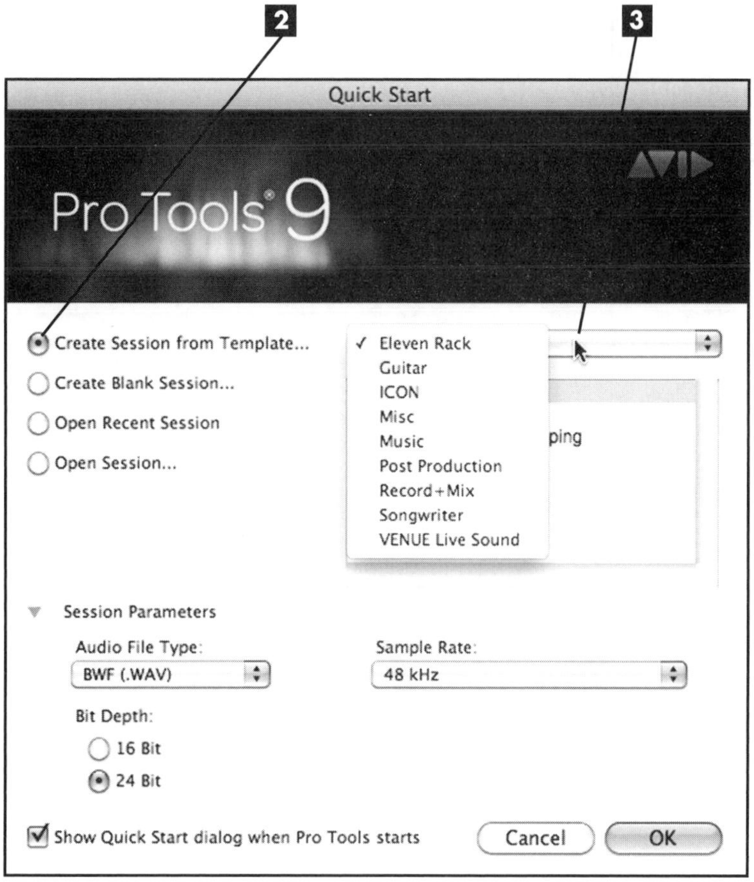

WHAT'S A TEMPLATE?

We'll get into that later in this chapter and book. For now, just know that opening a template session will create a new session complete with basic tracks, plug-ins, and so on, so that you can get straight to work.

4 Choose a category. The list below the menu will be populated by the templates in that category.

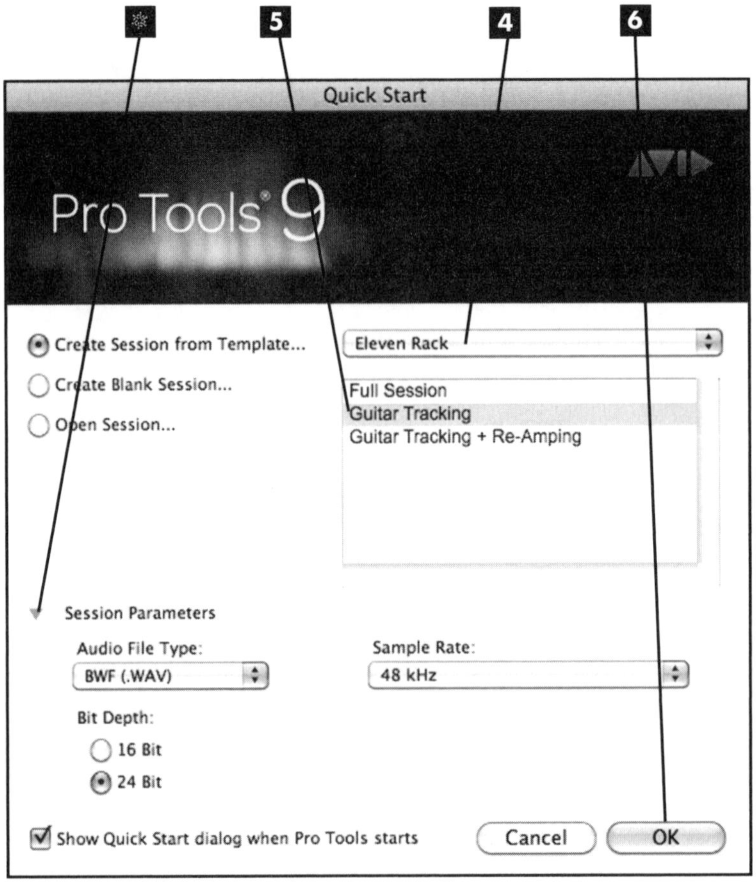

5 Click on the **template you want to load**.

- When you click a template, the session parameters will be updated in the lower section. If you want to change any aspects of the session, such as sample rate or bit depth (aspects we'll talk about later in this chapter), you can do it here.

6 **Click OK** to create the session. (Clicking the Cancel button will bypass the Quick Start dialog box.)

Alternatively, create a session by performing one of the following actions in the Quick Start dialog box:

- Click the Create Blank Session option button to create a session from scratch. We'll go through the details of creating a new session later in this chapter. Then click OK.
- Click the Open Recent Session option button to choose from a list of your most recently opened sessions (the list will appear to the right of the option buttons). Then click OK.
- Click the Open Session option button, then click OK to launch a standard File Open dialog box. This is the same dialog box you can access from the File menu in Pro Tools, which we'll go through in the next section.

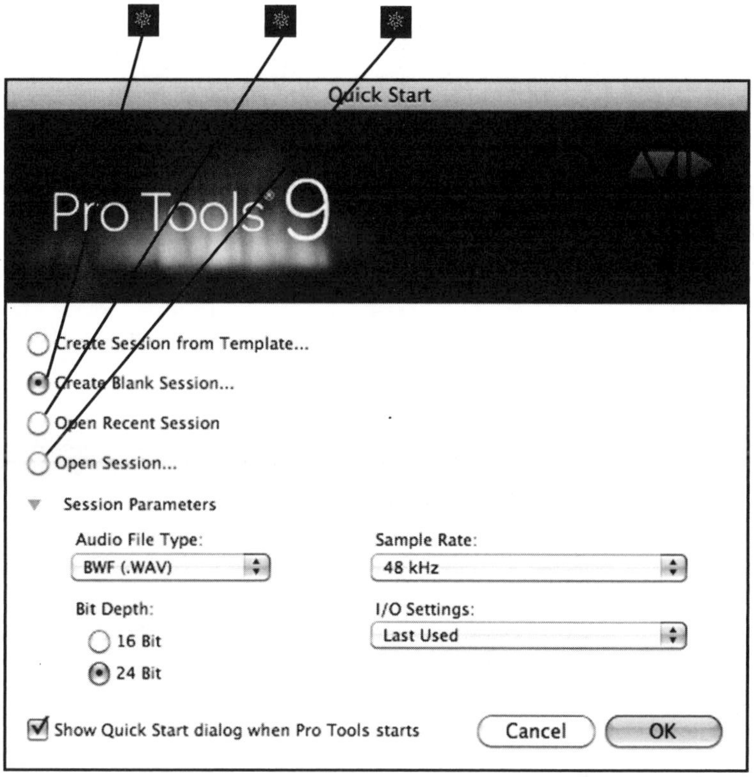

BYPASSING THE QUICK START DIALOG BOX

If you don't want to see the Quick Start dialog box when you start Pro Tools (in which case you'd go directly to Pro Tools with no session loaded), just click the Show Quick Start Dialog When Pro Tools Starts checkbox to remove the checkmark (this box is checked by default). Then click OK.

You can also prevent the Quick Start dialog box from being displayed when Pro Tools starts using the Preferences dialog box (which you'll learn quite a bit about as this book progresses). To do so, open the Pro Tools Setup menu and choose Preferences. The Preferences dialog box will open; click on the Show Quick Start Dialog When Pro Tools Starts checkbox in the lower-right corner of the Display tab to remove the checkmark. Then click OK.

Opening a Session When Pro Tools Is Running

Suppose Pro Tools is already running, and you've already gone past the Quick Start dialog box. Here's how to open a session:

1. **Click** on **File**. The File menu will appear.
2. **Click** on **Open Session**. A standard File Open dialog box will appear.

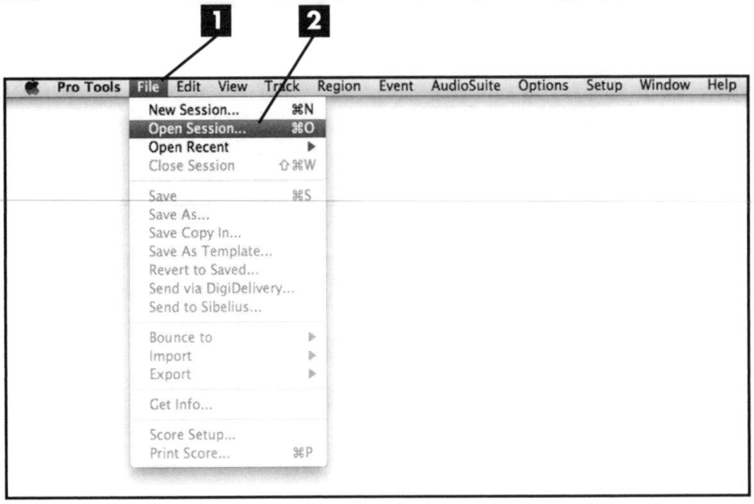

YOUR FIRST SHORTCUT

Pro Tools includes shortcut keys that enable you to work more efficiently. The shortcut for Open Session (Command+O on a Mac and Ctrl+O in Windows) is very useful—and easy to remember, as well!

3. If necessary, **select** the **drive** that contains the audio session. The drive will be selected, and the folders on that drive will appear.
4. **Click** on the **folder** that contains the session folder. The folder will be selected, and the scrollbar will automatically move to display the contents of that folder.
5. If necessary, **click** on the **subfolder** that contains the session file. The contents of the subfolder will be displayed.
6. **Click** on the desired **session file**. The file will be selected.
7. **Click** on **Open**. The session will be loaded into Pro Tools.

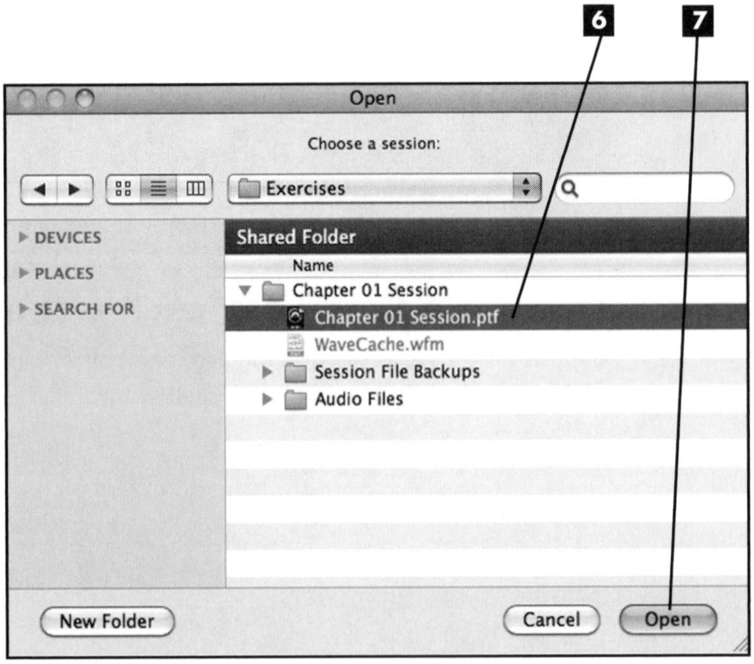

OPEN RECENT SESSIONS

The ability to select a recently opened file from a list is fairly common in the software world, and most users will be familiar with this idea from other applications. You've already seen the Open Recent Session option in the Quick Start dialog box, but you also have this available in Pro Tools itself. The Open Recent command can be found immediately below the Open Session command in the File menu. Simply click Open Recent, and you will see a list of up to 10 of your most recently opened sessions.

Opening a Session When Pro Tools Is Not Yet Launched

In this case, suppose Pro Tools is *not* yet launched. To open a session, follow these steps:

1. **Select** the **hard drive** that contains your session. On a PC, this will involve using My Computer or Windows Explorer. On a Mac, you can use the Finder or simply double-click on the hard drive icon on your desktop.
2. **Open** the **folder** that contains your session folder. The contents of the folder will be displayed.
3. **Open** the **folder** that contains the session file. The contents of the folder will be displayed.

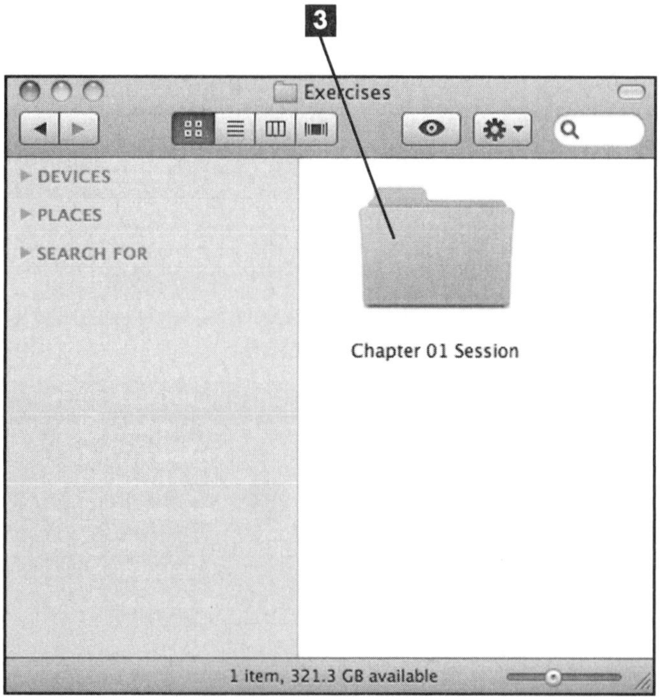

4 **Double-click** on the desired **session file**. Pro Tools will launch automatically, and the session will be loaded.

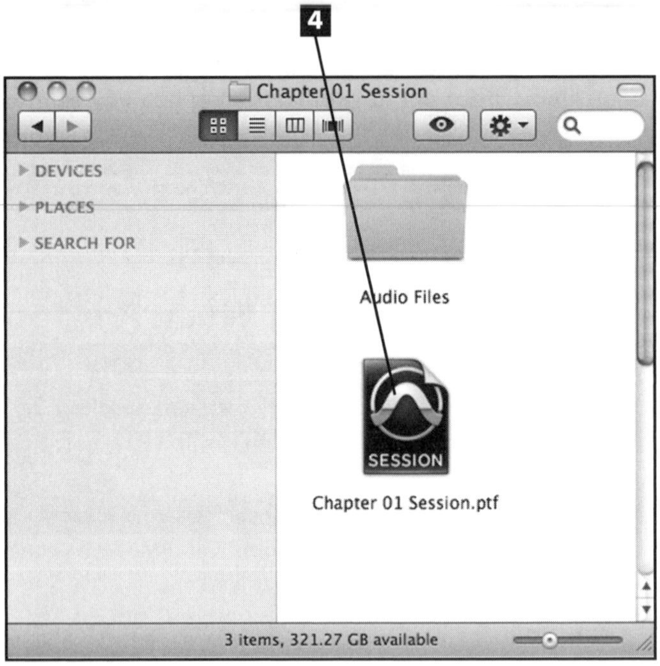

Creating a New Session

Now, let's take a closer look at the important process of creating a blank new session. (Many of these topics also apply to opening template sessions.) Once you've gotten your system together and everything working, your next step may be to create a new session (as opposed to opening a pre-existing session, as you did in the previous section of this chapter). Our earlier discussion of how Pro Tools works will come in handy here.

Starting the Process

In the previous section, you learned that you can create a blank new session from the Quick Start dialog box, but you can also create a new session from within Pro Tools itself.

1 **Click** on **File**. The File menu will appear.

2 **Click** on **New Session**. The New Session dialog box will open. In a sense, it is a smaller version of the Quick Start dialog box.

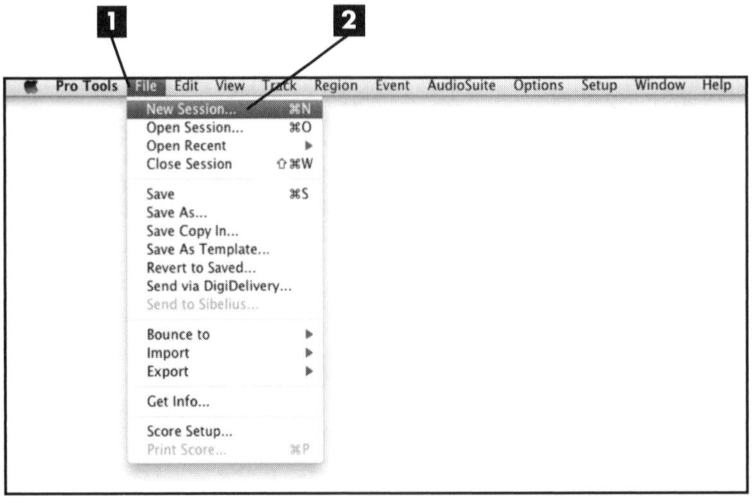

MORE SHORTCUTS!

As you explore Pro Tools further, you'll notice that many functions have shortcut keys associated with them. These shortcut key combinations are often displayed to the right of their functions, such at the shortcut for creating a new session—Command +N (Mac) or Ctrl+N (PC)—shown in the previous image. Although there are far too many shortcuts to learn all at once, learning the combinations for popular functions, such as opening or creating a session, can help you work more efficiently.

3a **Click** the **Create Session from Template option button** to gain access to your session templates, just as you did in the Quick Start dialog box.

OR

3b **Click** the **Create Blank Session option button** to create a new session, just as you can do in the Quick Start dialog box. Because that's what we'll be doing in the next section, this is the button you'll want to select.

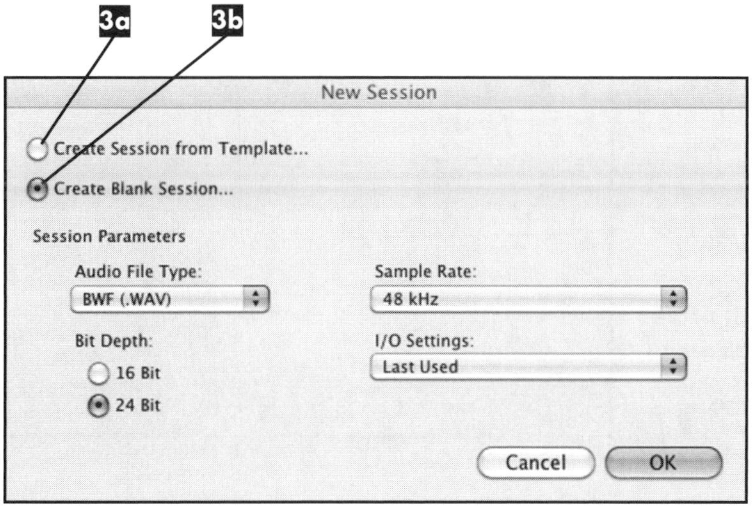

Choosing Session Parameters

Whether you're creating a new session from the Quick Start dialog box or from the File menu, your next task is to choose your session parameters.

1 **Click** on the **Audio File Type** arrows. A menu will appear. **Choose** a **file type** from the following options:

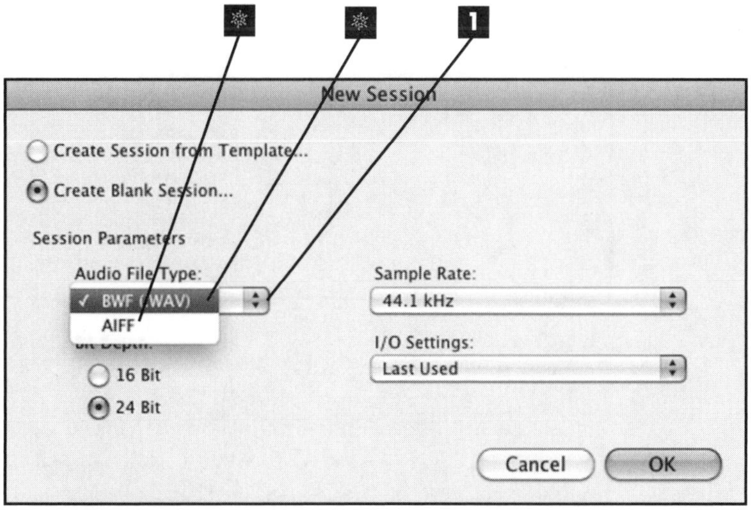

- **BWF (.WAV).** A WAV file is a Windows standard file, and the Broadcast Wave Format (BWF) is a version of this file type that is particularly suited to television and film production. (The file extension is still .wav.) This is a good format choice for session files that will be used in both Mac and Windows systems.
- **AIFF.** This was originally the standard file format for Mac computers.

CHOOSING A FILE FORMAT

Pro Tools' default file format is BWF (.WAV). This generally works well in most situations. If you are planning to share files between Mac and Windows systems, this is the preferred file format. There is no difference in audio quality between BWF (.WAV) and AIFF.

2 **Click** on the **Sample Rate** arrows. A menu will appear, showing the sample rates supported by your audio interface.

3 **Select** a **sample rate** for your session.

4 **Select** either **16 Bit or 24 Bit audio** as the bit depth for your session.

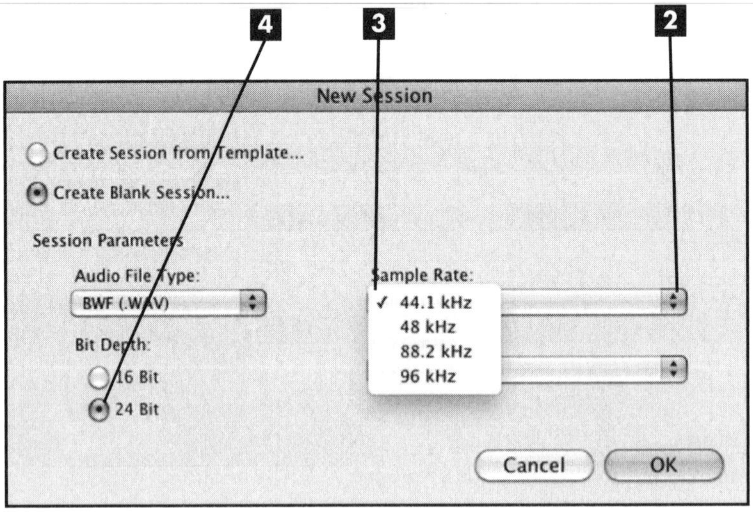

5 **Click** on the **I/O Settings** arrows. The I/O Settings menu will appear.

6 **Select** your **I/O (Input/Output) settings** for this session. For now, **choose Stereo Mix**. The option will be selected.

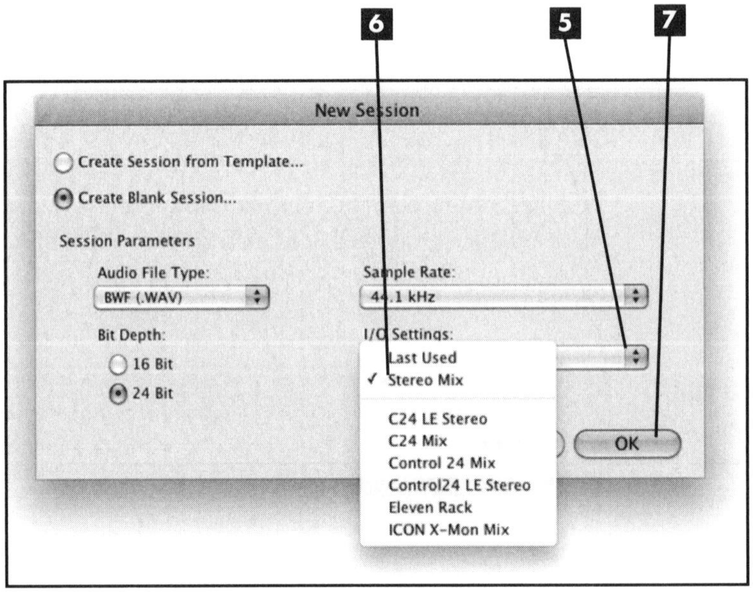

WHERE CAN I LEARN MORE ABOUT I/O SETTINGS?

Your I/O settings determine the assignments and names of inputs, outputs, inserts, and buses. Don't worry if this doesn't make a lot of sense now; you'll learn more about how to make the most of your I/O settings in Chapter 3, "Getting Started with Audio."

7 You've made some very important choices. The next step is to choose a name and location for your session. **Click OK** to proceed.

Choosing the Name and Place

Two of the most important skills you can learn as a DAW user are file management and documentation. Although these are fairly simple and straightforward tasks, you shouldn't underestimate their importance. The last thing you want is to misplace a session and waste valuable time trying to find it—or worse, inadvertently delete a session because it was in the wrong place!

1 At the end of the previous section, you opened the Save dialog box. The next thing you have to do is to choose the name of your session. **Type** the **name** in the Save As text box in the Save dialog box.

2 **Navigate** to the desired **drive**. If you have a hard drive devoted to digital audio, choose that drive.

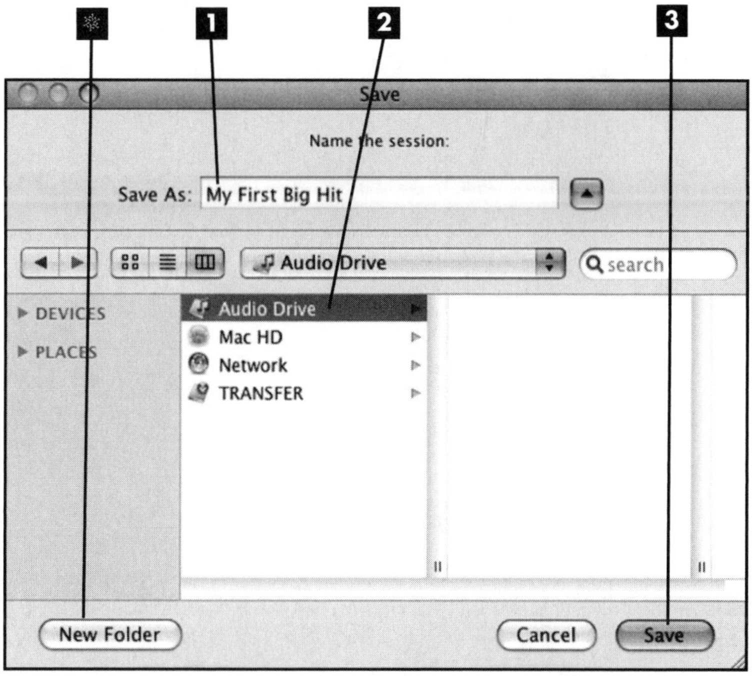

WHERE TO CREATE YOUR SESSION

According to the previous image, this new session will be created on my audio hard drive.

- In some cases, you might want to create a new folder in which to put your session folder (for example, when grouping sessions of a similar genre or artist). If you do, create a new folder according to the normal conventions of your operating system. Remember, Pro Tools will automatically create a session folder, as well!

3 Once you've set your name and location, **click** the **Save button**. Your session will be created and loaded into Pro Tools. Good job!

Playing a Session

Let's assume you have Pro Tools running and you've opened up a pre-existing session (for example, the Chapter 1 session you opened earlier). Wondering how to play it? No problem—it's easy!

You'll find a transport section in the top area of the Edit window (which you'll learn more about in the next chapters). It will help you with basic play and record operations. It looks very much like the controls you would find on almost any media player. Let's take a look at the basic functions:

HOW TO GET TO THE EDIT WINDOW AND TRANSPORT CONTROLS

If you're not seeing any transport-style controls at the top of your Pro Tools window, you've probably opened your session into the other main window (called the Mix window, which looks very much like a mixing console). Getting to the Edit window is very easy: Just open the Window menu at the top of the Pro Tools window and choose Edit.

If you are in the Edit window and you are still not seeing any transport controls, click the small triangular button in the upper-right corner of the Edit window and choose Transport from the list that appears. (This is a section of the Edit window that we'll go into in greater detail in Chapter 2, "Getting Around in Pro Tools.")

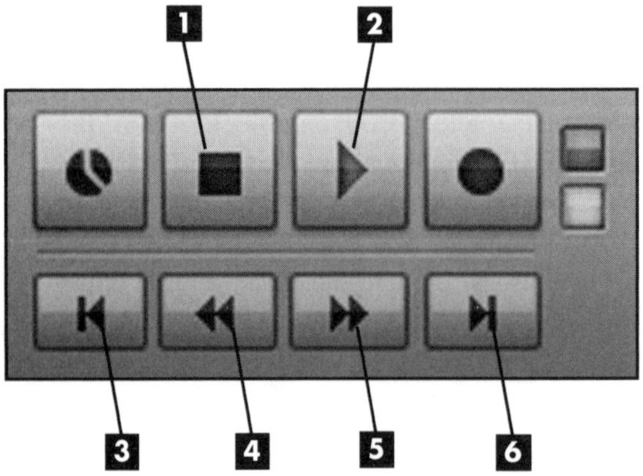

1 The Stop button—you guessed it—stops playback.

2 The Play button plays back your session from the current position.

3 The Return to Zero button takes you directly to the beginning of your session.

4 Rewind quickly moves your playback point earlier in your session.

5 Fast Forward quickly moves your playback point later in your session.

6 The Go to End button takes you directly to the end of your session.

Saving Your Work

Now that you have the basics down, it's time to think about how to wind things up. This is a crucial stage, and it's important to do the job correctly. There are a number of ways to save your work, each with its own specific advantages.

Save

This is a pretty standard feature and as straightforward as they come:

■ **Click** on **File**. The File menu will appear.

2 **Click** on **Save**. Your work will be saved, and you can continue to work on the saved session.

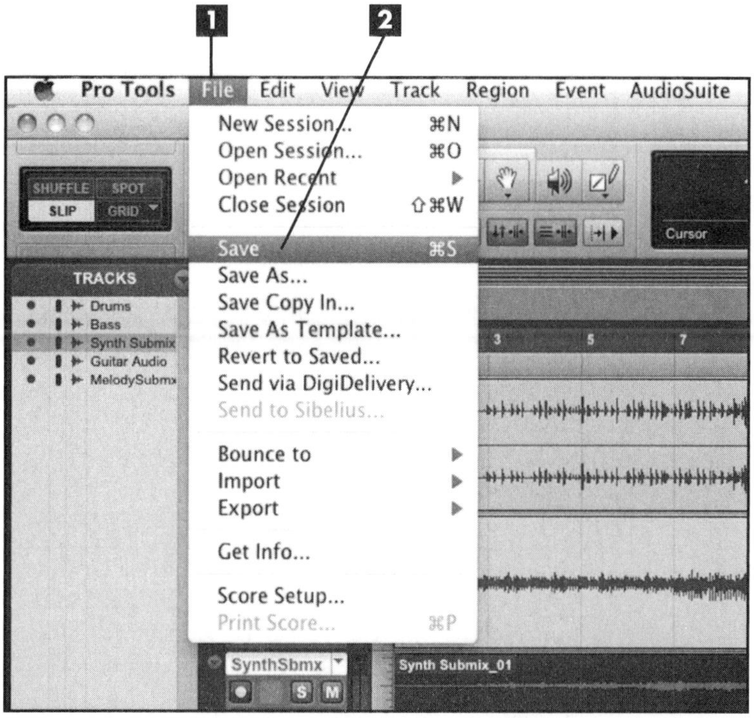

Save As

If you use the Save command, the previous version of the session will be overwritten with the current one. What if you don't want to overwrite the old session? That's where Save As comes into play.

■ **Click** on **File**. The File menu will appear.

2 **Click** on **Save As**. The Save Session As dialog box will open.

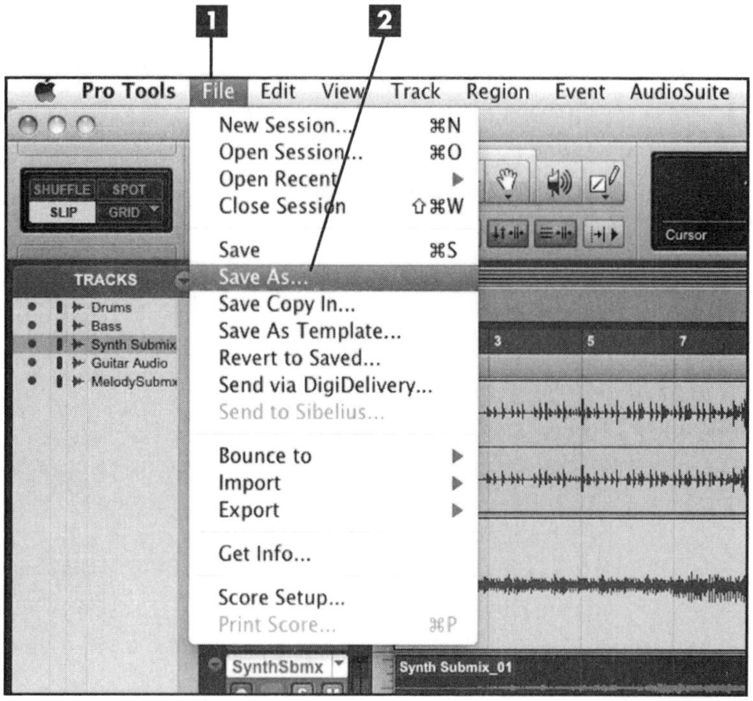

3 **Type** a **different name** for your session in the Save As text box to avoid overwriting the original session.

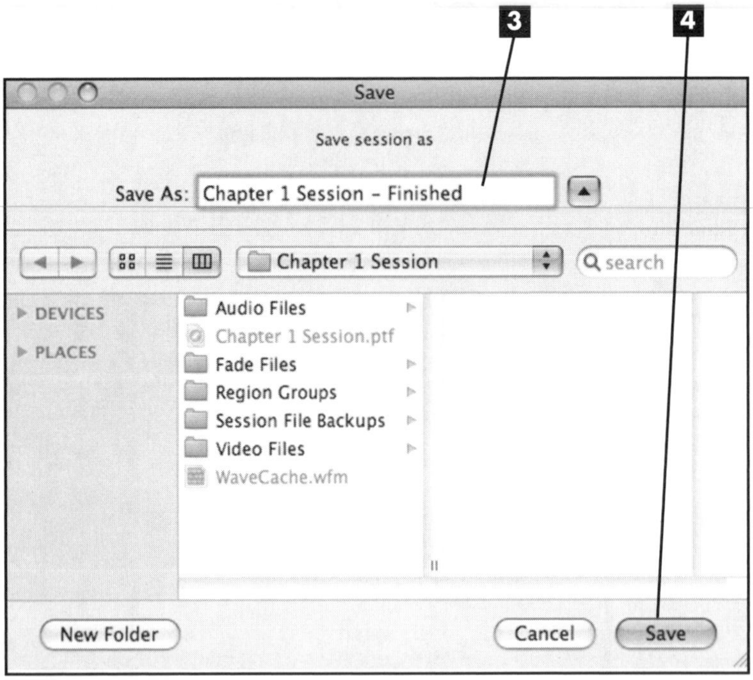

WHERE DO I SAVE THE NEW SESSION FILE?

It's important to note that both the original session file and the new version of the file can reside in the same session folder and can access the same source audio files. You just need to make sure they don't have the same name; otherwise, the old one will be overwritten by the new one.

4 **Click** on **Save**. The new version of the session will be saved with the name you specified in step 3. You are all set at this point to continue work on the newly saved session.

Save Copy In

If you want to save your session with a different name *and* create a new folder, complete with all the dependent audio files, the Save Copy In feature is for you! This is commonly a part of the final archiving process when a project is complete (which you'll learn more about later).

THE IMPORTANCE OF BACKING UP YOUR WORK!

Backing up (or *archiving*) your work is a tremendously important part of production. It might not be terribly exciting, but you'll be glad you established good file-saving habits when something unexpected happens. The Save Copy In feature is particularly suited to archiving because it makes copies of your original session in a separate (and hopefully safe) place. Additionally, this process can intelligently gather all the elements your session needs (assuming you selected them in the Items to Copy section) and save them in one central location. Bottom line: When you're backing up your session, Save Copy In is a very smart way to go!

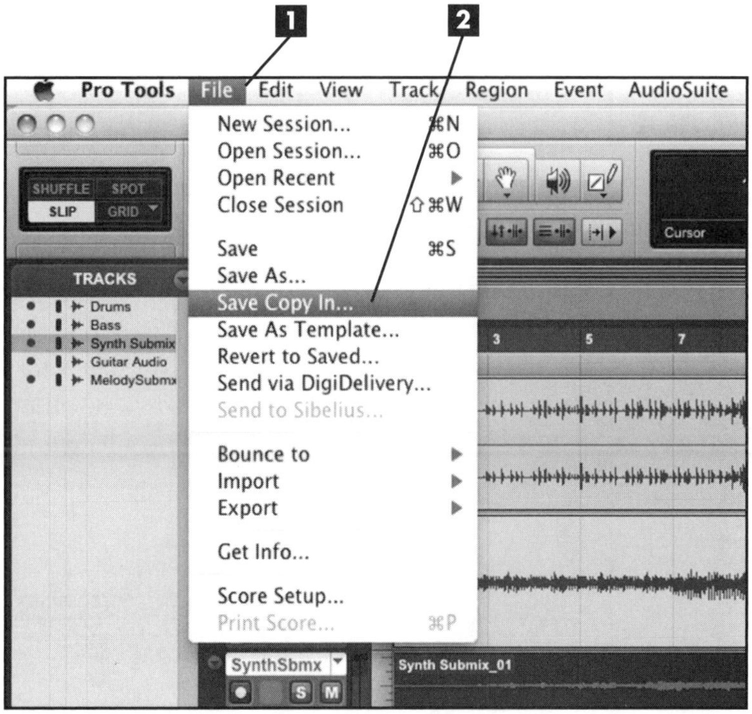

1 **Click** on **File**. The File menu will appear.

2 **Click** on **Save Copy In**. The Save Session Copy dialog box will open. Save Copy In enables you to save elements of your session (audio files, fade files, and so on), which gives you a whole new dimension of flexibility. Here are some things you can specify:

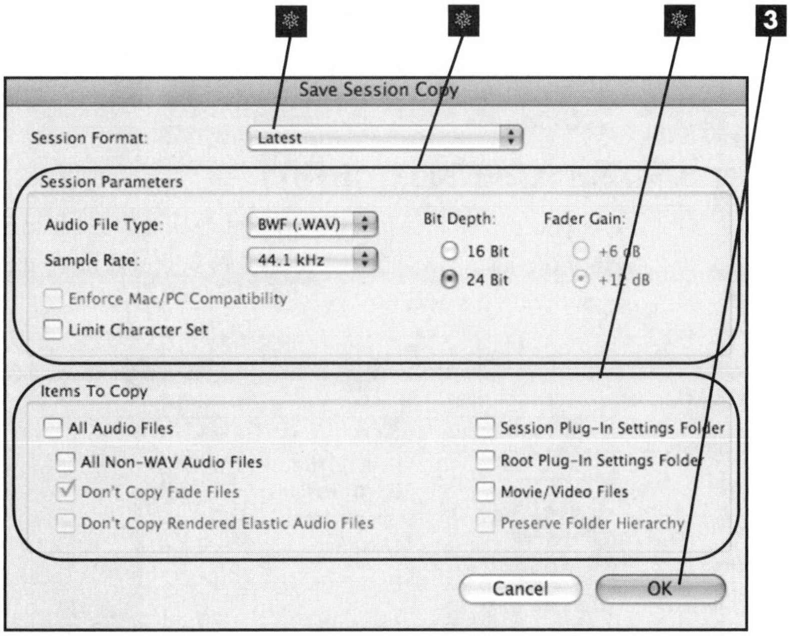

- **Session Format menu.** This menu contains options for previous versions of Pro Tools. Select one of these formats if you intend to open this session in an older version of Pro Tools.
- **Session Parameters section.** These are the same options you saw when you created your session. You can select different file types, sample rates, and/or bit depths for your session. Pro Tools will automatically convert audio files as needed in your new session's Audio Files folder.
- **Items to Copy section.** You can choose the elements of your original session that you want to copy over to your new session folder. Click the appropriate boxes to copy aspects of your old session to your new session folder.

3 When you've made the appropriate selections, **click OK**. The Save dialog box will appear.

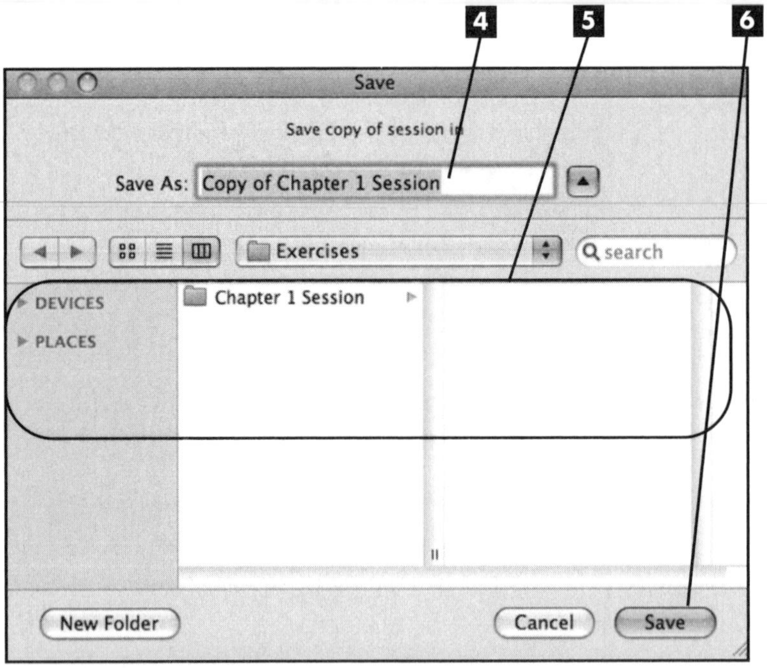

4 In the Save As text box, **type** a descriptive **session name** that is different from the original session name.

5 **Select** a **location** for your session. This section is identical to the related sections in the dialog boxes when you choose Save or Save As. This time, a new folder will be created for your new session, though.

6 **Click** the **Save** button.

PRESERVE FOLDER HIERARCHY

Sometimes, particularly in sessions with higher track counts, you'll want to record audio to multiple hard drives at once (something we'll discuss in Chapter 4, "Recording Audio," and in Chapter 10, "Moving to the Next Level: Tips and Tricks"). For now, leave the Preserve Folder Hierarchy checkbox unchecked.

Session Templates

As you saw in the Quick Start dialog box, you already have a list of useful templates that are installed with Pro Tools, but you also have the ability to create templates of your own. It's easy!

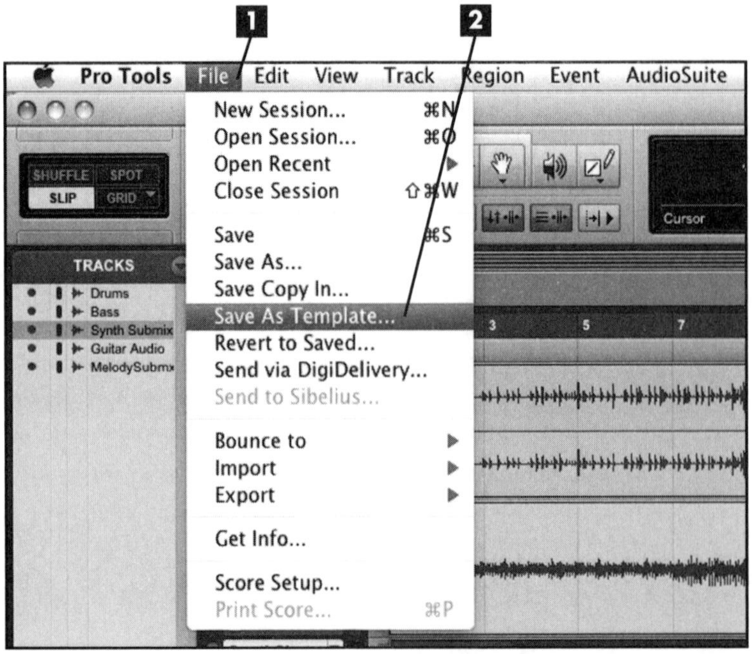

1 **Click** on **File**. The File menu will appear.

2 **Click** on **Save As Template**. The Save Session Template dialog box will open.

You have two options as far as location is concerned:

- Choose the Install Template in System option button to automatically create your template in the default system location. This will enable you to easily access the template from the Quick Start dialog box in the future.

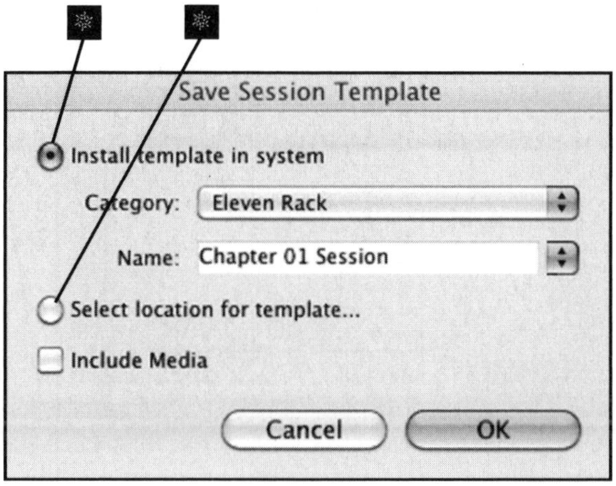

- Choose the Select Location for Template option button to be able to choose any name and location for your template file once you click the OK button. This is particularly handy for Pro Tools users who work in multiple studios. (An inexpensive USB drive can hold many session templates, and you can carry it with you easily.)

Let's assume that you want to create this template on your system, and that you've chosen the Install Template in System option button. Let's take a look at the different options you'll get:

1. **Click** the **Category** arrows. A list of category options will appear.

* The top section of the list shows you pre-existing categories, into which you can place your template. Just click the desired category to choose it.

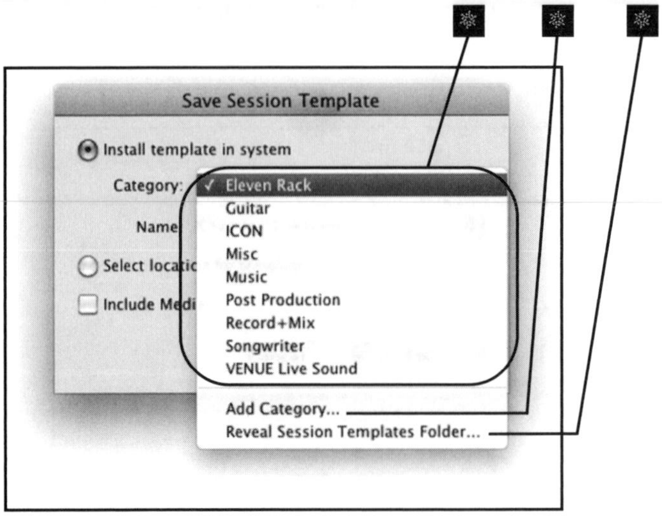

* The Add Category menu item enables you to create a new category and add it to the list shown in the top section. Click this option, and you will be prompted to name your new category.
* The Reveal Session Templates Folder menu item will open the template folder using your computer's file browser (Finder or Windows Explorer, depending on your platform). This is useful for managing your template files (renaming, deleting, and so on). It's worth mentioning at this point that Pro Tools template files are not session files themselves, and they have a .ptt file extension.

2 After you've chosen the appropriate category, **type** a **name** for your template in the Name text box. (Clicking the arrows button will display a list of all the templates currently in that category.)

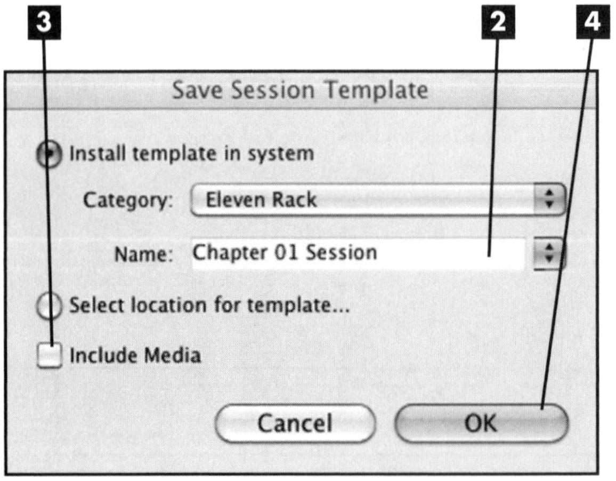

3 In many cases, you won't want your template to include any audio or video files. But if you do, **select** the **Include Media** checkbox.

4 When you're finished, **click** on **OK** to create your template.

Closing Your Session

The last basic procedure you have to complete is to close down your session.

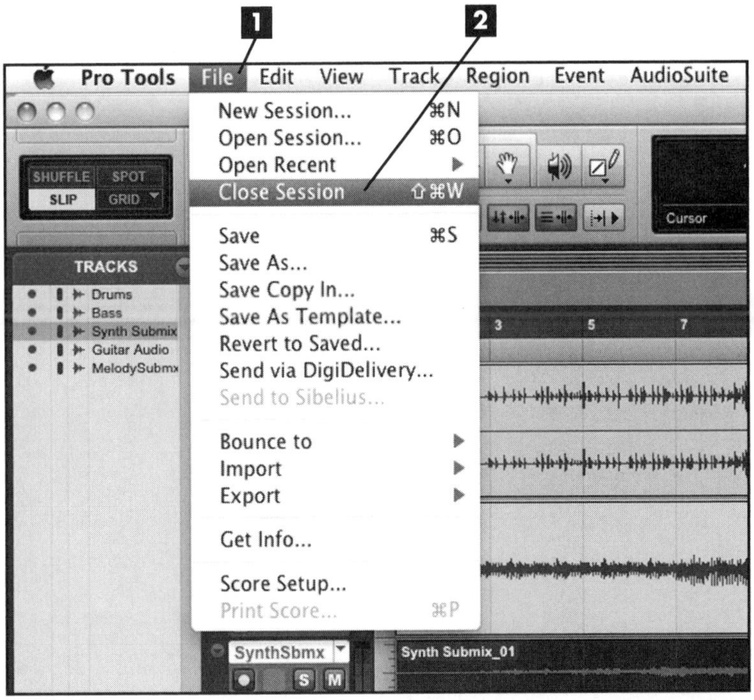

1 **Click** on **File**. The File menu will appear.

2 **Click** on **Close Session**. Pro Tools will shut down the current session and make itself ready for the next step.

> **DO YOU WANT TO SAVE YOUR CHANGES?**
>
> Before your session closes completely, a message box might prompt you to save your changes. This message box appears when you make any changes to your session and then try to quit Pro Tools before saving those changes. You can choose Save or Don't Save and move on.

Quitting Pro Tools

Actually quitting Pro Tools varies slightly depending upon the operating system you use. For Mac users, quitting Pro Tools is just like quitting any other application. Simply do the following:

1 **Click** on the **Pro Tools** menu.

2 **Select Quit Pro Tools.**

If you're using Pro Tools on a PC, closing the software is exactly the same as the process in virtually every other program you've used in Windows. Simply do the following:

1 **Click** on the **File** menu.

2 **Select Exit.**

That's it—good job!

2 Getting Around in Pro Tools

In Chapter 1, "Welcome to Pro Tools 9," you took some time to properly install and set up your Pro Tools system. You went the extra mile and learned how Pro Tools "thinks" about sessions and files. You even got to the point of creating, opening, and playing session files. Now let's go to the next level of using Pro Tools and get better acquainted with the layout of the Pro Tools environment.

Think of this chapter as a brief primer in the Pro Tools way of getting the job done. Based on the general architecture we'll discuss in this chapter, you'll be able to efficiently navigate the operations and features we'll go through later.

Some more experienced computer-based producers will immediately see similarities between Pro Tools 9 and other well-designed DAWs. If you're one such person, it will still be a good use of your time to learn the proper names and layouts of these new workspaces. There are a number of windows in Pro Tools, many with specific functions, and trust me: Getting acquainted with the most common ones will really pay off later.

In this chapter, you'll learn how to do the following:

- Recognize the main sections of the Edit window and how to customize them.
- Recognize the basic layout and functions of the Mix window.
- Access other useful windows, such as the Big Counter and System Usage windows.
- Make the most of your tracks and regions.

The Edit, Mix, and Transport Windows

When you open a session, Pro Tools displays the windows that were visible the last time you saved that session. In most cases, that will include one of Pro Tools' two main windows: the Edit window or the Mix window. It's important to know what these two windows do and how to navigate within them.

There's one more window that's crucial for all kinds of Pro Tools operation: the Transport window. (You used a smaller version of that window when you played a session in Chapter 1, "Welcome to Pro Tools 9.") Let's take a quick look at the general layout of these important windows.

> **A QUICK WAY TO CHANGE WINDOWS**
>
> You'll switch between the Edit and Mix windows often, so knowing how to do so as quickly as possible can be very useful. The shortcut to toggle between the Mix and Edit windows is Command+= (Mac) or Ctrl+= (PC).

Working with the Edit Window

If there's a primary window in Pro Tools, it's the Edit window. This environment is packed with useful tools and information about your Pro Tools session—so much so that it can be a little daunting at first! If you break it down into the basics, though, you'll find it easy to understand and use.

The Playlist Area

> **USING THE TUTORIAL SESSION**
>
> To follow along, just open the session named Chapter 2 Session, which is included on your book's disc. (Remember, you'll have to copy the session files to your computer's hard drive first.)

When you begin a new session from scratch, there will be an empty area in the middle of your Edit window. Any kind of track you create will appear in this area as a horizontal row. Here, for example, there are already four stereo Audio tracks and one stereo Instrument track (the Lead Line track). As discussed in Chapter 1, the colored blocks are called regions.

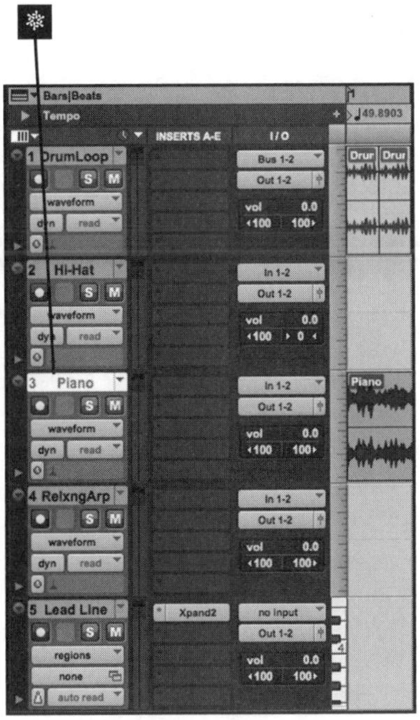

For each track, there is a specific track name (located in the upper-left corner of each track strip). You can select a track by clicking the track name button. Selected tracks are indicated with a highlighted name. (Here, the Piano track is selected.) Each track row shows a lot of information besides regions and track names, which we'll get into in Chapter 3, "Getting Started with Audio."

The Tracks and Edit Groups Column

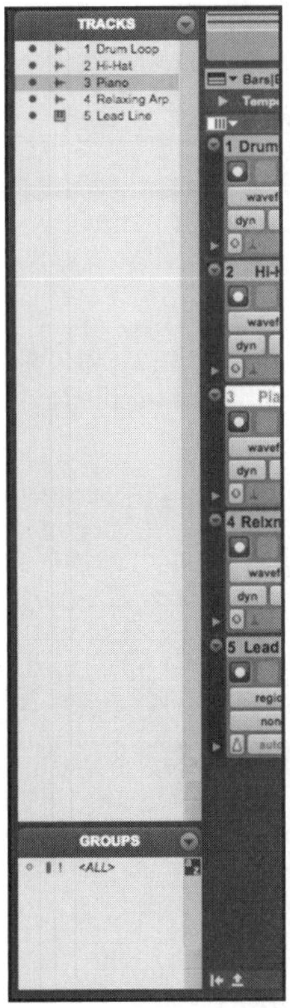

Immediately to the left of the tracks, you'll notice a column including the Tracks list and the Groups list. Let's take a look at the Tracks list first:

* You'll find the Tracks List button in the upper-right corner of the Tracks list. Think of this as a sort of command center for showing and hiding tracks. You have options to show or hide all tracks, only selected tracks, or track types. (For example, with the Show Only submenu, you can show only Audio tracks.) There is another submenu for sorting tracks (shown here), which enables you to arrange your tracks in a variety of ways.

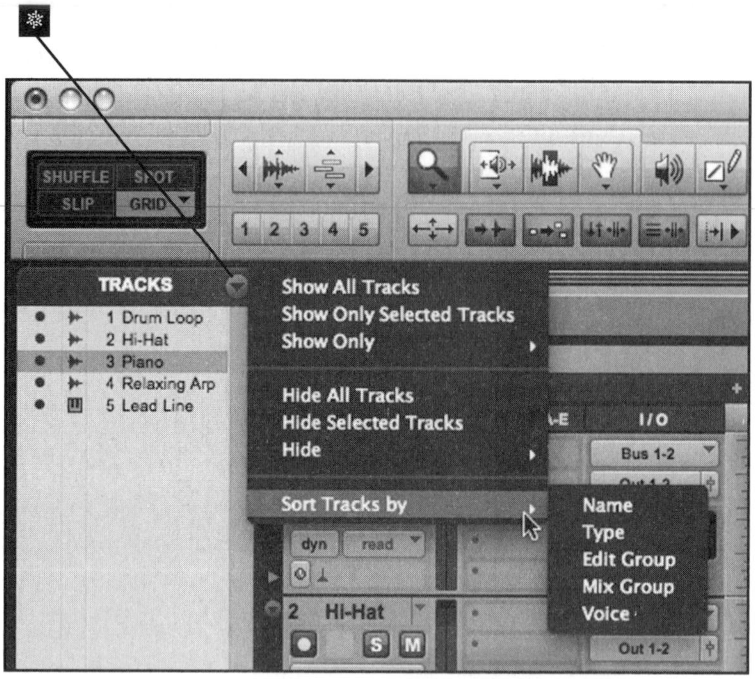

All the tracks in your session, whether visible or hidden, appear in the Tracks list. This list gives you important information about your session:

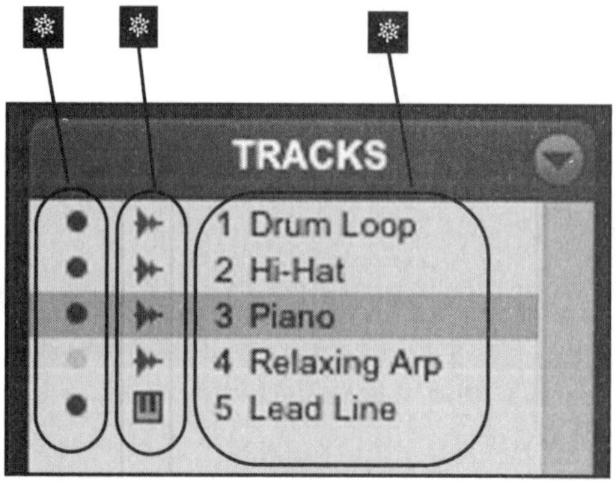

* The left column indicates which tracks are shown and which are hidden. Shown tracks are marked with a dark dot, and hidden tracks are indicated with a light-gray dot. (In this example, all the tracks are shown *except* the Relaxing Arp track.) This column not only gives you information, but control as well; just click any track's dot (technically called the Track Show/Hide icon) to change its state.
* Moving to the right, you'll see a column of icons indicating track type. (We'll go into track types in the next chapter.) In this case, the first four tracks are Audio tracks, and the bottom track is an Instrument track.
* Of course, you want to be able to see the track names, and you'll find them in the right column.

WILL HIDDEN TRACKS BE HEARD?

All active and unmuted tracks, whether they are shown or hidden, will sound during playback. The ability to hide or show tracks is simply to help you manage your editing and mixing desktop. It's a feature for which you'll be extremely grateful when your tracks start adding up!

TRACK COLOR COLUMN

In some cases, you may see a fourth column between the Show/Hide column and the Track Type column, indicating track color. We'll talk about track colors and how to use them later in this chapter.

Just below the Tracks list is the Groups list. An *edit group* is a selection of tracks that can be edited as one. (You'll learn more about edit groups in Chapter 6, "..And More Editing!") The layout of this list is similar to the Tracks list:

You'll find the Groups button in the upper-right corner of the Groups list. As with the Tracks List button, you'll see a list of group-related functions when you click on the Groups button.

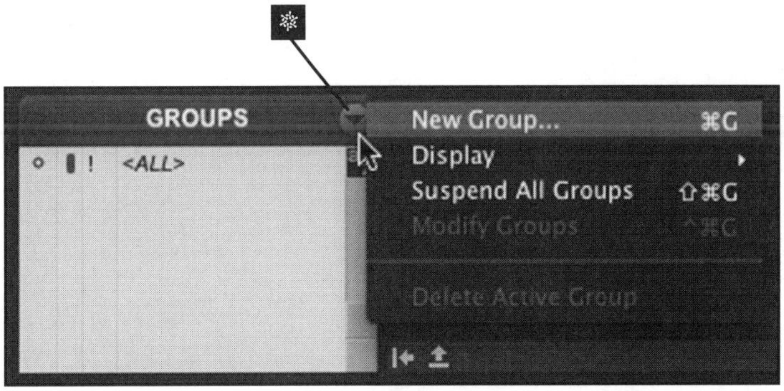

As you create edit groups, they'll show up in the Groups list. (Active groups are highlighted.) Here again, this list is divided into columns:

The left-most column indicates the tracks that are selected within the group. A circle (shown here) indicates that some members of that group are selected, but not all. A dot will tell you that all the members of that track are selected. A bull's-eye icon signifies that all the members of that group are selected, *plus* other tracks.

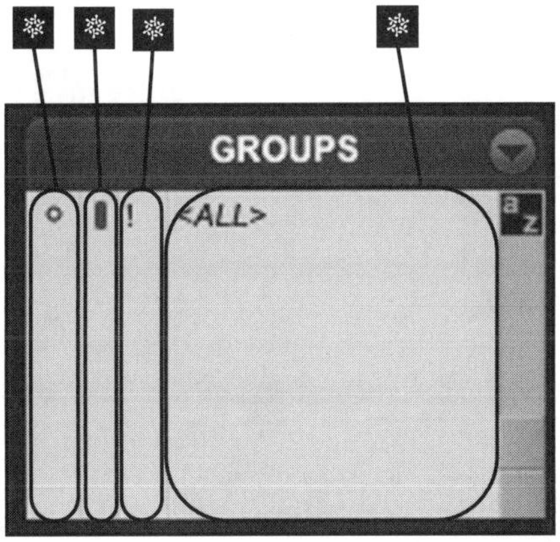

- The next column shows the group's color assignment. When a group is active, it is indicated in your Mix window, using this color.
- Immediately to the left of the group name is a column that will show the group's letter. Every group you create will have a letter assigned to it. (The All group shown here is special and is indicated by an exclamation mark.)
- Your group name should descriptively reflect the function of the member tracks in your session.

THE EVER-PRESENT ALL GROUP

When you create a new session, you'll notice that there's already a group shown in this list, even though you didn't create it. This group is named All, and includes all tracks in your session.

The Regions List

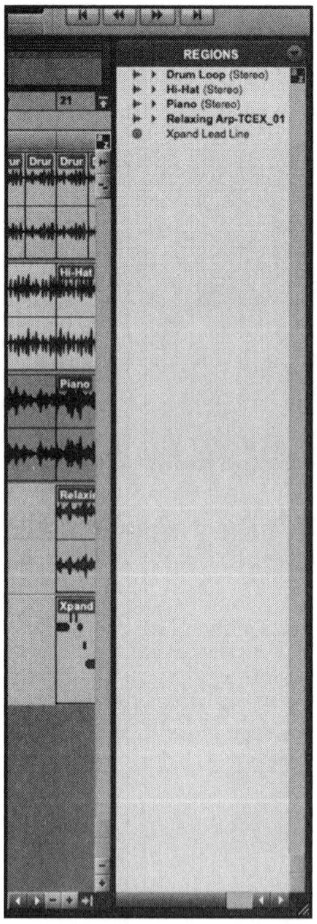

To the right of the tracks , you'll find another vertical column. This is the Regions list—a storage area for regions that are (or could be) used in your session.

Regions List button. At the top of the Regions list, you'll find the Regions List button. Clicking this button displays a drop-down menu of region-related functions.

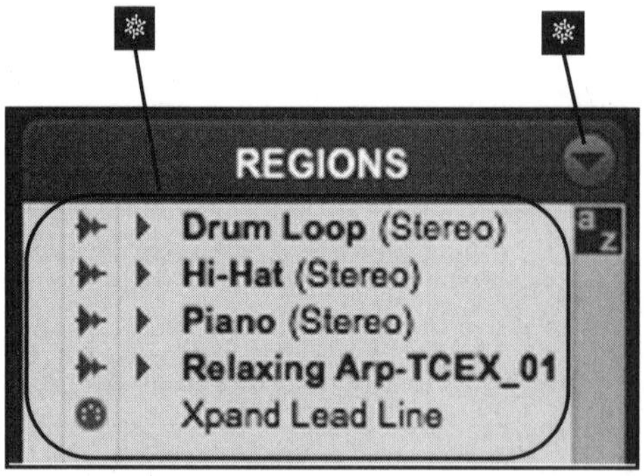

Regions list. This is a complete collection of all the regions (audio and MIDI) available in your session, regardless of whether they're being used actively in a track. From here, you can drag and drop regions onto the appropriate tracks. This list is broken down into columns, which can vary depending on the options you choose in the Regions List menu. (Click the Regions List button, open the Show submenu, and you'll see a number of different aspects that you can choose to show or hide.)

> **WHAT'S MIDI?**
>
> You might notice that I've been mentioning a thing called MIDI (*Musical Instrument Digital Interface*) from time to time. We'll go into MIDI and how to use it in Pro Tools in Chapter 7, "Using MIDI."

Rulers

The Ruler area enables you to view the passage of time in your session in a number of different ways. Different scales, such as minutes and seconds or bars and beats, can be useful to you depending on the kind of work you are doing in Pro Tools. Any combination of the following rulers can be shown:

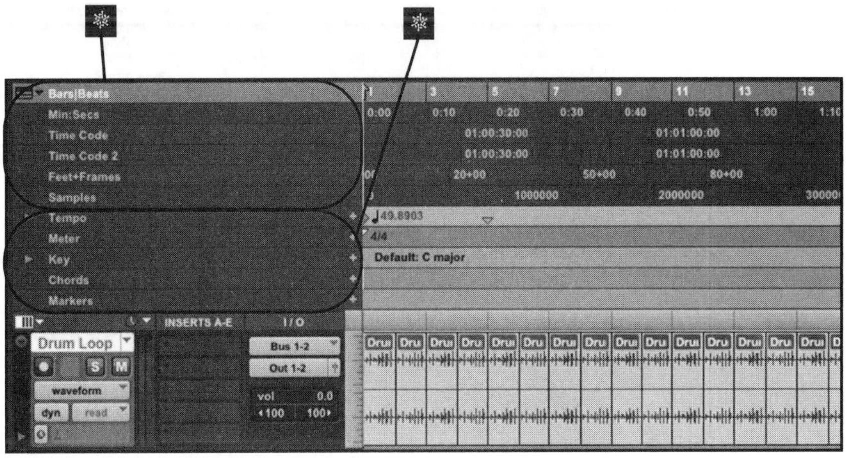

- Timeline rulers (Bars|Beats, Min:Secs, Time Code, Time Code 2, Feet+Frames, and Samples)
- Conductor rulers (Tempo, Meter, Key, Chords, and Markers)

You can display the timeline in many time scales simultaneously, with each visible ruler's format displayed to the left of the timeline.

Edit Tools

You can display a number of tools in the top row of the Edit window. What tools you see and their placement in this area is up to you to decide (and you'll do just that later in this chapter), but here are some basic tool clusters:

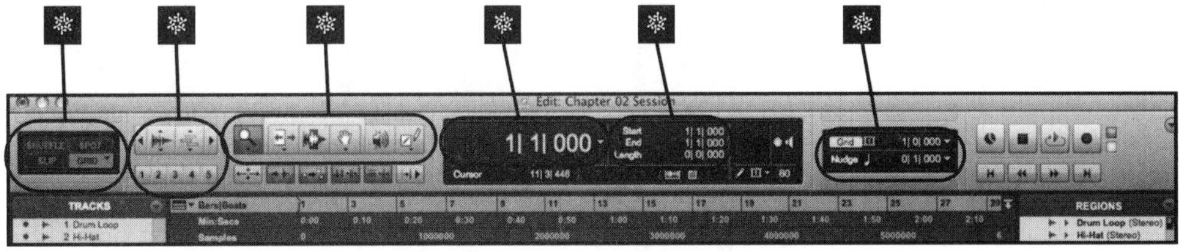

- Edit modes
- Zoom tools
- Basic Edit tools
- Grid and Nudge settings

In addition to these tool clusters, the location and selection displays give you location information.

- The time scale tells you exactly where you are in your session.
- The Edit selection area tells you the beginning, end, and duration of your selection. (The format for this section is based on the format you've chosen for the time scale.)

The Universe View

As you gain experience with Pro Tools, you'll find that one of the most time-consuming parts of production is navigating within your session. The Edit window's Universe view can make that process much quicker and easier. Take a look:

1. **Click** the **Edit Window button**. A list of display options will appear. Options that are currently shown will be indicated with a check-mark.
2. If it's not already selected, **Click** on **Universe**.

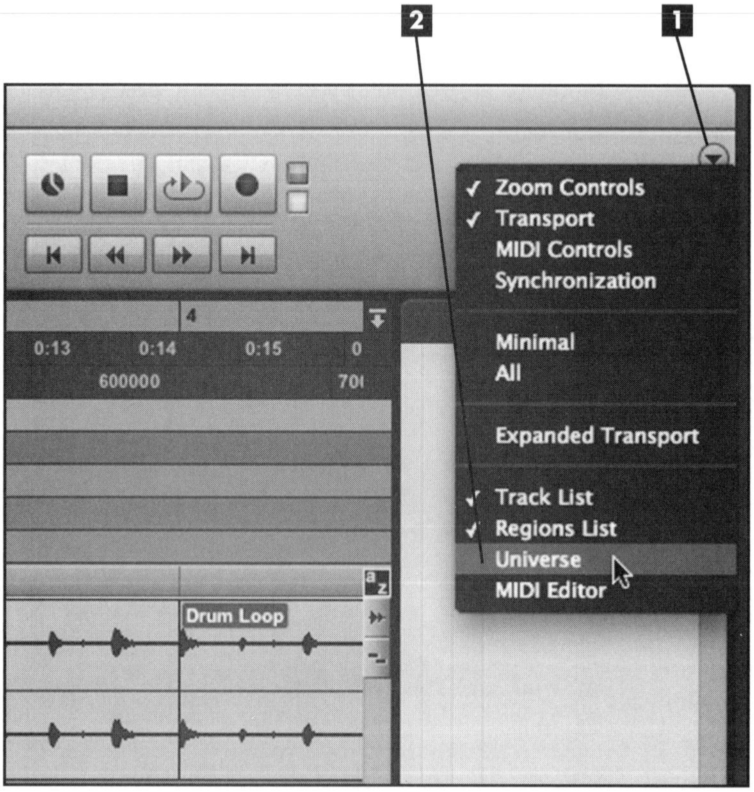

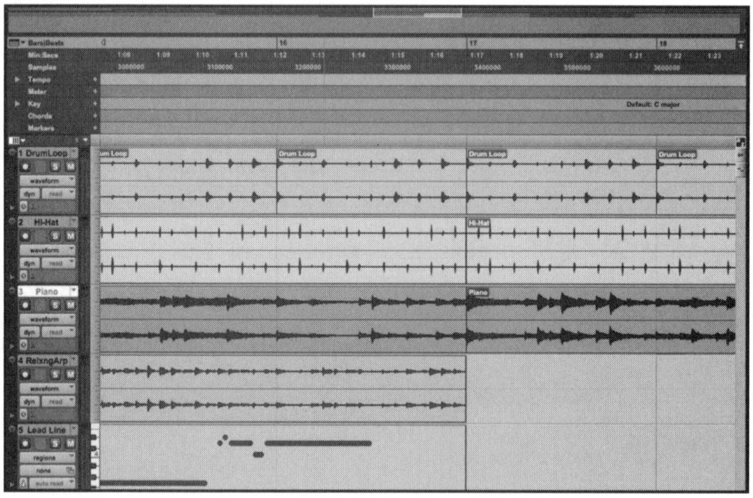

The Universe view will appear just above the ruler(s) and will show your session in its entirety. Let's take a closer look:

Regions in your sessions (audio or MIDI) will be represented as colored horizontal lines. Their color will reflect the color of the corresponding regions in your session.

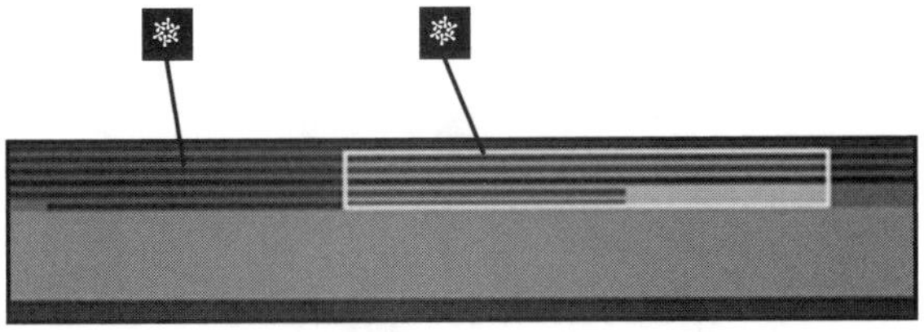

The Universe view is divided into a dark area and a light area, with the light area representing what you're actually seeing in your Edit window. Here's where it really gets interesting: Just click within this light area and drag it to the desired position in your session. You'll immediately see your Edit window update to reflect the movement of this light-colored area.

Customizing the Edit Window

Now that you've identified the overall layout of the Edit window, the following sections will describe a few ways to set up the window to make working easier.

Adjusting List Size

If your session calls for more groups than the Groups list can show at one time, you might want to give a little more space to the Groups list on your desktop. Here's how:

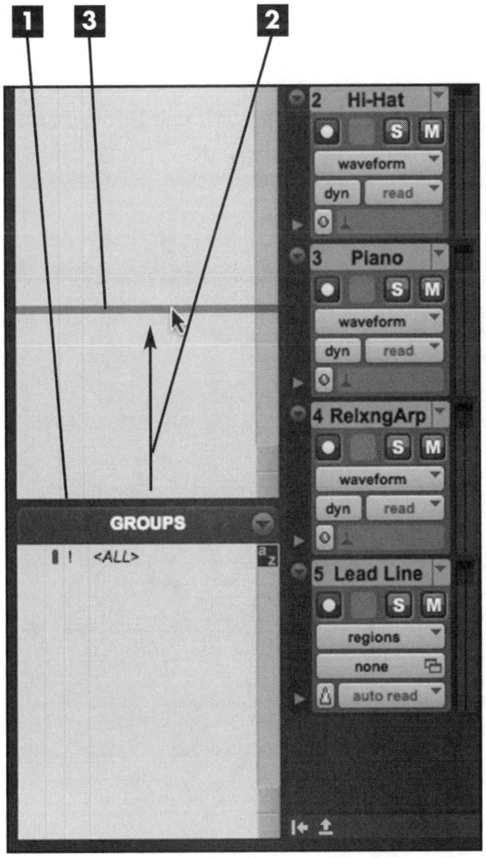

1. **Move** your **cursor** to the boundary between the Tracks list and the Groups list.
2. **Click and drag** the **boundary** up or down as needed. As you drag, you'll see a light-gray line marking the movement of the boundary.
3. **Release** the **mouse button**. The boundary will be "dropped," and the lists will be reorganized.

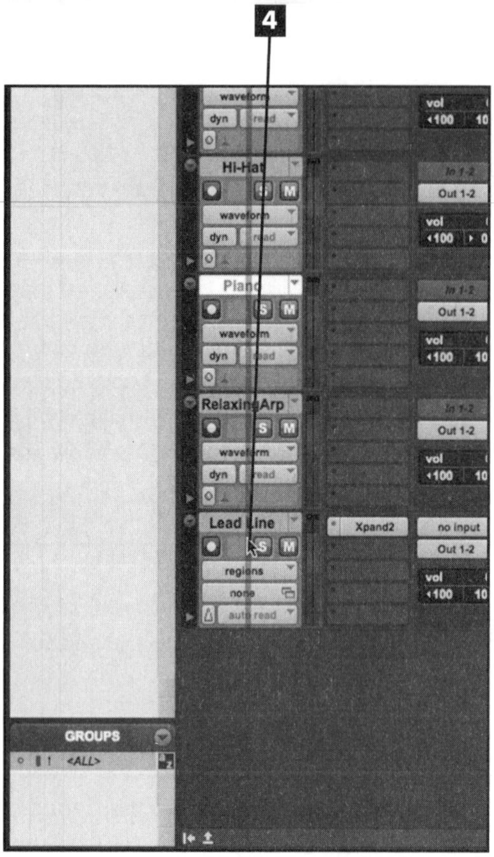

4 You can similarly **adjust** any of the **horizontal or vertical boundaries** for the Tracks list, Groups list, and Regions list. Be careful, though—adjusting the vertical edges of these areas can affect how much space you have on your screen for tracks.

Hiding Lists

In addition to adjusting the sizes of these lists, you can hide them entirely when you're not using them. Follow these steps:

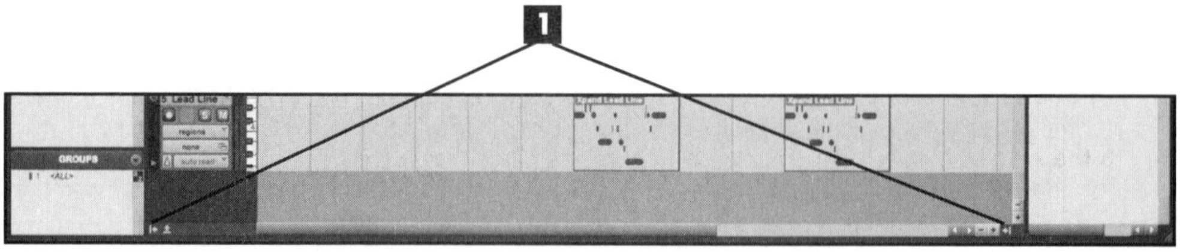

1 **Click** on the **arrow** at the bottom corner of either vertical section. Pro Tools immediately hides the appropriate column, making more of your Edit window available for your tracks.

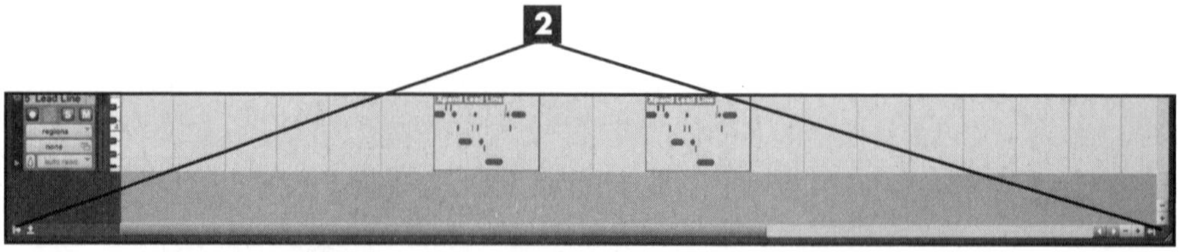

2 Not seeing your lists? That means they're currently hidden. **Click** on the **arrow** in either lower corner of the Edit window. The corresponding column immediately reappears.

WHAT WILL I SEE WHEN I OPEN A SESSION?

Remember, the window arrangements that appear when you open a session will be the same as they were in the session when you last saved it. It might be a bit surprising to open a session and see no Tracks or Regions list in your Edit window. Don't worry, though—you can always follow the previously mentioned steps to display the lists.

Displaying Track Columns

At the left of each track are one or more columns that provide track-specific information on such things as inputs, outputs, inserts, sends, comments, and more. We'll go into each of these in due course. For now, here's how to show or hide the columns you want:

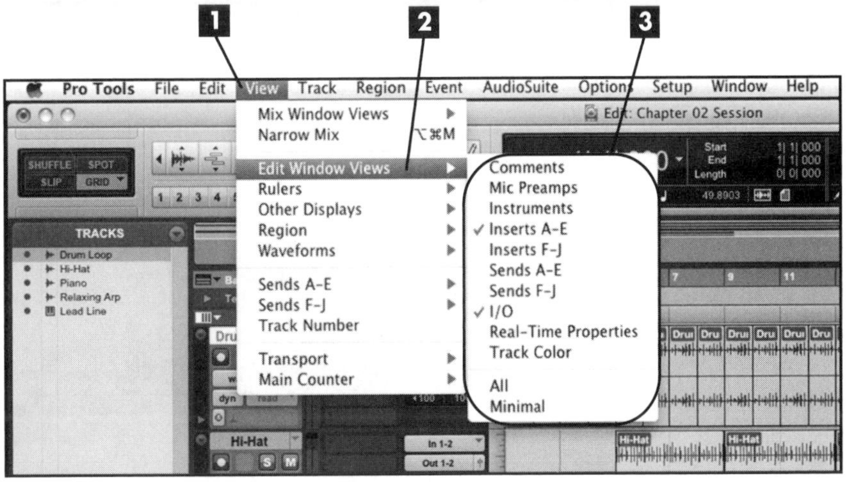

1. **Click** on **View**. The View menu will appear.
2. **Click** on **Edit Window Views**. A submenu containing the columns that can be shown will appear. Checked columns are currently displayed.
3. **Click** on any **menu item** to check or uncheck it; the appropriate column will be displayed or hidden.

Here's another way to get to the same list. Click the Edit Window View Selector icon, which you'll see just above the top track in your session and below the rulers section. Here again, you'll see a menu of viewable columns, with visible columns indicated with a checkmark.

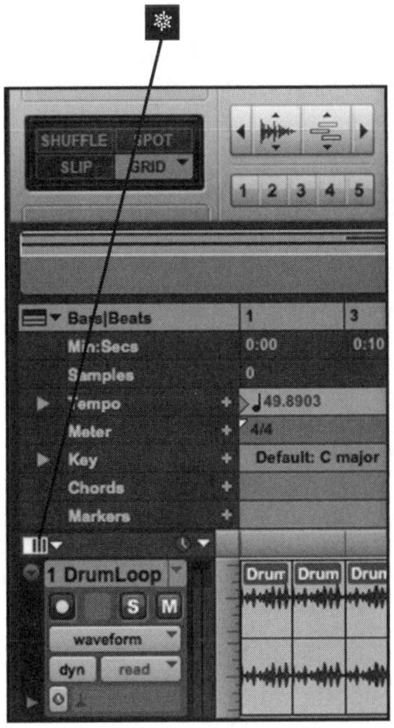

> **TOTALLY EXTREME VIEWING, DUDE!**
>
> In addition to selecting columns individually, you can select All or Minimal to show or hide all columns.

Displaying Rulers

You can also choose which rulers are to be shown. Here's how:

1. **Click** on **View**. The View menu will appear.
2. **Click** on **Rulers**. A list of available rulers will appear. (A checkmark by a ruler indicates that the ruler is being shown.)
3. **Click** any **ruler** to change its state (shown versus hidden).

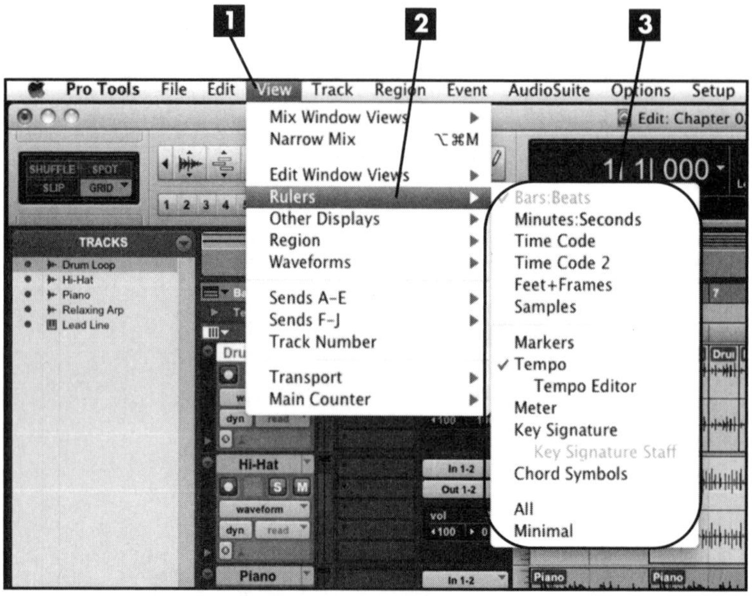

There's another way to get to the same list. Click the Ruler View selector to show the Ruler View menu. You'll find this button to the left of the highlighted ruler.

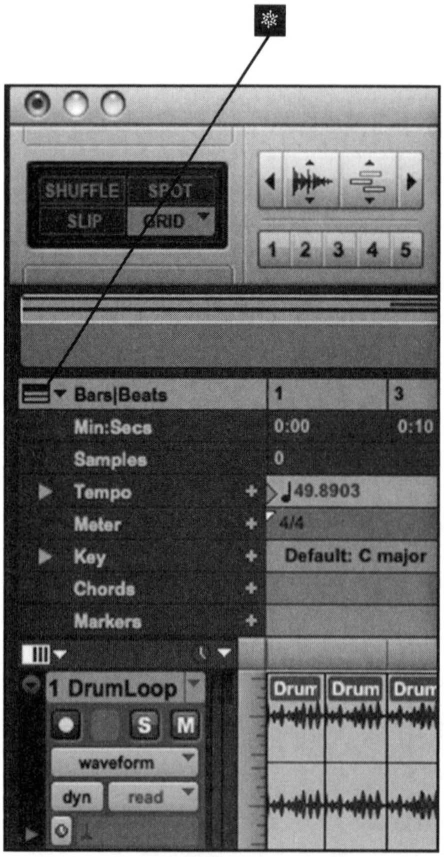

Adjusting Track Heights

In Pro Tools, you can change the height of individual tracks. This can come in handy, particularly when you have many tracks in your session and you want to see them all or conversely when you really want to do some microsurgery on one track in particular. Here's how:

1. To the right of each track's columns (I/O, Inserts, Sends, Comments, etc.) is a small vertical area (in this case, showing the amplitude scale). **Right-click** in this **area**. The Track Height drop-down menu will appear.

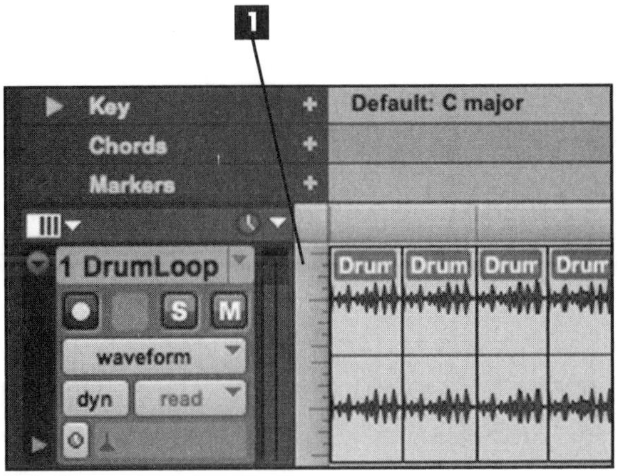

2. **Select** the desired **track height**. The track will immediately change to match your height choice.

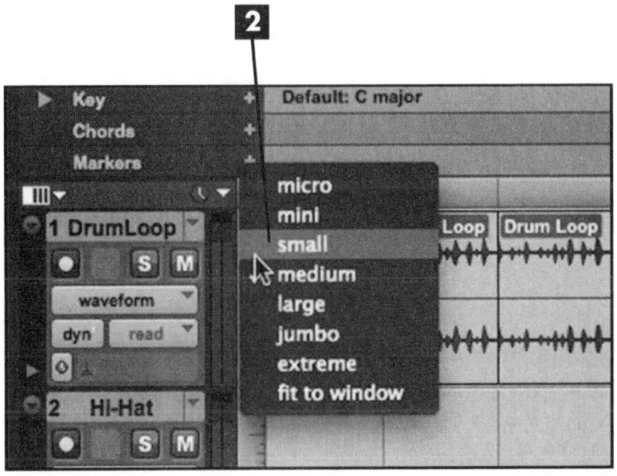

CHANGING THE TRACK HEIGHT FOR DIFFERENT TRACK TYPES

You can change the height of any Pro Tools track (including MIDI and Aux tracks, which you'll explore in later chapters). However, the thin vertical area for other types of tracks looks a little different from the amplitude scale of an Audio track. MIDI tracks, for example, show a keyboard-like display. In any case, right-clicking in this area will bring up the same Track Height menu.

❊ There's an even easier way to change track heights. Simply move your cursor to the bottom of the track you want to change, in the columns area. When your cursor turns into a double-arrow icon (shown here), click and drag up or down to decrease or increase that track's size.

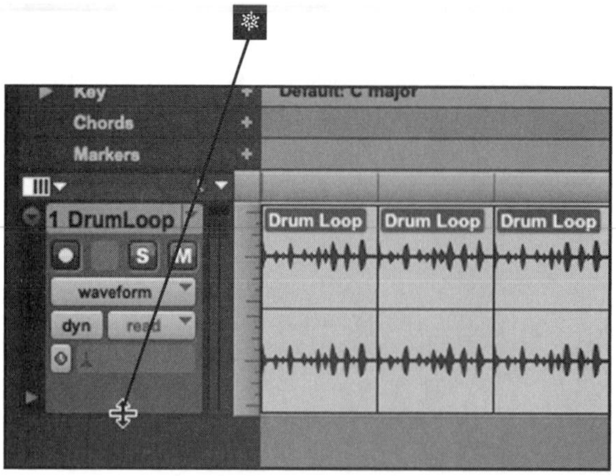

> ❊ **MAKING GLOBAL CHANGES**
>
> Here's another useful shortcut: Press the Option key (Mac) or the Alt key (PC) while you change the height of any one track, and the heights of all shown tracks will change at once.

Custom Colors

The ability to apply the color of your choice to a track, region, or group isn't a new feature in Pro Tools 9; it was introduced back in version 6. But like so many other features, it has been greatly improved upon since its introduction. Like other Edit window customizations, this won't change the *sound* of your session, but it can really help you work more efficiently. Users of all levels will find this sort of control a powerful ally in organizing tracks, regions, and more!

Let's take a look at how this feature can be used to mark your tracks. The first step is to make sure that you can view track colors:

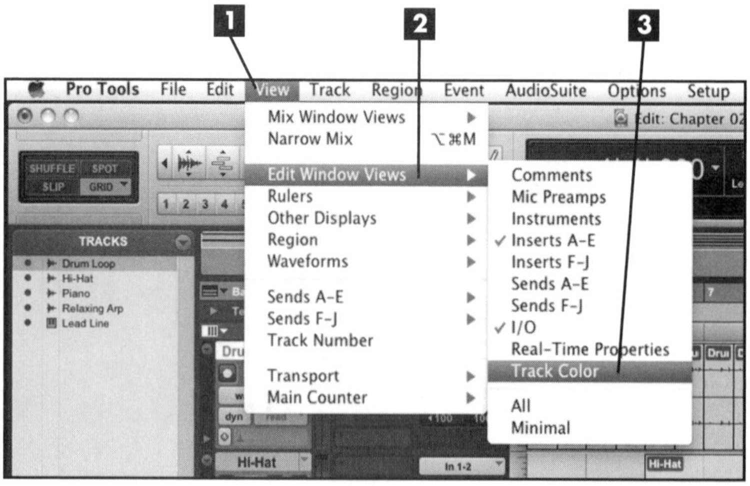

1. **Click** on **View**. The View menu will appear.
2. **Move your cursor** to the **Edit Window Views menu item**. The Edit Window Views submenu will appear.
3. **Click** the **Track Color menu item** if there is not already a checkmark by it. Track colors will only be visible if this menu item is checked.

You will now see a colored tab at the left of each track.

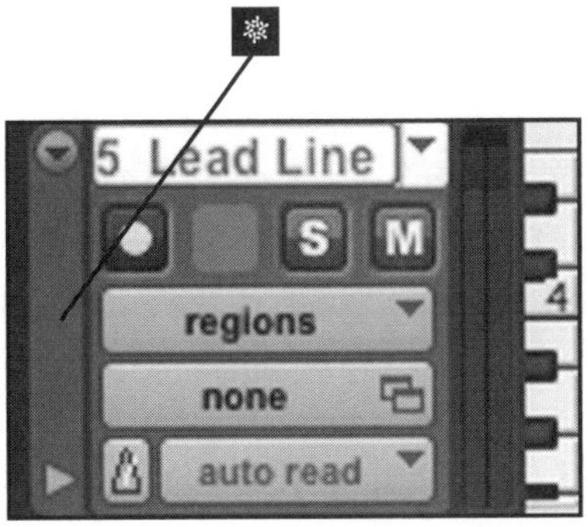

That's only the beginning of the power you have over the appearance of your tracks, however. Let's start off by changing the color of a specific track:

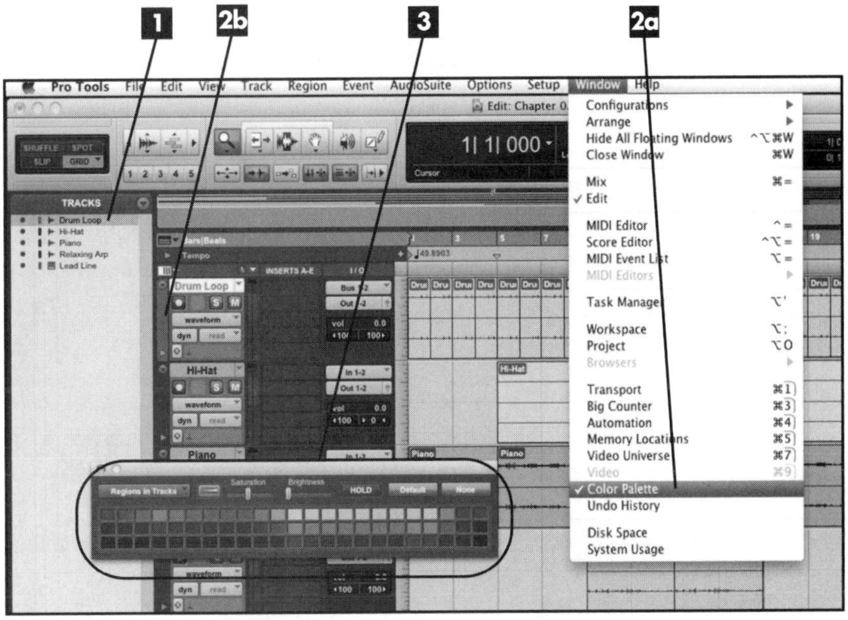

1 **Select** a track by clicking on the **track name** (or select multiple tracks using the modifier keys discussed earlier).

2a From the Window menu, **choose Color Palette**. The Color Palette window will appear.

OR

2b **Double-click** the **Track Color column** (at the left-most edge of the track). The Color Palette window will appear.

3 **Click** the desired **color box**. The selected track's color column will immediately change its color-coding to match.

But wait, there's more!

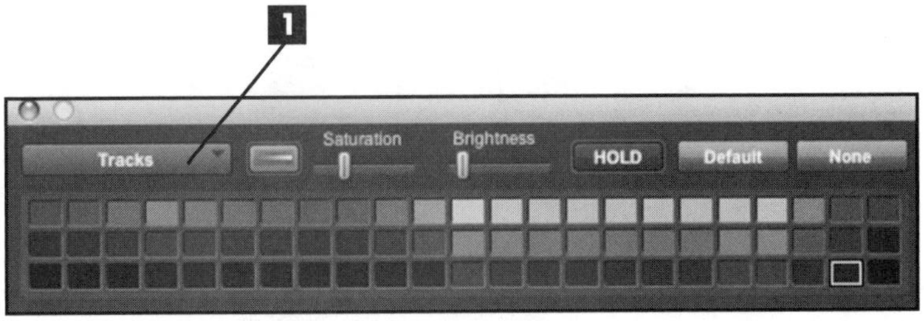

1 **Click** the **Apply to Selected menu** (which currently reads "Tracks"). This menu will enable you to color different elements of your session.

- **Tracks.** As you just saw, this menu item enables the Color Palette window to change a track's color tab.

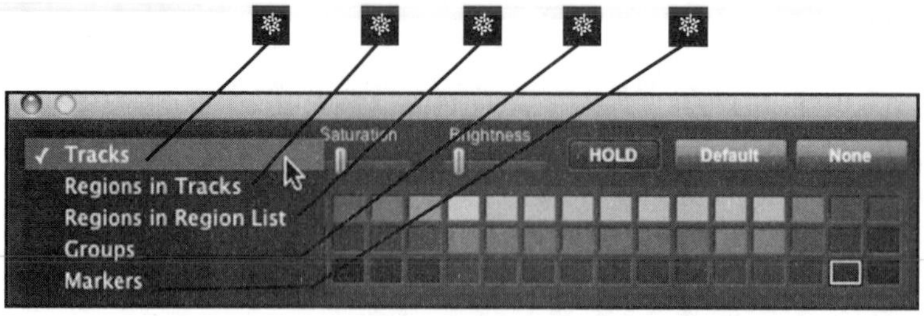

- **Regions in Tracks.** Choosing this option changes the color of regions selected in the Playlist.
- **Regions in Region List.** Selecting this menu item enables you to color-code regions selected in the Regions list.
- **Groups.** Choosing this menu item enables you to change the color-coding of selected groups.
- **Markers.** Markers can also be color-coded. (You'll learn about markers in Chapter 6.) If there are no markers in your session, this item will be grayed out.

Movable Tools

Not only can you show or hide different tool clusters in the top row of the Edit window (by clicking the Edit Window button in the upper-right corner), you can also move them to suit your particular work style. Follow these steps:

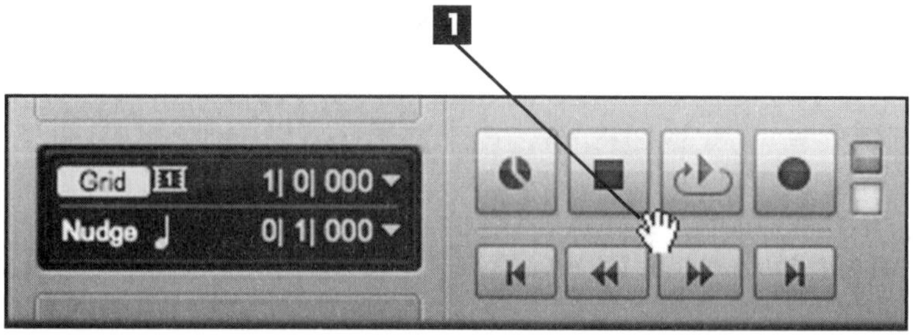

1. **Hold** down the **Command key (Mac)** or **Ctrl key (PC)** and move your cursor over the tool cluster that you want to move. (In this case, I want to move the Transport cluster.) The cursor turns into a hand icon to indicate that the cluster is ready to be moved.

2. **Click and drag** the **cluster** horizontally to the desired location. You will see a semi-transparent representation of the tool cluster as you drag it.

3. A vertical yellow line indicates where the cluster will be inserted. When you get to the desired location, **release** your **mouse button**. The clusters will be rearranged to reflect your changes.

Waveform Views

The graphic representation of audio within an audio region is technically referred to as the *waveform overview*. It's worthwhile to note that this overview is stored in the *wavecache* file (which we discussed briefly in Chapter 1). You can look at your waveforms in a number of different ways:

1. **Click** on **View**. The View menu will appear.
2. **Click** on **Waveforms**. The Waveforms submenu will appear. The top section of this submenu will enable you to view the waveform in two different ways:

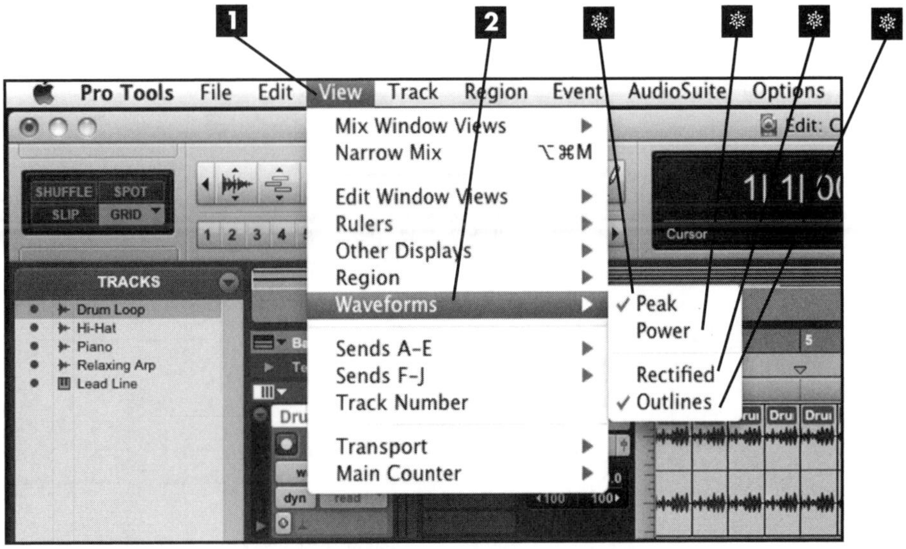

- **Peak.** This is the most common way of looking at your waveform. It is a faithful representation of the amplitude of each sample of your audio. This is important, because it gives you a sense of how you're using your dynamic range and when you're in danger of clipping (something that is particularly nasty when dealing with digital audio).
- **Power.** Although viewing your waveforms in Peak view is certainly useful, it sometimes doesn't match with the perceived loudness of a sound. For a waveform view that looks a bit more like it sounds, choose Power from the Waveforms submenu. I find this view quite useful for picking out beats (for music editing) or words (when editing dialogue for audio post-production).

In addition to these two ways of looking at your audio waveforms, you have a couple more view options:

- **Rectified.** Pro Tools has long had the ability to show you waveforms in a rectified manner, and has recently made this feature even more accessible by placing it in this submenu (introduced in Pro Tools 8). (If the term *rectified* doesn't sound familiar, check out the following sidebar.)
- **Outlines.** Particularly when working with a light-colored region, the difference between the color of the waveform and the background color of the region can be pretty subtle, and this can make the waveform a bit difficult to distinguish. Choosing the Outlines view enables you to view your waveforms with a very thin dark line. I think you'll appreciate how this makes your waveforms easy to read!

RECTIFIED WAVEFORMS

The term *rectified waveform* might be unfamiliar to many readers, but once you see one, it's easy enough to understand. To understand what a rectified waveform shows, though, it's useful to take a second look at the traditional un-rectified view:

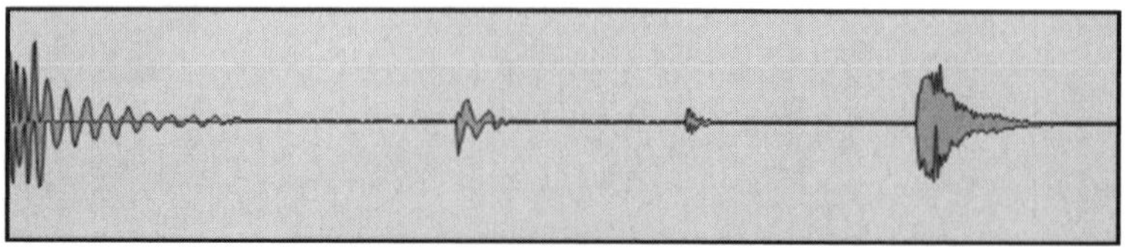

You'll notice that the waveform is centered around a virtual axis going through the middle of the wave. This axis represents zero volts, or silence. If you zoom into the waveform you'll find that the wave oscillates above and below this *zero-volt line*, indicating positive and negative voltage. Now let's take a look at a rectified waveform:

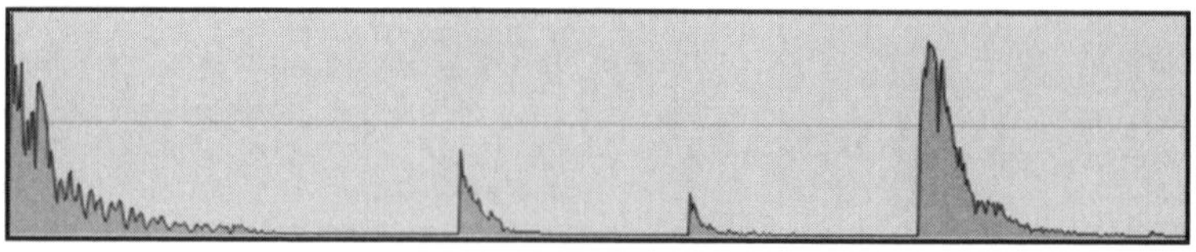

When you look at rectified waveforms, the zero-volt line is at the bottom of the waveform display. Whether the voltage is positive or negative, the visual representation ascends with increasing voltage. In many cases, this makes peaks and transients much easier to distinguish, particularly when working with drums or spoken words.

Working with the Mix Window

Along with the Edit window, another production environment you'll use extensively in Pro Tools is the *Mix window*. Although there's a good bit of common ground between the Mix and Edit windows, the layout and function of the Mix window is geared toward the mixing and automation phases of your session.

Understanding the Mix Window Layout

Much of the general layout of the Mix window is similar to the Edit window's layout.

HIDING THE LISTS COLUMN IN THE MIX WINDOW

As in the Edit window, you can click the double arrows in the corner of the Mix Groups list to hide the lists column. This can give you more space on your desktop for channel strips.

- **Tracks list.** This area functions identically in both the Edit and Mix windows. It enables you to select and show/hide specific tracks.
- **Mix Groups list.** As you create mix groups, they will show up in this area, just as edit groups showed up in the Edit window's Groups list.
- **Channel Strips.** When you create any kind of track (Audio, Aux, Master Fader, MIDI, or Instrument), it will appear here as a vertical strip. (You'll learn more about the elements that make up these channel strips in Chapter 8, "Basic Mixing.")

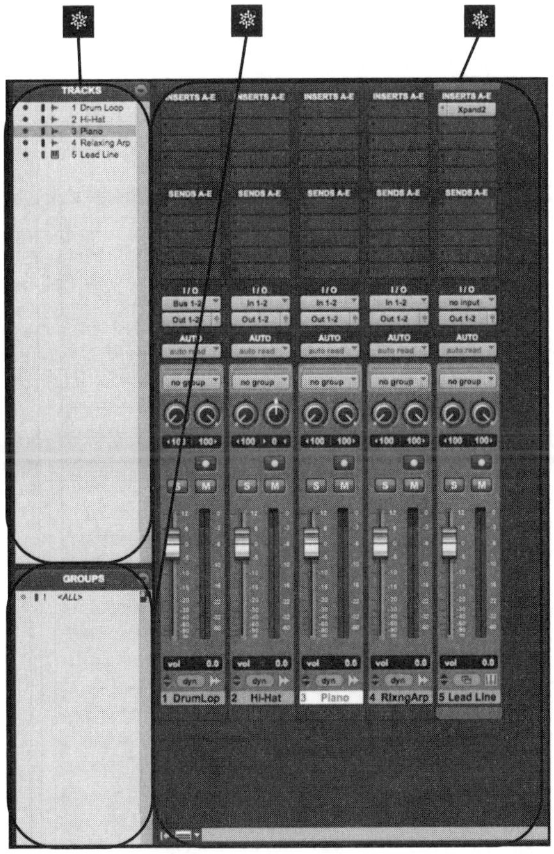

TRACK ORDERS IN THE EDIT AND MIX WINDOWS

Tracks that appear at the top of the Edit window will appear on the left side of the Mix window. As tracks descend in the Edit window, they move from left to right in the Mix window.

TRACK SHOW/HIDE IN THE EDIT AND MIX WINDOWS

Tracks that are shown or hidden in the Mix window are likewise shown or hidden in the Edit window (and vice versa). Also, remember that a track being shown or hidden doesn't affect that track's audibility.

Customizing the Mix Window

Tailoring your Mix window for maximum ease of use will make mixing much more efficient and fun. This section explores some of the most common customizations in the Mix window.

Just as with the Edit window, you have the ability to control the aspects of the Mix window that will be shown or hidden.

1a **Click** the **View menu** and then choose **Mix Window Views**. The Mix Window Views submenu will appear.

OR

1b **Click** the **Mix Window View Selector icon**. The Mix Window Views menu will appear.

2 **Click** on any **element** (Comments, Inserts, Sends, Track Color, or Instruments) to check or uncheck it. As with the Edit window, checked items will be shown.

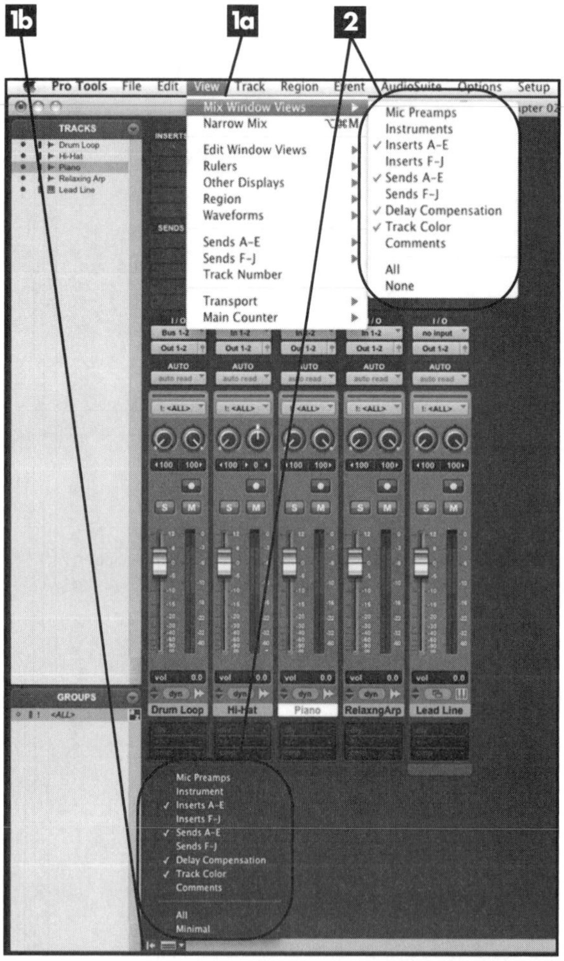

❊ SENDS AND INSERTS

Sends and inserts are essential to the mixing process, and the ability to show and hide them will be helpful as you tweak your mix. You'll learn more about mixing techniques in Chapter 8.

Suppose you have a lot of tracks in your session, and you'd like to see as many of them as possible in the Mix window. Here's how to squeeze more tracks onto a limited desktop:

1 **Click** on **View**. The View menu will appear.

2 **Select Narrow Mix.** Technically, the Mix window itself doesn't narrow, but the individual channel strips do, enabling you to fit more tracks within a given space.

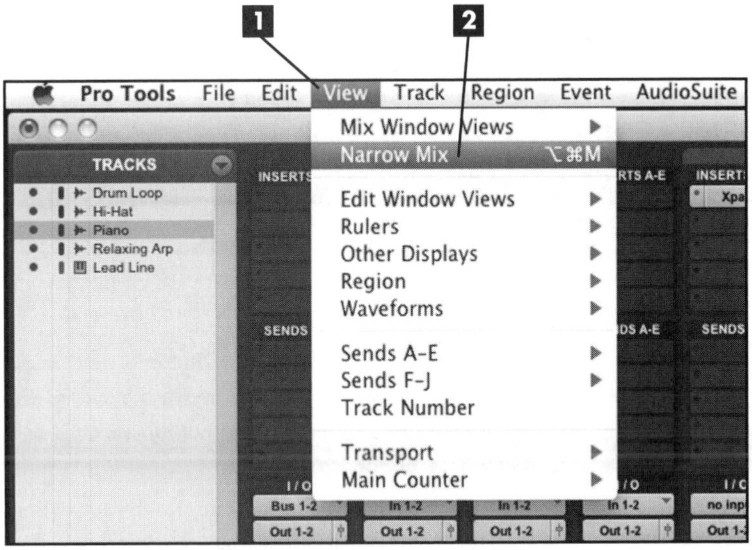

You might be wondering whether you can use track color-coding in the Mix window, as you did in the Edit window. The answer is a resounding yes. In fact, you'll find that coloring your channel strips will be particularly useful in organizing more complex mixes. You can apply color-coding to the Mix window in a few different ways:

- Double-click on either of the color-code areas of a given track to open the Color Palette window. From there, you can change the color-coding of selected tracks just as you did in the Edit window.
- You can also click the Window drop-down menu to access the Color Palette window (again, just as we discussed earlier with the Edit window).

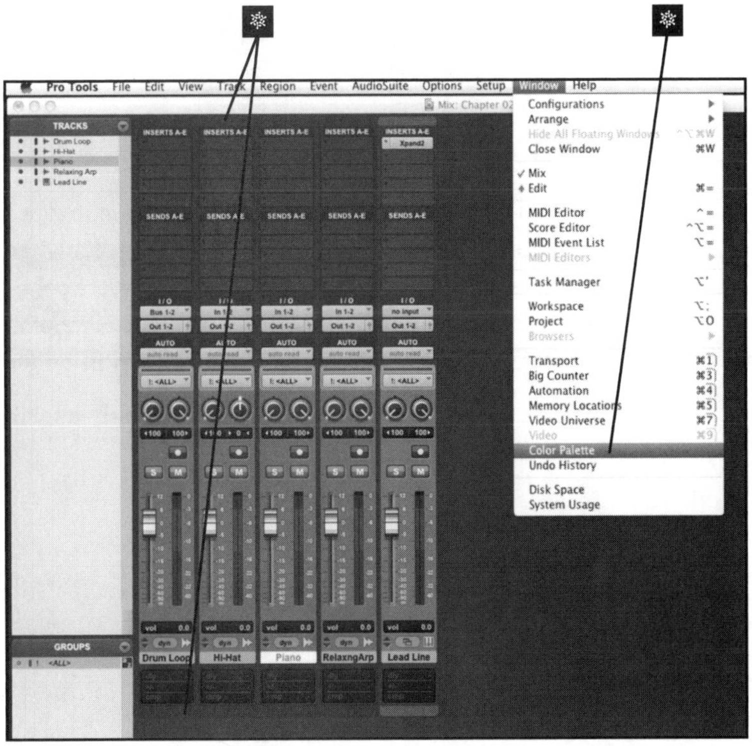

In addition to coloring the tabs on channels, you can also color the entire channel strip. This applies to the Edit window as well, but it's especially useful in the Mix window. You'll find the controls for doing this in the Color Palette window itself.

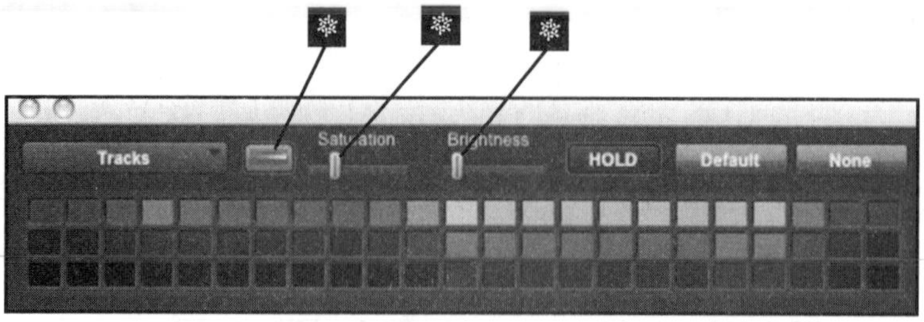

The Apply to Channel Strip button, when activated, applies the track's color to the entire track column (or the track row, in the case of the Edit window). The button will be blue when channel strip coloring is active.

- When the Apply to Channel Strip button is activated, you can choose the color's strength with the Saturation slider. As you move the slider from left to right, the channel strip's color becomes less subtle. (Note that this slider is accessible only when the Apply to Channel Strip button is activated.)
- You can change the overall brightness of your channel strips by adjusting the Brightness slider. (This control will affect your mix window whether you have chosen to color your channel strips or not.)

COLOR-CODING AND THE MIX WINDOW

Because the Mix window doesn't deal with regions, you will probably want to limit your color-coding to tracks and groups in this window. Color changes made in this window will be applied to the Edit window as well.

The Transport Window

Yet another window, called the *Transport window*, will be useful in playing your session. The Transport window is especially useful when you're working in the Mix window (the Mix window has no built-in transport controls). The shortcut to access the Transport window is Command+1 on your computer's numeric keypad on the Mac or Ctrl+1 on your computer's numeric keypad on the PC.

Although using the Transport window is fairly intuitive, this window bears discussion, as does how to customize it.

1 **Click** on **Window**. The Window menu will appear.

2 **Click** on **Transport**. The Transport window will appear. Like the Edit and Mix windows, the Transport window has a number of functions, but for now we'll just focus on basic transport controls:

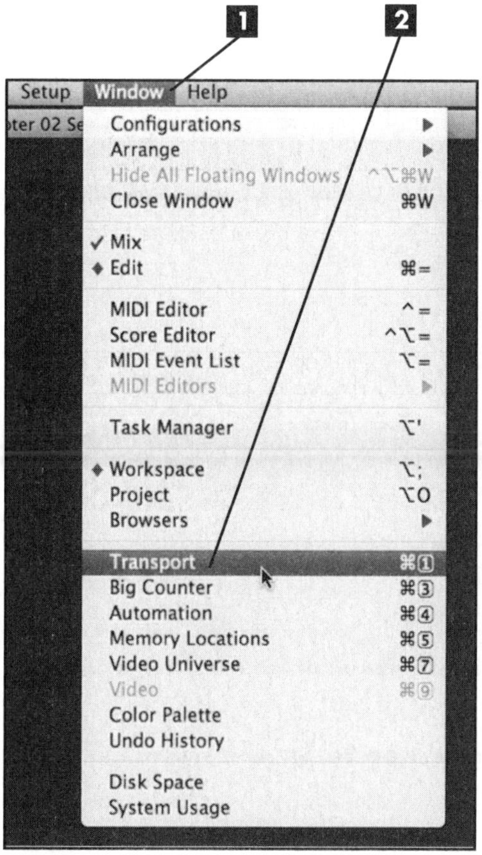

- Go to Beginning
- Rewind
- Fast Forward
- Go to End

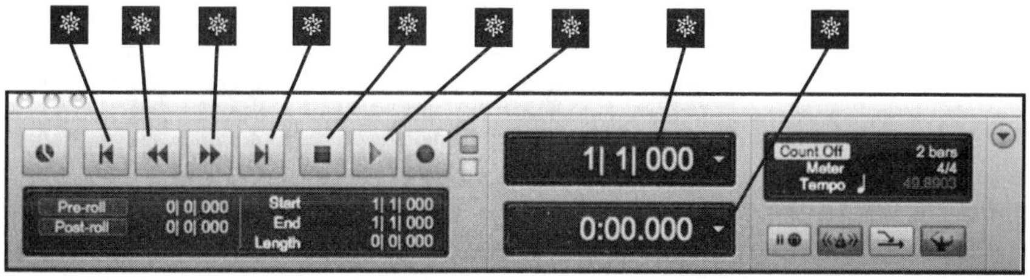

- Stop
- Play
- Record
- Main Time Scale
- Sub Time Scale

WHAT IS THE SUB TIME SCALE?

Think of the Sub Time Scale control as a way to view the passage of time in a different format from the Main Time Scale. You'll learn how to work with both scales in Chapter 5, "Editing."

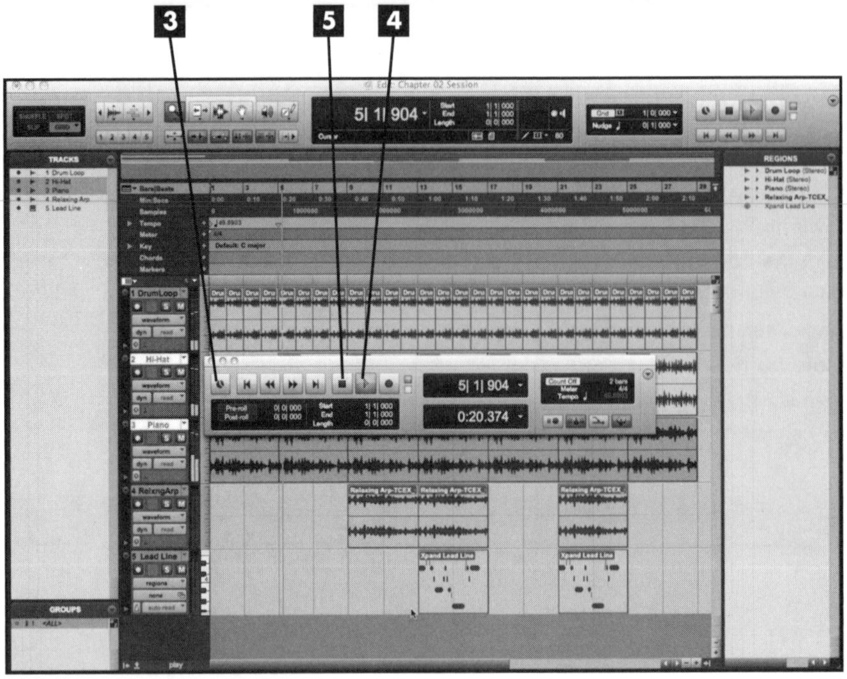

3 **Click** on the **Go to Beginning button** to make sure you're at the beginning of your session.

4 **Click** on the **Play button**. Your audio will begin playing, as shown here. You'll notice that a long vertical line travels from left to right in the Edit window. This is called the *timeline insertion point*. As it intersects with different regions, sound will be produced.

5 **Click** on the **Stop button** when you're finished. The playback will stop.

Customizing the Transport Window

Depending on the type of work you're doing, you may want additional transport-related control. Here's how to show (or hide) specialized Transport window sections.

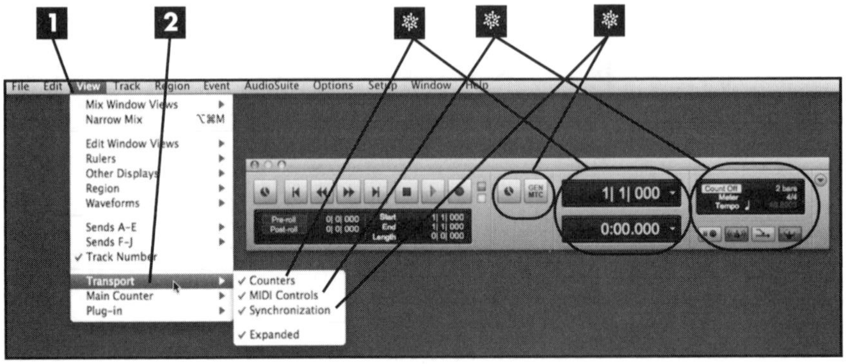

1 **Click** on **View**. The View menu will appear.

2 **Click** on **Transport**. The Transport submenu will appear with the following options:

- **Counters.** This option will add the main counter to the Transport window.
- **MIDI Controls.** This option will add basic MIDI controls to the Transport window. (These controls are discussed in detail in Chapter 7.)
- **Synchronization.** Choose this option if you are controlling Pro Tools remotely or using Pro Tools to control other devices. You'll learn how to use these features in Chapters 4, "Recording Audio," and 7, "Using MIDI."

- **Expanded.** This option shows secondary transport controls, including pre-roll and post-roll, the sub-counter, and secondary MIDI controls.

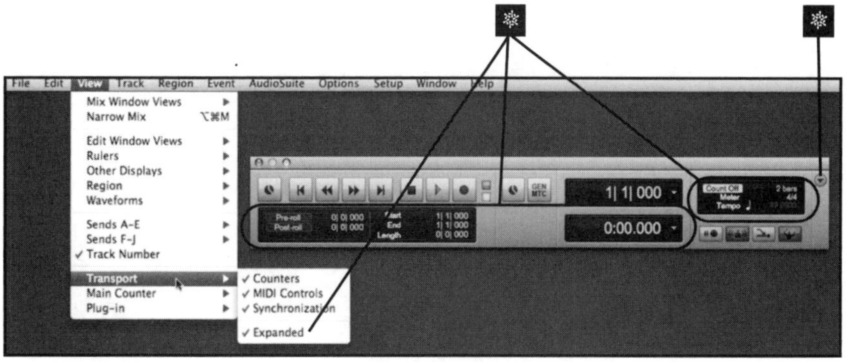

- Clicking the triangle icon in the upper-right corner of the Transport window is another way to display view options.

Other Useful Windows

Even though you'll spend the majority of your time in Pro Tools working in the Edit and Mix windows, there are a number of other windows that serve more specific purposes. These windows usually operate in conjunction with either the Edit or the Mix window (whichever one you're using). You can access these secondary windows through the Window menu, like so:

1. **Click** on **Window**. The Window menu will appear, displaying an assortment of choices.
2. **Click** on the **window** you want to display.

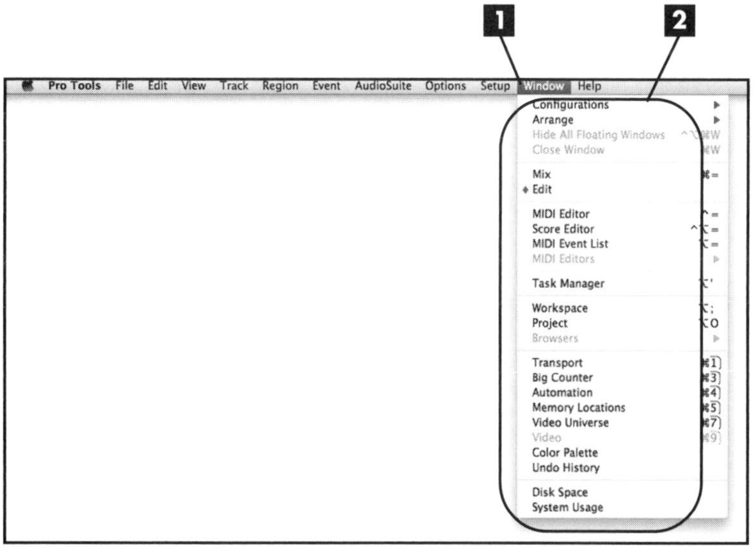

Before we move on, let's take a first look at two useful floating windows:

- **Big Counter.** The Big Counter window is simply a larger display of your main counter, but it really comes in handy when you want to watch your session's progress from across a room! The shortcut for the Big Counter window is Command+3 (on your computer's numeric keypad) on a Mac or Ctrl+3 (on your computer's numeric keypad) on a PC.

RESIZABLE!

You'll be very happy to hear that the Big Counter window is resizable. By dragging the lower-right corner of the window, you can adjust it to fill as much of your screen as you like!

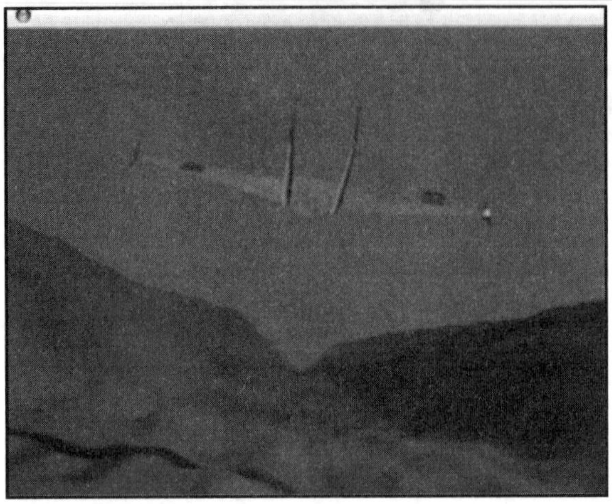

- **Video.** Pro Tools is an audio application, but that doesn't mean you can't use it to work with video. Importing video files into your session is easy, and viewing your movie as your session plays is as simple as opening the Video window from the Window drop-down menu. You can also get to this window quickly by pressing Command+9 on the numeric keypad (Mac) or Ctrl+9 on the numeric keypad (PC).

Session Setup

The Session Setup window displays useful information about your session's configuration, including synchronization and timecode settings for more-advanced workflows. Here's how to open the Session Setup window:

1. **Click** on **Setup**. The Setup menu will appear.
2. **Click** on **Session**. The Session Setup window will appear.

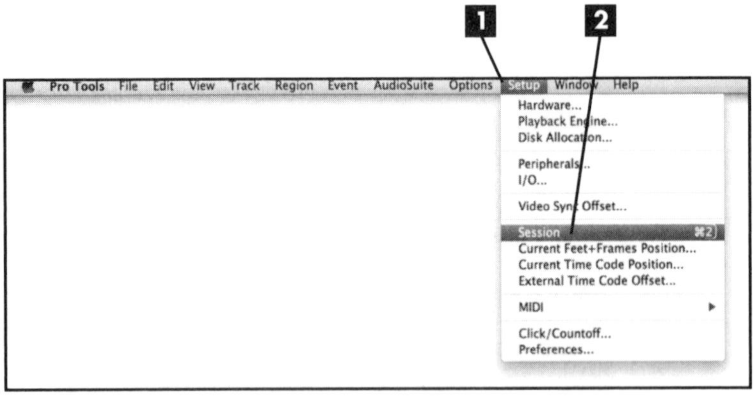

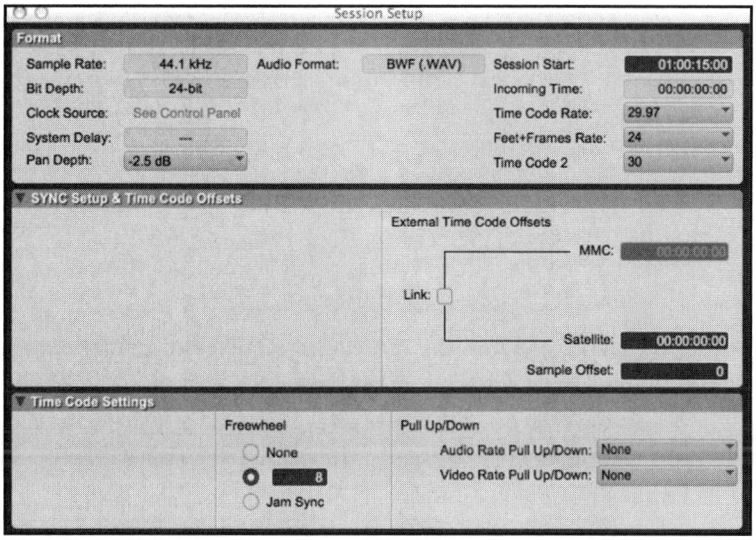

The shortcut for the Session Setup window is Command+2 on the numeric keypad (Mac) or Ctrl+2 on the numeric keypad (PC).

System Usage and Disk Usage

Last but not least among the traditionally popular windows, the System Usage and Disk Usage windows will give you important information about how your system is doing. There are no shortcut keys for these windows–you'll have to open them from the Window menu–but they're critical windows nonetheless!

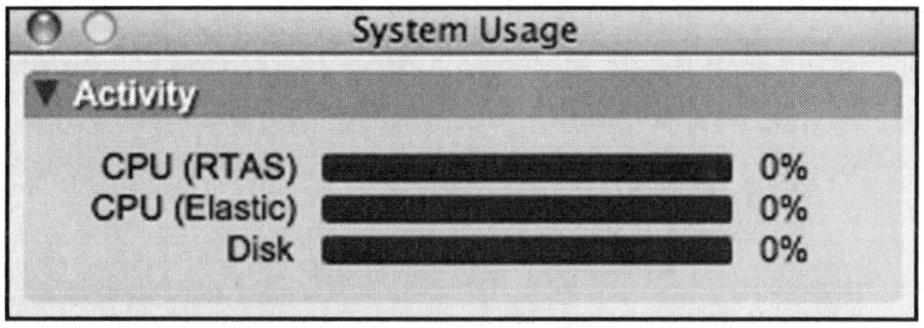

- **System Usage.** As you learn more about how to efficiently use Pro Tools, you'll want to refer to the System Usage window from time to time to see how your computer is dealing with the tasks associated with Pro Tools. This window gives a simple and efficient view of the workload your session is dealing with, broken down into categories.

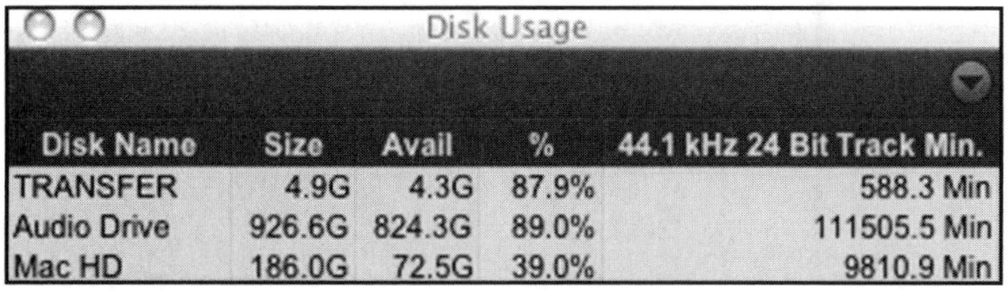

- **Disk Usage.** The size of a hard drive in a DAW is kind of like the amount of tape in an analog recording studio–the more you have, the more you can record. The Disk Usage window lets you know how much free space you have on each drive for recording audio and how much time that space represents (at your session's sample rate and bit depth).

❋ DISK SPACE VERSUS DISK ACTIVITY

You'll notice that there's a disk meter in the System Usage window as well as a standalone Disk Usage window. What's the difference? The System Usage window's disk meter tells you the activity of the hard drives in your system (in terms of data throughput), whereas the Disk Usage window gives you information about storage capacity.

MIDI Editor and Score Editor

Over the last few versions, Pro Tools has made impressive advancements in the world of MIDI. First introduced in Pro Tools 8, the MIDI Editor and the Score Editor windows provide powerful new environments for music creation (which we'll talk more about in Chapter 7).

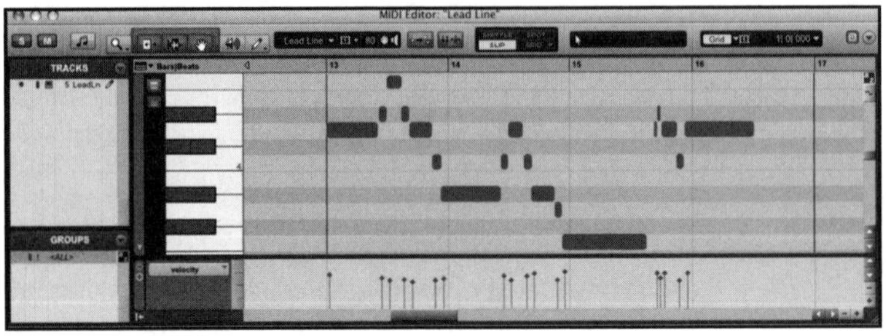

The MIDI Editor window is more than your typical floating window. For many users, it's their primary creative environment. To the left, you'll see the familiar-looking Tracks and Groups lists, and you'll be able to view MIDI data in a number of different ways in the main section of the window. The top row of the MIDI Editor window also shows you the same set of tools you saw in the Edit window.

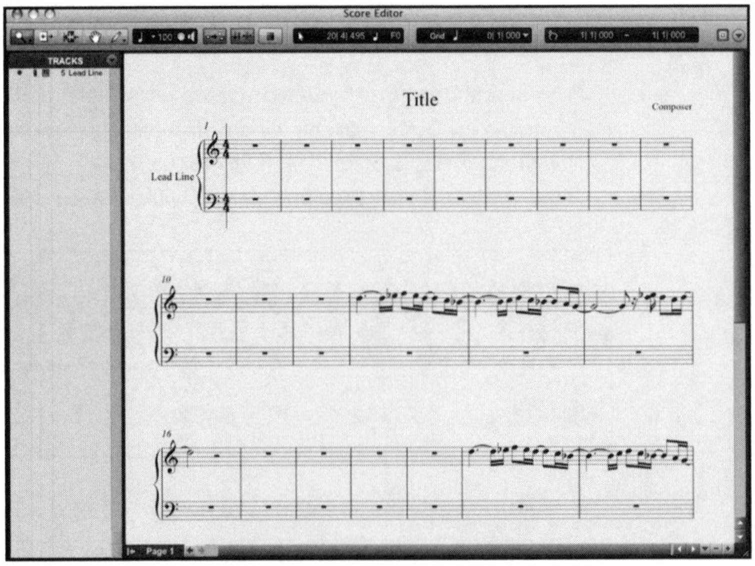

If you want to print music for your musicians (or even if you just prefer creating music in a more traditional environment), the Score Editor window will serve you well. Here, as with the MIDI Editor, you'll see the familiar Tracks list on the left side and editing tools on the top row. What makes the Score window unique, though, is its ability to add notational aspects—song title, composer, chord symbols, and so on—that musicians need to see in order to play your music.

Window Management

We've covered a lot of important introductory ground in this chapter, but if you'll indulge me just a bit longer, I'd like to walk you through some features you can use to get the most out of your desktop!

Window Configurations

A powerful (but sometimes underused) feature of Pro Tools is its ability to recall specific window arrangements. With window configurations, you can quickly change which windows are displayed, as well as their sizes and positions. The process is as simple as it is useful:

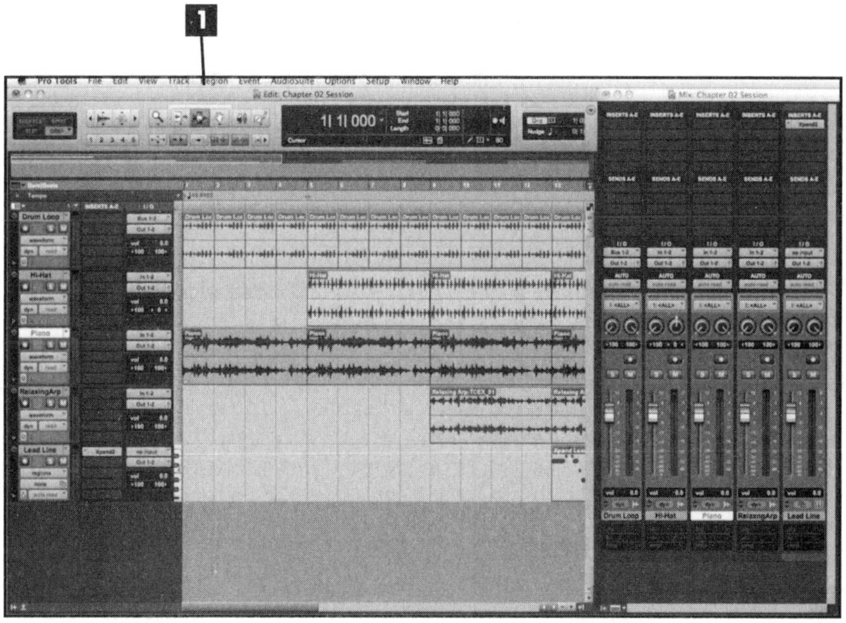

1 **Arrange** your **windows** in any way that suits your workflow. In this case, I've chosen a simple arrangement of both Edit and Mix windows.

2 Capture this arrangement of windows. From the Window menu, **choose Configurations**, and then **New Configuration**. The New Window Configuration window will appear.

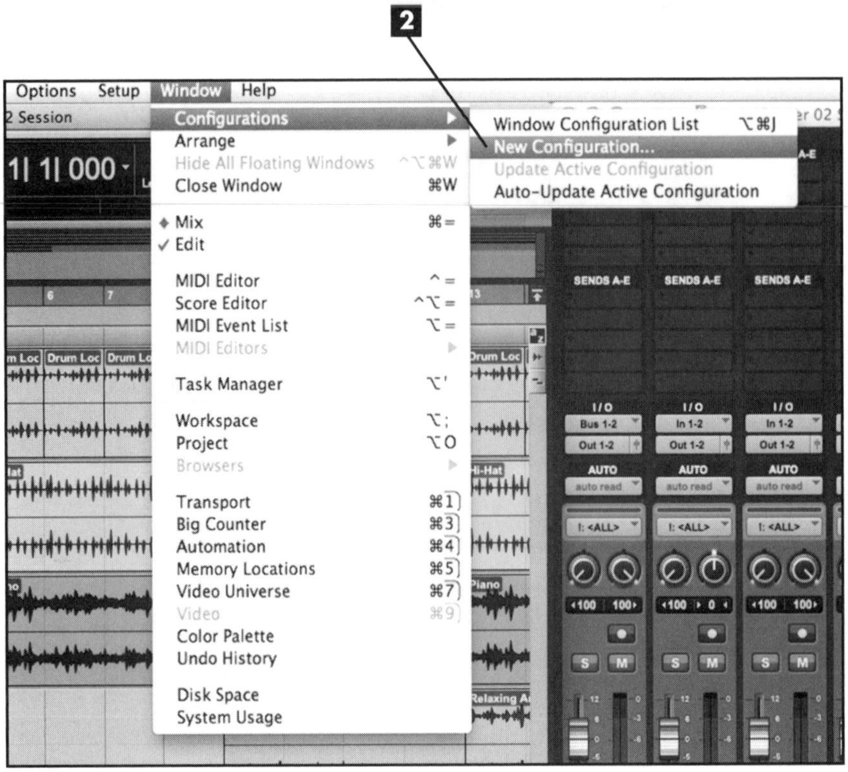

3 In the New Window Configuration window, you can click the top option button to capture the entire layout or open the drop-down menu next to the bottom option button to capture specific aspects of your desktop. In this case, **choose** the **top option button** and **type** a descriptive **name** in the Name field.

4 **Click OK.** The window closes. Now you can recall your screen arrangement at a moment's notice!

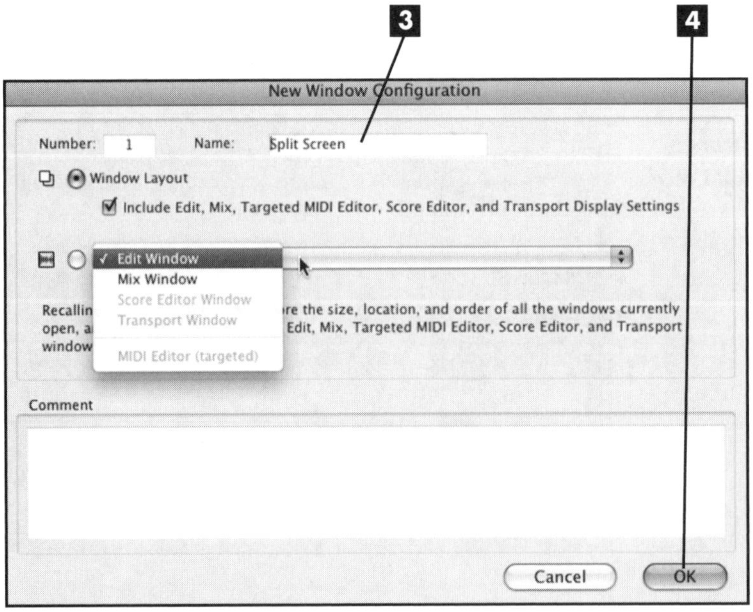

Recalling a window configuration is easy—and, as with most things in Pro Tools, there are a number of ways to do it. Here's one:

1 From the Window menu, **choose Configurations**. The Window Configurations submenu will appear.

2 Any existing window configurations appear at the bottom of the submenu. Just **click** the **layout** you want to recall.

3 There is also a convenient floating window that shows a list of your window configurations. **Choose Window Configuration List** to show this window.

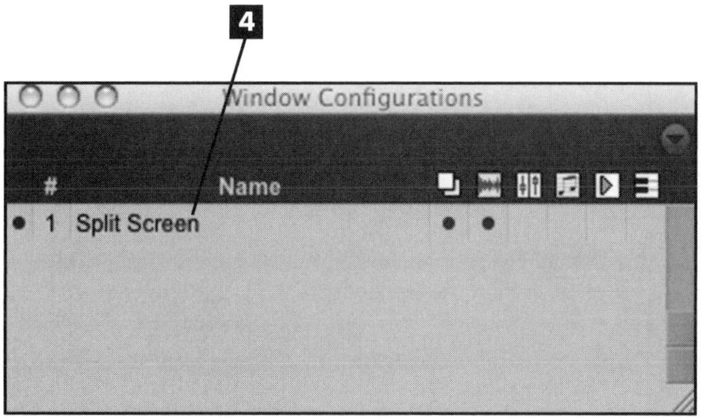

4 This window will not only show you a list of window configurations, it will also show you the aspects that are recalled with each configuration through the icons that are to the immediate right of the configuration name (window layout, Edit window, Mix window, Score Editor, Transport window, and MIDI Editor). Just **click** on the **configuration** you want to recall.

WINDOW CONFIGURATIONS SHORTCUT

Here's a shortcut for recalling a window configuration, but be careful—the key order is important. First, press the period key on your numeric keypad. Then press the number of the window configuration that you want to call up (again on your numeric keypad). Finally, press the asterisk key (yet again on your numeric keypad).

> **UPDATING A WINDOW CONFIGURATION**
>
> In the Window Configurations submenu, you'll notice that there is an Update "[configuration name]" option. This option enables you to change a given configuration to reflect the current window arrangement. Auto-Update Active Configuration will do this automatically.

Hiding Floating Windows

From time to time, your desktop may become a bit cluttered with floating windows, which get in the way of you seeing the Edit or Mix window clearly. There are two ways to quickly hide (and bring back) all floating windows in one fell swoop:

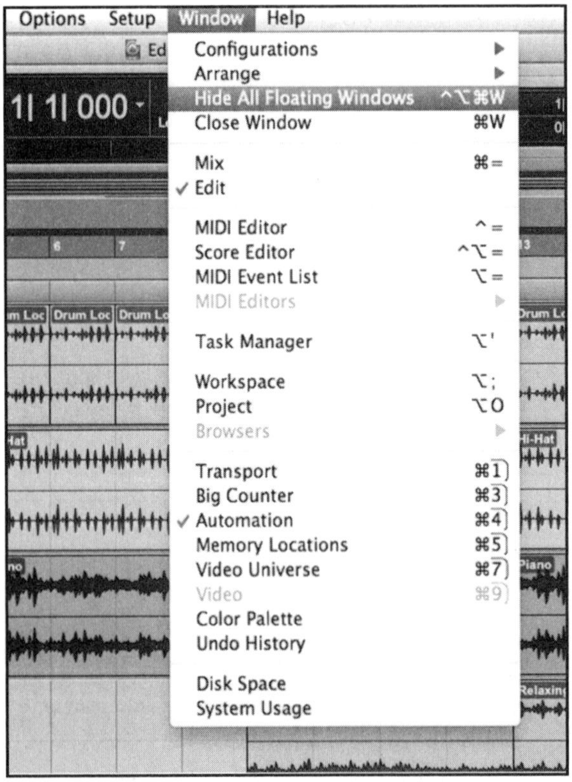

- From the Window menu, choose Hide All Floating Windows. All floating windows will immediately disappear, and the menu item will be checked. Re-clicking Hide All Floating Windows (when it is checked) will reveal all hidden floating windows.
- Press Command+Option+Control+W (Mac) or Ctrl+Alt+Start+W (PC) to hide or show all floating windows.

You'll find that this feature, though simple, is useful when you're using plug-in effects and virtual instruments, and it enables you to quickly shift your focus.

Window Arrangements

Like many multi-window applications, Pro Tools 9 gives you the ability to quickly arrange your windows in some standard configurations. This last bit is very straightforward, but let's take a look before we move on to the next chapter.

1 **Click** on **Window**. The Window menu will appear.

2 **Click** on **Arrange**. The Arrange submenu will appear.

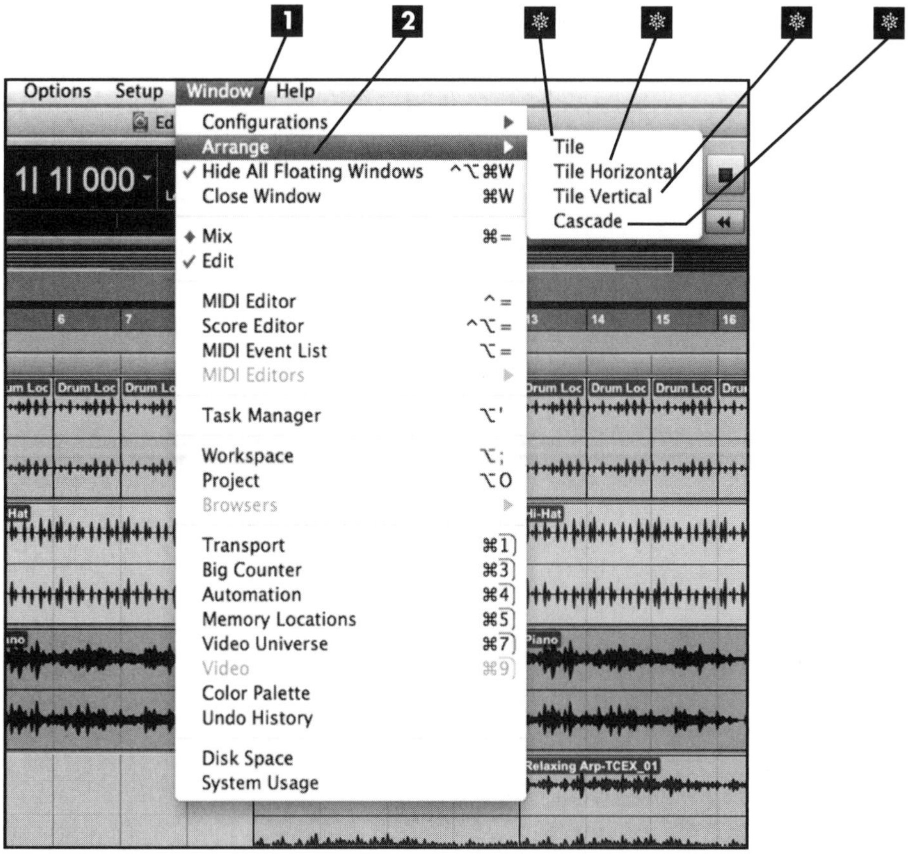

- **Tile.** Choose this option to arrange all active windows on the desktop in a standard tile pattern.
- **Tile Horizontal.** Choose this option to arrange windows from top to bottom. Note that this option is not available when too many windows are currently active.
- **Tile Vertical.** Select this option to arrange windows side by side. Here, too, this option will be grayed out if there are too many active windows in your session.
- **Cascade.** Selecting Cascade lays all active windows on top of each other, arranging them in a standard cascade pattern (showing the title bar of each window, so that you can easily see what windows are currently open).

Congratulations! You now have a fundamental understanding of what Pro Tools is and how it functions, which will help you be a more intelligent user as you delve more deeply into this powerful environment. Now you're ready to begin actively using Pro Tools and start working with audio!

3 Getting Started with Audio

Now that you have a basic understanding of what Pro Tools is and what it can do, it's time to start making things happen. The first step on the path to Pro Tools proficiency is to set up a session and start using audio. In this chapter, you'll learn how to do the following:

- Configure Pro Tools to make the most of your computer system.
- Set up and customize your inputs, outputs, inserts, and buses.
- Create Audio, Aux Input, and Master Fader tracks.
- Import audio into your session.
- Play your session in a variety of ways to suit different circumstances.

Setup

Before you can get your show on the road, you'll need to call upon knowledge that you gained in the first chapter to create a session upon which you can work.

1 Launch Pro Tools.

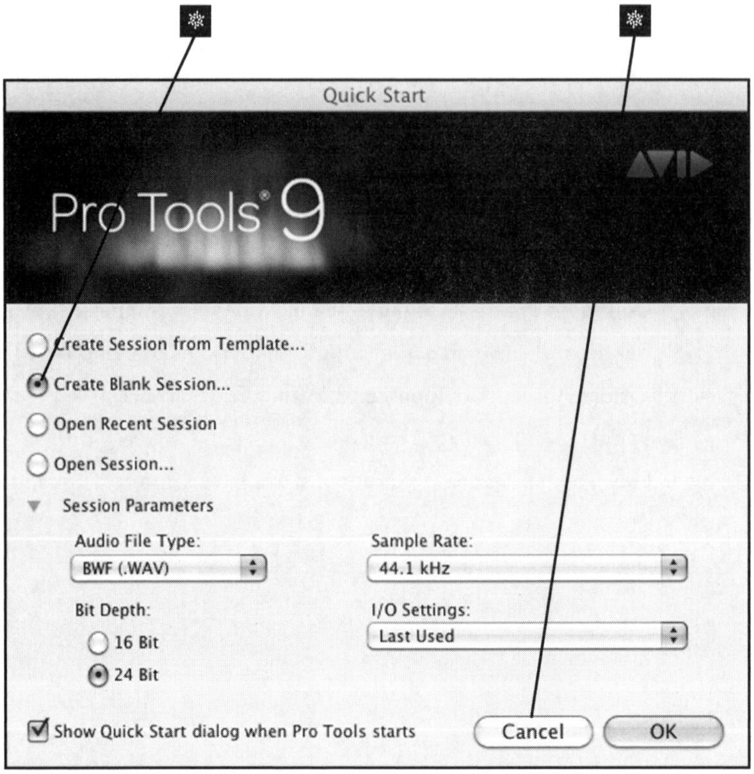

- At this point, you could click on the **Create Blank Session** option button in the Quick Start window. If you do that, be sure the Session Parameters are visible and jump down to step number 5.
- Alternatively, you can choose to exit from the Quick Start window by clicking the **Cancel** button and move on to step 2.

2 Click on **File.**

3 Click on **New Session.**

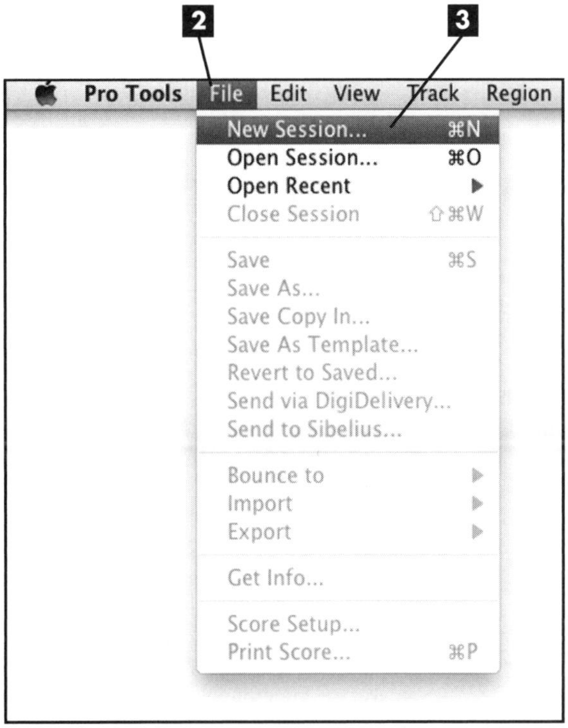

4 Choose the **Create Blank Session option button.**

5 Select BWF (.WAV) from the Audio File Type menu.

6 Select 44.1 kHz from the Sample Rate menu.

7 Select the **24 Bit option button** in the Bit Depth area.

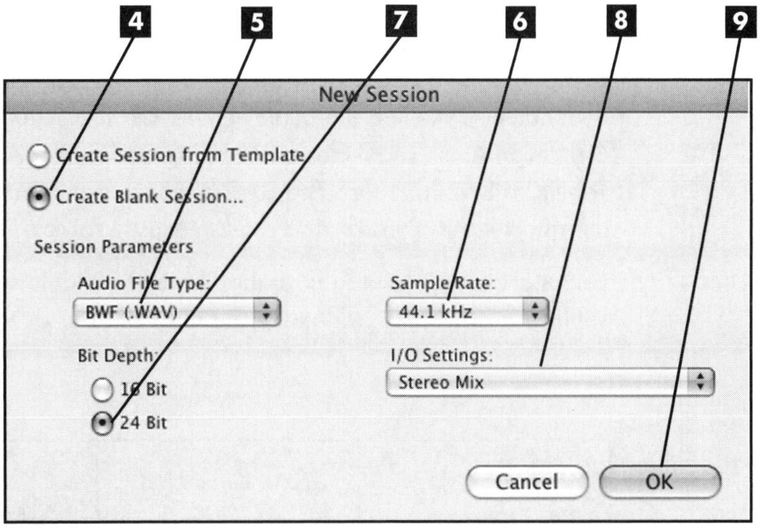

8 Select Stereo Mix from the I/O Settings menu.

9 Click on **OK.**

10 **Type** a descriptive **name** for your session in the Save As field.

11 **Choose** an appropriate **place** for your session. (In this case, I'm saving the session to my Audio hard drive.)

12 **Click** on the **Save button**. Pro Tools creates your session.

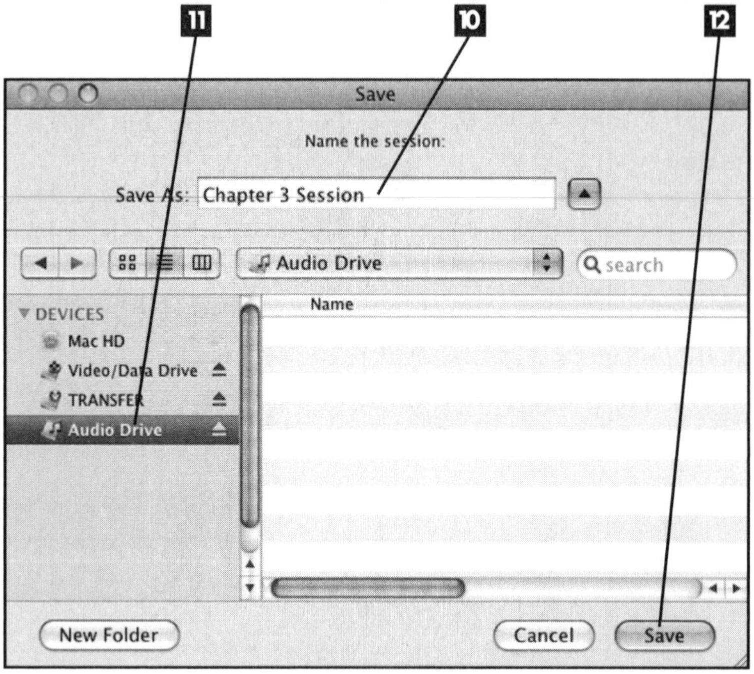

The Playback Engine Window

Every DAW application has a certain amount of code devoted to the tasks of digital audio recording and playback. This bit of programming is so important that it has its own name–it's called the *audio engine*. Pro Tools' audio engine is called the *Digidesign Audio Engine* (named for Digidesign, the Avid subsidiary that created Pro Tools), or DAE for short. The DAE is at the very heart of Pro Tools' operations, and the quality of its construction is a big reason for Pro Tools' popularity.

Let's start by taking a look at the Playback Engine window, where you can choose settings for the DAE and make the most of your overall system.

1 **Click** on **Setup**. The Setup menu will appear.

2 **Click** on **Playback Engine**. The Playback Engine window will appear. You saw this window before–back in Chapter 1, "Welcome to Pro Tools 9," when you chose an audio engine (from the menu at the top of the Playback Engine window). Let's take a deeper look, section by section:

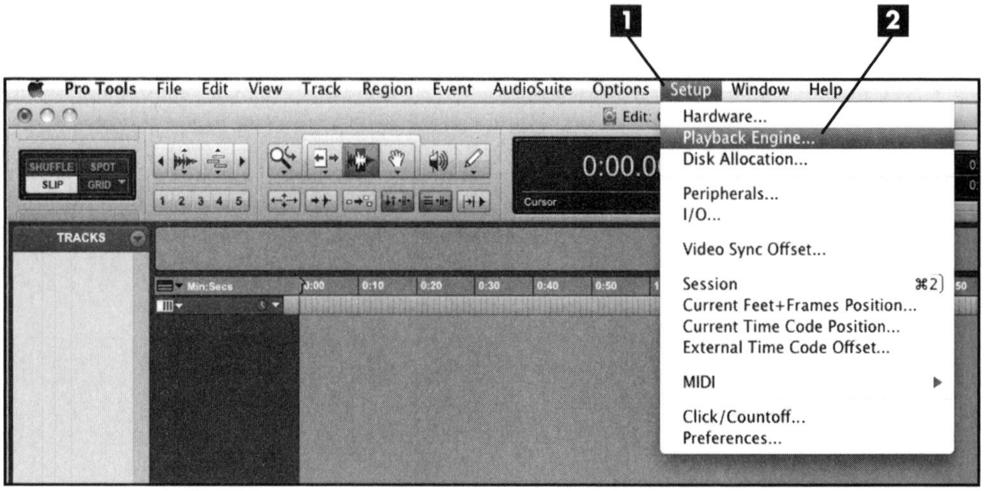

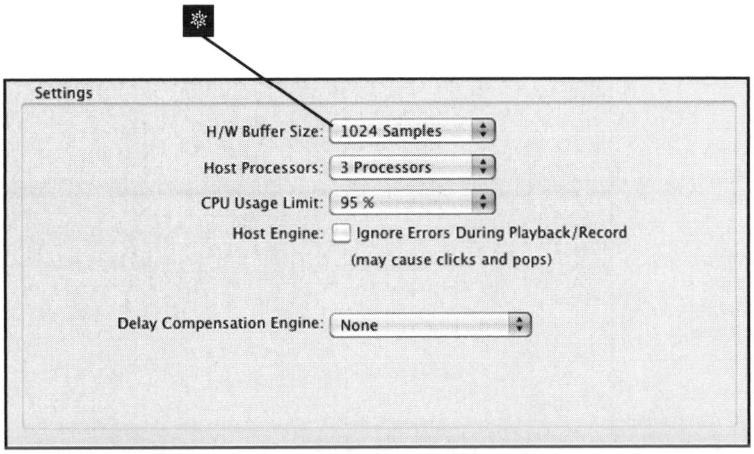

- The H/W Buffer Size (hardware buffer size) essentially affects all host-based real-time processes in your Pro Tools system. This is particularly important with host-based Pro Tools systems. With non-HD systems, your computer's CPU (the *host*) is responsible for all the processes, including recording, playback, and plug-in effects. The hardware buffer sets aside some memory to create a data buffer for these important tasks. Just click on the arrow button to the right of the setting to reveal a drop-down list of options.

WHAT'S A BUFFER?

You've probably heard the term buffer tossed about in discussions about computers, but you might be a bit foggy on what exactly a buffer is and what it does. A buffer is a certain amount of computer memory that is used for short-term data storage during operations.

Although buffers are used in different ways for different kinds of applications, as a general rule, buffers will enable a processor to work with large amounts of data more efficiently.

THE PROS AND CONS OF HARDWARE BUFFER SETTINGS

Having a higher hardware buffer setting can certainly allow for more simultaneous audio processes (such as plug-in effects, for example), but there's a catch: High buffer settings can also increase recording latency, or the delay between a signal going into Pro Tools and the audio heard out of the monitor speakers (in host-based Pro Tools systems). High recording latency can be a real bother during recording sessions. The delay can be very distracting to musicians when they are trying to hear their live performance through the headphones.

Here's a good rule of thumb: Set your hardware buffer as low as possible when recording. This may or may not be the first setting on the list, depending on your computer's power. After the recording phase of your project is finished, you can set the buffer higher so you can take advantage of more plug-ins during the editing and mixing stages.

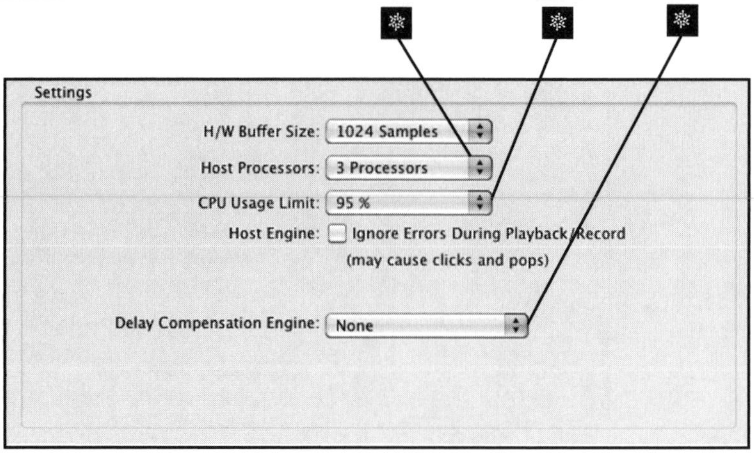

- The Host Processors list (which you can see if you click on the arrow button to the right of the setting) enables you to utilize any number of CPUs in a multi-processor system. If you have multiple CPUs, choosing to use them will give you the option of launching more Real-Time AudioSuite (RTAS) plug-ins. However, if other applications on your system (such as video-editing applications) have higher priority, or if your session has a great deal of mix automation, consider using fewer CPUs to free up processing power. In this example, I have four available processors in my system, but have chosen to use only three of them for Pro Tools. This frees up a single processor for more system stability.
- The CPU Usage Limit enables you to set a cap on the amount of CPU power that can be used by Pro Tools. When you click on the arrow button indicated, you'll see a menu showing a series of percentages. A higher percentage (for example, the 95% shown here) gives Pro Tools more power, although it may rob power from other applications (again, such as a video-editing application) that may also be running. A lower limit will restrict Pro Tools somewhat, but it can also ensure adequate power for other applications. This setting works in combination with the aforementioned Host Processors setting.
- One thing I like about the DAE is that it's a stickler for quality. If there are any errors in the recording or playing back of your audio, the DAE will stop everything and tell you about the problem. I do find, however, that these messages (which stop playback or recording) can get a bit bothersome when I'm working in a noncritical situation—for example, when I'm launching plug-ins during playback, just to see which effect suits my needs. In these situations, where a few clicks or pops are tolerable, check the Host Engine Ignore Errors During Playback/Record checkbox shown here.

WHEN *NOT* TO IGNORE THE ERRORS!

As a general rule, you should check Ignore Errors During Playback/Record only when you run into problems in noncritical situations (such as editing). When you' re in the important recording or final mixdown stages of your project, remember to uncheck Ignore Errors During Playback/Record. You certainly don' t want to hear clicks and pops then!

- The addition of a Delay Compensation Engine is new for host-based Pro Tools users and is a powerful new advance in terms of mix quality. Simply put, when activated, the Delay Compensation Engine automatically compensates for plug-in and other kinds of latency within your system, ensuring that your audio's timing is sample accurate across all tracks. This feature, called Automatic Delay Compensation (ADC), will be discussed in detail in Chapter 10, "Moving to the Next Level: Tips and Tricks."

3 Now let's take a look at the DAE Playback Buffer settings:

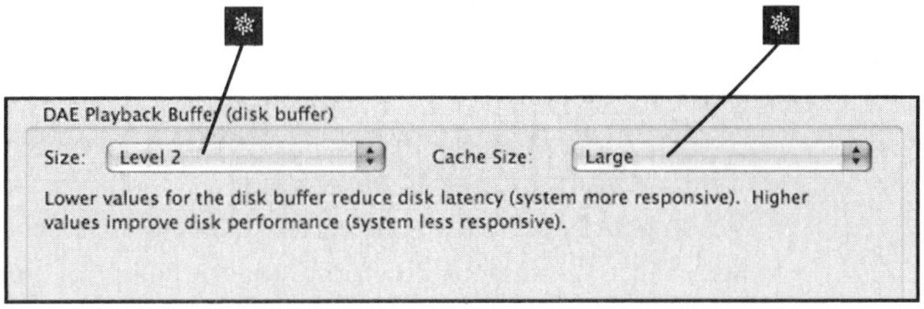

- The DAE Playback Buffer—not to be confused with the H/W Buffer—gathers audio from the hard drive and queues it up for playback. To change its size, simply click on the arrow button to the right of the Size value. The default value (Level 2, or 1500 milliseconds) is fine for the vast majority of situations. If you run into disk playback errors (errors telling you that your disk is too slow to continue playback of your session), however, you can choose a higher buffer setting to treat the symptom.

WILL THE DAE PLAYBACK BUFFER AFFECT RECORDING?

As the Playback Engine window states, higher buffer settings can make Pro Tools less responsive. In other words, you might perceive a bit of a lag between when you click on the Play button and when Pro Tools actually starts playback. This should not be confused with recording latency. In fact, the changes you make to the DAE Playback Buffer won' t affect recording latency one way or the other.

- The Cache Size setting is a relatively new addition to Pro Tools. Introduced in version 7.4, it enables the user to allocate memory specifically for Elastic Audio-related tasks. (We'll talk more about Elastic Audio in Chapter 10.) If you click on the arrow to the right of the Cache Size setting, you can choose from three settings: Minimum (reduces memory use), Normal, and Large (improves performance). If you rely on Elastic Audio in your projects, choose the Large cache setting.

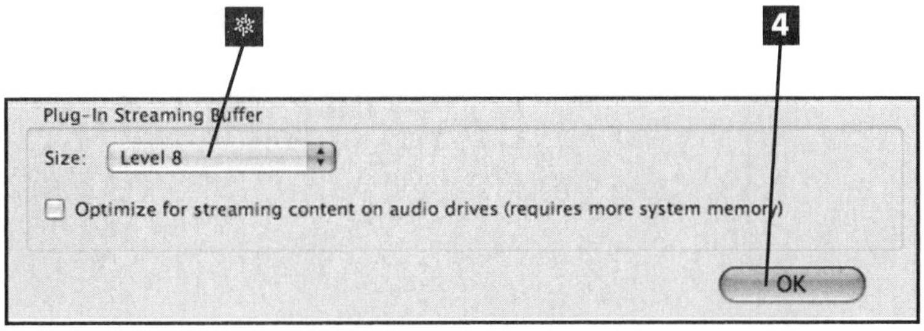

- If your system happens to be running Avid's Structure software sampler, you will also see a Plug-In Streaming Buffer Size section, which enables you to choose the amount of memory the DAE reserves for sample playback. If you don't see this section in your Playback Engine window, don't worry—that simply means you haven't installed Structure. Just like the DAE, the default settings are generally fine.

4 When you're finished, **click** on the **OK button** (at the bottom-right corner of the window), and your settings will take effect.

Customizing Your Session: I/O Setup

An understanding of Pro Tools' signal flow is critical to using this powerful DAW. At the heart of signal flow is the I/O (Input/Output) Setup window.

Setting Up Inputs

When you created this session, you chose Stereo Mix as your I/O (Input/Output) setting. This I/O setting is Pro Tools' generic setup for stereo work. Although it works fine as is, you can customize it to match your own studio's setup and boost your productivity right from the start! Let's begin by taking a closer look at the input setup for your studio—in other words, the connections going *into* your audio interface, and from there to the Pro Tools software environment.

1. **Click** on **Setup**.
2. **Click** on **I/O**. The I/O Setup dialog box will open.

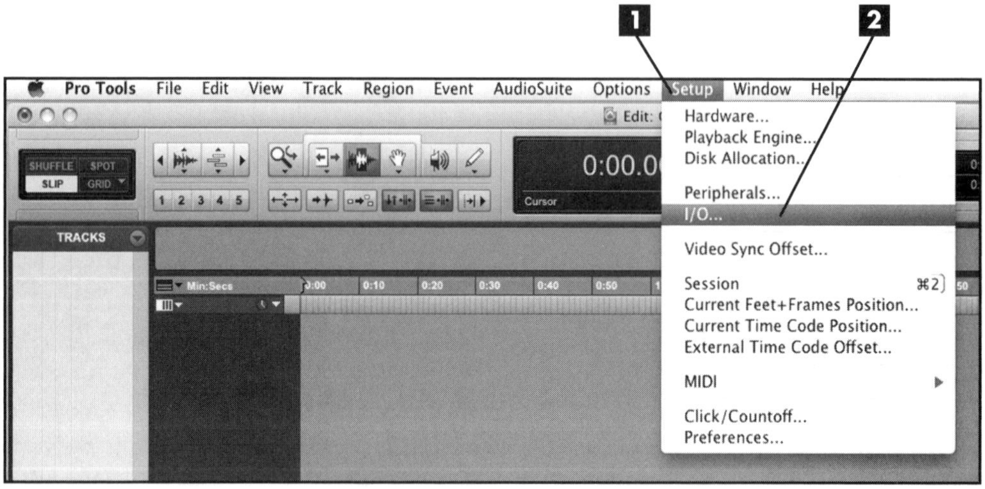

3. **Click** on the **Input tab**. The tab will move to the front.

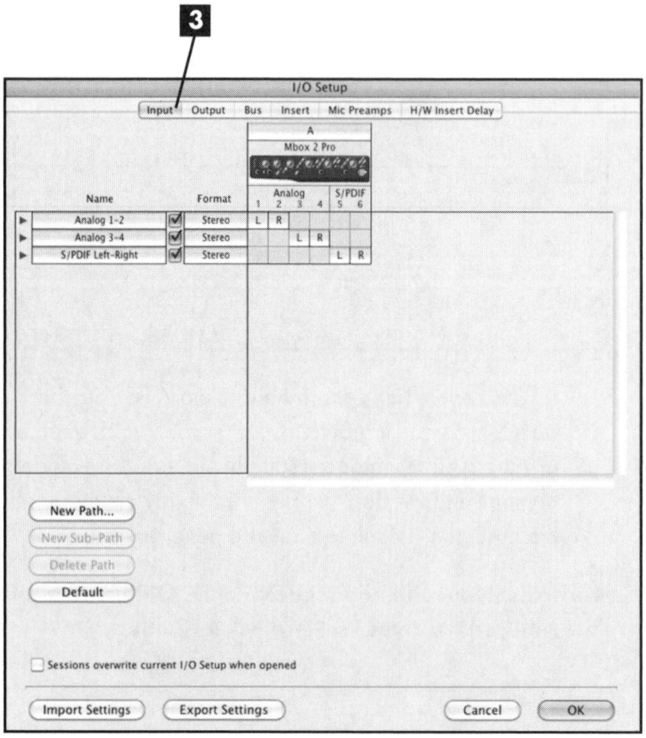

A WORD ABOUT THE SCREENSHOTS

The examples in this section show the windows you'll see if you have an Mbox2 Pro system. If you have any other kind of interface, the window will look a little different (although the functions will be the same). If your audio interface doesn't support the same number of I/O channels as an Mbox 2 Pro, you may not be able to create the same number of paths as described in the steps in this section.!

Customizing Your Inputs

The grid area and the labels to the left represent input paths, which enable you to match the virtual inputs in the Pro Tools software to the physical inputs of your audio hardware. The dialog box currently displays a default input setup. This section goes through the process of creating a custom I/O setup from the ground up. To make sure we're creating everything from scratch, let's delete the existing paths.

1. **Click** on the top **path name**.
2. **Press and hold** the **Shift key** and **click** on the remaining **path names** until all the paths are highlighted.
3. **Click** on the **Delete Path button**. All the input paths will disappear.

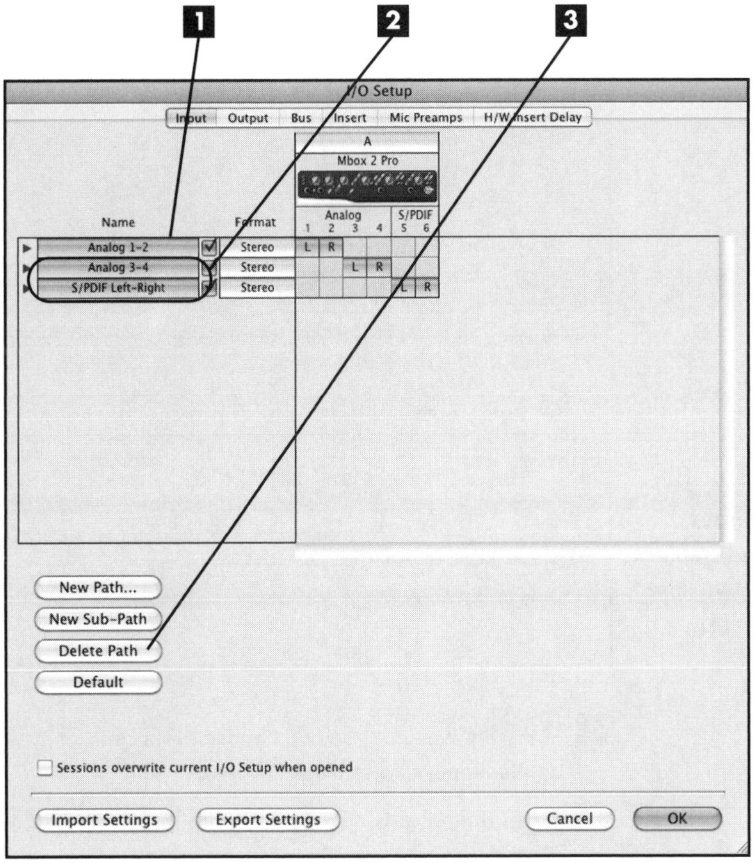

4 Now, let's create some new input paths. **Click** on the **New Path button**. The New Paths window will appear.

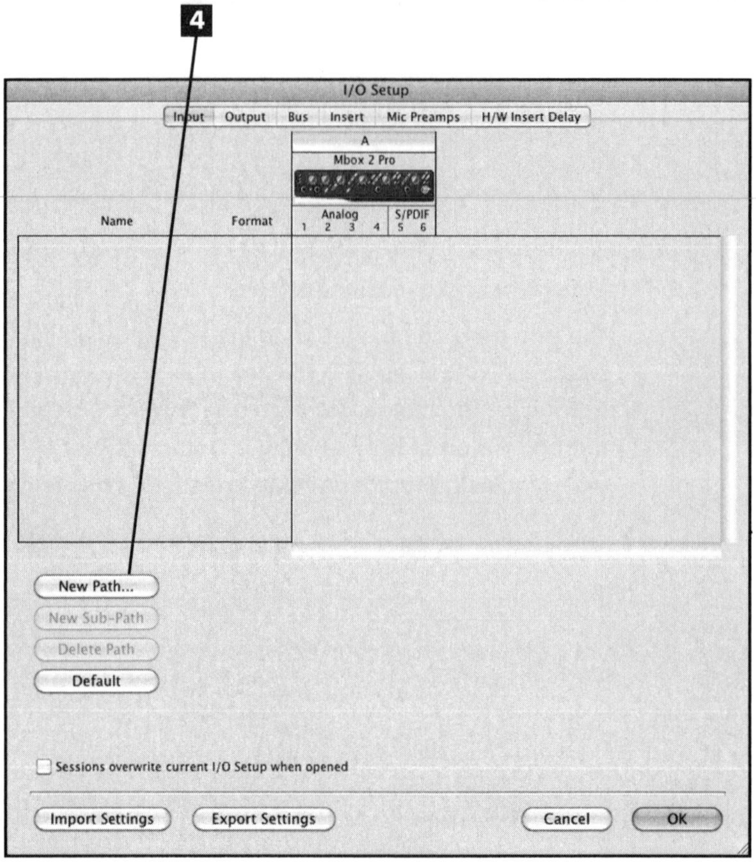

5 In the Create field, **type** the **number of input paths** you want to create. In this case, just leave this field at the default (1).

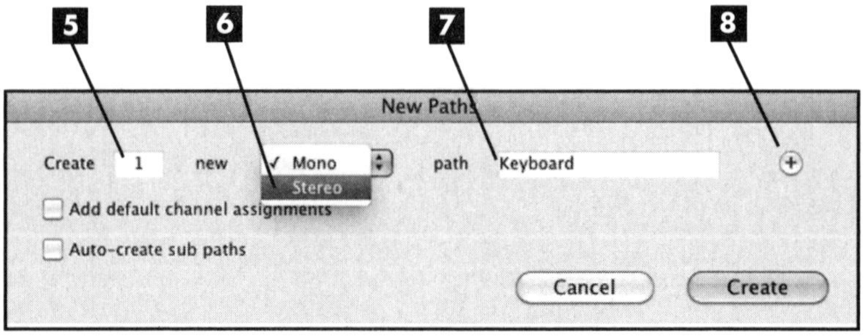

6 In the New menu, you can choose the format of your input path. For this example, click on the menu, and **choose Stereo**.

7 **Type** a descriptive **name** for your input path (In this example, I'll be using the path for recording a keyboard.)

8 At this point, you're poised to create a single stereo input path. Before you close that window, however, let's create a few more paths. **Click** on the **Add Row button**. A new row of input paths appears.

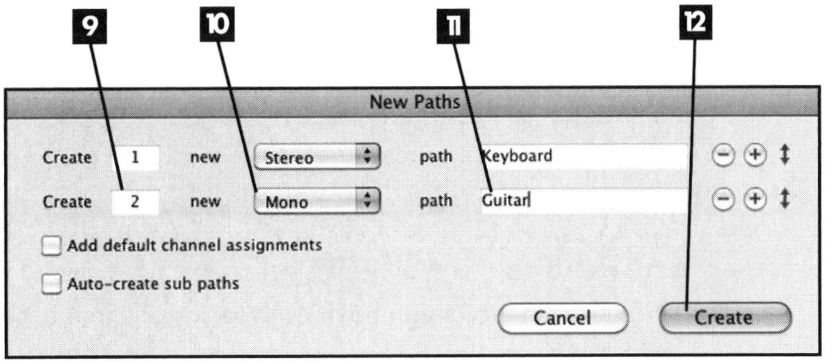

9 In the lower row, you'll be creating two paths, so **type 2** in the Create field.

10 For this example, you'll **create mono paths**, so you can leave the New menu alone.

11 For this I/O setup, these paths will be used for recording guitars, so **type Guitar** in the Path field.

12 **Click** on the **Create button**. Pro Tools will create the paths.

Now, you'll see a single stereo path and two mono paths in the I/O Setup window.

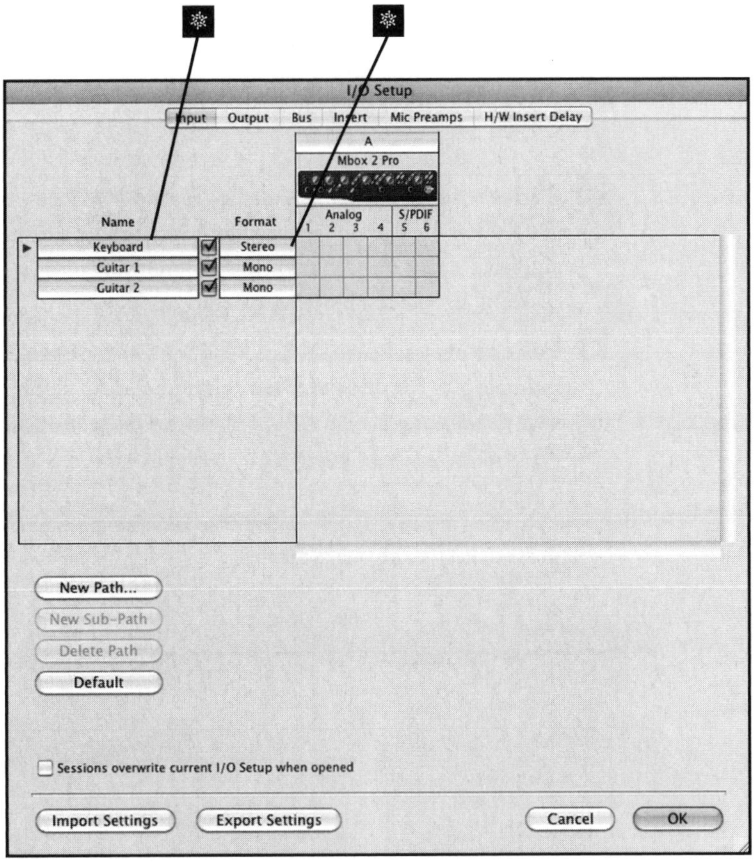

- If you decide you want to change the name of a path, double-click the path name, type a new name, and press Enter.
- To change a path's format after its creation, click on the appropriate button in the Format column and choose the format you want (i.e., Mono, Stereo, etc.) from the menu that opens.

HOW SHOULD I NAME MY INPUTS?

A good rule of thumb is to name your inputs for the devices that are connected to your system.

> **HOW I'VE ARRANGED MY INPUTS**
>
> In my system, I've set up my I/O window to reflect the devices that I've attached to the Mbox2 Pro in my home studio. The first path is reserved for a synthesizer (Stereo), followed by the bass and guitar (both mono inputs).

Assigning Your Path

Now it's time to assign each path to specific inputs of your audio interface. Let's start with the Keyboard path:

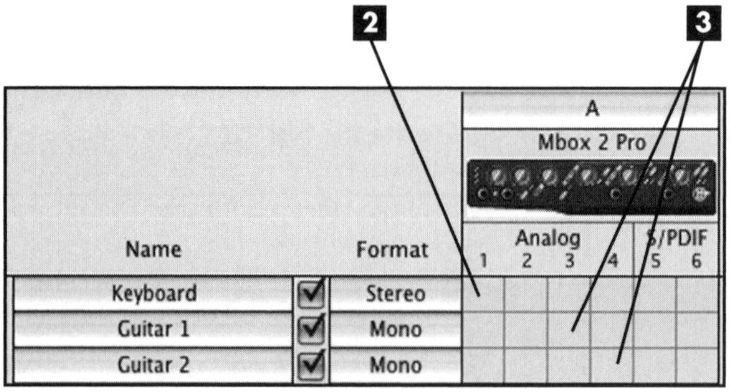

1. **Move** your **cursor** to the grid area in the top row. Your cursor will change from an arrow to a pencil.
2. **Click** on the **square** that matches the input you desire—in this case, click on the square in the Analog 1 column. Because this happens to be a stereo path, two blocks will appear, marked L and R (for left and right). Don't worry if you click on the wrong box; you can click and drag each block to the appropriate cell.
3. **Repeat steps 1 and 2**, assigning the Guitar 1 path to Analog 3 and the Guitar 2 path to Analog 4. For each of these, a single block will appear, labeled M (for mono).

> **ASSIGNING A STEREO PATH**
>
> In the case of a stereo path, click on the square that is assigned to the left channel. An L and an R block will be created automatically.

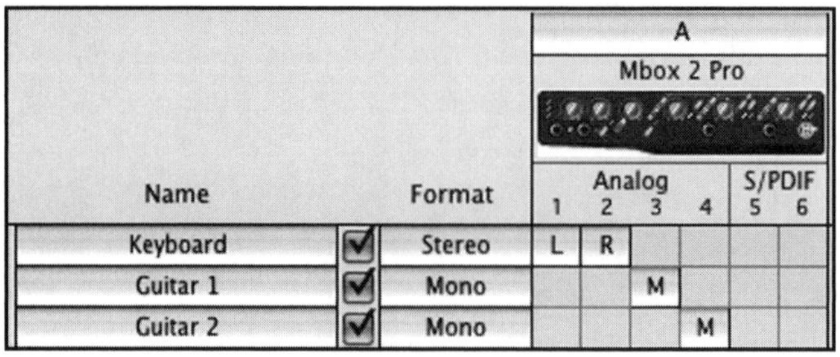

If you've followed the steps in this section (and assuming that your audio interface supports enough channels of I/O), you might see something like the image shown here. In this example, I have a stereo path dedicated to my keyboard (which is attached to inputs 1 and 2), a bass (using the Guitar 1 path, which is assigned to analog input 3), and a guitar (using the Guitar 2 path, which is mapped to analog input 4).

ADD DEFAULT CHANNEL ASSIGNMENTS

In the New Paths window, you might have noticed an Add Default Channel Assignments checkbox in the lower-left part of the window. Checking this box will automatically assign each track in turn to the first available input channel(s). If we had checked this box when we created our paths, it would have done our assignment work for us, but what fun would *that* be?

Setting Up Outputs

You've set up your system to deal with incoming audio—good job! The next step is to customize how audio *exits* your audio interface. For the examples shown in this section, we'll once again create a basic setup that works in my studio and that you can adapt to reflect your own needs and I/O capabilities. The good news is that the Output tab of the I/O Setup dialog box is laid out very similarly to the Input tab, so this should go a lot more quickly!

1. **Click** on the **Output tab** in the I/O Setup window. The tab will move to the front.
2. Just as you did in the previous section, select all existing paths, and **click** on the **Delete Path button** (technically, this isn't necessary, but for the sake of this example it'll make things clearer).
3. **Click** on the **New Path button**.

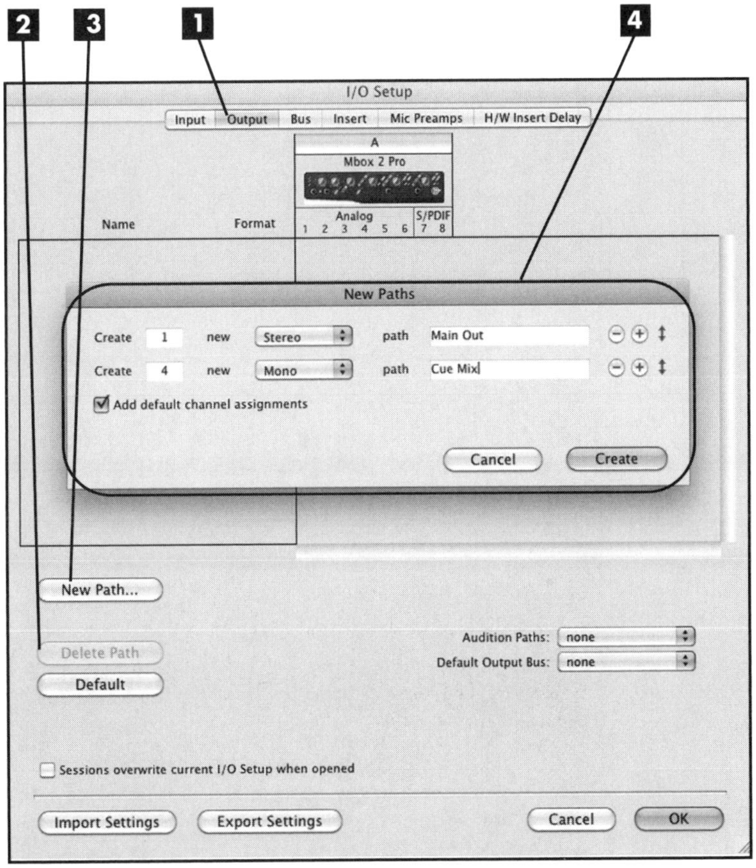

4. Following the same steps you took when creating input paths, **create one stereo path** (named "Main Out") and a **number of mono paths** (here, I'm creating four mono paths, which I've named "Cue Mix"). In this case, I'll check the Add Default Channel Assignments checkbox to make things easier.

When you're finished, your Output page should look something like this:

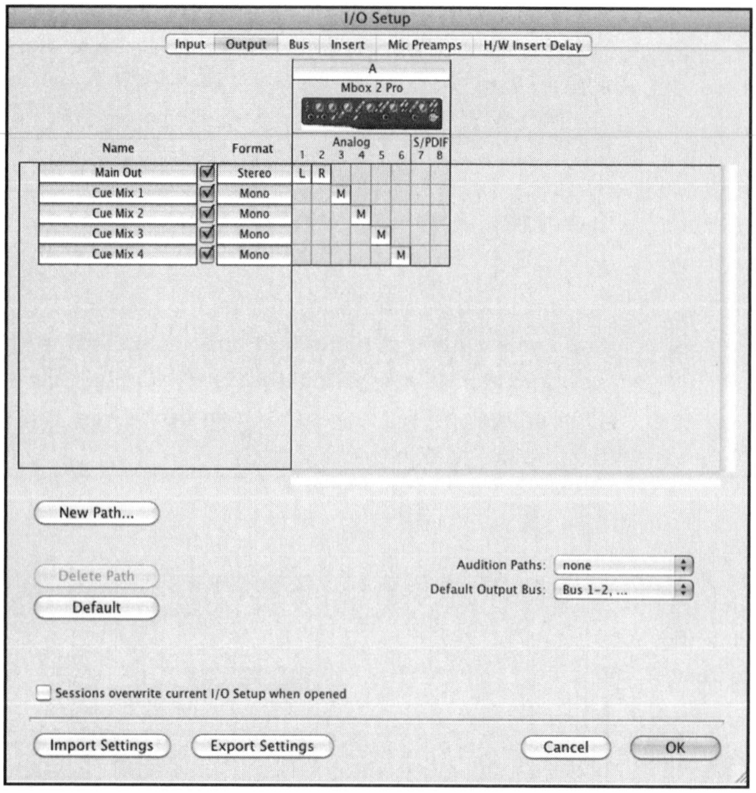

GENERAL RULES FOR OUTPUTS

This kind of setup is pretty common for stereo projects. In this case, you would typically use Main Output for your studio monitors. Use the Cue Mix outputs for individual headphone mixes for your recording musicians (these mixes can be stereo or mono, depending on the situation). Remember, though, that these are all line-level signals, and they will need amplification before they go to speakers or headphones.

OUTPUT PATHS AND PARTIAL OVERLAPS

When we refer to overlapping paths, we're talking about a situation in which multiple paths share physical inputs or outputs (like, let's say, a stereo path using outputs 1 and 2 and a mono path using output 2). In previous versions of Pro Tools, any kind of overlap with output paths was strictly prohibited. Pro Tools wouldn't even let you save your I/O settings if there was any kind of overlap whatsoever. Now, in Pro Tools 9, that ban has been lifted (yippee!) to some degree. Now, paths that completely overlap are possible. However, it's worth noting that partially overlapping paths (for example, a stereo path using outputs 1 and 2 and another stereo path using outputs 2 and 3) is still not possible in Pro Tools. In most cases, this limitation poses no real hardship.

Setting Up Buses

One of the aspects of Pro Tools that has changed most in the last few versions is the I/O Setup window's Bus tab. Longtime Pro Tools users will remember buses as virtual audio cables that you can use within the Pro Tools mixing environment. We use them for all sorts of internal routing, such as sending dry audio from an Audio track to a reverb on an Aux track. (Don't worry if this all sounds like Greek—you'll learn all about this starting in Chapter 8, "Basic Mixing.")

Although buses are still commonly used for this sort of internal signal routing, they are no longer limited to this internal function. They' re also now used as a bridge between your Pro Tools software and the output paths you set up in this chapter.

Although your Bus tab has made subtle alterations automatically to reflect the output paths you just created, perhaps the best way to illustrate the role of buses is to create a Bus tab from scratch:

1. **Click** on the **Bus tab**. The tab will move to the front.
2. Because we're building the Bus tab from scratch for the sake of illustration, select all existing paths, and **click** on the **Delete Path button**, just as you did in the previous section. The main area of the Bus tab will be blank, as shown here.

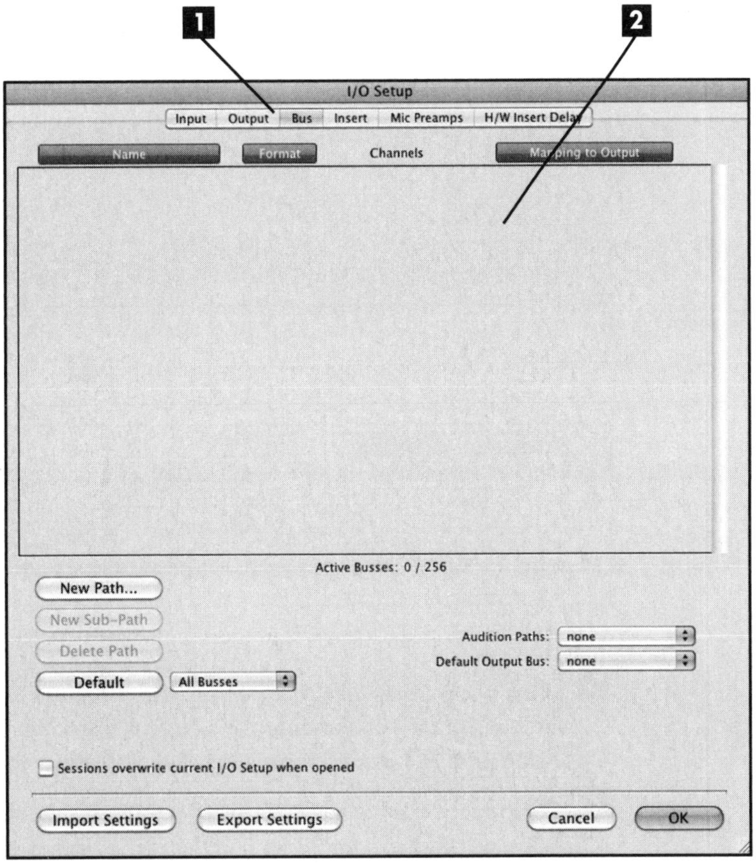

The basic idea behind buses is that they can be either assigned (or *mapped*) to a physical output path (in which case they're called output buses), or they can be unmapped to a physical output path (in which case they're called internal buses). Let's start out by creating some output buses so that we can use the output paths that we created earlier.

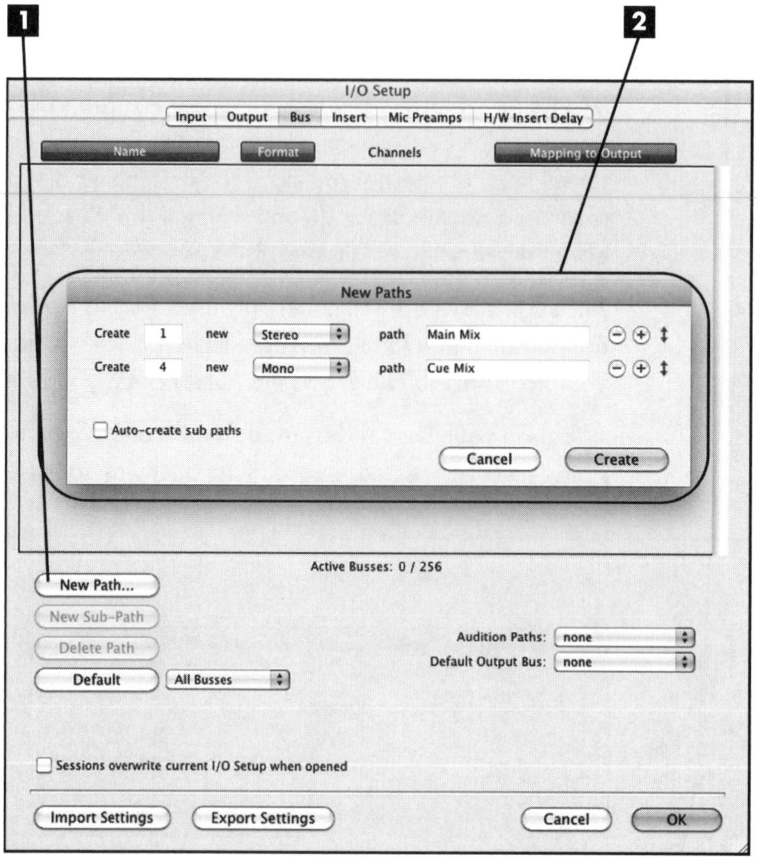

1 **Click** on the **New Path button**.

2 Using the same steps you used in the previous sections, **create** a **single stereo path** (which I've named "Main Mix") and **four mono paths** (which I've called "Cue Mix"). You might notice that these are the same numbers and types of paths that you created when we created our outputs—it's no coincidence! We'll be mapping these paths to physical output paths next.

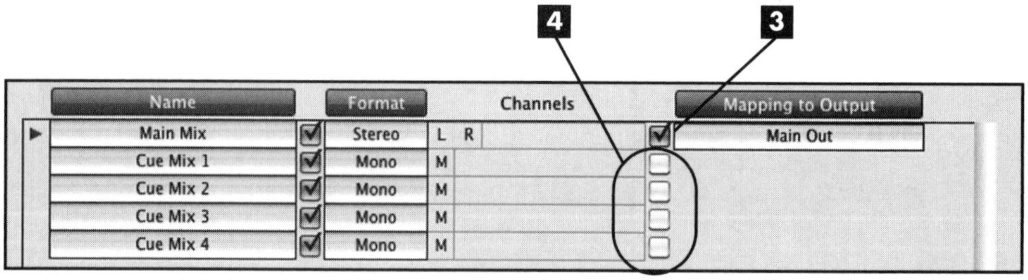

3 **Click** on the **Mapping to Output checkbox** in the first bus. If you've been following the steps so far in the chapter, this bus is a stereo bus. Because you've created only one stereo path, it'll automatically map to that stereo output path (named "Main Out").

4 **Click** on the remaining **Mapping to Output checkboxes**. Again, if you have been following the steps, the buses and the paths will naturally line up, and you'll see something like this:

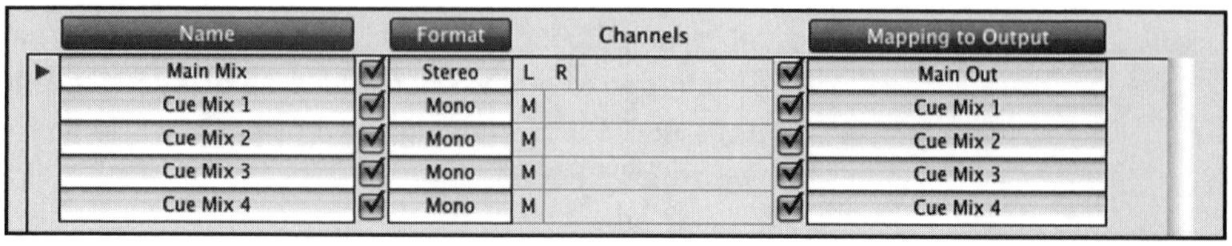

Now let's continue by creating a few internal buses—the kind that *aren't* assigned to physical output paths. You'll use these kinds of buses for all sorts of tasks, such as setting up reverb effects and submixes.

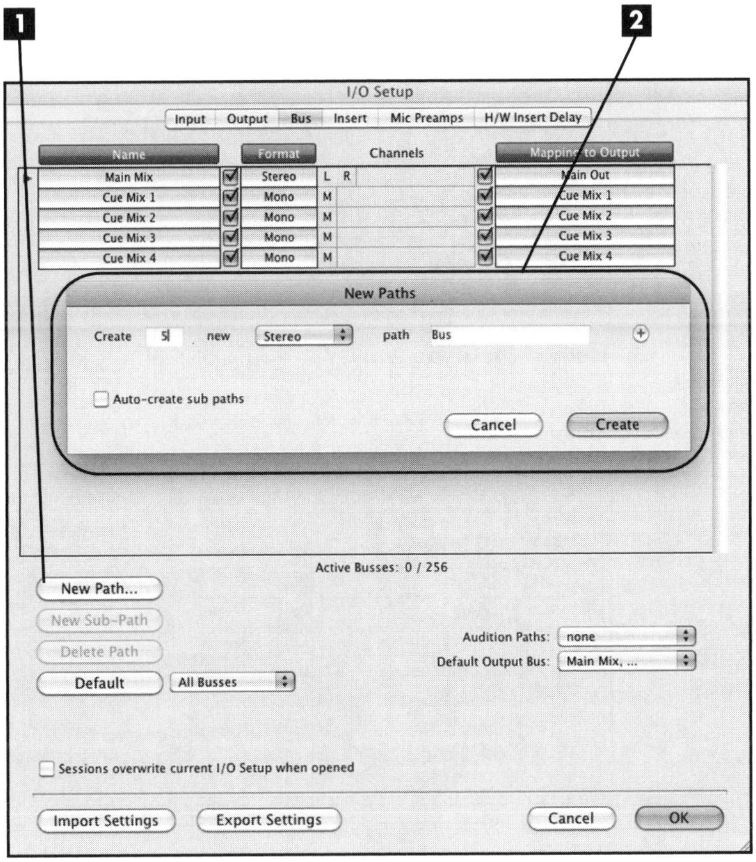

1 Once more, **click** on the **New Path button**.

2 This time, **create five new stereo buses**. In this case, don't worry about naming them. We'll do that individually this time.

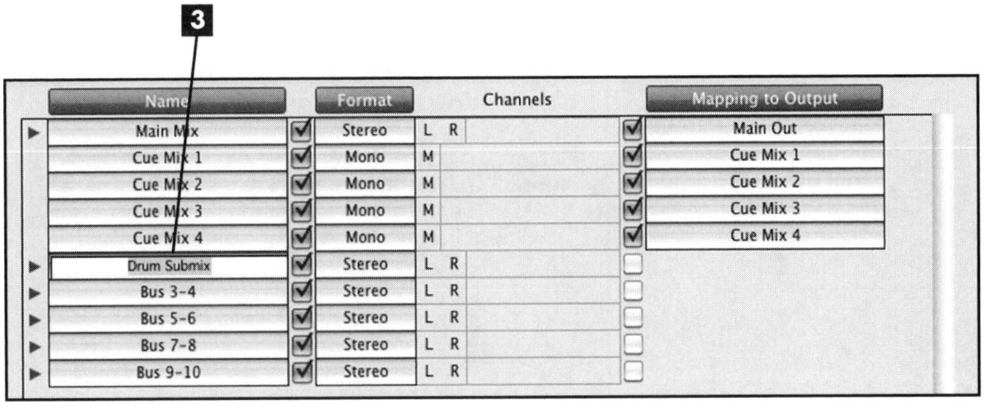

3 Individually naming paths is easy: Just **double-click** on the **path name** and **type** the **name** that you want to use. For the purposes of this exercise, let's use the following names for the buses you just created:

- Drum Submix
- GTR Submix
- Key Submix
- Vox Submix
- Reverb Bus

When you're done, press the **Enter** key. When you're finished, here's what you should see:

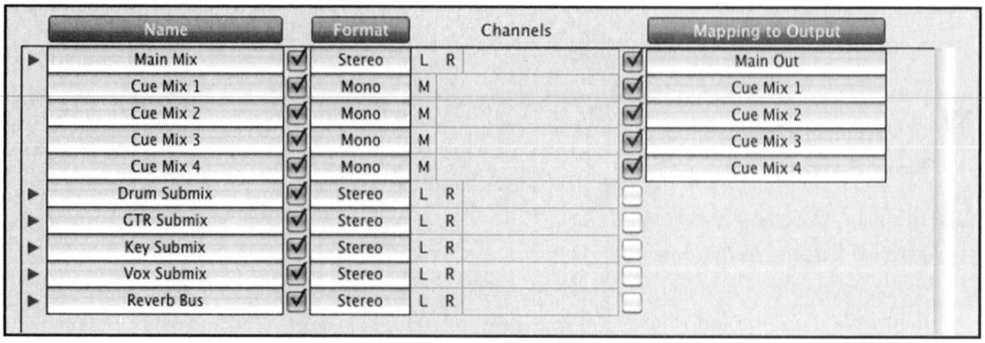

Here's where the work you've done will pay off:

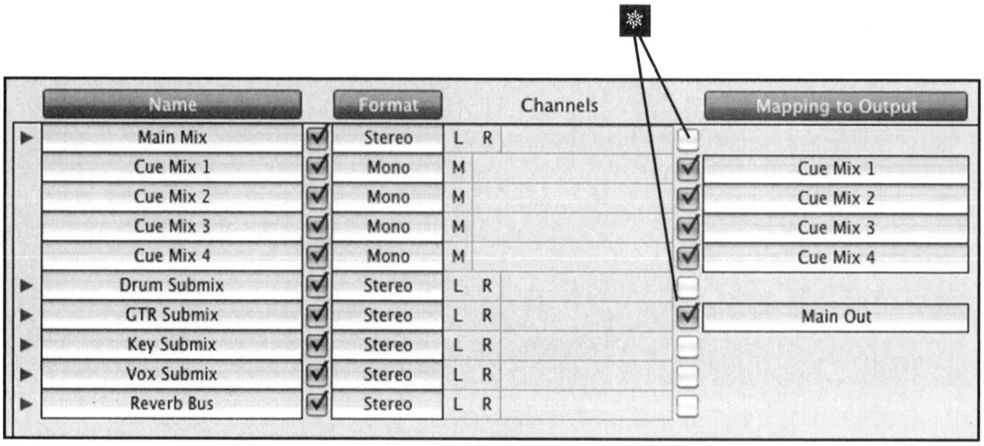

- Let's say that you want to play your Guitar submix through your main speakers, to hear how the parts blend. With buses, it's no problem—just assign the desired bus to the desired output path (in this case, you'd be assigning the GTR Submix bus to the Main Out output path). Basically, what you're doing is changing that bus from an internal bus to an output bus. Incidentally, in this case, you'd want to unassign the Main Mix bus, as shown here.

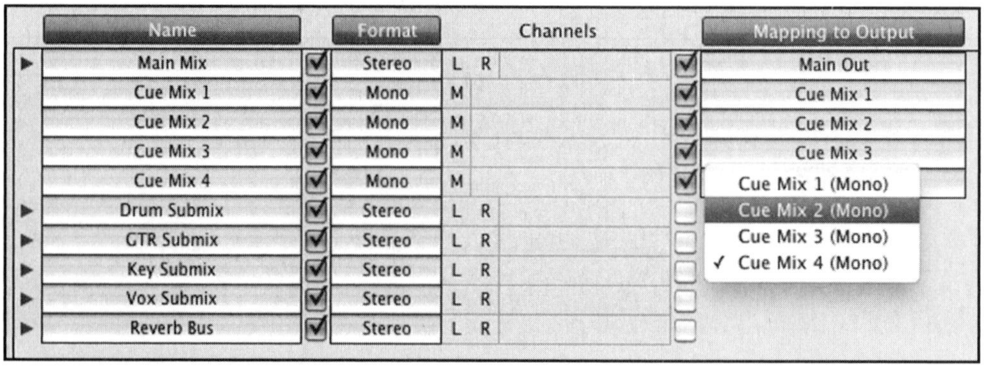

- If you want to reassign a bus that's already assigned to a physical output path, it's as easy as clicking on the desired **Mapping to Output** button. A list of available output paths will appear; you can choose the one that suits your needs.

MORE BUSES, MORE FUN!

The Bus tab that you set up here is pretty typical, but you'll almost certainly need more buses as your session grows. Don't fret—you can create up to 256 internal buses in your session.

GET YOURSELF SORTED

You can arrange your buses in a number of ways. One of the easiest ways is to sort them by name, format, or mapping to output. Just **click** on the appropriate **column heading** button to sort your buses. (Clicking the heading button a second time will invert the sorting.) If none of those automated sorting modes suits your needs, you can also manually drag your paths to the order you desire by clicking the path's name and dragging it up or down.

Setting Up Sub-Paths

You've set up your paths. Now it's time to think about *sub-paths*. Sub-paths are individual assignments within a path. For example, take a look at the Main Mix bus (a stereo path). If you will only ever have a stereo signal going into that pair of outputs, you're all set. However, if you want to also be able to use each output separately—for example, to send a signal to only the right or left speaker—you might consider setting up a couple of sub-paths within that stereo path.

1. **Click** on the desired **stereo path name**. The name will be highlighted.
2. **Click twice** on the **New Sub-Path button**. Two sub-paths will be created below the path, with default names (Path 1 and Path 2).
3. **Double-click** on each **sub-path** and **name it**, just as you did with the paths.
4. As you did with paths, you need to assign a channel to each sub-path. **Click** on the desired **grid square**. A block with an M (for mono) will appear.

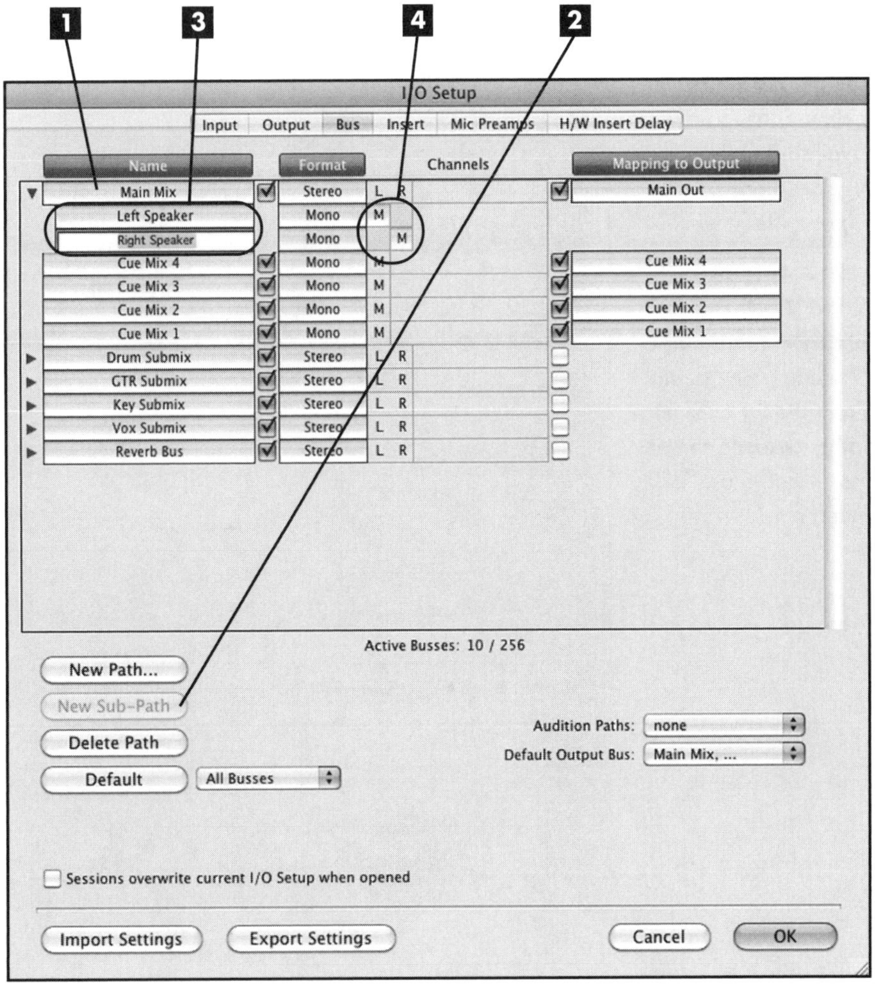

AUTO-CREATE SUB-PATHS

In the New Paths window, you might have noticed an Auto-Create Sub-Paths checkbox, located in the lower-left part of the window. Checking this box will automatically create the appropriate sub-paths for multichannel buses or inputs. (Output paths don't have sub-paths.)

AND SPEAKING OF SURROUND SOUND...

With a basic Pro Tools 9 (host-based) system, you're limited to creating mono or stereo paths, which effectively limits you to mono or stereo production. Actually, this isn't a serious limitation for many users, but there's a growing segment of LE users who crave the ability to create surround mixes. Don't despair—you can add surround functionality (up to 7.1 mixes!) by picking up the Complete Production Toolkit 2, an optional add-on for Pro Tools. You can learn more about the Complete Production Toolkit at http://www.avid.com.

Audition Paths and Default Outputs

From time to time, you'll want to "audition" audio files before you bring them into your session (this is something we'll talk about later in this chapter). You can choose to have this auditioned signal come out of any active output path you want. Here's how to set it up:

1. **Click** on the **Audition Paths down arrow**. A list of available paths will appear, based on your current output paths.
2. In this example (a default Mbox2 Pro I/O setup), there are four stereo output paths, including one digital path. From the list of available paths, **choose** the **path** you want to use for auditioning files.

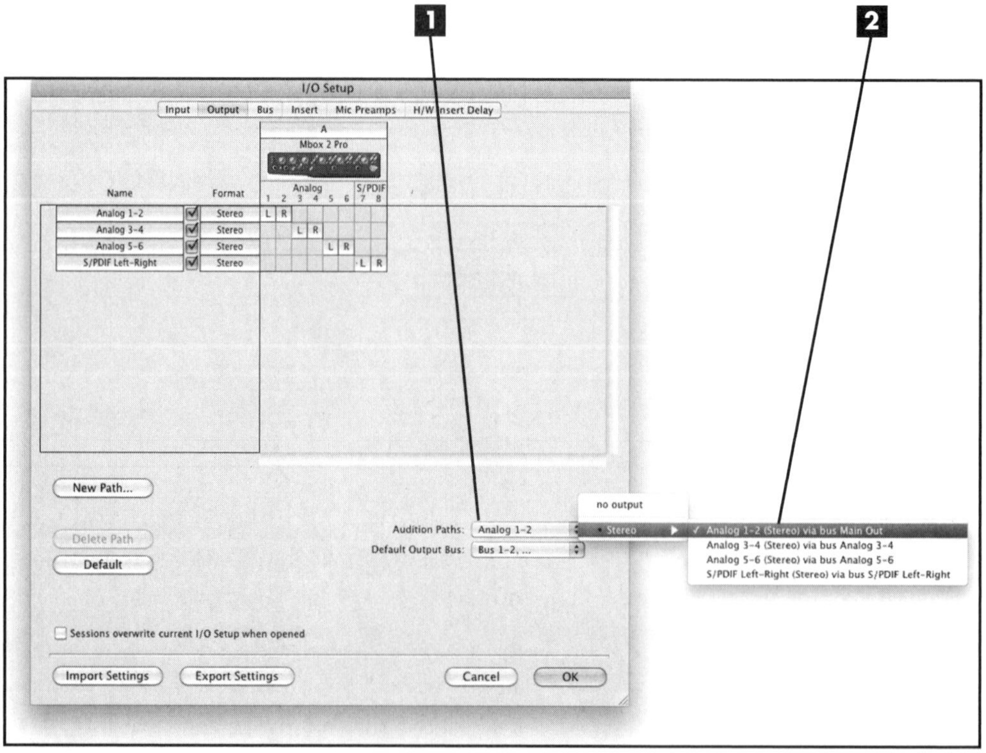

AUDITION PATH TIP

For many Pro Tools users, the main output path (the same one that you use to monitor your mix) is a good choice. You'll hear any auditioned files through your main monitor speakers.

Do you have a favorite output path—one you usually use when creating new tracks? You can configure Pro Tools so that new tracks are automatically set up with any output you desire!

1. **Click** on the **Default Output Bus down arrow**. A list of available paths will appear, based on your current output paths.
2. In this example (a default Mbox2 Pro I/O setup), there are four stereo output paths, including one digital path. From the list of available paths, **choose** the **path** that you want to be your default output path for newly created tracks.

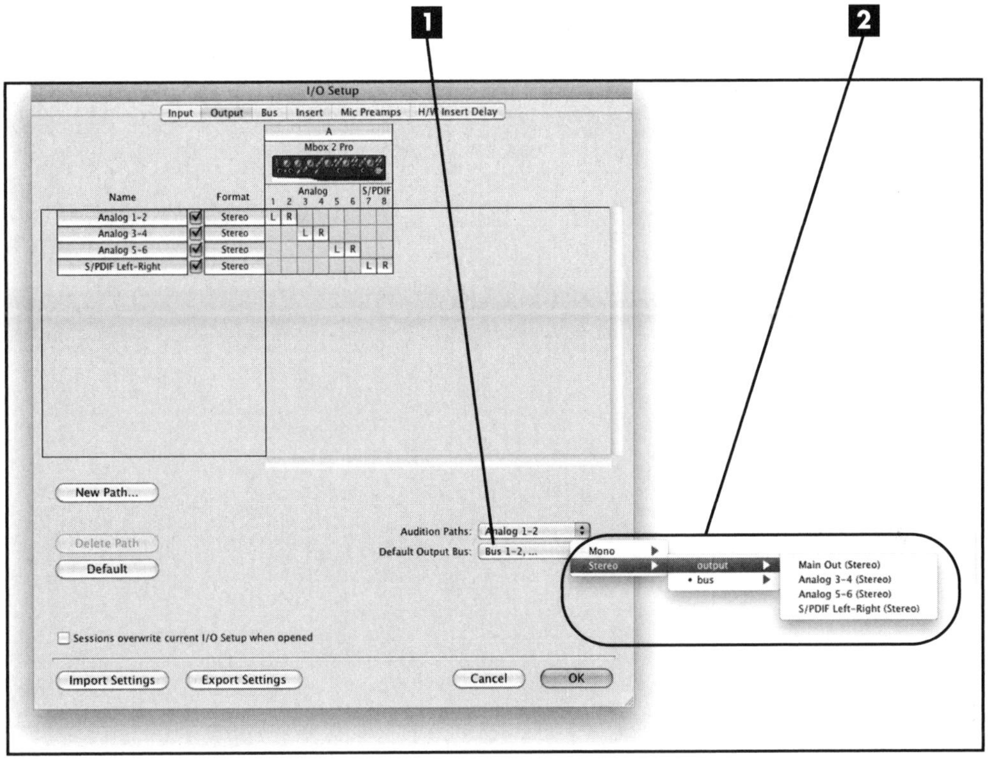

More I/O Tabs

Before we move on from this very important window, let's take a quick look at the remaining tabs.

Setting Up Inserts

In the world of DAWs, you can use a wide variety of software effects (reverbs, delays, and so on) called *plug-ins*. Does that mean you won't be able to use any of the rackmount effects you've got in your studio? Not at all—you can bring them into the Pro Tools environment through a configuration of your inputs and outputs called *hardware inserts* or *I/O inserts*. You'll learn more about inserts and how to use them in Chapter 8. Right now, our job is to set things up correctly.

One thing you need to know about hardware inserts is how to connect your gear. The rule is simple: Use the inputs that correspond to the ones you used for the outputs. For example, if you have a rackmount stereo reverb unit that you want to use with Pro Tools, and you use outputs 3-4 to send signal to the reverb unit, you have to use inputs 3-4 to get audio from the reverb back into Pro Tools.

In this example, I'll set up my system to use a digital reverb, with signal going to the unit from my S/PDIF outputs, and taking the processed signal back in through the S/PDIF inputs.

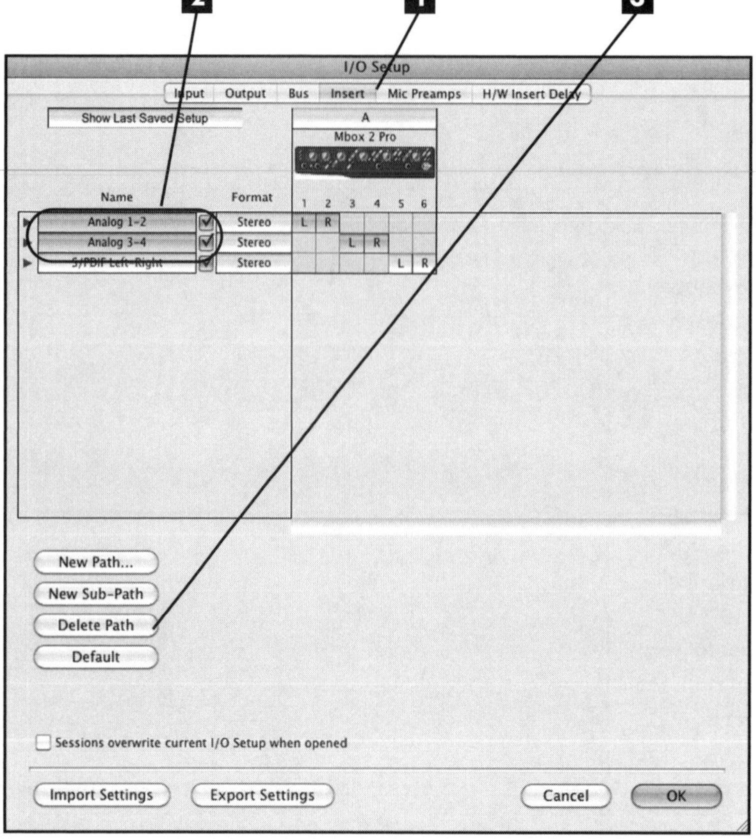

1. **Click** on the **Insert tab** in the I/O Setup dialog box. The tab will move to the front.
2. Because we're only going to be using the S/PDIF path for our reverb unit, let's delete all the paths that we won't need. Holding the **Shift** key, **click** on every **path name** that you *don't* plan to use for routing signal to and from your external gear.
3. **Click** on the **Delete Path button**. The paths you clicked will disappear.

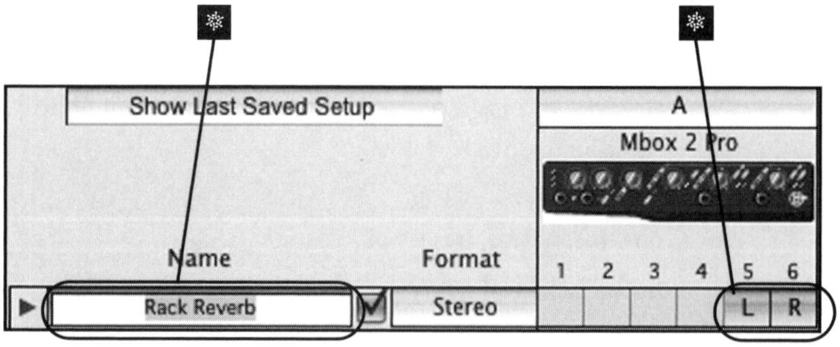

- Double-click on the path name and type a descriptive name for your Hardware Insert path. Technically, this is an optional step, but doing this will make working with your external gear easier and more straightforward.

- Similar to the Input and Output tabs, if you need to change the channel assignments, you can easily do this by clicking and dragging the channel icons to the desired position.

The Hardware Insert Delay Tab

On the topic of external effects units, it's important to mention that *all* devices exhibit some amount of delay (also caused *latency*). Although it might be overstating things a bit to say that this delay can sometimes wreak havoc on your mixes, even small amounts of latency can affect the phase alignment of audio within your system, which *will* affect the sound of your mix. Not to worry—the Hardware Insert Delay tab enables you to enter values that will compensate for the latency of your external devices. The details on how to enter the correct value is part of a larger discussion on Automatic Delay Compensation, which we' ll cover in detail in Chapter 10.

The Mic Preamps Tab

Certain external microphone preamp units—including the Avid PRE—can be controlled remotely directly from Pro Tools. This is a real convenience, particularly in situations where the microphone preamp is some distance from the Pro Tools user. It enables you to set up your preamp in the Mic Preamps tab of the I/O setup window. This sort of setup is beyond the scope of an introductory book, and is covered with your preamp documentation.

Managing Your I/O Settings

Now that you've created a tailor-made I/O setup, you might want to save your settings so you can use them in other sessions.

Saving Your I/O Settings

To save your I/O settings to an I/O settings file, follow these steps.

1. **Click** on **Export Settings**. The Save I/O Settings As dialog box will open.
2. **Type** a **name** for these settings in the Save As text box.
3. **Click** on **Save**. Your settings will be saved to Pro Tools' default I/O location.

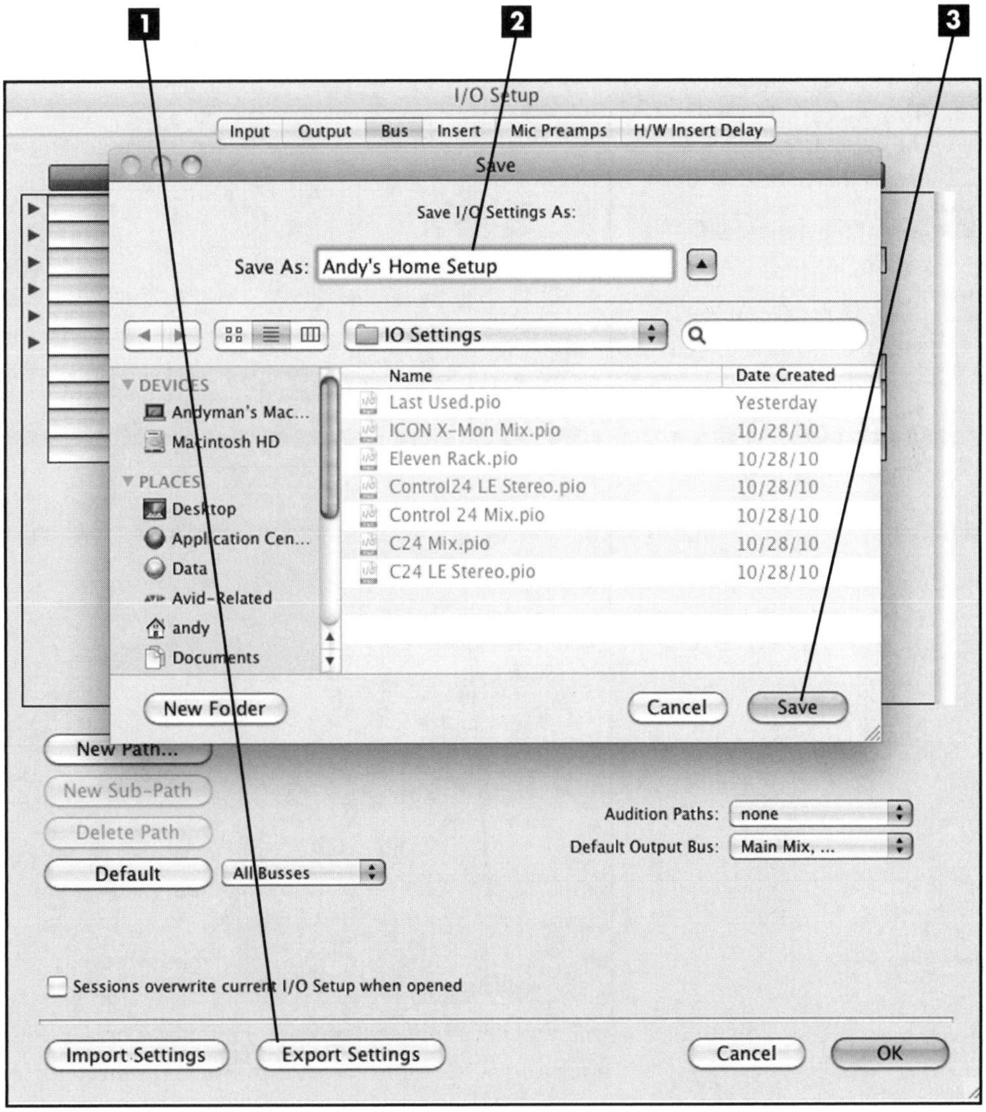

THE IMPORTANCE OF NAMING

Choose a descriptive name for your settings so you can recall them easily when you want to use them in another session.

I/O SETTINGS AND NEW SESSIONS

There's another benefit to exporting your tweaked I/O settings: If you save the I/O settings to the default location (which you just did if you were following the steps outlined here), your new setup will be an option in the I/O Settings drop-down menu when you create a new session.

Recalling Your Settings

After you've customized and exported your I/O settings, you can easily recall them. That means the time you spend tweaking your I/O settings to work in a variety of situations is easily integrated into any session.

1. To load previously saved I/O settings, **click** on the **Import Settings button**. The Select I/O Settings to Import dialog box will open.
2. **Select** the desired **I/O settings file**.
3. **Click** on the **Open button**. The I/O settings you selected will be loaded.
4. **Click** on **OK**. The dialog box will close. You're finished!

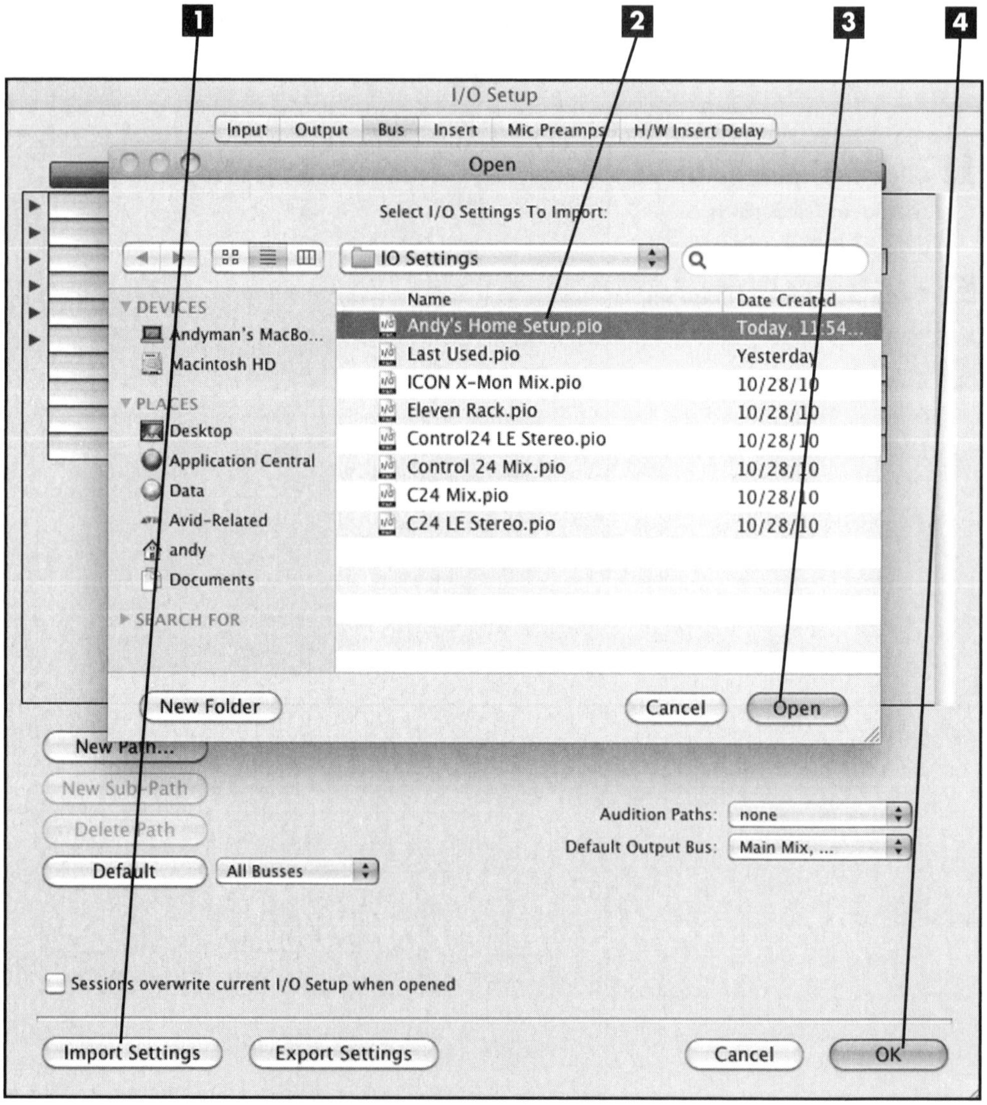

NEW IN PRO TOOLS 9: SELECTIVE IMPORTING

In previous versions of Pro Tools, when an I/O setup was imported (using the steps you just completed), the *entire* existing I/O setup would be affected. Thankfully, this has changed to allow users to target the aspects of I/O that you specifically want to alter. Starting with Pro Tools 9, the active page of the I/O window (the one you're currently looking at) will be the only one affected by the import. For example, if you are looking at the Input tab and you import an I/O Setting file, only the Input tab will be changed by the operation. Because of the special relationship between the Output tab and the Bus tab, sometimes importing into the Output tab will have some effect on the Bus tab.

NEW IN PRO TOOLS 9: SESSIONS OVERWRITE CURRENT I/O SETUP WHEN OPENED

In previous versions of Pro Tools, when a session was opened, the session's own I/O settings would overwrite any previously active I/O settings. While this worked well in some cases, it did pose some difficulties in other types of workflows—particularly in cases where sessions were moved from one studio to another. The Sessions Overwrite Current I/O Setup When Opened checkbox will enable you to choose which kind of behavior best works for you.

Tracks

Now that we've finished with the I/O Setup window (and if you haven't closed that window by now, do so by clicking the OK button), let's start making things happen within Pro Tools' main windows. Whether you're looking at the Edit window or the Mix window, you'll notice that your new session opened up without any tracks in it. It's up to *you* to create the tracks you'll need in your session.

Making Tracks

No matter what kind of track you want to create, you'll start with the following steps:

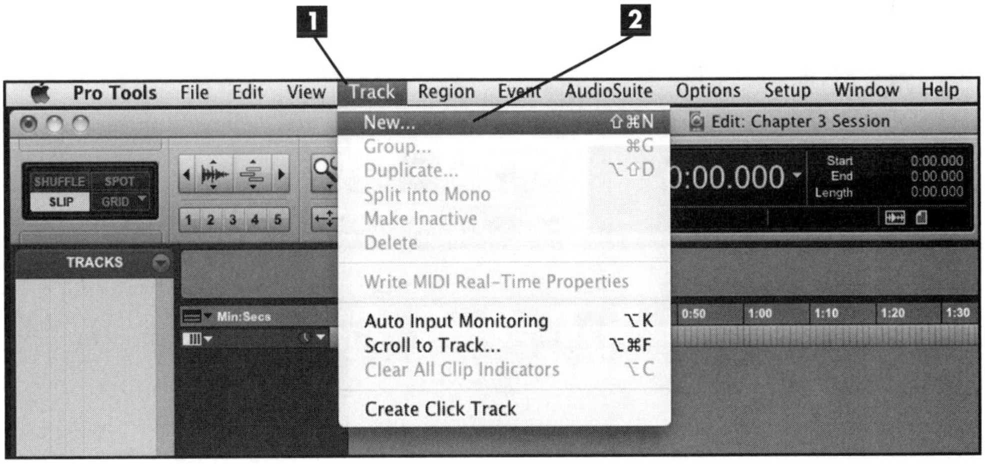

1. **Click** on **Track**. The Track menu will appear.
2. **Click** on **New**. The New Tracks dialog box will open.

NEW TRACK SHORTCUT

Because you'll be making many tracks as you work more and more in Pro Tools, you might want to learn the New Track shortcut. Command+Shift+N (Mac) or Ctrl+Shift+N (PC) will launch the New Tracks dialog box.

3 As soon as it's launched, the New Tracks dialog box is set up to create one mono Audio track (if you just finished the previous section, you'll see a great similarity between this dialog box and the New Paths dialog box in the I/O Setup window). For this example, let's create four tracks instead. **Click** in the **Create field** to highlight it (if it isn't already highlighted) and then **type** the **number of tracks** you want to create (in this case, you'll type 4).

MORE ABOUT THE NEW TRACKS DIALOG BOX

You'll notice that there are a few drop-down menus in the New Tracks dialog box. The first drop-down menu (the Track Format menu) enables you to specify whether your track will be stereo or mono. The second drop-down menu (the Track Type menu) enables you to select the *kind* of track you'll create. We'll be covering these menus (and what they mean) in just a bit, so read on!

4 **Click** on the **Create button**. The New Tracks dialog box will close, and the tracks will be created in your session.

Now let's create a couple of *stereo* Audio tracks.

1 **Open** the **New Tracks** dialog box as you did in the previous section.

2 **Type 2** in the Create field to create two tracks.

3 **Click** on the **Track Format drop-down menu.**

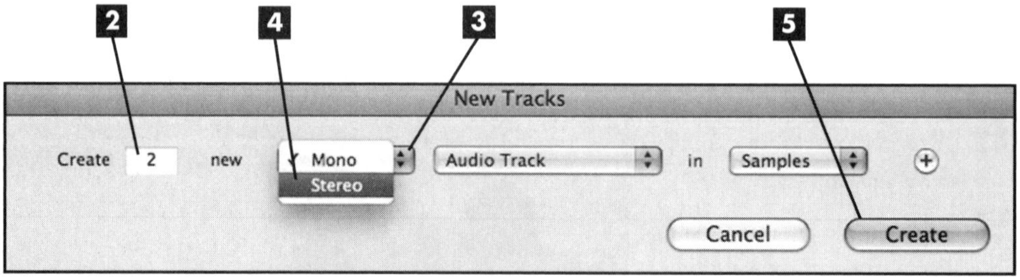

4 **Click** on **Stereo**. The option will be selected.

5 **Click** on **Create**. Two stereo Audio tracks will be created, just as you specified.

TRACK COUNT AND THE COMPLETE PRODUCTION TOOLKIT

You've just created six Audio tracks (four mono and two stereo). How many more can you make? Well, that depends. Here's what you'll get with a basic Pro Tools 9 system:

- If your session is at a sample rate of 44.1 or 48 kHz, you'll be able to use up to 96 active audio tracks.
- If your session is at a sample rate of 88.2 or 96 kHz, you'll be able to use up to 48 active audio tracks.
- If your session is at a sample rate of 176.4 or 192 kHz, you'll be able to have up to 24 active audio tracks.

We've previously talked about the Complete Production Toolkit 2, a software addition to Pro Tools that adds features and power to Pro Tools 9. In terms of active track count, here's what you'll get with the Complete Production Toolkit 2:

- If your session is at a sample rate of 44.1 or 48 kHz, you'll be able to use up to 192 active audio tracks.
- If your session is at a sample rate of 88.2 or 96 kHz, you'll be able to use up to 96 active audio tracks.
- If your session is at a sample rate of 176.4 or 192 kHz, you'll be able to have up to 48 active audio tracks.

Creating an Auxiliary Input Track

An Auxiliary Input track (also commonly called an *Aux Input* or simply an *Aux* track) is identical to an Audio track, except that it doesn't contain any audio regions. Its main function is to serve as a means of routing audio from a source to a destination or as a means to process one or more audio signals with plug-in effects.

You'll learn how to use Aux tracks in Chapters 7, "Using MIDI," and 8, "Basic Mixing," and you'll find them very handy indeed—particularly when you get down to the business of mixing. In this chapter, though, let's start with the process of creating a couple of stereo Aux tracks, a process almost identical to creating Audio tracks.

1. **Open** the **New Tracks** dialog box as you did in the previous sections.

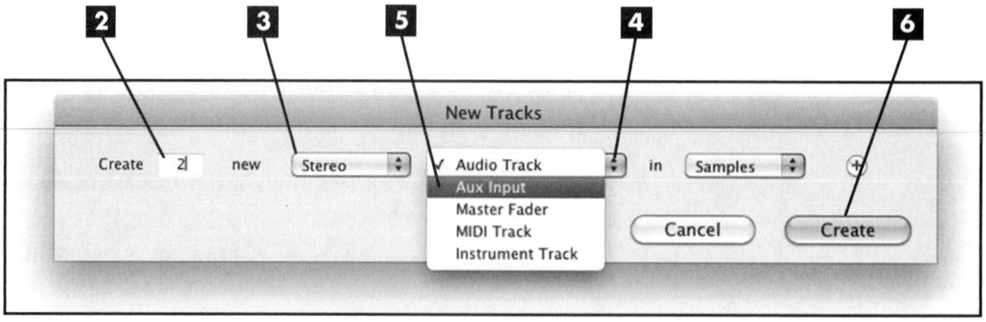

2. **Type 2** in the Create field to create two tracks.
3. **Click** on **Stereo** in the Track Format drop-down menu to make these Aux tracks *stereo* Aux tracks. The option will be selected.
4. **Click** on the **Track Type menu**. A list of all the different track types available in Pro Tools will appear.
5. **Click** on **Aux Input**. The option will be selected.
6. **Click** on **Create**. Two stereo Aux tracks will be created, just as you specified.

> **HOW MANY AUX TRACKS?**
>
> Although sometimes in larger sessions, you might find yourself concerned about running out of active audio tracks, you'll rarely find yourself in that position with Aux tracks. You have as many as 160 Auxiliary Input tracks at your disposal in Pro Tools 9, so you should be all set, even in very complex mix situations.

Master Faders, MIDI, and Instrument Tracks

As you probably noticed, there are three other kinds of tracks listed in the Track Type drop-down menu: Master Fader, MIDI, and Instrument tracks. Although you might not use these kinds of tracks in every session you create, they'll come in very useful when you need them.

If you've ever worked with a traditional mixing board, you know what a Master Fader does. These are the faders that control the overall volume of your entire mix after you have blended all the individual tracks. A Master Fader in Pro Tools does pretty much the same thing. Simply put, it's a fader that controls the overall volume of a given output path or bus. It will also enable you to add plug-in effects to the entire mix at once. You'll learn about Master Fader tracks in Chapter 9, "Finishing Touches."

When it comes to MIDI tracks, there's one thing to keep in mind: MIDI is *not* audio. Instead, it is a digital language that allows different musical devices to communicate—something like a network. You can record (and then edit) MIDI data on a MIDI track in Pro Tools. When combined with Pro Tools' powerful set of virtual instruments, this can open all sorts of creative doors!

There's another MIDI-related track, called an *Instrument track*, which can enable you to use MIDI and virtual instruments together in one convenient track. You'll learn about MIDI and Instrument tracks in Chapter 7 "Using MIDI."

The method of creating a Master Fader, MIDI, or Instrument track is almost identical to creating any other kind of track. The only difference is that you'll choose your type of track accordingly. Just for practice, try creating one new stereo Master Fader, using the steps outlined earlier. (Refer to the preceding image for your reference.)

MORE TRACK COUNTS!

Since we've talked about track counts for Audio and Aux Input tracks, here are some more details to keep in mind: In Pro Tools 9, you'll have up to 64 Master Faders, 512 MIDI tracks, and 64 Instrument tracks.

WHY CAN'T I CHOOSE A STEREO OR MONO MIDI TRACK?

When you choose to create a MIDI track, you'll notice that there is no stereo or mono option available. Don't worry, it's not a malfunction of Pro Tools. Rather, it's because MIDI isn't audio, so the terms *stereo* and *mono* don't really apply in this case.

Managing Your Tracks

This section contains a few techniques you can use to make the creation of tracks even easier and to set tracks up for efficient use after they've been created.

Creating Multiple Tracks

If you completed the previous sections on the I/O Setup window, you'll note a striking similarity between the New Tracks dialog box and the I/O Setup window's New Paths dialog box. Just as you can in the I/O Setup window, you can create multiple types of tracks in a single pass—here's how:

1 If you've opened up the New Tracks dialog box, and you want to create more than one type of track, simply **click** on the **Add Row button** at the right end of the dialog box. A second row of track parameters will appear.

- You can continue creating different kinds of tracks by repeatedly clicking the plus sign, as shown here.
- Did you go one step too far, and do you now want to remove one of the rows? It's easy—just click on the minus (−) sign to the right of the row you want to delete.

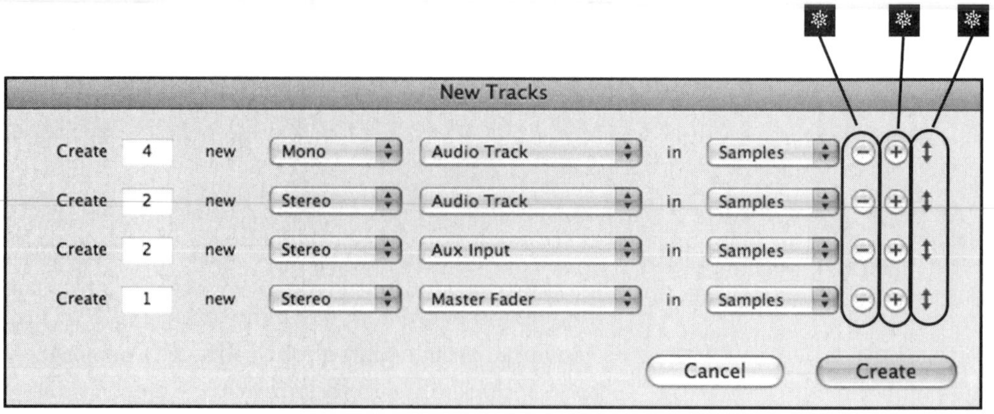

- The tracks will be created in your session from top to bottom, as shown in this dialog box. If you want to reorder the tracks, just click and hold the double-arrow icon at the far right of the row that you want to move. A blue box will appear around that row (the Master Fader, in this case), indicating that it's ready to be moved. Still holding down your mouse button, drag the row up or down. A line will appear, displaying where the track will be deposited when the mouse is released.

MORE SHORTCUTS!

There's also a shortcut to create or delete rows in the New Tracks dialog box. If you're a Windows user, you can press the Ctrl+Plus/Minus(+/−) keys on the numeric keypad or the Ctrl+Shift+Up/Down Arrow keys. If you're a Mac user, you can use the Command+Plus/Minus(+/−) keys on the numeric keypad or the Command+Shift+Up/Down Arrow keys.

Naming Your Tracks

One of the most important aspects of working in a DAW is documentation. (It may be *the* most important, depending on whom you talk to.) Keeping track of your sessions, files, tracks, patches, and so on is absolutely critical, especially as your sessions become more complex.

When Pro Tools creates a new track, it assigns a generic name (such as "Audio 1") as a default. Descriptively naming your tracks is a big part of session documentation—and the good news is, it's easy.

1. **Double-click** on the **Track Name** of the track you want to rename. A dialog box will open.
2. **Type** a **name** for the track in the Name the Track field.
3. If you want to continue naming tracks, **click** on **Next** to name the track below the current track or **click** on **Previous** to name the track above the current track.
4. When you're finished naming tracks, **click** on **OK**. The dialog box will close.

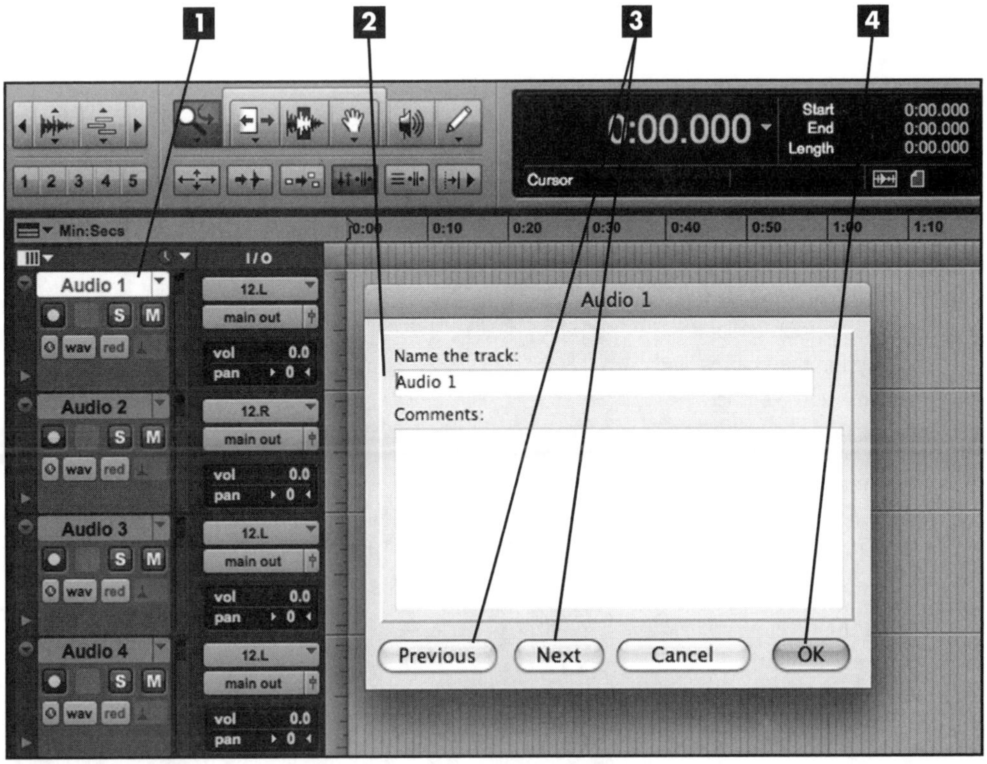

NAMING YOUR TRACKS FOR THE TUTORIAL SESSION

If you've been following along with this chapter's examples, you should have four mono Audio tracks, two stereo Audio tracks, two stereo Aux tracks, and one stereo Master Fader. To keep the ball rolling, name each of the tracks as follows: Bass, Guitar, Vocal, Sax, Drums, Keyboard, Vocal Reverb Aux, Drum Reverb Aux, and Master Volume.

Moving Tracks

After you've assigned names to all your tracks, you might want to reorganize them so that related tracks are near each other. Although moving tracks around in the Edit or Mix window won't change how they play back, a logical arrangement of tracks can make the entire production process much easier. There aren't any hard and fast organizational rules—each session is unique, and you'll have to decide how to arrange your tracks so they make sense to *you*.

In this example, I want to move my Drums track to just below my Bass track:

1. **Click and hold** on a **track nameplate**. The track will be selected.
2. **Drag** the **track** up or down to the desired location. As you drag the track, a gold line will appear, indicating the position the track would assume if you were to release the mouse button.
3. **Release** the **mouse button** when you have the gold line at the desired position. The tracks in your session will be reorganized.

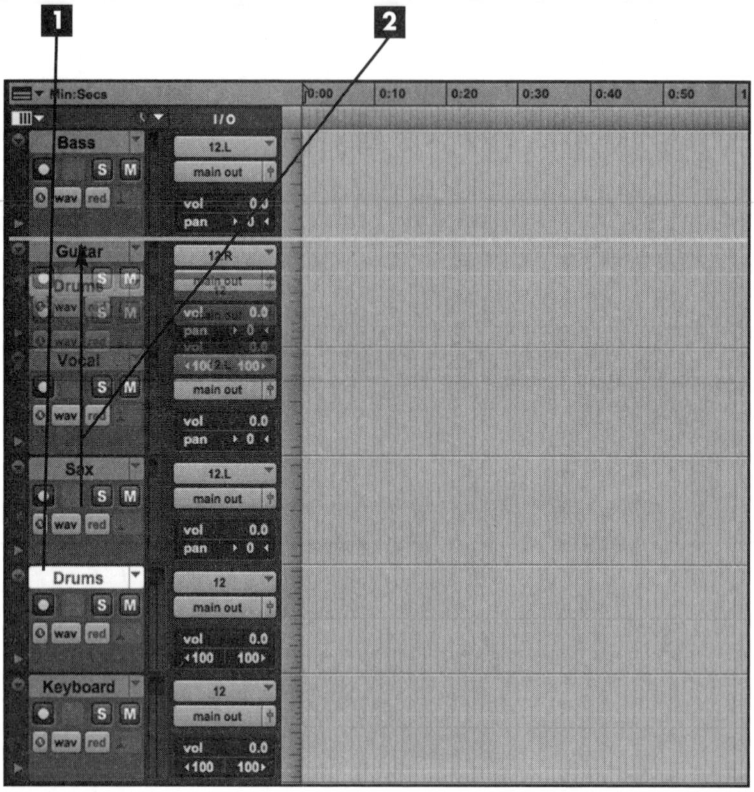

ANOTHER WAY TO MOVE TRACKS

Here's another way to move tracks: Click and hold the track name in the Track Show/Hide list, and then drag the track up or down to the desired position. A thin line will indicate where the track will be moved; when you release the mouse button, your tracks will be reordered.

In the Mix window, as in the Edit window, you can click and hold to drag any track to a new location. Of course, instead of dragging up or down, you drag left or right.

1. **Click and hold** on a **track nameplate**. The track will be selected.
2. **Drag** the **track** left or right to the desired location. As you drag the track, a gold line will appear, indicating the position the track will assume when it is dropped in its new location.

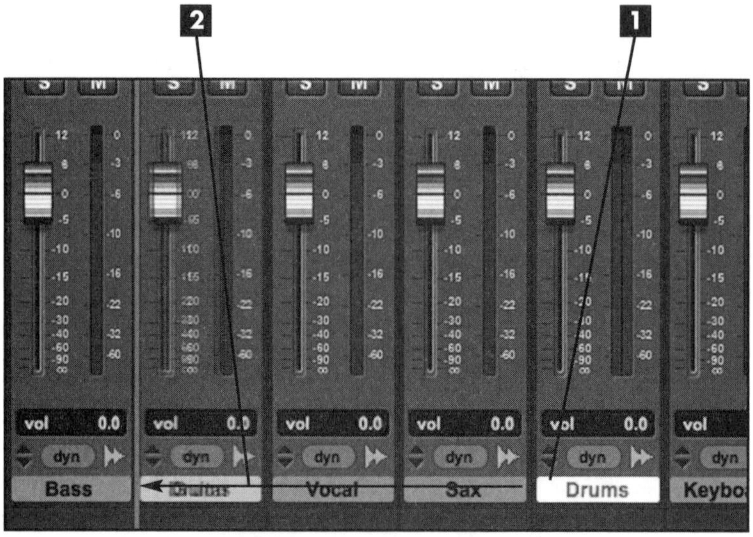

3. **Release** the **mouse button** when you have the track at the desired location. The tracks in your session will be reorganized.

Duplicating Tracks

From time to time, you might want to do a little more than simply create a new blank track. In some cases, you might want to clone your track, making an exact copy (including any regions that are on the track). Here's how it's done.

1 **Select** the **track(s)** you want to duplicate by clicking the track nameplate(s).

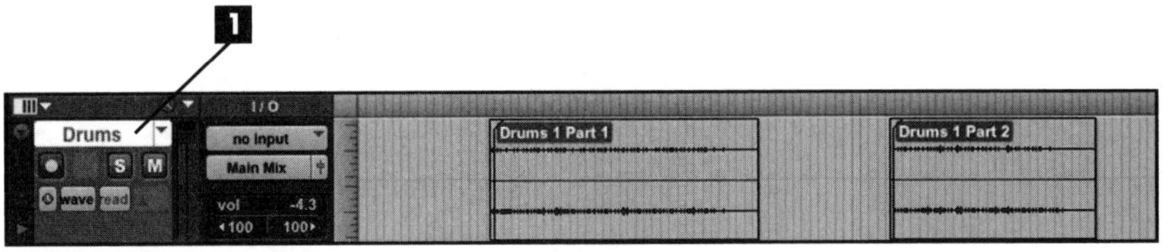

2 **Click** on **Track**. The Track menu will appear.

3 **Click** on **Duplicate**. The Duplicate Tracks dialog box will open.

4 In the Number of Duplicates field, **type** the **number of duplicates** you want to make.

5 In the Data to Duplicate section, **choose** the **aspects** of the track that you want to copy. (If these terms have little meaning to you, don't fret; we'll explore their meanings in later chapters.) To make a complete duplicate of the selected track(s), select *all* the checkboxes in the Data to Duplicate section.

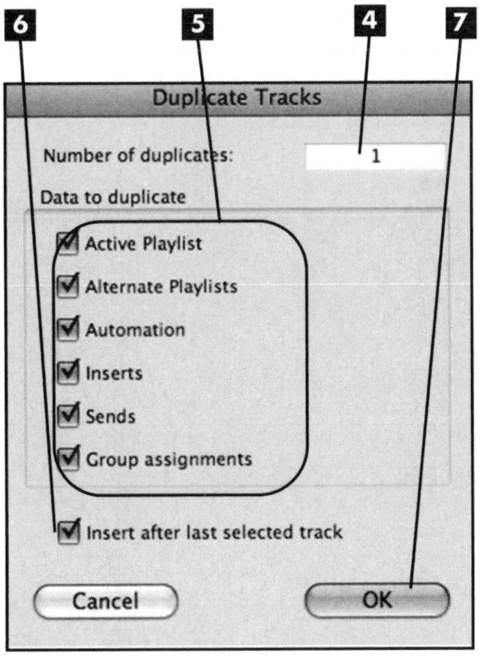

6 **Check** the **Insert after Last Selected Track checkbox** if you want to have your duplicate tracks created directly adjacent to your selected tracks. If you leave this box unchecked, your new tracks will be created at the bottom of your Tracks list.

7 When you' re finished, **click OK**. The duplicate track(s) will be created.

Deleting Tracks

Suppose you've created a duplicate track (as you have just done), and then you decide it was a bad idea. No worries—deleting tracks is nearly as easy as creating tracks.

1. **Select** the **track(s)** you want to delete by clicking the track name(s).
2. **Click** on **Track**. The Track menu will appear.
3. **Click** on **Delete**. The track(s) will be deleted.

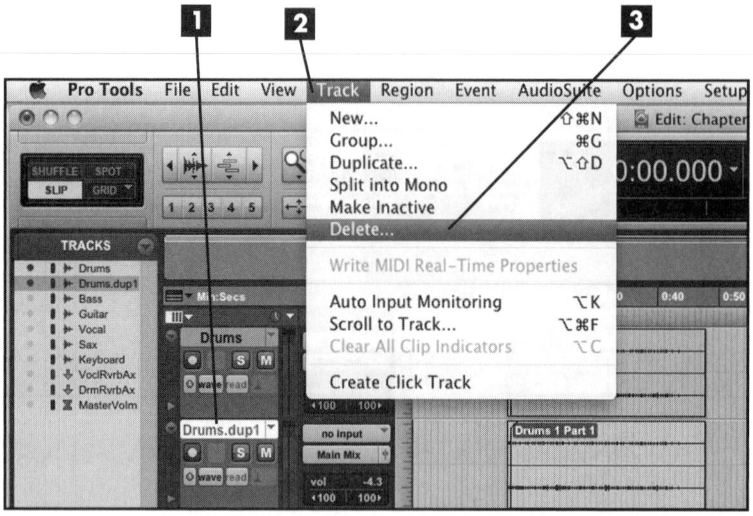

Note that there's no shortcut for deleting tracks, as there is for creating them. This is deliberate, so that you don't accidentally delete tracks.

RIGHT-CLICK POWER

If you have a mouse that has a right-click button (which is virtually all PC mice and quite a few Mac mice as well), I have some great news for you: Pro Tools has incorporated many common operations into right-click commands. This makes already-easy jobs even easier.

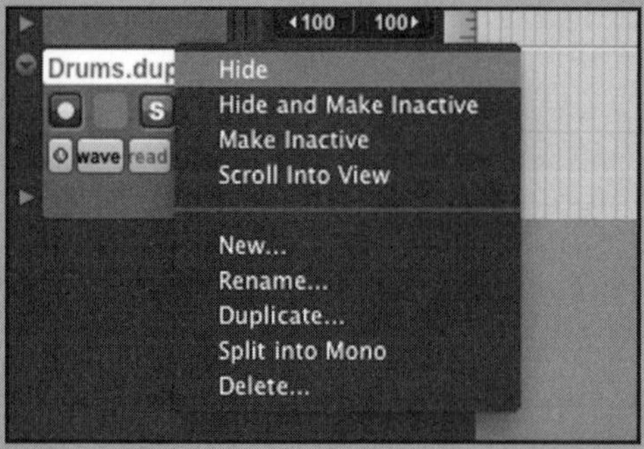

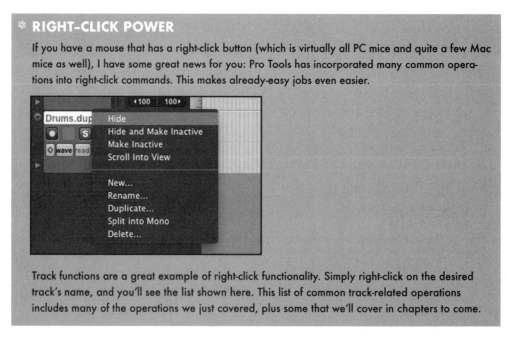

Track functions are a great example of right-click functionality. Simply right-click on the desired track's name, and you'll see the list shown here. This list of common track-related operations includes many of the operations we just covered, plus some that we'll cover in chapters to come.

Importing Audio

Although you can certainly record live audio into Pro Tools (it wouldn't be much of an audio workstation if you couldn't!), that's not the only way to get sounds into your session. Indeed, one of the big advantages of a computer-based DAW is that you can import digital audio files into a pre-existing project, bypassing the recording process entirely.

Importing files into Pro Tools is a quick and easy way to get started, and as with so many of Pro Tools' operations, there are a number of ways to get the job done. In this section, we'll explore the two basic methods: using the File menu and using the Workspace Browser.

USING YOUR TUTORIAL SESSIONS

The examples shown in the remainder of this chapter are using the Chapter 3 import materials. You'll find the files for this next section on your book's CD, in the Chapter 03 Import Materials/Source Audio for Import folder. You should leave the current session open, so that you have a session to import into!

Importing from the File Menu

Importing audio using the File menu is a tried-and-true way to get the files you want into your session. The first thing you need to do is locate the file you want to import into Pro Tools.

GETTING STARTED

Although you can use the File menu while viewing either the Mix window or the Edit window, it's typically done while working in the Edit window. For the purposes of this demonstration, if you're currently looking at the Mix window in Pro Tools, switch to the Edit window. (From the Window menu, choose Edit; the Edit window will open.)

1. **Click** on **File**. The File menu will appear.
2. **Choose Import**. The Import submenu will appear.
3. **Choose Audio**. The Import Audio dialog box will open.

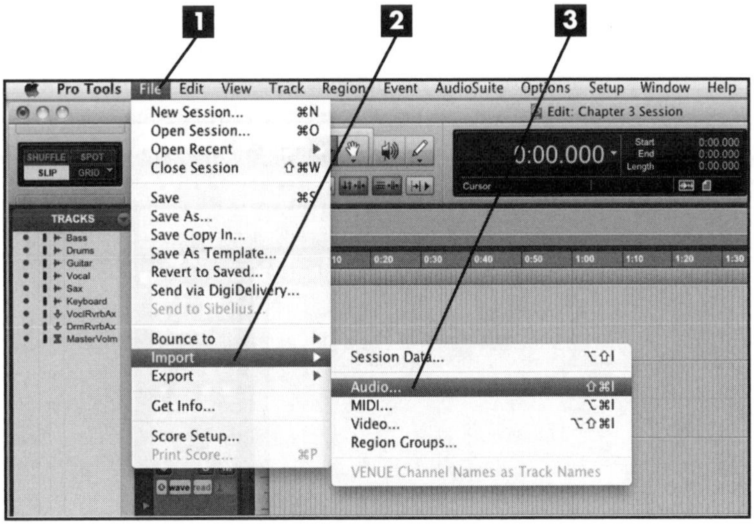

4 **Navigate** to the **folder** that contains the audio you want to import. (If you're using the disc that came with your book, find the Chapter 03 Import Materials/Source Audio for Import folder.)

5 **Click** on the **audio file(s)** you want to import into your Pro Tools session. The file(s) will be selected. If you're working with the materials set up for this book, select the two Synth Only Mix files.

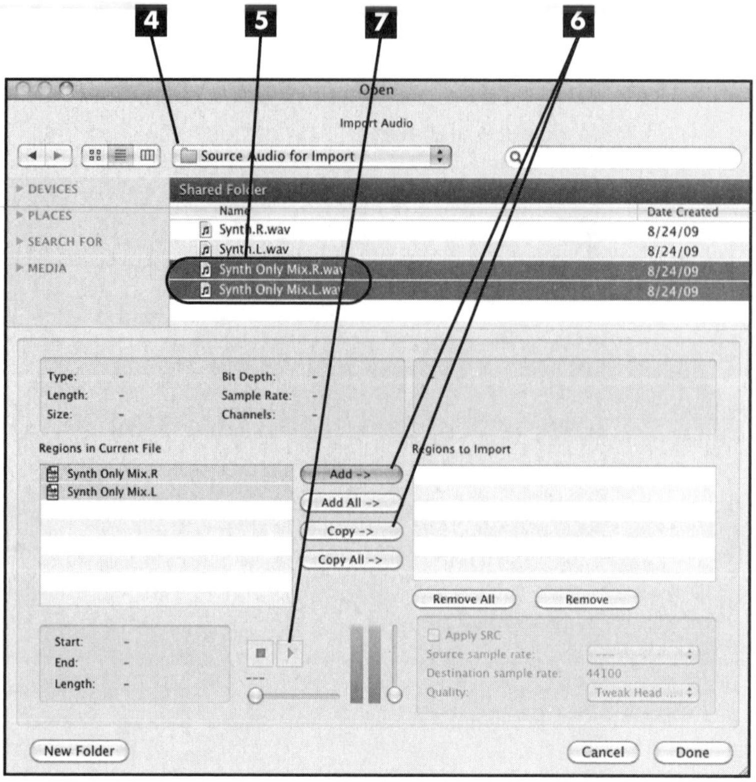

6 The box in the lower left shows regions in the audio files you've selected, but those regions haven't actually been incorporated into your session yet. To do that, you'll need to add those regions to the box on the right (called Regions to Import). **Select** the **regions(s)** you want to import, and then **click** on the **Add button** or the **Copy button**. The regions will be added to the right box, (see the following note to learn the difference between adding and copying audio to your session).

7 To audition any single region before importing, **select** the desired **audio region** (in the Regions in Current File area) and then **click** on the **Play button** to preview it. (Note that multiple regions can't be previewed simultaneously.)

ADDING FILES VERSUS COPYING FILES

You'll notice that there are Add buttons and Copy buttons in the bottom-center section of the Import Audio dialog box. Clicking the Add button will simply add regions to your Pro Tools session, and Pro Tools will play the audio file from its original location on your hard drive, wherever that may be. Clicking Copy, on the other hand, will actually make copies of those files and place the copies in your session's own Audio Files folder.

You'll notice that sometimes the Add buttons are grayed out and not clickable. Whenever any sort of conversion must happen (for example, when you're importing audio files with different sample rates or bit depths than that of your session), those files must be copied (and converted). Also, as in this example, Pro Tools will have to make copies whenever importing from CD discs.

WHAT IF I CAN'T HEAR ANYTHING WHEN I TRY TO PREVIEW A FILE?

If you don't hear your selected audio, you might want to check the Audition Paths setting in the I/O Setup dialog box. Review the "Audition Paths and Default Outputs" section earlier in this chapter for more information.

Before you proceed, let's take a look at a couple of things:

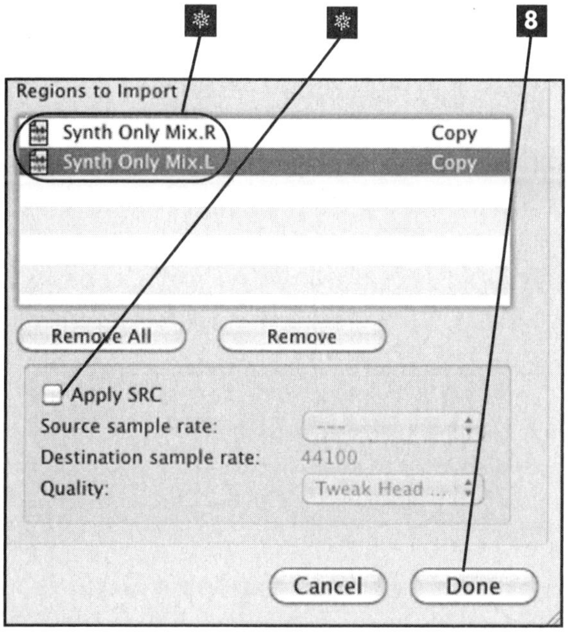

- You'll notice that one file has an .R listed before the file extension (in this case, it's a WAV file), and the other file has an .L in the file name. This indicates to Pro Tools that these files are two halves of a stereo region. (The L is for left, and the R is for right.) When these files are imported, they'll be listed in your Regions list as a single stereo audio region.

- Although Pro Tools will automatically convert sample rates and bit depths when necessary, checking the Apply SRC checkbox will enable you to manually specify the source file's sample rate, even if it's different from the reported sample rate shown in the middle-left area. You can also specify a conversion quality setting, which will override the Pro Tools default setting. Manual sample rate conversions like this are most commonly necessary when converting between NTSC, Pal, and Film video sessions.

8. **Click** on **Done** when you're finished. If you chose to add audio to your session, the imported audio will immediately be added. If you chose to copy the audio into your session or were required to convert it, you'll have to choose a destination folder for your copied files—read on!

Choosing Where to Import To

If you clicked the Copy button (as opposed to the Add button), you'll need to specify a location for your new files.

1. By default, Pro Tools will choose to copy the audio files to your session's own Audio Files subfolder, as shown here. You can, however, choose to place them anywhere on your hard drive. If you want to change the location of the copies, simply **navigate** to the desired **location**.
2. **Click** on **Choose**. The audio files will be copied to the folder and imported into your session.

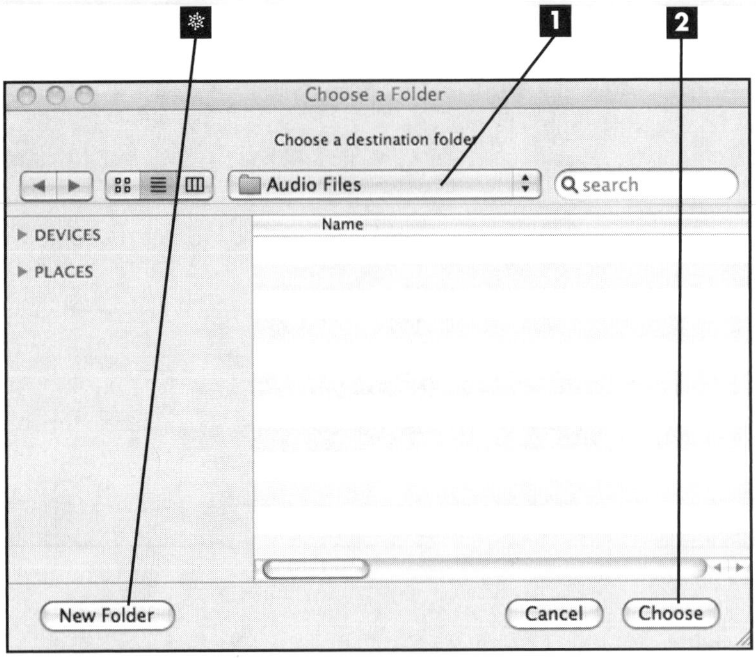

If you want to create a new subfolder for your audio, click on New Folder. You'll be prompted to name your new folder, and you'll be moved into it. Once you've reached your desired location, click on the Choose button, and you're finished.

Importing to the Regions List

Regardless of whether you chose to copy audio files or simply add regions to your session, the next window will enable you to add regions to the Regions list or create a brand-new Audio track. For starters, let's run through the steps involved in importing to the Regions list only.

1. In the Audio Import Options dialog box, **click** on the **Region List option button**.
2. **Click OK**. The region(s) will be created in your session.

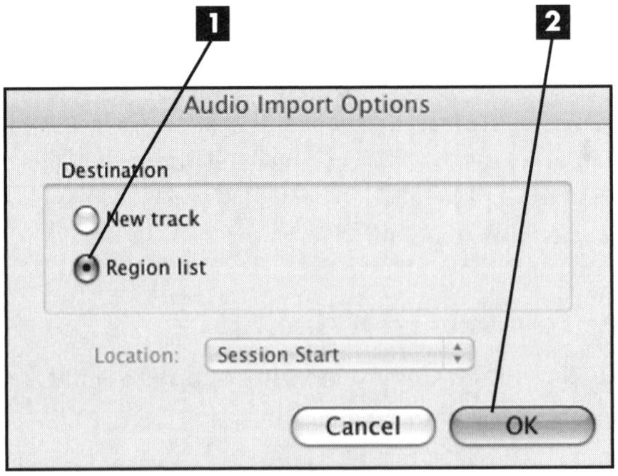

You'll notice that although the audio region is added to the Regions list, it hasn't been added to any of the Audio tracks you've created. Don't worry—that's the way this method of importing is supposed to function. Later, you'll drag this audio file onto an Audio track and use it as an element of your session.

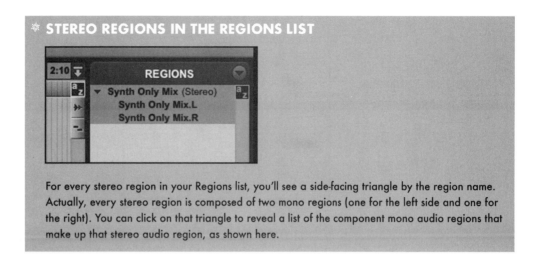

STEREO REGIONS IN THE REGIONS LIST

For every stereo region in your Regions list, you'll see a side-facing triangle by the region name. Actually, every stereo region is composed of two mono regions (one for the left side and one for the right). You can click on that triangle to reveal a list of the component mono audio regions that make up that stereo audio region, as shown here.

Importing Audio to a Track

Sometimes, instead of importing an audio region to the Regions list and using it later, you'll want to import the region onto a new track directly. Just for practice, let's import the synth audio into a brand-new Synth track. The steps for importing audio to a track are, for the most part, the same as importing to the Regions list.

1. **Click** on **File**. The File menu will appear.
2. **Choose Import**. The Import submenu will appear.
3. **Choose Audio**. The Import Audio dialog box will open, just as you've seen before.

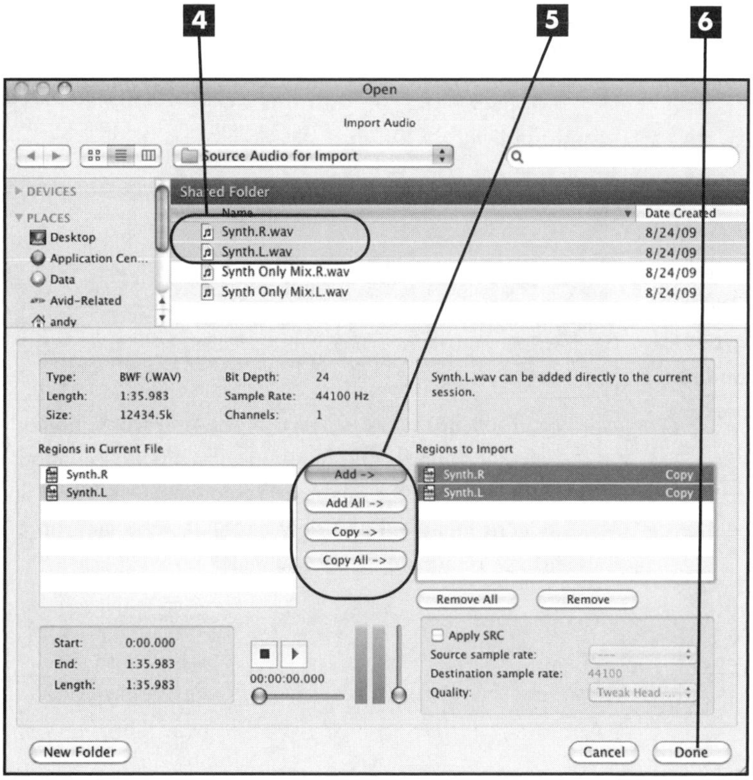

4. **Select** the **audio file(s)** to import into your session. In this example, you'll want to choose Synth.L and Synth.R.
5. For the purposes of this example, you can choose to either **Add** (if that's an option for you) or **Copy** your **audio**.
6. **Click** on **Done** when you're finished making your choices. If you choose to copy files, you will see the Choose a Destination Folder dialog box. Otherwise, (or thereafter) the Audio Import Options dialog box will open.

7 In the Audio Import Options dialog box, **choose** the **New Track option button**.

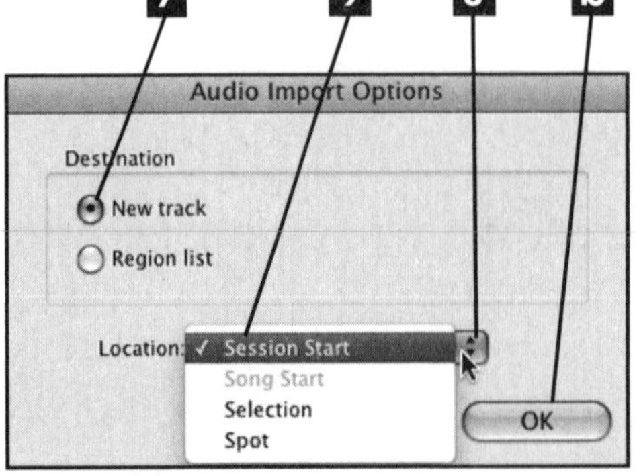

8 **Click** on the **Location button** to view a number of placement options.

- **Session Start.** This will place the audio region at the very beginning of the new track.
- **Song Start.** You can set your song to start at a place other than the beginning of your session (something we'll explore in Chapter 6, "...And More Editing"). If your song start is anywhere other than the beginning of your session, the option to place your audio at the song start will become available.
- **Selection.** Choosing this option will place your audio at the beginning of any selected area. (You'll learn more about making selections in your session later in this chapter.)
- **Spot.** The term "spot" (usually used in a video context) is used to describe the placement of audio at a specific point in time. Choosing this option will open the Spot dialog box, where you can type a specific time location for your audio. You'll learn more about using the Spot window in Chapter 5, "Editing."

9 For the purposes of this exercise, **choose Session Start**.

10 **Click** on **OK**. The dialog box will close, and your track will be created.

You'll notice that Pro Tools has done a couple of significant things with the click of a single button:

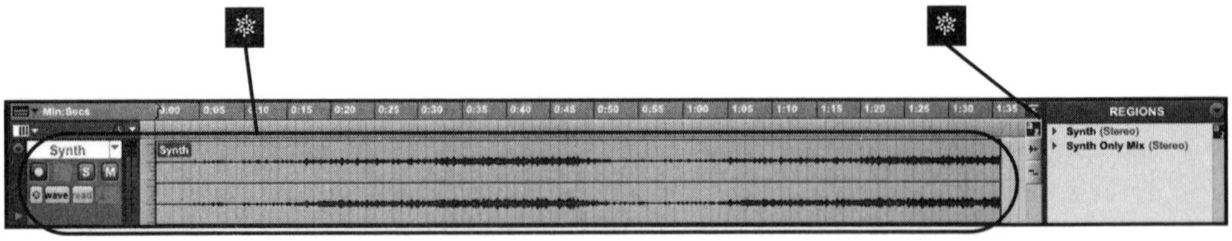

- Pro Tools has imported the desired region (in this case, Synth) into the Regions list. That means you can use this region in your session.

- Pro Tools has *also* created a brand-new track, named Synth (named for the audio file being imported), and automatically placed the imported region at the beginning of that track. Because the imported regions had an L and an R after them, Pro Tools recognized them as being left and right channels, and incorporated them into a single stereo Audio track. Pretty cool, don't you think?

> **MIXED FILE FORMATS**
>
> Prior to Pro Tools 8, all audio used in your session needed to be of one type. (For example, in a session set up to use WAV files, any non-WAV file needed to be converted to WAV when it was imported.) Those days are over. Now, WAV, AIFF, and SD2 files can peacefully coexist within a single session. That means you can import any of these types without having to convert them on the basis of their file format.
>
> However, it's important to remember that Pro Tools sessions still need to use a single bit depth and sample rate. That means if you import audio of a different sample rate or bit depth than the one you chose when you created your session, that audio will be converted and copied into your Audio Files folder.

The Workspace Browser

A powerful window called the Workspace Browser was added to Pro Tools in version 6, and it has gotten even better in more recent versions of Pro Tools. Think of the Workspace Browser as being similar to the Mac Finder or Windows Explorer window, but with added features specifically for Pro Tools. In this section, you'll see how the Workspace Browser provides you with yet another way to import audio into your session, and more!

1. **Click** on **Window**. The Window menu will appear.
2. **Click** on **Workspace**. The Workspace Browser will appear.

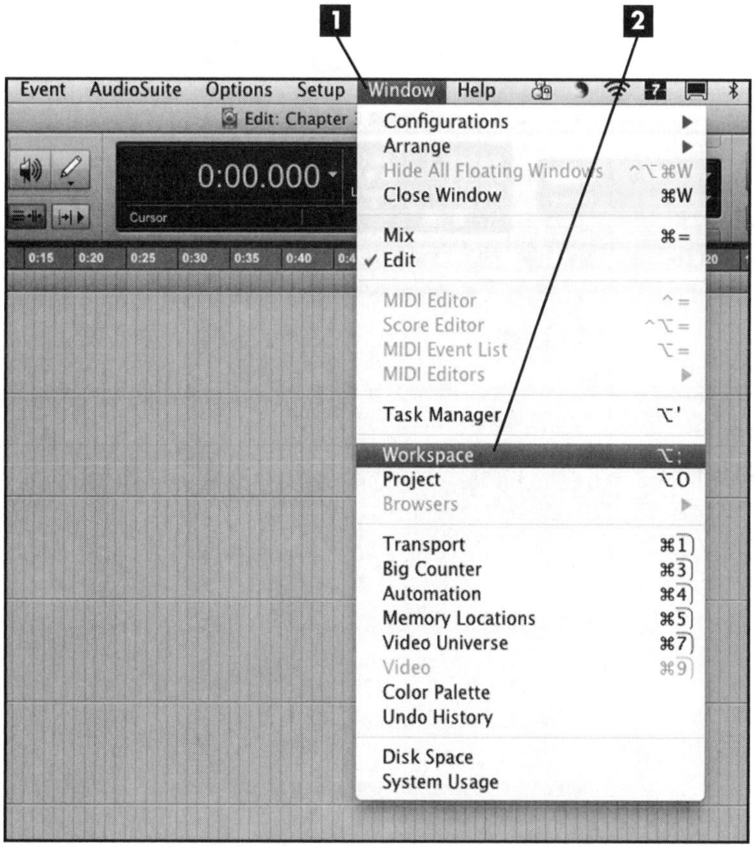

Searching for Audio Using the Workspace Browser

Finding the file you want is easy, and it's one of the Workspace Browser's special advantages.

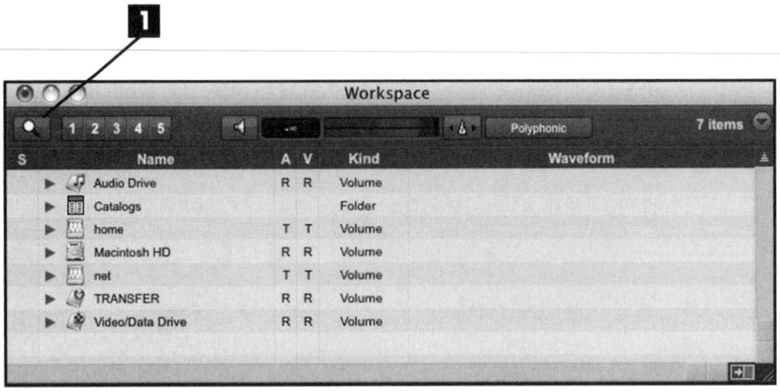

1. **Click** on the **magnifying glass button**. The Find section of the Workspace Browser will appear.

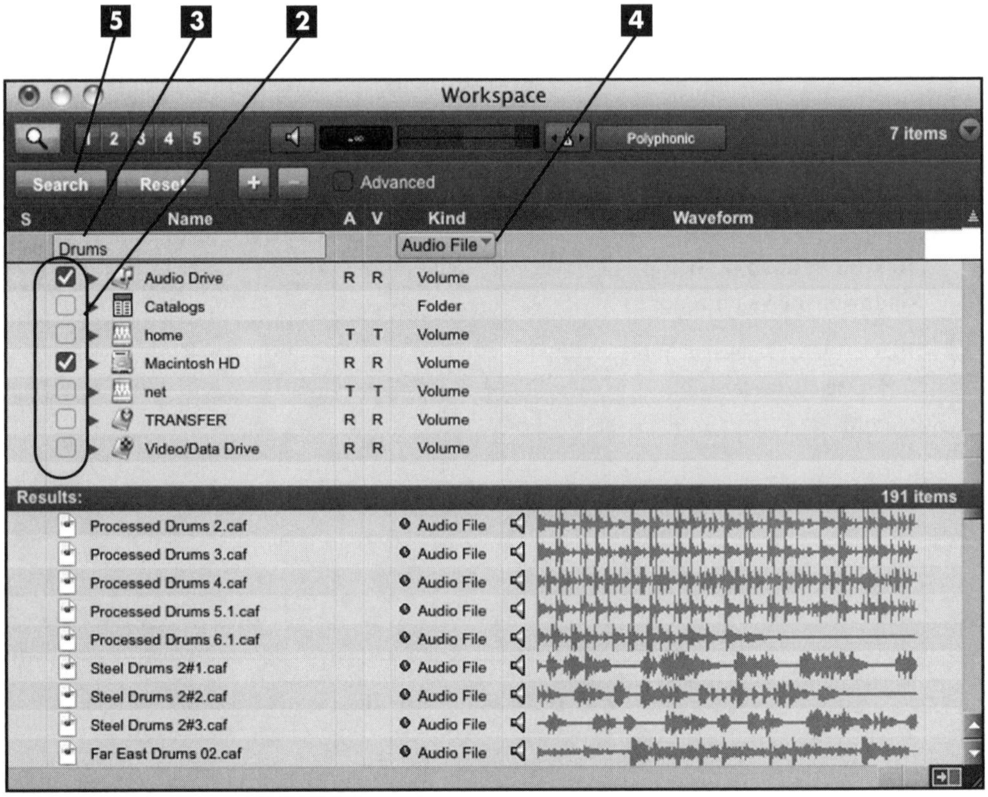

2. **Click** on the appropriate **checkboxes** to select the drives you want to search.
3. **Type** the **name** of the file (or keyword) you want to search in the text box.
4. You can further refine your search by specifying the *kind* of file you're searching for (audio files, video files, session files, and so on) from the Kind drop-down menu. For the purposes of this exercise, **choose Audio File** from the list.
5. **Click** on the **Search button**. Matching results will appear in the bottom section of the Workspace Browser.

> **SEARCHING BY MULTIPLE CRITERIA**
>
> Right next to the Search button, you'll see a Reset button (which as you expect, clears the search). Next to that button, you'll see plus (+) and minus (−) buttons. Clicking those buttons will add or remove lines in your search area, enabling you to refine your search.

You can also navigate in a more traditional way, if you know where to look for a specific file.

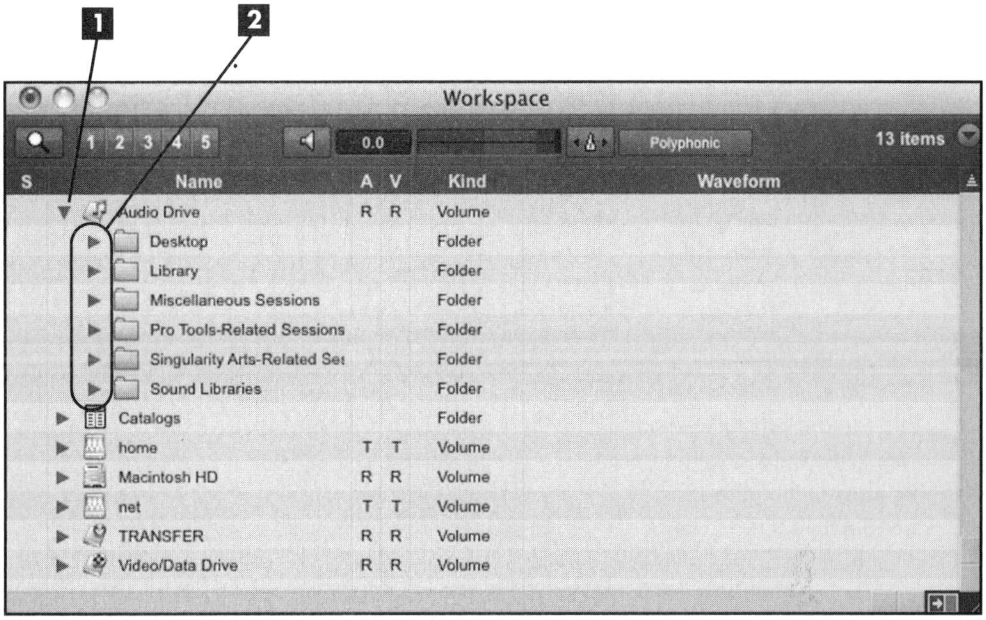

1 **Click** on the side-facing **triangle** next to the drive you want to search. The triangle will immediately point downward, and the folders within that drive will be revealed.

2 In a similar manner, **navigate** through the **folders** and **subfolders** until you locate the file you want.

THE VOLUME BROWSER

If you've used the Mac Finder or Windows Explorer, you should find the behavior of the Workspace Browser fairly straightforward. As with most file browsers, you can view the contents of a specific drive (or folder) by double-clicking the drive's or folder's name. The browser that opens will have the location name in the title bar, and will enable you to easily navigate through only the files in that drive or folder. The proper name for this type of browser is the Volume Browser.

The Workspace Browser has a few more nifty features:

- Click on the Show/Hide button in the bottom-right of the window to reveal (or conceal) a second pane in the Workspace Browser. This pane contains a wealth of information about the files displayed in the main pane, such as sample rate, duration, and even comments about the files.

- In either pane, you can scroll through the different columns easily by using the appropriate scrollbar at the bottom of the browser.
- Suppose you want to move the Waveform column from the secondary pane to the primary pane. That's easy: Just click on the column heading (the cursor will turn into a hand) and drag it to the desired location. You can drag columns not only from one pane to the other, but also to different locations within a single pane.

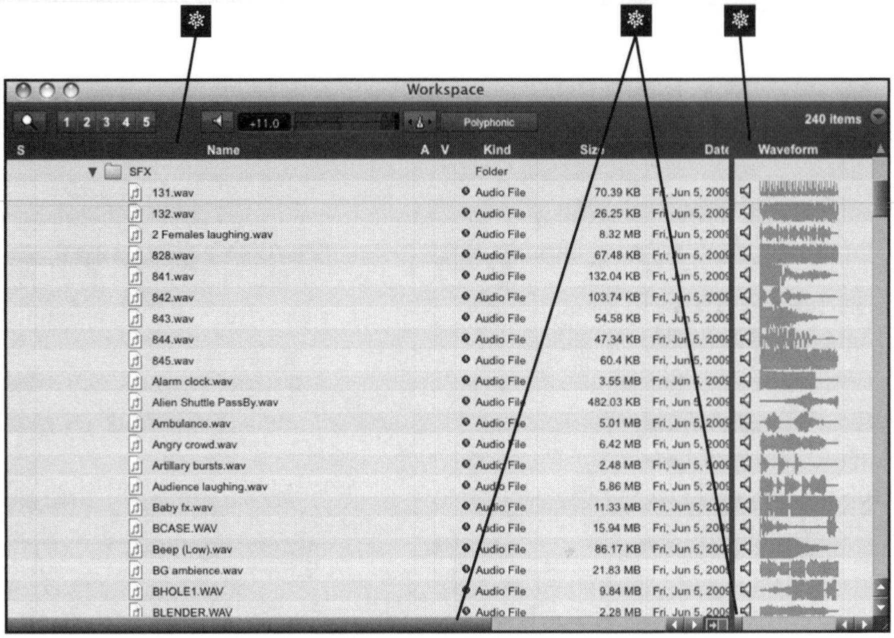

- You can easily show or hide specific columns by right-clicking on any column's heading. A list of available columns will be shown, with displayed columns indicated with a checkmark. Just click on the desired menu item to change its state.

- You can audition an audio file by clicking on the speaker icon to the left of the waveform overview. The waveform will give an indication of the file's characteristics. To stop playback, simply click on the speaker icon again.

> **AUDITIONING LONG FILES**
>
> If you're auditioning a particularly lengthy audio file, you can click at any point within the blue audio waveform to begin playback from that point.

If you click on the browser menu button (in the upper-right corner), you'll find a list of useful options. Let's take a look at some that are specifically relevant to auditioning audio:

- **Loop Preview.** If you select this option, the file will automatically repeat when you preview it. This is especially useful when you are previewing drum beats and other kinds of files that are typically repeated in a mix.

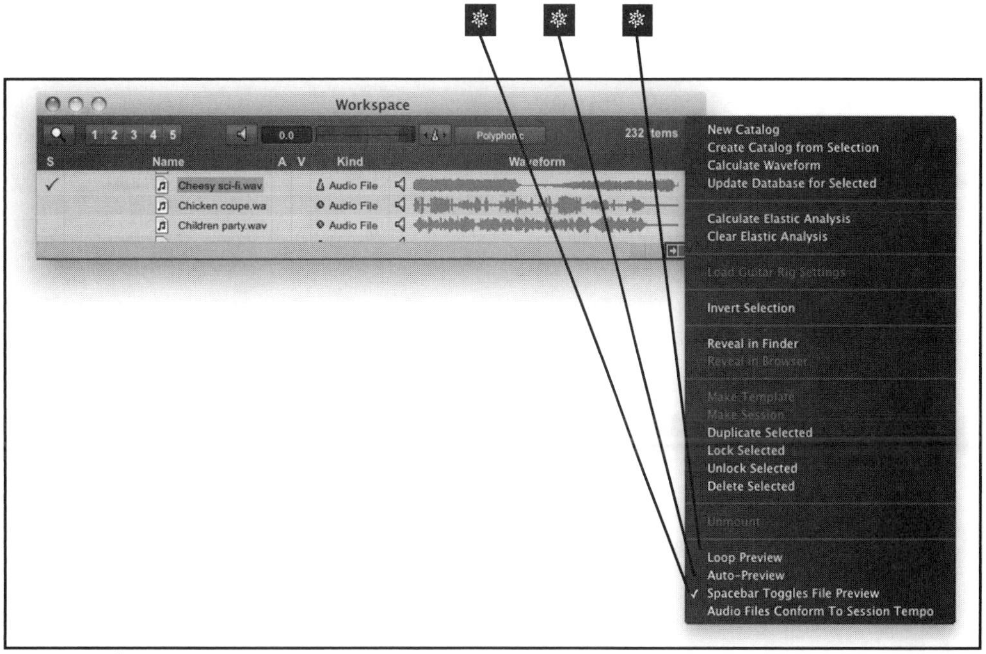

- **Auto-Preview.** Choosing the Auto-Preview option will set up the Browser to automatically play an audio file as soon as it has been selected in the Workspace Browser. This means you won't have to click on the speaker icon to hear it. It also means, however, that files will always start playing as soon as you select them, which can be distracting to some users.
- **Spacebar Toggles File Preview.** In the normal Pro Tools environment, pressing the spacebar will start or stop playback in your session. It' s one of Pro Tools' most fundamental shortcuts (and one we' ll cover later in this chapter). If you enable this option, the spacebar will have a similar behavior in the Workspace Browser. Just select a file and press the spacebar to start or stop playback of the audio.

In earlier versions of Pro Tools, previewed files would play at their full volume. This was often a shock to the ears and could potentially even damage speakers! Thankfully, those days are over!

- **Preview Volume Control.** Simply click and hold on the volume field (indicated here), and a volume slider will be revealed. Just drag the slider up or down to increase or decrease the volume of the previewed audio.

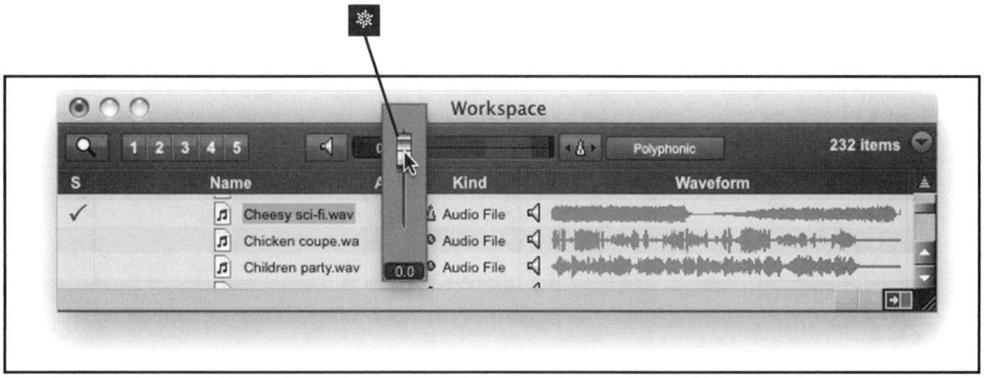

> **PREVIEW AND PLAYBACK**
>
> Another nice feature of using the Workspace Browser is the ability to preview audio while your session is playing. Doing this in conjunction with adjusting the preview volume control can give you a great sense of how the audio works with your session before you commit to importing it. The process is easy—just start playback of your session, open the Workspace Browser, and preview to your heart's content!

Importing Audio Using the Workspace

Once you've located the audio you want to use in your session, the Workspace Browser will give you a few options for importing.

1. **Click** and **hold** the **file** you want to import into your session.
2. Your next step will be to **drag** and **drop** the **file** into your session, but *where* you drag it will affect *how* it will be imported.

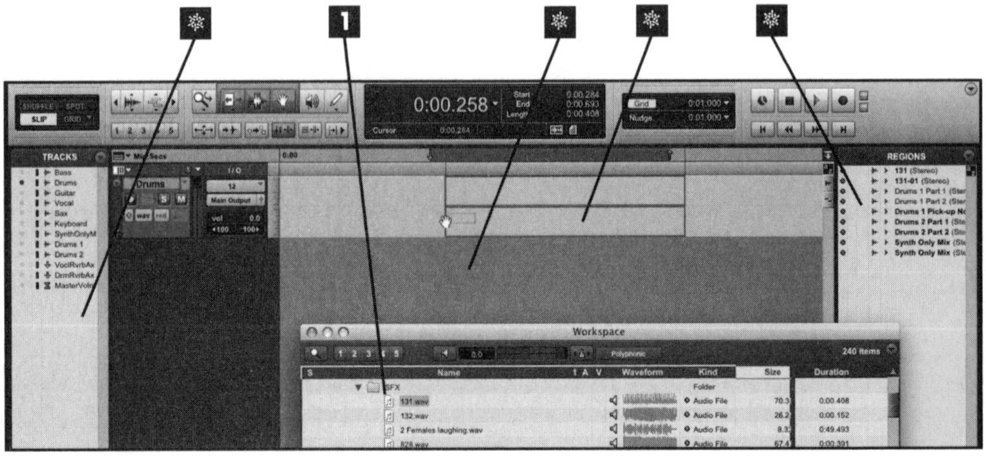

- If you drop the file into the session's Regions list, a new region will appear in the Regions list. When you move your mouse into the Regions list, the list will be outlined in gray, indicating that you can release the mouse button.
- If you drop the file onto an existing track, a new region will appear on that track. As shown here, a rectangle will indicate where the region will be placed when your mouse is released. The region will also appear in the Regions list.
- If you drop the file into an area with no track, a new track will be created, and a region will be placed on that new track. The region will also appear in the Regions list.

> **IMPORTING AND EDIT MODES**
>
> When you drag a file onto either an existing track or a blank area where there is no track, the placement of the region will depend on the Edit mode you're currently using. You'll learn more about the edit modes in Chapter 5.

- If you drop the file into the Tracks list, a new track will be created, and a region will be placed at the beginning of that track (regardless of the edit mode you're using). The region will also appear in the Regions list.

3. Once you've dragged your mouse to the desired location, just **release** the **mouse button** to complete the importing process—easy!

FILE CONVERSION

Did you notice that you weren't prompted to do any sample-rate or bit-depth conversion? Pro Tools automatically converts the file if it's necessary!

Preference: Automatically Copy Files on Import

Importing audio from the Workspace Browser is certainly very convenient, but there's one thing you should be aware of when you do it. By default, Pro Tools will *refer* to audio files dragged from the Workspace Browser, which means that the audio will *not* automatically be copied into your Audio Files folder (as though you had used Add from the Import Audio dialog box). Instead, Pro Tools will access the audio from its original location (unless sample rate or bit depth conversion is needed; in those cases, files are always copied into your Audio Files folder). Sometimes, especially for new Pro Tools users, this can lead to confusion about where your audio files actually are!

This leads us to a very important window in Pro Tools, the Preferences window, which enables you to decide how Pro Tools will behave in a wide range of situations. Let's take a quick first look at this window and a preference that will enable you to *always* copy files when you import them.

1. **Click** on **Setup**. The Setup menu will appear.
2. **Choose** the **Preferences menu item**. The Pro Tools Preferences window will open.

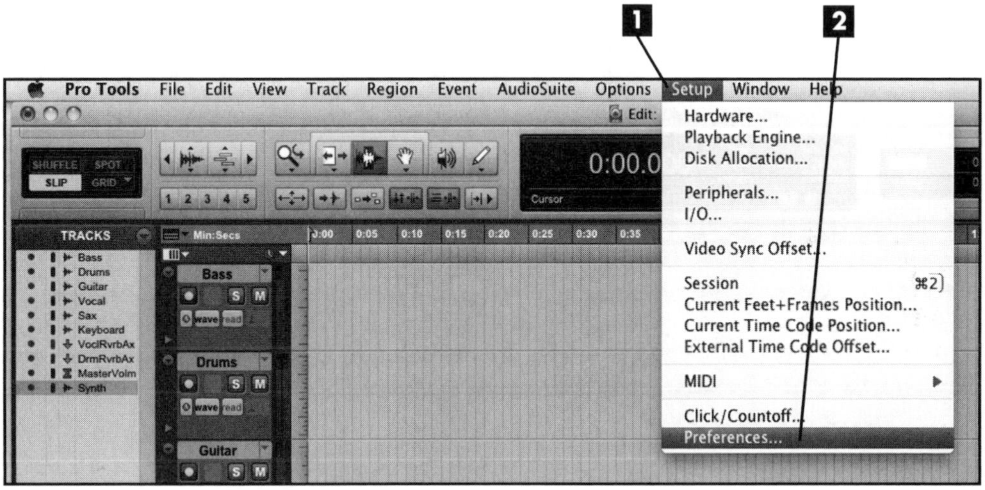

3 **Click** on the **Processing tab**. The Processing preferences will be revealed.

4 **Click** on the **Automatically Copy Files on Import checkbox** to select it. It's that simple! Now your dragged-and-dropped files will always be copied to your Audio Files folder, even if no file conversion is required.

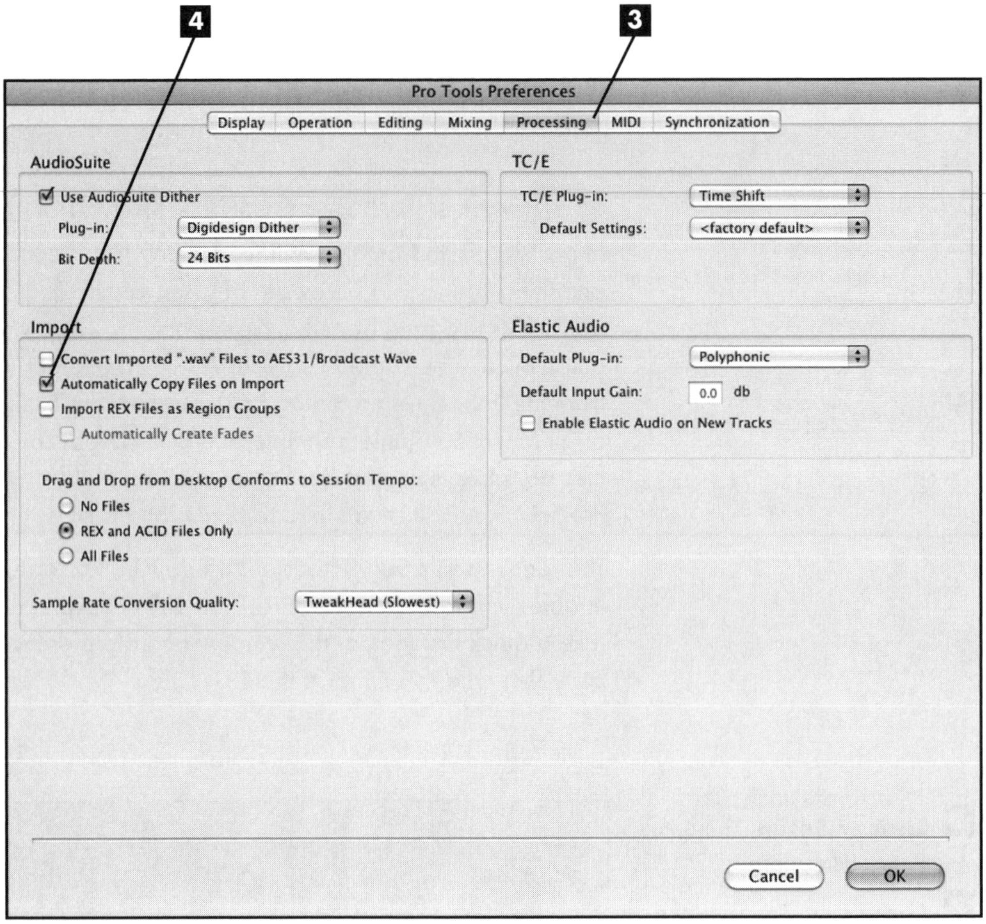

Using Catalogs

Catalogs have been part of higher-level Pro Tools systems for some time, but with the release of Pro Tools 9, this convenient new feature is now part of *all* Pro Tools systems. But what is a catalog anyway? Essentially, a catalog is a user-definable collection of audio, sessions, effects—basically anything you find yourself using frequently. A catalog doesn't include the files per se, but actually is a collection of file aliases, or shortcuts.

Using catalogs is very straightforward. Let's take a quick look at the basics:

1 From the browser menu (which you can access by clicking the browser menu button in the upper-right corner of the Workspace Browser, **choose New Catalog**.

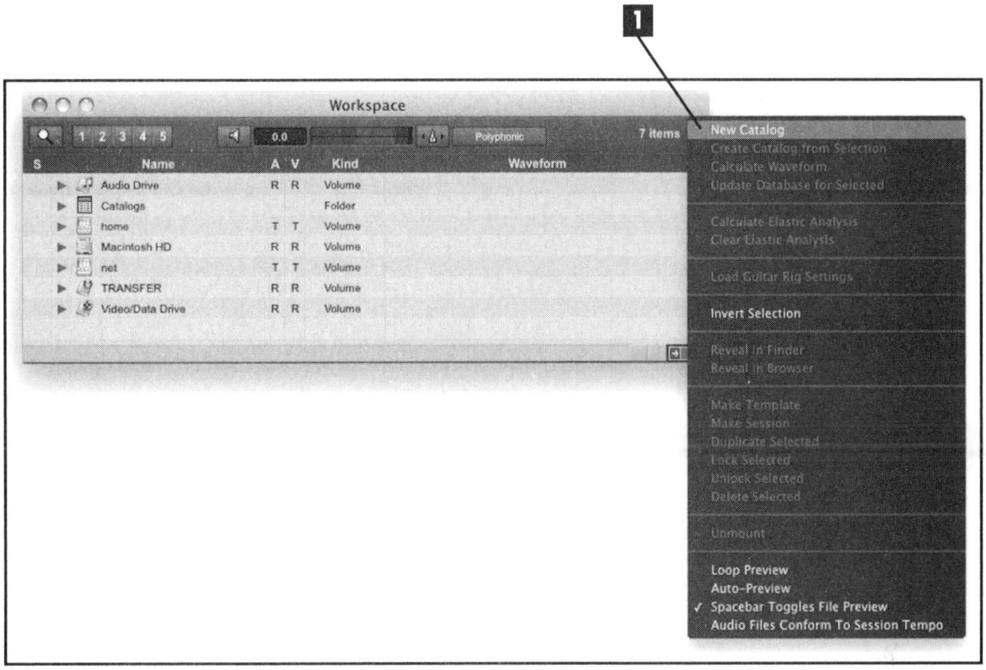

2 **Type** a **descriptive name** for your catalog.

3 **Click** on **OK**. The catalog will be created.

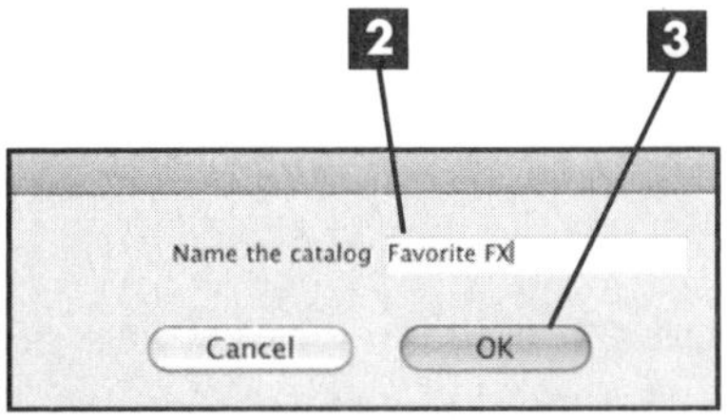

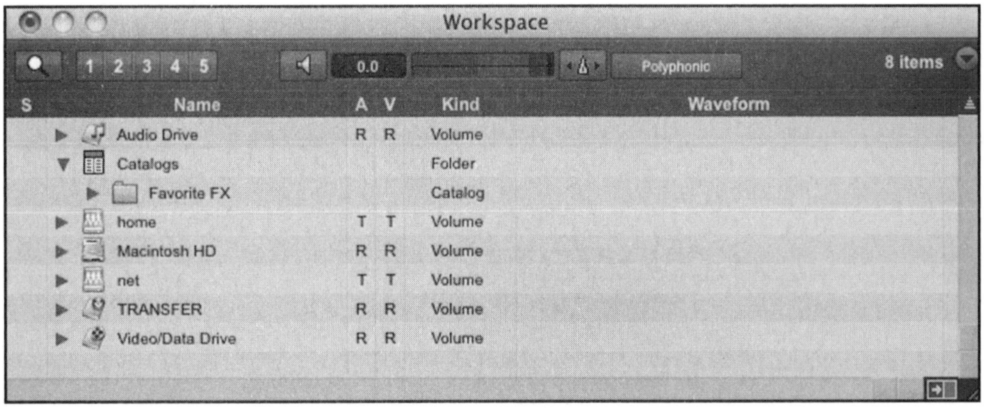

You'll see now that a subfolder has been created under the Catalogs device. Here are a couple of ways to get files into your catalogs:

- Drag and drop selected files into the desired catalog folder.
- Create a catalog and import files into that catalog by selecting the files you want to put into a catalog and then choosing Create Catalog from Selection from the browser menu.

Once you've created a catalog, you can easily search and import files from that catalog, just as if it were a folder on your computer. You'll find this especially useful with often-used files, such as sound-library audio and commonly used effects.

Importing Tracks

Importing audio to a track is certainly an easy way to get started, but there is a limitation—the region that you import will simply be placed at some point on your track's timeline, with no specific editing or mixing. But what if you want to import a fully tweaked-out track that you created in *another* session? No problem—Pro Tools can import tracks from other sessions, including all edits, volume, panning, and so on, for you to use in your current session!

1. **Click** on **File**. The File menu will appear.
2. **Choose Import**. The Import submenu will appear.
3. **Choose Session Data**. The Open dialog box will open.

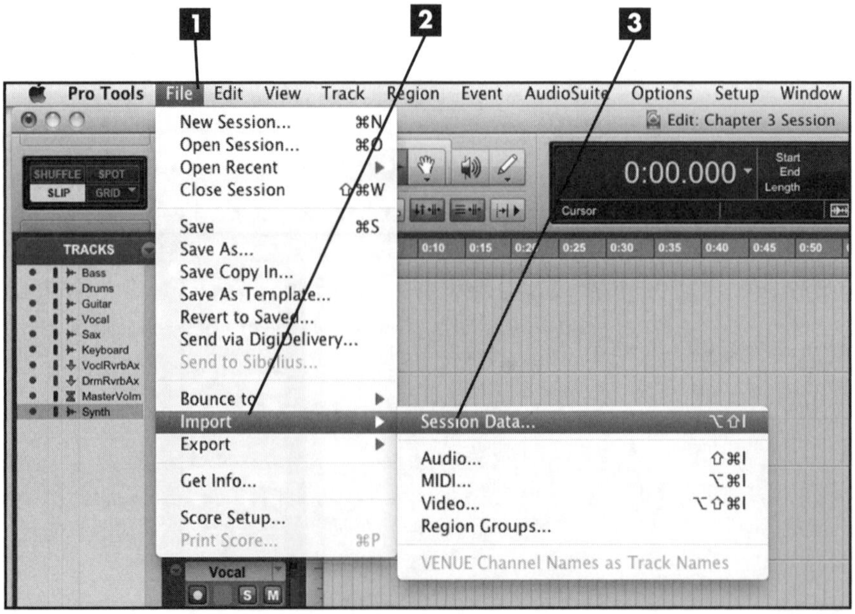

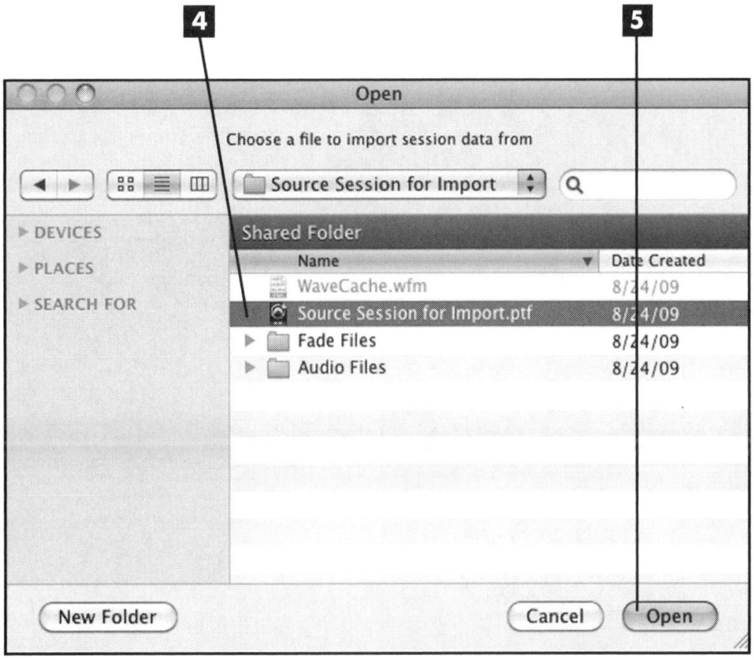

4 **Navigate** to the **session file** from which you want to import. Remember, you're not importing just audio anymore, but rather an entire track. That track exists in the session file, which is why you're selecting a session file, not an audio file. If you're following the example shown here, you'll find a folder named Source Session for Import within the Import Materials folder on the CD that was included in your book. Select the session named Source Session for Import.

5 **Click** on **Open**. The Import Session Data dialog box will open.

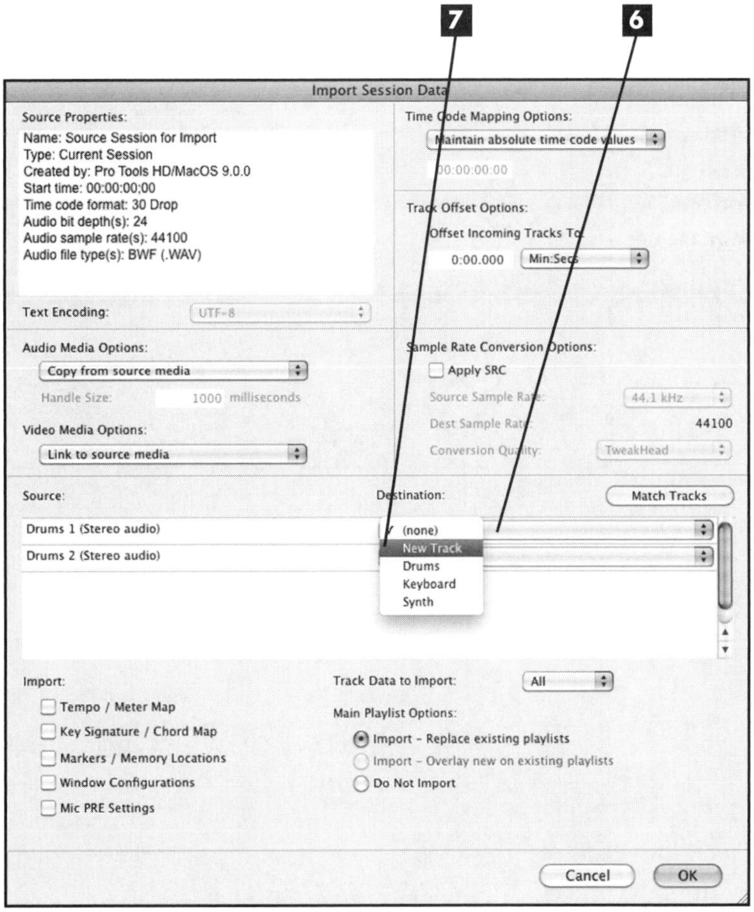

6 The Source Properties section (in the upper-left corner) of the Import Session Data dialog box provides a wealth of information about the session from which you'll be importing. The bottom of the dialog box contains a list of all tracks in this session, and that's where we'll pick our tracks. **Click** on the **button** in the destination column of the Drums 1 (Stereo Audio) track. The destination menu will appear.

7 **Choose New Track** to create a new track in your session without overwriting any pre-existing tracks.

IMPORTING TO EXISTING TRACKS

If you're following along with the steps in this chapter, you'll see that in addition to the option for creating a new track, there's an option to import the track into any existing track of the same type (mono, stereo, etc.). If you choose any of these pre-existing tracks, the track in the session will be replaced by the track being imported.

You can go one step further, however: By clicking the **Match Tracks** button (just above the tracks list on the right side), imported tracks will automatically be mapped to tracks of the same name and type (in other words, a stereo audio track named "drums" would be imported to an existing stereo audio track named "drums" and so on).

8 It's possible to import more than one track at a time. **Click** on the **Drums 2 (Stereo Audio) Destination menu** and **select New Track** here also.

9 You can choose whether to simply add the tracks' audio regions to your session or copy their audio files to your Audio Files folder (similar to what we did in the Import Audio dialog box earlier in this chapter). **Click** on the **Audio Media Options button**. A drop-down menu will appear.

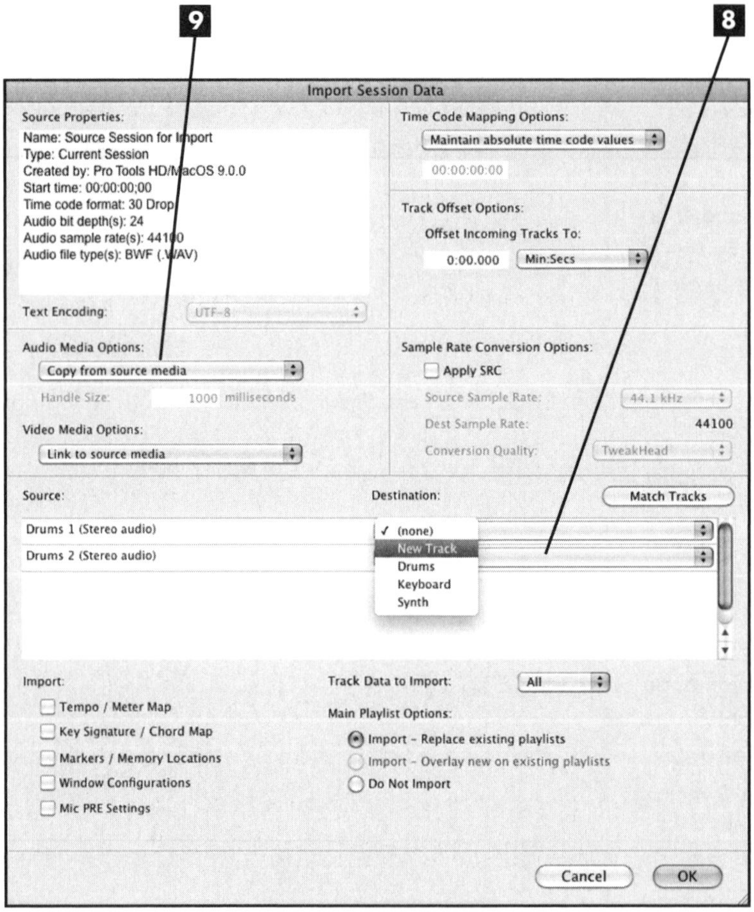

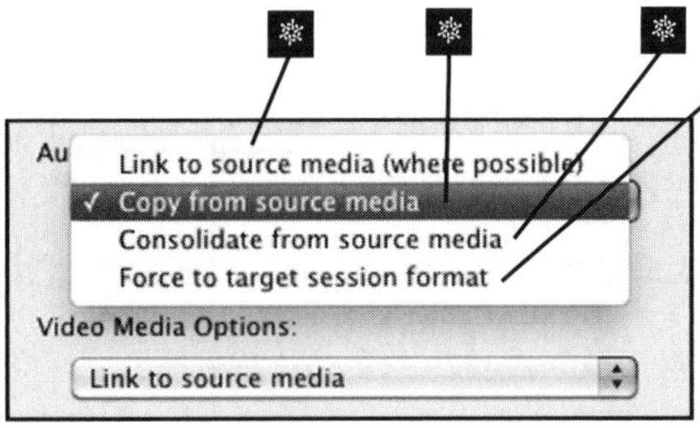

- **Link to Source Media (Where Possible).** Linking to source media will not make a copy of any audio files, but rather will direct the session to refer to the audio files in their original location if their sample rate and bit depth match the current session.
- **Copy from Source Media.** Copying from source media, on the other hand, will copy any audio files used in the imported tracks into the session's Audio Files folder.
- **Consolidate from Source Media.** Consolidating from the source media is another type of copying, but in this case, instead of copying entire files associated with tracks, only the portion of those files actually being used in a track will be imported. In many cases, this can be a more efficient copying option and can save space on your hard drive.
- **Force to Target Session Format.** This option takes a hybrid approach to importing audio. In cases where the imported audio matches the session's audio file format, the audio will be linked. In cases where the audio doesn' t match, the audio files will be converted and copied.

10 The Link to Source Media (Where Possible) and Copy from Source Media options are the most commonly used. For the purposes of this example, **choose Copy from Source Media**.

11 There are a few more advanced features that you can take advantage of. Let's start out by taking a look at the different Time Code Mapping and Track Offset Options (you'll find this in the top-right corner of the window). These are mostly used in situations involving SMPTE timecode.

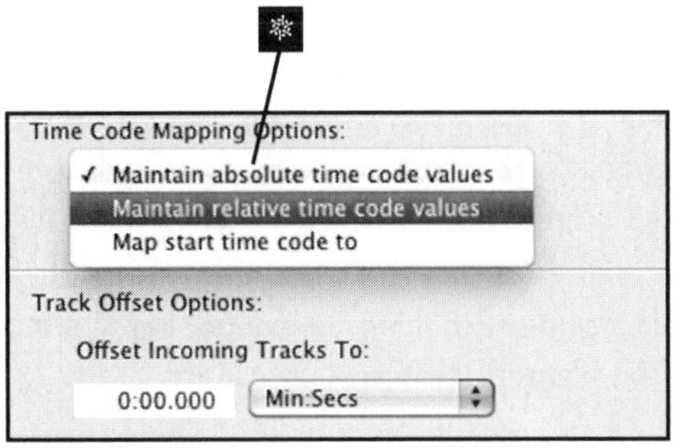

- **Maintain Absolute Time Code Values.** This will ensure that the timecode location of regions on your imported tracks will remain unchanged (for example, a region that has a SMPTE time of 01:01:15:06 will keep that value). In cases where the two sessions have different SMPTE start times, this will result in the regions having different positions on the Pro Tools timeline.

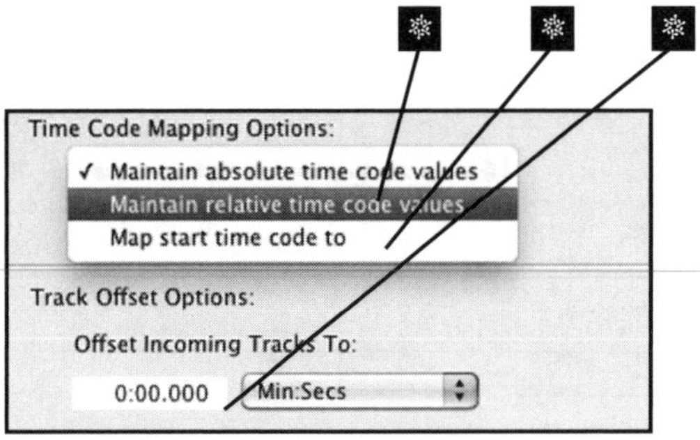

- **Maintain Relative Time Code Values.** This will keep regions in the same position on your Pro Tools timeline. In other words, a region that is at the beginning of a session will continue to be at the beginning of the timeline once it's imported. In cases where the two sessions have different SMPTE start times, this will result in the regions having different SMPTE times.
- **Map Start Time Code To.** This setting enables you to specify a timecode time for your imported tracks to begin.
- **Offset Incoming Tracks To.** You can choose to offset incoming tracks to any time you choose. This offset time can be in a number of time scales (including SMPTE timecode).

You also have a number of options in terms of what *kinds* of session data to import:

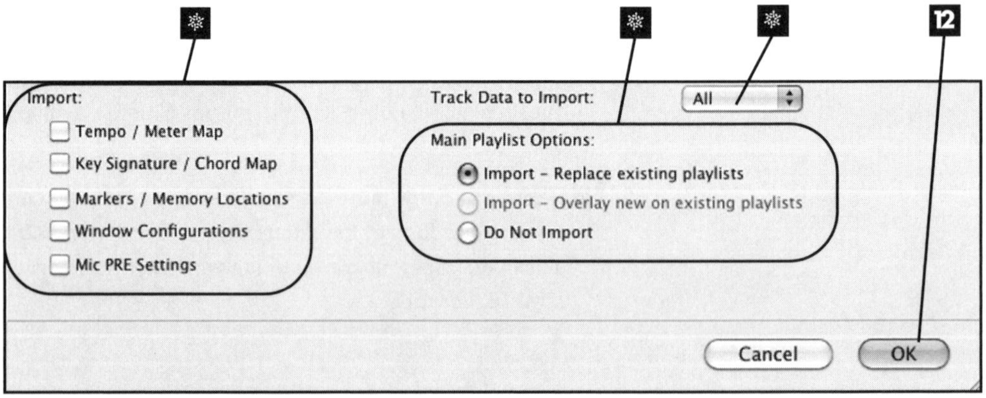

- In the Track Data to Import menu, you'll see a list of the aspects of the tracks that you want to import (regions, plug-ins, automation, and so on). From this list, you can specify precisely what parts of your tracks to import.

- You can choose how to address your Edit Playlists in this section. We'll talk about Edit Playlists in Chapter 5.
- There are some aspects of a session that are global. That is, they apply to the entire session. These include such things as tempo, key signatures, and so on. In this section, you can choose to import these session aspects.

12 When you're finished, **click** on **OK**.

Again, you'll see that Pro Tools has done a number of operations with one user command.

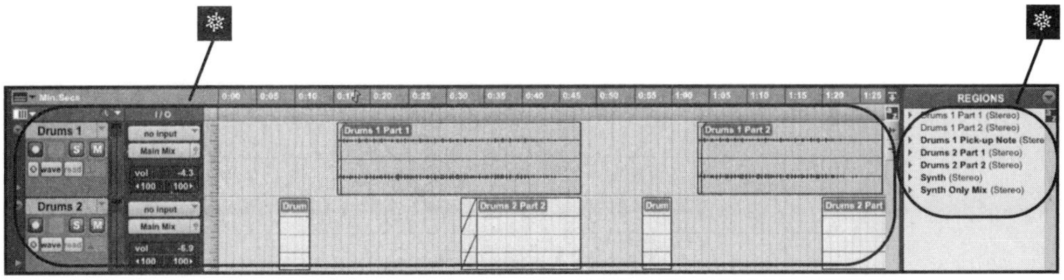

- New tracks will be created in your session. The interesting thing about these tracks is that you've imported a number of audio regions, and they are already arranged at specific times in your session.
- Each separate region in each of the tracks is listed individually in the Regions list to the right.

Working with Tracks

This next section will put some things we discussed in the first chapter into a more practical situation.

Selecting and Moving Tracks

Let's start by moving your newly created tracks to the top of the Edit window.

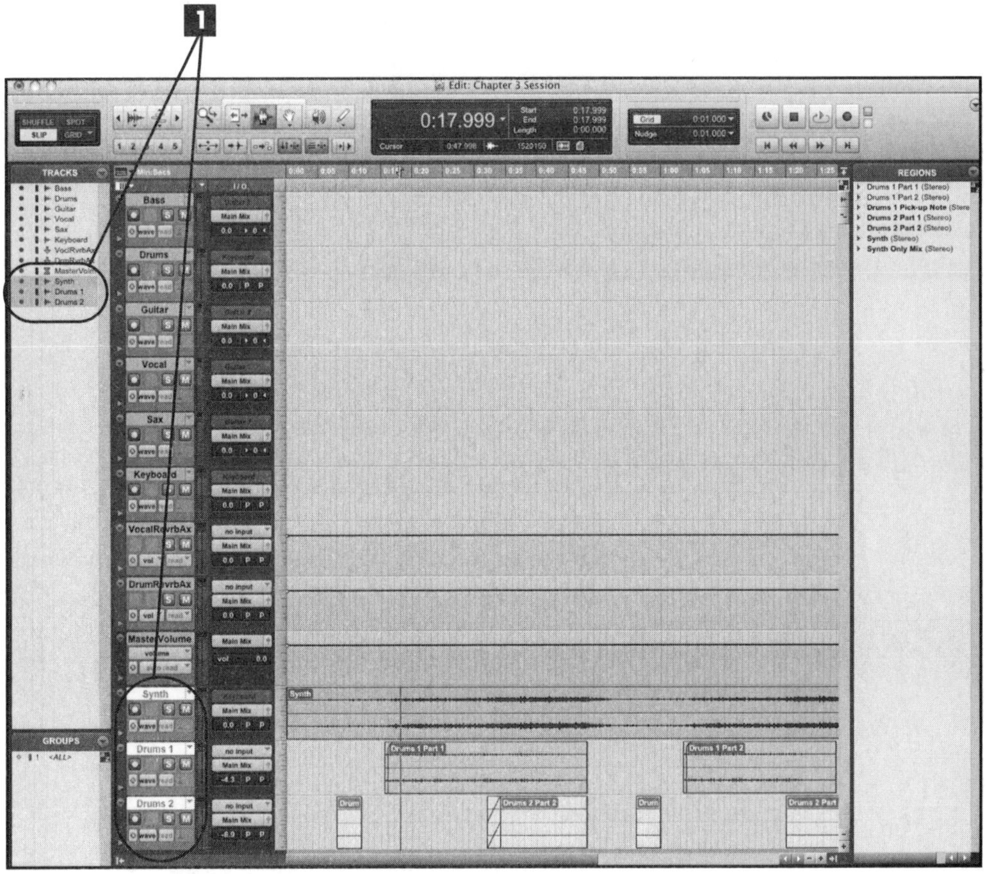

1 To select a range of tracks, **hold down** the **Shift key** and **click** on the **track names** of the tracks you want to select. You can make this selection either on the tracks themselves or in the Tracks list. In this case, I've selected the Synth Only Mix, Drums 1, and Drums 2 tracks.

SELECTING NONADJACENT TRACKS

The Shift key is handy for selecting a range of tracks, but what if the tracks you want to select aren't next to each other? No problem. Just hold down the Command key (Mac) or the Ctrl key (PC) and click on the individual track names that you want to select.

2 Just as you did when you moved a single track, **click and drag** the **group of tracks** to the desired location in your Edit window.

Deleting Tracks

If you've been following the steps throughout this chapter, you'll notice that you have two imported drum tracks, plus the Drums track that you originally created. We don't really need that original Drums track; let's delete it.

1 **Click** on the **track name** of the track that you want to delete (in this case, the Drums track).

2 **Click** on **Track**. The Track menu will appear.

3 **Click** on **Delete**. The track will be removed permanently.

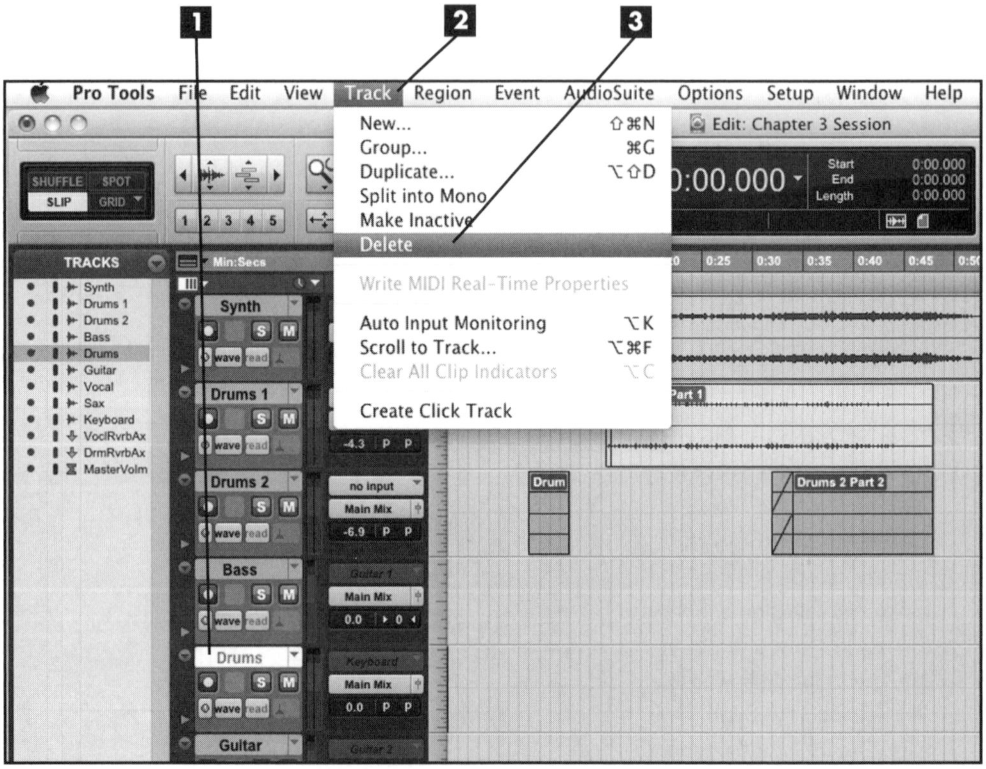

If you have a mouse with a right-click button, you can easily delete any track from that track's individual menu. (If you don't have a right-click button on a Mac mouse, you can reveal the menu by Control-clicking the track name.)

1 **Right-click** on the **track name** of the track you want to delete in either the track itself or the Tracks list. The Track Name Right-Click Menu will appear.

2 **Click** on **Delete**. The track will be removed permanently.

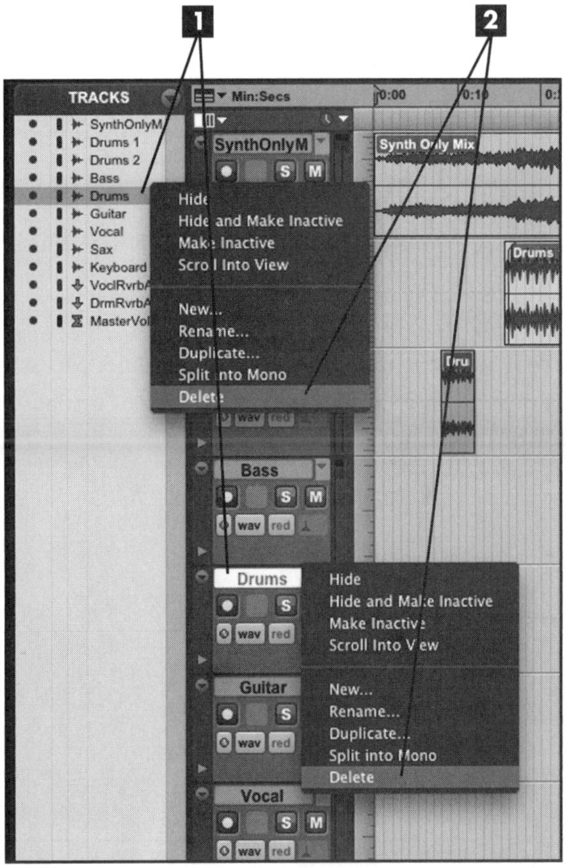

Muting and Soloing Tracks

Mute and solo are two of the most traditional functions in audio production, and they are used in a variety of situations (some of which we'll explore as this book progresses). Many readers already know what these terms mean, but here are some definitions for those who don't know what exactly *mute* and *solo* mean.

- **Mute.** Tracks that are muted will be inaudible.

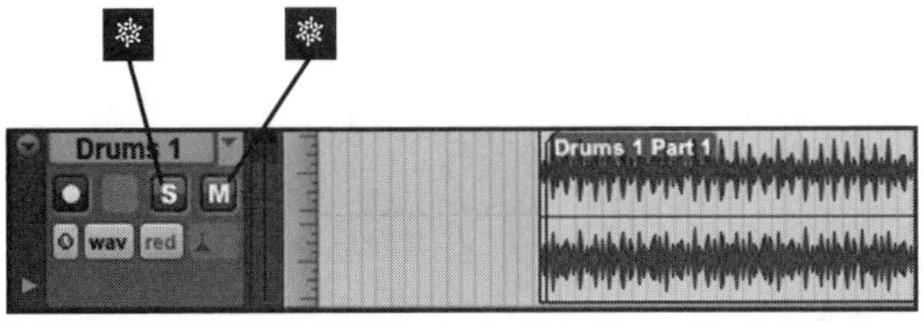

- **Solo.** Tracks that are soloed will be heard, and any non-soloed tracks will be inaudible.

> **MUTE AND SOLO ON MULTIPLE TRACKS**
>
> Clicking the M (mute) or S (solo) button on multiple tracks will enable you to mute or solo more than one track at a time.

> **MUTE AND SOLO SHORTCUTS**
>
> Shift+M will mute, and Shift+S will solo, any tracks that contain an Edit Cursor (the vertical play line, which indicates your current location).

Making Selections and Playing Audio

Being able to play your session in different ways (in addition to being able to play it from the beginning) will enable you to be flexible in your work. In this section, we'll take a look at the two primary variations—playing a selection and loop playback.

Playing a Selection

Playing a selection may just be the easiest process we'll discuss in this chapter, but being able to do it correctly is an absolutely essential skill. First, let's start with a basic playback scenario.

1 **Click** on the **Selector Tool button**.

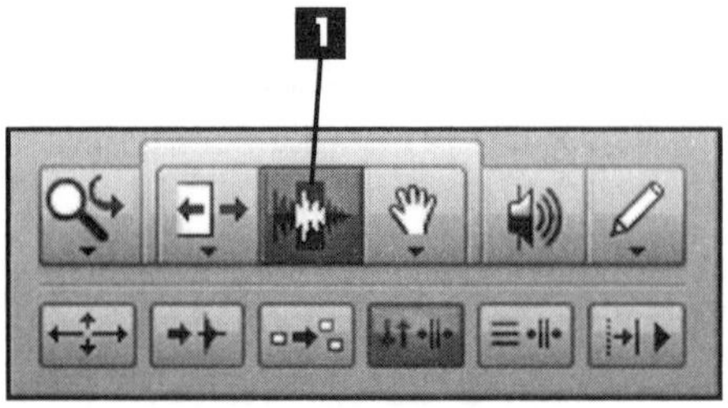

2 In this case, we just want to operate in a basic playback mode, so let's make sure that Loop Playback (which we'll talk about in just a bit) is disabled. In the Options menu, **uncheck** the **Loop Playback menu item** if it is selected.

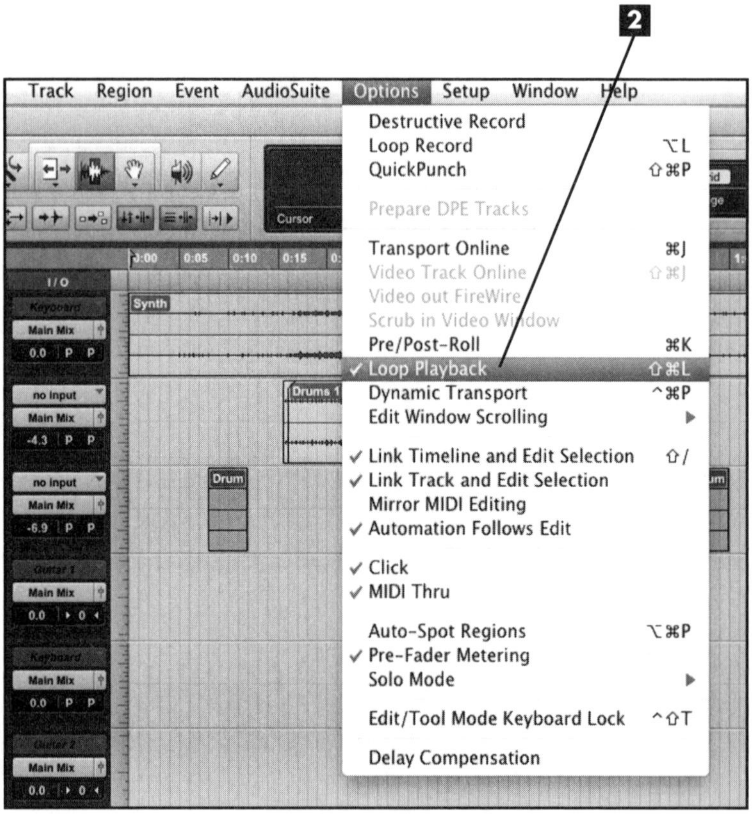

3 With the Selector tool chosen, **click and drag** over any **section** in your session. (This can be done in a track or in a ruler.) Alternatively, to select an entire region, as shown here, just double-click on the desired region. The area you select will appear dark.

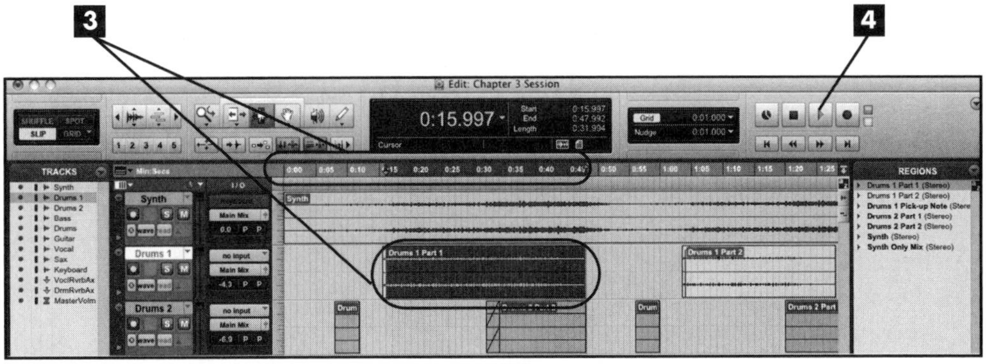

EDIT AND TIMELINE SELECTIONS

Note that any selection you make in the Playlist (this is called your *edit selection*) is mirrored in your rulers (this is called your *timeline selection*), and vice versa. This is a default setting for Pro Tools, and it is useful in the vast majority of cases. If you find that this is *not* the case in your session, please refer to the section in Chapter 10 called "Timeline Versus Edit Selection."

4 **Click** on the **Play** button. The selected area will play back one time and then stop.

WHERE'S MY PLAY BUTTON? (ANOTHER USEFUL SHORTCUT)

The transport section at the top of your Edit window can be moved, as you saw in Chapter 2, "Getting Around in Pro Tools," or even hidden completely! No worries–you can press the **spacebar** instead of clicking on the Play button to play the selection.

Loop Playback

Loop playback does just what it says: It will loop, or repeat, any selected area of your session until you stop playback.

1. **Click** on **Options**. The Options menu will appear.
2. **Select Loop Playback**. The option will be checked, and a curving arrow will be shown on the Play button of your transport controls.
3. **Click** on the **Play button** (or **press** the **spacebar**) to begin loop playback of your selection. The selection will repeat until you click on the Stop button (or until you press the spacebar again).

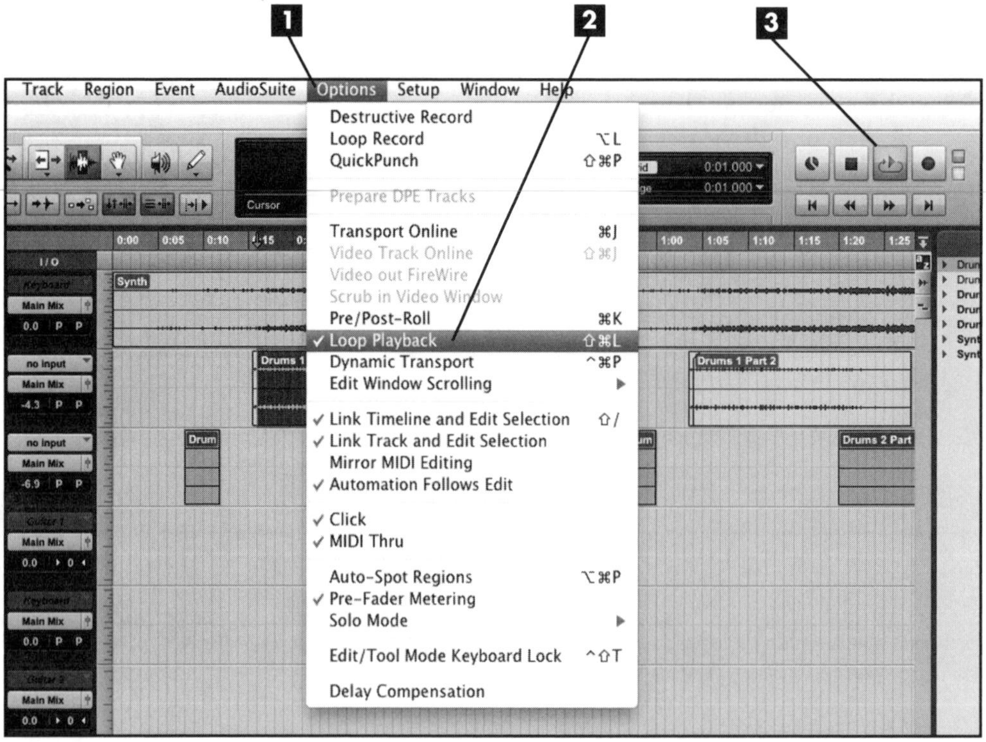

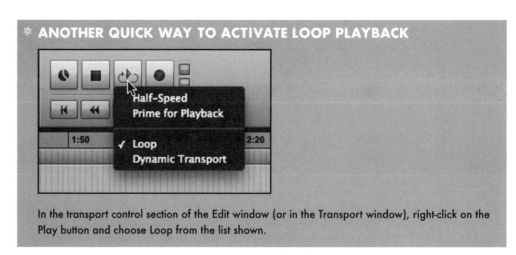

ANOTHER QUICK WAY TO ACTIVATE LOOP PLAYBACK

In the transport control section of the Edit window (or in the Transport window), right-click on the Play button and choose Loop from the list shown.

RESTORE LAST SELECTION

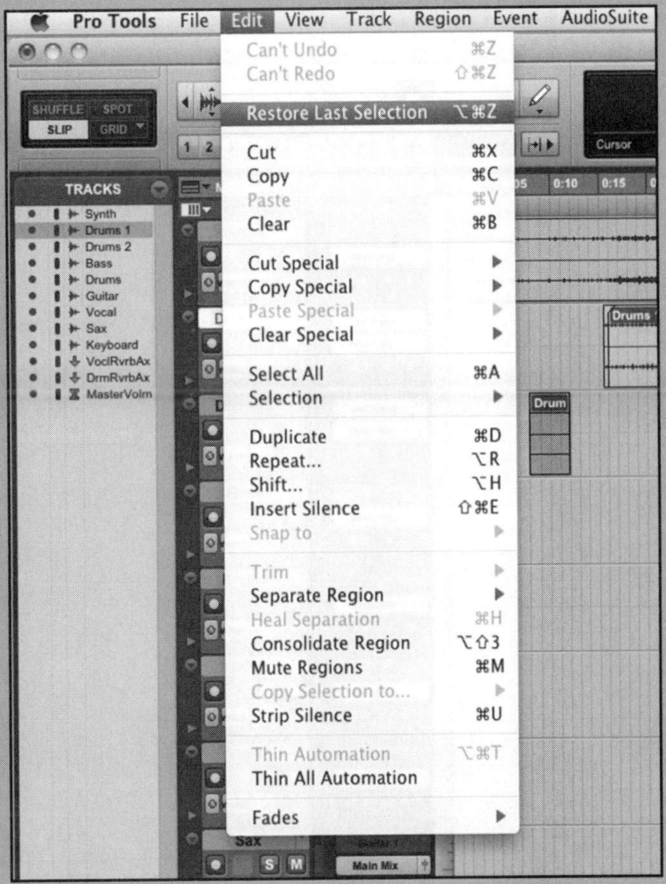

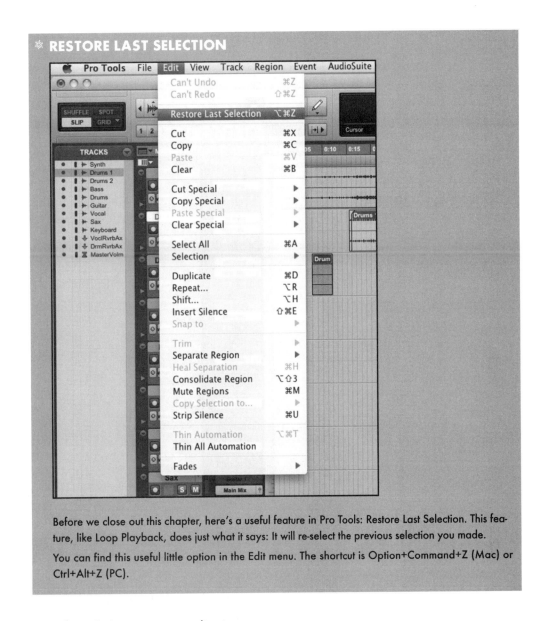

Before we close out this chapter, here's a useful feature in Pro Tools: Restore Last Selection. This feature, like Loop Playback, does just what it says: It will re-select the previous selection you made.

You can find this useful little option in the Edit menu. The shortcut is Option+Command+Z (Mac) or Ctrl+Alt+Z (PC).

Good work! Next up..recording!

4 Recording Audio

The things you've learned in previous chapters are some of the most important parts of becoming a strong Pro Tools user. Sooner or later, though, you'll want to move beyond simply importing audio and actually *record* an audio performance. The ability to record quickly and easily is a key area where Pro Tools really shines, and the flexibility this software offers has helped it earn its place as a leader in the field. In this chapter, you'll learn how to do the following:

- Set up a click track.
- Make your first recording.
- Use punch-in/punch-out recording and other recording options.
- Make the most of your monitoring options.

Getting Started: Signal Flow 101

We took a good first look at the Edit window in the first few chapters. Now it's time to dig deeper. First, though, you'll need to create a new blank session. (Refer to Chapter 1, "Welcome to Pro Tools 9," for a complete rundown of this process.)

If you don't have any musicians on hand to record, don't worry—I've got you covered. The CD included with your book is actually an enhanced CD, which means it's a data disc *and* an audio CD. Just pop the disc in a regular CD player, and you'll hear the following tracks:

1. Kick
2. Snare
3. Hi Hat 1
4. Hi Hat 2
5. Drum Stem
6. Bass
7. Blorp
8. Synth Pad 1
9. Synth Pad 2
10. Synth Pad 3

You can connect the line outputs of your CD player to line inputs of your audio interface. It's imperfect, but it'll simulate a live musician well enough to suit our purposes. Here is a typical setup to use in connecting your CD player to your system:

1. **Connect** the **left output** of your CD player to the first available input of your audio interface (for example, input 1).
2. **Connect** the **right output** of your CD player to the next available input (for example, input 2).
3. In the I/O setup window, **create** a **stereo input path** that corresponds to the two physical inputs (this is the path you'll use for stereo recording). Also, **create** one **mono subpath** (typically, this would be mapped to the left input, but in this case, either channel would do). This is what you'll use for mono recording.

Then do the following:

1. **Create** a **new session**. (From the File menu, choose New.)

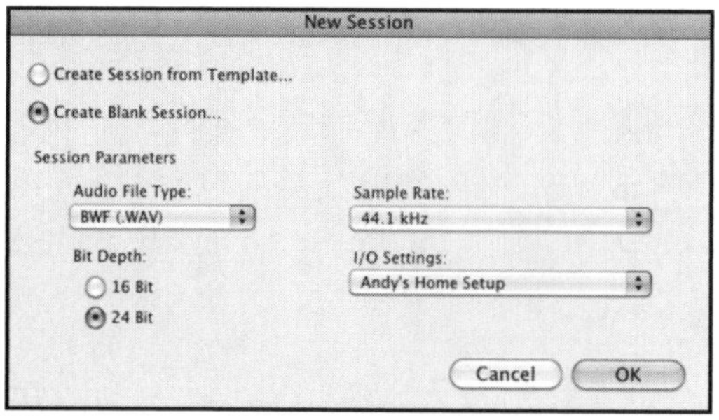

2 **Create** a **new blank session** with the settings shown here. (In this case, I'm using the I/O setup that we created back in Chapter 3, "Getting Started with Audio.")

> **SHOULD I USE THE LAST USED I/O SETTINGS?**
>
> By default, Pro Tools' New Session dialog box opens with Last Used as an I/O setting. These are the settings last used by Pro Tools on a given system. Especially in cases of multi-user facilities, users might not know just what they'll get with Last Used, so it's a good general practice to specify an I/O setting of your own (like the I/O settings you created in Chapter 3).

3 **Choose** your **new session's name** and location and then **click** the **Save** button.

Since we're going to be recording audio, you need to create an Audio track upon which to record.

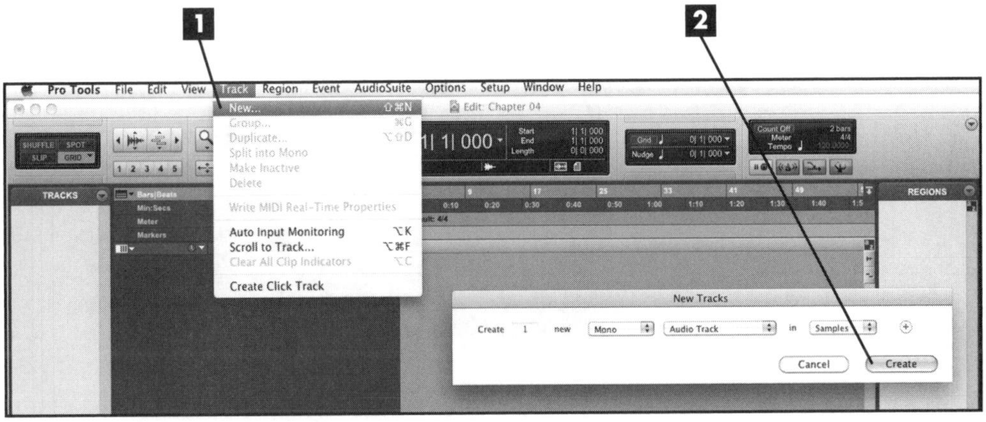

1 From the Track drop-down menu, **choose New**. The New Tracks dialog box will open.

2 **Click** the **Create button**. A single mono Audio track will be created.

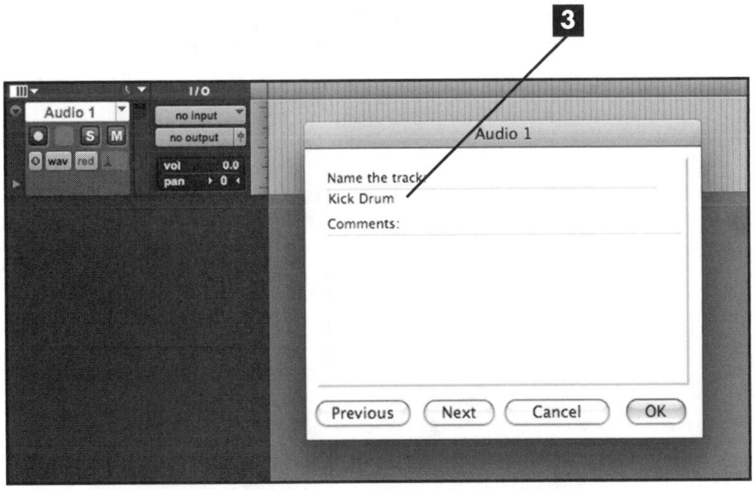

3 **Double-click** on the **track name** and **type** a descriptive **name** for the track in the Name the Track text box. (If you're going through the tutorial steps in this chapter, "Kick Drum" would be a good name to use.)

How I/O Settings Affect Your Session

It's time for the work you put into your I/O settings to start paying off. Your configuration of the I/O setup will determine how your tracks receive and output audio.

Setting Up the Output

There is an output assignment button in the I/O column of each track. (You learned how to show or hide columns back in Chapter 2, "Getting Around in Pro Tools.") By default, each track will be assigned to the Default Output as specified in the I/O Setup dialog box. In a typical studio setup, this output might be connected to your studio monitors. In any case, setting the output is easy—just follow these steps.

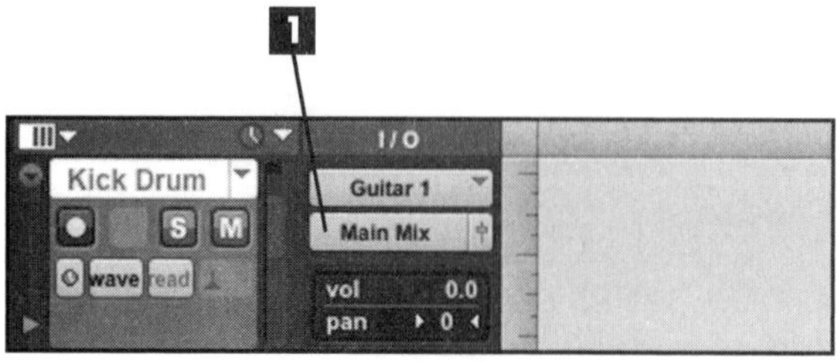

1 **Click** on the **Output button** for the track you want to change. An Output drop-down menu will appear.

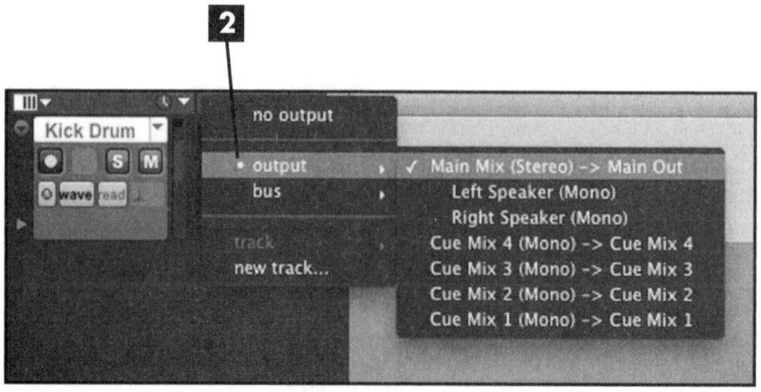

2 **Move your cursor** to **Output**. A submenu will appear, from which you can select any output path or sub-path that you created earlier in your I/O setup. In the case of recording sessions, you can change the output of any given track to be routed to your musicians' individual (or cue) mixes (you'll learn more about setting up cue mixes in Chapter 10, "Moving to the Next Level: Tips and Tricks"). If you're using the tutorial materials, you should choose your main output path.

Setting Up the Input

The top button in the I/O column of each track shows the *input* of that track. From here, you can select the desired input for your track.

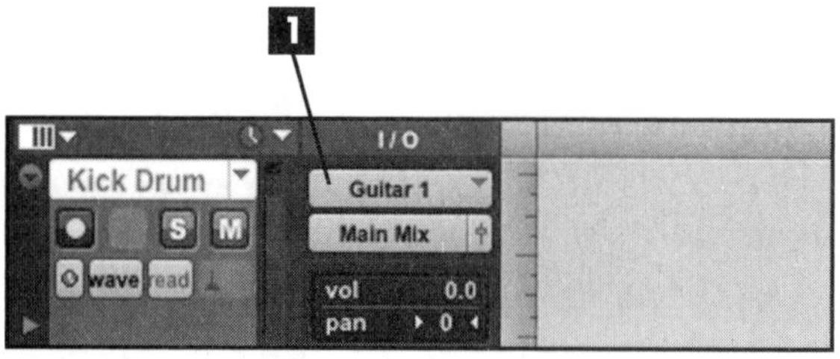

1 **Click** on the **Input button**. A drop-down menu will appear.

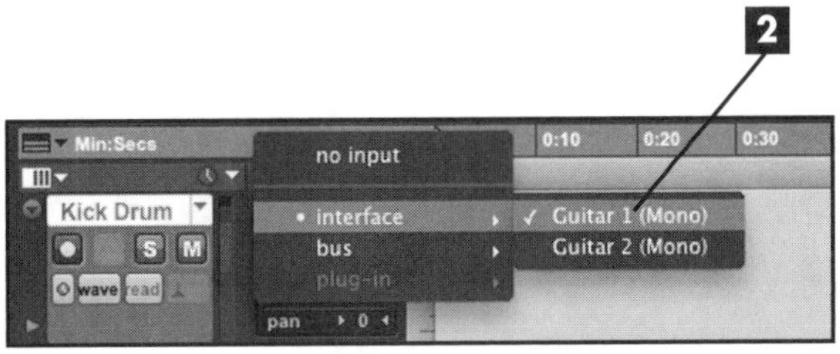

2 **Select** the **physical input or bus** that your audio will be coming from (as specified in your I/O settings). As you did when setting up outputs, move your mouse to the appropriate type of input (interface or bus), and from there choose the specific path that you want to use. The input will be selected. If you're following the tutorial, that will be where your CD player is connected. If you're recording a live musician, the input you choose for a track in a typical recording session should match the physical input on your audio interface to which his or her instrument or microphone is connected.

INPUT OPTIONS

Because the track in this example is a mono track, only mono input paths (and sub-paths) will be displayed. (If you're following the tutorial example, you created a mono subpath early in this chapter.)

INPUT VERSUS OUTPUT PATH NAMES

If you take a close look at the names of your inputs and outputs, you'll notice that the inputs are named for the paths you created in the Input tab of the I/O window. In contrast, the output paths are named for the paths you created in the Bus tab, followed by the output path to which the bus is assigned.

RIGHT-CLICK RENAMING

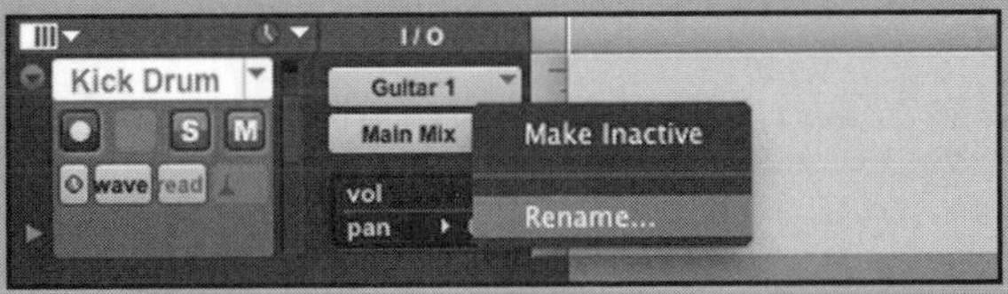

Here's a recent addition to Pro Tools: the ability to rename inputs, outputs, and buses *without* having to go into the I/O Setup dialog box. Simply right-click on either the Input or the Output button (depending on which one you want to rename), and you'll see the drop-down menu shown here. Choose Rename from the list. The Rename I/O window will appear; type a new name and click the OK button. The changes you make there will be reflected in the I/O window.

Setting the Output Volume

Right below the Output selector button, you'll see a display showing you the output volume of the track. You can easily adjust the volume by clicking in this field.

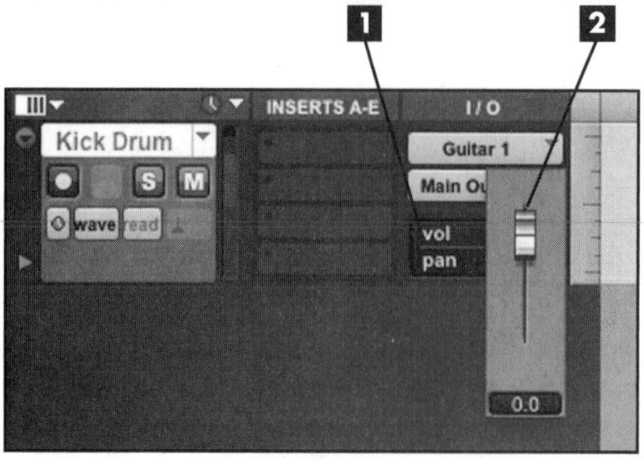

1 **Click and hold** in the **Volume field**. A volume fader will appear.

2 Still holding down your mouse button, **drag** the **fader** to the volume level you desire and then **release** the **mouse button**. The volume will be changed.

Setting the Output Pan

Just below the Volume field, you'll find a display showing you the pan value (the placement of the audio between the left and right speakers) for the track. You can adjust the pan setting by clicking in the field.

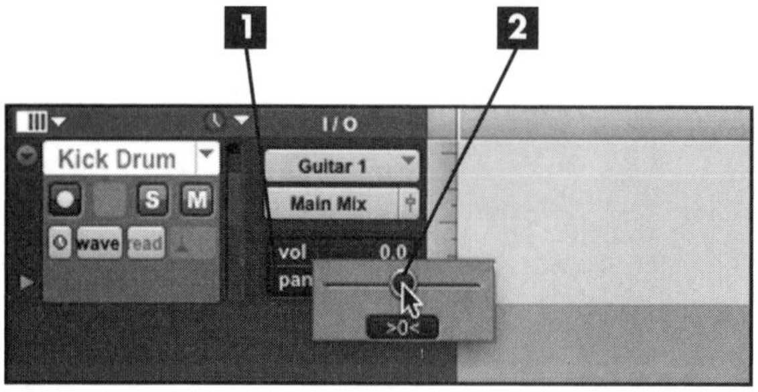

1 **Click and hold** in the **Pan field**. A horizontal slider will appear.

2 Still holding down your mouse button, **drag** the **slider bar** to the pan you desire and then **release** the **mouse button**. The output pan will be set.

> **IMPORTANT: RECORDING LEVELS VERSUS TRACK OUTPUT LEVELS**
>
> The changes you make to the output volume and output pan controls will affect the track's output only, not its input level. That means if you're recording an especially loud signal that is clipping (distorting) your input, you'll need to bring down the level of your sound source (instrument, microphone, and so on) rather than the volume fader on the track.

Using an Output Window

There's another way to view and manipulate essential track-related data. A track's Output window (sometimes called a *tear-away strip*) enables you to adjust many of your track's parameters through a single mixer-like interface. You can launch the Output window from either the Mix or Edit window; it is particularly useful when adjusting mix settings in the Edit window.

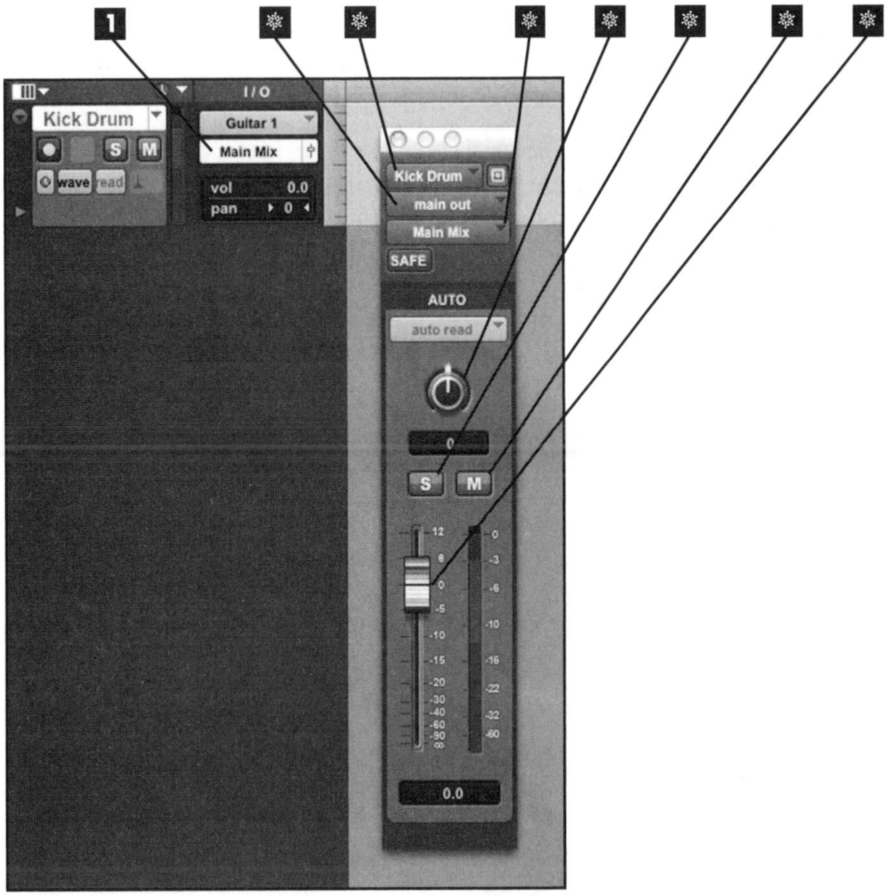

1 **Click** on the **Output Window button** at the right of the output selector. (The icon looks like a tiny fader.) The track's Output window will appear. Note that much of the track-related data you set up earlier in this chapter is shown here as well.

- Output View selector (which enables you to quickly switch over to one of that track's sends—something we'll discuss in Chapter 8, "Basic Mixing")
- Track selector
- Output Path selector
- Pan knob
- Solo button
- Mute button
- Volume fader, with a volume meter to its right

QUICK RESET SHORTCUT

You can quickly reset your volume to unity (0.0) or your pan to center (0) by holding the Option key (Mac) or Alt key (PC) while you click on the volume or pan controls in either the track' s display fields or the Output window.

Synchronization

In many recording scenarios, you'll have to make sure that the timing of your musicians—and sometimes even the timing of other machines—lines up with the timing of your Pro Tools session. This is an essential skill for all sorts of work and is generally referred to as *synchronization*. In this section, we'll examine a number of ways to get everything in sync.

Setting Up a Click Track

You might be wondering just what a click track is. Fair question. Even though it's a common term within recording circles, it's surprising how many musicians don't know what a click track is or what it's used for. The answer is pretty straightforward: A *click track* is an audible track that indicates the tempo of a song through a series of short tones (usually click sounds, hence the name). This is similar to what a metronome does when it helps a musician keep tempo in the practice room, and the two terms are often used interchangeably.

This feature is not specific to Pro Tools. Click tracks have been used for decades, dating back to the earliest analog recording studios, when multiple musicians would all listen to the same click track in their headphones as they played in order to stay in time with each other. Although you certainly won't need a *click track* every time you work with Pro Tools, you'll find that using one is a convenient way to keep everything in sync, and the ability to work with one is considered an essential skill.

Creating a click track is very simple:

1. **Click** on **Track**.
2. **Choose Create Click Track**. A click track will be created.

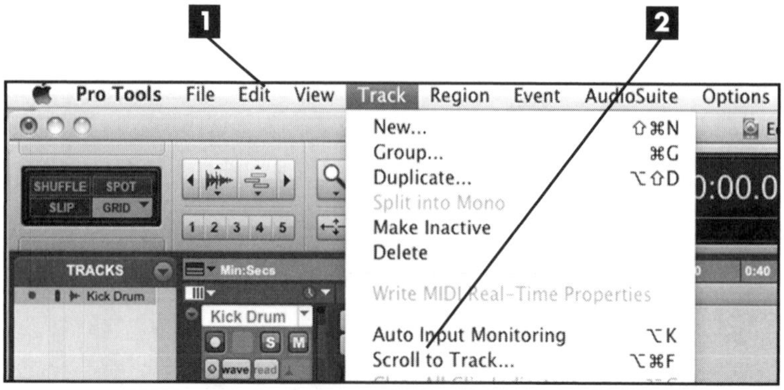

ANATOMY OF A CLICK TRACK

In case you' re curious, here' s what you' ve created: a mono Auxiliary Input track. On this track, you' ll see a small box in the Inserts column. This is a very simple virtual instrument plug-in called Click. This primitive instrument has one simple job: to make clicks that follow the session' s tempo. Despite its simplicity, you do have a few options at your disposal.

3. **Click** on the Click plug-in's **Insert button** (on this track, it is the small box with the C on it, for Click). The Click plug-in window will open.

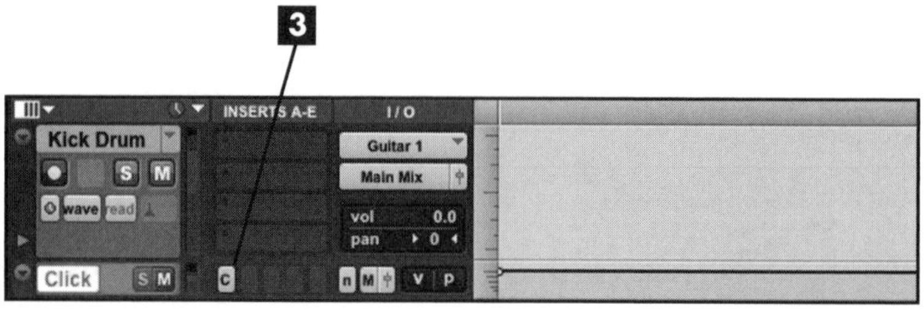

4a **Adjust** the **Accented** (for each measure's Beat 1) and **Unaccented** (for the other beats) **sliders** to get the best overall volume. You can change these values at any time in your session.

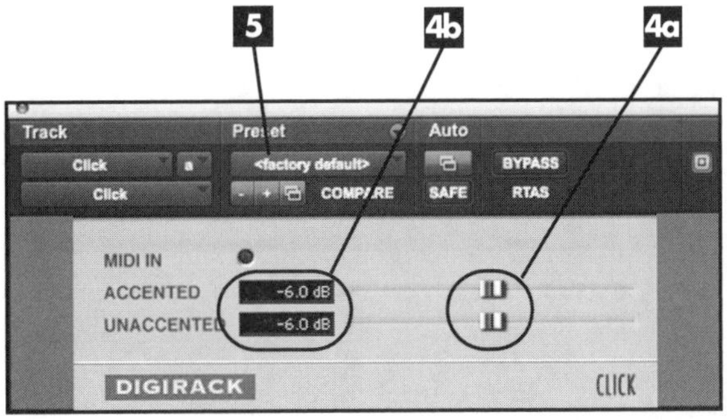

OR

4b **Type** a **value** in the Accented or Unaccented field. **Press Return** when you're finished to confirm your entry.

5 If you want a different sound for your metronome, **click** on the **plug-in preset name**. A preset drop-down menu will appear, from which you can choose the best tone for your click.

6 **Choose** a **tone** for your click track. The sound of your click track will change to reflect your selection.

7 When you're finished, **click** on **Close**. The Click plug-in window will close.

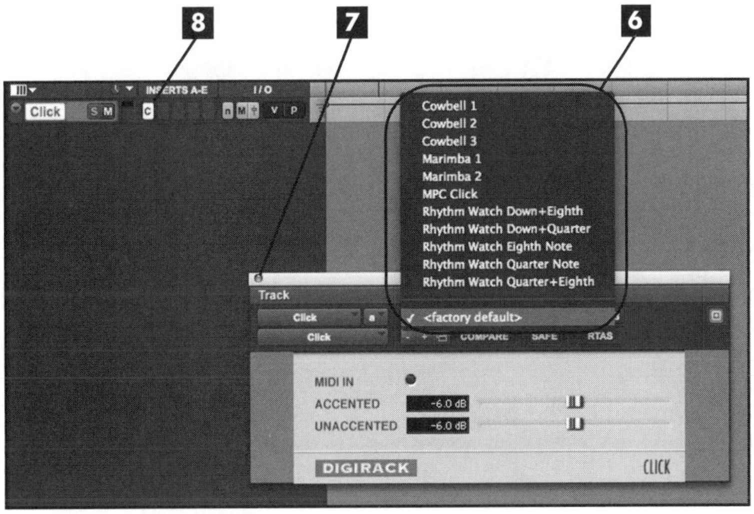

8 If you want to change your settings at some later point, **click** on the **Insert button** to reopen the Click plug-in window.

The next thing you'll need to do is set up how your click track will behave.

1 **Click** on **Setup**.

2 **Choose Click/Countoff**. The Click/Countoff Options dialog box will open.

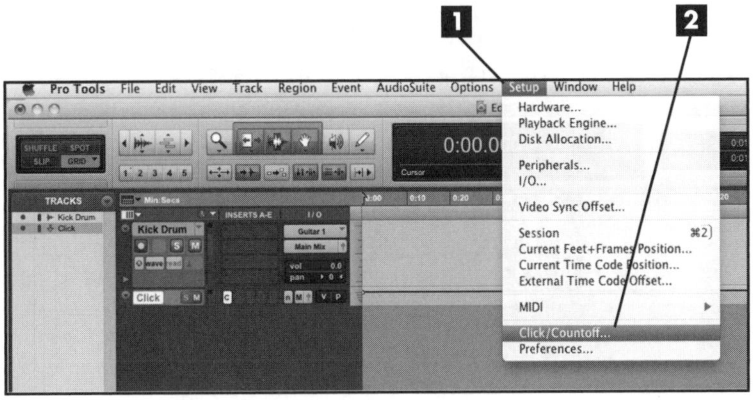

ANOTHER WAY TO OPEN THE CLICK/COUNTOFF OPTIONS DIALOG BOX

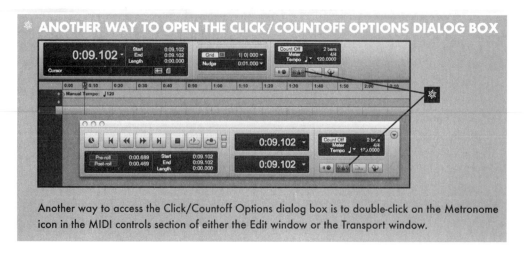

Another way to access the Click/Countoff Options dialog box is to double-click on the Metronome icon in the MIDI controls section of either the Edit window or the Transport window.

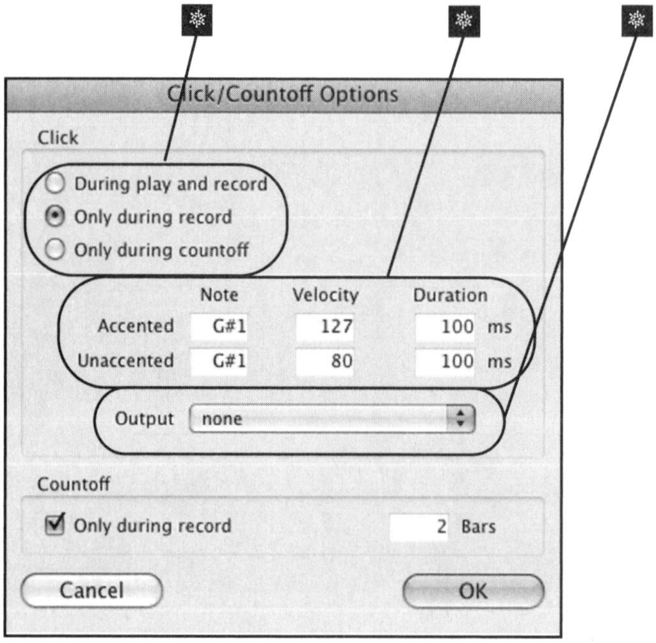

- The top three option buttons enable you to control the fundamental behavior of your click. The most common way to use a click is to hear the click when you're recording audio, but not when you're only playing your session. To set up your click in this manner, select the Only During Record option button.

- You have the option to send click information to a MIDI synthesizer (something we'll discuss in greater depth in Chapter 7, "Using MIDI"). In the case of using a MIDI synth for a click, you can enter specific notes, velocities, and durations for the accented and unaccented click sounds, according to the layout of your specific MIDI device.
- If you're using a MIDI synthesizer for your click source, you'll need to click on the Output menu and select a MIDI output port for your click information.

CLICK PLUG-IN CONVENIENCE!

If you're using the Click plug-in (which is probably the most common way of working these days), you don't need to worry about assigning specific MIDI notes, velocities, durations, or MIDI output ports, because the Click plug-in is not a MIDI synthesizer in the traditional sense. If you followed the steps earlier in this section and created a click track from the Track menu, settings in the Accented, Unaccented, and Output rows of the Click/Countoff Options dialog box won't affect your click track one way or the other.

- In the Countoff section, select the Only During Record checkbox to ensure that your countoff will only be heard before recording. During regular playback, you won't be bothered with the countoff.
- Enter the number of bars you want for your countoff in the Bars field. Two measures is a common setting.

3 **Click** on **OK**. The Click/Countoff Options dialog box will close.

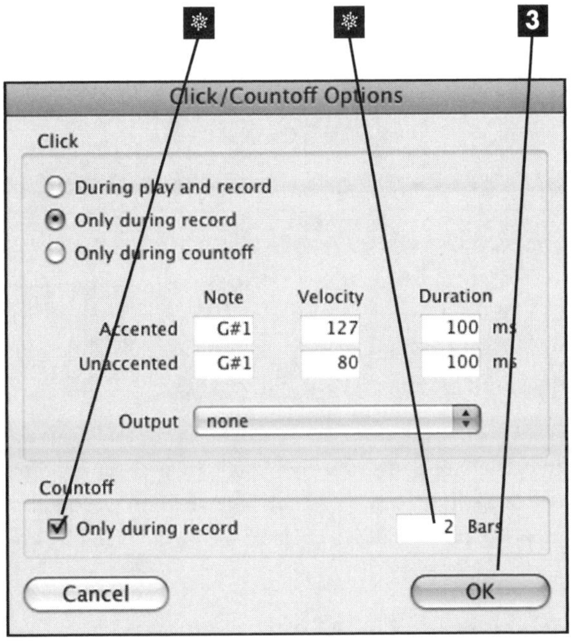

Now that the parameters of the click have been set up, the last step is to make sure that the click is actually *enabled*. The Options menu is a good place to check on the status of your click (and many other features in Pro Tools as well).

1 **Click** on **Options**. The Options menu will appear.

2 If your click is enabled, you'll see a checkmark next to the Click menu item. If there's no checkmark shown, just **click** the **menu item** to turn it on.

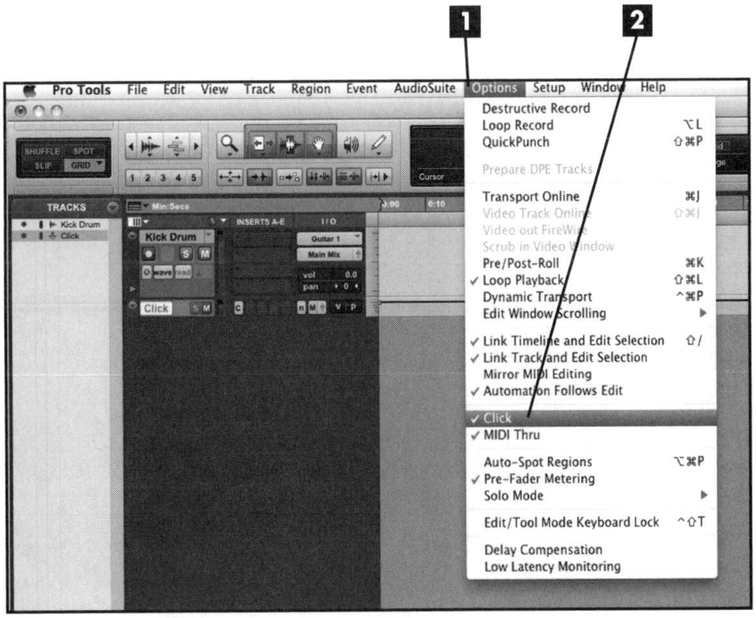

If you've followed the steps in this chapter so far, you're all set—but as with many things in Pro Tools, there's more than one way to get the job done. You can also enable the click (and the countoff) from the MIDI controls section of the Edit or Transport window.

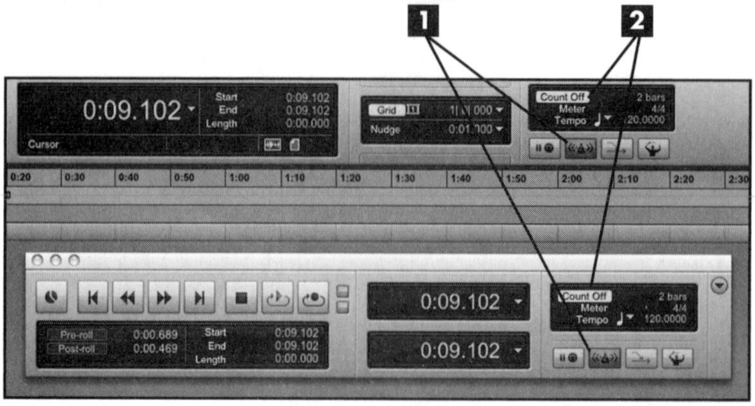

1 **Click** on the **Metronome icon** in the MIDI controls section to activate the click. When active, the button will have a blue color.

2 To activate or deactivate your countoff, **click** on the **Count Off indicator** in the MIDI controls section. An active countoff (shown here) will be displayed in black text with a green background, and an inactive countoff will be indicated by green text with a black background.

Tempo and Meter

Now that you have your click track set up, you'll need to choose the tempo and meter of your song—the two main factors controlling your session's metronome.

Basic Tempo Setup

A Pro Tools session's tempo can operate one of two ways: Either the session will follow a single tempo value (giving you a static tempo), or it will follow the tempo ruler (which will allow you to have your song speed up and/or slow down as it plays). In this chapter, let's choose to use a static tempo. (You'll learn how to use the tempo ruler in Chapter 7.)

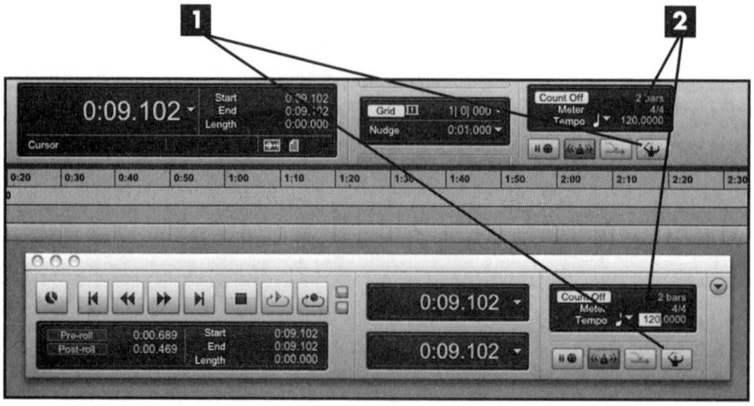

1 If the Conductor Track button is highlighted in blue, **click** the **button** to deactivate the Conductor. With the Conductor inactive, a numeric tempo display will be shown in green just above it.

2 **Click** the **Tempo value area**, which will highlight the tempo number. At this point, you have a number of options as to how to set your session's tempo.

3a **Type** a **tempo** in the numeric Tempo value field, and then press Return.

OR

3b **Click and drag** your **mouse** up or down to increase or decrease the tempo value.

OR

3c **Press** the **T key** on your computer keyboard in tempo, and press Return when you are done. The numeric display will change to reflect the tempo of your taps.

Basic Meter Setup

As with tempo, you can have a constant meter (time signature) throughout your session, or you can make metric changes during the course of your song—something we'll discuss in Chapter 7. For now, though, let's set a single meter for our session. There are two ways to get the ball rolling.

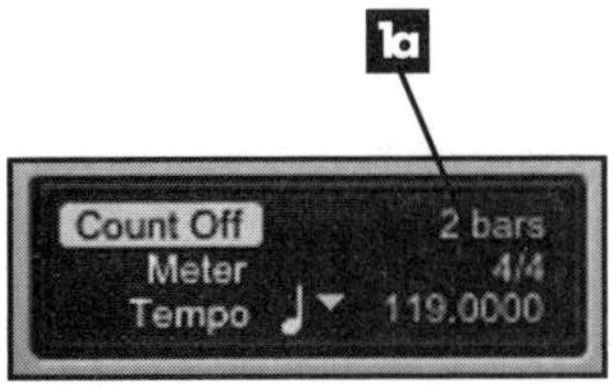

1a In the MIDI controls section of either the Edit window or the Transport window, **double-click** on the **Meter display**. The Meter Change dialog box will open.

OR

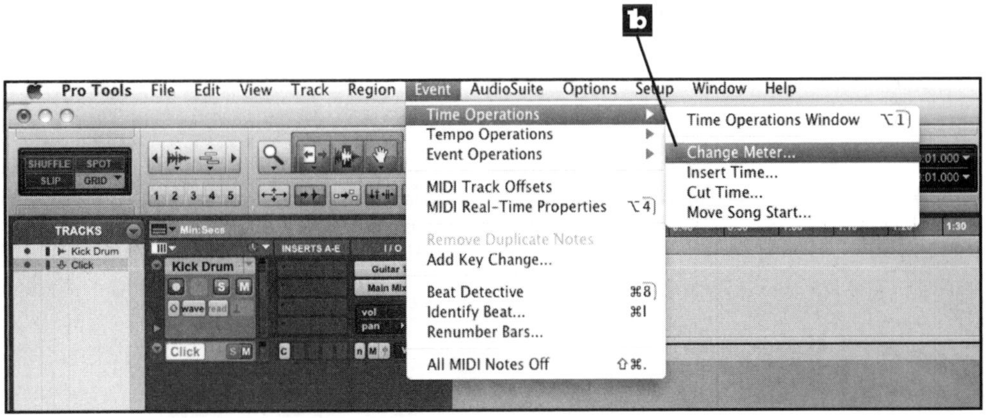

1b From the **Event** menu, **choose Time Operations** and then **Change Meter**. The Time Operations window will appear.

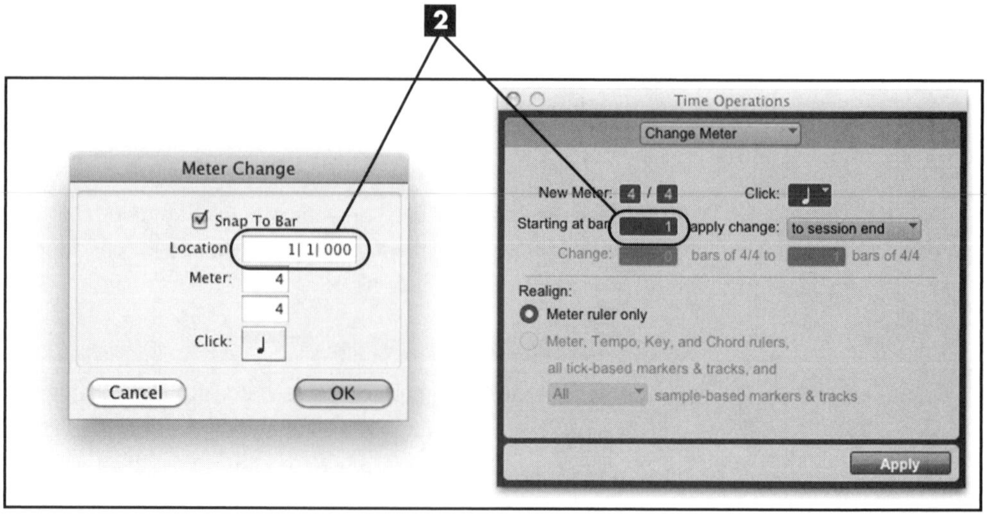

2 Although the Meter Change and Time Operations windows appear to be quite different, they do the same thing. Regardless of which window you're looking at in your session, setting your meter is a straightforward process. **Type** a **location value** to indicate where the meter change should take place. In the Meter Change dialog box, the value is displayed in bars|beats|ticks. For this example, we want our meter to start at the beginning of the song, so enter a value of 1|1|000 in the Meter Change dialog box or simply 1 in the Time Operations window.

3 **Type** a **value** in the Meter field to select the meter you want to use.

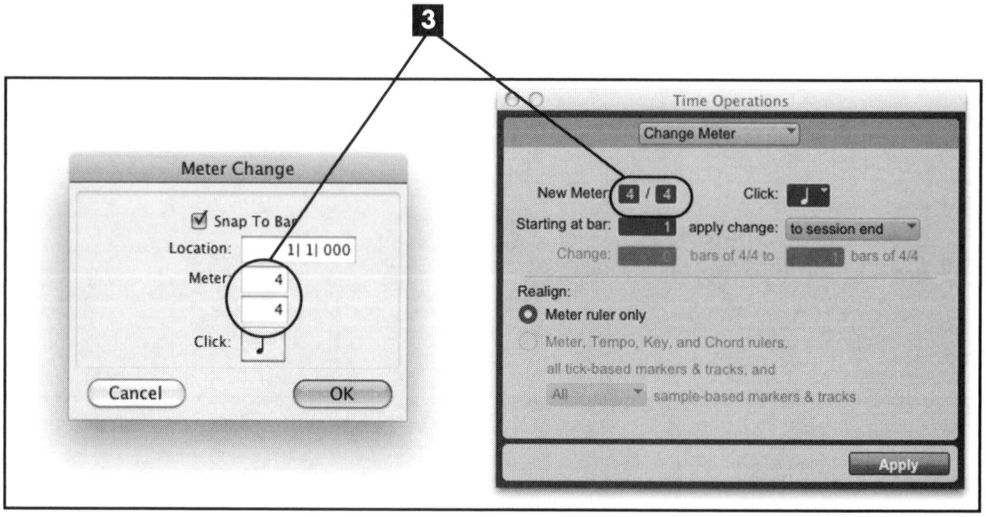

SNAP TO BAR

When dealing with meter changes, it's *very* unusual to have a metric change at any point other than the beginning (beat 1) of a bar. In the Meter Change dialog box, checking the Snap to Bar checkbox will place the meter change at the beginning of the bar indicated in the Location field.

4 Although a quarter note is most commonly used in click tracks, you can choose any note value for your click. **Click** on the **Click button** (or in the Click field, if you're working in the Time Operations window). The click resolution menu will appear.

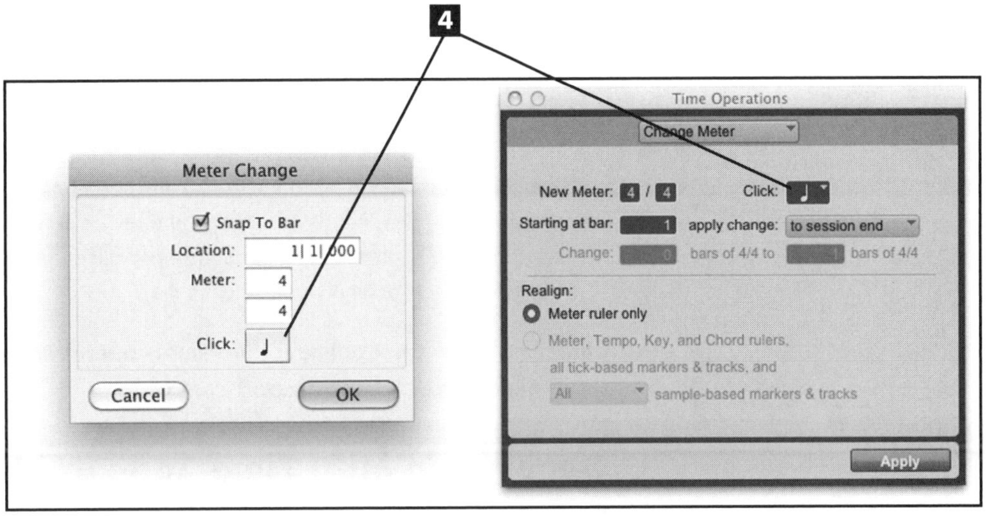

5 **Click** on the **note value** that matches the desired value of your click.

6 Additionally, you can **click** on the **dot** if you want to use a dotted-note value for your click.

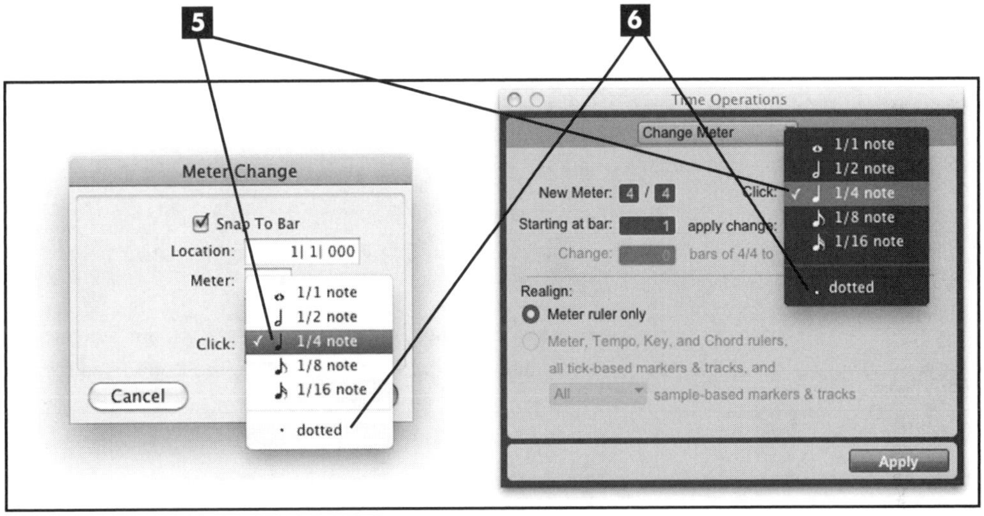

7 Once you're satisfied with your settings, **click** on **OK** in the Meter Change dialog box or **click** on **Apply** in the Time Operations window. Your meter changes will be applied.

Online Mode

In some complex recording scenarios, Pro Tools must operate in concert with other hardware systems. Commonly, this means that Pro Tools must be set up to work with tape-based devices (video or audio) in such a way that all devices start, stop, and play together. For this sort of arrangement to work, they must be *synchronized*—in other words, when a master device starts and stops, the slave devices will follow.

Although the complexity of such setups is beyond the scope of this book, enabling Pro Tools to operate as a synchronization slave device is an easy matter—it's called *Online mode*.

You'll find the Online button in your Transport window or in the Synchronization tool cluster of the Edit window. When active, the button will appear blue. With this option enabled, Pro Tools will follow the master device (which you can determine from Setup > Peripherals > Machine Control).

Once Pro Tools is put online, all transport operations will be carried out remotely. You won't need to touch the transport controls.

Generating MIDI Time Code (MTC)

Pro Tools can operate as a synchronization master device. One of the most common ways for Pro Tools to control a complex setup is through the use of *MIDI Time Code,* also known as MTC. For those technical readers, MTC is a digital form of SMPTE time code and is transmitted to slave devices via MIDI (which you'll learn more about in Chapter 7).

You'll find the Generate MTC button in the Synchronization tool cluster of the Edit or Transport window. When active, the button will appear blue. When Pro Tools is acting as an MTC master device, all devices configured to follow MIDI Time Code will follow your Pro Tools session.

FOLLOWING MTC

Setting up an external device to follow MIDI Time Code is a very straightforward process, and one we'll go through in Chapter 7.

WHAT ABOUT MIDI BEAT CLOCK?

Pro Tools can use two kinds of MIDI synchronization: MIDI Time Code, which we've just touched on here, and another type of synchronization called MIDI Beat Clock. Beat Clock is used to keep different MIDI musical devices working at the same tempo. This is a bit different from MTC, which deals with synchronization in terms of hours, minutes, seconds, and divisions of seconds called *frames.* You'll learn more about Beat Clock and how to use it in Chapter 7.

Basic Recording

You're all set—let's go! Now you're ready to record some audio from the outside world into the Pro Tools environment.

> **TRACKS FOR RECORDING PRACTICE**
>
> Here's where the included disc's audio CD tracks can help. If you don't have a live musician on hand, just play the audio CD. In this chapter, you'll be recording a number of tracks in series, and it's recommended that you mute each track after it's been recorded so you can listen to the track you're recording without distraction.

1. **Click** on the **Track Record Enable button** to "arm" the desired track for recording. Bear in mind that as soon as the track is armed, its input will be active, so take care to avoid situations that can cause feedback.

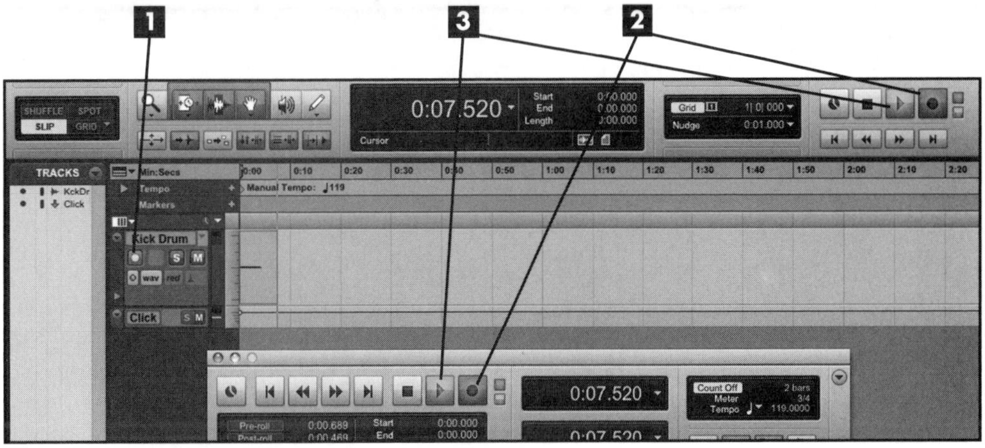

2. **Click** on the **Record button** in the Transport window or in the Edit window's transport controls. The Record button will begin to flash.
3. **Click** on the **Play button**. Recording will begin. If you're following the tutorial, begin the playback of the CD after recording has started.

> **RECORDING SHORTCUT**
>
> The shortcut for record/play is Command+spacebar (Mac) or Ctrl+spacebar (PC).

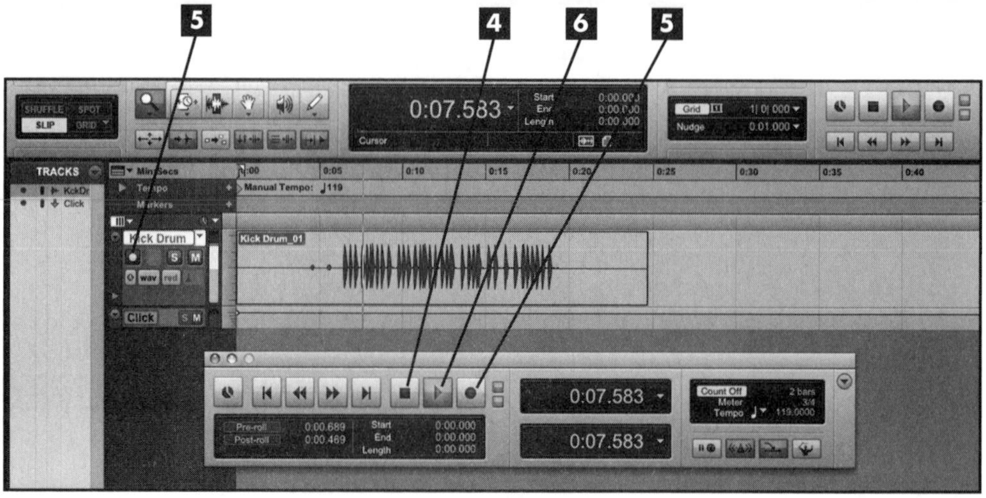

4 **Click** on the **Stop button** when you want to stop your recording. A new region will be shown in the track and will also be listed in the Regions list.

5 Before you listen to your track, **click** the **Track Record Enable button** (to disarm the track), and make sure the Record button is not highlighted.

6 **Click** on the **Play button** or **press** the **spacebar**. You will hear your newly created track. Woo hoo!

Other Recording Options

Congratulations! You've taken another important step down the Pro Tools road. Now let's explore some different ways to record audio that can come in useful in specific situations.

Punching In and Punching Out

Suppose you recorded a perfect take, except for just one problem section. It's something that happens in recording sessions again and again. Don't worry—with Pro Tools, you can specify a section of your track and redo it, a technique commonly called *punching in*. Remember, too, that Pro Tools generally operates *nondestructively*, so you don't have to worry about losing any of your original take!

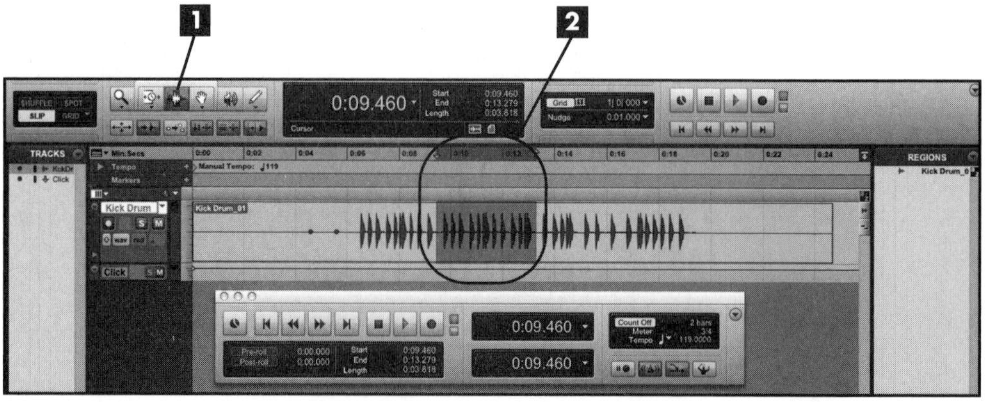

1 **Click** on the **Selector tool**. The tool will be highlighted (in blue).

2 **Mark** the **area of audio** that you want to re-record by clicking and dragging with your mouse.

3 If your track isn't record-armed already, **click** the **Track Record Enable button** on the track you want to redo. The track will be armed for recording. Note that the selected area in the Ruler area, which is usually bordered by blue arrows, is now bordered by red arrows. These indicate that there is a track in your session that is record-armed.

4 If you want to hear a little bit of your original track before you start recording (before you punch in), you'll want to set up some pre-roll. **Click** on the **Pre-Roll indicator.** When active, it will be black text against a green background (as shown here).

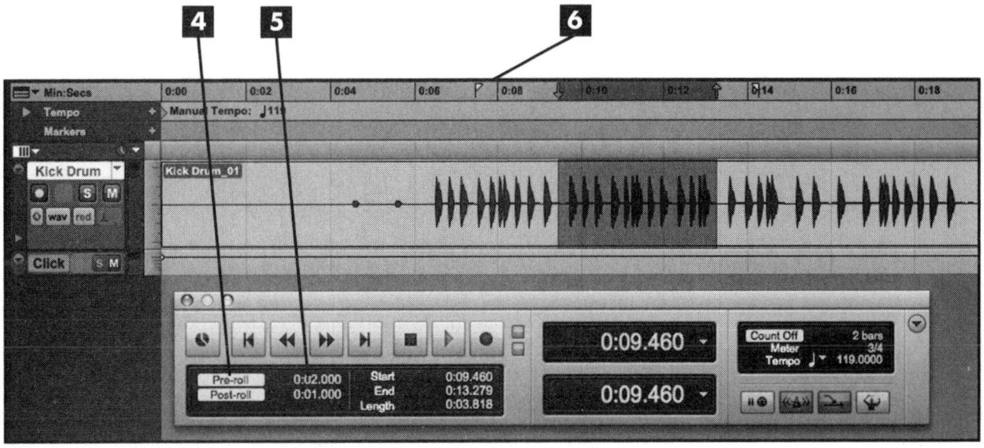

5 **Click** inside the **numeric display** to the right of the Pre-Roll button and **type** the **length** of your pre-roll. Bear in mind that the scale of this value follows the Main Counter display.

6 **Press Enter** to confirm your entry. A small gold flag in the Ruler area will represent your enabled pre-roll.

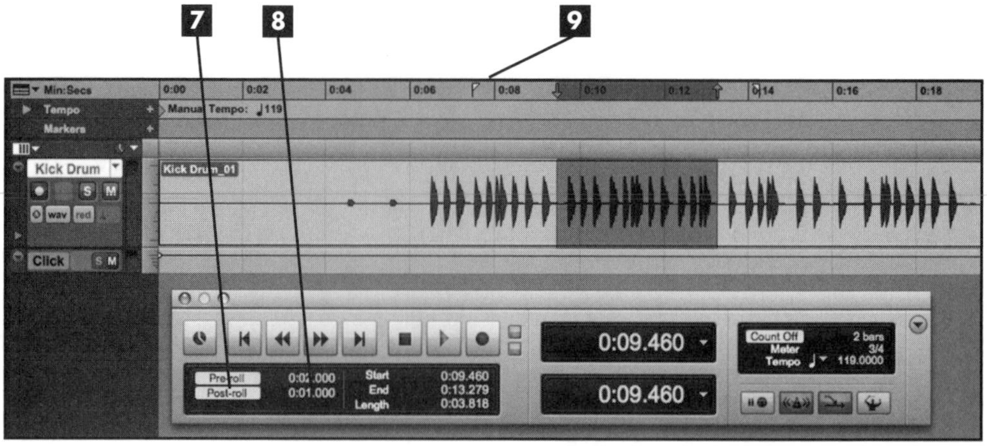

7 If you want to hear a little bit of your original track *after* your recorded section is finished (after you punch out), you'll want to set up some *post*-roll. **Click** on the **Post-Roll indicator**. When active, it is black text against a green background (as shown here).

8 **Click** inside the **numeric display** to the right of the Post-Roll button and **type** the **length** of your post-roll. Bear in mind that the scale of this value follows the Main Counter display.

9 **Press Enter** to confirm your entry. A small gold flag in the Ruler area will represent your enabled post-roll.

> **MAKING CHANGES**
>
> You can click and drag the arrows and flags on the Ruler timeline to change your selection, pre-roll time, or post-roll time. Using the Selector tool, you can also hold the Option (Mac) or Alt (PC) key and click in a track before or after a selection to instantly move your pre- or post-roll to that location.

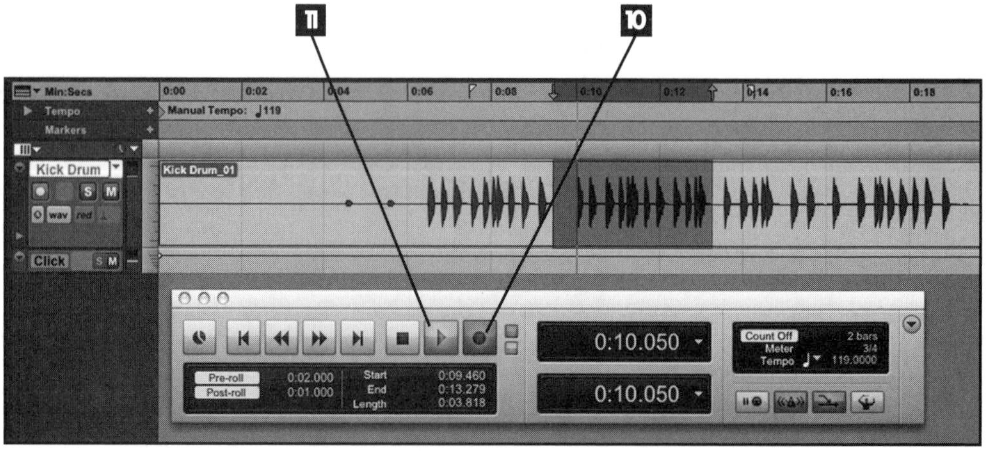

10 **Click** on **Record**.

11 **Click** on **Play**. If you've selected a pre-roll value, your session will begin playback from the pre-roll position. If no pre-roll is selected, recording will begin immediately at the selected area.

If you've set up a pre-roll, Pro Tools will automatically start recording when the timeline insertion reaches the selected area. Pro Tools will continue recording until the end of the selection and then switch back to normal playback and continue playing for the post-roll duration (if any). When the timeline insertion reaches the end of the post-roll duration, playback will stop.

Here's what you'll end up with:

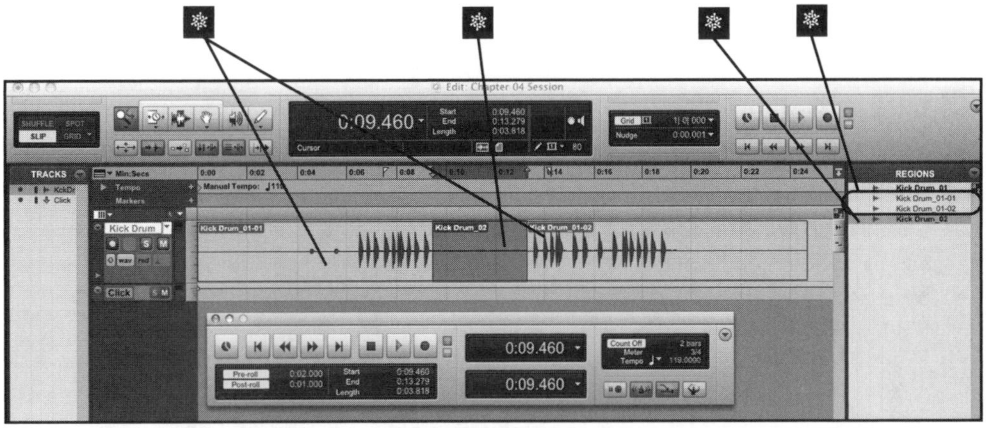

- Two new regions will be created, representing the "good" parts of the original take.

- Both of these new regions also appear in the Regions list. However, these regions are not shown in bold text because they are only incomplete parts of a whole file. Note that the original take is still in the Regions list as well, and it is displayed in bold type (since it does represent a whole file).
- Your punch has been recorded as a new region. For this example, I've recorded silence for visual effect.
- Your punch region appears in bold text in the Regions list because it is a whole-file region, which means that it represents an entire file in your Audio Files folder.

> **WHOLE-FILE REGIONS VERSUS SUBSET REGIONS**
>
> When using Pro Tools, audio files fall into one of two categories—*whole-file* regions and *subset* regions. This is a simple but important distinction:
>
> - Whole-file regions are regions that represent entire audio files. In other words, the region begins at the very beginning of an audio file and ends at the very end of that file. Whole-file regions are most commonly created during the recording process and are displayed in bold text in your Regions list.
> - Any region that represents anything *other* than an entire audio file is called a subset region. Subset regions are commonly created during the editing process, when unwanted sections are trimmed from a region. Subset regions are also automatically created when punching in and out, as shown in the preceding example.

QuickPunch Recording

The main limitation of the basic punch-in and punch-out workflow is that it's a one-time thing. You punch in, you punch out, and you're done. So what if you want to punch in and out more than once in a single pass? Rejoice—QuickPunch mode is for you!

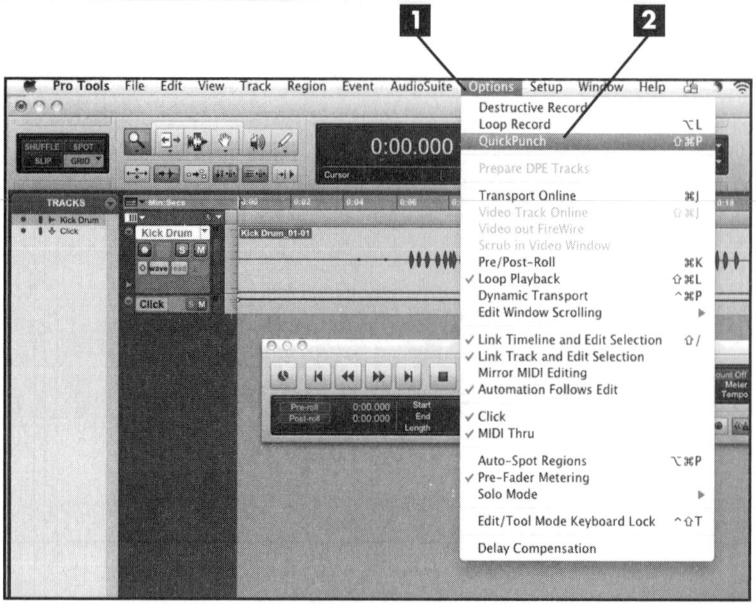

1. **Click** on **Options**. The Options menu will appear.
2. **Click** on **QuickPunch**. QuickPunch record mode will be enabled, indicated by a letter P displayed inside the Record button.

QUICKPUNCH SHORTCUT

Here's another way to access QuickPunch mode: Right-click on the Record button to reveal a list of the various recording modes. Just select QuickPunch from that list.

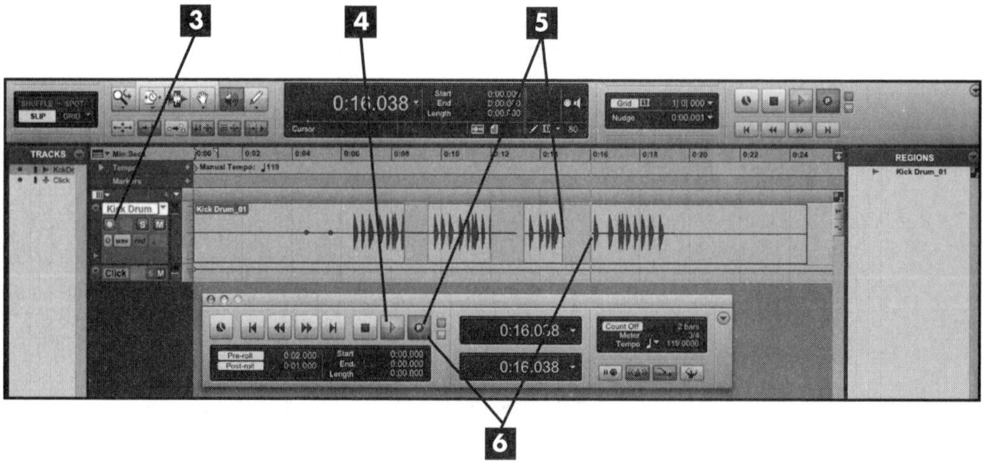

3. If your track isn't record-armed already, **click** the **Track Record Enable button** on the track you want to redo. The track will be armed for recording.
4. **Click** on **Play** at any point prior to when you want to record new audio. In this case, I'll start from the beginning of the session. Your session will play as normal.
5. When you want to punch in, or begin recording, **click** on **Record**. Recording will start.
6. **Click** on **Record** again when you want to punch out, or *stop* recording. Recording will stop, and playback will continue. To start recording again, simply click the Record button when you wish to resume recording.

> **ANOTHER QUICKPUNCH SHORTCUT**
>
> Here are a few ways to punch in and out in QuickPunch mode: During playback, press Command+spacebar (Mac) or Ctrl+spacebar (PC), press the 3 key on the numeric keypad, or press the F12 key.

Here's what you'll end up with:

New regions will be created in your track to reflect each time you engaged and disengaged recording. As before, new regions are also created that represent the "good parts" of the original take.

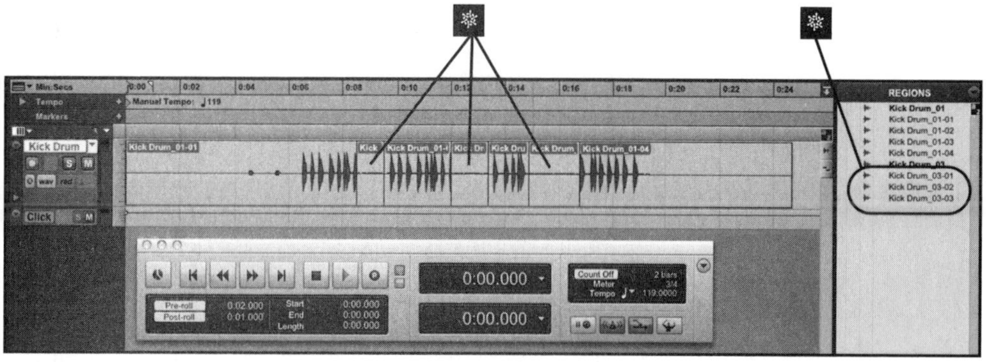

As you might expect, new regions will also be added to the Regions list. The regions created in the track are not whole-file regions, although a whole-file region is also created in your Regions list.

Loop Recording

Suppose you want to record several passes of a certain section (a guitar solo, for example) and then pick the best one. In cases like this, you'll want to use Pro Tools' Loop Record function. Loop recording essentially records a selected area over and over, enabling the artist to create as many takes as desired without stopping. When you're finished, you can choose the best take or even combine takes (a process called *comping* a track, which we'll discuss in Chapter 5, "Editing").

Although loop recording has existed in Pro Tools for quite some time, how you work with loop-recorded tracks—especially in the editing phase of a project—has changed massively. We'll go through these new features and workflows in depth in Chapter 5; for now, let's lay the foundation for those workflows by setting a few preferences *before* we start loop recording.

1. **Click** on **Setup**.
2. **Choose Preferences**.

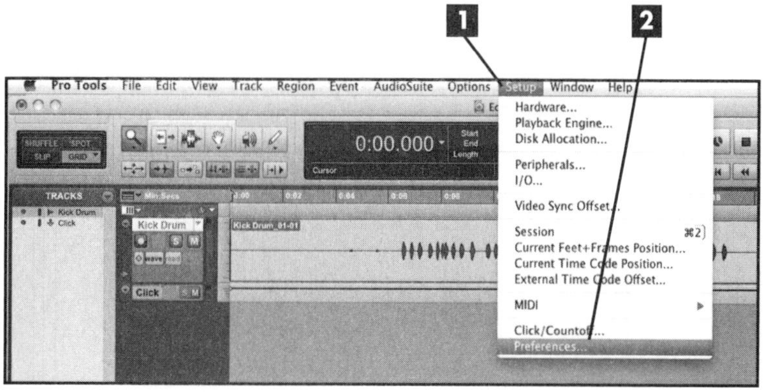

3 In the Pro Tools Preferences window, **click** the **Operation tab.**

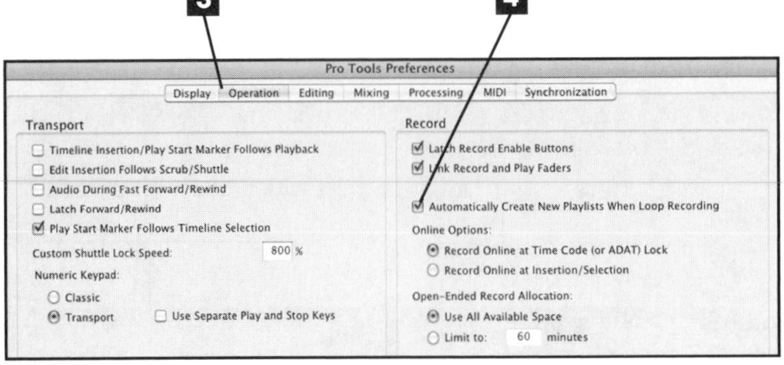

4 In the upper-right area of the Pro Tools Preferences window, **click** the **Automatically Create New Playlists When Loop Recording checkbox** to select it. (When it is selected, a checkmark will appear in the checkbox.) You'll learn more about the effect of this preference in Chapter 5.

Now that you've laid the groundwork for more effective editing later on, you're all set to go through the normal process of loop recording.

1 **Click** on **Options**.

2 **Click** on **Loop Record**. The Loop Record feature will be enabled (as indicated by a looped arrow around the Record button icon).

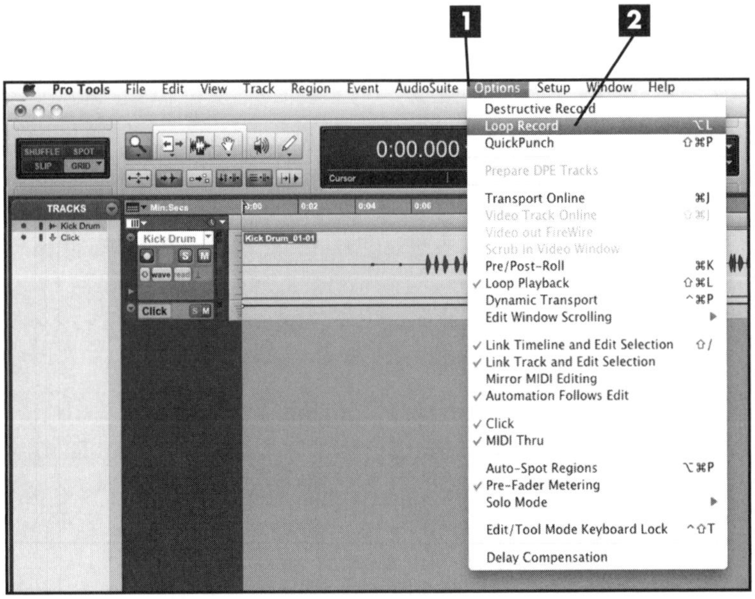

LOOP RECORDING SHORTCUT

Alternatively, you can right-click the Record button and choose Loop from the menu that will appear.

3 **Use** the **Selector** tool to click and drag over the section you want to loop.

4 If your track isn't record-armed already, **click** the **Track Record Enable button** on the track on which you want to loop record. The track will be armed for recording.

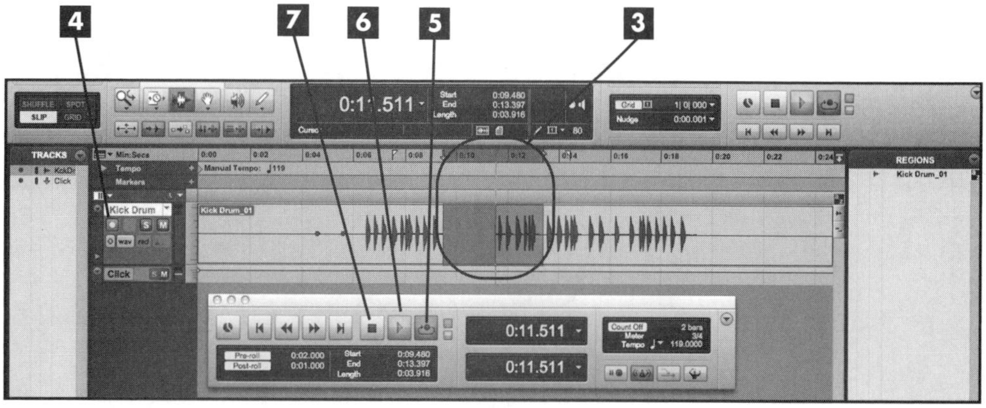

5 **Click** on **Record**.

6 **Click** on **Play**. Playback will begin at the pre-roll position (if pre-roll is enabled). When the selected area is reached, Pro Tools will begin recording. At the end of the selection, recording will immediately begin again from the beginning of the selection (even if pre-roll is enabled).

7 When you have enough takes, **click** on **Stop**. The last take will appear in the selected area.

WHOLE-FILE REGIONS AND LOOP RECORDING

When you're finished with a loop-recording pass, you'll notice that there are new regions in the Regions list representing each time you looped—plus one. In the list, note that there is a whole-file region (in bold text) in addition to the subset regions that represent individual takes. Although it's not specifically used in the track, it represents the parent file in which all the individual takes reside in sequence. Below the whole-file region are individual takes numbered sequentially in the order in which they were recorded.

8 After your loop-record passes, you might want to check your takes to see whether you captured a good one. With the Selector tool chosen, **Command-click (Mac)** or **Ctrl-click (PC)** on the **loop-recorded region**. A menu of alternate takes will appear.

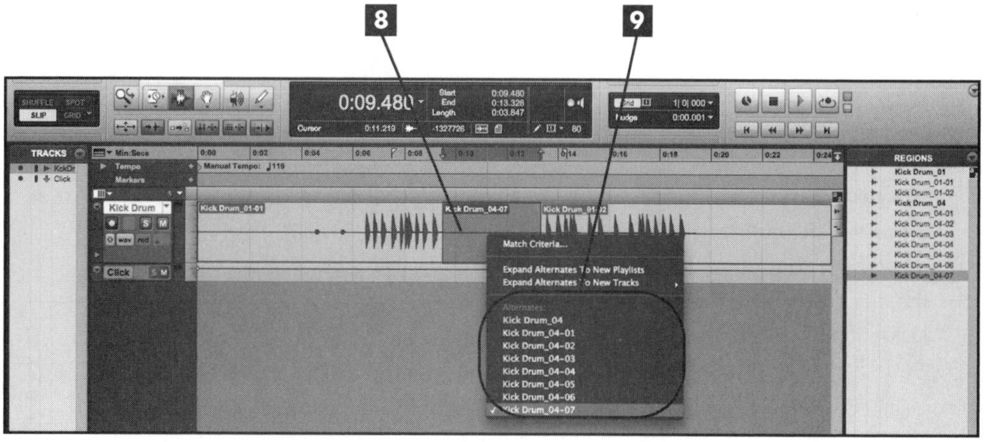

9 **Click** on the **take** you want to use. The take will be selected, and the region will be replaced. This is a great way to audition different takes to find just the right one.

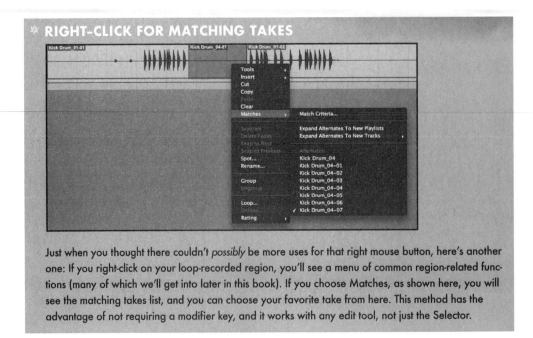

RIGHT-CLICK FOR MATCHING TAKES

Just when you thought there couldn't *possibly* be more uses for that right mouse button, here's another one: If you right-click on your loop-recorded region, you'll see a menu of common region-related functions (many of which we'll get into later in this book). If you choose Matches, as shown here, you will see the matching takes list, and you can choose your favorite take from here. This method has the advantage of not requiring a modifier key, and it works with any edit tool, not just the Selector.

For the Brave: Destructive Recording

Thus far, you've only seen nondestructive recording modes, meaning that you never actually erase any audio in the process of punching in, punching out, or looping, and you can always recover your original recording pass with no loss. This is a huge advantage over working with tape, and it was one of the initial advantages of DAWs in general. With Destructive Record mode, however, you can record directly—and permanently—onto a pre-existing audio file. Be careful, though; there's no way to undo what you've done if you make a mistake!

1. **Click** on **Options**.
2. **Click** on **Destructive Record**. Destructive Record mode will be enabled (indicated by a checkmark by the menu item and a letter D inside the Record button).

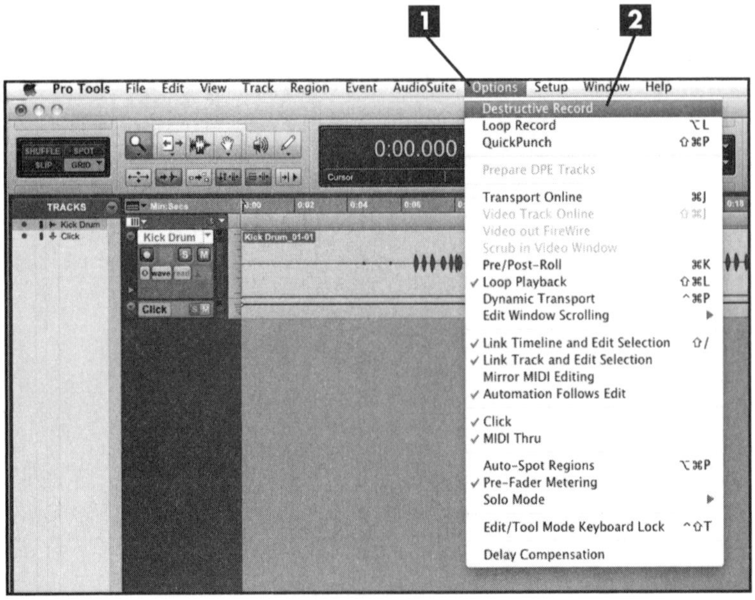

3 Use the Selector tool to **choose** the **section** of the Audio track that you want to overwrite.

4 If your track isn't record-armed already, **click** the **Track Record Enable button** on the track on which you want to record. The track will be armed for recording.

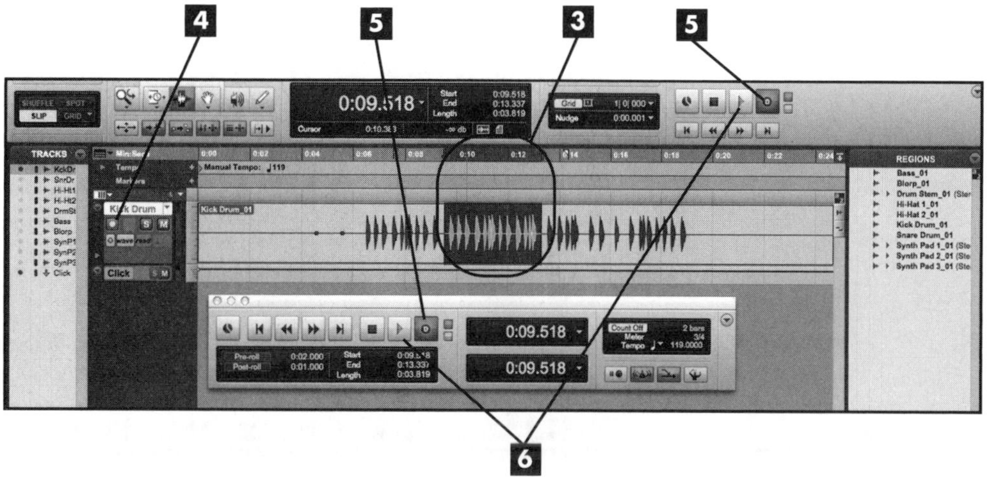

5 **Click** on **Record**.

6 **Click** on **Play**.

At this point, the process works much the same as basic punch-in and punch-out recording—with one important difference. Just as you saw when you did basic punch-in/punch-out, your session will begin playing at the pre-roll position (if you've enabled pre-roll), and then it will automatically begin recording at your selected area. It will stop recording at the end of your selection and play for the post-roll amount (if post-roll has been enabled).

The important distinction between Destructive Record mode and the other modes becomes apparent when the recording pass has finished.

Unlike the other record modes in Pro Tools, with Destructive Record mode, *no new regions* have been created—in the track itself or in the Regions list. What you've done is permanently changed the file you originally recorded!

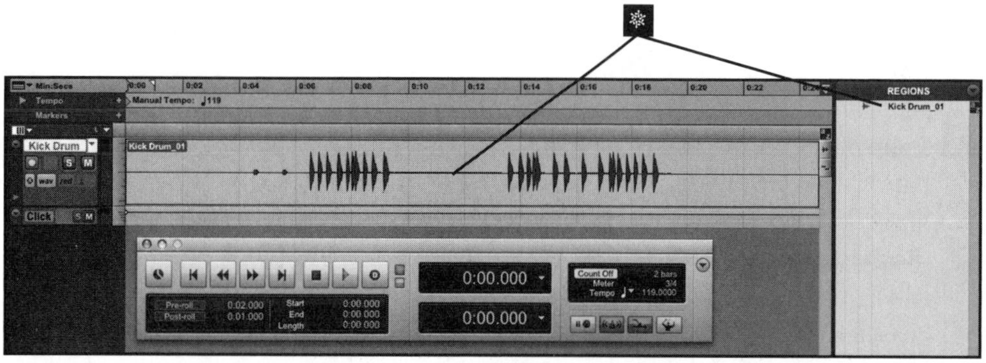

RECORD-ARMING SHORTCUT

If you've read the previous chapter, you know that Pro Tools includes shortcuts for mute and solo—Shift+M and Shift+S, respectively—for any tracks that contain a timeline insertion (the vertical "play" line that indicates your current location). Well, you can add another shortcut to that list: Shift+R will record-arm any tracks that contain an Edit Cursor.

✻ FILE SIZE LIMITATIONS

This might be a little technical for most users, but it bears mentioning: Prior to version 8, Pro Tools only supported audio file sizes up to 2 GB (admittedly, a very *long* audio file!). Starting with Pro Tools 8, however, single file sizes up to 3.4 GB were supported. In a typical studio situation, you're not likely to run into either of these file-size ceilings. However, if you're recording a lengthy live performance, this might become an issue. It's an easy fix: At some point before you reach the maximum file size (at about 7.66 hours if you're recording at a sample rate of 44.1 kHz and a bit depth of 24 bits), just quickly stop and restart recording. This will automatically create a new file.

Tips, Tricks, and Troubleshooting

Fantastic! You're on your way to running a great recording session! Before we close this chapter, here are a few tidbits to call on when you need them.

Naming Regions and Files

When it comes to good file-management practices, remember this: The names of regions and files that you create during recording will follow the names of the tracks upon which they're being recorded. For example, a track named Drums will yield recording passes named Drums_01, Drums_02, and so on. Bottom line: The best work habit is to name your tracks *before* you start recording. However, if you ever forget to do this, or if you ever want to change the name of a region after that region has been created, it's easy to do.

1 **Double-click** on the **region** you want to rename (either in the Regions list or in a track with the Grabber tool selected). The Name dialog box will open.

2 **Type** a new **name** for the region in the Name the Region text box.

3a To rename the region only and leave the audio file's name unchanged, **click** the **Name Region Only option button**.

OR

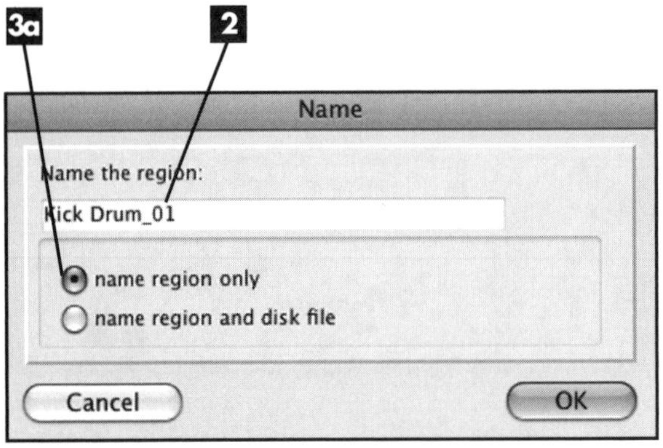

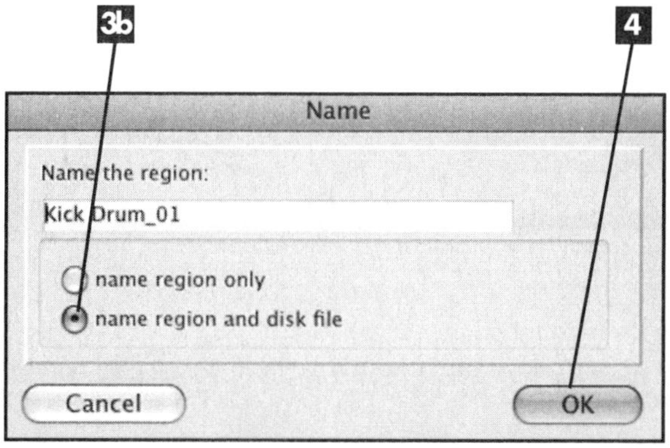

3b To rename the region in the session *and* the audio file's name, **click** the **Name Region and Disk File option button**. Note that this option will only be available if the region you are renaming is a whole-file region. (A whole-file region corresponds to an audio file from start to finish, making this twofold naming possible.)

4 **Click OK**. The Name dialog box will close, and the region will be renamed.

Understanding the Monitor Modes

In addition to all the different record modes you've learned about, there are two monitor modes that affect how you hear your audio during the recording process. The two modes, Auto Input Monitoring and Input Only Monitoring, will be useful in different situations.

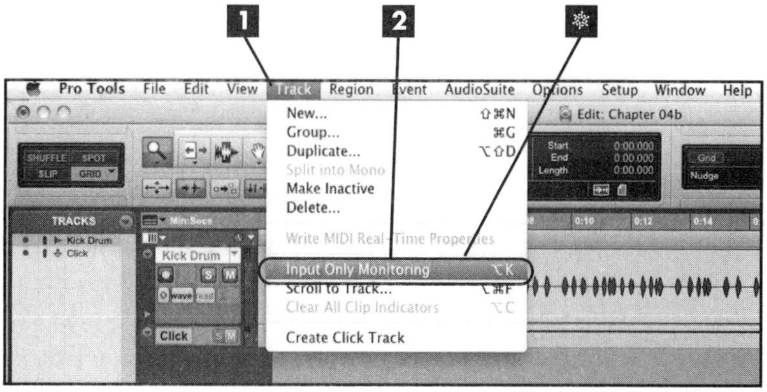

1 **Click** on **Track**. The Track menu will appear. The monitor mode that you're *not* in will be shown as an option in this menu. In the case of the image shown here, the menu item reads Input Only Monitoring, which indicates that the *current* monitoring mode is Auto Input Monitoring.

2 **Choose** a **monitor mode**.

- Choose Auto Input Monitoring mode if you want to hear what was previously recorded right up to your punch-in point. Pro Tools will behave as if it is in playback mode during any pre-roll and post-roll and will automatically switch over to monitoring your live input in the selected area only. Although both monitoring modes are useful, Auto Input Monitoring mode is more frequently used for many users.

- To the right of the transport controls (in the Edit window or the Transport window), the Input Status LED will be off (the checkbox will be gray) when you're in Auto Input Monitoring mode.

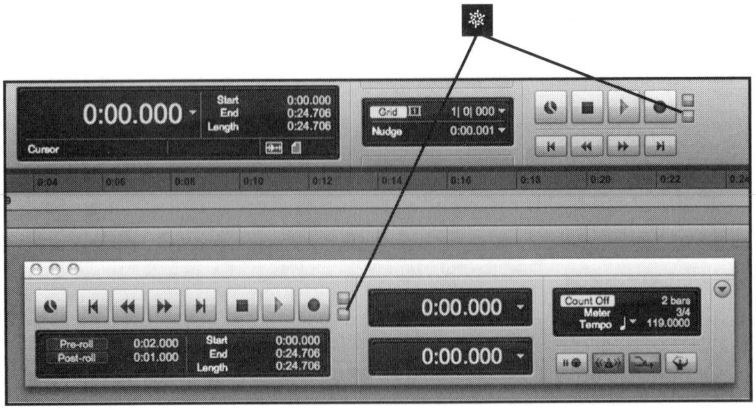

- Choose Input Only Monitoring mode if you *don't* want to hear what you've already recorded during a punch-in/punch-out situation. Pro Tools will still only record during the selected area, but for the pre-roll and post-roll durations, you' ll hear live input rather than the previously recorded track.

- With Input Only Monitoring enabled, the Input Status LED will be on (the box will be green) to indicate that you're in Input Only Monitoring mode.

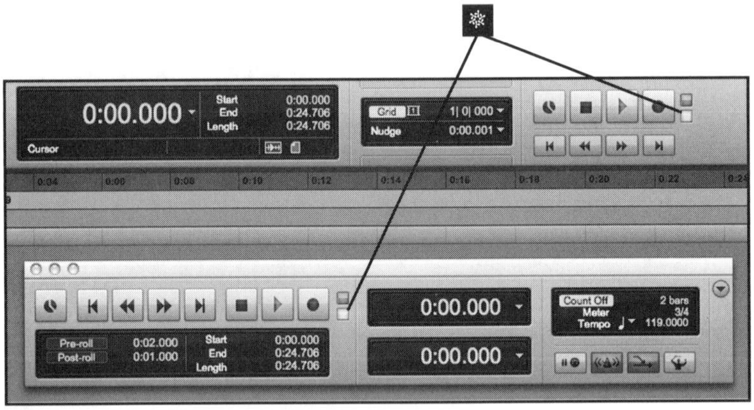

Low-Latency Monitoring

When you're recording, you might sometimes notice a bit of delay between when a note is played and when it is heard through your monitor speakers or headphones. This is called *latency*, and it's an unavoidable part of host-based DAWs in general. In Chapter 3, "Getting Started with Audio," you learned that reducing your H/W buffer during recording can help minimize latency. There's another option available when using interfaces like the Mbox Pro, however: *low-latency monitoring*. This monitoring mode minimizes the process of running audio through the host computer's CPU, reducing the delay you hear.

Low-latency monitoring is only available in Pro Tools software running in conjunction with Digi 002, Digi 003, Mbox2 Pro, and Mbox Pro hardware. For Mbox and Mbox Mini users, there's a different solution, which we'll discuss in the next section.

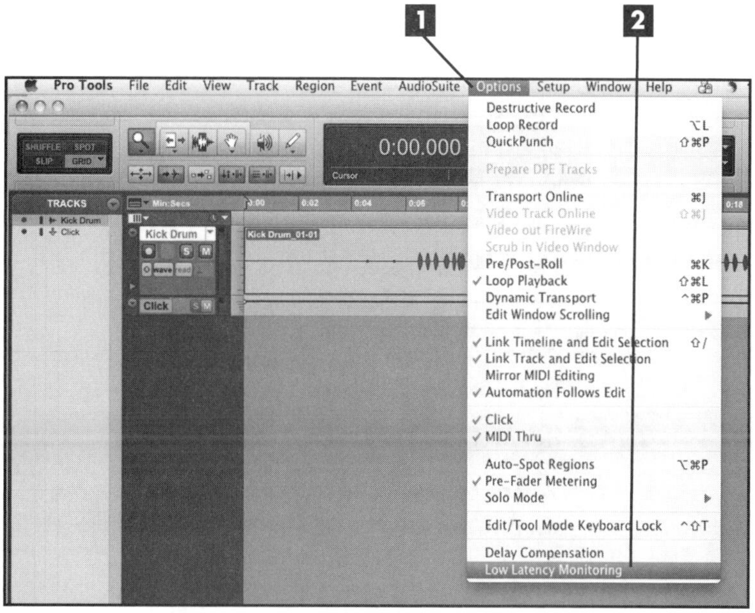

1. **Click** on **Options**. The Options menu will appear.
2. **Click** on **Low Latency Monitoring**. That's it!

The good news is that your latency situation just got a lot better, but there's a small price to pay for low-latency monitoring. All inserts on any record-enabled tracks will be bypassed. For example, if you need to have an EQ plug-in on the track's insert while you're recording, low-latency monitoring isn't for you. Fortunately, having inserts on your recorded tracks is fairly rare in normal situations.

LATENCY AND HD

Recording latency is an issue that must be dealt with in all host-based systems. Regardless of whether you reduce the H/W buffer or use Low Latency mode, there are concessions that must be made in terms of the quantity and quality of the low latency recording experience. One of the advantages of Pro Tools|HD systems is that the business of recording isn't managed by your computer's CPU, but rather by dedicated processors that reside on cards that are added to the host computer. The result is that latency is typically not an issue when recording audio, with no need for low hardware buffer settings or low-latency modes.

Mbox Mini No Latency Operation

If you're working with an Mbox Mini (or an Mbox or the previous generation Mbox 2 or Mbox 2 Mini) audio interface, you'll notice that the Pro Tools software doesn't give you a low-latency monitoring option. Does that mean you're out of luck? No way! The solution lies in the Mbox Mini's Mix knob, which is on the front panel of your Mbox Mini interface. When the knob is all the way to the input side (fully counterclockwise), you'll be monitoring signals coming directly into the interface *only*, and you won't hear the Pro Tools software play back at all. When the Mix knob is set all the way to playback (fully clockwise), you'll *only* hear audio coming from the Pro Tools software. Here's how to eliminate the latency problem using the Mbox Mini's Mix knob:

1. **Set** the **Mix knob** to 12 o'clock as a starting point, giving you an even balance between input and playback.
2. **Record-arm** the **Audio track** upon which you wish to record. If you play now, you should hear a doubled signal. The earlier signal is from the input side of the Mix knob; the latent (delayed) signal is coming from the Pro Tools software, routed through the playback side of the Mix knob.
3. **Mute** the **track** upon which you wish to record. You can still record onto the track, but you won't hear that annoying delayed signal.
4. **Adjust** the **Mix knob** to get the desired balance between your live input and the Pro Tools software playback.
5. **Record** as normal.
6. When you're finished recording, you can **change** your **mix** fully to play back (clockwise) so you won't be distracted by any audio going into your Mbox or Mbox 2.

RECORDING WITH BUSES

So far, we've only dealt with physical inputs as being sources for audio recordings, but what about buses? Actually, using a bus as an input is done all the time, especially when working with virtual instrument plug-ins. (We'll explore that scenario in Chapter 7.) Don't worry if you're not a MIDI whiz; the section "Recording MIDI Instruments to Audio Tracks" shows a classic bus recording scenario.

A SETUP FOR RECORDING PRACTICE

In this chapter, we've been working with only a single track, recorded from the first track of the audio CD portion of your book's disc. There are nine more tracks that you can practice with. Try recording tracks 1, 2, 3, 4, 6, and 7 to mono audio tracks and tracks 5, 8, 9, and 10 to stereo audio tracks. If you want to check your work, you'll find a Chapter 04 Session-Finished session in the data portion of your book's disc to give you an idea of what your recording session might look like when you're finished.

I have two recommendations for working though this exercise. First, when you're done recording each track, mute that track before moving onto the next one. That way, you'll be able to focus on the track you're currently working on. Second, when you're finished, you'll notice that the timing of the tracks will not be lined up properly. Don't fret—in Chapter 10, you'll learn a very powerful technique that'll make lining up these tracks a breeze!

Next step: editing!

5 Editing

Audio production can be broken down into a number of phases: recording (or *tracking*), editing, mixing, and mastering to name but a few. Like many DAWs, Pro Tools perhaps shines brightest in the editing phase. In its nonlinear environment, you can accomplish in seconds what used to take minutes or hours with tape-based systems. And of course, there is always the Undo function if you make a mistake. Even among DAWs, Pro Tools has led the pack in the world of audio editing.

In this chapter, you'll learn how to do the following:

- Take advantage of the Pro Tools Edit window.
- Use the edit modes, and know the best one to choose in any given situation.
- Work with Pro Tools' basic editing features.
- Use processes such as Cut, Copy, and Paste to create your own arrangements.
- Use Pro Tools' Playlist lanes to work with loop-recorded tracks.

TUTORIAL NOTE

For the purposes of this chapter, I'll be reconstructing a song from rough elements. If you want to follow the screenshots, just copy the Chapter 05 Session folder from the included disc and launch the Chapter 05 Session file.

Understanding the Edit Window

We took a good first look at the Edit window in Chapter 2, "Getting Around in Pro Tools." Now it's time for a closer examination of this powerful editing environment.

Using the Tools of the Trade

Some of Pro Tools' most useful tools are located in the top row of the Edit window. Let's start with the tool clusters included with the minimal tool set.

The four edit modes—Shuffle, Spot, Slip, and Grid—are at the heart of the editing process. The mode you choose will determine how regions can be moved in time within your session. You'll learn more about these modes in the section "Moving Regions on the Timeline: The Edit Modes," later in this chapter.

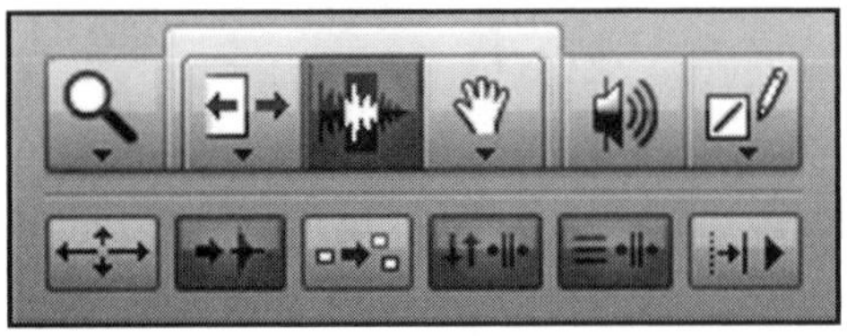

The Edit tool cluster includes the most popular editing tools in the Pro Tools arsenal. From left to right on the top row, the tools are as follows:

- Zoomer
- Trimmer
- Selector
- Grabber
- Scrubber
- Pencil

These tools can operate directly on specific regions within your session. The bottom row of the Edit tool cluster includes different features that you can enable or disable. These are as follows:

- Zoom Toggle
- Tab to Transients
- Mirrored MIDI Editing
- Link Timeline and Edit Selection
- Link Track and Edit Selection
- Insertion Follows Playback

You'll learn more about these in the section "Basic Tool Functions" later in this chapter.

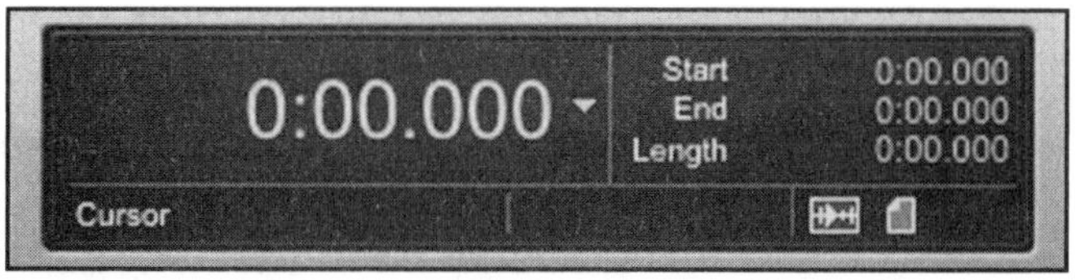

The Counters and Edit Selection indicators give you a variety of information about both your session and where you are within it. On the left side, you'll see your session's Main Counter display, which shows you exactly where you are in your session. To the right are the Start, End, and Length displays, which show you the beginning, end, and duration of any selected area. Other displays in this cluster are related to session status.

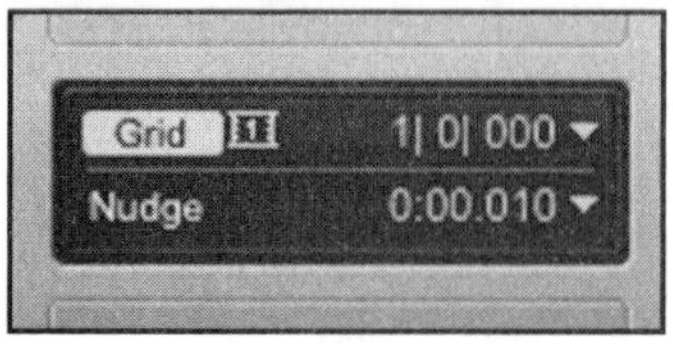

I've already mentioned the Grid edit mode. Here's where you can choose the size of the grid (a topic we'll go through later in this chapter). There's also a feature that enables you to move regions by very small amounts, called *nudging*, and you can choose your nudge amount right below the grid amount. We'll talk about nudging regions in Chapter 6, "And More Editing."

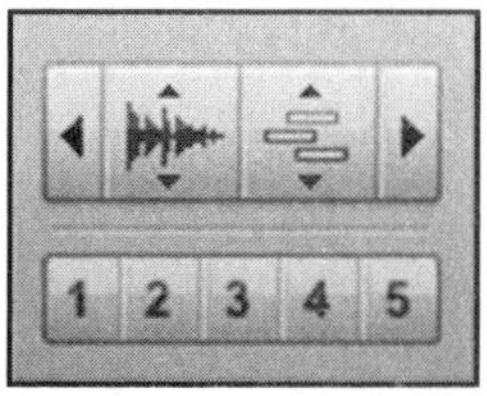

Though they're not part of the minimal tool set, I personally find the Zoom Controls cluster particularly useful. The Zoom Controls cluster enables you to quickly zero in on a very brief section of your session (useful for fine editing) or zoom out to view longer sections in your project. The numbered buttons on the bottom of the Zoom Controls cluster enable you to save your favorite zoom settings as zoom presets.

You can also zoom in or out using other methods, which will enable you to view your regions in different ways. We'll discuss these later in this chapter.

Navigating Your Session

Before you can do anything else, you need to know the basics of how to get around. You'll find that the Selector tool is well suited to this task. Along with this tool, you'll want to use the location displays to their best advantage.

1 Right now, the Main Counter scale is set to display time in terms of minutes and seconds. You can view time in a number of other ways, however. **Click** on the **arrow** to the right of the Main Counter display. A drop-down menu will appear.

2 **Choose** the desired **scale** for your session. For this example, choose Bars | Beats. The time scale of the Main Counter display will change to reflect your selection.

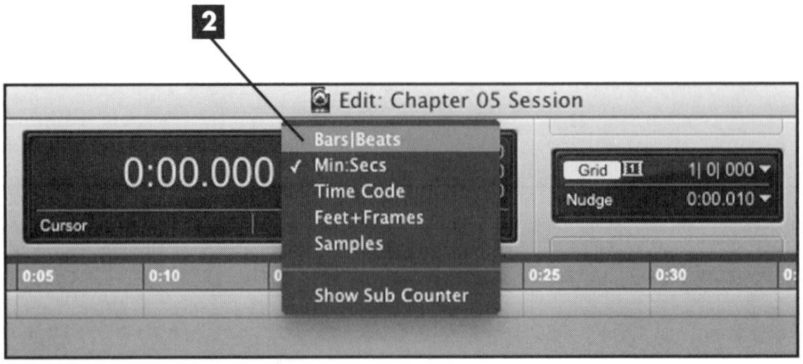

SELECTION DISPLAY SCALE

The scale of the Edit Selection indicators (to the right of the Main Counter display) will change to match the Main Counter's scale. For example, if you change the Main Counter's scale to Bars | Beats, any selections you make will also be shown in bars and beats in the Edit Selection display area.

In many cases, you might want to see the passage of time in a number of ways simultaneously. In the case of a music project, you might be working in terms of bars and beats, but you might also want to see where you are in the real-time scale of minutes and seconds. That's where the Sub Counter can help.

1 **Click** on the **arrow** to the right of the Main Counter display. A drop-down menu will appear.

2 **Choose Show Sub Counter**. The Sub Counter display will appear in the Counter display.

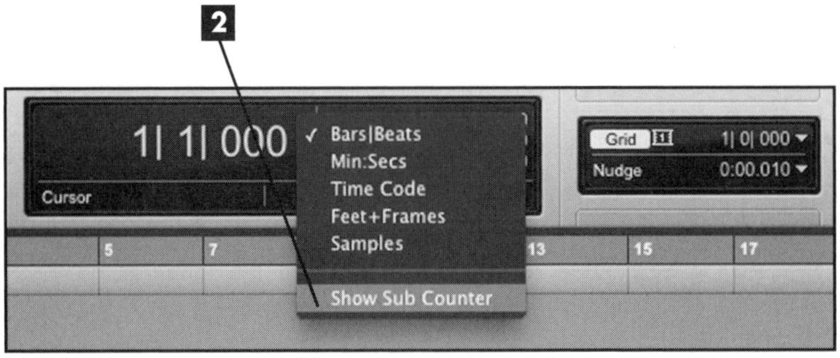

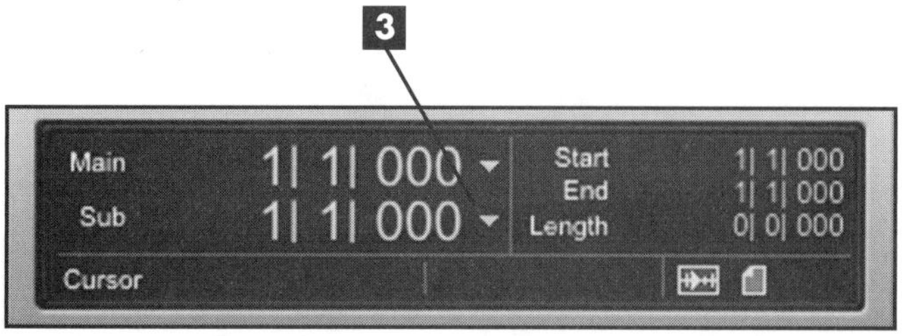

3 In this case, my Sub Counter is showing exactly the same value as my Main Counter. That doesn't help at all, so I'll need to change the Sub Counter's time scale. **Click** on the **arrow** to the right of the Sub Counter display. A drop-down menu will appear.

4 **Choose** the desired **scale** for your Sub Counter. In this case, I'll choose minutes and seconds (displayed as Min:Secs) so that I can view my position in terms of not only bars and beats (in my Main Counter), but in real time as well.

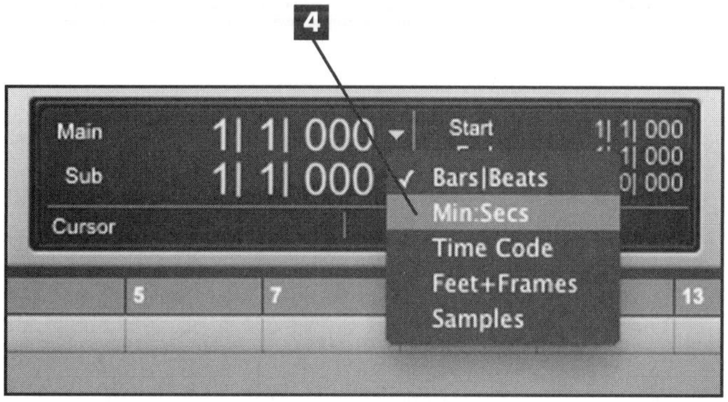

Now that you have your counters set up, you're all set to roam your session!

1 **Click** on the **Selector tool**.

2 **Click** anywhere in the **session's Edit area**. A small line (called the *timeline insertion*) will appear where you clicked. Your timeline insertion's location is precisely noted in the Main Counter and Sub Counter displays.

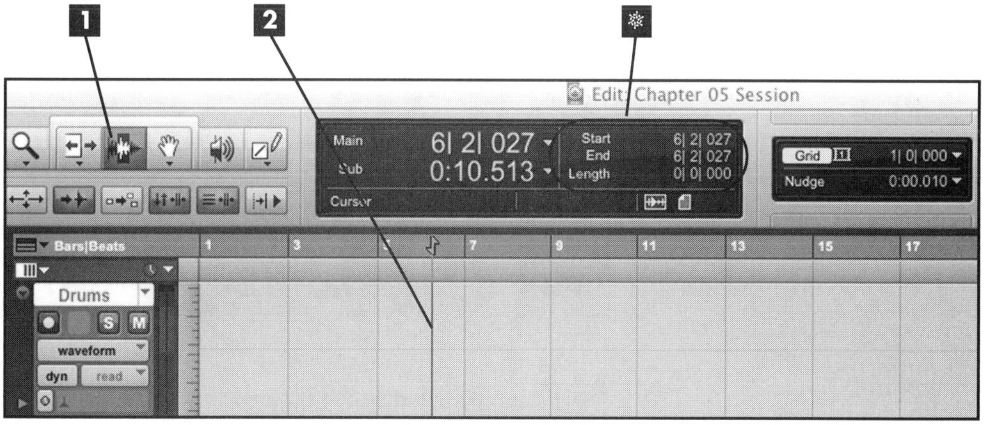

The Edit Selection Start display will also show the timeline insertion location. Because you've selected only a single location, the End value is identical to the Start, and the Length value is zero.

Now, try to make a different kind of selection:

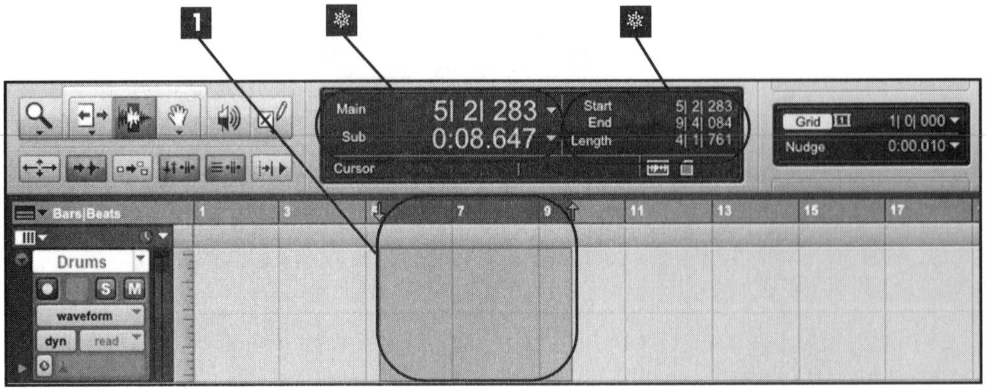

1 Still using the Selector tool, **click** and **drag** (to the left or right) in a track to make a selection with a length greater than zero. The selection you make in the track is mirrored in the Ruler. A blue down arrow in the ruler indicates the beginning of the selection, and an up arrow indicates the end.

- The Main Counter and Sub Counter displays show the start of your selection.
- The Edit Selection indicators show the start, end, and length of your selection.

Navigating with the Tab Key

The Selector tool is one way to get around your session, but it's not the *only* way. For example, the Universe section of the Edit window (which we explored back in Chapter 2) is a way to navigate as well. There's also the Tab key (on your computer's keyboard), which can really be useful in a number of different ways. Let's take a look.

The Tab key can be set up to operate in one of two different modes. We'll take a look at the most basic mode first, so we need to make sure that the Tab to Transients mode is *disabled*.

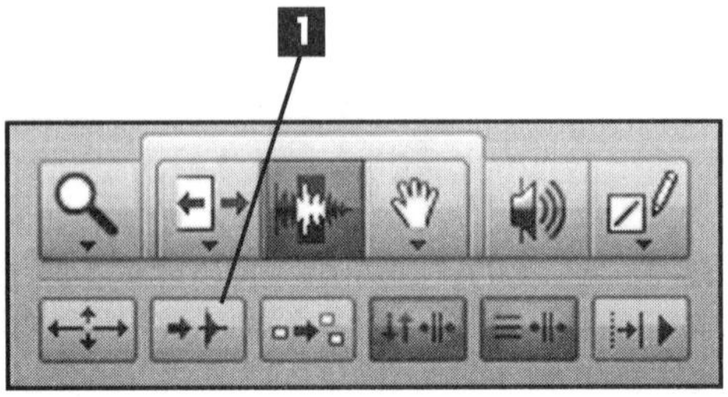

1 Immediately below the Trimmer tool in the Edit tools cluster, you'll find the Tab to Transients button. When enabled, this button will be colored blue. Since we want this mode to be *disabled* for the time being, **make sure** the **button is toggled off** and is shown in a basic gray color.

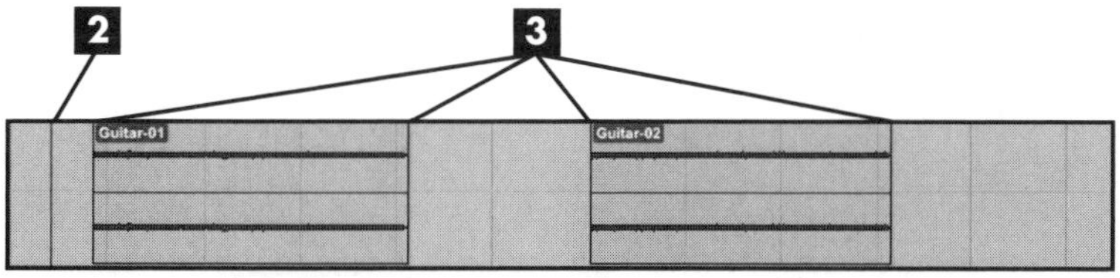

2 Using the Selector tool, **click** on a **track** with a number of regions before any of the regions. (If you're working with the tutorial session, the only track that has multiple regions is the Guitar track.) The timeline insertion will appear wherever you click.

3 **Press** the **Tab key**. The timeline insertion will move to the next region boundary (in this case, the start of a region). Each additional time you press the Tab key, the timeline insertion will move to the next region boundary (moving from left to right).

MODIFYING THE TAB KEY BEHAVIOR

Here's a twist on using the Tab key: Hold the Ctrl key (PC) or the Option key (Mac) while you press the Tab key to move the timeline insertion to the *previous* region boundary (moving right to left).

With Tab to Transients enabled, the Tab key will continue to jump to region boundaries, but it will also stop at each *transient*. The first step in the process is to turn Tab to Transients mode on.

SO WHAT THE HECK IS A TRANSIENT, ANYWAY?

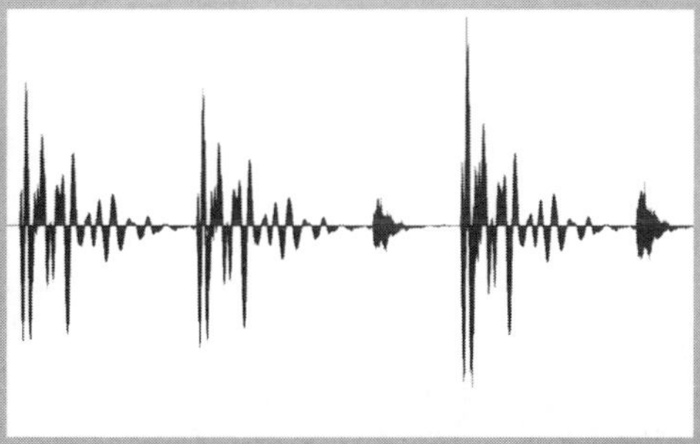

Simply put, a transient is a rapid increase in amplitude (loudness). Commonly, transients are found at the beginning of a percussive waveform, such as a pick or a hammer hitting a string or a drumstick hitting the head of a drum. Different types of instruments have different kinds of transients, but they tend to be good visual cues when editing, indicating the beginnings of notes (or words, in the case of a vocal track).

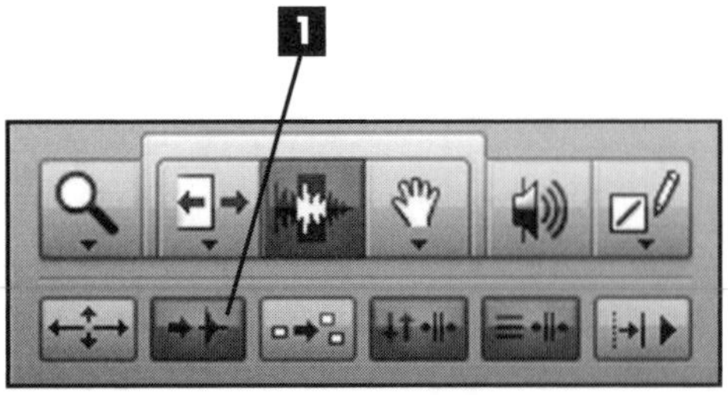

1 The Tab to Transients button will let you know if it's enabled or disabled. When enabled, this button will be colored blue. If the button is disabled (the color will be a basic gray), just **click it** to turn Tab to Transients mode on.

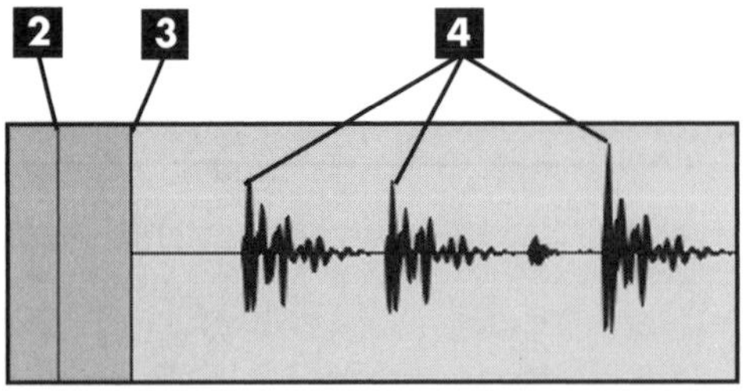

2 Using the Selector tool, **click** on a **track** with at least one region, and before a region, as shown here. (If you're using the tutorial session, the Bass track shows this feature well.)

3 **Press** the **Tab key**. The timeline insertion will immediately jump to the start of the region. Regardless of whether Tab to Transients is enabled or disabled, the Tab key can always be used to quickly move to region boundaries (start or end).

4 **Press** the **Tab key** again. Here's where Tab to Transients differs in its behavior: This time, instead of moving directly to the next region boundary, the timeline insertion will jump from transient to transient as well. This is a fantastic way to locate drum hits and other transient-based audio.

MODIFYING TAB TO TRANSIENTS

Again, the Ctrl key (PC) or the Option key (Mac) will move the timeline insertion *backward* in time, this time to the *previous* transient peak.

MAKING SELECTIONS WHILE TABBING

If you want to make a selection while you're moving with the Tab key, just hold down the Shift key as you tab. This is particularly useful in combination with Tab to Transients and is a quick and effective way to select transient-heavy phrases (such as drum beats, for example).

MOUSE-BASED SCROLLING

If you have a mouse equipped with a scroll wheel, you have some additional navigational power at your disposal. You'll find that your scroll wheel will move you up and down through your shown tracks. (This will only work when you have more shown tracks than can be seen at once in your Edit window.) Holding down the Shift key as you use the scroll wheel will enable you to scroll horizontally along the timeline. Bear in mind, however, that this horizontal scrolling will *not* move the timeline insertion.

Zooming

Sometimes, when you're editing a specific section (such as when you're working with transients, for example), you'll want to get a close look at your audio. Also, when you're finished, you might want to take a step back and get an overview of your entire session. To do either of these things, you'll need to know how to use the Zoom tools.

1. If your Zoom cluster isn't showing, **click** the **Edit Window Toolbar Menu button** (in the upper-right corner of the Edit window). The Edit Window Toolbar menu will appear.
2. **Choose Zoom Controls**. The tools currently displayed in your Edit window will be indicated by a checkmark.

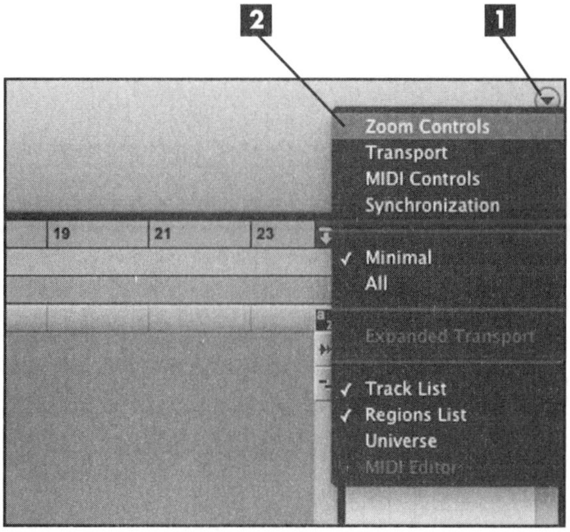

1. **Click** on the **left zoom arrow** to zoom out. Each time you click on this button, the Edit window will show you a greater span of time.

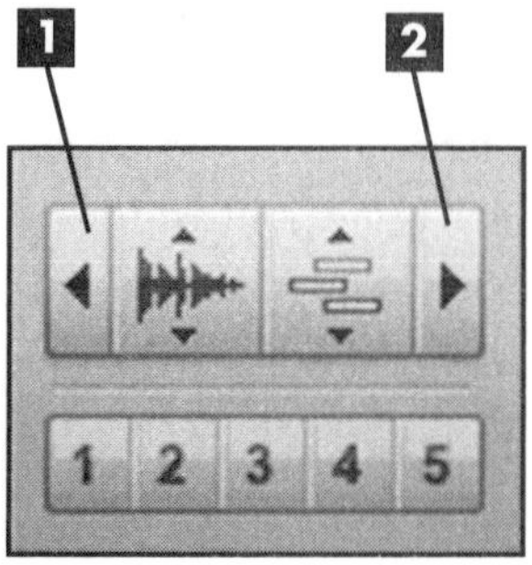

2. **Click** on the **right zoom arrow** to zoom in. Each time you click on this button, you will gain a finer view of your session's timeline.

ZOOMING BEHAVIOR

Notice that your zooming centers on your timeline insertion's location.

ZOOMING SHORTCUTS

You might use these shortcuts more than any others covered in this book: On PCs, it's Ctrl+] (right bracket) to zoom in and Ctrl+[(left bracket) to zoom out. On Macs, Command+] will zoom in and Command+[will zoom out. You can also use the T key to zoom out and the R key to zoom in.

> **SCROLL WHEEL ZOOMING**
>
> Here's even more scroll-wheel power: If you hold down the Alt key (PC) or the Option key (Mac), you'll be able to smoothly zoom in and out, centered on the timeline insertion point. Scrolling up will zoom you in, and scrolling down will zoom you out. This is a very handy new addition, and you'll find that this new mouse power will speed up your editing processes!

Even if you don't have the Zoom cluster shown at the top of the Edit window, you still have access to Zoom buttons. You'll find them in the lower-right corner of the Playlist area in the Edit window.

- Click the Minus (–) button to zoom out.
- Click the Plus (+) button to zoom in.

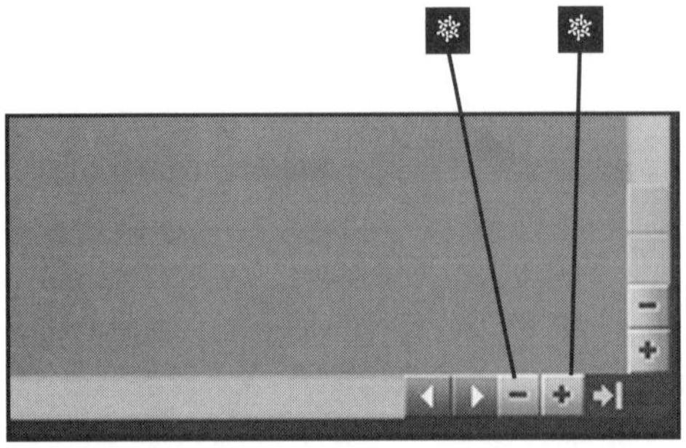

> **CONTINUOUS ZOOMING**
>
> Clicking any of these Zoom buttons (either at the top or the bottom of the Edit window) will incrementally zoom you in or out, but you can also smoothly zoom by clicking and holding on any horizontal Zoom button and dragging your mouse to the left or right.

Here's another way to zoom in on a specific section.

1. **Click** on the **Zoom tool**.
2. **Click and drag** horizontally on a **track** to select an area.
3. **Release** the **mouse button**. The view will zoom in on the selected area.

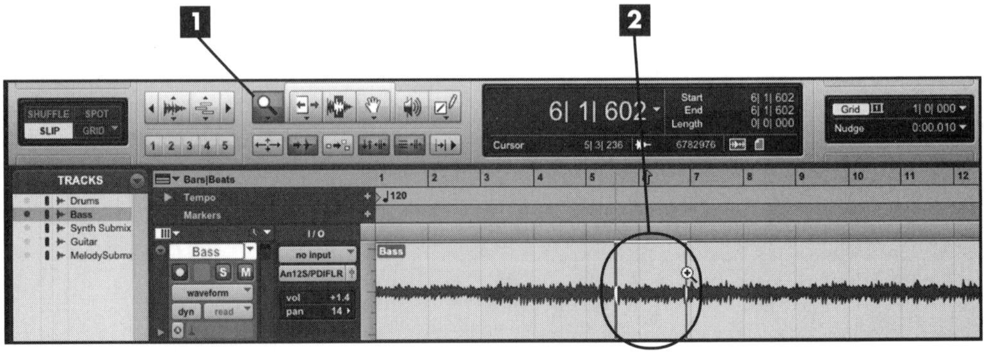

Moving Regions on the Timeline: The Edit Modes

Pro Tools has four basic edit modes that determine how regions can be moved in your session. Each mode is unique. As you gain experience with each of them, you'll get a feeling for which mode is best suited to any given task. To demonstrate how each mode works, we'll work with the drum track of the Chapter 5 tutorial session.

Using Slip Mode

When you need flexibility, Slip mode gives you the most freedom of region movement.

1. **Click** on the **Slip Mode button**. The mode will be selected (indicated by the word "Slip" being shown in black text against a green background).

2. **Click** and **hold** a **region** in the Regions list. (In this case, I've chosen the Drums region.)

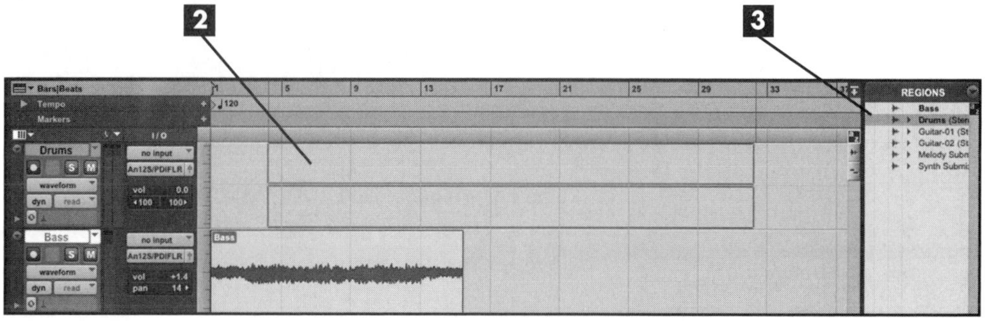

3. **Drag** the **region** onto a track. You will see an outline of the region, indicating where it will be placed when you release the mouse button.

SOME RULES ON MOVING REGIONS

It's important to remember that when you're working with mono regions, you can only drop them onto mono tracks. However, when you drag stereo regions onto the timeline, they can occupy a single stereo track *or* two mono tracks.

HEY, WHERE AM I?

It might seem unusual, but your Main Counter display will not be much help while you're moving regions; it will continue to show your current timeline insertion position. However, the Edit Selection indicators (to the right of the Main Counter display) will reflect the beginning, end, and duration of the dragged region as you move it, helping you get it to the desired position.

Using Grid Mode

Sometimes, it's convenient to have your regions snap a grid of user-definable increments. This can be particularly useful when you're working on a music-based project, when it's often helpful to have your regions align themselves to bars and beats. Pro Tools actually gives you *two* ways of doing this sort of grid-based work, which we'll cover here.

Absolute Grid Mode

First, let's take a look at Grid mode in a typical music context.

> **IF YOU'RE USING THE TUTORIAL SESSION**
>
> If you're following along with the steps so far in this chapter, you should have a selected region on your drum track that you just deposited using Slip mode. Let's get that region out of there before we move on. Because the region is probably still selected, all you have to do is press the Delete key to remove it. If the region is *not* selected, just double-click with the Selector tool or single-click with the Grabber tool to select the region and then press the Delete key. (Note that the region is still present in the Regions list, so you're not losing anything.)

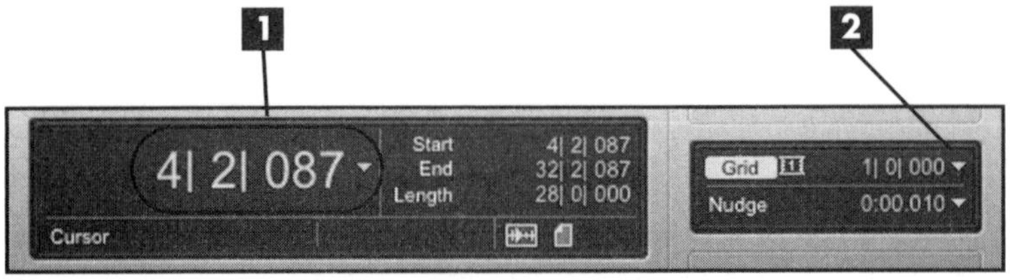

1 You'll want to make sure that your Main Counter display is showing you the kind of information you need. In this example, we'll want to view our location in terms of bars and beats. If that's not what you're seeing in your Main Counter display, just **click** on the **Main Counter display's down arrow** and **change** the **display** to Bars | Beats. The scale will be shown in Bars | Beats | Ticks. Notice that the Edit Selection indicators will also change scale.

2 The next thing you need to do is check your grid value to make sure it's what you want, and make the appropriate changes if needed. **Click** on the **Grid Value arrow**. The Grid Value menu will appear.

3 **Select** the desired **scale** for your grid. Because we're working with music in this case, Bars | Beats is a good fit. The scale will be selected, indicated by a checkmark.

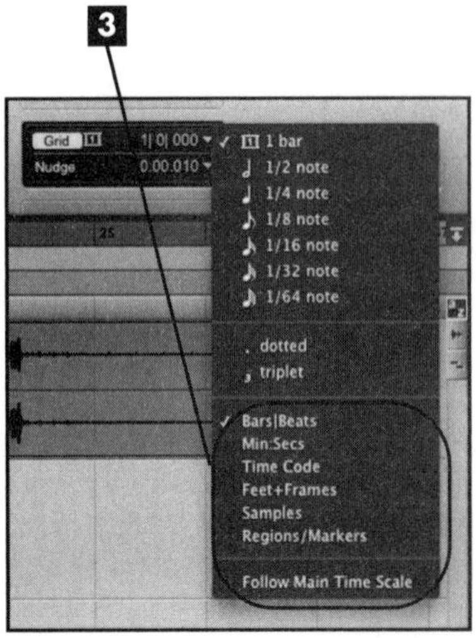

FOLLOW MAIN TIME SCALE

At the very bottom of the Grid Value menu, you'll find an item called Follow Main Time Scale. When you choose this (indicated by a checkmark), the grid scale will automatically change whenever you change the Main Counter display's scale. For many users, it's a very convenient way to work.

4 **Choose** the desired **resolution** for your grid. For the purposes of this example, 1 bar will do the trick.

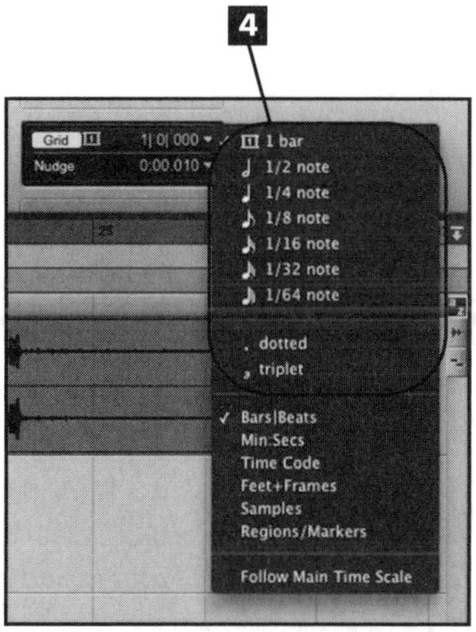

BARS|BEATS GRID INCREMENTS

Because this scale is musical, you will see grid resolutions such as bars, half notes, quarter notes, and so on. At the bottom of the resolution section of the menu, you'll also see options for dotted-note and triplet-based grids.

HEY, WHERE ARE MY GRID LINES?!?

Normally, you'll see a series of vertical lines to indicate your grid positions. If you're not seeing them, just click the word "Grid" in the Grid Value display. When grid lines are being shown, the word "Grid" will be shown in black text against a green background. On the other hand, if you ever want to hide your grid lines for any reason, you can click the word "Grid" to toggle the lines off. (When the grid lines are hidden, the word "Grid" appears in green text against a black background.)

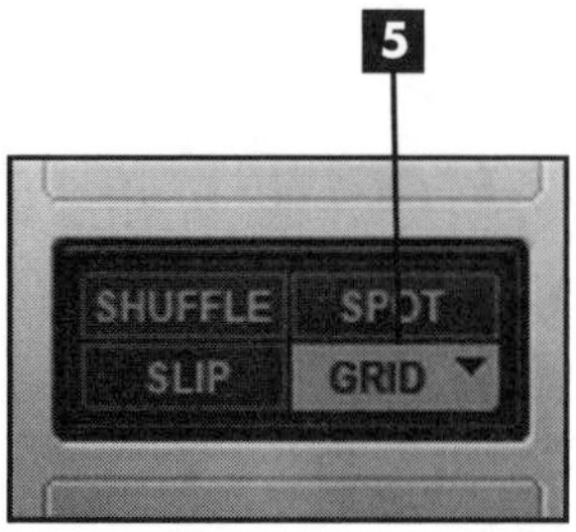

5 In the Edit Modes tool cluster, **click** on **Grid**. When Absolute Grid mode is active, the word "Grid" will appear in black text against a blue background.

6 Just as you did before, **drag a region** from the Regions list onto the Track area. With Absolute Grid mode, however, the region will snap to the nearest bar as you drag it.

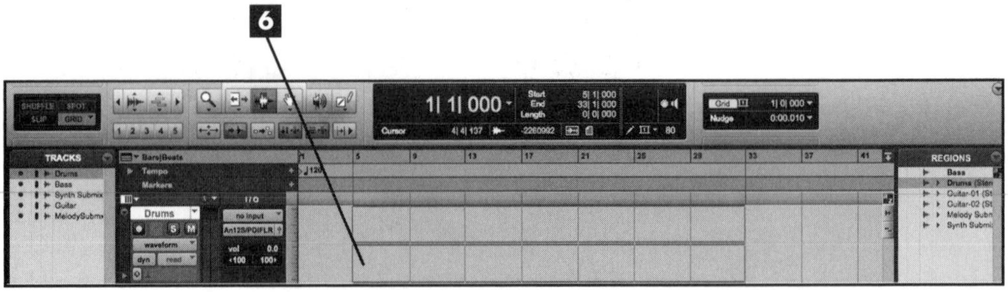

The essence of Absolute Grid mode is simple: Regions will strictly align themselves with the grid values. In this case, with our grid value being 1 bar, the start boundary of any region moved from the Regions list (or even regions moved within tracks) will always jump to the beginning of a bar. (In this case, the start of the region will be x|1|000, with x representing a bar number.)

Relative Grid Mode

There's a second Grid mode available to you, called *Relative Grid mode.* This mode won't move regions *to* the nearest grid line, but rather it will move regions *by* the grid value that you set. Here's a hypothetical situation that shows the operation of Relative Grid mode.

> **TAKING A BREAK FROM THE TUTORIAL SESSION FILE**
>
> The demonstration of Relative Grid mode that follows isn't based upon the Chapter 05 Session file that you've been working with up to now. If you'd like to follow along with the steps here, save and close the Chapter 05 Session file and open the session named "Chapter 05–Relative Grid Mode Session," which is included on your disc.

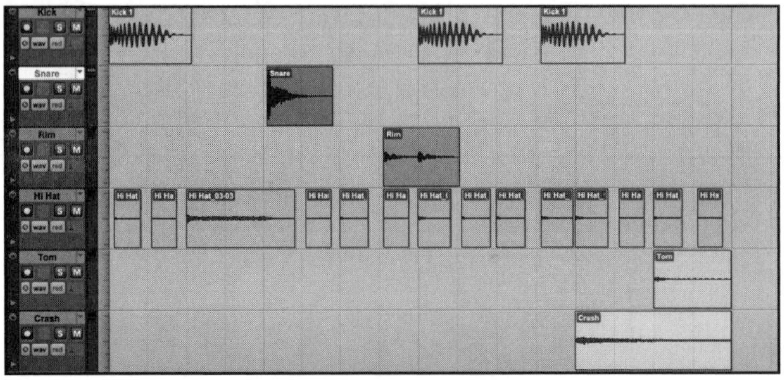

In this example, we have a number of drum tracks. On the Snare track, we have a single snare drum hit. Using Slip mode, I've dragged this region a little to the right of the beat 2 grid line. (If you're working with the tutorial session, you'll see that the region has been placed at 1|2|077.) This is to "lay back" and give the beat a bit of a groove.

We want to move that snare region to the fourth beat, but we don't want to lose that laid-back feel. Relative Grid mode will enable you to do just that: Move the region and maintain a consistent distance from the grid line.

1 **Click and hold** the **Grid Mode button**. The Grid Mode menu will appear.

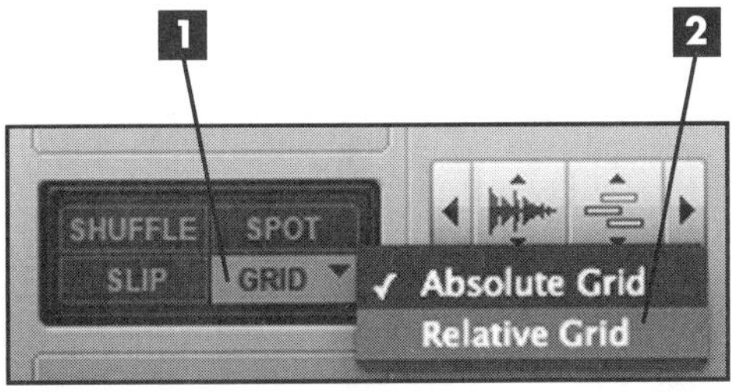

2 **Choose Relative Grid** from the menu shown. The Grid Mode button will now appear in purple and will read Rel Grid.

3 If it's not already selected, **choose** the **Grabber tool** from the Edit Tool cluster at the top of the window.

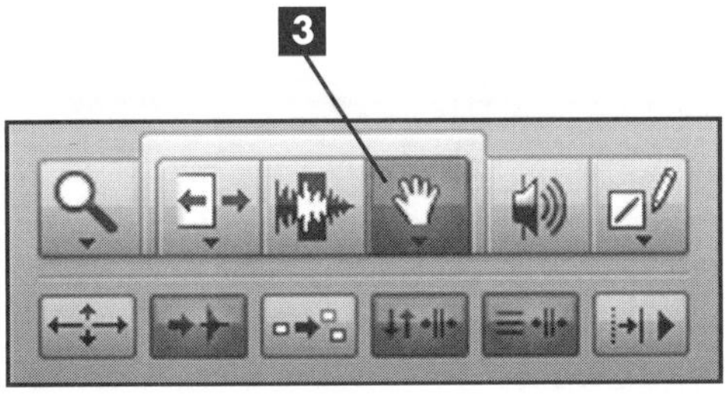

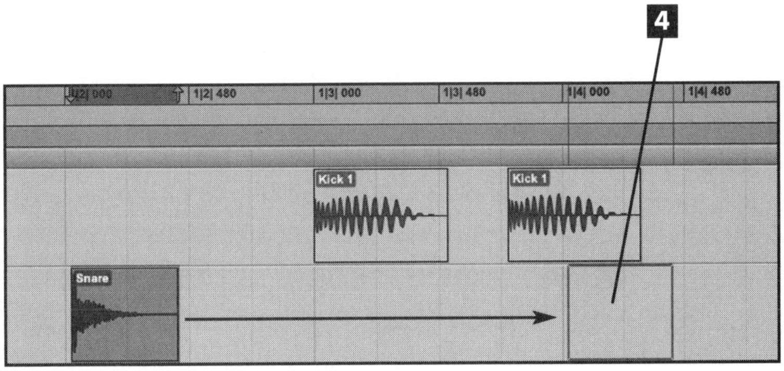

4 With Relative Grid mode selected, **click and drag** the **region** to its new position. (In this case, I've dragged it to just after the fourth beat.) You'll see that as you drag your region, it moves by the sixteenth-note grid value, maintaining its offset from the grid lines.

COPYING WHILE DRAGGING: A NEW KEY COMMAND

We'll talk more about editing in the next two chapters, but there's one thing you might like to try with this example. Hold the Option (Mac) or Alt (PC) key as you drag a region with the Grabber tool to make a copy of the region as you drag it.

Using Shuffle Mode

Shuffle mode operates in a much different way from both Slip mode and Grid mode. In Shuffle mode, regions move end to end with each other. When you see how this mode works, you'll see how it can be useful for stitching together verses, choruses, and so on into a seamless final product!

> **BACK TO THE TUTORIAL**
>
> If you're following the steps outlined here, you should move back to Chapter 05 Session file that you saved before working with Relative Grid mode.

1 **Click** on **Shuffle**. The mode will be selected.

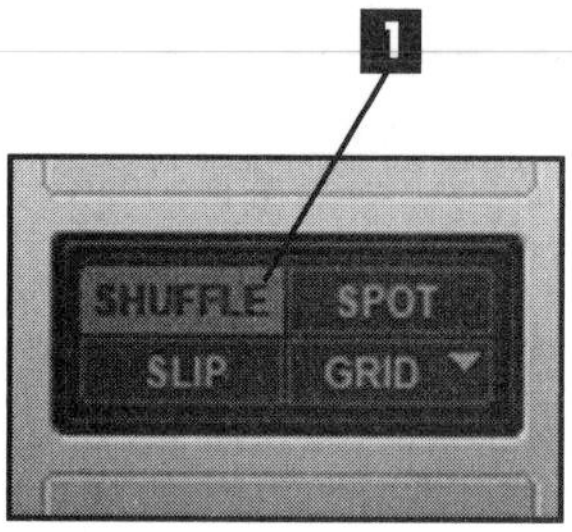

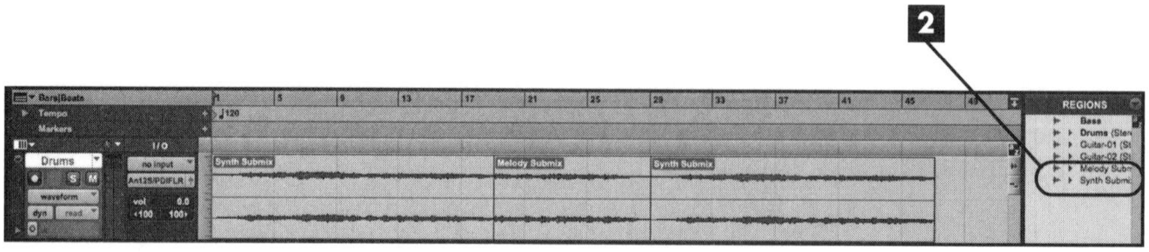

2 One by one, **drag and drop** various **regions** from the Regions list onto a single track. For the purposes of this example, try dragging Synth Submix onto a stereo track, followed by Melody Submix, and finally Synth Submix again. Wherever you drop these regions, they will snap end to end with the previous region, starting with the first region, which automatically snaps to the beginning of your track.

3 Now let's "shuffle" the regions a bit. **Click** on the **Grabber tool** if it's not already selected.

4 **Click and hold** on a **region** that you want to move.

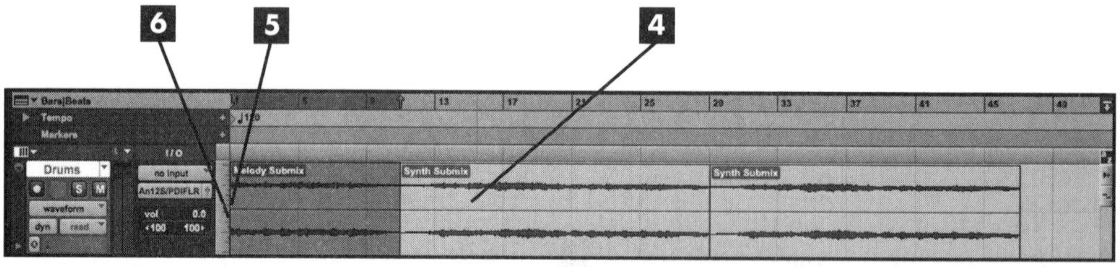

5 **Drag** the **region** over another region on the track. A gold-colored line will appear at the region boundaries, indicating where the region would be repositioned if the mouse were released.

6 **Release** the **mouse button** when the region is at the desired location. The regions will be reorganized.

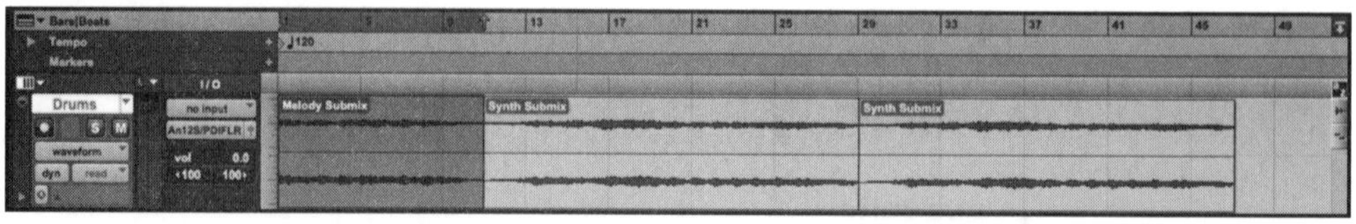

Note that all regions are still adjacent to each other, despite the fact that their order has been changed. Of course, you can move more than one region at a time. In fact, you can shuffle regions forward and backward at will and create new arrangements of these regions, while keeping all the regions snugly end to end.

SHUFFLE LOCK

In some cases, users want to make sure they *can't* enter Shuffle mode inadvertently. (This is most common in audio post-production situations, where Shuffle mode is rarely used.) If that fits with your workflow, it's easy to lock yourself out of Shuffle mode. While you're in any mode *other* than Shuffle mode, Command-click (Mac) or Ctrl-click (PC) on the Shuffle Mode button. A small lock icon will appear in the lower-left corner of the Shuffle Mode button. To unlock Shuffle mode, simply Ctrl-click (PC) or Command-click (Mac) on the Shuffle Mode button again.

Using Spot Mode

Spot mode is very popular in audio post-production situations, where users commonly want to assign a region to a specific place in time. For example, if a producer wants a specific sound effect to occur at a specific point, with Spot mode, you can just type in the location for your region.

SETTING THINGS UP (AGAIN)

Once more, you'll want to clear the drum track for this next section. Here's a quick way to do it: With the Selector tool, **triple-click** anywhere in the track you want to clear. All the regions in that track will be selected, and you can now remove them by pressing the **Delete** key.

1. **Click** on the **Spot button**.

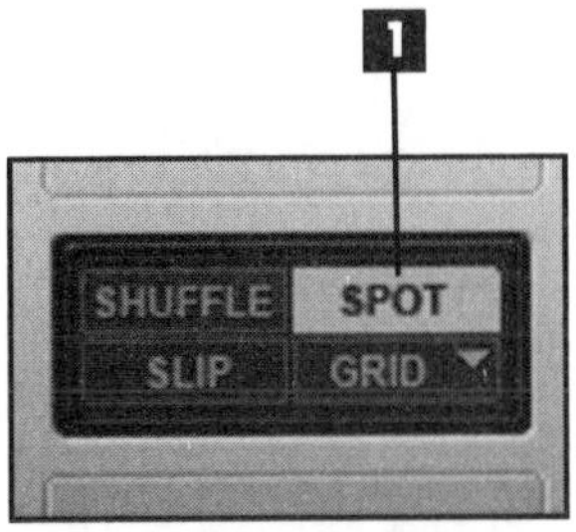

2. **Select** a **region** and **drag it** onto an appropriate track.

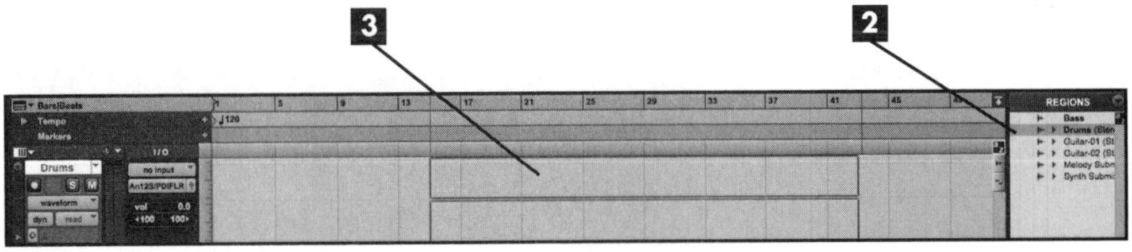

3. **Release** the **mouse button** to drop the region on the track. The Spot dialog box will open.

4 **Click** on the **Time Scale menu button** and **select** the **time scale** you want to use in positioning your region. (You can choose Bars|Beats, Min:Secs, or Samples.)

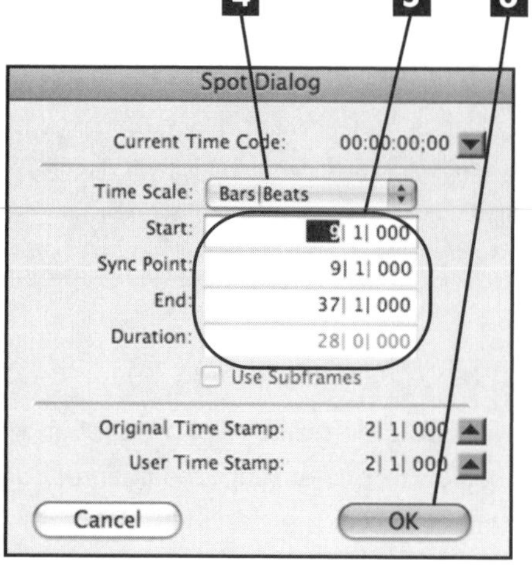

5 You can choose to place your region's start, end, or sync point to a position that you type into the appropriate field. (We'll talk about sync points in Chapter 10, "Moving to the Next Level: Tips and Tricks.") Very often, users are most concerned about the placement of the start of the region, so let's try moving the region's beginning to a specific point in time. **Type** exactly **where you want your region** to **begin** in the Start field.

6 **Click** on **OK**. The region will be placed on the track at the specified location.

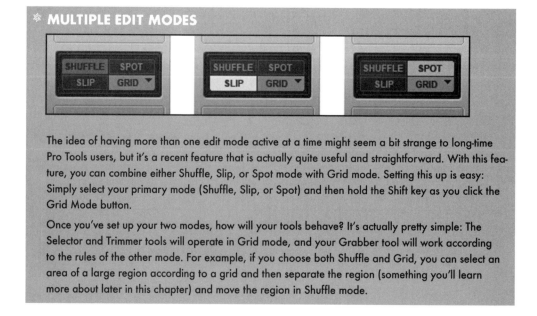

MULTIPLE EDIT MODES

The idea of having more than one edit mode active at a time might seem a bit strange to long-time Pro Tools users, but it's a recent feature that is actually quite useful and straightforward. With this feature, you can combine either Shuffle, Slip, or Spot mode with Grid mode. Setting this up is easy: Simply select your primary mode (Shuffle, Slip, or Spot) and then hold the Shift key as you click the Grid Mode button.

Once you've set up your two modes, how will your tools behave? It's actually pretty simple: The Selector and Trimmer tools will operate in Grid mode, and your Grabber tool will work according to the rules of the other mode. For example, if you choose both Shuffle and Grid, you can select an area of a large region according to a grid and then separate the region (something you'll learn more about later in this chapter) and move the region in Shuffle mode.

Basic Tool Functions

The three main edit tools you'll use are the Trimmer, Selector, and Grabber tools. We've touched on some of their functions already, but let's go just a bit deeper so you can make the most of them.

Understanding the Trimmer Tool

The first tool we'll look at is the Trimmer tool. Its basic function is to change the left or right boundary of a region.

MAKING THINGS GO A BIT MORE SMOOTHLY

This tool can get a little tricky when you're working in Spot mode. Just for simplicity's sake, change your edit mode to Slip mode.

1 **Click** on the **Trimmer tool**.

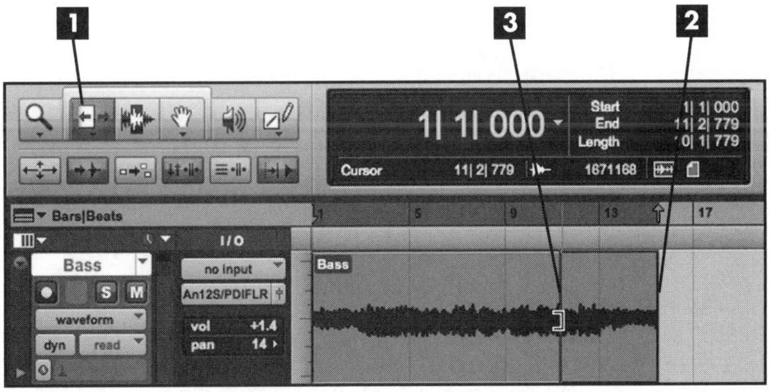

2 **Position** your **cursor** near the beginning or end of a region that you wish to change. The cursor will take on the appearance of a bracket, indicating that the Trimmer tool is ready to be used. The direction the cursor is facing depends on your cursor's position within a region.

3 **Click and drag** the **region boundary** horizontally. You will see a graphic representation of how your region will be altered as you drag.

4 When you have reached the desired position, **release** the **mouse button**. The region will be changed accordingly.

SOME NOTES ON THE TRIMMER TOOL

There are a few things to keep in mind when you're using the Trimmer tool:

- Trimming a region is nondestructive. It only changes the part of the audio file you are choosing to hear in your session.
- When you use the Trimmer tool on a whole-file region, a new region will be created in the Regions list.
- When you're in Grid mode, your trimming will snap to the current grid values. This is particularly useful when you're editing drum beats and other musical material.

Understanding the Selector Tool

You've already used the Selector tool to choose a section of your session to play. You can do other things with the Selector tool as well. For example, let's try removing several regions over a number of tracks all at once.

1 **Click** on the **Selector tool**.

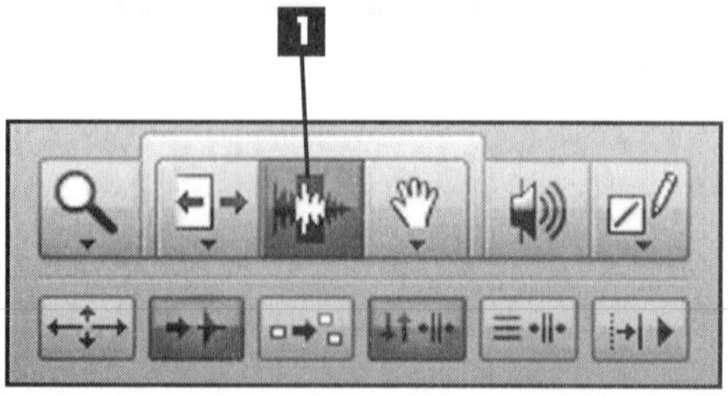

2 Starting in one corner, **click and drag** a **square area** that includes the elements you wish to remove from your session. A gray box will indicate what you've selected.

3 **Press** the **Delete key**. The regions (or portions of regions) will be removed from your tracks.

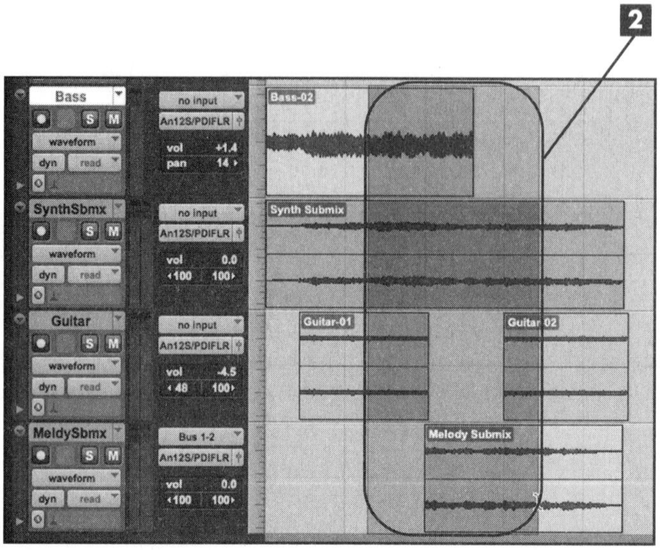

> **THE POWER OF A NONDESTRUCTIVE ENVIRONMENT**
>
> Remember that Pro Tools is (for the most part) a nondestructive DAW. The regions you clear from your tracks won't be removed from the Regions list or your hard drive. Nondestructive also means that you can easily undo what you've done (by choosing Undo from the Edit menu), which you should do right now, to set up the next section.

Link Track and Edit Selection

There's another way to easily make selections over a number of tracks or to move a selected area from one track to another. It's a feature called Link Track and Edit Selection, which enables you to assign edit selections based upon track selections and vice versa. In a nutshell, here's how it works:

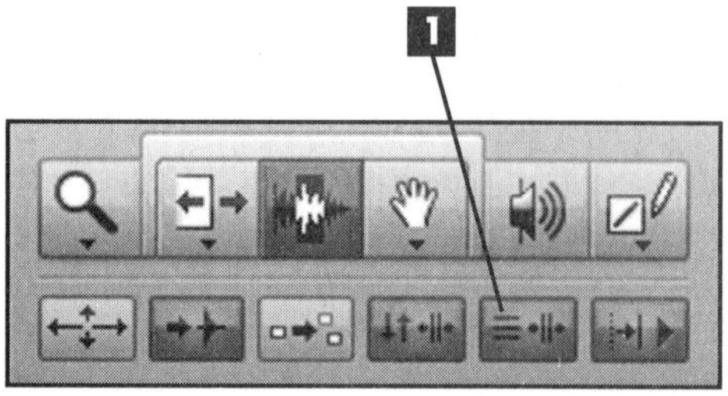

1 The first thing to do is to enable this feature. The Link Track and Edit Selection button is just below the Scrub tool. Just **click** this **button** to enable or disable the feature. (When enabled, the button will appear blue.)

❊ Note that any track that has a selected area is also selected.

2 To move the selected area to another track, simply **click** the target track's **nameplate**.

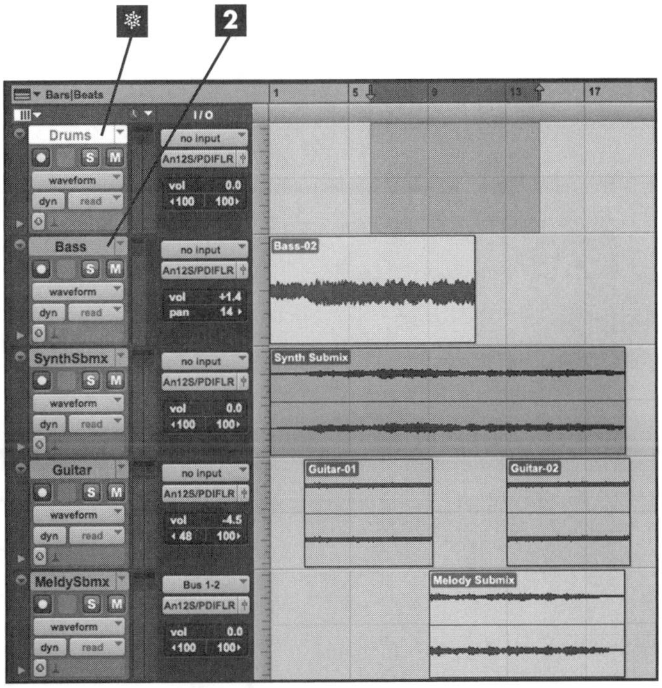

❊ Here's what you'll get: The selection will migrate immediately to the newly selected track.

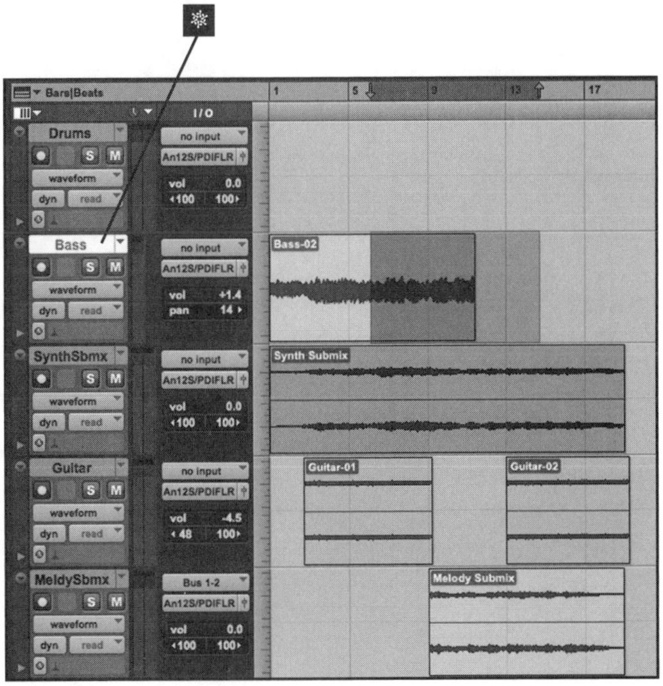

❊ SELECTING A BLOCK OF TRACKS

If you want to select a consecutive block of tracks (and hence a selected area that spans those tracks), just hold down the Shift key when you click the tracks' names. If you want to add or remove track selections individually, just hold the Ctrl (PC) or Command (Mac) key while you click the desired track name(s).

Understanding the Grabber Tool

Last but not least, you have the Grabber tool. We've used it before, but this section will show you how to move more than one region at a time.

1 **Click** on the **Grabber tool**.

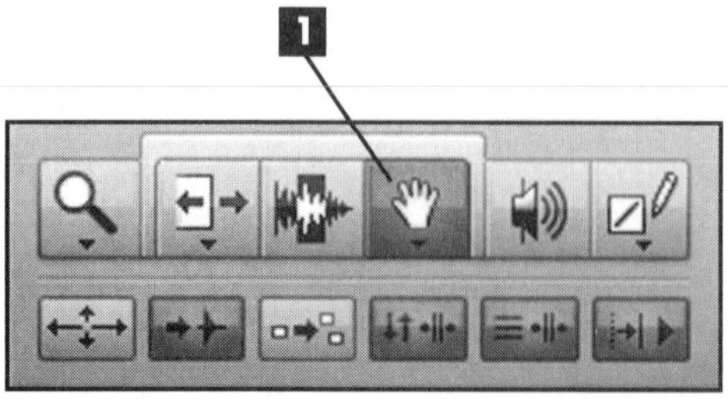

2 **Click** on a **single region** that you wish to move. The region will be highlighted.

3 **Press and hold** the **Shift key** and **click** on **additional regions**. The regions will be highlighted.

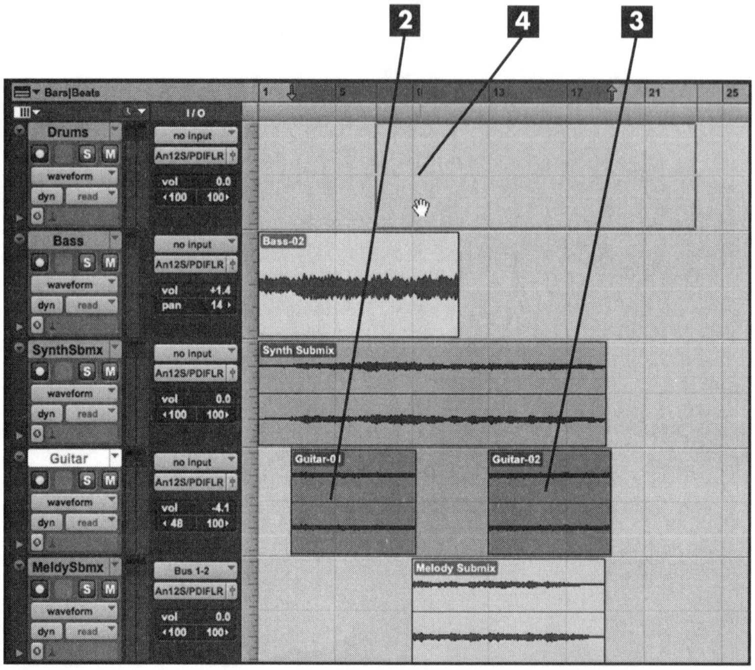

> **GRABBING A BLOCK OF TIME**
>
> As you grab additional regions using the Grabber tool, a shaded area will appear. This area will include not only all the regions you have selected, but also all regions that fall within that shaded area. This is the normal operation of the basic Grabber tool, which is more accurately known as the Time Grabber. There are variations of the Grabber tool (the Object Grabber and the Separation Grabber), which we'll explore in Chapter 6.

4 **Drag and drop** the **regions** you selected. As you drag, a box shows you where your regions will be deposited.

> **SETTING THINGS UP FOR THE NEXT SECTION**
>
> Once more, please undo any changes you've made before progressing to the next section.

Assembling a Track

Now we're going to combine a number of tools you've already worked with, plus a few editing tricks, to re-create the bass line from the session in Chapter 1, "Welcome to Pro Tools 9." In addition to tools from this chapter, you'll be drawing on some knowledge you picked up in earlier chapters as well. When you're finished, you'll have a good idea of how you can assemble tracks of your own!

Creating Regions

We've already created regions through the process of importing and recording audio, but that's only the beginning of the story. In this section, you'll create new regions for your track based upon pre-existing regions.

Capturing a Selection

In this example, you have a source track (named Bass), which simply contains a single region. The task at hand is to build a complete bass track from this single region.

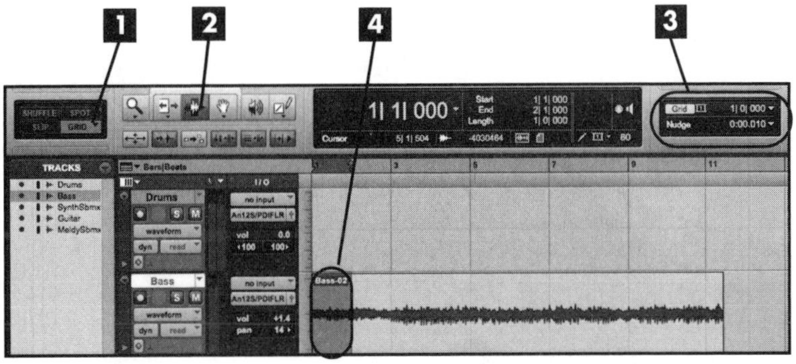

1. **Click** on **Grid**.
2. **Click** on the **Selector tool**.
3. **Double-check** the **grid resolution** to make sure it is 1 bar.
4. Using the Selector tool, **select** the **first measure** on the Bass Audio track. When you've selected the right amount, your Edit Selection indicators will show a start time of 1 | 1 | 000, an end time of 2 | 1 | 000, and a length of 1 | 0 | 000.

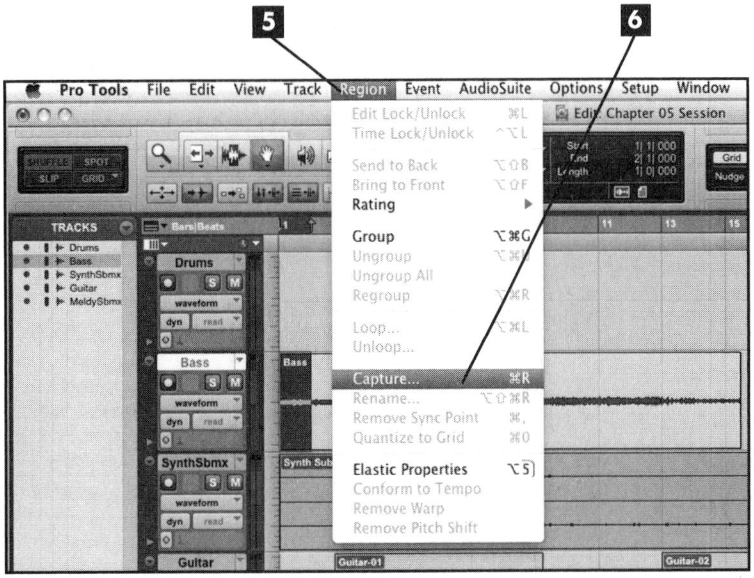

5. **Click** on **Region**. The Region menu will appear.
6. **Click** on **Capture**. The Name dialog box will open.

7 **Type** a descriptive **name** for your new region in the Name the Region text box.

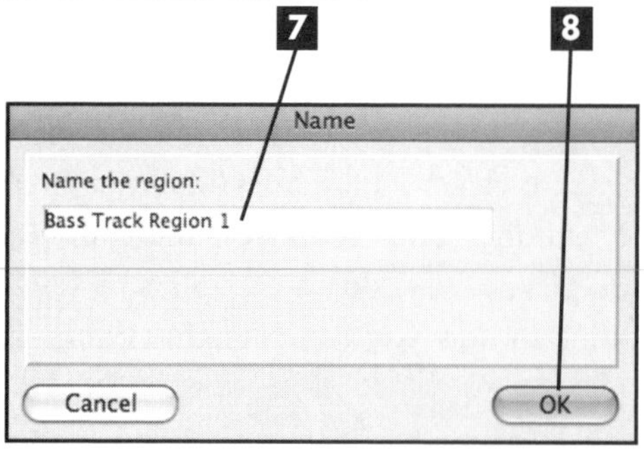

8 **Click** on **OK.** The Name dialog box will close, and the new region—a copy (or capture) of the area you selected—will be created. You can see your newly created region in the Regions list.

Separating a Region

Here's another way to create a region from a selected area. This time, instead of *capturing* a selection, you're simply going to start chopping up your big region into smaller, more manageable bits. Visually, these two methods might appear quite similar, but by separating a region, you'll be creating a new region in the Regions list *and* in your track simultaneously. (Capturing will only create a new region in the Regions list.)

1 Still using the Selector tool, **select measures 3 and 4** on the Bass track. It's easy when you're in Grid mode with a whole-measure grid!

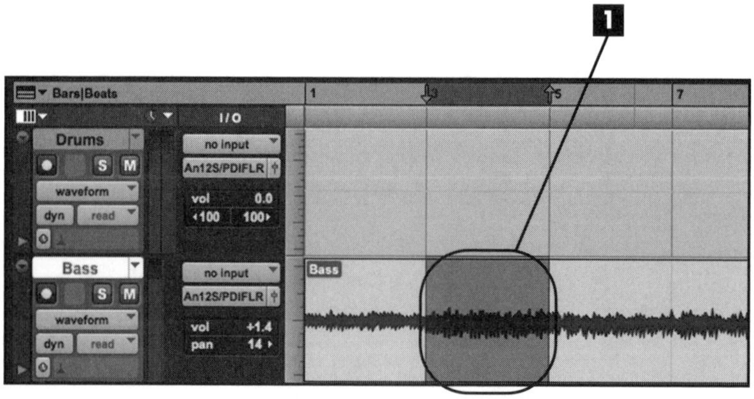

2 **Click** on **Edit**. The Edit menu will appear.

3 **Move your cursor** to **Separate Region**. A sub-menu will appear.

4 **Choose At Selection**. A new region will be created.

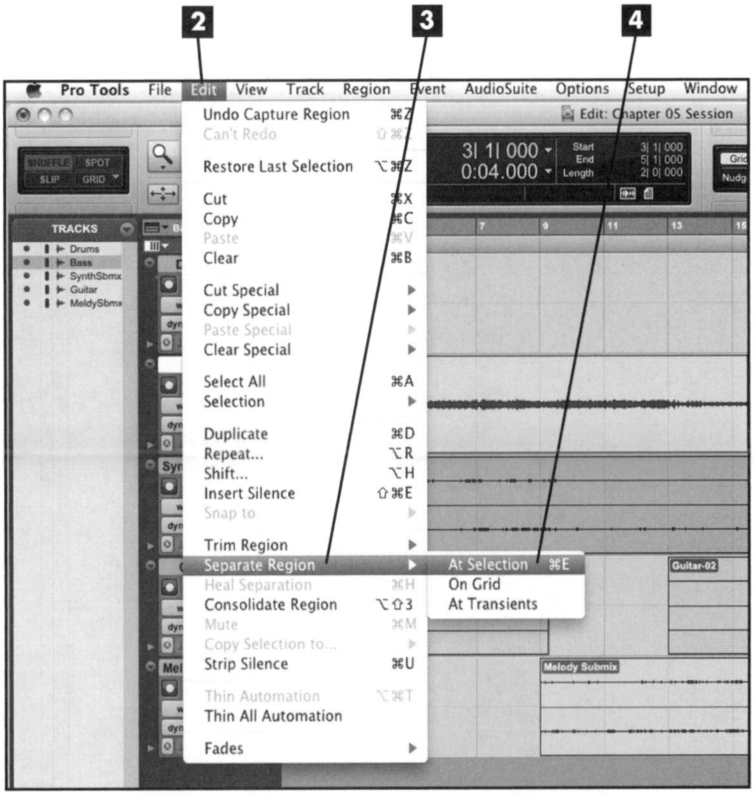

AUTO-NAMING REGIONS

At this point, Pro Tools *might* ask you to name your new region—something that can wind up taking a good deal of time in a busy editing session. You can remove the need to manually type names for regions with a feature called *Auto-Name*. You can disable or enable the Auto-Name feature by selecting the Setup menu, choosing Preferences, and then clicking on the Editing tab. Look for the Auto-Name Separated Regions checkbox; when this feature is enabled, this checkbox will be checked.

Your original region has been separated into three smaller regions. The region that matches your selection will be in the middle.

❄ CONSTRUCTING THE BASS TRACK: STAGE ONE

If you've been working with the Chapter 5 session and following the steps in this chapter, you're well on your way to building this bass part from scratch. Good for you! Now you're ready to do some work on your own and get some good ear-training practice in the process. To get to the next step, you need to use either the Capture Region or the Separate Region function to create the next three regions—in addition to using your ears. The next steps will be a rough guide for you:

1. Import the Reference Bass track from the Reference Bass Track Session file (in the Session 05 Import Materials subfolder on the disc included with your book). This will be your guide in rebuilding the bass track. Please refer to the "Importing Tracks" section in Chapter 3, "Getting Started with Audio," for directions on importing session data.
2. Listen to the region beginning at measure 9 on the Reference Bass track. Select a section on the Bass track that matches it, and then capture or separate a region. Name this region Bass Part Reassembly 3 (if prompted for a name).
3. Listen to the region beginning at measure 12 on the Reference Bass track. Select a section on the Bass track that matches it, and then capture or separate a region. Name this region Bass Part Reassembly 4 (if prompted for a name).
4. Finally, create a region that matches the region on the reference track that starts at measure 15 and ends at measure 20. (Keep in mind that this section is five measures long.) Name this region Bass Part Reassembly 5 (again, if prompted).

One thing to keep in mind: Although either capturing or separating will do the job as far as this example is concerned, there are differences in the way each method works. Capturing will leave the original region intact on the timeline and will only create a new region in the Regions list. Separating a region will alter the region in your track in addition to creating new regions in the Regions list.

Cropping a Region

You have nearly all the regions you'll need to assemble the Bass track. To finish the job, we'll be trimming a region—but in a new way. The last thing we need to do is to create a region based on measure 14 on the Bass track. You know by now that there are a number of ways you could create this region: capturing, separating, or trimming with the Trimmer tool. In this section, we'll trim the region, but in a different way.

1. **Click** on the **Selector tool**.
2. **Select** the **area** of the audio region that you want to retain. (In this case, it will span from 14|1|000 to 15|1|000.)

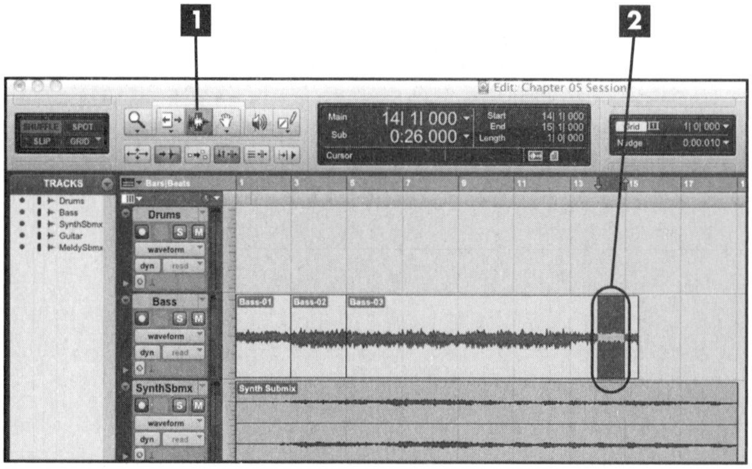

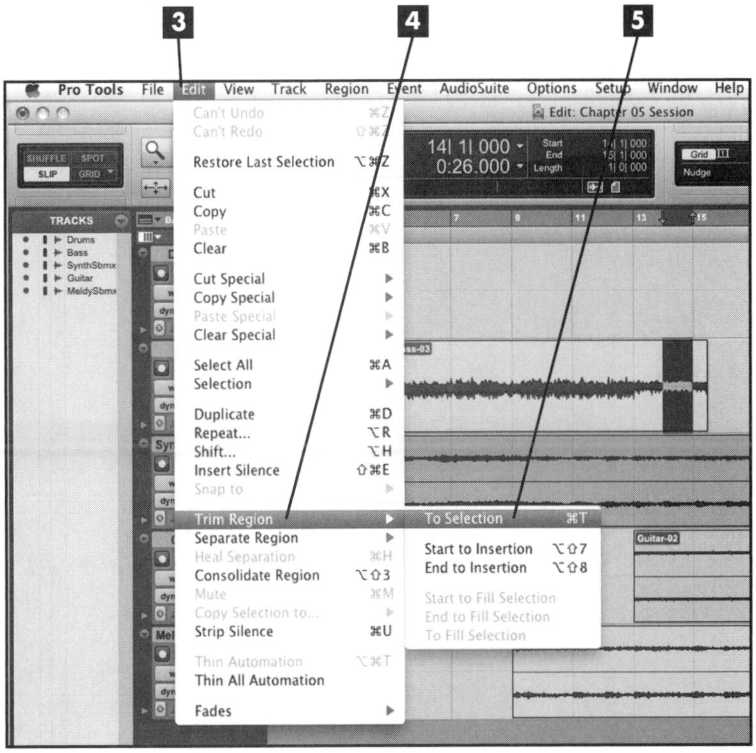

3 **Click** on **Edit**. The Edit menu will appear.

4 **Click** on **Trim Region**. A submenu will appear.

5 **Choose** the **To Selection menu item**. The region will be trimmed to your selection on the track, and a new region will be created in your Regions list.

Renaming a Region

At any time in the editing process, you might want to rename a region in your session. Here's how to do it.

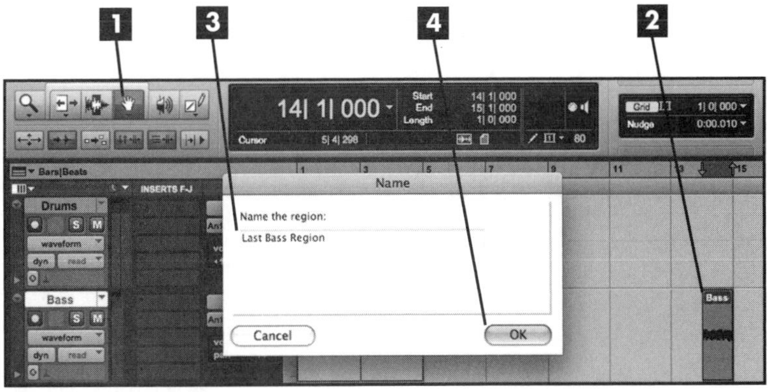

1 **Click** on the **Grabber tool**.

2 **Double-click** on the **region** you want to rename. The Name dialog box will open.

3 **Type** the **name** you want for the region in the Name the Region text box.

4 **Click** on **OK**. The Name dialog box will close, and the region will be renamed.

Arranging Regions

Now that we've created the regions we need, the next step in the process is to organize them on the track. In this part of the process, what you've already learned about the edit modes will serve you well, and a couple additional tricks will make the process even easier!

> **CONSTRUCTING THE BASS TRACK: STEP TWO**
>
> If you're following the steps so far in this chapter, the next step is to select all remaining regions on the Bass track and press the Delete key, leaving a blank track on which to assemble your newly created regions.

Working in Shuffle mode makes the job easy!

1 **Click** on **Shuffle** if you're not already in Shuffle mode.

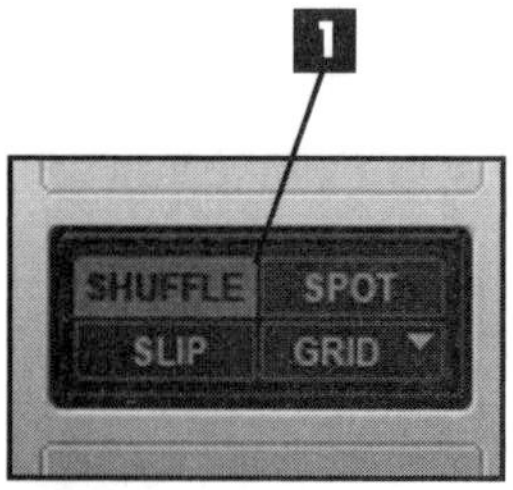

2 One by one, **drag regions** onto the desired track in the order that you want them to be played back.

> **CONSTRUCTING THE BASS TRACK: STEP THREE**
>
> If you're following the example in this chapter, drag Bass Track Region 1 onto the track six times. Then find the region that sounds like the region on the Reference Bass track at measure 7 (you'll have to use your ears, and you may find that the region lengths aren't the same!) and drag it onto the Bass track twice. Last but not least, find the region that sounds like the Reference Bass Track at measure 9 and drag it to the Bass track once. Remember that in Shuffle mode, it doesn't matter where you drop your regions; drop them anywhere *after* the existing regions, and they'll automatically move to the edge of the preceding region.

Duplicating Regions

Of course, you *could* just drag the same region onto a track over and over to create a looping phrase, but that can get really boring very quickly. Here's another way to make a copy of a region or selection and place it immediately after the original:

1. **Select** the **region** you want to duplicate (either by single-clicking with the Grabber tool or by double-clicking with the Selector tool).
2. **Click** on **Edit**. The Edit menu will appear.
3. **Click** on **Duplicate**. A duplicate of the selected region will appear immediately after the selection.

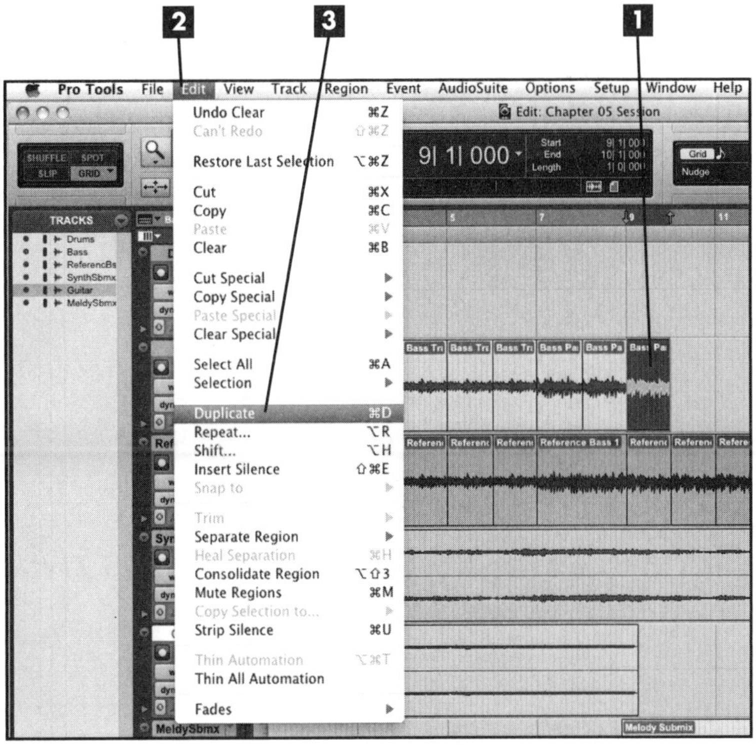

DUPLICATE SHORTCUT

The shortcut for the Duplicate function is Command+D (Mac) or Ctrl+D (PC).

FINISHING UP THE BASS TRACK

If you've been following the steps in this chapter, you'll want to duplicate the region named Bass Part Reassembly 3 (if you've named your regions manually) two times and then add the Bass Part Reassembly 4 region at bar 12. After that, you'll add the Bass Part Reassembly 3 region another two times. When that's done, add the region named Bass Part Reassembly 5 at measure 15. Last but not least, add the region named Last Bass Region at measure 20, and you're ready to continue on to the next section.

THE EFFECT OF AUTO-NAMING

If you have Auto-Naming enabled, you might find that some of the region names I've listed here don't match the regions in your Regions list. In that case, you'll want to audition the regions in the Regions list. You can do this by holding down the Option key (Mac) or the Alt key (PC) and clicking and holding on the desired region's name. You'll be able to hear the highlighted region and use your ears to find the right ones (which is a great practice for beginning editors).

Repeating Regions

Repeating regions is similar to duplicating regions, but with a twist. Instead of repeating the process for each additional loop, you can get create multiple loops in one quick process.

1 **Select** the **region** you want to repeat (either by single-clicking with the Grabber tool or by double-clicking with the Selector tool). In this case, you should select the region named Last Bass Region.

2 **Click** on **Edit**. The Edit menu will appear.

3 **Click** on **Repeat**. The Repeat dialog box will open.

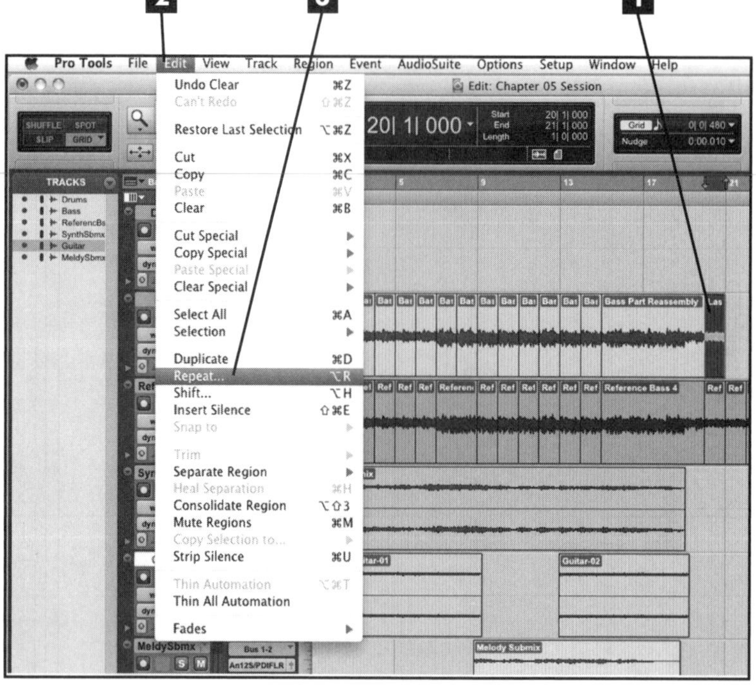

4 **Type** the **number of times** that you want the region to repeat in the Number of Repeats text box. (In this case, type 8.)

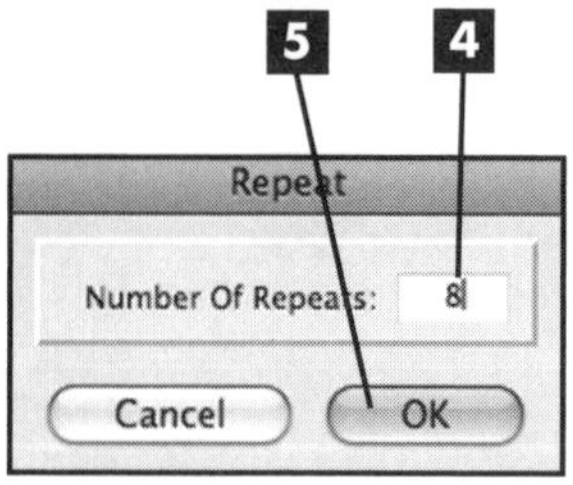

5 **Click** on **OK**. The selected region will be repeated the specified number of times, just as if you had used the Duplicate command multiple times.

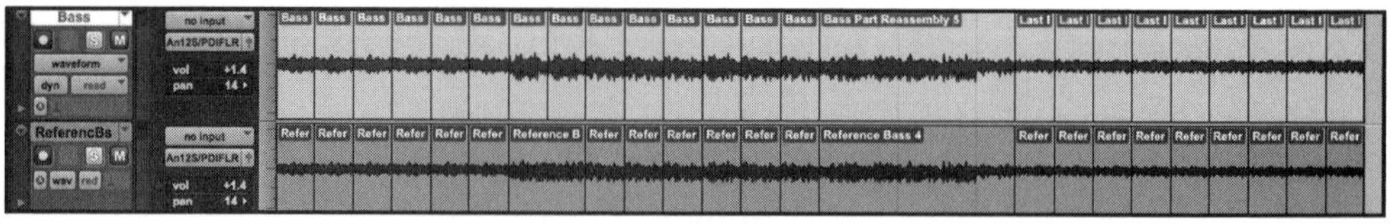

Solo both bass tracks (if you haven't already) and play them together. They should sound identical. If they do, you're finished! If they don't, then it's time to take a closer look at the Reference Bass track and the Bass track you just created, find where they disagree, and then make the necessary changes.

Working with Grids

By now, you're getting a good sense of the usefulness of working in Grid mode. However, using a grid value as large as a whole measure might not work for you in all situations. Changing the grid value will open new possibilities.

If you've listened closely to the melody track, the timing should seem a bit off. The good news is that the tempo isn't the problem—the entire melody is just an eighth note too late. You can still use Grid mode to fix the problem, but we'll need to make a finer adjustment than a whole-measure grid can provide. Read on...

1 **Click** on the **arrow** next to the grid value. The Grid Value menu will appear.

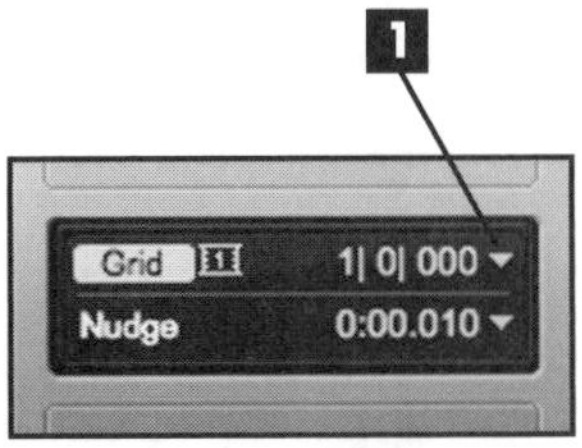

2 **Select** the **scale** (for example, Bars|Beats or Min:Secs) if you want to change the scale of your grid. If you want to continue in the same scale (as I do in this case), just **click** on the **grid value** you want (in this case, choose the 1/8 note option). The grid will immediately change in the Edit window.

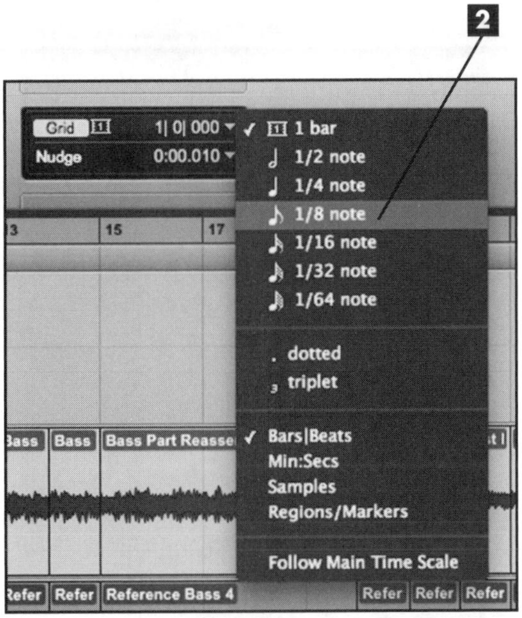

3 If you're not in Grid mode already, **click** the **Grid Mode button**.

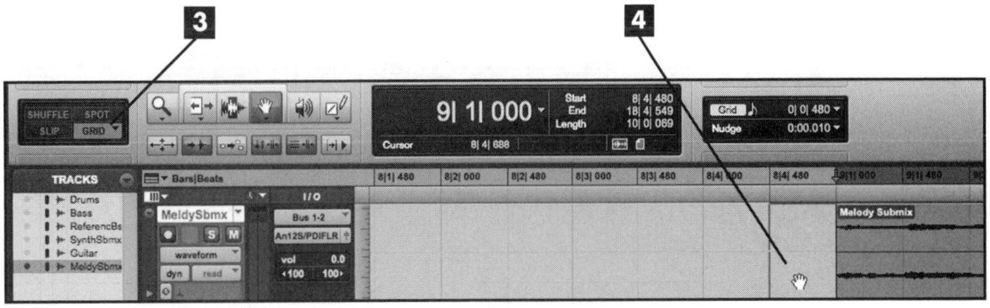

4 **Drag** the **Melody Submix region** one eighth note earlier. (You may want to zoom in a bit so that you can see the individual grid line clearly.) As you drag the region in the track, a box will show you where your region will be deposited when you release the mouse button (moving in eighth-note increments). This region will sound a *lot* better if it begins at 8|4|480.

5 **Drop** the **region** at the desired location.

Cutting, Copying, and Pasting

Cutting, copying, and pasting are tried-and-true staples of many kinds of software, and Pro Tools is no exception. These processes are very straightforward and easy to use.

Copying a Region

1 **Select** the **region** you want to copy.

2 **Click** on **Edit**. The Edit menu will appear.

3 **Click** on **Copy**. The region will be copied to the Pro Tools clipboard, ready to be pasted.

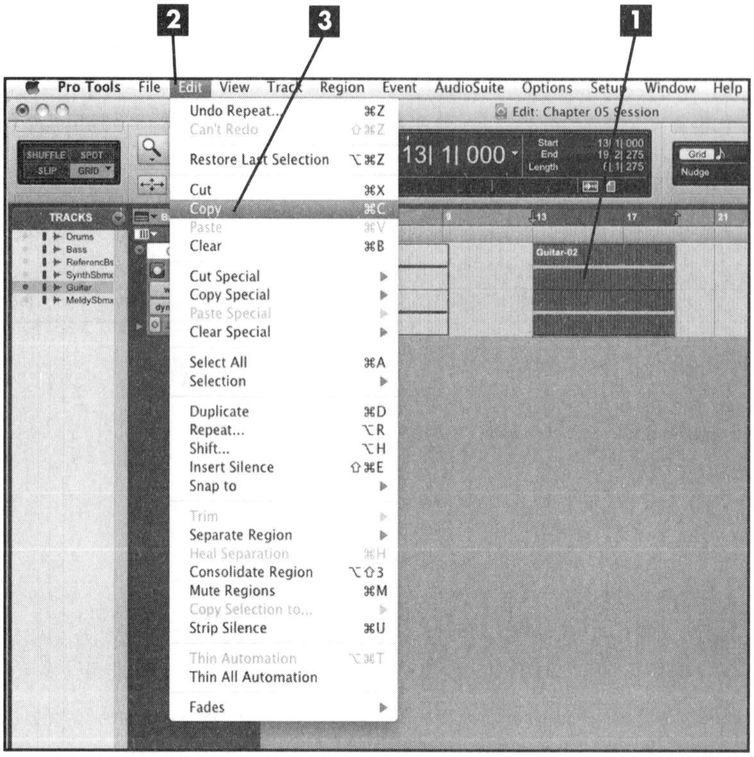

COPY SHORTCUT

The shortcut for the Copy command is Command+C on a Mac or Ctrl+C on a PC.

Pasting a Region

A copied region means nothing until it's *pasted* to a new location. Here's how to do it:

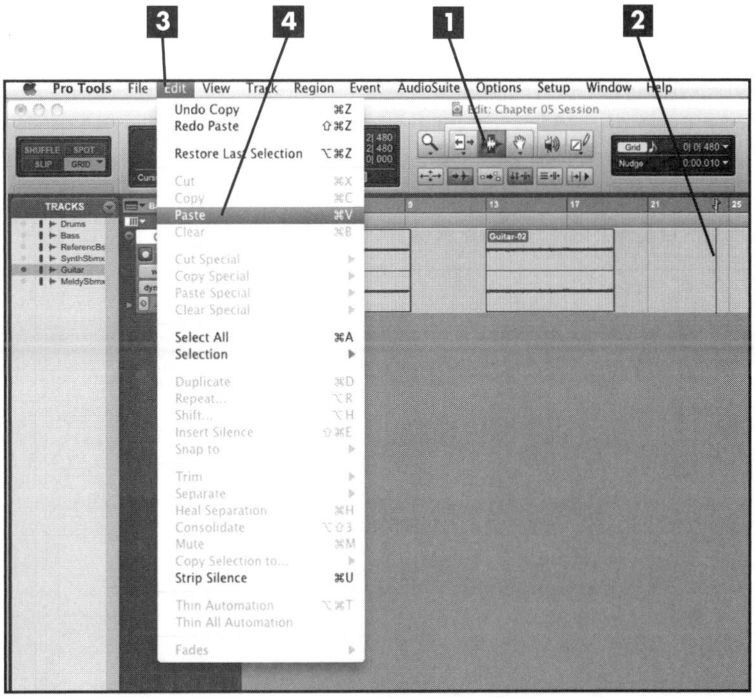

1. **Click** on the **Selector tool** if it's not already selected.
2. **Click** in a **track** at the location where you want the pasted region to begin.
3. **Click** on **Edit**. The Edit menu will appear.
4. **Click** on **Paste**. The region will be pasted at the location you selected.

> **PASTE SHORTCUT**
>
> The shortcut for the Paste command is Command+V (Mac) or Ctrl+V (PC).

Cutting a Region

Because you're not going to use that region you just pasted, let's go ahead and cut it:

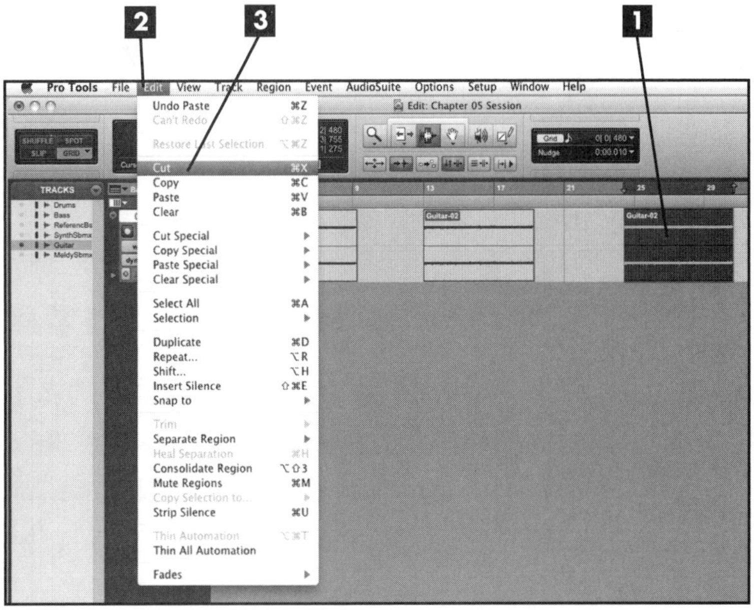

1. **Select** the **region** you want to cut.
2. **Click** on **Edit**. The Edit menu will appear.
3. **Click** on **Cut**. The region will be cut and placed in the Pro Tools clipboard (for pasting, if desired).

CUT SHORTCUT

The shortcut for the Cut command is Command+X (Mac) or Ctrl+X (PC).

Working with Overlapping Regions

From time to time, you'll want to move one region so that it partially overlaps another region. This is absolutely not a problem—it happens all the time—but there are some things you should be aware of. First, you will only hear the region that's "in front," meaning that you won't hear both audio regions play together. Second, this sort of action is nondestructive, meaning that when you overlap regions, no audio is being removed from your audio files.

NOW'S A GOOD TIME TO SAVE YOUR WORK

We're going to work with the Guitar track a little bit to show how overlapped regions work, but you won't want to keep these changes. If your session sounds good (and it shouldn't sound too bad if you've been following the steps in this chapter), you should save your work before moving on.

CHECK YOUR WORK

The steps covered so far in this chapter have been saved to a session named Chapter 05 Session—Finished, which is on the disc that is included with your book.

First, let's take a look at the normal behavior of overlapped regions:

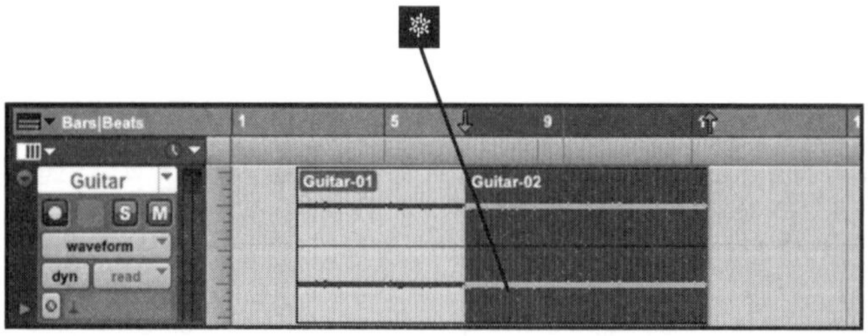

- Drag a region over another region using the Grabber tool (in this case, the second region on the Guitar track is dragged over the first), and you'll notice that when you play back the track, only the region (or portions of a region) that is immediately visible will be heard.

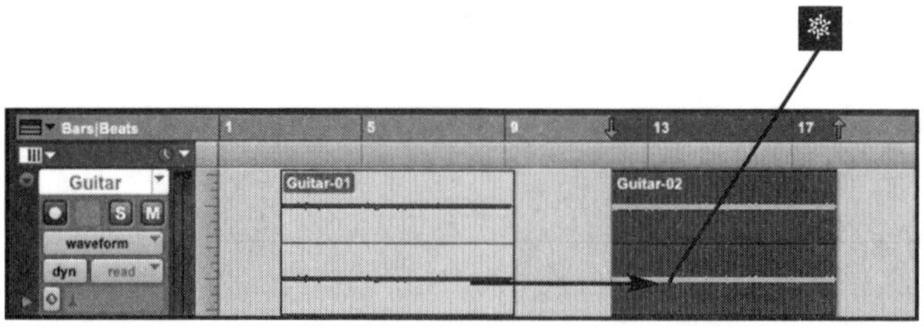

- Move the region that was "on top" out of the way, and you'll see that the region that was partially blocked hasn't changed at all!

OVERLAPPING REGIONS' BEHAVIOR

If only one region boundary overlaps another region, then you'll see the same nondestructive behavior that you've just seen here. If, however, a smaller region is dragged completely over a larger region and dropped (in other words, both region boundaries are overlapping), a hole will be left when that smaller region is moved away again. Last but not least, if a larger region completely covers a smaller region, that region will be removed from the track (although it will still be in the Regions list).

Sometimes it's hard to visually determine when regions are overlapping versus when they are simply next to each other. It would sure be easier if there were some sort of visual cue to show an overlapped arrangement. No sooner said than done!

1. **Click** on **View**. The View menu will appear.
2. **Click** on **Region**. The Region submenu will appear.
3. This submenu is a checklist of region-related attributes that can be shown or not shown. **Click** on **Overlap**. (It will appear checked when activated.)

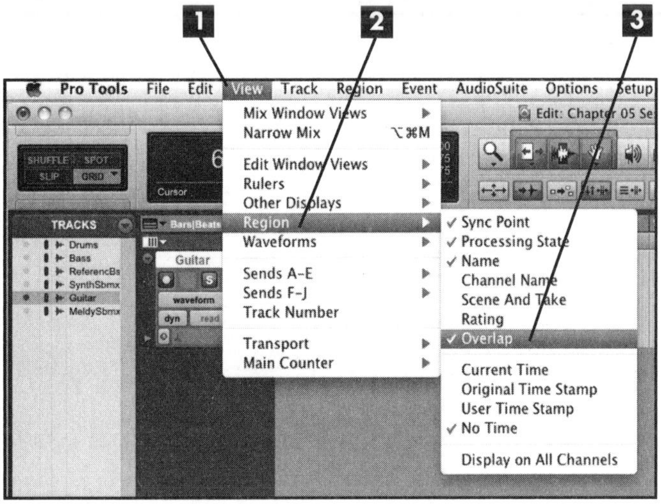

- Note that now you'll see a small bevel in the overlapping upper corner of a region that is covering another region.

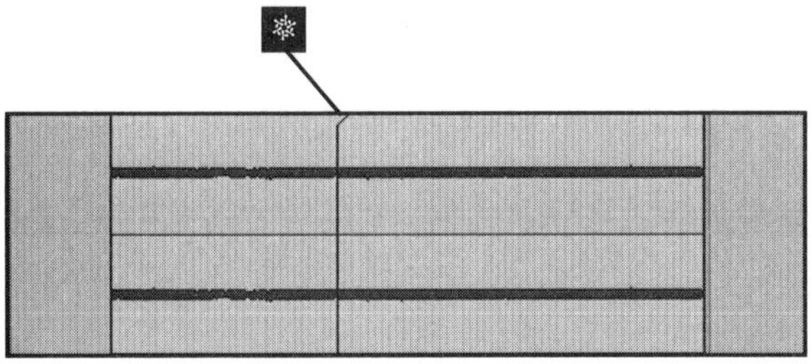

But wait, there's more! What if you want to reverse the way the regions are overlapped *without* moving either of the regions?

1 **Select** the **region** in front.

2 **Click** on **Region**. The Region menu will appear.

3 **Click** on **Send to Back**. The selected region will be moved *behind* the first region and will now be partially covered by it. Here again, there will be a beveled upper corner to indicate the overlap (although it is now in the first region, indicating that *it* is covering another region).

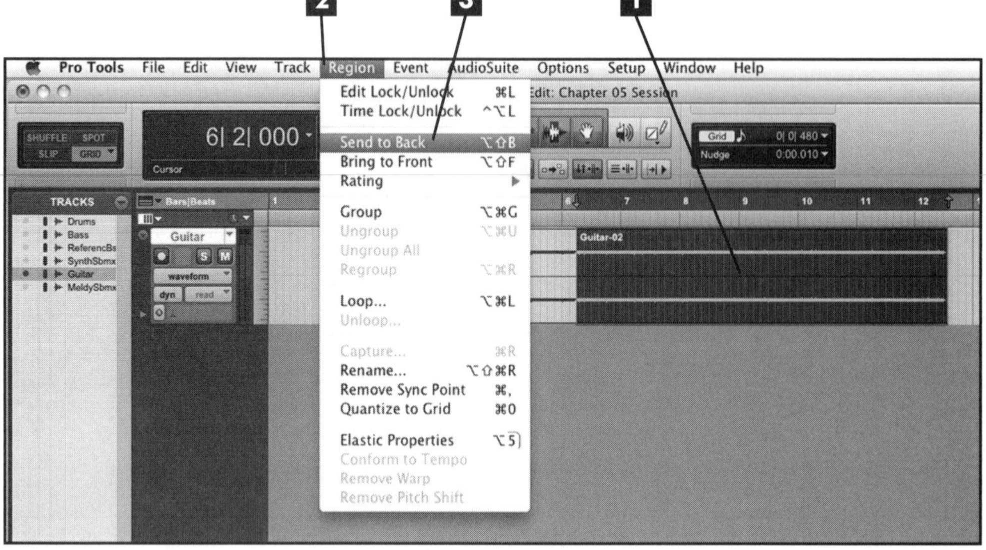

You can similarly choose a region that is in *back* and choose Bring to Front from the same menu. Again, the relationship between these two overlapping regions has been reversed, while leaving their timing untouched.

Edit Playlists

An Edit Playlist is perhaps best defined as a sequence of regions on a track. For example, any given mono audio track may have regions that sound like a bassist or a saxophonist. The track is the same—only the Edit Playlist is different. Although Edit Playlists are among the most unsung of Pro Tools' features, they're easy to use. Better still, there's no limit to the number of Edit Playlists you can have, so you have a whole new dimension of editing flexibility to work with.

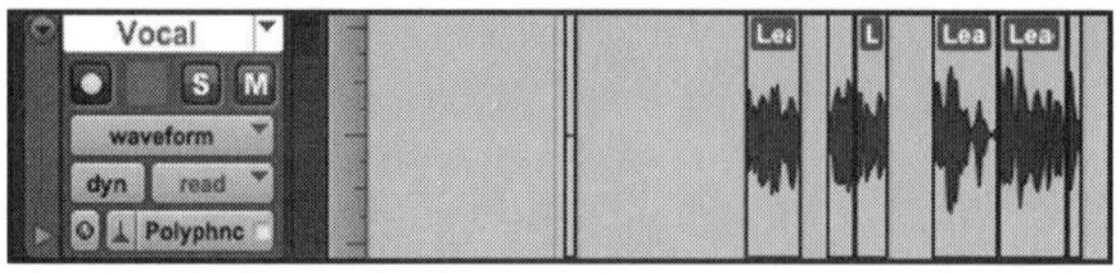

Here's an example of how Edit Playlists can be used. The track shown here is a mono audio track with a number of vocal regions on it. Normally, we would say that the track name is Vocal, but that's not 100-percent accurate. It is actually more technically accurate to say that the Edit Playlist name is Vocal and describes the sequence of audio regions on this track.

Suppose we want to make a few changes on this track but keep the original version as well. No problem—that's just what Edit Playlists are good at!

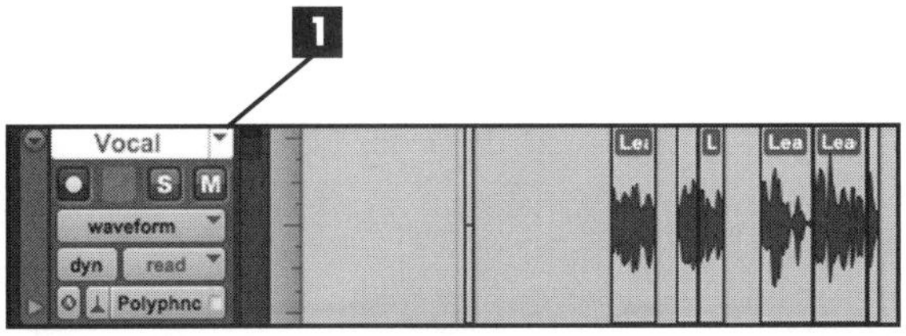

1 **Click** the **Playlist Selector** on the track you want to change. A menu will appear.

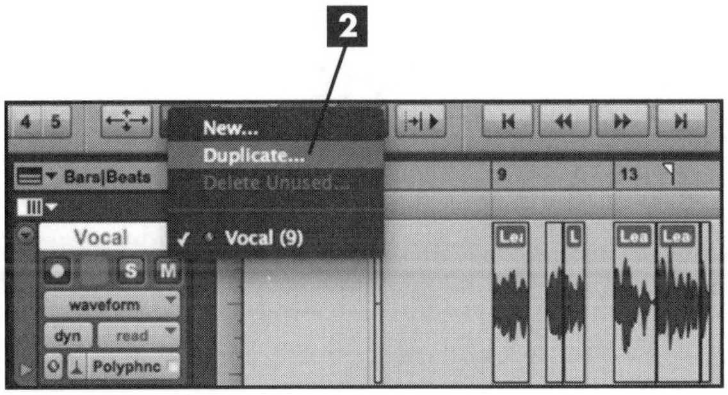

2 Because in this case we want to make a change on an existing playlist, **choose** the **Duplicate menu item**. Effectively, what you'll be doing is copying this sequence of regions. A dialog box in which you can name your duplicated playlist will appear.

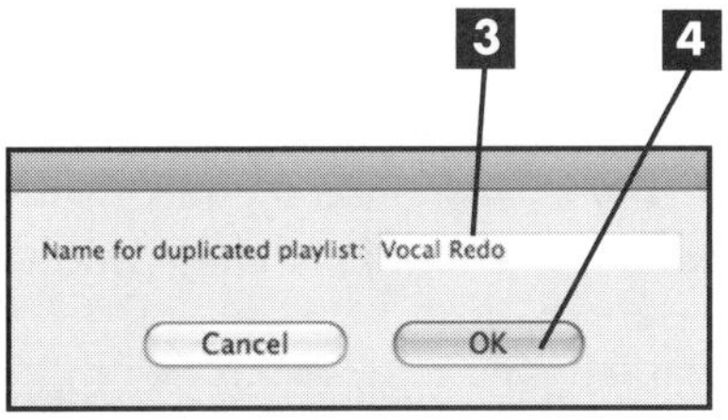

3 **Type** a descriptive **name** for your new playlist.

4 **Click** on **OK**. The dialog box will close, and your new playlist will be created.

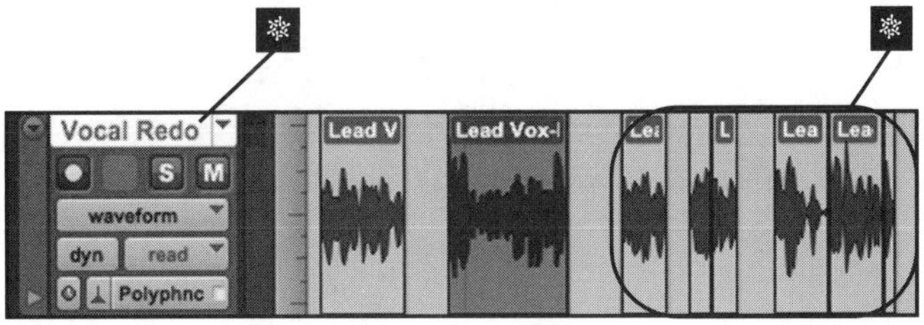

- Note that your "track name" (which you now know is actually the Edit Playlist name) has changed to match your new Edit Playlist.

- Now you're free to make whatever changes you like to your regions.

Here's the coolest part: You can change between playlists anytime and compare the two different edits!

✻ Now, if you click the Playlist Selector button, you'll see both of the Edit Playlists that you've created, and you can choose the desired one at any time—even during playback! Edit Playlists are a great way to explore different creative directions and compare multiple versions.

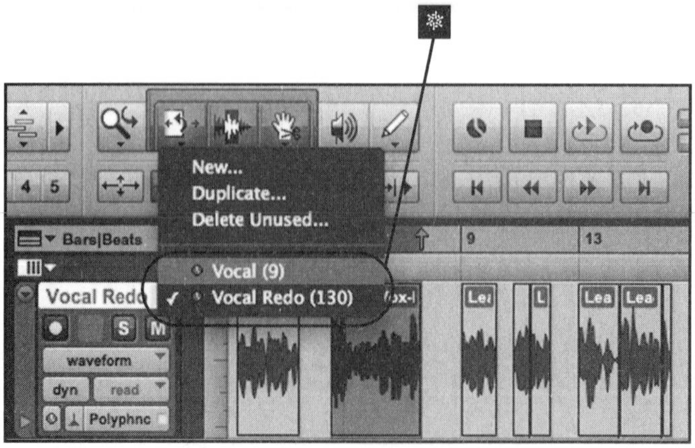

Of course, you can use Edit Playlists for more than just creating multiple versions of a given track. If you like, you can create entirely different playlists on a given track.

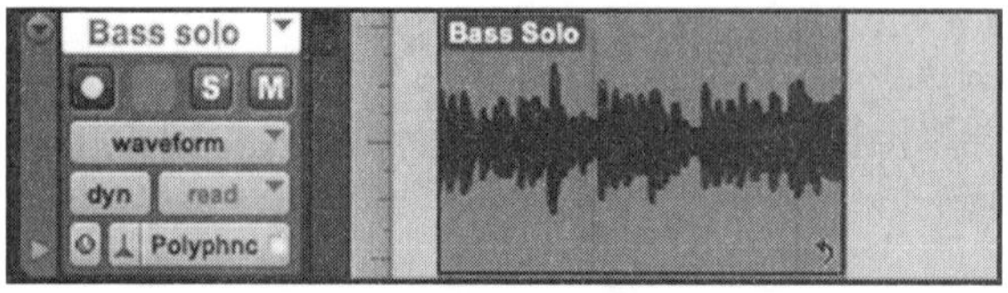

Let's try a different scenario: Again, we have a mono Audio track, this one with one bass solo region on it. The Edit Playlists name (which we commonly would refer to as the track name) is Bass Solo. What if we wanted to try something completely different on this track?

1 **Click** the **Playlist Selector button**. The Edit Playlist menu will appear.

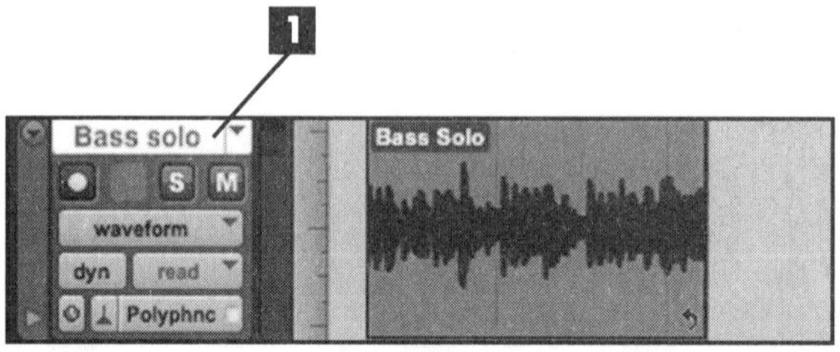

2 In this case, we want to create a blank playlist—one with no regions on it—so that we can do something completely different. **Click** on **New** to do this. A dialog box in which you can name your new playlist will open.

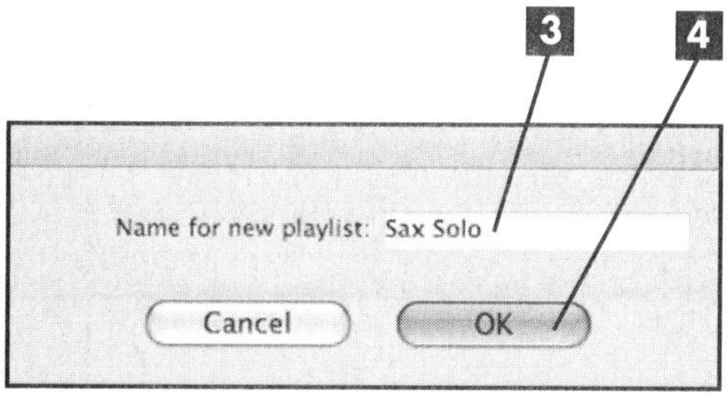

3 **Type** a descriptive **name** for your new playlist. (In this case, I want to type Sax Solo.)

4 **Click** on **OK**. The dialog box will close, and your new playlist will be created.

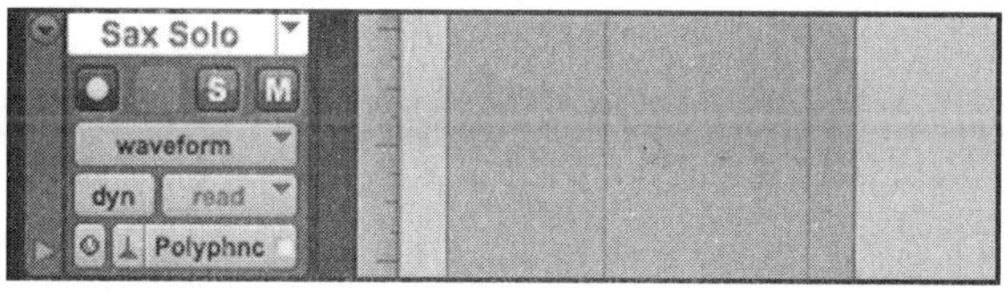

We still have our mono Audio track, but now we have one with a brand-new Edit Playlist—a blank track ready for us to work with. In this particular case, I would record my saxophone solo on this track.

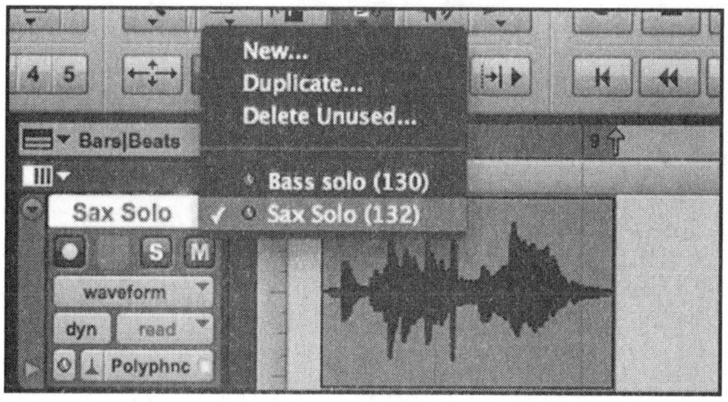

Once you've recorded your sax solo, you can switch between the different Edit Playlists by again clicking on the Edit Playlist selector button. You can change between the two Edit Playlists at any time, even during playback, so that you can determine which fits best.

Track-Comping Tools

Let's say you've just finished multiple takes of a section (either by recording a number of times or through loop recording). In most cases, the next step is to compile a final track that includes the best parts of each take. This process is called *comping* a track, and it is one of the cornerstones of professional editing.

As with many other processes in Pro Tools, there are a number of ways to comp a track, with different methods appropriate for different situations. However, some recent new features in Pro Tools (added in Pro Tools version 8) have revolutionized the way Pro Tools editors assemble a comped track. We'll discuss how these features are used in this section.

This new workflow relies heavily on the knowledge you've just gained about Edit Playlists. Essentially, what we'll be doing is putting the best parts of the different takes, each of which will reside on individual edit playlists, to a blank track (which you now know is simply an Edit Playlist with no regions on it). How you record your individual takes is important; it will enable you to utilize these new track-comping tools during the editing phase of your process, so let's start there.

If you're recording multiple takes without loop recording:

1. **Record** the **first take** normally.
2. Before recording the second take, **create** a **new Edit Playlist** (using the steps outlined in the previous section). The track will now be empty, because the first take's region resides on a different Edit Playlist.
3. **Record** the **second take** normally.
4. For each additional take, **create** a **new Edit Playlist** before recording. This will ensure that each recording pass will be represented individually on its own Edit Playlist.

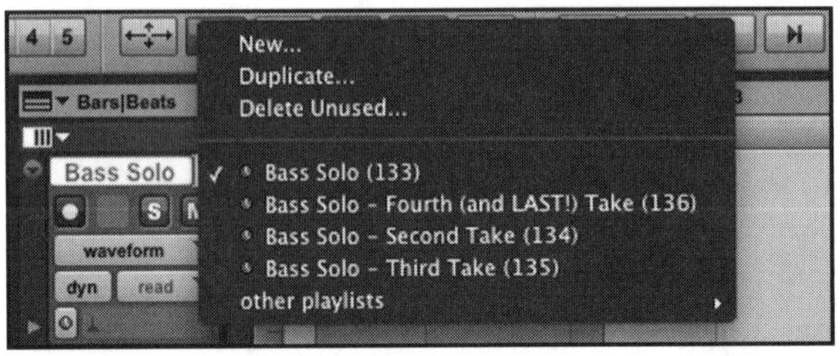

After recording, you can access each individual take by clicking the Playlist Selector button (again, as discussed in the previous section) and choosing the desired take from the list of Edit Playlists.

If you are recording multiple takes *with* loop recording:

1. In the Preferences window (which you access from the Setup menu), **click** the **Operation tab** and **check** the **Automatically Create New Playlists When Loop Recording checkbox**.
2. **Click** the **OK button** to close the Preferences window.
3. **Loop record normally.**

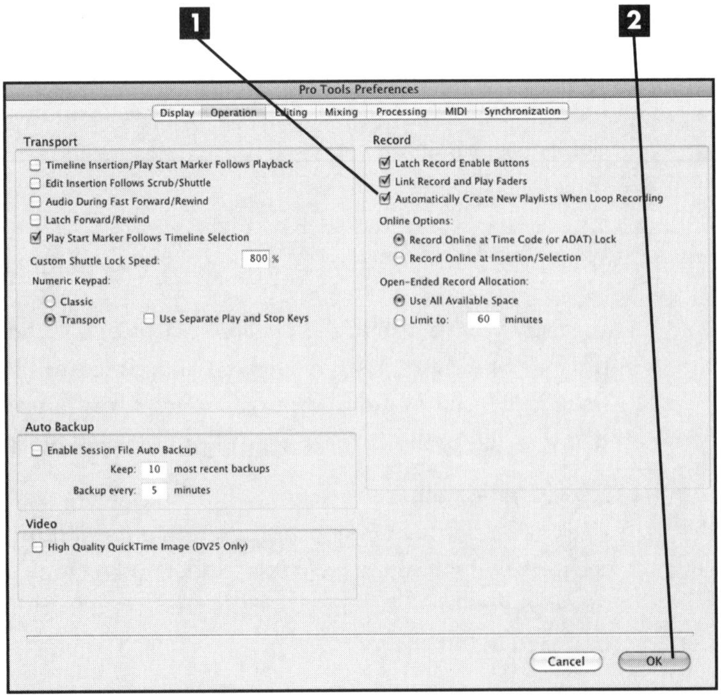

Here again, you'll wind up with a dedicated Edit Playlist for each time the section was recorded. In this case, though, each new playlist has been automatically created and named.

Viewing Playlists in the Edit Window

Now that you have all your takes separated into individual playlists, you can get down to some serious comping. In this example, we have a single mono audio track, upon which was recorded four different takes of a keyboard solo. In this case, it doesn't matter whether we recorded the solo using Loop Record; our job is to pull out the best parts of each take and make a final comped track.

COMPING PRACTICE

If you don't have any material of your own for track-comping practice, don't worry—just open the Chapter 05—Track Comping Session file, which you'll find on your book's disc.

1 **Click** the **Playlist Selector button** to reveal a menu of Edit Playlists.

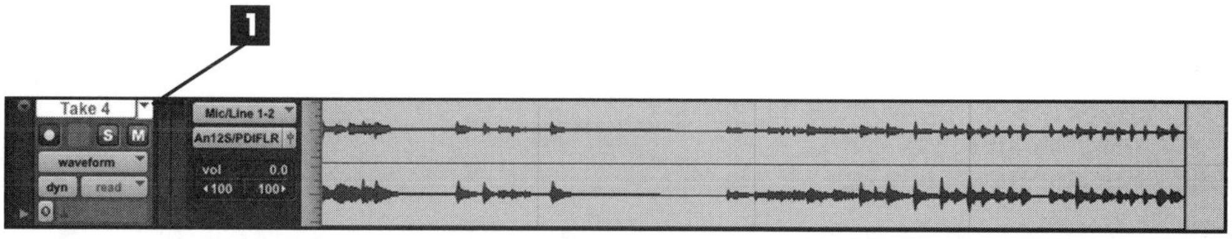

As you've done before, you can choose the take you want to view. Once you see a take you like, you can select an area, copy it, change playlists, and paste the section to the new playlist. Although that's an effective way of editing, it's not the most efficient way of working.

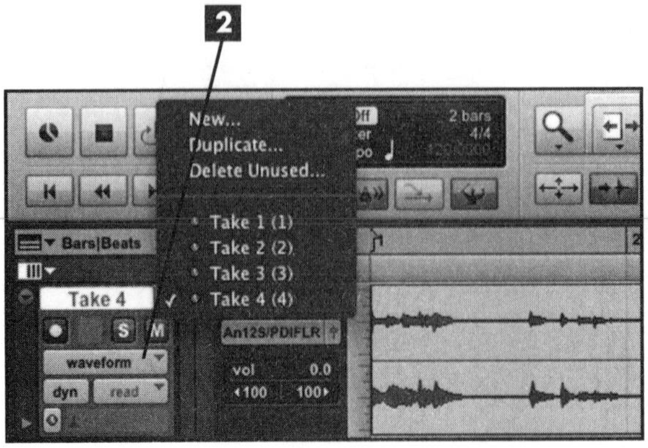

2 It would be great if we could see *all* the Edit Playlists for a given track at one time and create our comped track without having to switch playlists all the time. That's exactly what Pro Tools 8 allows you to do. **Click** the **Track View selector** (which reads Waveform in this example) on the desired track. A menu will appear.

3 **Click** the **Playlists menu item**.

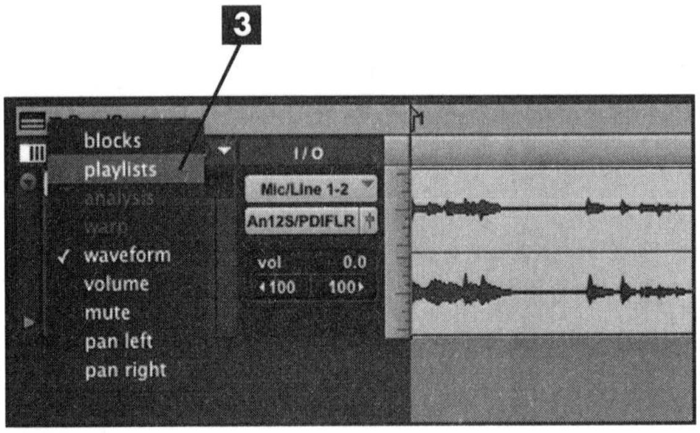

* In Playlists view, you'll see all the Edit Playlists associated with a given track, displayed as different lanes.

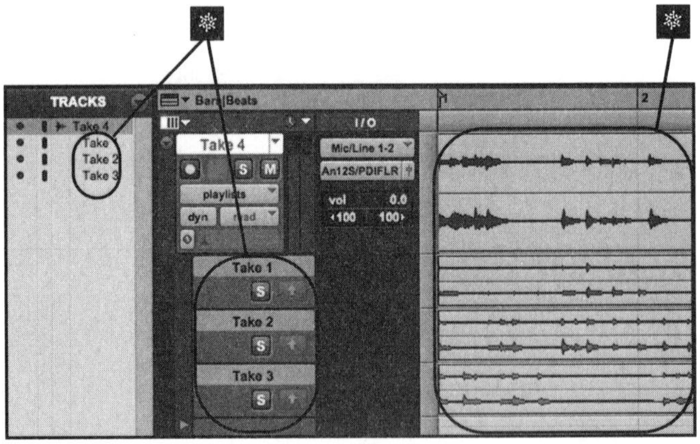

* Working in Playlists view—especially when you're using this view with multiple tracks simultaneously—can result in a pretty complicated-looking Edit window. To let you know which lanes are associated with which tracks, alternate playlists lanes are indented (both in the Playlist area and in the Tracks list).

Basic Track Comping

Now the fun starts. The first thing to do is to create a *new* playlist, giving you a blank track to comp to. Playlists view makes this easy!

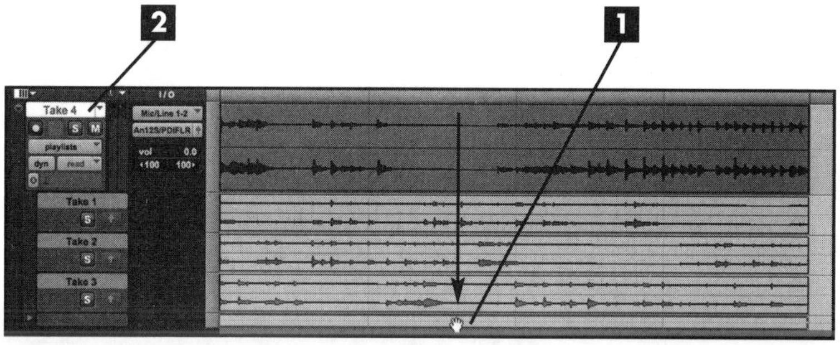

1 Using the Grabber tool, **drag** the desired **region(s)** to the empty lane at the bottom of the track. When the region has been dragged to the proper place, you'll see an empty box. **Release** the **mouse button**, and the region will be moved to a new playlist, leaving a blank area at the top for comping.

2 You can **double-click** on the track's **nameplate** to rename the main playlist if you wish. Similarly, you can click on the alternate playlists' names to name individual takes.

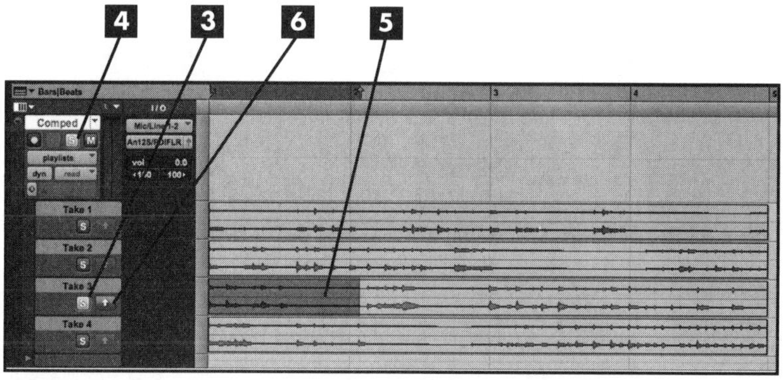

3 To preview alternate playlists, **click** the **Solo button** for the desired Playlist lane. The soloed playlist will be heard instead of the active Edit Playlist.

4 If you **click** the track's main **Solo button**, all the other non-soloed tracks in your session will be muted.

5 With the Selector tool, **mark** an **area** that you wish to use in your comped track.

6 **Click** the **Copy Selection to Main Playlist button**.

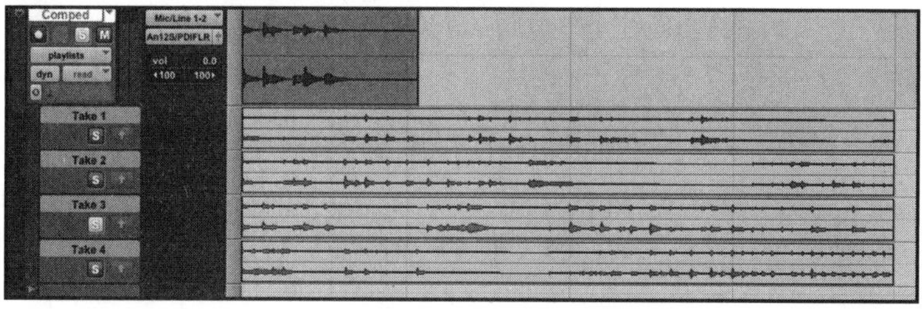

As you can see here, the selected area has been copied from the original playlist and automatically pasted to the main playlist. At this point, you can audition other sections, pick your favorites, and send them from the alternate playlist to the comped track playlist as well, creating a new track that represents the best parts of each take. Because this is all nondestructive, you can still adjust boundaries with the Trimmer tool or move segments around with the Grabber tool. If a particular transition from one region to another is abrupt, you can use crossfades to smooth things out. (You'll learn more about crossfades in the next chapter.)

> **COMPING SHORTCUT**
>
> Instead of clicking the Copy Selection to Main Playlist arrow button, you can press Control+Option+V (Mac) or Start+Alt+V (PC) after selecting an area on a Playlist lane to paste the selected area up to the main Edit Playlist.

Beyond the Basics

As if this radical improvement in the editing process wasn't enough, Pro Tools also has more ways to organize and view your takes!

Region Ratings

In the preceding example, we had four takes. In a normal comping situation, you might have dozens! It might be hard to believe, but the mere act of separating the good takes and sections is often an important and time-saving step. With the new comping tools, Pro Tools has some important features to help with this as well, in the form of region rating.

The first thing to do is make sure you can see the ratings of regions.

1 **Click** on **View**. The View menu will appear.

2 **Click** on **Region**. The Region submenu will appear, showing different display options for regions.

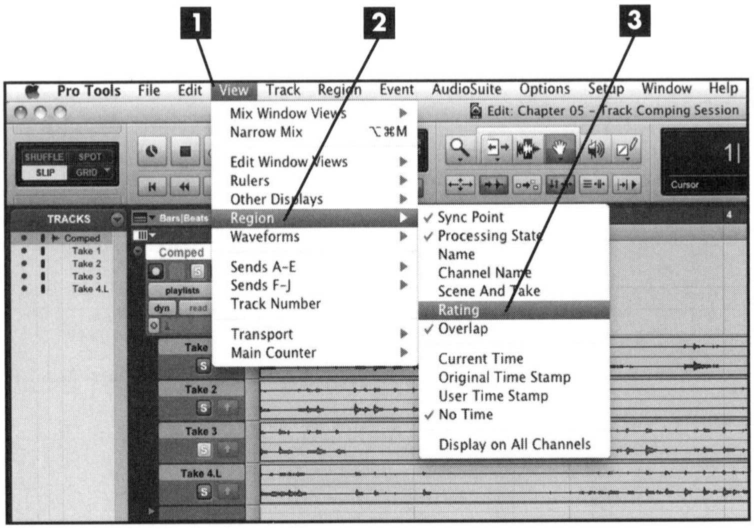

3 As with other menus you've seen so far, aspects that are shown are indicated with a checkmark. Because we want to see regions' ratings, **click** the **Rating menu item** to check it (assuming that it's not already checked).

- You'll see that all the regions on your track show an initial ranking of none.

4 When you find a section of a region that you want to rank, simply **separate** the **section**, creating a new region. This new region also has an initial ranking of none.

5 **Right-click** the **region** you want to rank. A menu will appear.

6 **Choose** the **Rating menu item**. The Rating submenu will appear.

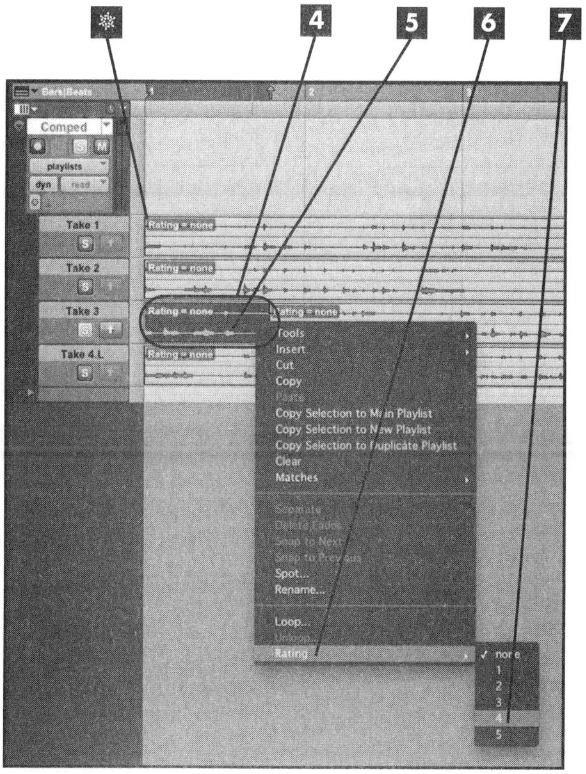

7 **Choose** the desired **ranking** for the region. It's up to you whether 5 or 1 is the best ranking, but it's important to be consistent with your method.

> **RATING SHORTCUT**
>
> Instead of right-clicking the region to rank it, you can press Control+Option+Command+[number from 1–5] (Mac) or Ctrl+Start+Alt+[number from 1–5] (PC) after selecting a region.

Filtering Lanes

When you've picked out the best takes, you can show only the lanes containing good takes and hide the lanes that you don't want to include in the comping process.

1 **Right-click** the **name-plate** of any lane. A menu will appear.

2 **Choose** the **Filter Lanes menu item**. The Filter Lanes submenu will appear.

3 In this menu, you can show or hide all lanes or show/hide lanes based on their ranking. Here's where your ranking system will make a difference:

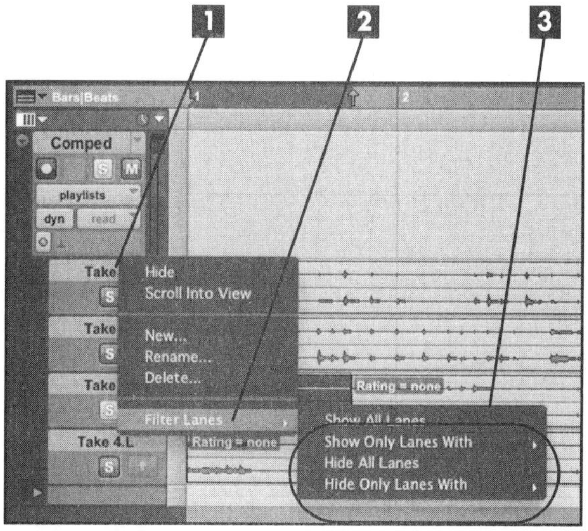

* If your ranking system is set up so that your best takes are ranked higher (the best being ranked a 5), you'll want to choose Show Only Lanes With and then choose Regions Rated >= 1–5. In this case, I've chosen 3, which means only lanes with regions ranked 3, 4, or 5 will be shown.

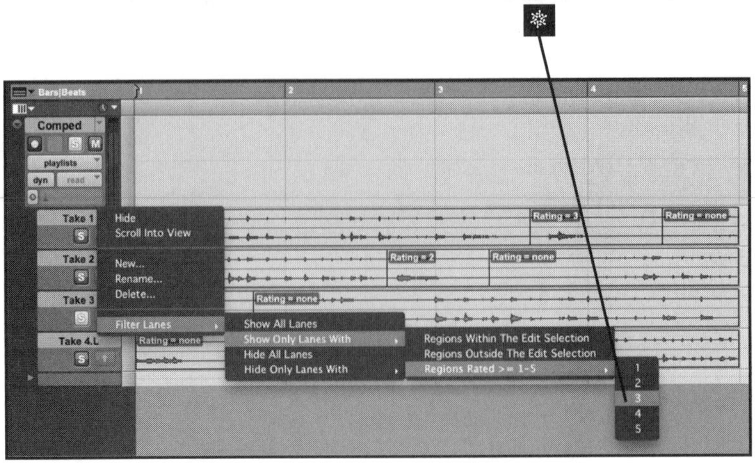

* If your ranking system is set up so that your best takes are ranked lower (the best being ranked a 1), you'll want to choose Hide Only Lanes With and then choose Regions Rated >= 1–5. In this case, I've chosen 3, which means only lanes with regions ranked 3, 2, or 1 will be shown.

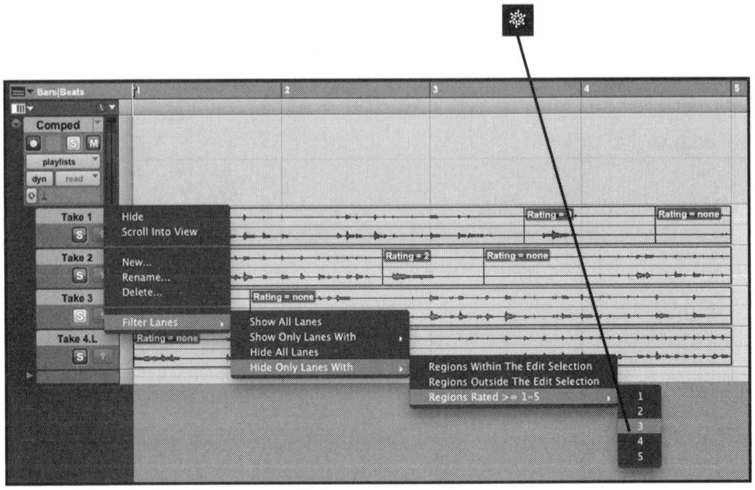

That's it for beginning editing! Now on to some of the more "tweaky" features!

6 And More Editing

Although the editing power of a DAW like Pro Tools is impressive indeed, the editing process in and of itself is rarely glamorous. A good editor knows that editing essentially boils down to a few simple functions done many, many times. In the editor's world, patience is a virtue, and attention to detail is put to the test when you cut and paste, drag and drop, and switch editing tools time and time again. Indeed, it's not uncommon for a professional editing session to involve thousands of individual editing operations!

The good news is that you already learned the basics of editing in Chapter 5, "Editing." The next step is to expand upon the basic editing tools you've already begun to use and learn more flexible and efficient ways to work. The idea behind these techniques is that the time you'll save with each editing function will accumulate, saving you a sizable amount of time by the end of the day. Better yet, you'll not only save time, but you'll also become a better and more creative editor in the process! In this chapter, you'll learn how to:

- Navigate your session with greater ease.
- Use alternate methods of zooming and customized zoom settings to boost efficiency.
- Use variations of the Trimmer and Grabber tools.
- Boost your editing power by using the Smart tool.
- Put new region-based features (region looping, region groups) to use in your session.
- Protect your regions from accidental change by locking them.

More Organization: Memory Locations

As your session gets more complex, organizing and navigating the maze of regions and tracks can become a real issue. This is not only true of the editing phase, but in the mixing stage as well, when you're mainly working in the Mix window and you don't have the convenience of clicking on a specific time on a track (although you will still have the Transport window when you want it). The good news is that you can make navigation significantly easier by setting up a few memory locations.

Memory locations are user-defined presets that enable you to recall a variety of settings with a single click of a button. Not only will you be able to instantly jump to important places in time, but you can also change zoom settings, track visibility, track height, and more!

> **USING THE TUTORIAL SESSION**
>
> For this section, please use the session named Chapter 06 Session—Part 1 included on the disc that came with your book. Remember, you'll want to copy the folder to a location on your computer's hard drive before working on it.

Creating a Memory Location

Before you can use memory locations, you have to create them! Typically, the first step is to set up the Edit window in a way that you would like to be able to recall. In this case (and this is something I commonly do), I want to set up the window in a sort of default state. Here's what I do:

1. **Set** the **timeline insertion cursor** to the beginning of the session (1|1|000).
2. **Show all the tracks** in the session.
3. **Zoom out** horizontally to see the entire length of the session.
4. **Set** the **track heights** to see all the tracks in the session.

Once you have your Edit window set up in a way that you'd like to save to a memory location, you're ready to begin the process of creating the memory location itself.

1. **Click** on the **Window menu**.
2. **Click** on **Memory Locations**. The Memory Locations window will appear.

3. **Click** on the **Memory Locations Menu button** in the upper-right corner of the Memory Locations window. A menu will appear.
4. **Click** on **New Memory Location**. The New Memory Location dialog box will open.

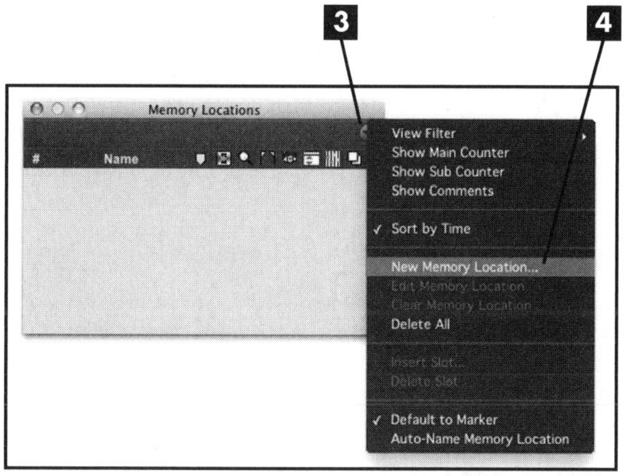

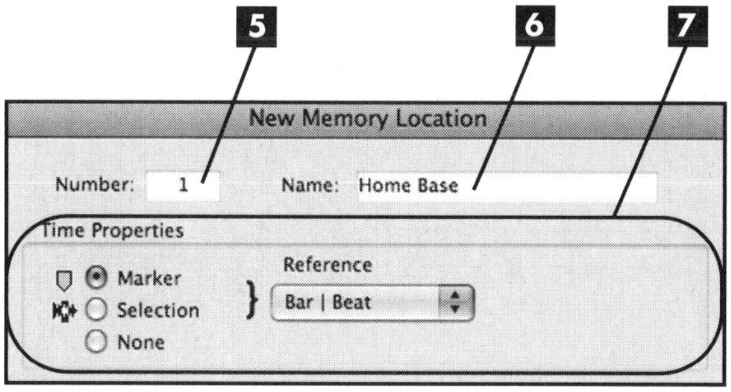

5. Although Pro Tools will automatically assign a memory-location number when you create a new memory location, you can **type** a different **number** in the Number field. This number will determine the ranking of the new memory location and the shortcut you will use to recall it (which we'll cover later in this section).
6. **Type** a descriptive **name** for your new memory location in the Name text box. In this case, I'm calling my memory location Home Base, because it recalls some basic settings for my session.
7. **Select** the **time property** that you want this memory location to recall. The choices are as follows:

* **Marker.** The timeline insertion cursor will jump to a specific location when the memory location is chosen. (In this case, it will go to the beginning of my session.) This is the kind of memory location I want for this example.

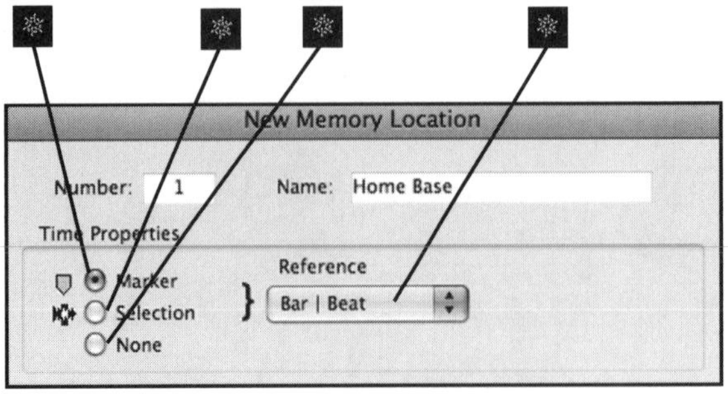

* **Selection.** A selected area will be recalled when the memory location is chosen.
* **None.** The timeline insertion/selection will not change when the memory location is chosen.
* **Reference button.** Clicking the Reference menu button will reveal two basic modes for your time properties:
  * **Bar|Beat.** If you choose Bar|Beat, your memory location's position on the timeline will be anchored to a specific bar and beat position and will move on the timeline if the tempo is changed. This is most useful in musical situations.
  * **Absolute.** If you choose Absolute, your memory location will be anchored to a sample-based location and will not move if your session's tempo changes. This is most commonly used when working with video soundtracks (since video typically doesn't deal with musical tempo).

8 **Check** the **General Properties checkboxes** that match the settings you want to recall with this memory location. In this example, when the Home Base memory location is chosen, the current zoom settings, track show/hide, and track heights will be restored. Other characteristics, such as pre-/post-roll and group enables, will not change when you recall this memory location.

9 **Type** a descriptive **comment** in the Comments field to describe the memory location. This is an optional step, but can save you when things get complex!

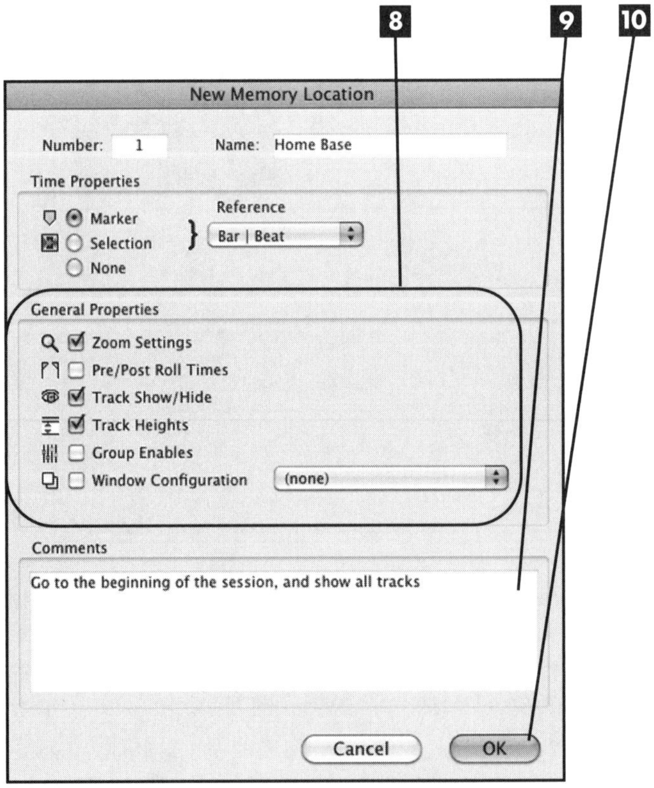

10 **Click** on **OK**. Your memory location will be saved, and the New Memory Location dialog box will close.

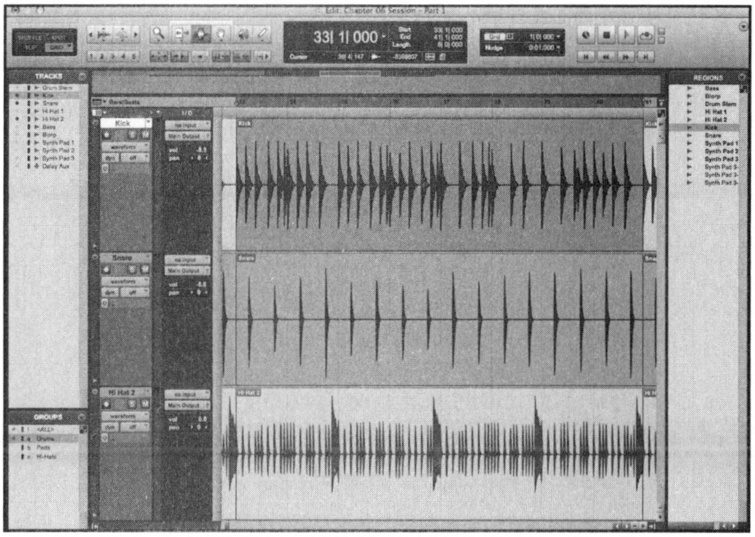

11 Now let's try setting up a different memory location. **Select** a different **area** (in this image, I selected from bar 33 to bar 41), and different **zoom settings, track heights, and track show/hides**. (In this image, I am showing only the Kick, Snare, and Hi Hat 2 tracks.) And this time, **enable** a **group**. (I've enabled the Drums group by clicking the word Drums in the lower-left area of the Edit window.)

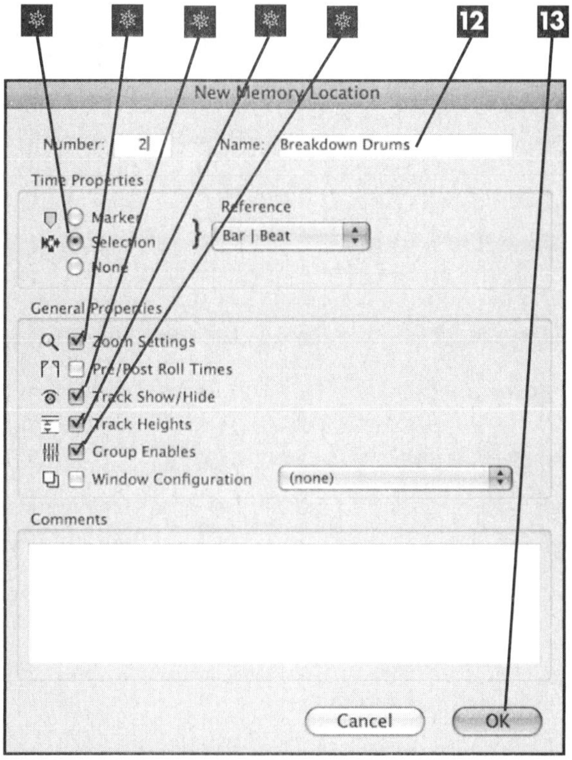

12 **Create** a new **memory location** by repeating steps 3 and 4. If you're following this example, name the new memory location Breakdown Drums and choose the following settings in the New Memory Location dialog box:

- Choose the Selection option in the Time Properties section. When this memory location is recalled, the selection will be as well.
- Select Zoom Settings.
- Select Track Show/Hide.
- Select Track Heights.
- Select Group Enables. This will activate the currently active groups (in this case, the Drums group) when this memory location is recalled.

13 **Click** on **OK** when you're finished.

If you're following along with the steps so far in this chapter, your session will now have two different memory locations, and you can begin to get a sense of their usefulness.

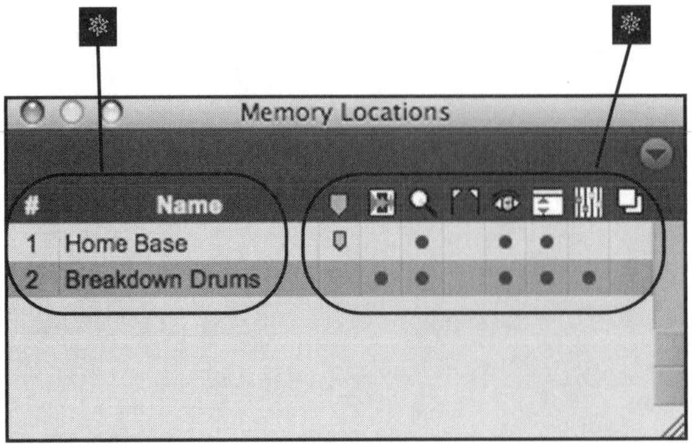

By clicking on the desired memory-location name, you will instantly recall all the aspects associated with that memory location.

If you're ever unclear as to what parameters are stored in a specific memory location, you can find out just by noting the icons that are shown to the right of the memory-location name. From left to right, the icons are Marker, Selection, Zoom, Pre-/Post-Roll, Track Show/Hide, Track Heights, Group Enables, and Window Configurations (something we'll talk about in just a few pages).

MEMORY-LOCATION SHORTCUT

You can easily recall a memory location from your keyboard. Just press the period (.) key on your keyboard's numeric keypad, then the number of the memory location you want to recall (again, on your computer's numeric keypad), and then the period key again. This works identically for both Mac and PC systems.

ANOTHER WAY TO CREATE MEMORY LOCATIONS

You can also create memory locations by pressing the Enter key on your computer keyboard's numeric keypad. You can even do this on the fly as your session is playing. After creating the memory locations, you can then go back and edit them by right-clicking the desired memory location or double-clicking the memory location that you want to change.

Using Memory Locations

There's no big mystery to creating and using memory locations, but before we delve into the next section, let's take a quick look at some of the various options available to you.

1 **Click** on the **Memory Locations Menu button**.

- When you select the Show Main Counter option, the location of each memory location in relation to the main time scale will be shown in a column in the Memory Locations window.

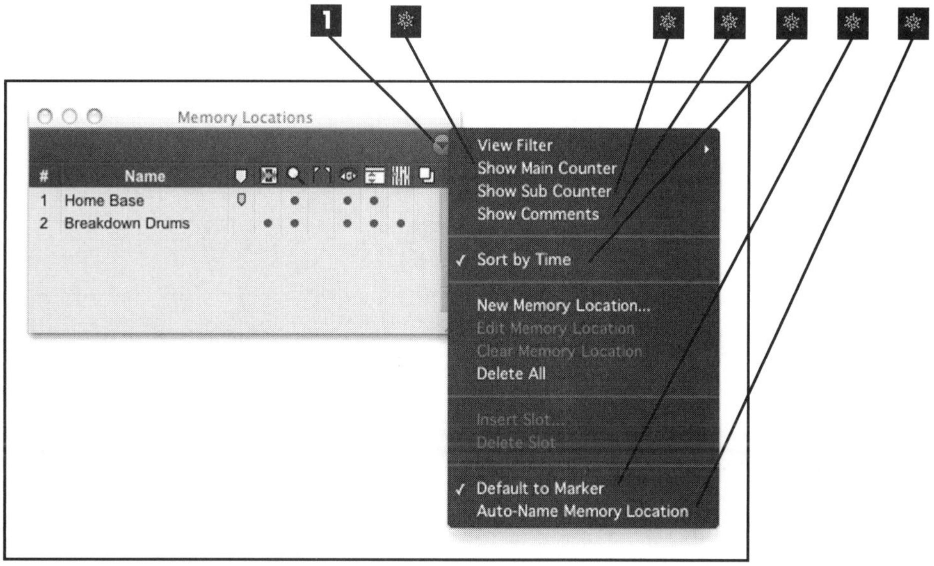

- When you select the Show Sub Counter option, the location of each memory location in relation to the sub time scale will be displayed.
- When you select the Show Comments option, any comments you've entered for your memory locations will be shown.
- When you select the Sort by Time option, your memory locations will be sorted depending on how early or late they are in your session rather than by the order in which they were created or their numeric ranking.
- When you select the Default to Marker option, the Memory Locations dialog box will open with the marker option chosen by default. This is particularly useful when you're creating memory locations while your session is playing. (See the earlier note "Another Way to Create Memory Locations".)
- The Auto-Name Memory Location option is also very handy when you're creating memory locations on the fly. It will remove the need to type in a name for your memory location. In fact, the dialog box will not even open, making the creation of a memory location a one-click (or one-keystroke) operation.

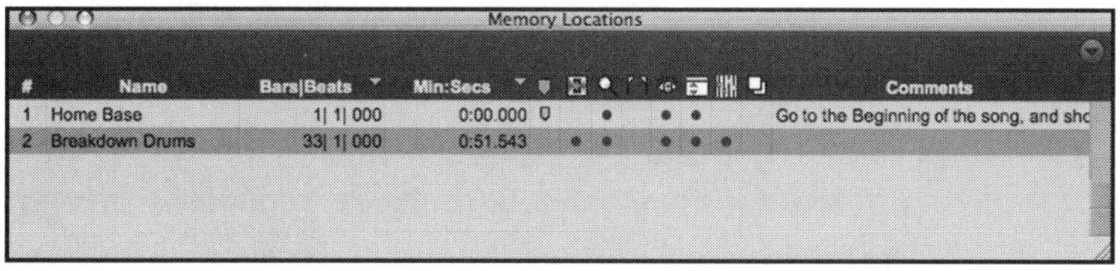

Here's what the window will look like when the main counter and sub counter are shown, as well as the comments. Note the two new columns created, and that their time scales reflect the currently selected main and sub time scales. Either (or both) of these columns can come in mighty handy, particularly when you're working in the Mix window, where it's harder to visualize your time position in your session.

Inserting a Memory-Location Slot

For those of you who have been using memory locations for some time already, you'll appreciate a relatively new bit of functionality to the Memory Locations window. The Insert Slot feature will enable you to create a new memory location *between* two existing memory locations. Here's how it's done.

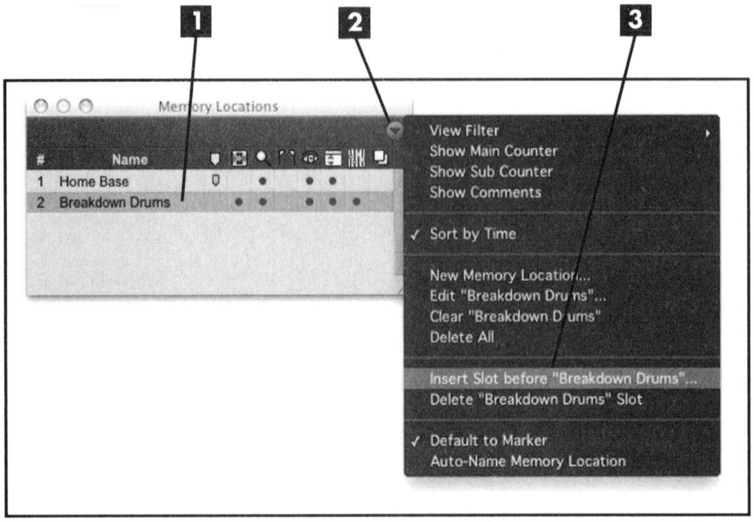

1. **Select** the **memory location** that you want to be *after* the new memory location. In this image, I've selected memory location 2, because I want to create a new slot 2 and shift the existing slot to position 3.
2. After you set up your desired memory-location settings (selections, zoom settings, track show/hide, and so on), **click** on the **Memory Locations Menu button**. The menu will appear.
3. **Select Insert Slot before "[memory location name]"**. Once you click this menu item, the New Memory Location dialog box will open, and you'll be able to create the new memory location as usual. When you're finished, this new memory location will be inserted in the desired slot, and the appropriate existing memory locations will be moved to later slots.

Window Configurations

In our discussion of memory locations, you may have noticed a property called Window Configurations and wondered what the heck it was. Well, a window configuration is just what it sounds like: a recallable arrangement of windows that you can create to make your editing work go even more smoothly.

Creating a Window Configuration

Creating a recallable window configuration is even easier than creating memory locations. For purposes of illustration, let's start with the Edit window. Here are the steps.

1 **Arrange** your **windows** as desired, including any columns, rulers, and lists that you want shown in the Edit and Mix windows. For this example, let's set up a basic Edit window layout. (If you're using the tutorial session, the Edit window is already set up this way.)

2 **Click** on the **Window menu**.

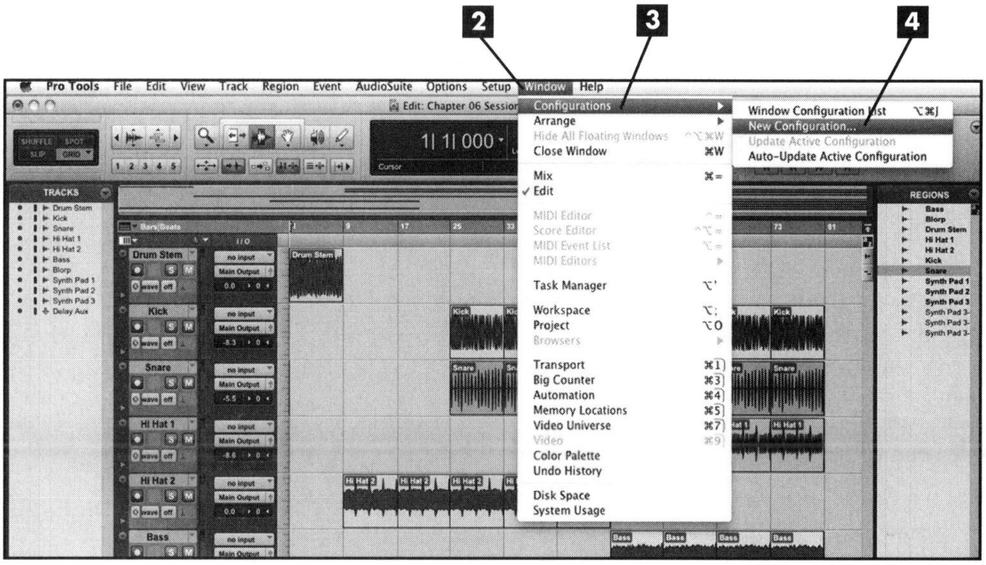

3 **Click** on **Configurations**. The Configurations submenu will appear.

4 Because you want to create a *new* window configuration, **click** on **New Configuration**. The Edit Window Configuration dialog box will open.

Now you have to choose what aspects of your layout you want to be able to recall. The two option buttons will enable you to choose what aspects of your desktop will be incorporated into the window configuration (similar to the General Properties section of the New Memory Location dialog box). The choices are pretty simple:

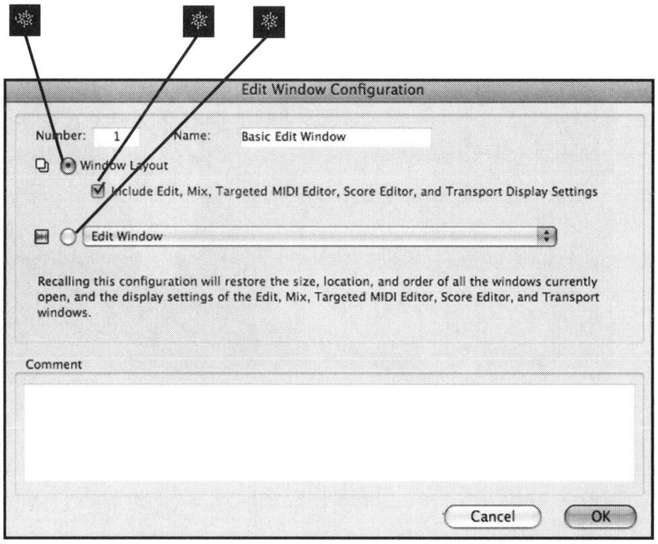

- Clicking the Window Layout option button will set up your window configuration to recall all the windows you see on your desktop, sized and positioned as they are right now. In this example, since I want to recall the entire desktop, I'll choose this option.
- If you additionally check the Include Edit, Mix, Targeted MIDI Editor, Score Editor, and Transport Display Settings checkbox, the view settings that you've chosen for these windows (things such as column show/hide settings) will also be recalled.
- The second main option button allows for finer control. It will enable you to recall settings for only the Edit, Mix, Score Editor, Targeted MIDI Editor, or Transport windows. For example, if you only want to recall your ruler settings for the Edit window, you would click this option button and then select Edit Window Display Settings from the drop-down menu. The Edit window would be changed, but any other active windows would be unaffected.

5 **Type** a **name** for your window configuration in the Name text box.

6 This is an optional step, but a useful one: **Type** a **description** for your window configuration in the Comment section.

7 That's it—just **click** on **OK**, and you're finished!

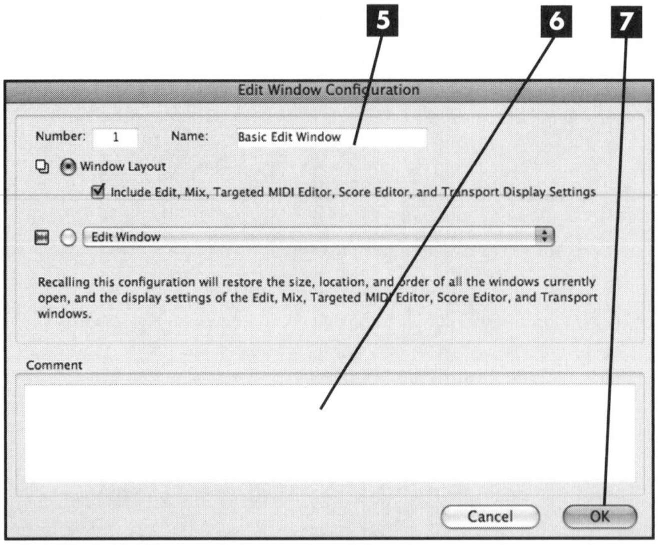

Now that you've created a basic configuration for your Edit window, let's set up a basic Mix window view (you can use the one shown here for reference) and create a second window configuration by repeating the previous steps. Name the new window configuration Basic Mix Window. For a refresher on how to customize the Mix window, you can refer to Chapter 2, "Getting Around in Pro Tools."

Window configurations aren't limited to single-window views only. In fact, the ability to arrange multiple windows as you please and save that arrangement is where window configurations really shine. Try this: Create a layout that has the Edit window across the top of your monitor and a minimal Mix window along the bottom. (This is a personal favorite desktop arrangement of mine.) Once that's done, create another new window configuration and call it Edit/Mix Split.

Recalling Window Configurations

Now that you've created a few window configurations, you can recall them easily, much as you did with memory locations. There are three main ways that you can do it.

1. **Click** the **Window menu**.
2. **Choose Configurations**. The Configurations submenu will appear.
3. At the bottom of the submenu, you'll see a list of all the session's window locations. (The currently targeted one will be indicated with a diamond to the left of the name.) Just **click** the **window configuration** that you want to recall, and your desktop will be instantly rearranged.

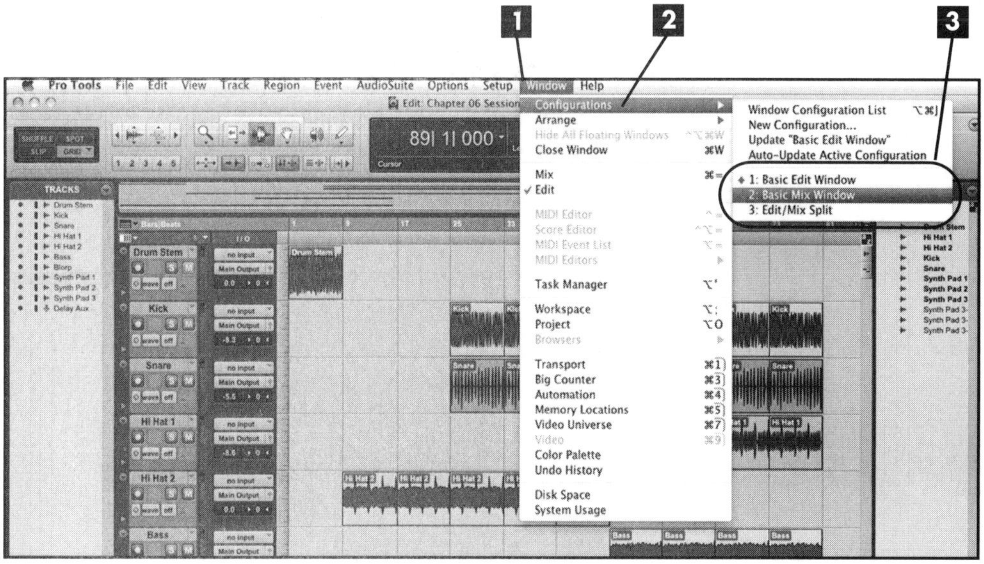

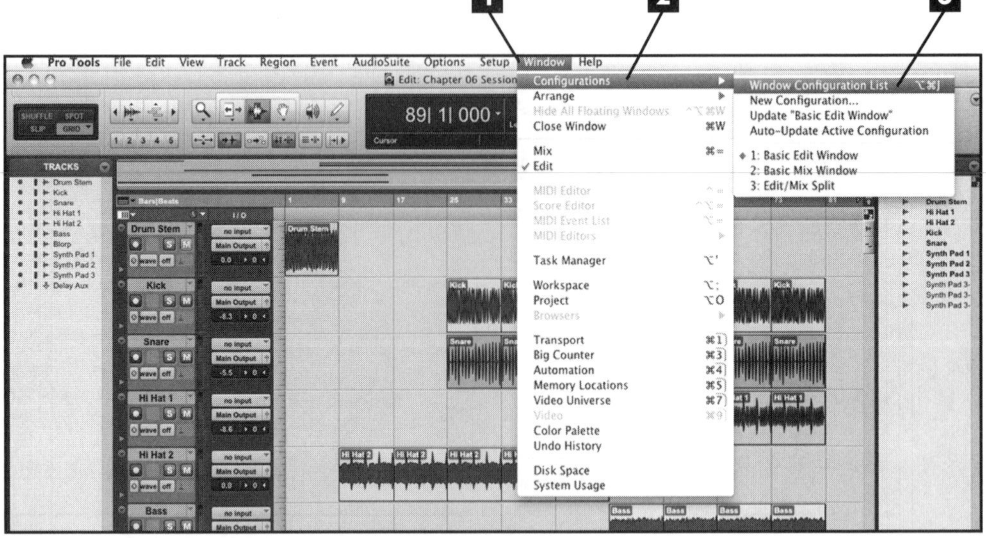

1 **Click** the **Window menu**.

2 **Choose Configurations**.

3 **Choose Window Configuration List**. The Window Configurations window will appear.

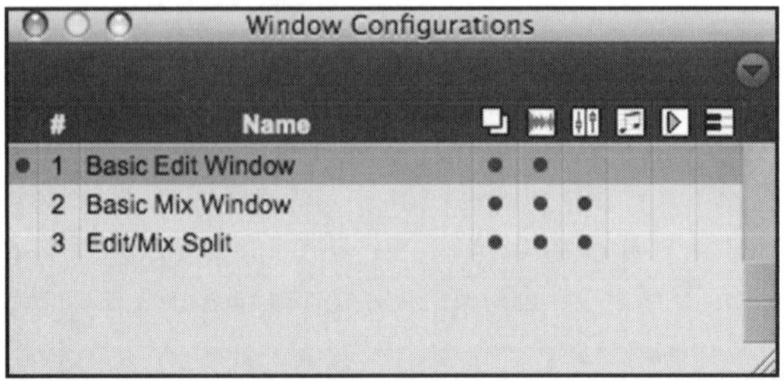

The Window Configurations window not only looks like the Memory Locations window, it acts like it as well. Just click the window configuration you want to recall. The dots to the right of the window configuration's name will let you know what settings have been stored in it (window layout, Edit window settings, Mix window settings, Score Editor settings, Transport window settings, and targeted MIDI Editor settings).

In addition to these two methods, you can also recall a window configuration as a property of a memory location. Basically, this means you can associate a window configuration with a memory location and change not only your desktop's layout, but any memory-location property as well, all in one click! Here's how:

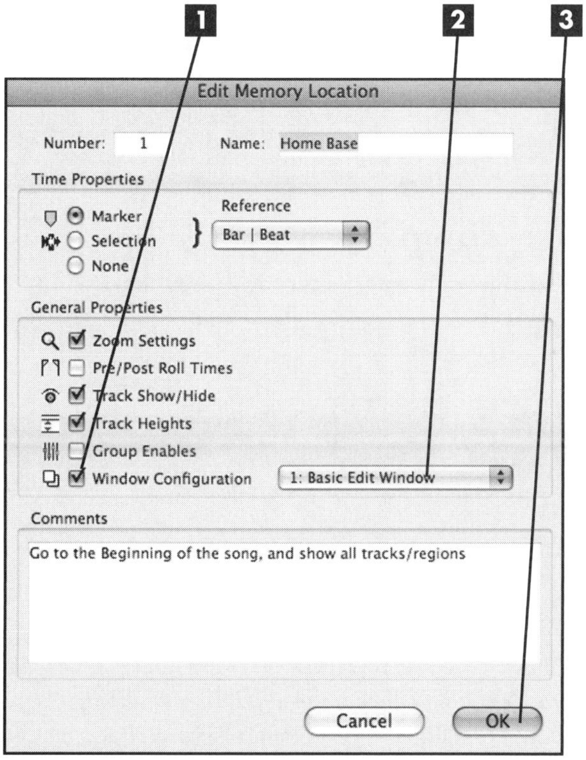

1 In the Edit Memory Location window, in the General Properties area, **click** the **Window Configuration checkbox**. This will configure the memory location to recall a window configuration along with any other properties that you've chosen to associate with that memory location.

2 Once the Window Configuration checkbox is marked, the next step is to **choose** which **window configuration** will be recalled with that memory location. Just select the desired window configuration from the Window Configuration drop-down list. (Click on the menu button to reveal a list of all the window configurations that you have created in the session.)

3 Once you're done, **click** the **OK button**.

WINDOW CONFIGURATION SHORTCUT

Here's yet another way to recall a window configuration: Just press the period (.) key on your keyboard's numeric keypad, then the number of the window configuration you want to recall (again, on your computer's numeric keypad), and then press the asterisk (*) key on your computer's numeric keypad. This works identically for both Mac and PC systems.

Zoom

Zooming is not only one of the most basic of operations; it's also one of the most frequent things you'll do in any editing session. In Chapter 5, "Editing," you learned the basics of zooming. The following sections discuss other ways to zoom and how to use them.

TIME TO CHANGE TUTORIAL SESSIONS!

For the next section of this chapter, we'll take advantage of what you just learned about memory locations. Please copy the Chapter 06 Session—Part 2 folder to your audio hard drive and launch the session. Once it's launched, go to memory location 1, named Selections.

More Zoom Tools

Let's start from what you already know and work from there.

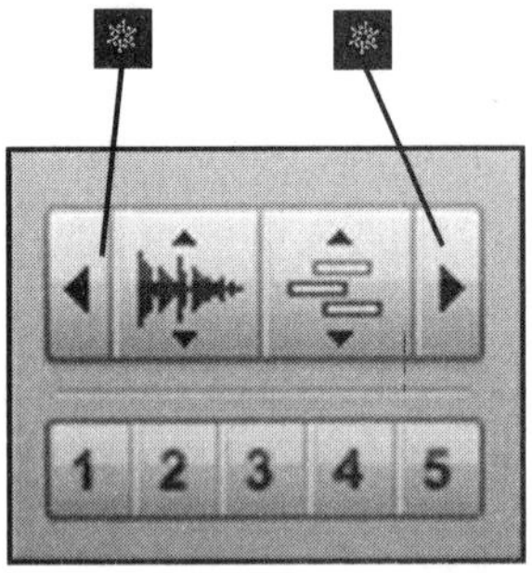

- Click on the Zoom Out button of the Zoom cluster. As you've seen before, your view of your session's timeline will expand, and a longer duration will be shown in your Edit window. Note that this horizontal zooming affects all tracks in your session.
- Click on the Zoom In button. Again, you'll see that Audio and MIDI tracks are zoomed at the same rate. The Zoom In and Zoom Out buttons will enable you to zoom in on the time scale, and although they won't affect the speed at which your session will play back, they will enable you to view your regions and data differently to suit different kinds of editing.

Remember that even if your Zoom cluster isn't being displayed in the top row of the Edit window, you still have access to Zoom controls, in the lower-right corner of the Edit window:

- Click the minus sign on the bottom of the Edit window to zoom out.
- Click the plus sign on the bottom of the Edit window to zoom in.

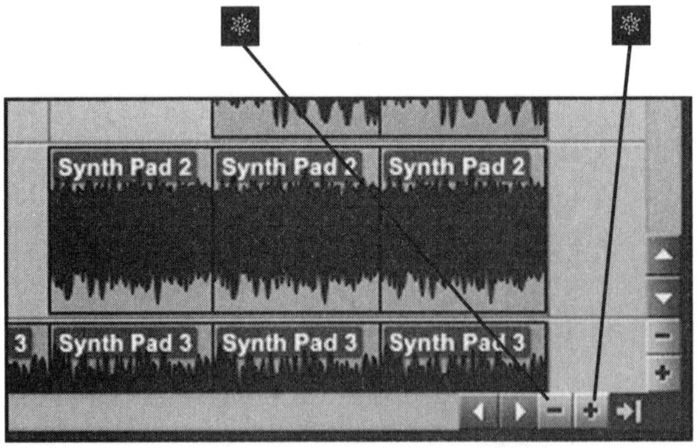

In addition to these basic horizontal Zoom controls, you have the ability to zoom in and out *vertically* as well.

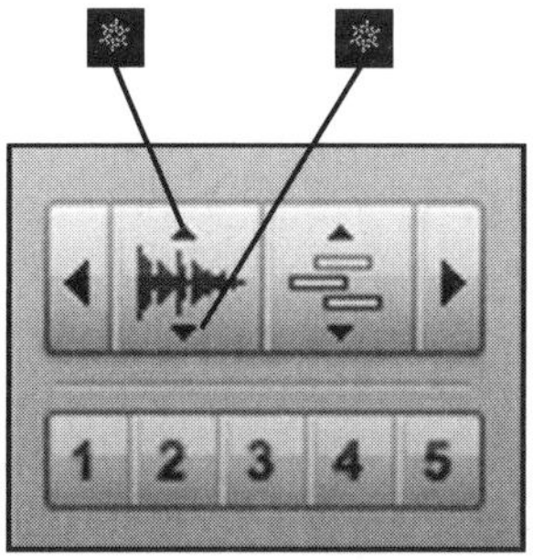

- Click on the top half of the Audio Zoom button. With each click, your audio data will zoom *up* vertically, allowing you to more clearly see low-level signals.
- Click on the bottom half of the Audio Zoom button. The height of your audio waveforms will be reduced with each click of this button.

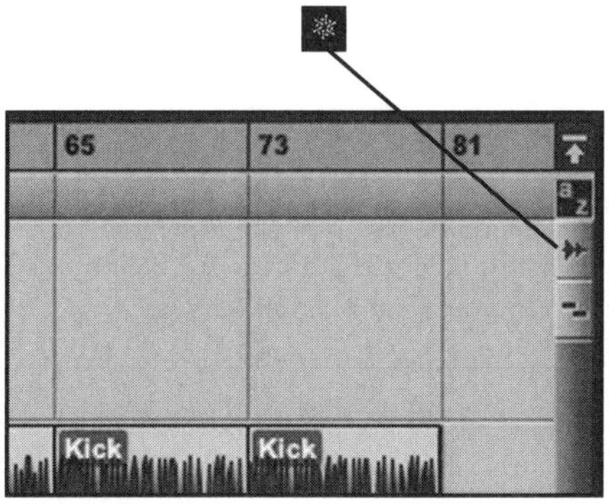

The Zoom cluster's Audio Zoom button is duplicated in miniature in the upper-right corner of your Edit window's Playlist area. Click on the top or bottom half of this button to zoom up or down on your audio regions.

VERTICAL ZOOM (AUDIO) SHORTCUT

Although vertical zooming is not quite as common as horizontal zooming, the shortcut keys are still useful to know. On a Mac, the shortcut is Command+Option+] (right bracket) to zoom up and Command+Option+[(left bracket) to zoom down. On a PC, it's Ctrl+Alt+] (right bracket) to zoom up and Ctrl+Alt+[(left bracket) to zoom down.

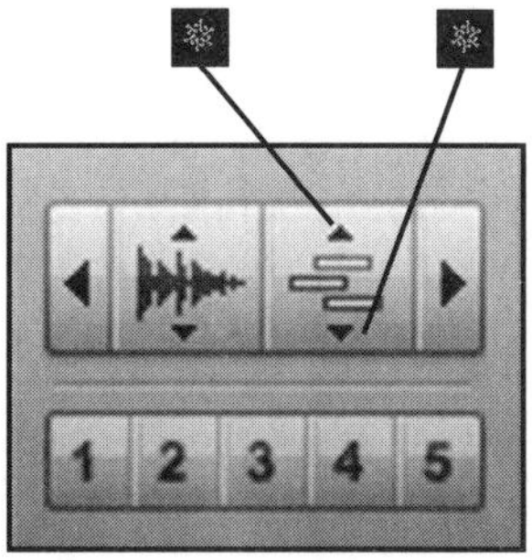

- Click on the top half of the MIDI Zoom button. With each click, your MIDI data will zoom up vertically, allowing you to more clearly see individual notes. Note that all your MIDI regions have zoomed up at the same time, but audio regions are left unchanged.
- Click on the bottom half of the MIDI Zoom button. Your MIDI data will zoom down, allowing you to see a greater range of notes at one time in the Edit window.

You'll also find a MIDI Zoom button in the upper-right corner of your Edit window's Playlist area, just below the small Audio Zoom button. Click on the top or bottom half of this button to zoom up or down on your MIDI regions.

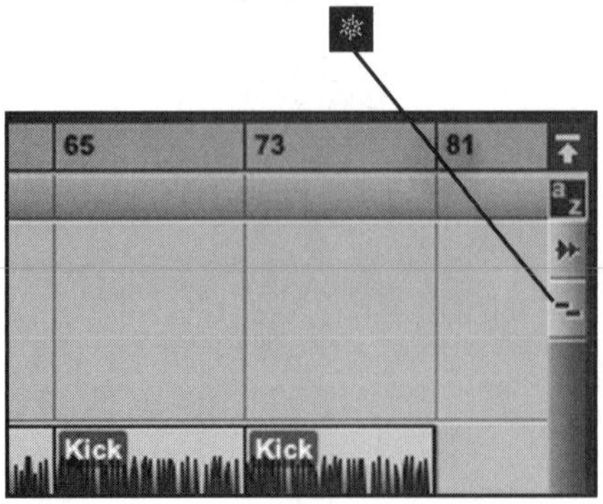

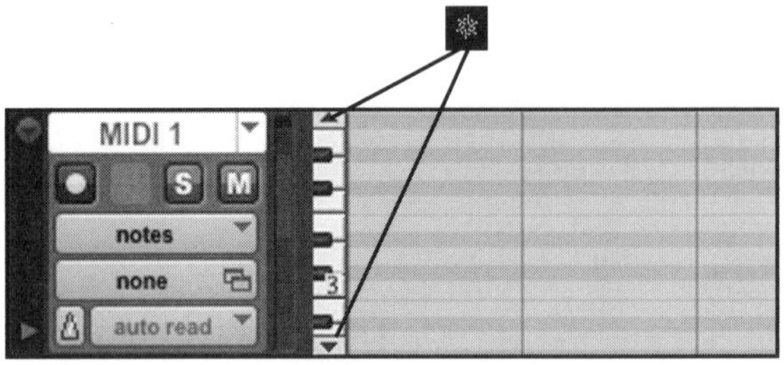

As you zoom up or down, you will see less or more of the keyboard graphic on the left edge of each MIDI track. You can use this display as a reference point to see how broad (or narrow) of a tonal range you're viewing. Low pitches are displayed toward the bottom of each MIDI track, and high notes are toward the top.

You can scroll up and down the MIDI note range by clicking on the up and down arrows at each end of the keyboard graphic.

VERTICAL ZOOM (MIDI) SHORTCUT

Here are the shortcuts for vertical zooming for MIDI data: On a Mac, the shortcut is Command+Shift+] (right bracket) to zoom up and Command+Shift+[(left bracket) to zoom down. On a PC, it's Ctrl+Shift+] (right bracket) to zoom up and Ctrl+Shift+[(left bracket) to zoom down.

Zoom Presets

Okay, I'm going to go out on a limb with this comparison, but bear with me. Take the average car radio. If you're a music lover, you probably use it quite a bit. On most car radios, there are a number of buttons (usually below the main display) that you can use to quickly get to the stations you listen to most often. Once you set up these presets, you can simply press a button and immediately jump to your favorite station.

Many Pro Tools users find that, although they use all the zoom tools a *lot*, they tend to use certain zoom settings more frequently than others do. Like on a car radio, you can set up your most common zoom presets and recall them with the click of a button. In fact, setting these zoom presets is pretty similar to setting the presets on your car radio!

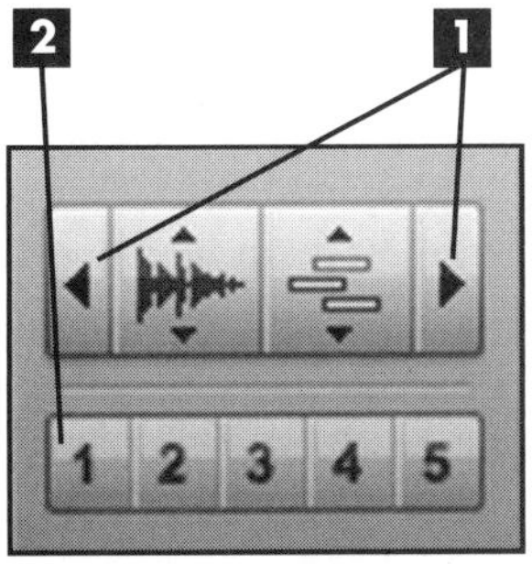

1 Using the horizontal zoom tools, **adjust** your **zoom level** until you arrive at a setting that you want to be able to recall.

2 **Hold down** the **Command key (Mac) or Ctrl key (PC)** and **click** on the **Zoom Preset button** that you want to assign to the current zoom level. The button will flash briefly to let you know that the preset has been stored.

From this point on, it's easy. Simply set the five presets for the five zoom settings you use the most. To recall any preset, you can click on the desired Zoom Preset button.

WILL ZOOM PRESETS RECALL BOTH HORIZONTAL AND VERTICAL ZOOM SETTINGS?

The Zoom Preset buttons will recall only the horizontal (time) zoom amount, not the vertical zoom levels for Audio and MIDI tracks.

ZOOM PRESET SHORTCUTS

The shortcuts to switch between your presets are pretty straightforward. While pressing Control (Mac) or Start (PC), press 1, 2, 3, 4, or 5 on your computer's keyboard (above the alphabet section).

Zoom Toggle

Over the last few versions of Pro Tools, Digidesign has added some new functionality to a feature called *zoom toggle*. Zoom toggle does just what its name would suggest: It enables you to quickly take a close-up look at a section and then get back out to the previous zoom level. In truth, this feature has been a part of Pro Tools for some time, but with the new power that's behind it, it's even more useful!

Actually, using zoom toggle is very easy when you use the Zoom Toggle button.

FOLLOWING ALONG

Although zoom toggle can be used in a variety of situations, the illustrations shown in this section are based upon the Chapter 06 Session—Part 2 tutorial session. Once you open that session, go to Memory Location #8—Getting Specific. You'll find that this view will give you a very clear idea of what zoom toggle is all about.

1 **Select the area** on which you want to zoom in.

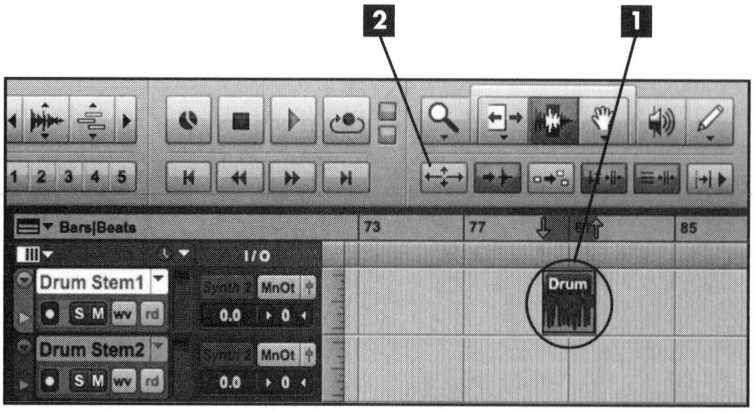

2 **Click** the **Zoom Toggle button**. The selection will zoom in according to the zoom toggle settings (which we will talk about in just a moment). When active, the Zoom Toggle button will be colored blue to show that you are indeed zoomed in.

3 To zoom back out to your previous zoom level, just **click** the **Zoom Toggle button** again. You'll be zoomed back out, and the Zoom Toggle button will be displayed in its inactive gray color.

> **ZOOM TOGGLE SHORTCUT**
>
> There is also a shortcut for zoom toggling: Just press Control+E (Mac) or Start+E (PC).

What makes the zoom toggle function particularly useful is the customization you can get through the setting of preferences. Here's how.

1 **Click** the **Setup menu.**

2 **Choose Preferences.** The Preferences window will appear:

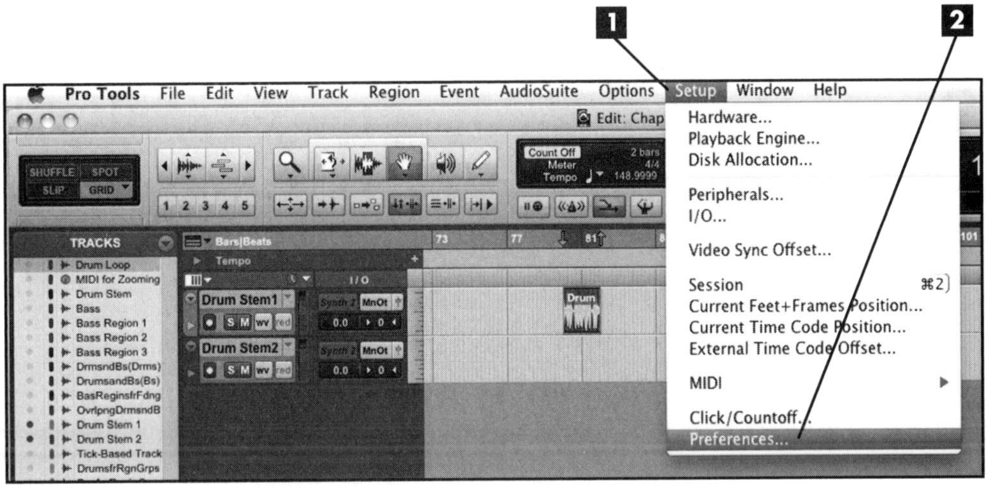

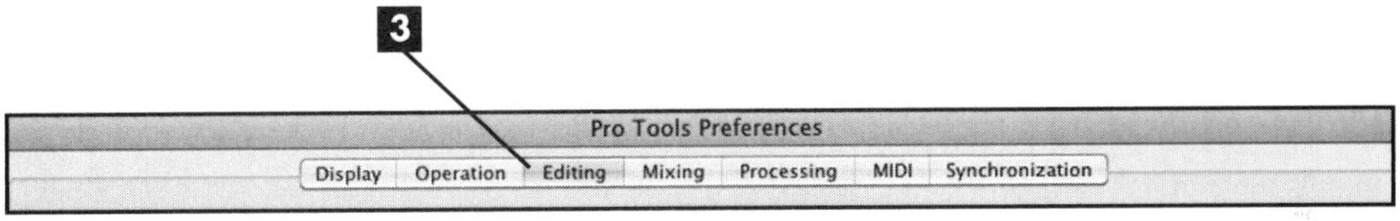

3 If your Preferences window isn't already showing the Editing page, **click** the **Editing tab** at the top of the Preferences window.

You'll find the Zoom Toggle section in the lower-right corner of the Preferences window's Editing page. The settings you establish here will determine how the zoom toggle feature will behave when you engage it. The first set of choices you need to make covers just how much you want to zoom in!

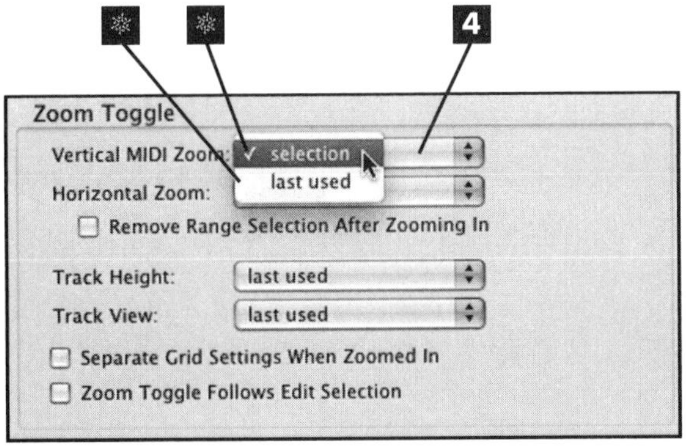

4 MIDI is a topic we'll tackle later, in Chapter 7, "Using MIDI." For now, it's sufficient to know that you can view MIDI data in fundamentally different ways than you view audio. If you **click** the **Vertical MIDI Zoom drop-down menu**, you can control zoom toggle behavior when MIDI data is selected. You have two options in this list.

- **Selection.** This option configures Zoom toggle to zoom into only the note range that is currently selected in the Edit window.
- **Last Used.** This option will recall the MIDI vertical zoom level that you used last time zoom toggle was engaged.

5 The Horizontal Zoom setting that you choose will control how the Zoom Toggle tool deals with zooming in on the time axis. Again, there are two options.

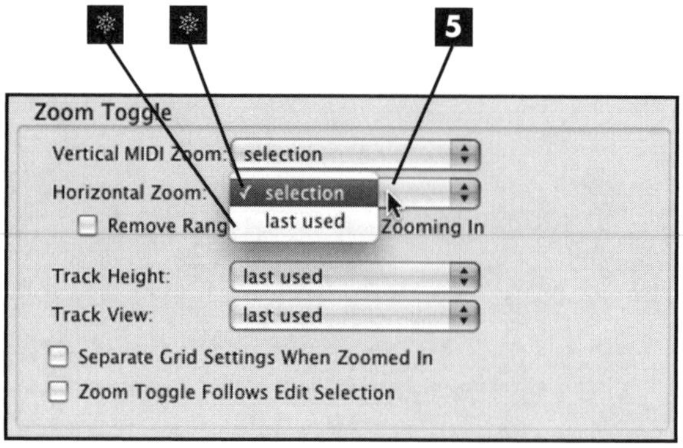

- **Selection.** With this option selected, the selected area will be zoomed in so that the selected area spans from the left edge to the right edge of the tracks area.
- **Last Used.** This option will recall the horizontal zoom level that was used when zoom toggle was last engaged.

- When the Remove Range Selection After Zooming In checkbox is checked, as soon as you engage zoom toggle, your selected area will be deselected, so that you can quickly make a different selection.

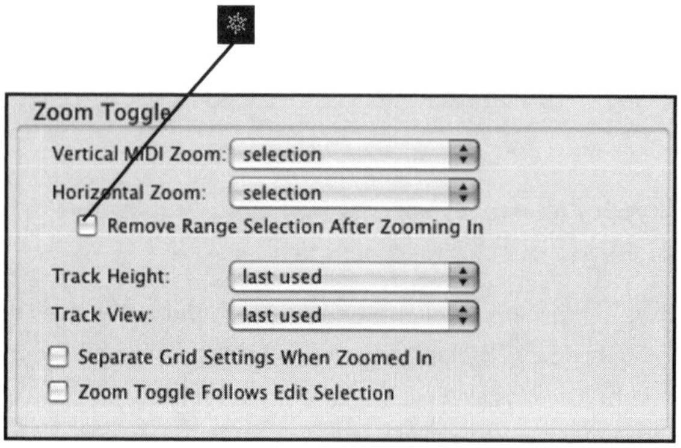

6 But wait—there's more! The Track Height drop-down menu will enable you to choose the track height that will be recalled when zoom toggle is engaged. Here's a tip: The Fit to Window setting is a favorite of mine for this sort of work.

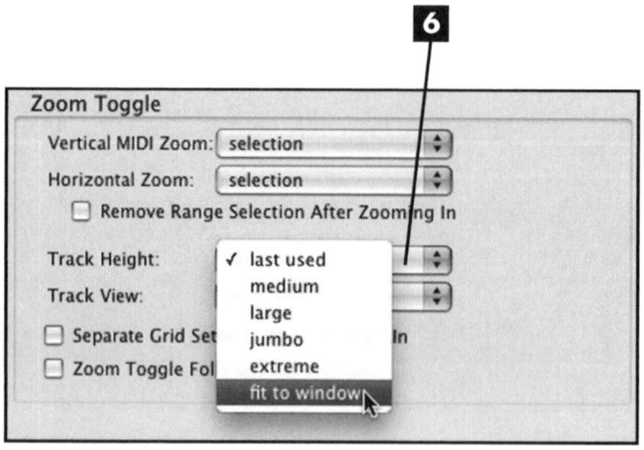

7 The Track View drop-down menu can change your Track view to a desired view when zoom toggle is engaged. Here are your options:

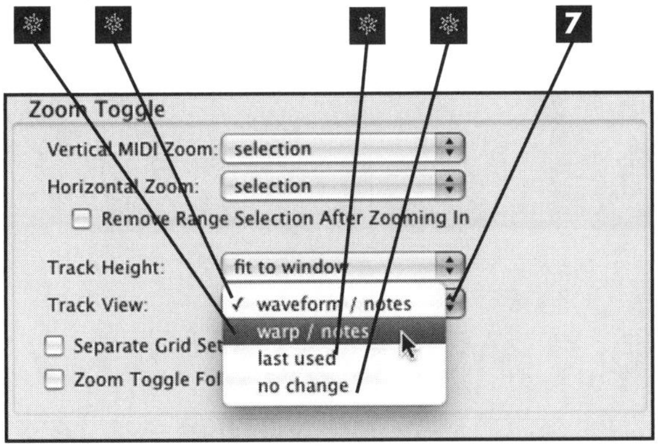

- **Waveform/Notes.** This is Waveform for Audio track, and Notes view for MIDI tracks.
- **Warp/Notes.** This is Warp view for Audio tracks, and Notes view for MIDI tracks.
- **Last Used.** This will recall the format view that you used when you used zoom toggle last on that track.
- **No Change.** This will make no view format change when you zoom toggle.

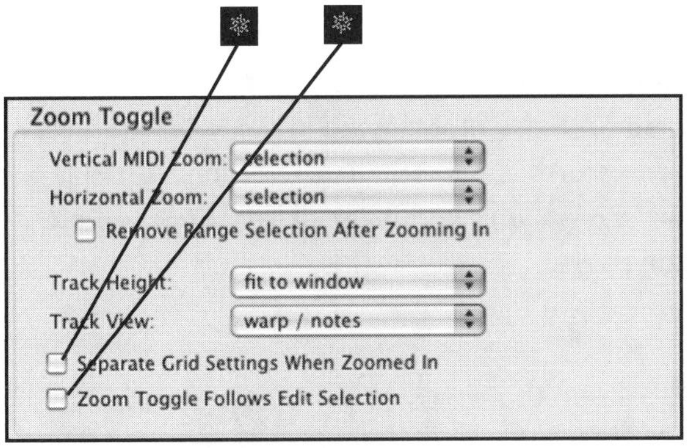

- If you check the Separate Grid Settings When Zoomed In checkbox, it will enable you to choose two different zoom resolutions—one that you see when you're toggled in and one when you're in your normal mode. To set the zoom toggle zoom resolution, just activate zoom toggle and then select the grid resolution that you want to use. It's really that easy! When you zoom back out, you'll see the grid resolution change back.
- This last checkbox—Zoom Toggle Follows Edit Selection—is an option that requires a bit of explanation. With this option selected, aspects such as track height and horizontal zoom settings will continually follow any tracks or regions that you have selected. For example, suppose you select a region on the top track in your session and then turn on zoom toggle. Your chosen zoom toggle settings will be recalled. Now, suppose you click a region on *another* track while zoom toggle is still engaged. With Zoom Toggle Follows Edit Selection checked, *that* track will immediately change its track height to the zoom toggle level. (Admittedly, this can be a little distracting from time to time!)

8 Once you've made your desired selections, just **click** the **OK button**, and you're ready to rock!

USING "LAST USED"

The Last Used option found in many of the zoom toggle menus might be a bit puzzling at first, but it's actually pretty straightforward. Practically speaking, this means that if you zoom toggle in, change your settings (zoom level, track view format, etc.), and then toggle out, the next time you engage zoom toggle, you will recall those last-used settings.

More Ways to Work with Selections

Now that you're comfortable with these more flexible ways of zooming, let's take a look at some different ways of making selections.

SETTING THINGS UP

For this section, go to Memory Location #1—Selections. For a refresher on recalling memory locations, take a look at the "More Organization: Memory Locations" section earlier in this chapter.

Making Selections Using the Arrow Keys

In Chapter 3, "Getting Started with Audio," you learned that the boundaries of a selected area are represented in the Ruler area (above the tracks) by a down arrow and an up arrow, representing selection start and end points, respectively. Using the arrow keys on your computer's keyboard is an easy way to make a selection as your session plays.

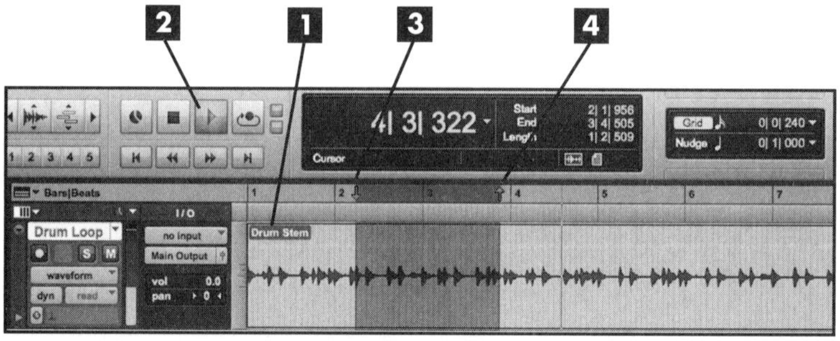

1 **Choose** a **starting point** for playback, making sure that it is *before* the spot where you want your selection to start.

2 **Start playback**. (Remember, you can click the Start button on the transport controls, or you can press the spacebar.)

3 As your session continues playing, **press** the **down arrow key** on your keyboard at the point where you want to begin your selected area.

4 With your session still playing, **press** the **up arrow key** on your keyboard when you want your selection to end.

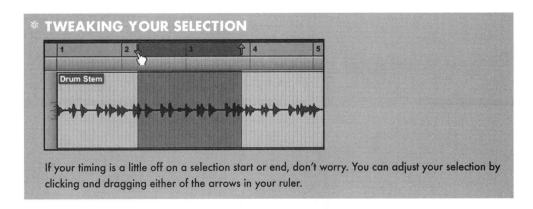

TWEAKING YOUR SELECTION

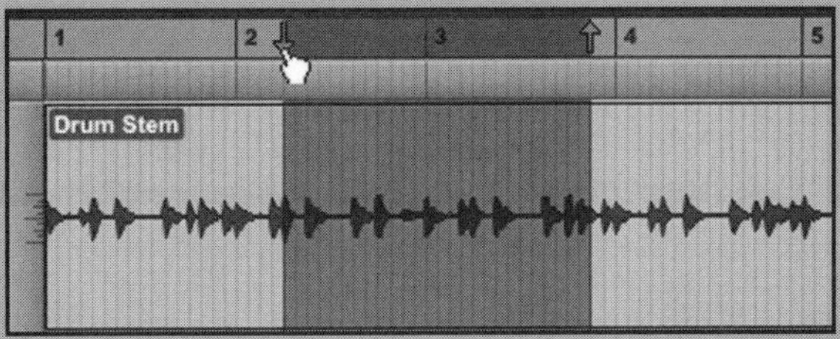

If your timing is a little off on a selection start or end, don't worry. You can adjust your selection by clicking and dragging either of the arrows in your ruler.

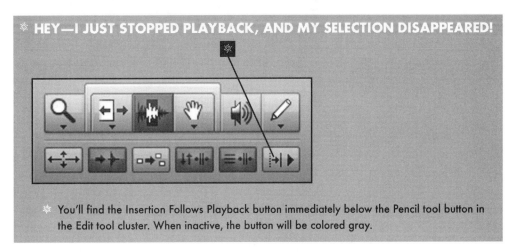

HEY—I JUST STOPPED PLAYBACK, AND MY SELECTION DISAPPEARED!

You'll find the Insertion Follows Playback button immediately below the Pencil tool button in the Edit tool cluster. When inactive, the button will be colored gray.

Making Selections Using the Return Key

You've already learned that pressing the Return key (on a Mac) or the Enter key (on a PC) will send the timeline insertion back to the beginning of the session. Here's a useful variation, which will enable you to make a selection from the beginning of your session to a specified point:

1 **Choose** the **Selector tool**.

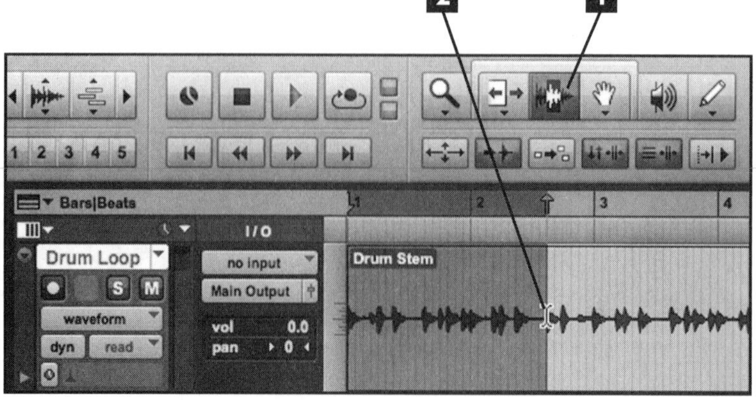

2 **Click** on the **point** on a desired track (or ruler) at which you want your selection to end. A flashing timeline insertion will appear where you clicked. (If you click on a ruler, a flashing timeline will appear on all the shown tracks in your session.)

3 **Press and hold** the **Shift key** and then **press** the **Return key (Mac) or Enter key (PC)**. A selection will be made from the timeline insertion back to the beginning of your session (as shown here).

Here's a variation of the same technique that will enable you to make a selection from a specified point to the *end* of your session.

1 **Click** on the **Selector tool** if it is not already selected.

2 **Click** on the **point** on a desired track at which you want your selection to start.

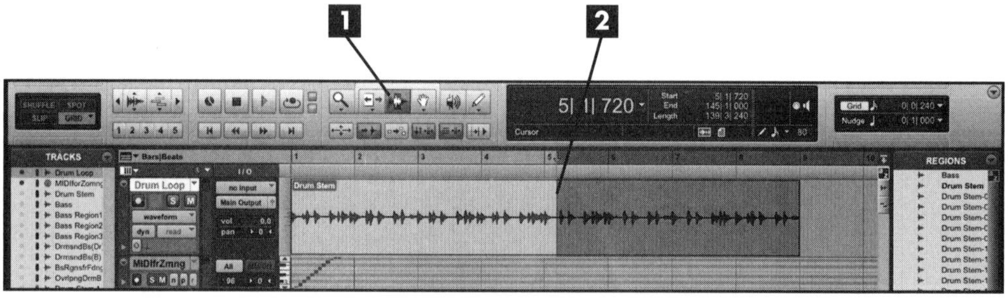

3 **Press and hold Option+Shift (Mac) or Control+Shift (PC)**, and **press** the **Return key (Mac) or Enter key (PC)**. A selection will be made from the timeline insertion the end of your session.

Making Selections Using Tab to Transients

The Tab to Transients feature is a great way to make selections with transient-based audio, particularly for those of us who enjoy chopping up beats into loopable segments.

1 **Click** on the **Tab to Transients tool**. When active, it will be colored blue.

2 **Use** the **Selector tool** to set a timeline insertion a little before the transient with which you want to start your selection.

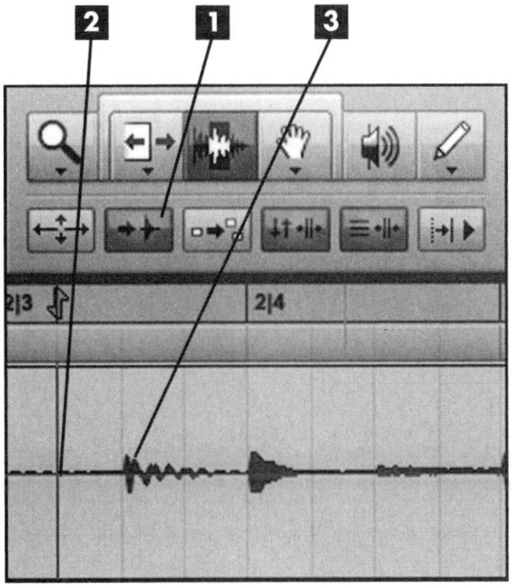

3 Press the **Tab** key once. The timeline insertion will jump to the next transient (where you want to begin your selection).

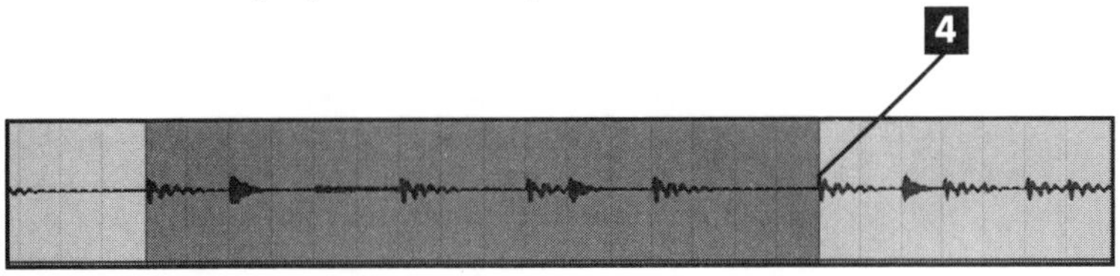

4 **Press and hold** the **Shift key** and **press** the **Tab key**. As you've seen before, the timeline insertion will jump from transient to transient each time you press the Tab key, but the addition of the Shift key will cause a selection to be made in the process.

5 When you reach the end of your desired selection, **stop pressing** the **Tab key**. You've now made a selection based upon Pro Tools' analysis of the transients, which can help you find the right start and end points quickly and accurately!

Timeline Insertion Follows Playback

Consider this scenario: You've selected a nice, loopable selection. You wisely put yourself into Loop Playback mode to hear your selection in the proper context. Sounds great, doesn't it? Then you click Stop, and the selection goes away! Is this a bug within Pro Tools? Nope—it's the effect of a mode of operation called Timeline Insertion Follows Playback, which you can set in the software in a number of ways. You can either enable or disable this mode to fit your circumstance, but it's important to understand how it works so you'll know when to use it and when not to!

One of the ways to enable or disable this mode of operation is from the Preferences window. You've opened the Preferences window before, so let's take a look at that method first.

1 **Click** on the **Setup menu**.

2 **Click** on **Preferences**. The Pro Tools Preferences window will open.

You'll find the preference you're looking for in the Transport section, located in the upper-left corner of the Operation tab.

3 **Click** on the **Operation tab**.

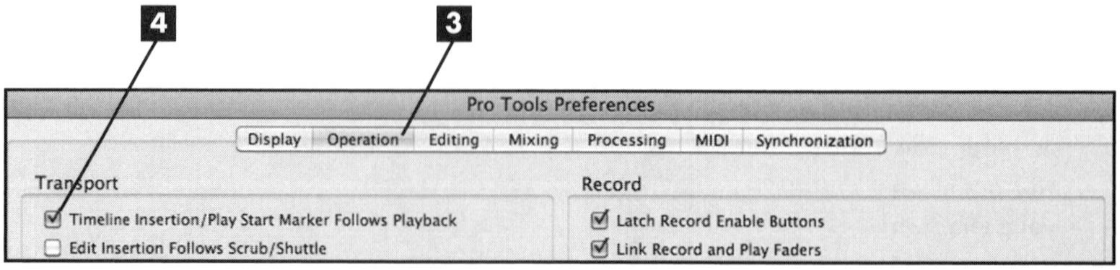

4 **Select or deselect** the **Timeline Insertion/Play Start Marker Follows Playback checkbox**. Here's what the options mean:

- **Checked (enabled).** Playback will begin wherever the timeline insertion is set. When playback is stopped, the timeline insertion will jump to the point where playback ended. When you start again, playback will pick up where you left off. If you have a selected area in your timeline, that selection will be lost when you click Stop.
- **Unchecked (disabled).** Playback will begin wherever the timeline insertion is set. When playback stops in this mode, the timeline insertion will stay where it was originally set. When you start playback again, it will start from this original position. If you have a selected area in your timeline, that selection will be maintained when you click Stop, making this the ideal mode for editing loopable selections.

Prior to Pro Tools 8, there was no way to visually check to see whether Timeline Insertion/Play Start Marker Follows Playback was enabled or disabled—until you stopped playback and observed Pro Tools' behavior. Now, we not only have a visual cue to find out the mode we're working in, but we have a quick and easy way to enable or disable this feature.

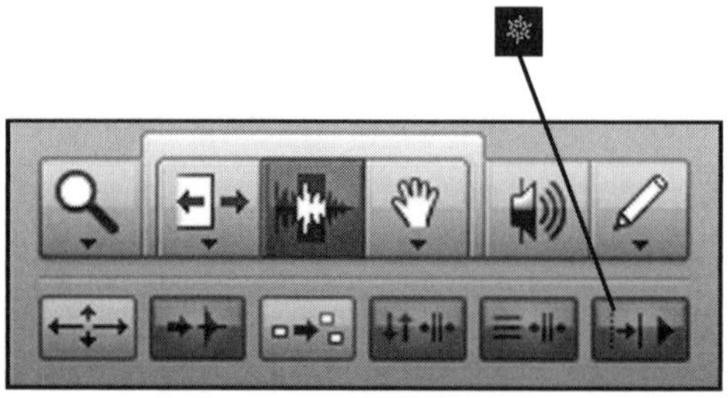

- You'll find the Insertion Follows Playback button immediately below the Pencil tool. When the mode is active, the button will be colored blue. You can toggle the mode on and off simply by clicking the button.

Separate Regions Options

Once you've made a selection within a region, you can separate your regions based upon that selection, as you've done already in Chapter 5. Let's take a quick look at two more new ways to use your selected area to separate your region.

SETTING THINGS UP

For the purposes of this example, select the entire Drum Stem region shown in Memory Location #1—Selections.

Separate Region on Grid

As the name might suggest, Separate Region on Grid will chop up your region on every grid point. In the case of the tutorial session, our grid value is 16th notes, so this will create new regions in 16th-note increments.

1. **Click** on the **Edit menu**.
2. **Click** on **Separate Region**. The Separate Region submenu will appear.
3. **Click** on the **On Grid menu item**. The Pre-Separate Amount dialog box will open.

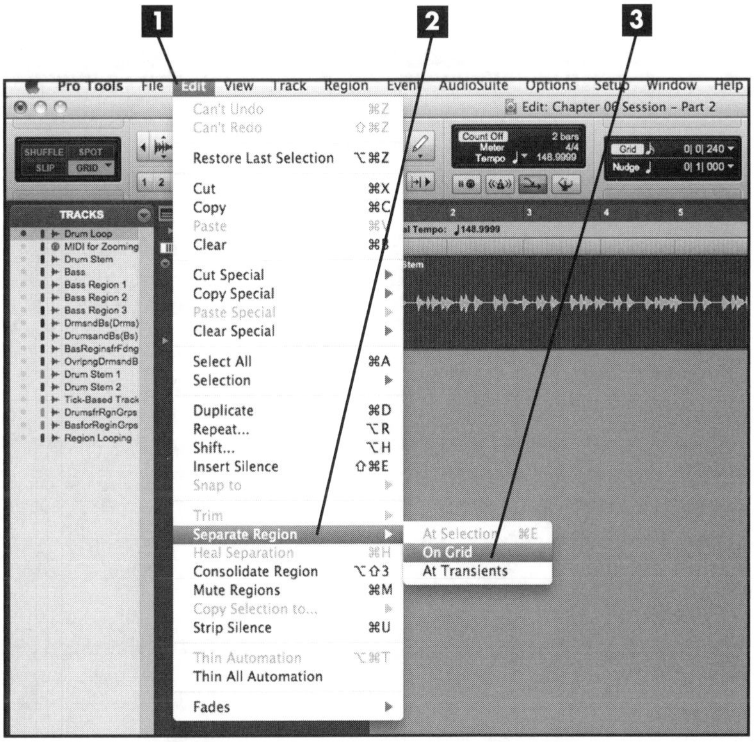

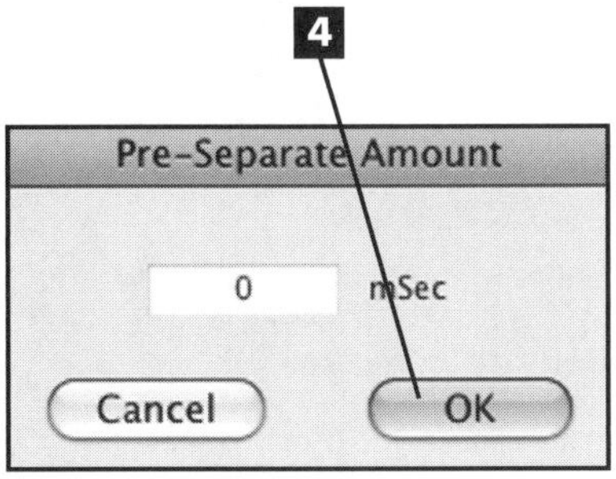

4. Setting any value above zero in the Pre-Separate Amount dialog box will shift the created region boundaries earlier. The greater the value, the farther ahead of the grid the separations will be. To separate regions exactly on the grid lines, **choose 0**. When you're finished, **click OK**.

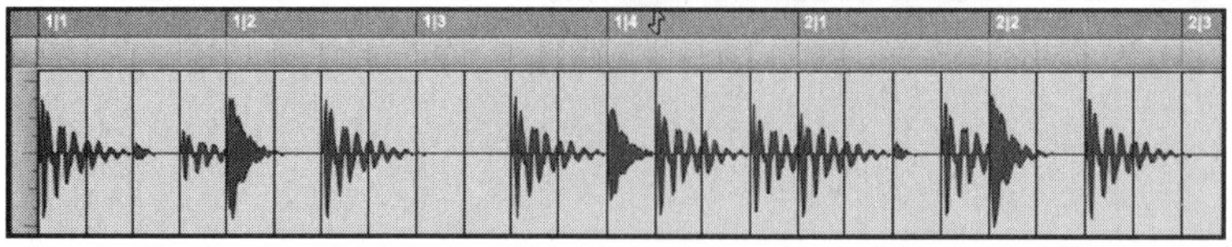

The result is immediate: Your region will be separated regularly according to the grid value you have and any Pre-Separate amount you've entered. If you look at your Regions list, you'll see that you've created new regions as well (in the case of the tutorial session, *lots* of them).

Separate Region at Transients

A variation on the theme, this is a handy little feature that creates a new region boundary at each detected transient. Take a look.

SETTING THINGS UP

If you're going through this chapter and have just separated the Drum Stem region on the grid, please undo that separation before proceeding.

1. **Click** on the **Edit menu.**
2. **Click** on **Separate Region**. The Separate Region submenu will appear.
3. **Click** on the **At Transients menu item**. The Pre-Separate Amount dialog box will open.

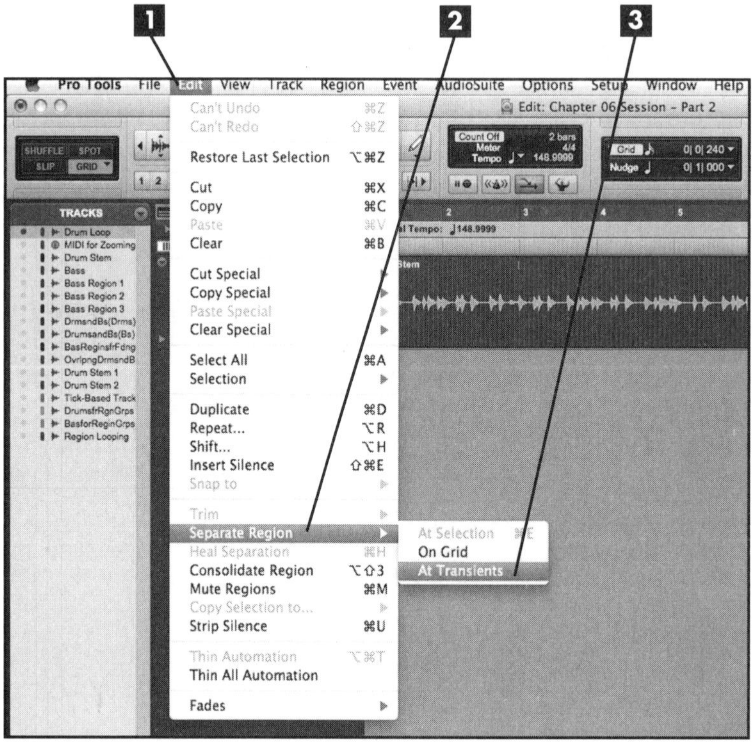

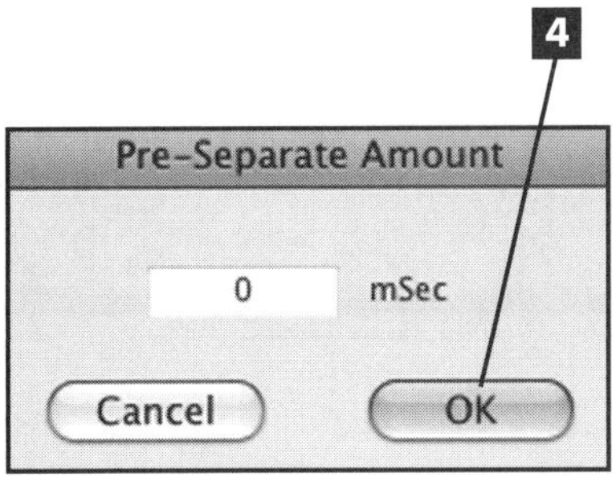

4 Setting any value above zero in the Pre-Separate Amount dialog box will shift the created region boundaries earlier. The greater the value, the farther ahead of each transient the separations will be. To separate regions exactly at the beginning of each transient, **choose 0**. When you're finished, **click OK**.

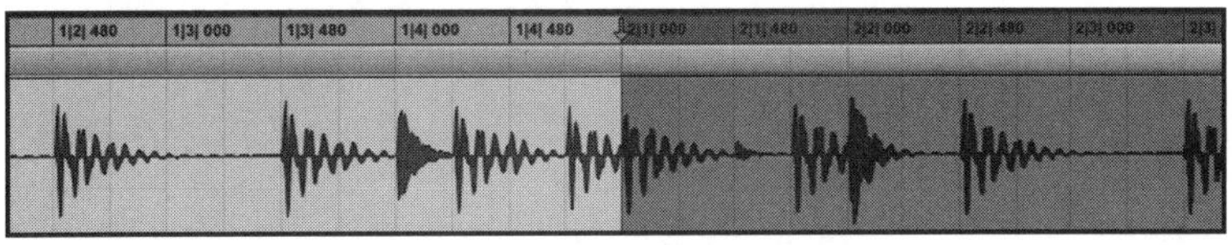

Again, you'll see your region immediately separated into a number of regions. Each new region will be represented in the Regions list, but the placement of the region boundaries will be a little different from when you separated at each grid line. This time, you'll see that your region has been separated at each transient (just ahead of the transient if you entered a Pre-Separate amount).

Navigating and Auditioning a Selection

Usually, when making a selection, the most important parts to get right are the beginning and the end. You'll listen to the boundaries of your selections many times, just to make sure you have everything you want and nothing you don't.

> **SETTING THINGS UP**
>
> For this section, go to the second memory location of the tutorial session, named Navigating a Selection.

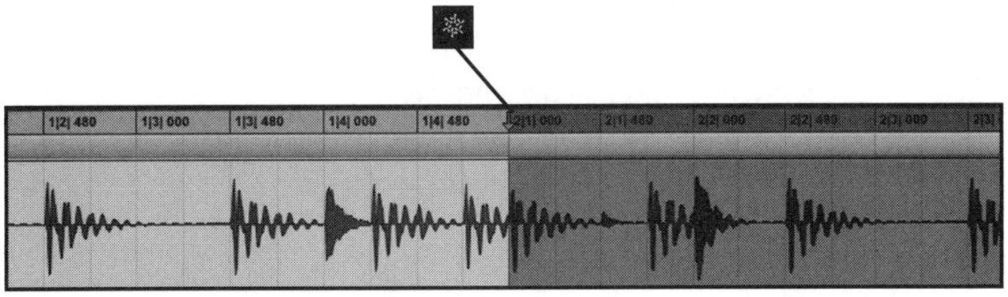

- Press the left arrow key. The Edit window's focus will move to the beginning of the selection, as shown in this image.

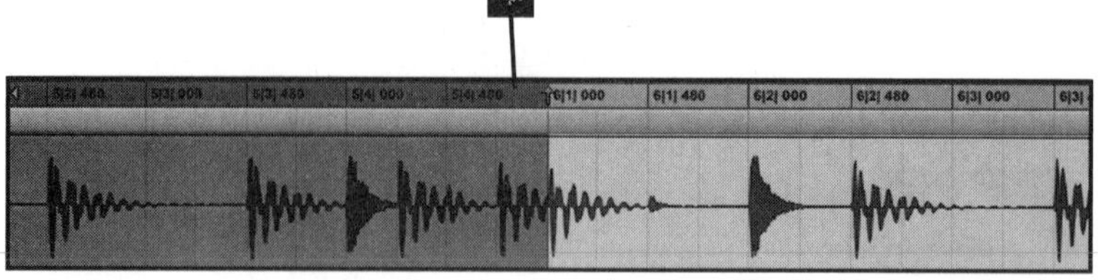

- Press the right arrow key. The Edit window's focus will move to the end of the selection and center that boundary in your Edit window.

The next shortcuts depend upon the value entered for your pre-roll and post-roll:

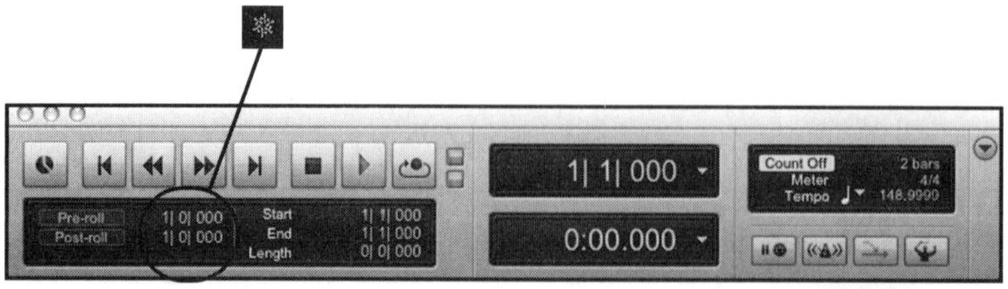

- As you learned in Chapter 4, "Recording Audio," you can set the values for both of these by typing the desired number in the appropriate fields in the lower-left corner of the Transport window. You don't have to enable pre-roll or post-roll—just set a value.

Now it's time to audition the boundaries of your selection.

- Press and hold the Option key (Mac) or the Alt key (PC) and press the left arrow key. Your audio will play up to the beginning of your selection by the pre-roll amount. Because the pre-roll amount is set as one measure in this image, playback will start one measure before the beginning of the selection and stop when the selection begins.
- Press and hold the Option key (Mac) or the Alt key (PC) and press the right arrow key. Your audio will play up to the end of your selection by the pre-roll amount.
- Press and hold the Command key (Mac) or the Ctrl key (PC) and press the left arrow key. Your audio will play from the beginning of your selection by the post-roll amount.
- Press and hold the Command key (Mac) or the Ctrl key (PC) and press the right arrow key. Your audio will play from the end of your selection by the post-roll amount.

Beyond the Basics

You've already worked with the basic editing tools, and things such as trimming, selecting, and grabbing are starting to become familiar by now. Some of these tools have secondary layers to them, giving them added functionality. And then there's the Smart tool...

The TCE Trimmer Tool

First on the list is the Time Compress/Expand (TCE) Trimmer tool. This useful variation of the Standard Trimmer tool enables you to stretch or compress the duration of an audio region without changing the pitch!

SETTING THINGS UP

To follow with this demonstration, go to Memory Location #3—TCE Trimmer Tool.

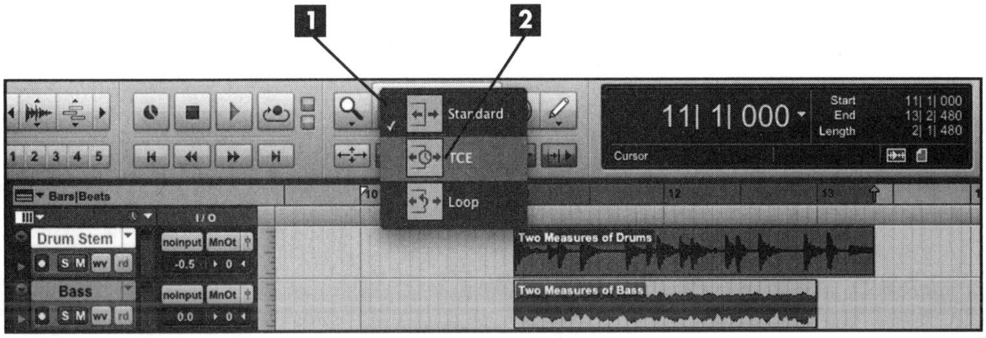

1 **Click and hold** the **Trimmer tool button** until the Trimmer tool pop-up menu appears. The currently selected version of the Trimmer tool will be indicated by a checkmark.

2 **Move your cursor** to **TCE**, and **release** the mouse button to change to the TCE Trimmer tool. The icon for the Trimmer tool will change to reflect the currently active version of the tool.

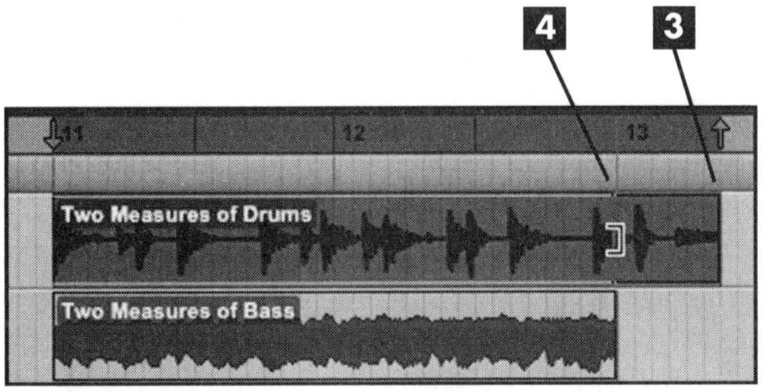

3 **Click and hold** the **boundary** that you want to adjust. In this example, I want to time-compress the *end* of the upper region so that it matches the bottom one, so I'm clicking on its right boundary.

4 **Drag** the **boundary** left or right, just as if you were using the Standard Trimmer tool. When you release the mouse button, a new audio region will be created with a different duration from the original region, but with its pitch unchanged.

TRIMMER TOOL TIP

The TCE Trimmer tool is really useful in Grid mode. Suppose you've imported a drum loop that doesn't match the tempo of the rest of your session. Just make sure your grids are a musical unit (such as quarter notes, for example) and use the TCE Trimmer tool. The edges of the region will snap to the nearest grid point when released, and you'll be perfectly in tempo!

The Object Grabber Tool

Up to this point, you've used the Grabber tool to move a block of time (and all the regions that are contained within that block)—hence the tool's proper name, Time Grabber. But what if you want to select more than one region without selecting all the regions between them? That's where the Object Grabber tool comes into play!

> **SETTING THINGS UP**
>
> For this section, go to Memory Location #4—Grabbers.

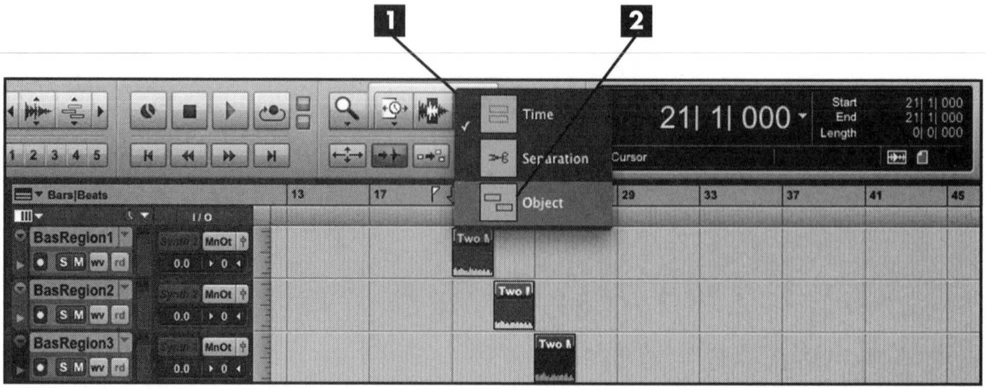

1 **Click and hold** the **Grabber tool button** until the Grabber tool pop-up menu appears. The currently selected version of the Grabber tool will be indicated by a checkmark.

2 **Move your cursor** to **Object**, and **release** the mouse button to change to the Object Grabber tool. The icon for the Grabber tool will change to reflect the currently active version of the tool.

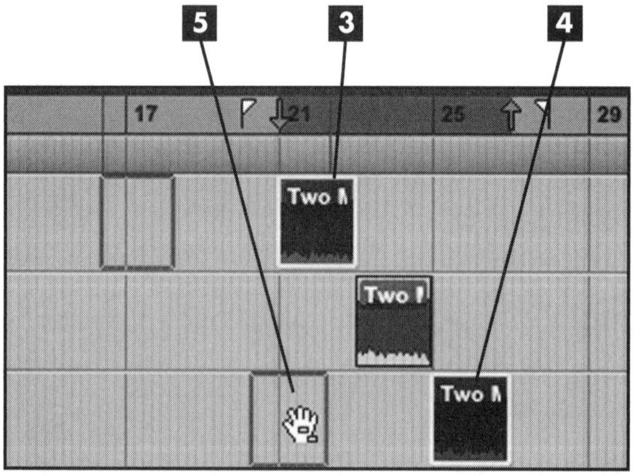

3 **Click** the first **region** that you want to move. You'll note that when you're using the Object Grabber, the region isn't highlighted, but rather a gold border is displayed around the edge of the region.

4 **Hold** the **Shift key** and **click** additional **regions** that you want to move. Note that only the regions (objects) you click are selected, and not a rectangular block of time between them (as would be the case if you were using the Time Grabber tool).

5 **Drag and drop** the **regions** you want to move to the desired location. As you drag, you'll see an outline indicating where the regions would be placed if you were to release your mouse button.

The Separation Grabber Tool

Either the Time Grabber or the Object Grabber tool will enable you to move regions around in your session, albeit in different ways. The Separation Grabber tool goes a step further, allowing you to take a selection from within a single region and move just that selected area. This is a cool trick (and a real timesaver as well), but there are a few steps in using this tool most effectively.

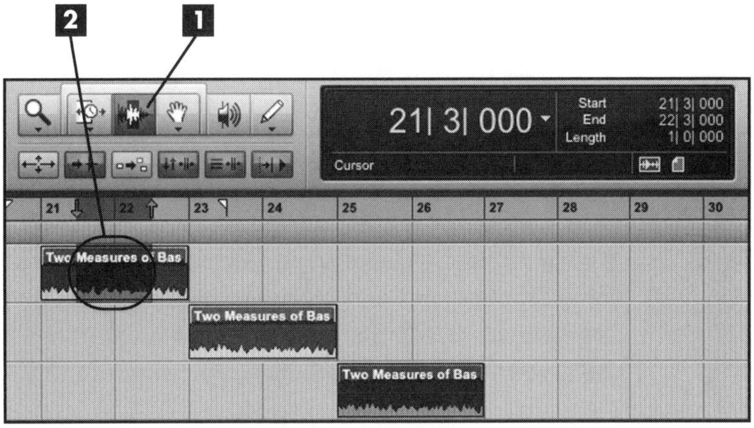

1 **Click** on the **Selector tool**. (Have faith—we're going somewhere with this.)

2 **Select** the **section** of a region that you want to separate and move.

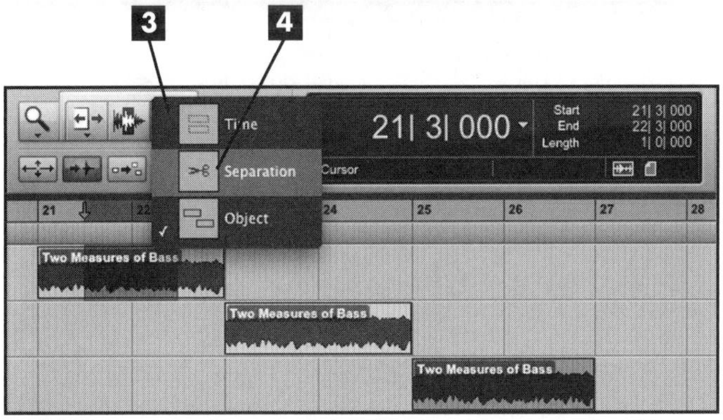

3 **Click and hold** the **Grabber tool button** until the Grabber tool Options menu appears. The currently selected version of the Grabber tool will be indicated with a checkmark.

4 **Move your cursor** to **Separation**, and **release** the mouse button to change to the Separation Grabber tool. The icon for the Grabber tool will change to reflect the currently active version of the tool.

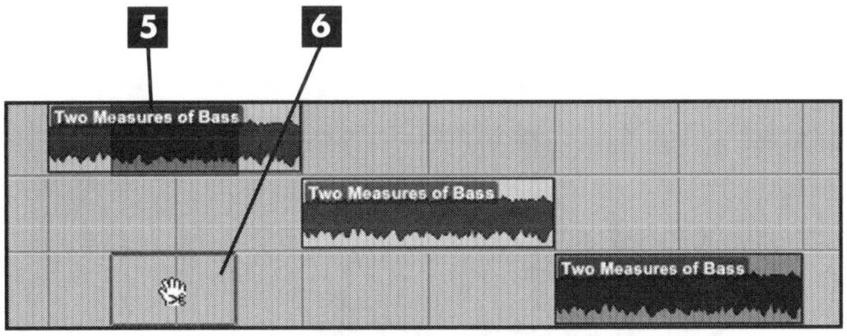

5 With the Separation Grabber tool selected, **click and hold anywhere** in the selected area.

6 **Drag and drop** the **selection** to the desired destination. As you've seen with other variations of the Grabber tool, you'll see an outline indicating where the selected area will be placed when you release your mouse button.

The selection will be removed from the original region and will become its own region, represented on the track and in the Regions list.

A TWIST ON THE SEPARATION GRABBER

If you want to drag out a selection of a region but leave your source region unchanged, hold down the Option key (Mac) or the Alt key (PC) as you drag.

The Smart Tool

The Smart tool is a real timesaver, combining the editing power of the Trim, Selector, and Grabber tools and adding some extra functionality for good measure. It might take you a while to get used to using the Smart tool, but once you have it under your belt, you'll be able to work more efficiently.

SETTING THINGS UP

For this section, go to Memory Location #5—Smart Tool.

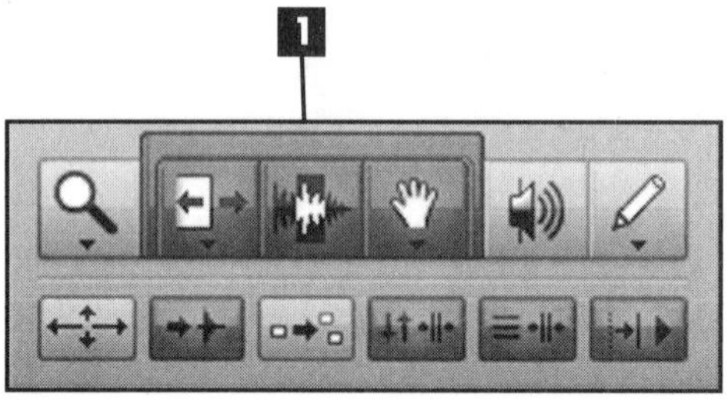

1 **Click** on the **Smart Tool bracket**, which arches over the Trim, Selector, and Grabber tool buttons. The button will be highlighted (blue) when the Smart tool is active, as will the three tools below it.

The concept behind using the Smart tool is simple: Your cursor will take on different tool behaviors based upon its location within a track.

When your cursor is in the *upper* half of a track, it will take on the function of the Selector tool.

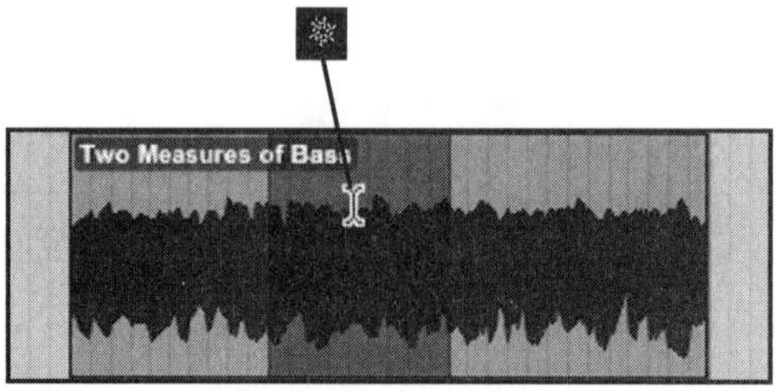

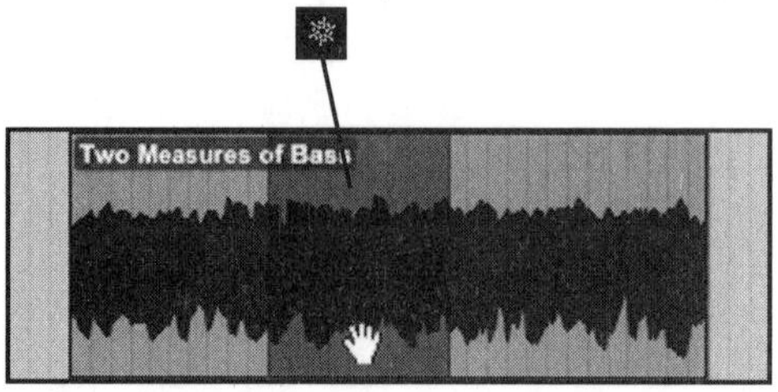

When you move your cursor to the *lower* half of a track, the cursor will take on the behavior of the currently active version of the Grabber tool.

THE SMART TOOL AND THE SEPARATION GRABBER

The Smart tool works particularly well when you have the Separation Grabber tool selected. Just move your cursor to the top half of a track to make your selection, and then move your cursor to the bottom half of the track to drag the selection to its new location. Easy!

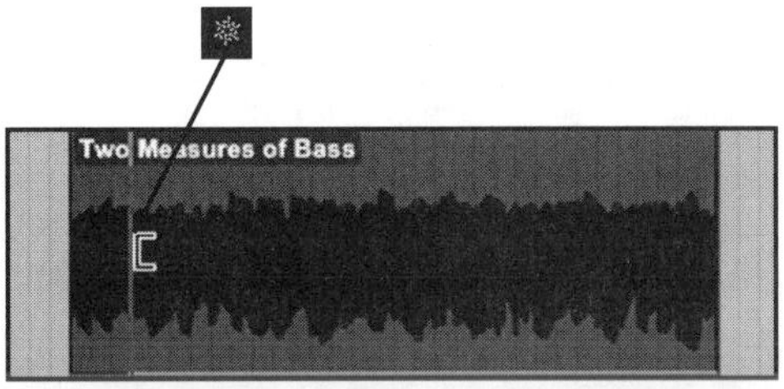

- When you move your cursor to either end of a region, the cursor will change its function to that of the currently active version of the Trimmer tool.

MORE SMART TOOL FEATURES

You might have discovered that if you move your cursor to the corner of a region, it takes on a different function, beyond that of the Trim, Selector, or Grabber tool. Be patient—we'll get to that in a couple of pages!

THE SMART TOOL AND TRACK HEIGHTS

Because the position of the cursor within a track is so critical when you're using the Smart tool, shorter track heights can be a little tricky to work with at first. As you get used to using the Smart tool, medium track height (or greater) is a good way to practice.

Edit Groups

Hopefully, you've found the edit tools you've explored to be powerful and easy to use. Now let's boost your effectiveness by enabling you to edit a number of tracks at the same time. To do this, we'll create an edit group.

SETTING THINGS UP

For a simple run-through of how to use an edit group, go to Memory Location #6—Edit Groups.

GROUPS AND MIXING

You'll notice that there are some features we'll pass over in this section. Not to worry—these are features more relevant to the process of mixing, so we'll cover them in Chapter 8, "Basic Mixing."

1 **Click** the **Groups list menu button** (which is in the upper-right corner of the Groups list in your Edit window). A menu will appear.

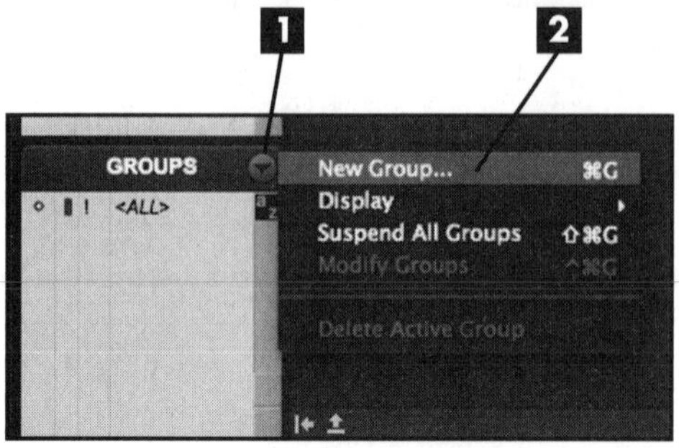

2 **Choose** the **New Group menu item**. The Create Group dialog box will open.

3 **Type** a descriptive **name** for your group in the Name text box at the top of the Create Group dialog box.

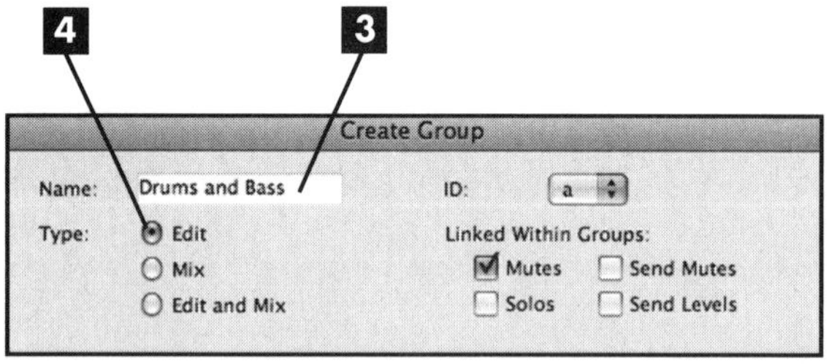

4 You can choose to have your selected tracks available as an edit group (active only in the Edit window), as a mix group (active only in the Mix window), or as an edit and mix group (active in both windows). In this case, we'll only be using these tracks as an editing exercise, so **choose Edit** in the Type section.

5 Initially, any currently selected tracks will be placed in the Currently in Group area, but that doesn't mean you have to select the tracks you want to group before creating the group. If you want to add more tracks to your group, just **select** the desired **tracks** in the Available area and then **click** the **Add button**. Conversely, if you want to remove a track from the group, just **select** the **track** in the Currently in Group area and then **click** the **Remove button**.

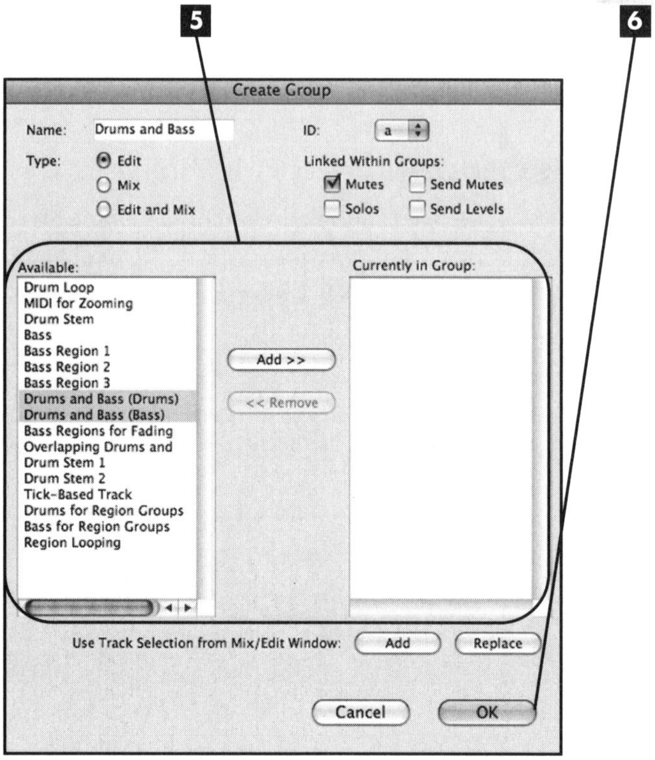

FOLLOWING ALONG?

If you're following the steps with the book's tutorial session, make sure the Drums and Bass (Drums) and Drums and Bass (Bass) tracks are the only tracks shown in the Currently in Group area.

A TRADITIONAL TECHNIQUE

In some previous versions of Pro Tools, group membership was solely determined by the tracks that were selected *prior* to creating a new group. Once the Create Group dialog box was open, group membership couldn't be changed. Even now, the Currently in Group area defaults to containing the currently selected tracks. As a result, many long-time users of Pro Tools make it a point to select the tracks they want to use in their group *before* creating the group, often saving themselves a few steps in the process.

USE TRACK SELECTION

Just below the track-selection area of the Create Group dialog box, you'll see two Use Track Selection from Mix/Edit Window buttons. Clicking the Add button will add the currently selected tracks to any tracks already in the Currently in Group area. Clicking the Replace button will clear the Currently in Group area and populate it with the currently selected tracks only. These two buttons can come in handy not only when you're creating a new group, but also when you're modifying a group that you've previously created. To modify an existing group, just choose Modify Groups from the Groups list pop-up button, or right-click the group you want to change.

6 **Click** the **OK button**. The dialog box will close.

- Your new edit group has been added to the Edit Groups list. By default, a newly created group is immediately made active, indicated by a gray highlight around the group name. To make the group inactive, just click the group name to un-highlight it.

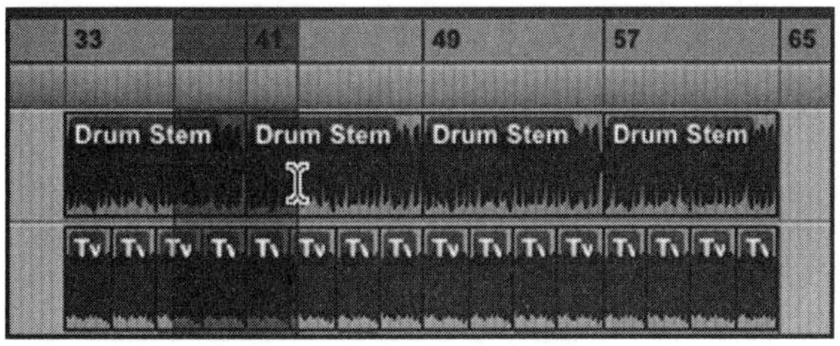

When you apply any edit tool to a member of an active edit group, you'll see that the effect of the tool is mirrored on all members of that group. This is particularly handy when you are assembling or tweaking tracks together (commonly done for drum kits, string or horn sections, and multiple vocal tracks). Shown here, I've made a selection on one of the tracks in a group, and that selection is mirrored on all members of this active edit group (named Drums and Bass).

Creating and Customizing Fades

Fade-ins and fade-outs are used to gradually transition into or out of a region. Additionally, you can create *crossfades* between regions to make a smooth transition from one region into another. Of course, this is nothing new in the world of DAWs, but Pro Tools makes fades easy to create and tweak. You can even use the Smart tool to create them!

SETTING THINGS UP

For our discussion of fades, go to Memory Location #7—Fades.

Creating a Fade-In

Everybody has heard fade-ins used on a mix, such as when a song starts from a silent beginning and gradually gets louder until it reaches its running volume. In Pro Tools, however, you can create a fade-in for an individual region *within* a mix. Here's how:

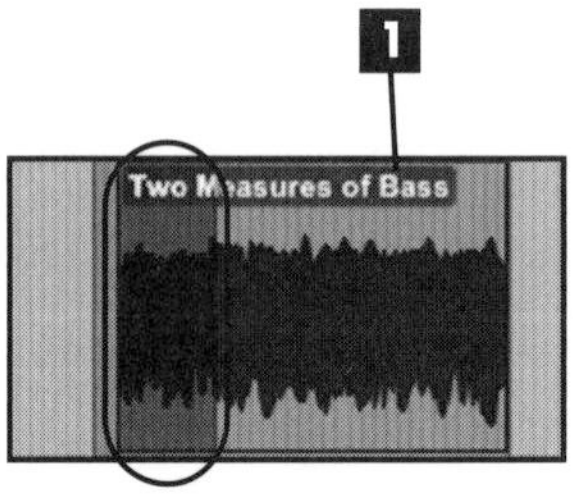

1 Using the Selector tool (or the Selector mode of the Smart tool), **select** the **area of a region** that you want to turn into a fade-in.

ABOUT YOUR SELECTION

It's important to make sure your selection starts *at* or *before* the region begins, and that it ends where you want the fade-in to end.

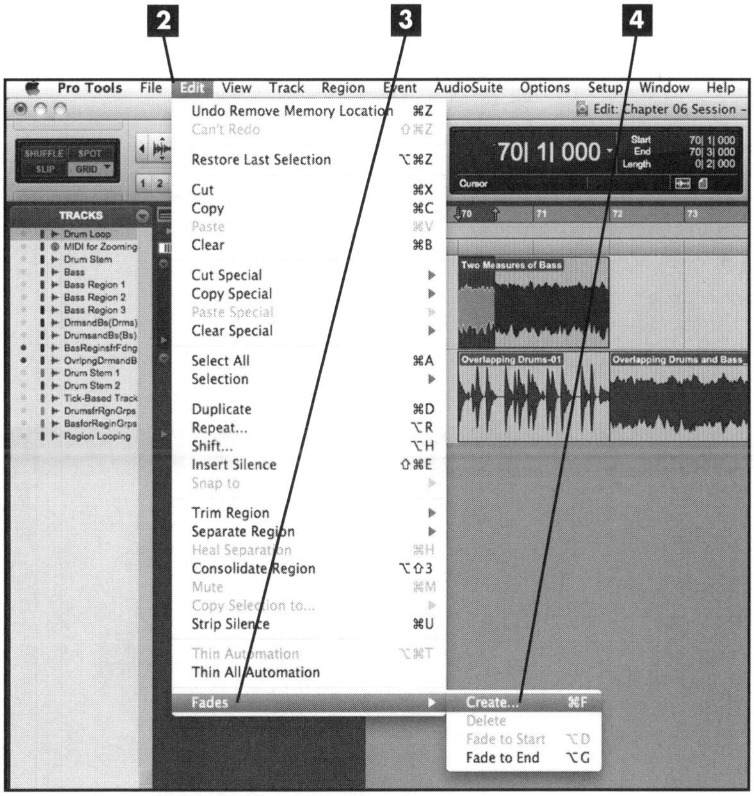

2 **Click** on the **Edit menu.**

3 **Click** on **Fades**. The Fades submenu will appear.

4 **Click** on **Create**. The Fades dialog box will open.

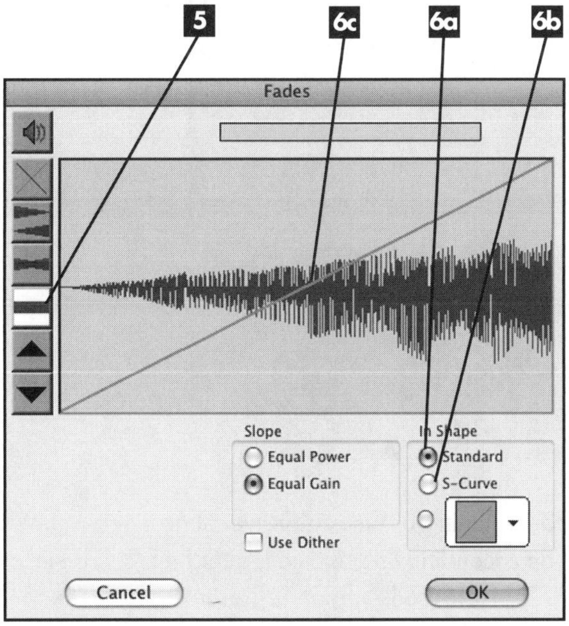

5 **Click** on the **Waveform Display button** to show a graphic view of the audio you will be fading in.

The next step is to choose the contour (often referred to as the *curve*) of the fade you will be creating. There are a number of ways to get the shape you want.

6a **Click** on the **Standard option button** in the In Shape section to select a basic exponential or logarithmic curve for the new fade.

OR

6b **Click** on the **S-Curve option button** in the In Shape section to select an S curve for the new fade.

6c Once you've chosen either the Standard or S-Curve option button, **click** on the **fade curve** and **drag horizontally** with your mouse to change its shape.

OR

6d **Click** on the **Preset Curve option button** to use a standard fade curve.

6e **Click** on the **Preset Curve Selection down arrow**. A menu of fade-in curve presets will appear.

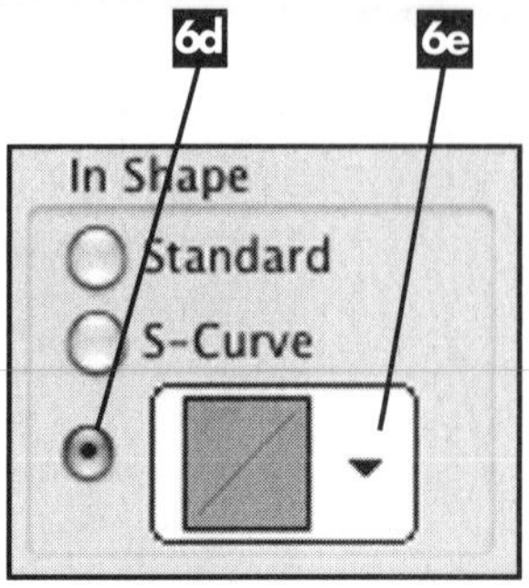

6f **Click** on the desired **fade-in curve preset** from the menu.

7 Once you have the fade curve you want, **click** on **OK**. The Fades dialog box will close.

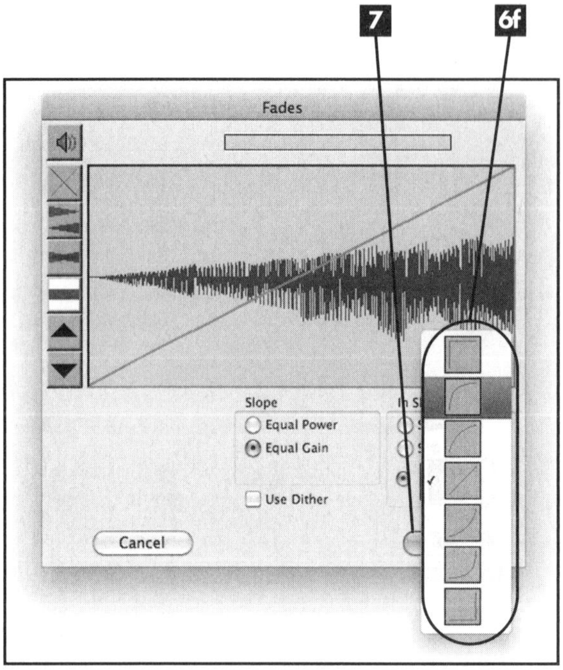

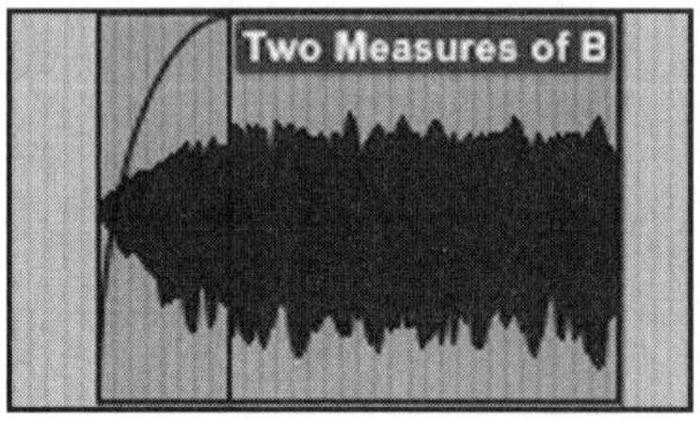

At the beginning of the region, you'll now see a new fade region. This region is shown with an ascending line, indicating that it is a fade-in, as well as indicating the curve of the fade-in. This fade region represents a fade file located in the Fade Files subfolder on your hard drive. Although this is certainly a region and an audio file, it will not be displayed in the Regions list.

AUDITIONING FADES

Often, when creating a fade, it's useful to preview the sound of the fade *before* you've created it. In the Fades dialog box, you'll see a small button in the upper-left corner (shown here) that will do just that. Click the button to hear the effect of the fade curve on the audio region. You won't hear any other tracks in your session—just the fade that you're creating.

Creating a Fade-Out

After you've created a fade-in, creating a fade-out will be easy. As you might expect, it's essentially a mirror image of the fade-in process.

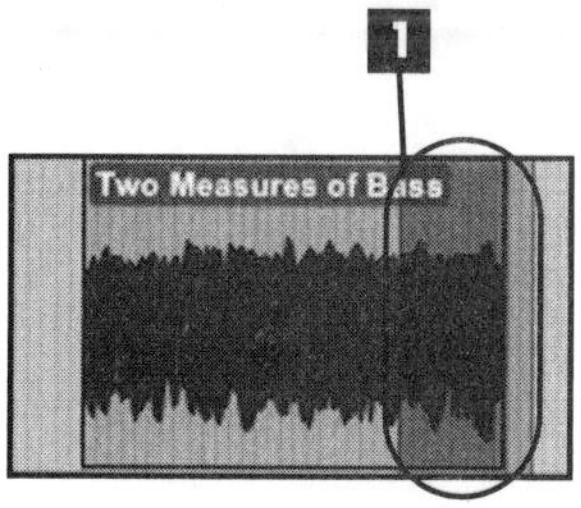

1. **Select** the **area of a region** that you want to become a fade-out. Make sure your selection starts at the point that you want your fade-out to begin and ends *at* or *after* the region boundary.

   The next steps are identical to the ones you took in creating a fade-in:

2. **Click** on the **Edit menu**.
3. **Click** on **Fades**. The Fades submenu will appear.
4. **Click** on **Create**. The Fades dialog box will open.

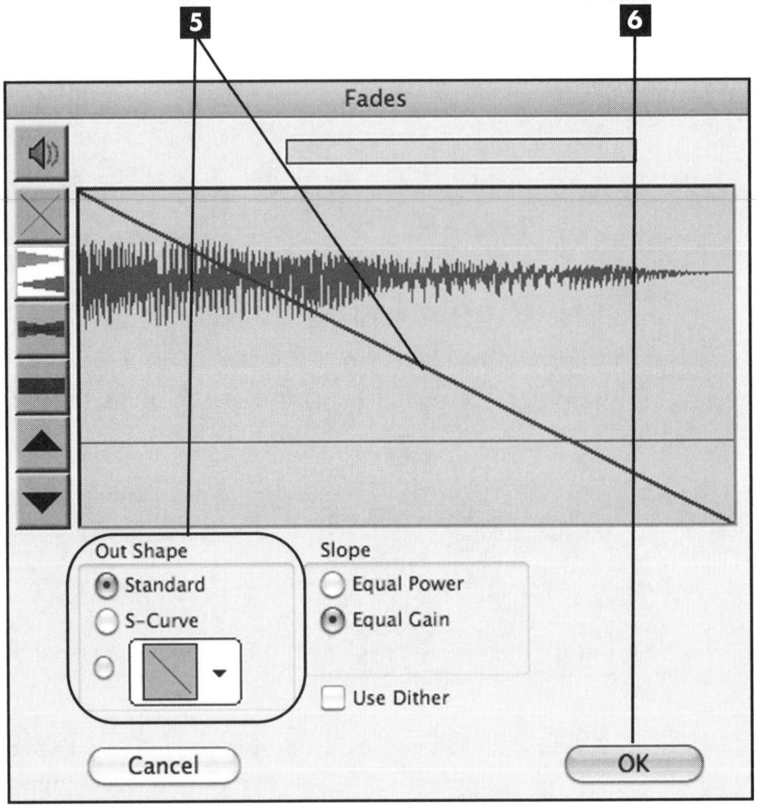

5 **Use** the **shaping options** of the Fades dialog box to customize your fade-out curve, just as you did when you created your fade-in. The tools operate in the same way, just in the opposite direction!

6 **Click** the **OK button** when you're finished. The Fades dialog box will close.

FADE-IN OR FADE-OUT?

Here's something to be careful about when creating fades: If you don't select to the end (or beginning) of a region, Pro Tools will get confused about what you want to do. Even if you go to the Edit menu and select Fades, the Create option will be grayed out and unavailable.

Crossfades

For readers who are unfamiliar with the term *crossfade*, it's a simultaneous fading out of one sound while another sound fades in, creating a smooth transition from one sound to the other. Here's how to create a crossfade between two overlapping regions.

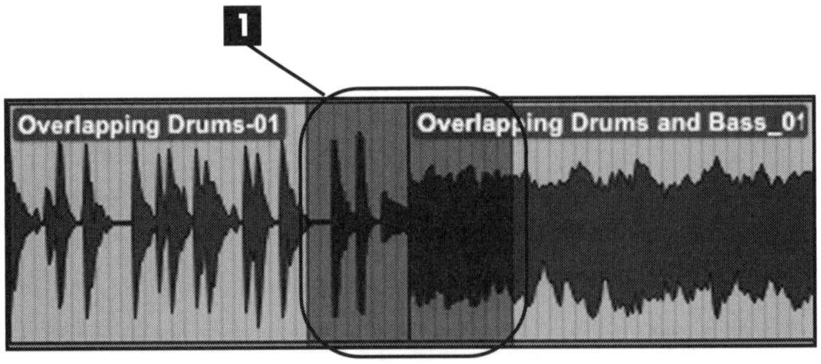

1 **Select** an **area** of two overlapping regions that you want to become a crossfade. (If you're following the tutorial session, I've created a track of alternating bass and drum regions so that you can easily hear the transition from one region to another.)

Once more, the next steps you'll take to create a crossfade are the same that you took to create a fade-in or fade-out:

2 **Click** on the **Edit menu**.

3 **Click** on **Fades**. The Fades submenu will appear.

4 **Click** on **Create**. The Fades dialog box will open.

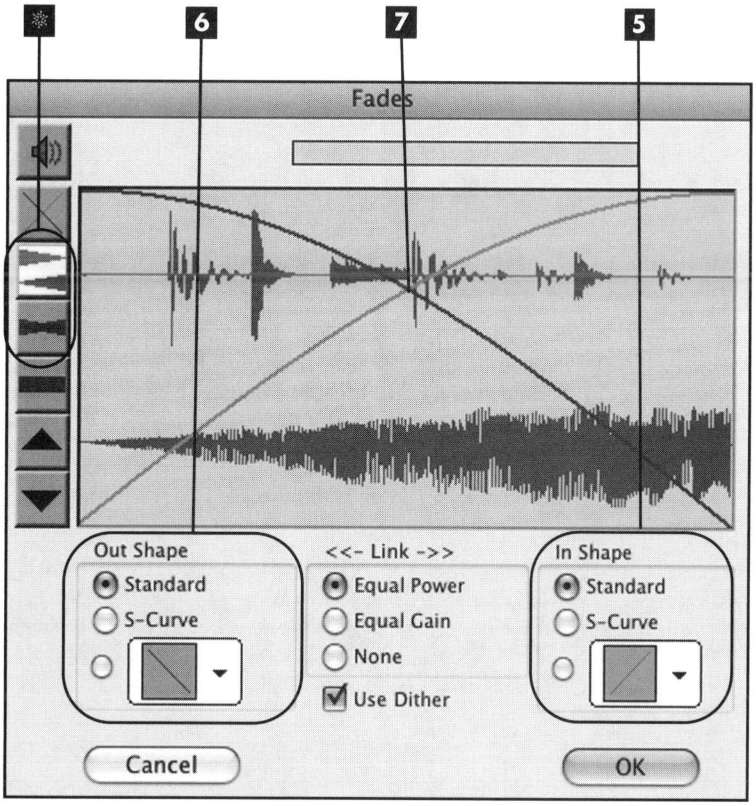

When dealing with crossfades, you have a number of different display options. The 2nd and 3rd Waveform Display buttons are commonly used for this sort of work.

5 **Set up** the **fade-in portion** of your crossfade the same way you would a standalone fade-in.

6 **Set up** the **fade-out portion** of the crossfade the same way you would a standalone fade-out.

7 **Drag** the **crossing point** of your crossfade earlier or later, depending on your preference for this particular crossfade.

You'll notice that the fade-in and fade-out curves are linked. Changes made to either curve will affect the other. Let's take a look at the different fade-linking options. (Let your ears be your guide as to which is the best in any given situation.)

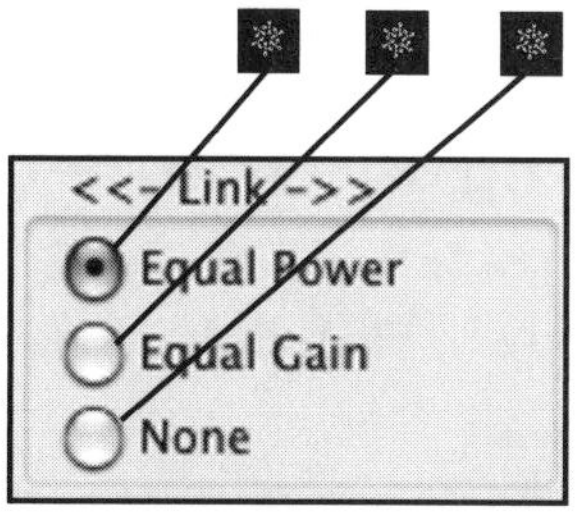

- **Equal Power.** This linking option will compensate for the volume drop that can sometimes occur when significantly different waveforms are combined, and it is usually heard as a smooth transition between dissimilar regions.
- **Equal Gain.** When you select this as a linking option, the midpoint of the crossfade will not be boosted in any way. When you are crossfading identical or very similar audio, this linking will often give you the desired smooth transition from region to region.
- **None.** This will enable you to change one half of a crossfade without changing the other half. Although it's the least commonly used of all the linking options, it will give you a degree of flexibility that the other linking options don't provide. Let's take a look at how to use this linking option.

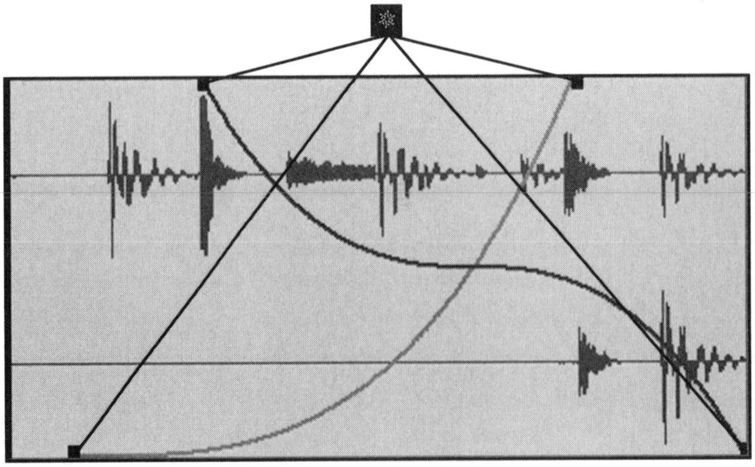

- With linking set to None, you have the ability to move the beginning or end of either curve independently. Just click on the small black handle at the beginning or end of a fade curve and drag it to the desired position. These handles are small and can be a little difficult to click on with your mouse, but once you do get them, you'll be able to drag and drop them anywhere you want, with all other aspects of the crossfade remaining unchanged.

THE ADVANTAGE OF "NONE" LINKING

Although the None link mode might not be the most commonly used mode of crossfading, it is often the mode of choice if you need a specific nonlinear transition.

DITHER

In the world of digital audio, the concept and application of dither is pretty deep stuff, and tends to stand outside of an introductory book like this one. Put very simply, it's a mathematical formula, which many refer to as a low-level noise that is applied to audio to combat some of the nasty things that can happen with very quiet signals. (Low-level signals are created whenever you create a fade.) You'll learn more about dither in Chapter 9, "Finishing Touches."

Creating Fades Using the Smart Tool

In addition to the triple benefit of Trim, Select, and Grabber tools that you get with the Smart tool, you can also quickly create fade-ins, fade-outs, and even crossfades!

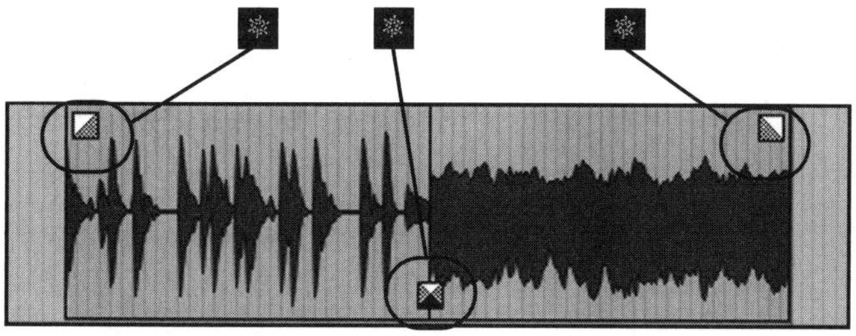

- **Fade-in.** If you move your cursor to the upper-left corner of an audio region, the cursor will change to a small square with an ascending diagonal line through it (looking something like a fade-in region). Just click and drag your cursor to the right to quickly create a fade-in region. Release the mouse button at the point where you want your fade-in to end, and the region will be created.
- **Fade-out.** If you move your cursor to the upper-right corner of a region, the cursor will change to a small square with a descending diagonal line through it. Just click and drag your cursor to the left to quickly create a fade-out region. Release the mouse button at the point where you want your fade-out to begin.
- **Crossfade.** If you move your cursor to the bottom corners of two adjacent or overlapping regions, the cursor will change to a small square with two diagonal lines through it (looking like a crossfade region). Just click and drag your cursor to the left or right to quickly create a crossfade region. Release the mouse button at the point where you want your crossfade to begin or end. Your crossfade will be created and centered on the regions' boundaries.

You'll notice that when you create a fade or crossfade using the Smart tool, the Fades dialog box does not appear. The shape of the fade is automatically determined by the default fade setting. Customizing this default is easy to do and will make the Smart tool even more useful. Once more, the Pro Tools Preferences window comes to the rescue!

1. **Click** on the **Setup menu**.
2. **Click** on **Preferences**. The Pro Tools Preferences window will open.

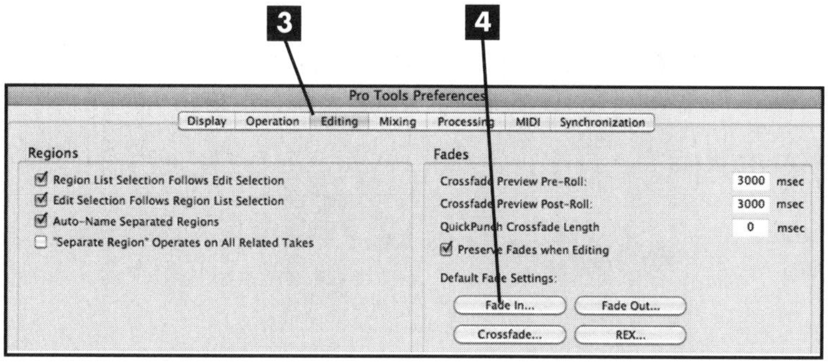

3. **Click** on the **Editing tab** at the top of the Preferences window, if it's not already selected. The editing preferences will be displayed.

The Fades section is located in the upper-right corner of the Editing tab, and it's in this section that you can set up your default fade settings (the ones that the Smart tool will apply when creating a fade or crossfade). The process of setting up default fade settings is identical to the process of creating fades themselves.

4. **Click** on the **Fade In button** to open the (by now familiar) Fades dialog box. From here, you can configure your default fade-in curve. **Click** the **OK button** to close the Fades dialog box.

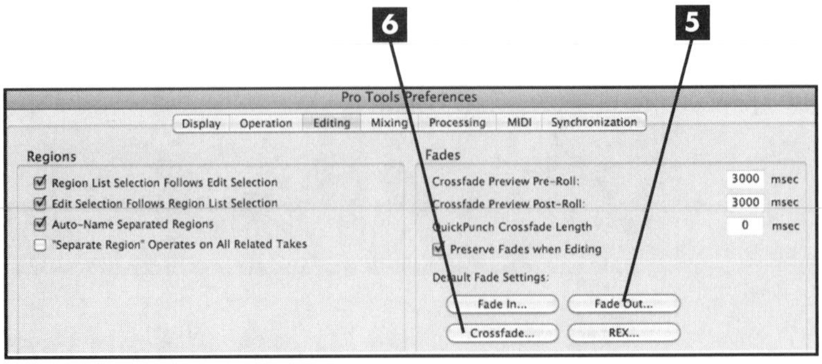

5 **Click** on the **Fade Out button** to open the Fades dialog box again, and **choose** your default **fade-out curve. Click** the **OK button** to close the Fades dialog box.

6 **Click** on the **Crossfade button** to open the Fades dialog box and **set up** your default **crossfade settings**. Once more, **click** the **OK button** to close the Fades dialog box.

7 Once you've set up your default fade settings, just **click** on the **OK button** in the lower-right corner of the Preferences window. Your settings will be saved, and the window will close.

> **CHANGING FADE REGIONS**
>
> If you create a fade in your session, and decide later that you want to change its contour, just double-click on the fade region with the Grabber tool. The Fades dialog box will open again so you can adjust the individual fade. Note that any changes you make in this dialog box will not affect the defaults you've set in the Preferences window. Deleting a fade is even easier; just select the fade region you want to remove (either single-click with the Grabber tool or double-click with the Selector tool) and press the Delete key.

Getting Specific: Nudging Regions

Using the Nudge function, you can move regions (or region boundaries) by incremental amounts, enabling you to get very specific with your timing. First, though, you'll have to choose a nudge value. Setting up your nudge value is nearly identical to setting up your grid resolution (which you learned back in Chapter 5):

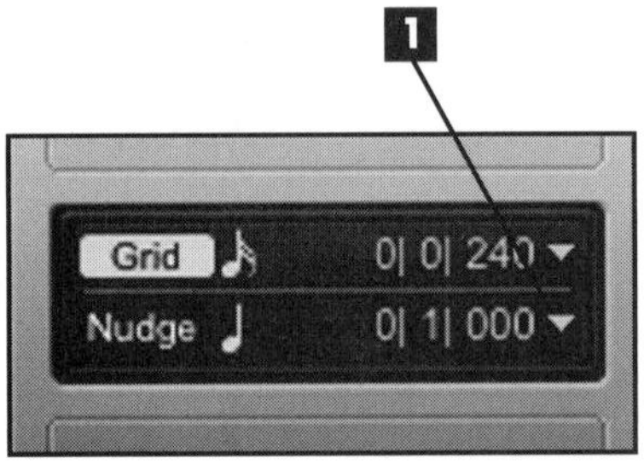

1 **Click** on the **downward-facing triangle** to the right of the nudge value. The Nudge menu will appear.

2 **Select** the **scale** with which you want to nudge your region. The currently chosen scale will be indicated by a checkmark. (In this image, Bars|Beats is chosen, which is well suited for music sessions.) Based upon the scale you choose, the options at the top of the list will change.

3 **Select** the **increment** by which you want to nudge your region. The currently chosen increment will be indicated by a checkmark.

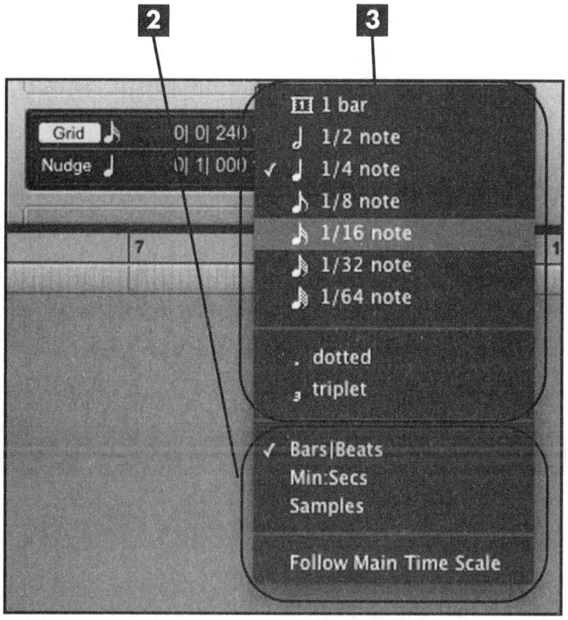

Once you have the nudge value you want, using the feature is very straightforward.

1 **Select** the **region(s)** you want to move.

2a **Press** the **+ (plus) key** on you keyboard's numeric keypad to move your selected region(s) *later* in time (to the right) by the nudge amount.

OR

2b **Press** the **– (minus) key** on your keyboard's numeric keypad to move your selected region(s) *earlier* in time (to the left) by the nudge amount.

NUDGING SHORTCUTS

Holding down the Option key (Mac) or Alt key (PC) while pressing the plus or minus key will nudge only the left boundary of a region. Holding down the Command key (Mac) or Ctrl key (PC) while pressing the plus or minus key will nudge only the right boundary. Holding down the Shift key while pressing the plus or minus key will move only the selected area and will leave the selected region in its original position. (If you want to get really creative, you can add the previous modifiers to the Shift key and nudge just the beginning or end of the selected area.)

Cool Editing Tools

Before we move on, let's take a look at four features that can kick your editing up a notch!

Tick-Based Audio Tracks

In most cases, you'll want your audio regions securely anchored to an absolute time location, right down to the sample. In this kind of scenario, audio regions' timing will not change if you change your session's tempo. MIDI notes and regions (which we'll talk about in the next chapter), on the other hand, typically *do* change along with tempo, their position being locked to your session's bars, beats, and ticks. With Pro Tools, you have the option of breaking away from this default behavior, setting up an Audio track's regions to be locked to a tick-based location. In this sort of tick-based Audio track, when you change your tempo, your regions will move accordingly.

> **SETTING THINGS UP**
>
> If you go to Memory Location #9—Tick-Based Audio, you'll see a familiar-sounding drum part, separated at each transient.

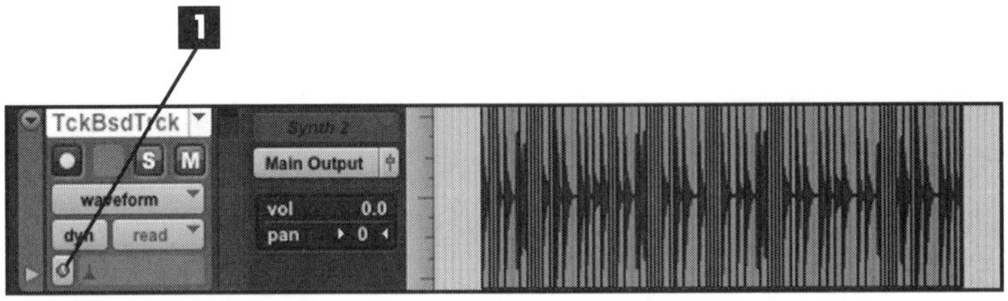

1 **Click** the **Timebase Selector button**. A menu will appear.

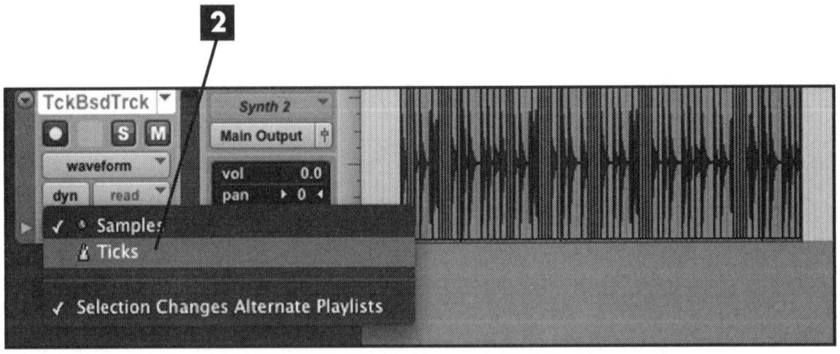

2 In this menu, you choose between having a sample-based or a tick-based timebase for your track. The currently selected timebase is marked with a checkmark. In this image, the Audio track shown is currently set to Samples, meaning that the placement of regions on the track is based upon a real-time location and won't move if the tempo (which is tick-based) is changed. To change the track to be tick-based, **click** the **Ticks menu item**.

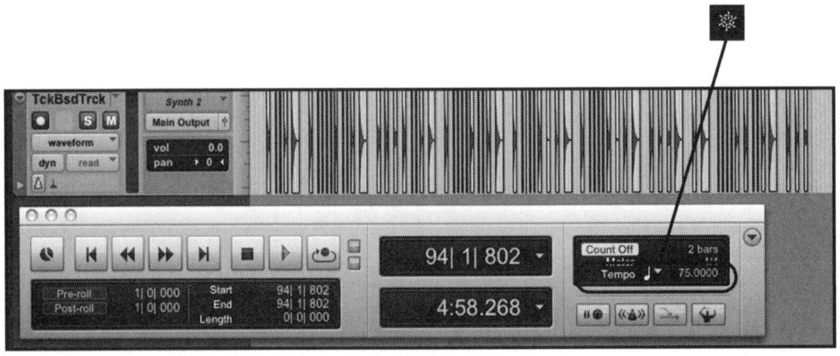

Now that you have a tick-based Audio track, all the regions on this track are locked to bar|beat|tick-based locations, which means if you change the tempo in your session, each individual region (in this image, each individual transient) will move accordingly. In this example, I've reduced the tempo from 150 beats per minute down to 75 beats per minute. The regions have moved, and the drum beat now plays at half-tempo.

FIXING THE CLICKS (AND THE ZERO-CROSSING RULE)

If you're following the steps using the tutorial session, you might be hearing clicks and pops when you change the tempo (especially if you slow the tempo down, as I have here). This is not uncommon in this sort of situation. The cause of the problem is that some regions have been separated at a point *other* than the zero crossing. Let me explain.

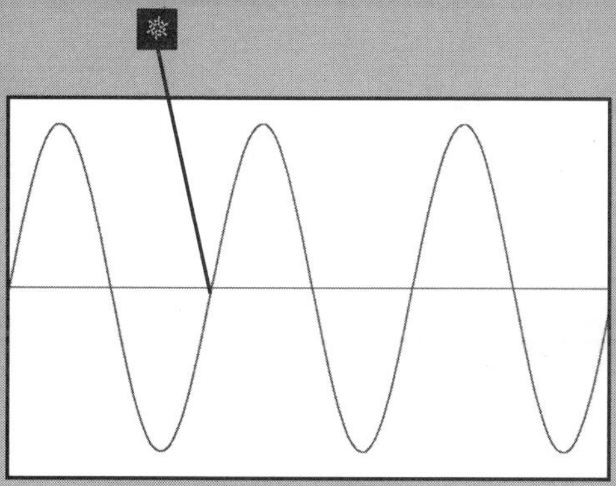

As your audio waveform oscillates, it intersects the line in the center of the Waveform view. This line, commonly called the *zero* line, represents no voltage being sent to a speaker—a speaker at rest.

When a region begins and ends with the waveform at the zero line, there will be no unwanted clicks and pops. If, however, the waveform has been cut at a point *other* than the zero volt line, clicks and pops may be heard (as a result of the speaker suddenly receiving a radical change in voltage). Cutting regions at the zero-volt line, with the waveform ascending, has become the general convention when editing.

You can use the Trimmer tool to change a region's boundary so that it begins and ends on the zero line, but this is sometimes prohibitively time-consuming. Not to worry—you can also treat the problem by creating fade-ins or fade-outs for the regions, which will create a zero crossing at the beginning or end of the region.

Region Groups

Region groups are a way to link regions together so they move and behave as a single unit, even though they may span multiple tracks. Similar to edit groups, region groups give you the power to have a single edit applied to multiple tracks, but with even more individual control.

SETTING THINGS UP

For this section, go to Memory Location #10—Region Groups.

1 **Select** the **regions** that you want to assign to your region group. It's worth mentioning that any type of region (audio, MIDI, and even video) can be part of a region group. If you're following the tutorial session, your regions have been selected for you.

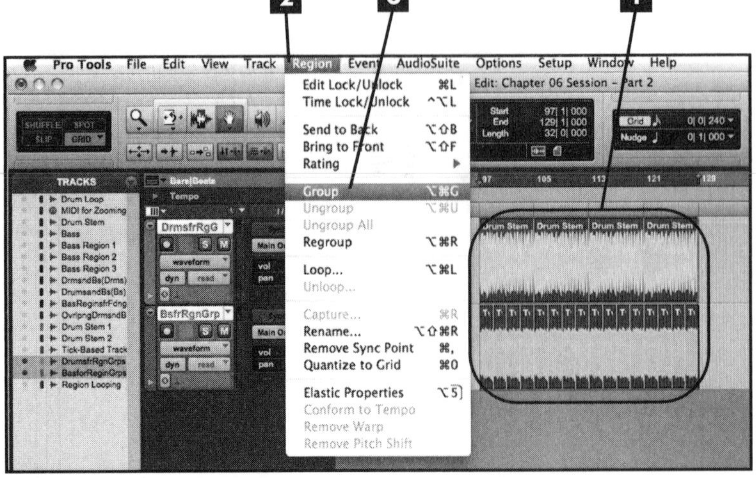

2 **Click** on the **Region menu.**

3 **Click** on **Group.**

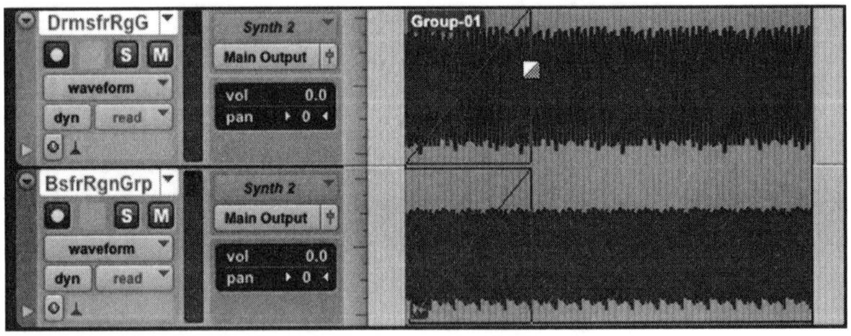

The region group is a single object that contains all the regions you've selected. It will have its own name and will appear in the Regions list at the right edge of your Edit window. Even though it may span many regions and tracks, you can edit the region group as a single object, such as creating a long fade, as shown here.

Region Looping

The ability to loop regions is very useful when you're working with repetitious material, such as drum beats. Here's how it works.

> **SETTING THINGS UP**
>
> For this section of the chapter, recall Memory Location #11—Region Looping.

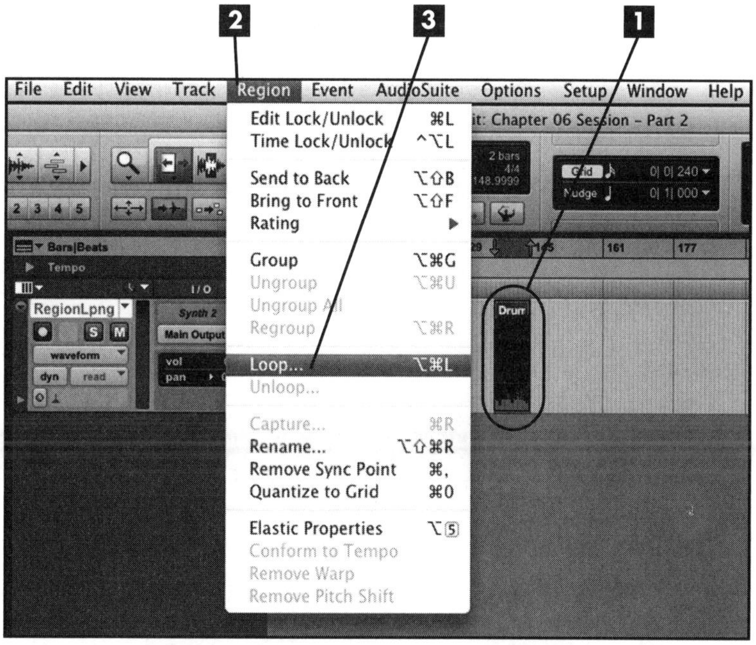

1 **Select** the **region** you want to loop. If you're following the tutorial session, your region has been selected for you.

2 **Click** on the **Region menu**.

3 **Click** on **Loop**. The Region Looping dialog box will open.

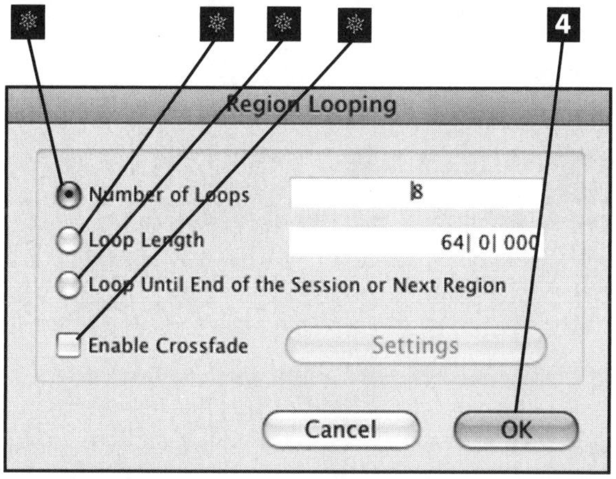

You have a number of choices when it comes to how you want your region to loop. You can:

- Choose the number of repetitions you want your region to have. This number includes the original instance of the region.
- Specify a length of time (based upon the main time scale) that you want to fill with these loops.
- Loop until the end of the session or until the next region (whichever comes first).
- Check the Enable Crossfade checkbox to create crossfades between each loop iteration. When this checkbox is checked, you can adjust the crossfade curve by clicking the Settings button (which will open the same kind of Crossfades dialog box that you worked with earlier in this chapter).

4 Once you've chosen how you want your region to loop, just **click** the **OK** button. The dialog box will close, and your region will be looped.

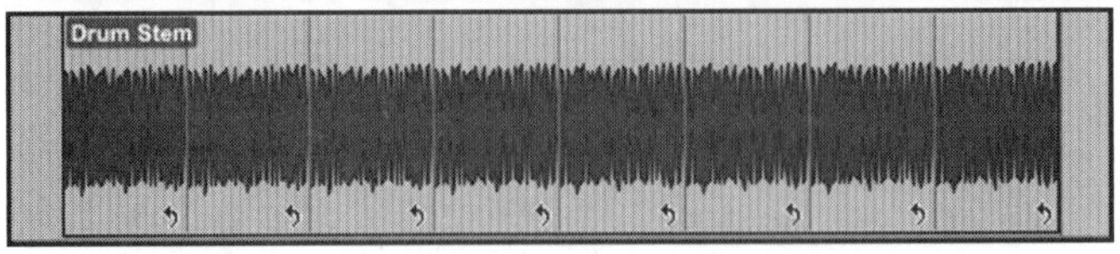

In this example, I've chosen to repeat this region eight times, and here's the result. This series of looped regions, like region groups, functions in many ways like a single unit and can be moved and edited with great flexibility.

The Loop Trimmer tool

As if region looping wasn't easy enough already, the Loop Trimmer tool will give you even more functionality. For example, you can use the Loop Trimmer tool to quickly create just the right amount of looping.

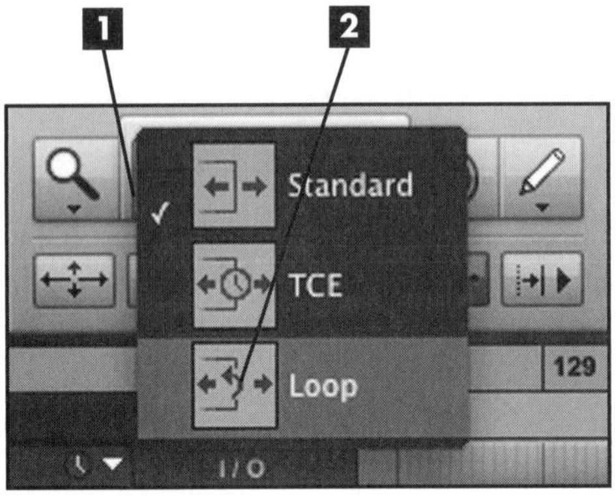

1 **Click and hold** the **Trimmer tool button** until the Trimmer tool Options menu appears. The currently selected version of the Trimmer tool will be indicated with a checkmark.

2 **Click** on **Loop** to change to the Loop Trimmer tool. The icon for the Trimmer tool will change to reflect the currently active version of the tool.

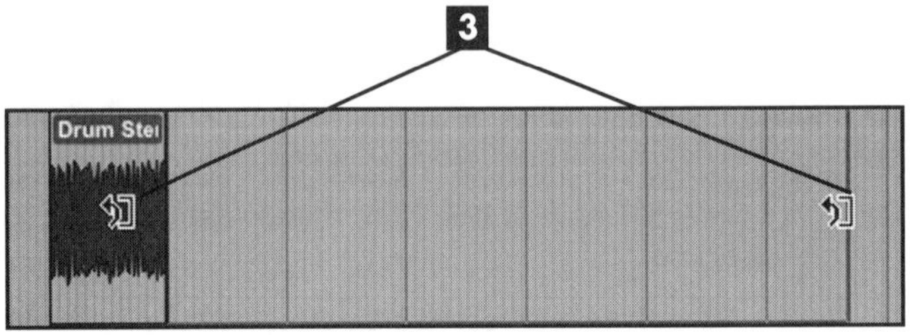

3 The rest is pretty simple. When you see the Trimmer tool with the curved arrow icon (as shown in this image), just **click and drag** the desired **region boundary**. (You can drag either the left or the right boundary to loop forward or backward.) As with other versions of the Trimmer tool, all you have to do is **release** the **mouse**, and you'll have your new looped region.

There's another side of region looping that's particularly interesting: Using the Trimmer tool with a looped region object, you can change the length of the member regions without changing the total length of the looped region object. Sound confusing? Take a look, and I think it'll become clear.

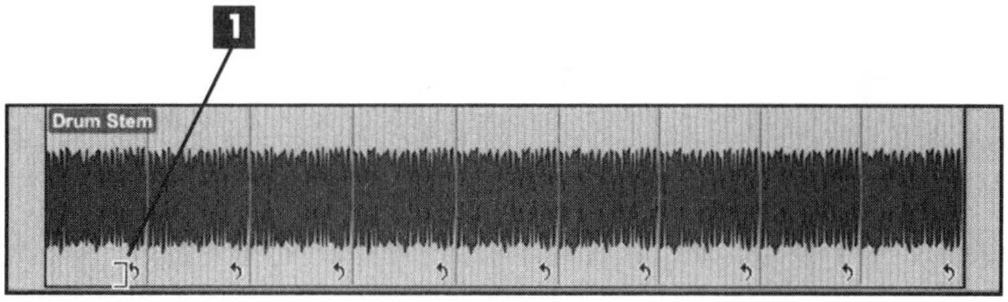

1 With the Trimmer tool selected (actually, any version of the Trimmer tool will do the trick), **move** your **cursor** to a lower corner of any member region of your region loop object. The Trimmer tool will be displayed as a basic Trimmer tool, as shown here.

2 **Click and drag** your **mouse** horizontally to adjust the boundary of the member region, just as if you were trimming a normal region.

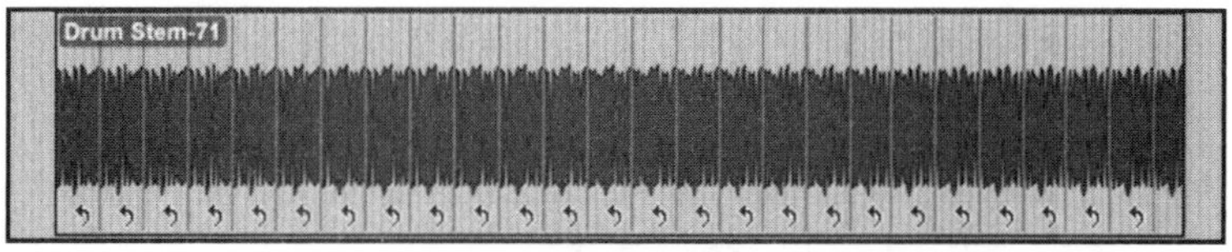

The difference becomes apparent when you release your mouse. You'll notice that the overall length of the looped region object is the same, but the length of member regions within it has changed! This technique can be particularly useful when you are dealing with drum beats, and it can often yield interesting results!

Region Locking

When you're finished editing a section of a project, you might want to make sure that your regions don't inadvertently move or change. Region locking will do just that. It's been a fixture in Pro Tools for quite some time, and has benefited from some improvements in recent versions of Pro Tools. Whether you're a new user or an experienced editor, it's worth taking a look at the different ways you can protect your work!

Edit Lock

The first kind of region locking to look at is edit lock. It will prevent your locked regions from being moved or edited accidentally.

1. **Select** the **region(s)** you want to lock.
2. **Click** on the **Region menu**.
3. **Choose Edit Lock/Unlock**. The region will be locked.

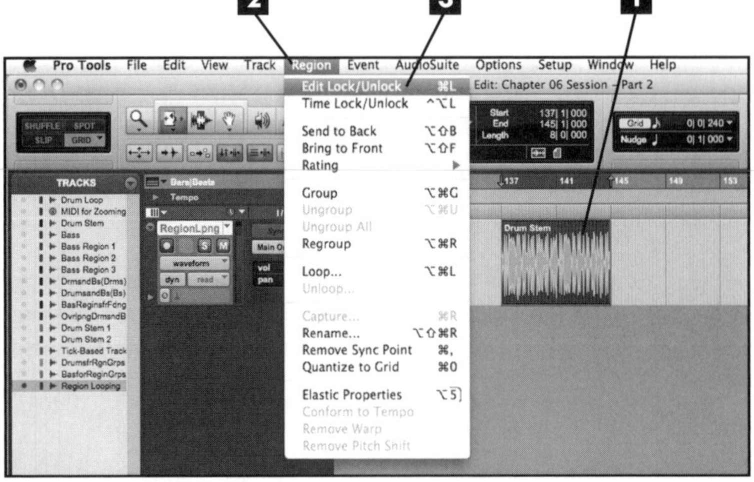

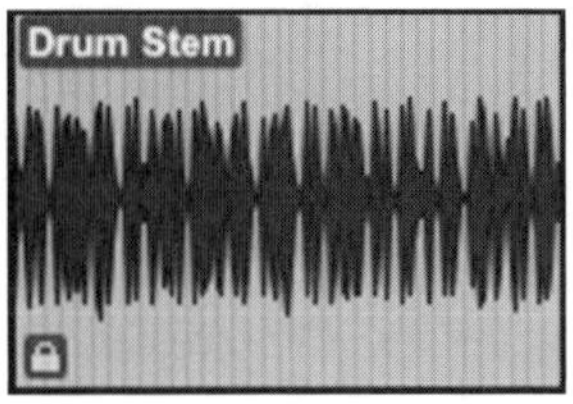

An edit-locked region will be indicated by a small lock icon in the bottom-left corner of the region.

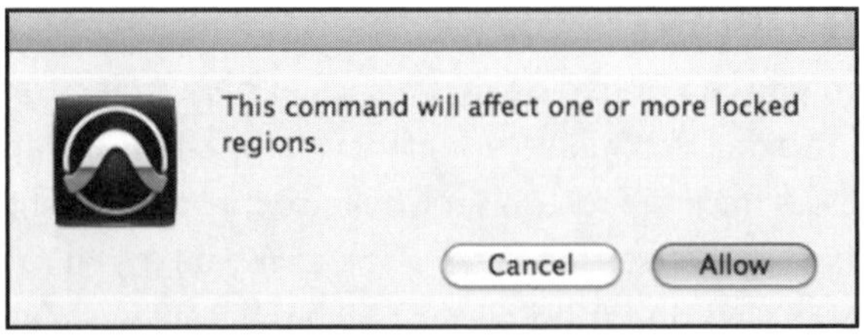

If you attempt to change the region in any way (including moving the region to another location), you will see a window that will enable you to apply this change or leave the locked region unchanged.

Time Lock

When a region is time locked, it can be freely edited in all ways *other* than moving the region to a different location.

1 **Select** the **region(s)** you want to lock.

2 **Click** on the **Region menu**.

3 **Choose Time Lock/Unlock**. The region will be locked.

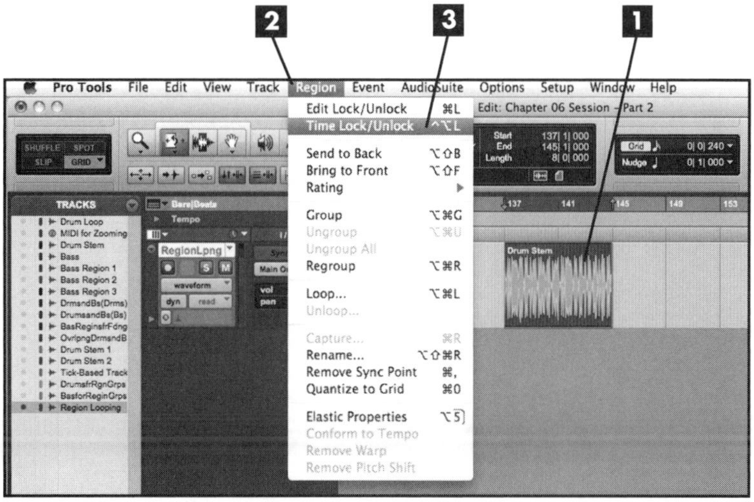

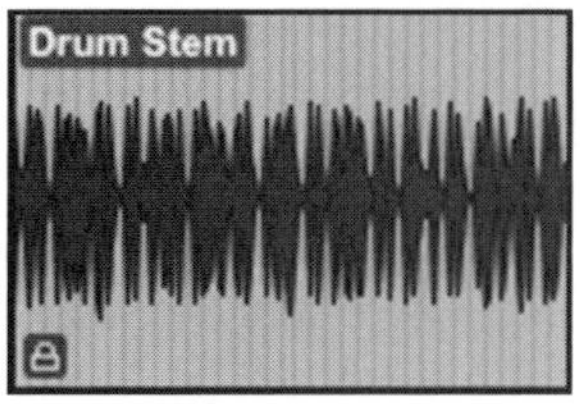

A time-locked region will be indicated by a small lock icon in the bottom-left corner of the region. Notice that the edit-lock icon is solid-colored, whereas the time-lock icon is an outline of a lock.

When a region is time locked, all editing processes can be applied normally, *except* dragging the region. This new variation of region locking is particularly useful, allowing a region to be tweaked and faded, but maintaining the position of the audio within the region.

That's all for now. Next..MIDI!

7 Using MIDI

MIDI, which stands for *Musical Instrument Digital Interface*, is a language that enables keyboards, synthesizers, and other musical devices to interact with one another. Since its inception in the early 1980s, MIDI has proved to be an invaluable creative tool to musicians of all kinds, and it has changed the face of the music industry.

Not too long ago, music software worked with *either* audio *or* MIDI, but usually not both. Thankfully, those days are over. Now, there are a number of DAW products, including Pro Tools, that incorporate the creative power of MIDI and the advantages of digital audio. Pro Tools in particular has made impressive gains in its MIDI power functionality, while remaining a solid audio workstation. In this chapter, you'll learn how to:

- Set up your MIDI studio.
- Route MIDI and audio signals so you can work with synthesizers in Pro Tools.
- Record and edit MIDI data.
- Work with your MIDI data intelligently, including importing to and exporting from Pro Tools.
- Use Pro Tools' MIDI Editor and Score Editor windows.

MIDI RESOURCES

A mastery of MIDI is a study in and of itself, upon which volumes of information have been written. For the purposes of this chapter, a fundamental understanding of MIDI will necessarily be assumed. Here, we'll focus on how to use MIDI in the Pro Tools environment rather than on the underlying principles of MIDI itself. For a good book on the subject of MIDI, check out *MIDI Power! Second Edition: The Comprehensive Guide* (Thomson Course Technology PTR, 2005).

This chapter is dedicated to the types of MIDI skills that any engineer might call upon when working with a MIDI musician in their studio. For more detail on advanced MIDI features (like the dedicated MIDI and Score Editor windows), please see Appendix A, "More MIDI Power," which is included as a PDF file on the CD-ROM that came with your book.

VIRTUAL INSTRUMENTS

For the purposes of this chapter, you'll be dealing with *virtual* instruments—in other words, instruments that are software-based rather than physical devices. The list of free instruments included with Pro Tools is impressive:

- **Boom**: Vintage drum-machine emulation
- **DB-33:** Tonewheel organ emulation
- **Mini Grand:** Acoustic piano emulation, featuring a number of piano models and ambient effects
- **Vacuum:** Vintage monophonic tube synthesizer emulation
- **Xpand2!:** Workstation synthesizer, featuring a wide variety of useful sounds
- **Structure Free:** Sample playback instrument

Again, these instruments are free, and installation files are included on your Pro Tools 9 installation disc (listed as the Pro Tools Creative Collection). If you haven't installed them already, now would be an excellent time to do so!

When we were working with audio, one of our first steps was to configure inputs and outputs (in the I/O Setup window). You'll want to do this with MIDI as well, using the MIDI Studio Setup window, identifying your MIDI devices before proceeding. Don't worry; it's easy!

Setting Up Your MIDI Studio

Before you can record any MIDI data, you'll need to physically attach your external MIDI device(s) to your system's MIDI interface. (Refer to the documentation that came with your MIDI gear for more information.) Let's assume you've physically connected your MIDI gear in a traditional configuration—in other words, you've connected the output of your MIDI interface to the MIDI input of your device and then connected the MIDI output (*not* the Thru) of your device into an input on your MIDI interface. Once that's done, you'll need to set up Pro Tools to recognize that connection.

1. **Click** on the **Setup menu**.
2. **Click** on **MIDI**. The MIDI submenu will be displayed.
3. **Choose MIDI Studio.** The Audio MIDI Setup window will appear.

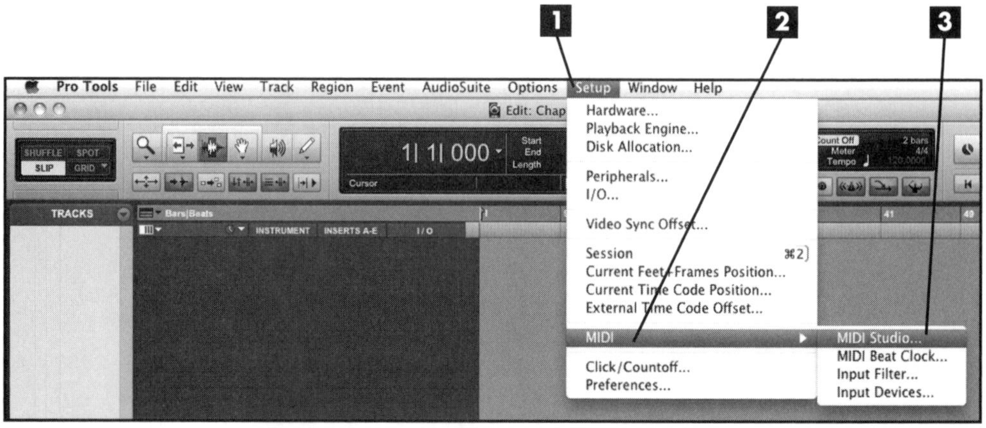

PC AND MAC MIDI SETUPS

The process of configuring your MIDI studio varies a bit between Mac systems and PCs. For example, the window you'll use to configure your MIDI devices on a PC is called MIDI Studio Setup, whereas it's just called MIDI Studio on a Mac. Where appropriate, both Mac and PC screenshots will be shown.

MIDI Studio Setup on a Mac

The Audio MIDI Setup window will give you an overview of the devices attached to your system. Initially, it might show you only your MIDI interface (the device to which you'll attach any external MIDI devices). The next step is to add a device to your system.

1. **Click** the **Add Device button**. A New External Device icon will appear.

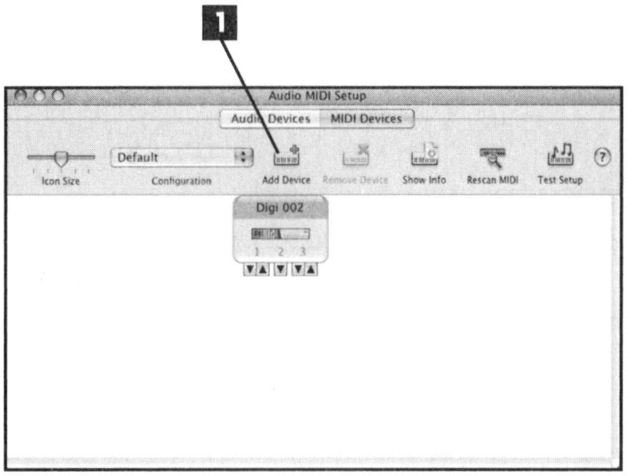

2. **Click and hold** on the **MIDI OUT port** of the MIDI interface that is connected to your external device.

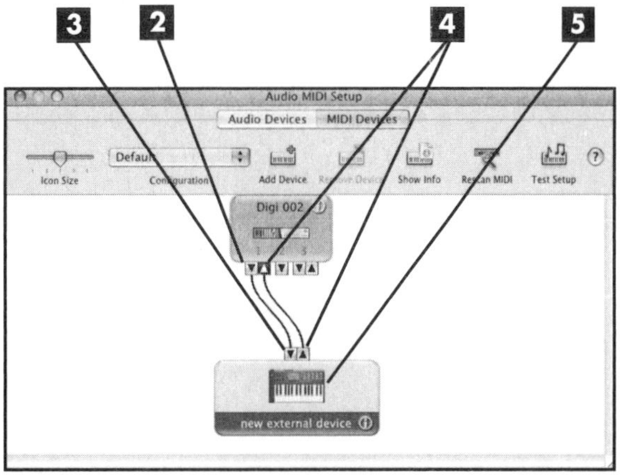

3. **Drag** with your mouse to the **MIDI IN port** of your external device. You'll see a line connecting the MIDI interface icon and the New External Device icon.
4. **Repeat steps 2 and 3** for the connection from the MIDI OUT port of your external device to the MIDI IN port of your interface, if applicable.
5. **Double-click** the **New External Device icon**. The New External Device Properties dialog box will appear, enabling you to customize the connection.

❋ The top section enables you to type a descriptive name for your device and choose the manufacturer and model that match your gear. If you don't see your manufacturer or model, don't worry—just leave the fields blank.

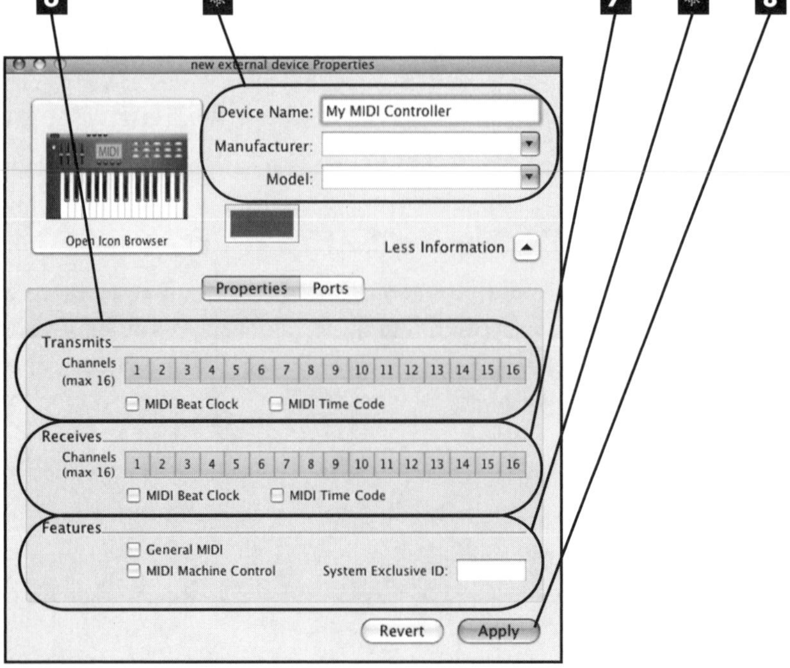

6 **Click** the **Transmits channels** that you want to make available to your device. (Enabled channels will be colored blue.) You can also choose to enable the device to transmit MIDI Beat Clock and/or MIDI Time Code. (Enabled options will be indicated with a checkmark.)

7 **Click** the **Receives channels** that you want to make available to your device. (Enabled channels will be colored blue.) You can also choose to enable the device to receive MIDI Beat Clock and/or MIDI Time Code. (Enabled options will be indicated with a checkmark.)

❋ Finally, you can enable your device to operate as a General MIDI device or a MIDI Machine Control device (to control transport of Pro Tools), or you can assign a System Exclusive ID number (if you have multiple devices of the same model).

8 When you've set up your device, **click** the **Apply button**. The dialog box will close. When you've created and configured all your external gear, just quit the Audio MIDI Setup application.

MIDI Studio Setup on a PC

To add a device to your PC, follow these steps:

1 **Click** the **Create button**. A new device, initially named New Instrument 1, will be created.

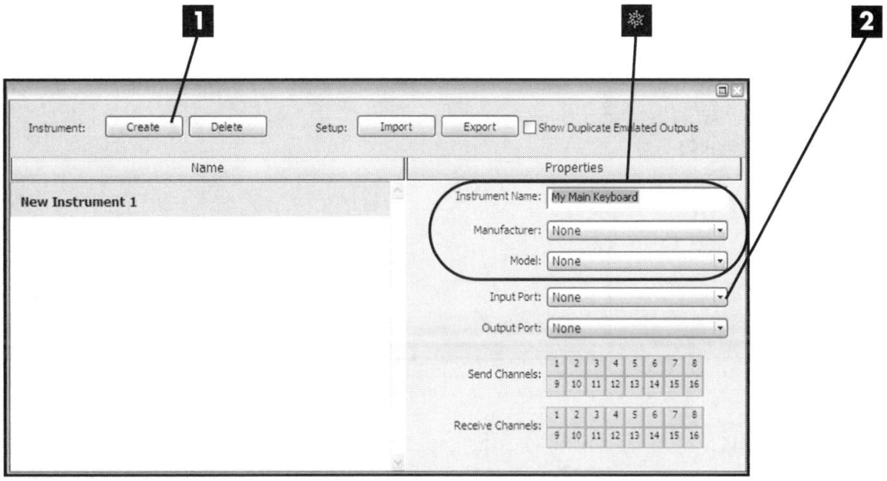

The top section will enable you to type a descriptive name for your device, plus choose the manufacturer and model that match your gear. If you don't see your manufacturer or model, don't worry—just leave the fields blank.

2 **Click** the **Input Port button**. A menu will appear.

3 **Choose** the appropriate **MIDI In** port on your MIDI interface (the MIDI In port that is connected to your external device).

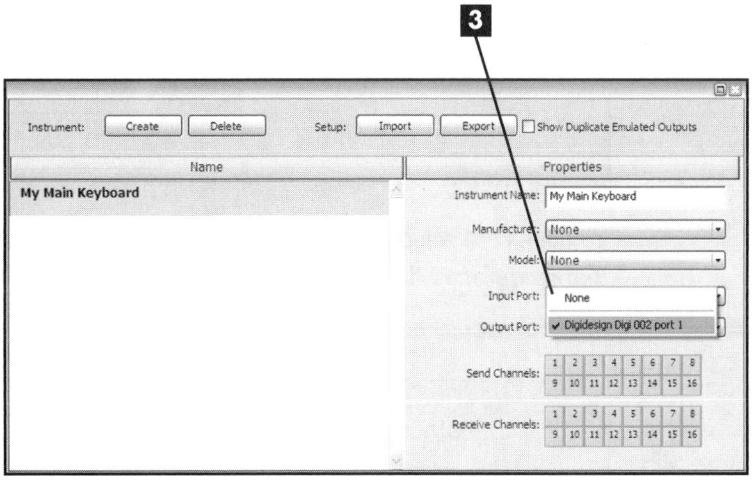

4 Now it's time to choose how your system will *send* MIDI information to the device. **Click** the **Output Port button**. A menu will appear.

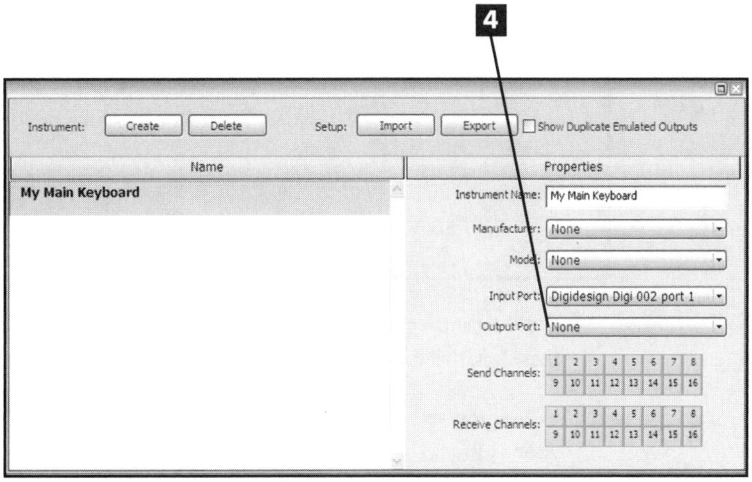

5 **Choose** the appropriate **MIDI Out** port on your MIDI interface (the MIDI Out port that is connected to your external device).

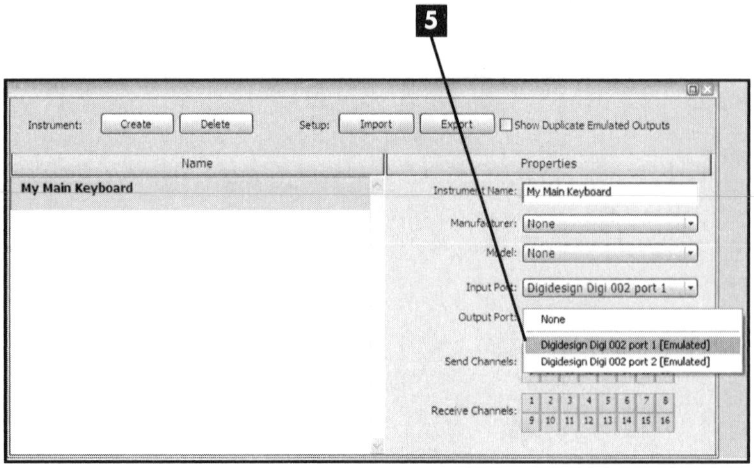

6 **Click** the **send channels** that you want to make available to your device. (Enabled channels will be colored blue.)

7 **Click** the **receive channels** that you want to make available to your device. (Enabled channels will be colored blue.)

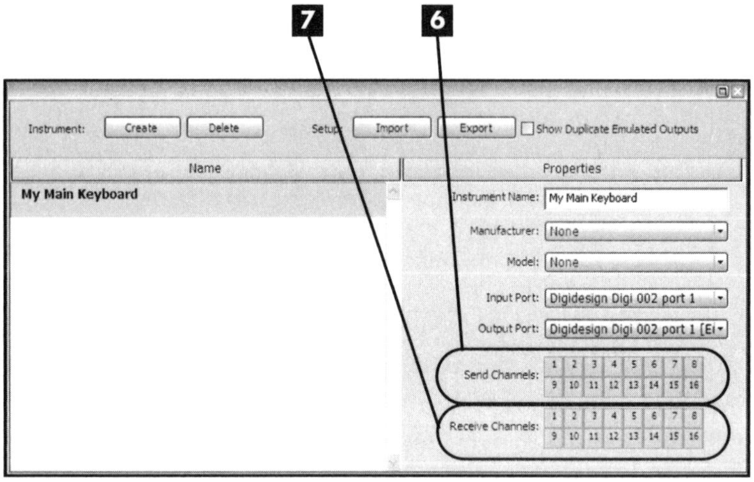

You can repeat this process for each of the external MIDI devices in your system. Before we leave this window, though, let's take a look at some of its other features:

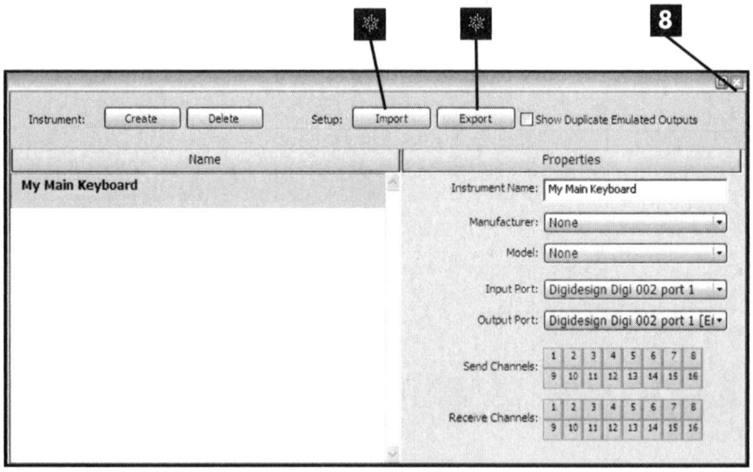

- The Import button will enable you to open any MIDI setup file (stored with a .dms file extension) that has been previously created. Be careful, though—this will overwrite your current settings.

- Want to store the setup you have now for future use or to transplant to another system? Just click the Export button. You will be prompted to save your settings as a DMS file.

8 When you're finished, just **close** the **window**, and your settings will be applied to your system.

Signal Flow 201: MIDI versus Audio

If there's one important thing to remember about MIDI, it's this: MIDI is *not* audio. MIDI isn't even audible—it's a digital language that enables musical devices to communicate with each other on a fundamental level. It's a common (and dangerous) misconception that MIDI and audio are somehow related, and this probably stems from the fact that the use of MIDI enables musical gear to make sound.

Given that MIDI and digital audio are fundamentally different, it should come as no surprise that MIDI has its own rules for signal flow. The good news is that if you know the rules, setting up your instruments is easy, and you can manage MIDI signal paths and audio signal paths simultaneously in a single Pro Tools session.

Managing the MIDI Signal Path

We've already gone through the process of basic audio signal routing. You'll find that managing your MIDI tracks has a familiar look and feel.

1 **Create** a **MIDI track** and **name it** descriptively. (Refer to Chapter 3, "Getting Started with Audio," if you need a refresher on how to do this.)

You'll notice that the overall layout of a MIDI track is consistent with other tracks you've seen so far:

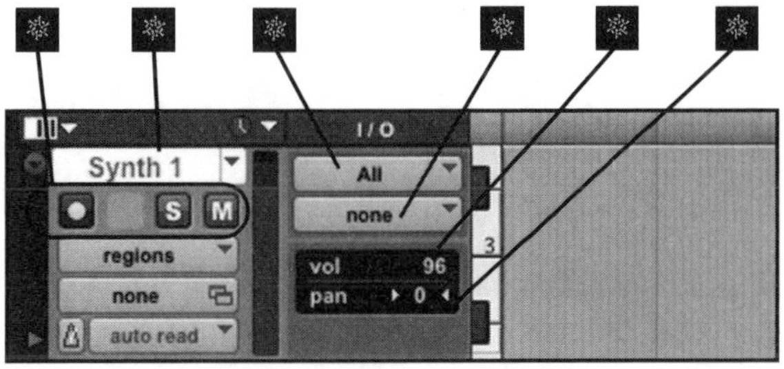

- Track name
- Record, Solo, and Mute buttons
- Input selector
- Output selector
- Volume control
- Pan control

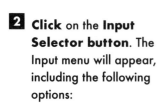

2 **Click** on the **Input Selector button**. The Input menu will appear, including the following options:

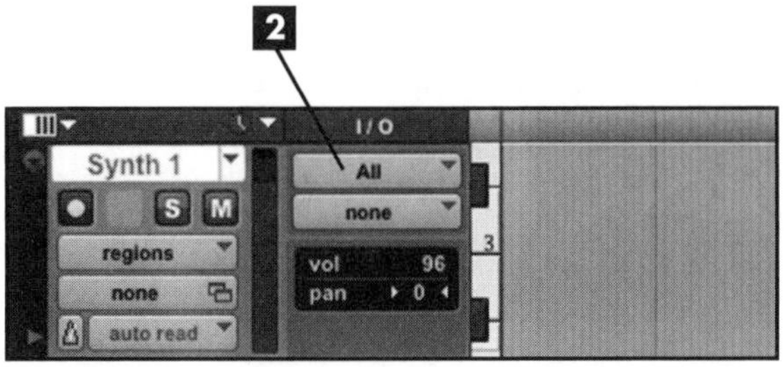

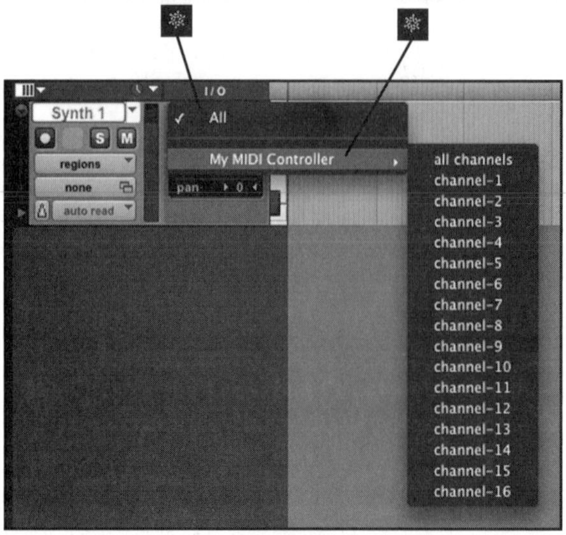

- By default, a new MIDI track will have All set as the input and will enable the track to accept MIDI data from any port and on any channel. This is a particularly convenient way to work if you're a single user in a multi-keyboard studio. With All selected as an input, you can play any MIDI device in your studio and have it recorded to the track, without having to change your input selection.
- Additionally, each input device you've specified in your MIDI setup will appear as an input option. You can choose a single device or even a specific MIDI channel as an input for your track. This is useful in multi-keyboard setups in which you have multiple musicians playing simultaneously. You can assign multiple tracks to accept input from specific MIDI sources, isolating each musician's performance to separate tracks.

3 **Select** the **input** that suits your situation.

4 **Click** on the **Output Selector button**. The Output menu will appear.

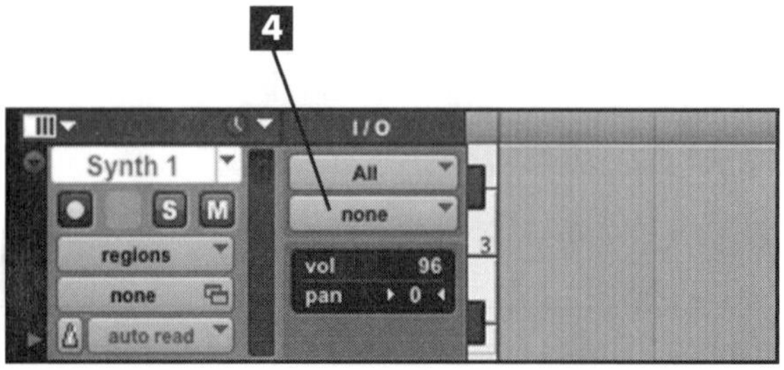

5 **Select** the **device and MIDI channel** that are routed to the device you want to use for this track.

> **USING MIDI CONTROLLERS**
>
> With MIDI, the device you physically play does *not* necessarily have to be the device that you hear. In these cases, where the performance device and the device making the sound are different, the device you actually play is called a *MIDI controller*.

Now your MIDI track is set up to route MIDI data from a source (for example, a MIDI controller) to a destination (for example, an external sound module). When you play your MIDI instrument, you should see an indication on the destination device that it is receiving MIDI data. At this point, that device should respond to the MIDI data by making sound.

Occasionally, you'll need to adjust your MIDI track's volume. This is also a straightforward process.

1. **Click and hold** on the **Volume display area**. A small fader box will appear.
2. Still holding down the mouse button, **drag** the **fader** on the fader box to adjust the volume to suit your session.

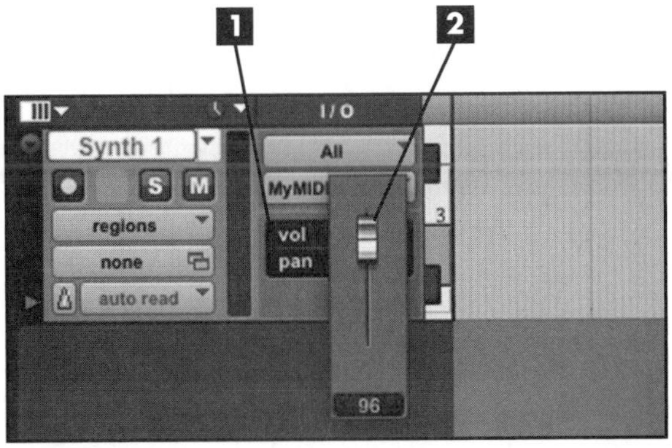

MIDI VOLUME RESOLUTION

MIDI volume has a range of 128 steps, from 0 to 127.

Similarly, you can adjust a track's pan settings.

1. **Click and hold** in the **Pan display area**. A small slider box will appear.

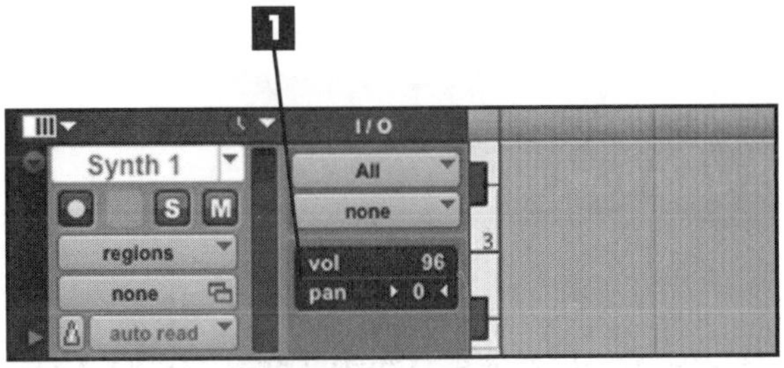

2. Still holding down the mouse button, **drag** the **slider** to adjust the pan to suit your session.

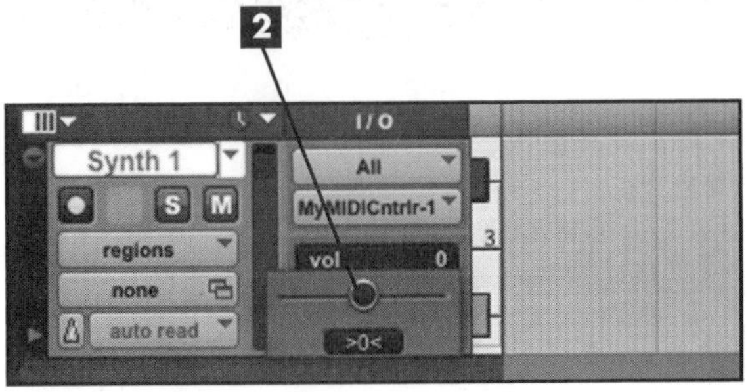

MIDI PAN RESOLUTION

MIDI volume has a range of 128 steps, from 64 left to 63 right.

Setting Up an Aux Track to Monitor Your MIDI Gear

We discussed the idea of Aux tracks (or more formally *Auxiliary Input* tracks) back in Chapter 3. Aux tracks are the track type of choice when you need to manage an audio signal, but you don't need to record audio to your hard drive. In this example, we'll use an Aux track to hear an external MIDI sound module through Pro Tools.

> **AUX TRACKS VERSUS AUDIO TRACKS**
>
> Even though an Aux track is an *audible* track, it certainly isn't an *Audio* track. The main difference between the two is that an Audio track can play back regions in your session (as you've already seen), whereas an Aux track cannot. Although you technically *could* use an Audio track to monitor an external MIDI device's output, Aux tracks usually are generally more suited to the task, and using Aux tracks whenever possible will conserve resources so you can get the maximum performance out of your system.

Once you've connected the audio outputs of the MIDI sound module to the appropriate audio input(s) of your Pro Tools interface, follow these steps.

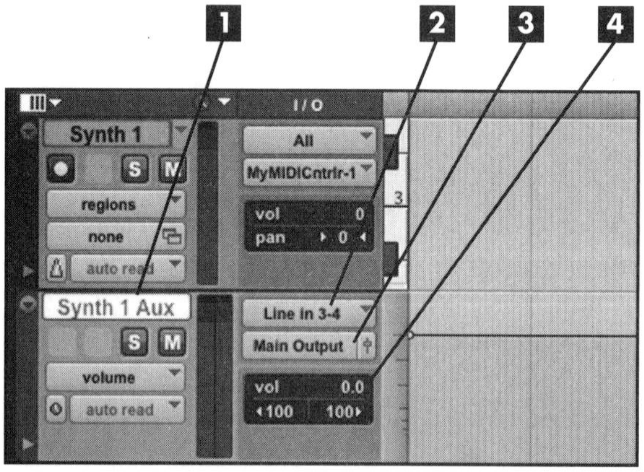

1. **Create** a new **Aux track** and **name it** descriptively. (This is the track you'll use to hear your MIDI device.)
2. **Assign** the **input** of this Aux track to match the *audio* inputs to which your external MIDI sound module is attached.
3. **Assign** the **output** of this Aux track to the audio outputs to which your monitor speakers are attached.
4. **Adjust** the **volume** of the Aux track to suit your session.

At this point, you've completely configured your MIDI signal flow, as well as the audio signal routing that will enable you to listen to your sound-producing device. When you play your controller device (with the MIDI track record armed), you will trigger your slave device (with MIDI data traveling through the MIDI track and recordable on that track) and listen to the audio output of your sound module through the Aux track.

Using Virtual Instruments

A relatively recent addition to the world of music creation, virtual instruments have really boosted the power of the modern DAW. Virtual instruments are real-time plug-ins, but whereas most plug-ins *process* sound, virtual instruments *make* sound!

Think of them as the marriage between software plug-ins and MIDI synthesizers, giving you the best of both worlds. With virtual instruments, you not only have the power of a MIDI synth without the bulk of physical hardware, you also have the ability to automate its parameters just like any plug-in. (Don't worry; we'll talk more about that in the next chapter.)

The secret to using virtual instruments is in the setup, which is really just a variation of the traditional MIDI setup that you learned in the previous section. Here again, you can use two tracks to get MIDI and sound to work together within Pro Tools—a MIDI track (for the MIDI data) and an Aux track (for your virtual instrument).

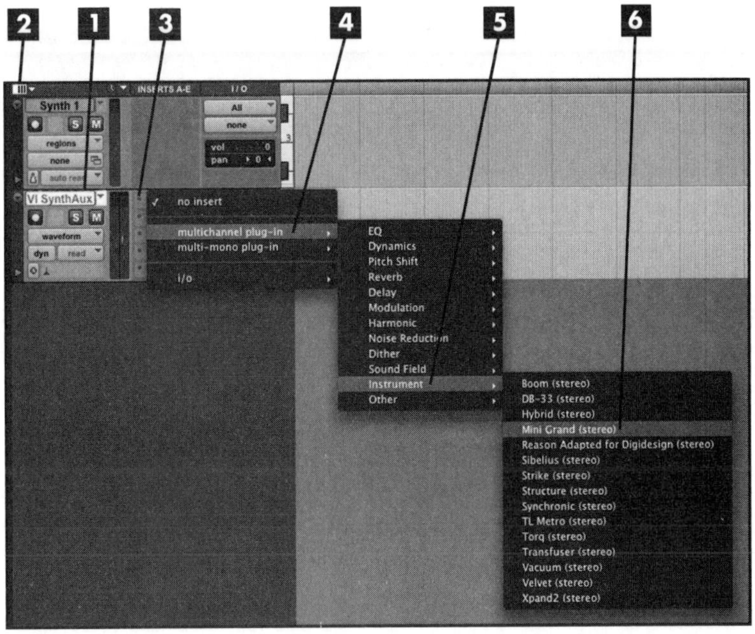

1 **Create** a new **stereo Aux track** and **assign** its **output** to your system's monitor speakers.

2 Because we'll be using a plug-in and because plug-ins are used via inserts, you'll want to make sure you can see an Inserts column in your Edit window. If you're not seeing an Inserts column, **click** the **Edit Window View** selector and choose an Inserts view from the list. (In this image, I'm showing Inserts A–E.)

3 **Click** on an **Insert Selector button**. A menu will appear.

4 **Select** either **multichannel plug-in** or **multi-mono plug-in** (based on the kind of instrument you want to use—I've chosen multichannel). A submenu will appear.

5 **Move your cursor** to **Instrument**. Yet another submenu will appear.

6 **Choose** your desired **virtual instrument**. (In this image, I've chosen the Mini Grand plug-in.) The plug-in's window will appear.

7 Next, you'll need to create a MIDI track (if you haven't already) and set up the output to be routed to your new virtual instrument. **Click** on the **Output Selector button** of the MIDI track. A menu will appear.

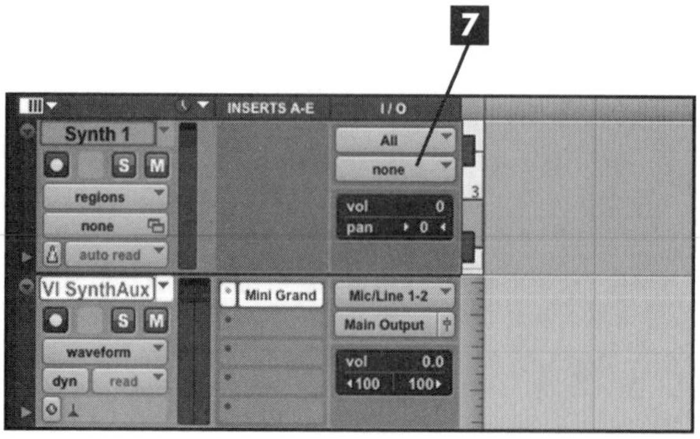

8 You'll notice that, once you've launched a virtual instrument plug-in, it will appear as an output option for your MIDI track (in addition to your physical MIDI outputs). **Select** the **instrument** you want to control from the Output drop-down menu.

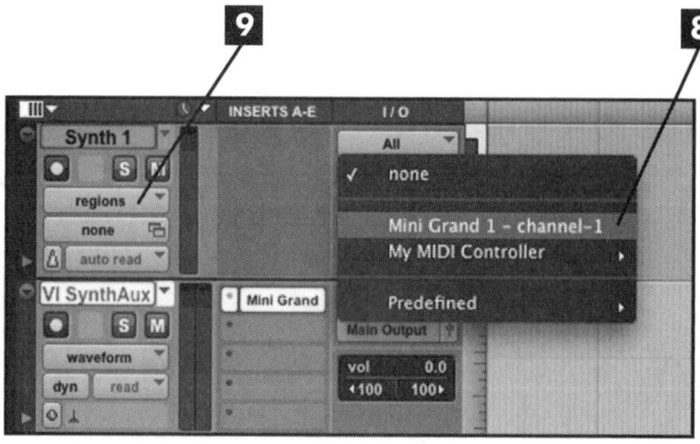

9 Now let's test your setup. **Click** the MIDI track's **Track View Selector button** (which will initially read "Regions"). A menu will appear.

10 The Track View list will show you the available view options for this track, with the currently active view indicated by a checkmark. **Choose Notes** from the list.

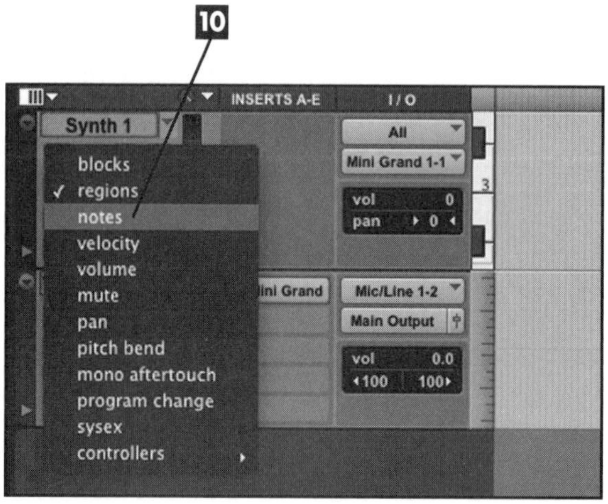

11 **Click** on any **note** on the mini keyboard to the left of your MIDI track's Playlist area. If everything is set up properly, MIDI data will be created, the data will be sent to the virtual instrument, and the instrument will sound.

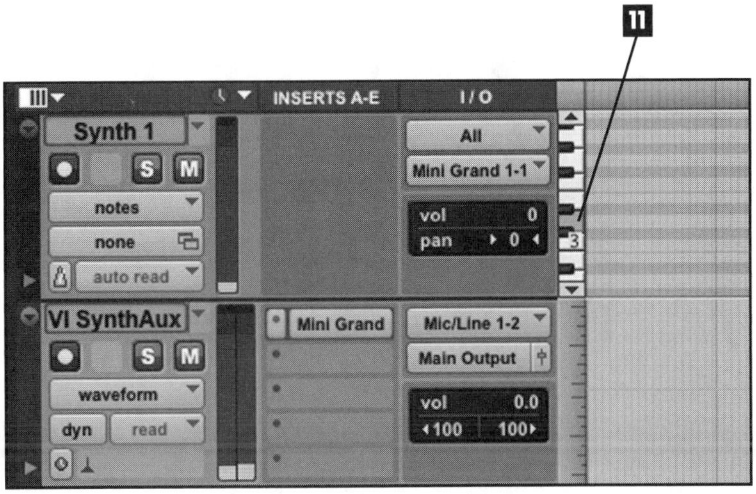

MIDI METERING

As you click on the mini keyboard, you will see activity in your MIDI track's level meters. What you're seeing is *not* audio, but rather control data (note messages) being sent to the virtual instrument on your Aux track. The levels you see on the Aux track's meters are the audible signals being routed to your monitor speakers.

Instrument Tracks

Instrument tracks are real timesavers for MIDI production, combining the power of a MIDI track *and* an Aux track in a single unit. Let's delete the two tracks you created in the previous virtual instrument scenario and redo the whole job with just one track.

1 **Open** the **New Tracks dialog box** and create a **stereo** track. (Refer to Chapter 3 if you need a refresher on how to do this.) From the Track Type menu, **select Instrument Track**. When you click Create, a new Instrument track will be created.

2 **Name** your **track** descriptively.

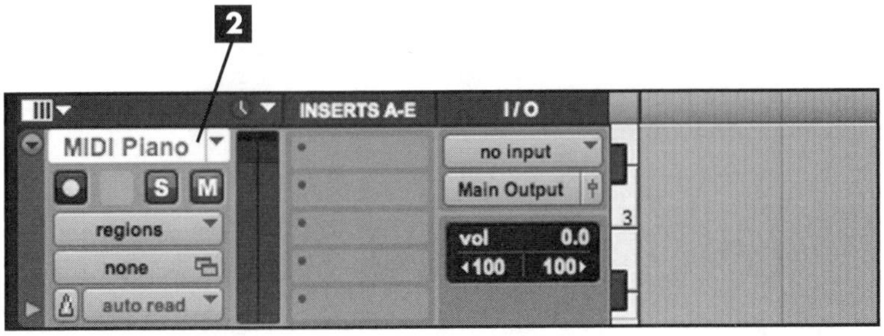

Below the track name, you'll see some familiar-looking buttons.

- Track Record Enable
- Solo
- Mute
- Track View Selector
- Patch Select

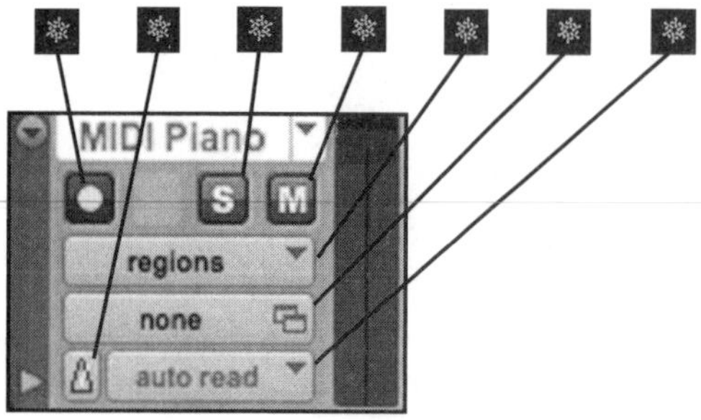

- Timebase Selector
- Automation Mode Selector (We'll discuss this in the next chapter.)

3 If you're not seeing the Instrument column, **click** the **Edit Window View selector** and **click** the **Instrument menu item**. (Visible columns will be indicated by checkmarks.) The Instrument column contains the functionality of a MIDI track's I/O column.

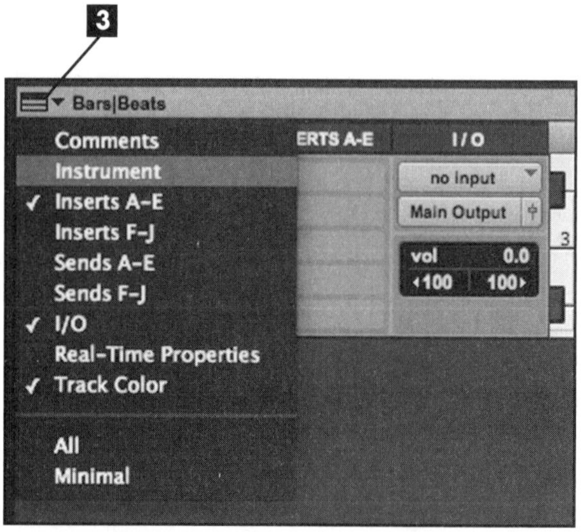

- MIDI Input Selector
- MIDI Mute
- MIDI Output Selector
- MIDI Volume
- MIDI Pan
- MIDI Level Meter

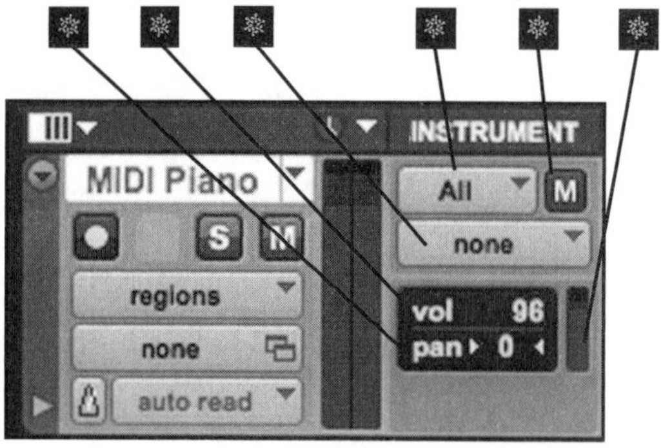

4 The Inserts column of an Instrument track functions just like the Inserts column of an Aux track. Simply **choose** the desired **virtual instrument plug-in** on this track, just as you did before with an Aux track. Your plug-in will launch, and the plug-in window will be displayed.

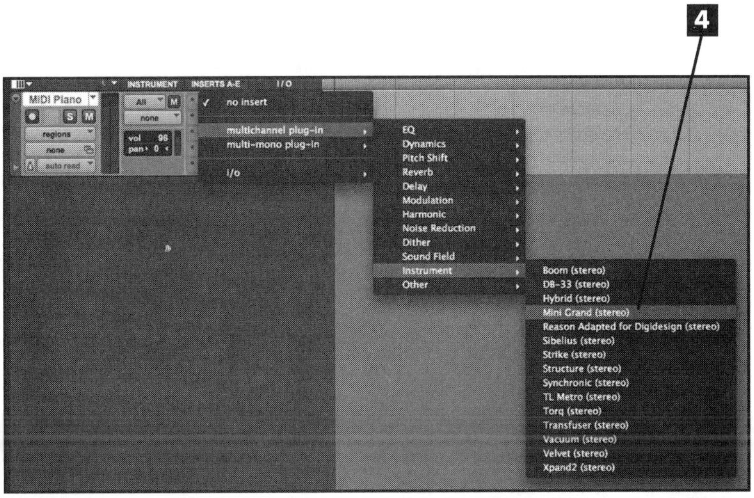

As soon as your virtual instrument is launched, the MIDI Output button of the Instrument track automatically changes to match the plug-in, making an Instrument track even more convenient. If you need to change that MIDI output for any reason, you can do it easily by clicking the MIDI Output button.

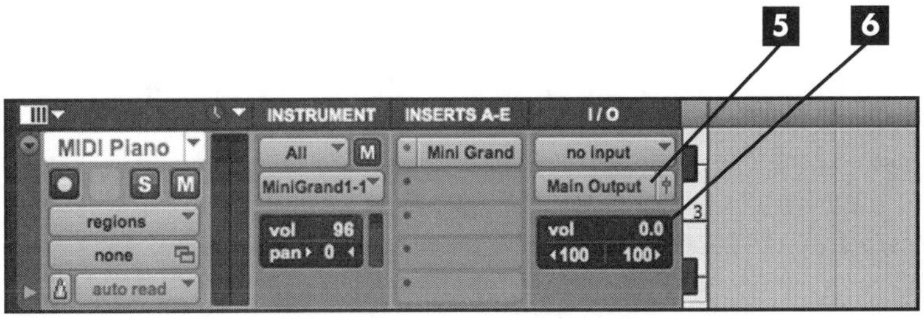

5 The I/O column of an Instrument track is identical to the I/O column of an Aux track, and you'll use it the same way. **Set** the **output** of the Instrument track.

6 Last but certainly not least, **adjust** your track's **output level** as needed. Note that it is standard practice to control the volume level of an instrument track from the *audio* volume fader rather than the MIDI volume fader.

Now your track should look something like the image shown here. Initially, the Instrument track view will be set to Regions (similar to the MIDI track you worked with earlier). As with a MIDI track, you can change the view to Notes and click your mini keyboard to test your setup, as you did in the previous section of this chapter.

MIDI and Instrument Tracks in the Mix Window

The Mix window is well suited to the task of routing and combining individual signals to achieve a pleasing total mix. We'll take a closer look at mixing in the next chapter, but for now let's take a look at how MIDI and Instrument tracks appear in this environment.

First, you need to make sure you're seeing the appropriate aspects of each track strip in the Mix window:

1. **Click** the **View menu**.
2. **Choose Mix Window Views**. A submenu will appear.

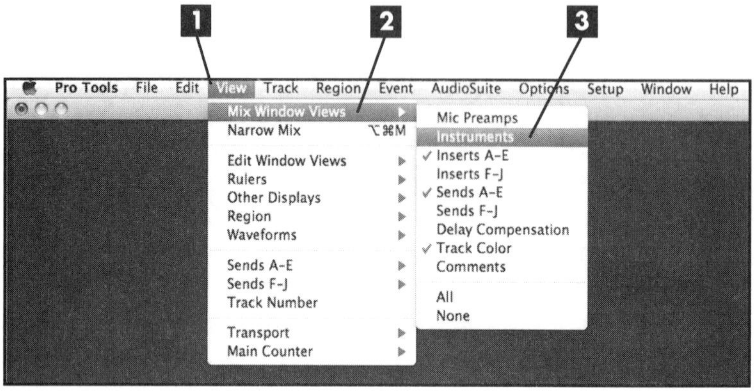

3. Displayed elements of your session's tracks will be indicated by a checkmark. If the **Instruments** menu item isn't checked, **click it** now.

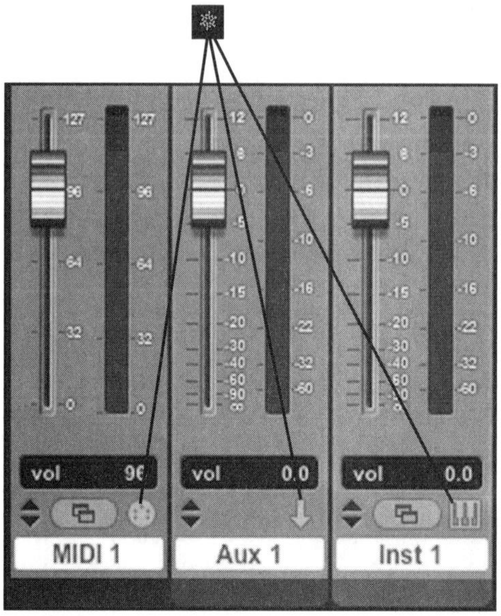

The icons at the bottom-right corner of each channel strip indicate track type (a MIDI plug for a MIDI track, an arrow for an Aux track, and a keyboard for an Instrument track).

- The Instrument row (at the top of the channel strip) mirrors the functionality of the Instrument column that you saw earlier in the Edit window (MIDI input, output, volume, pan, and mute). Note that the area is blank in any track other than an Instrument track.

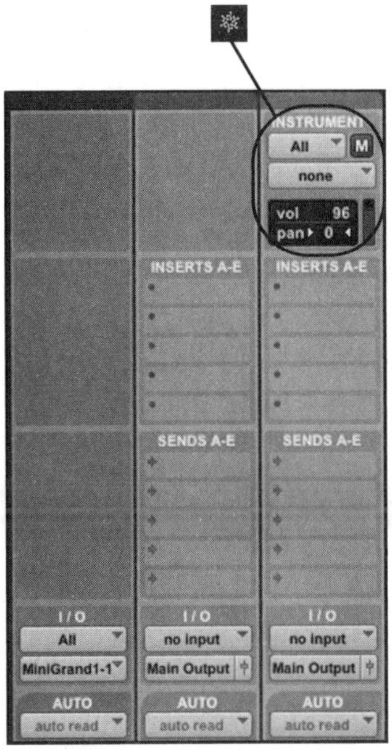

- The I/O section of a MIDI track enables the user to choose the MIDI input and output assignments. The I/O section of an Instrument track is the same as the I/O section of an Aux track, and it is here where you will set up your audio ins and outs.
- The bottom section of each of these track types enables you to adjust positioning with pan controls and includes record (when applicable), solo, mute, and volume controls.

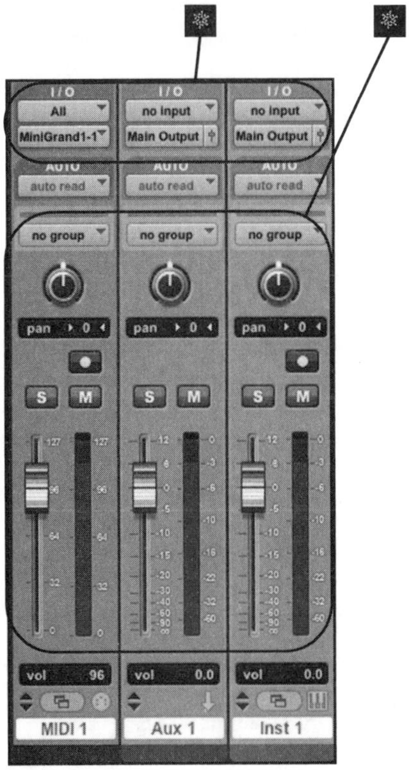

Recording MIDI

The process of recording MIDI is similar to audio recording in many respects, but with some additional flexibility.

Choosing a Sound

Usually, your first step is to pick a sound that you want to use. Doing this varies slightly depending on whether you're using an external MIDI device or a virtual instrument plug-in. Let's start with the external device.

Choosing a Sound for an External Device

To choose a sound for an external device, follow these steps:

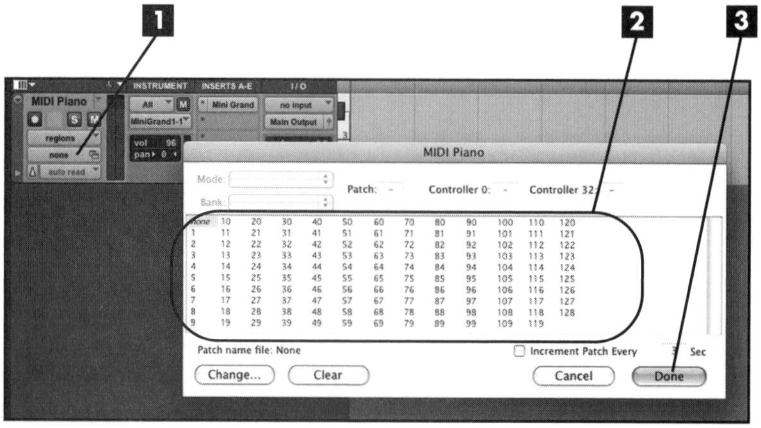

1 **Click** on the **Patch Select button**. (Conveniently, it's in the same position on MIDI tracks and Instrument tracks.) A dialog box containing a patch list for the MIDI device will open. Depending on the device you configured in your MIDI setup, the patch list displayed will consist of numbers and/or text names.

2 **Click** on the **patch** you want to use.

3 **Click** on the **Done button**. The dialog box will close, and the program number or name will appear on the Patch Select button.

Choosing a Sound for a Virtual Instrument

If you're using a virtual instrument (such as Mini Grand), you'll need to choose a sound directly from the plug-in's window:

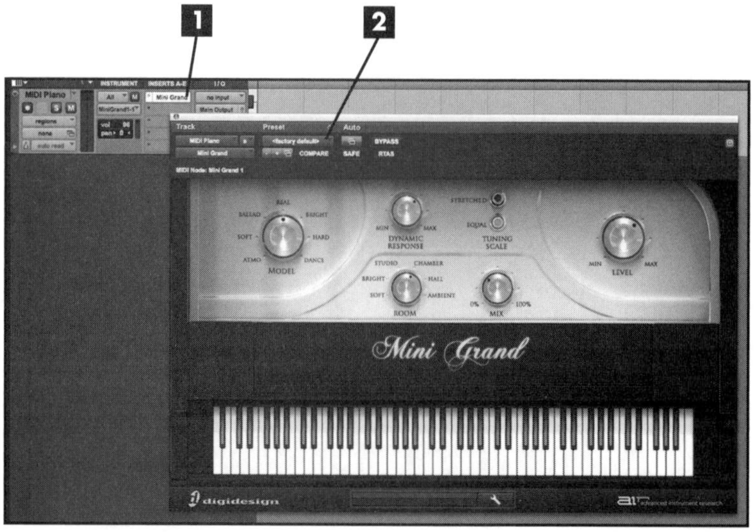

1 If the plug-in window isn't open already, **click** on the virtual instrument's **Insert button**. The Insert button will be highlighted, and the plug-in window will open.

2 **Click** the **Librarian Menu button** (which will be displaying the currently active sound). A menu of available sounds will appear.

3 **Choose** the desired **sound** from the menu. The menu will close, and your choice will be applied.

Here's an alternative method:

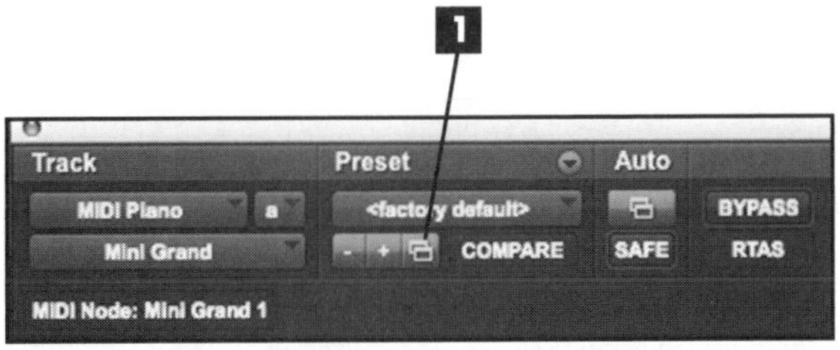

1 **Click** the **Plug-In Settings Select button**. The plug-in settings window will open.

2 If your plug-in presets are organized into submenus, **click** the **Folder menu**. The subfolder hierarchy will be displayed. Once shown, **select** the desired **subfolder** from the list that is displayed. When you make your selection, the programs in that subfolder will be displayed in the window.

3 **Select** the desired **sound**.

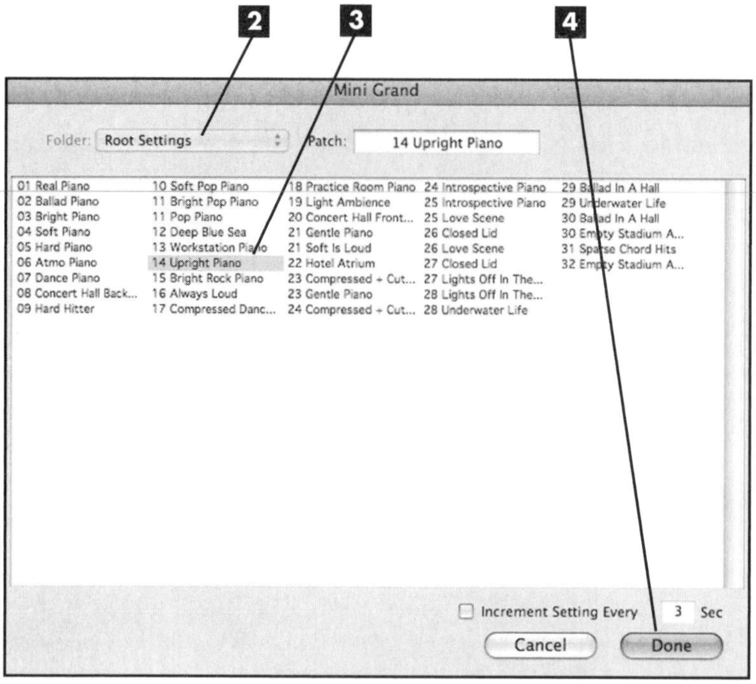

4 When you've settled on the best sound, **click** the **Done button**.

INCREMENT PATCH

If you're searching for just the right sound, the Increment Setting Every *n* Sec checkbox (in the bottom-right corner of the plug-in settings window) can come in handy. Just enable the feature to cycle through all the sounds in this window automatically, enabling you to keep playing while the patches change.

HEY, I'M NOT HEARING ANYTHING!

If you're playing your keyboard, but can't preview sounds, just record-enable the track. This will route incoming MIDI data to the appropriate instrument.

Basic MIDI Recording

Before you start recording, you might want to set up a click track (which you learned about in Chapter 4, "Recording Audio"). Remember to click on the Metronome icon to enable your click track. Now it's time to actually record the MIDI. The process of recording MIDI is nearly identical to recording audio.

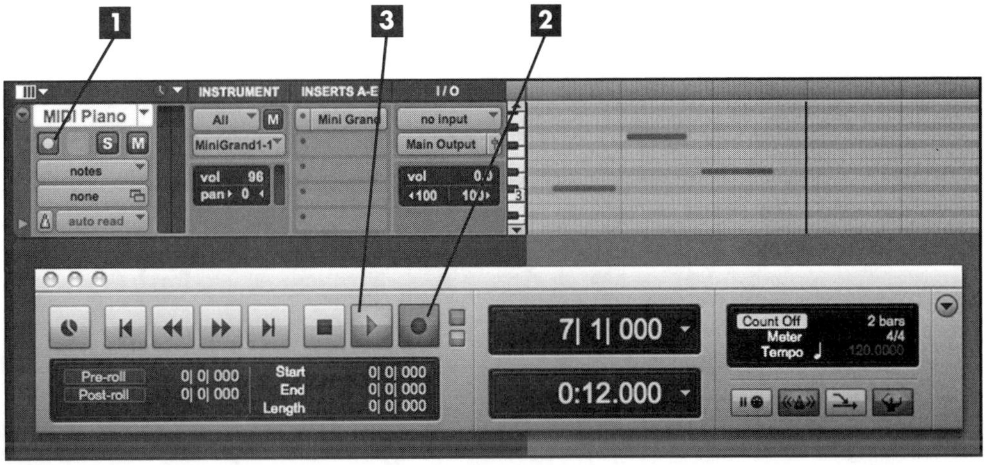

1 **Click** on the **Track Record Enable button** to arm the track for recording.

2 **Click** on the **Record Enable button** in the Transport window (or in the transport controls at the top of the Edit window).

3 **Click** on the **Play button**. Recording will begin. It operates the same as when you record audio, with pre-rolls, post-rolls, and so on.

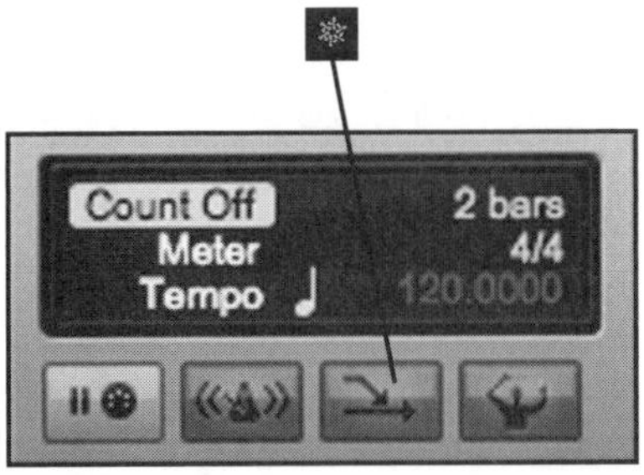

Here's a nifty feature: MIDI Merge enables you to record on a MIDI track without overwriting any pre-existing MIDI data. It's an especially useful feature when you're working in Loop Playback mode.

When you're finished, you'll have a region, as you did when you recorded audio. This time, however, you'll see MIDI note data within the region rather than audio waveforms!

Recording MIDI Instruments to Audio Tracks

Suppose you've created a killer track using your favorite MIDI hardware, and you want to send the session to a friend so that he or she can lay down tracks of his or her own. There's a potential problem: If your friend doesn't have the same MIDI hardware (or virtual instrument) that you have in your studio, he or she won't be able to hear your killer track the way it's meant to be heard. The solution is to record your MIDI instrument to an Audio track and then send your session out for collaboration.

The process is simple enough. You'll use a bus to connect the output of your MIDI instrument's Aux or Instrument track to the input of an Audio track to which you'll record.

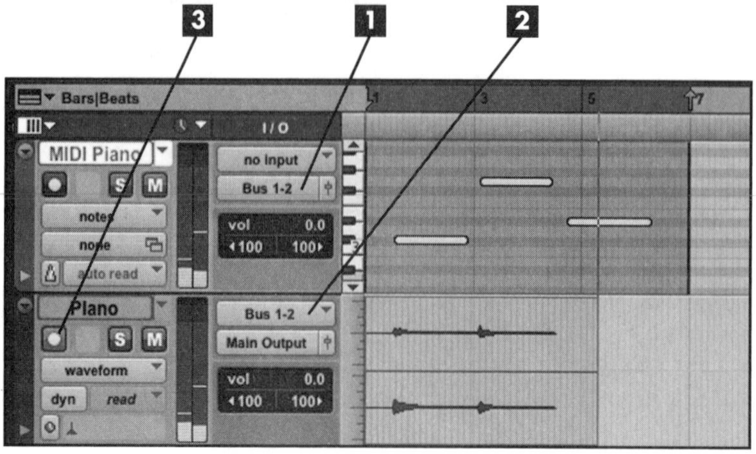

1 **Assign** the **output** of your instrument's Aux or Instrument track to an available bus. (In this image, I've chosen Bus 1–2.)

2 After creating an Audio track to record to, **assign** the **input** of that track to the same bus that you chose for the output of the Aux or Instrument track (again, Bus 1–2 in this example).

3 Now that you have your signals routed properly, you can **record** your **Audio track** normally (which we covered in Chapter 4). You'll see that the level meters of the two tracks are identical.

> **TRACK OUTPUT**
>
> Pro Tools 9 introduces a very useful track-output feature, enabling you to choose either an existing or a new track as an output destination. This can be especially useful when recording virtual instruments to audio tracks, and is a feature we'll dig into in Chapter 9, "Finishing Touches."

> **CHECKING YOUR WORK**
>
> To review some of the concepts discussed in this chapter thus far, take a look at Chapter 07 Session - Part 1 Finished.ptf, included on your book's disc.

Editing MIDI

Editing operations that would be extremely difficult with audio, such as fixing a single note in a chord, are easy with MIDI—if you know how to use the tools available to you. That's what we'll discuss in this section.

> **SETTING THINGS UP**
>
> If you've recorded any MIDI tracks in previous sessions, then you'll have some material with which to practice editing. If not, just launch the Chapter 07 Session - Part 2.ptf session, which you'll find on your book's disc.

Editing with Tools

There are a number of ways to edit MIDI data, giving you a greater degree of control over specific notes than you might have when working with Audio tracks. Of course, you'll still have all the region-editing tools that you've come to know in the previous editing chapters; Selector, Grabber, and Trimmer (including the TCE Trimmer tool) work with MIDI regions in the same way they work with audio regions. In the interest of efficiency, I won't rehash these basic (but powerful) ways of working in the Edit window, but do take some time to reacquaint yourself with these tools when you get the opportunity.

The interesting thing about working with MIDI is the specificity of control you have over your tracks. You can go beyond the relatively large region level and work with individual notes themselves, and beyond. Even at these deeper levels, you still have use of the editing tools that are already familiar to you, although their behavior will be somewhat different. The first thing to do, though, is to change your Edit window's view so that you can actually see what you're working with.

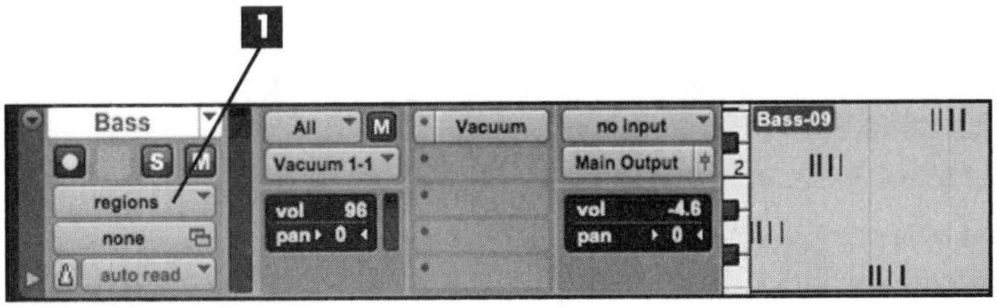

1 **Click** on the **Track View selector** on the desired track. (In this example, I've chosen the Bass track.) The Track View menu will appear.

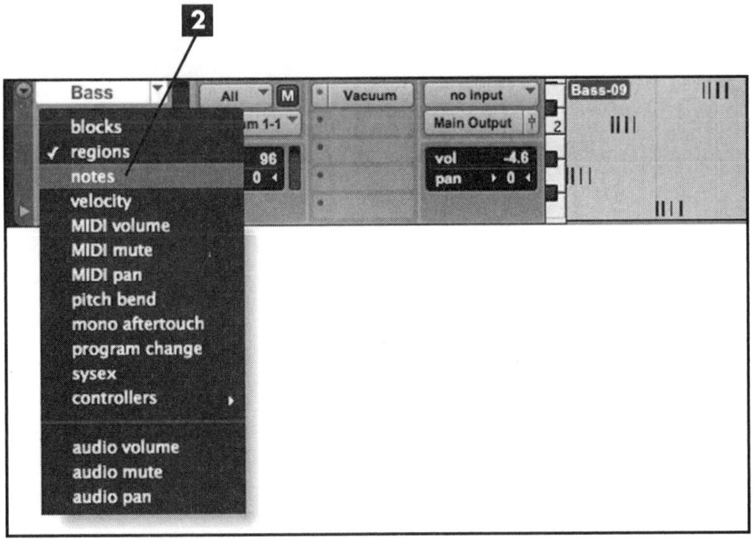

2 The Track View menu enables you to choose the kind of data you will view and manipulate. Because this is an Instrument track and contains MIDI data, the menu will display all editable aspects of MIDI in Pro Tools, including controllers and system-exclusive data. You'll be working on note data first, so **click** on the **Notes menu item**.

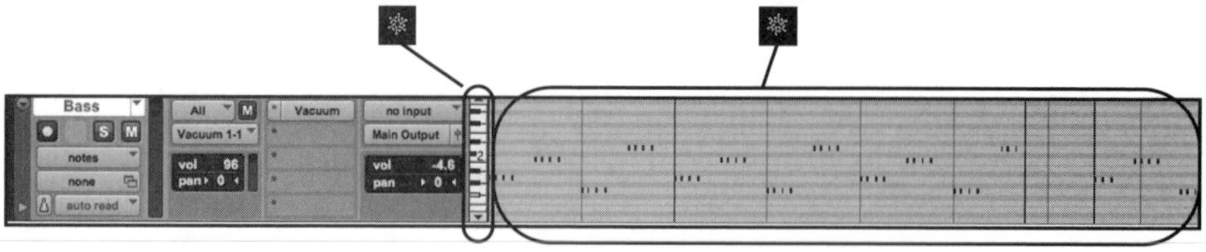

- The regions will fade out a bit, and a series of blocks will gain prominence. Each of these blocks represents a MIDI note.
- On the left edge of the MIDI track's Playlist area, you will notice an image of a piano keyboard. This side-facing keyboard indicates the pitches of the MIDI notes on the track.

Depending on the kind of track you're working with, your next step is to get your MIDI data into easy view. There are a few ways to do this, using some familiar tools:

- Use the horizontal zoom buttons to see more or less of your timeline.

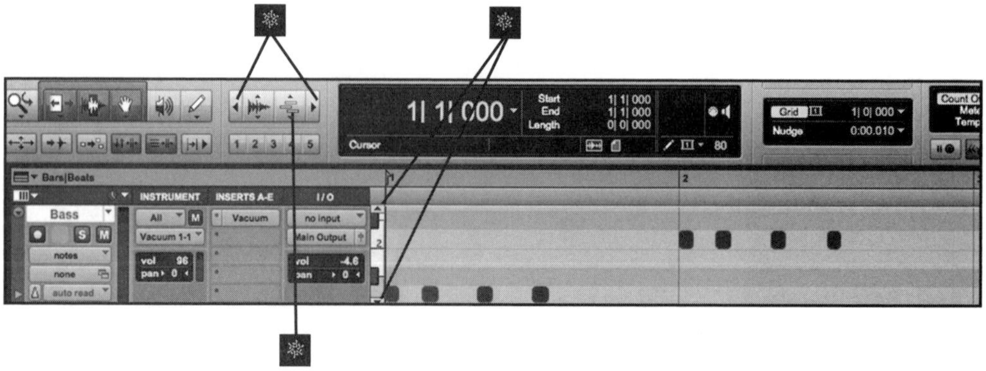

- Use the MIDI Zoom buttons to zoom *vertically* on your MIDI data. Note that the keyboard image to the left of the Playlist area will expand and contract accordingly.
- Click on the arrow at either end of the keyboard image to scroll the register of the track up or down.

The Grabber Tool

The Grabber tool does just what it says: It enables you to *grab* data objects in the Edit window and move them. Since we're working with a MIDI track in Notes view, your "objects" in this case are individual notes!

1 If the Grabber tool isn't already selected, **click** the **Grabber tool** to activate it.

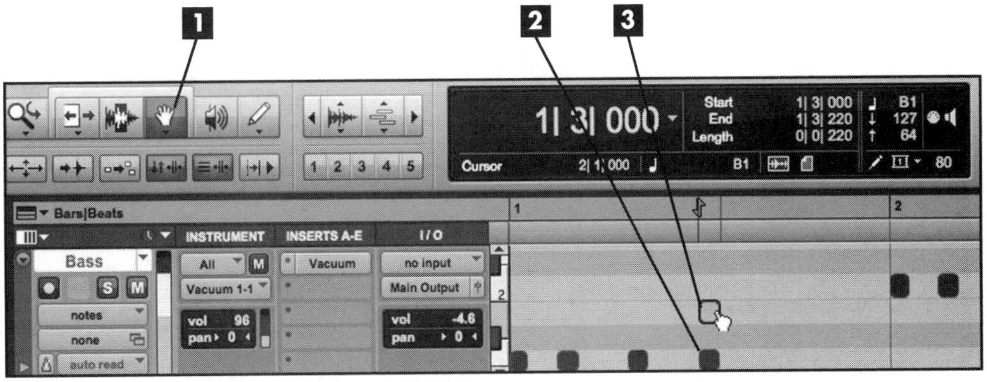

2 **Click** on a **single note** in your track. The note will be highlighted, indicating that it has been selected and is ready to be moved.

3 **Drag and drop** the **note** to a different pitch or timing, as desired.

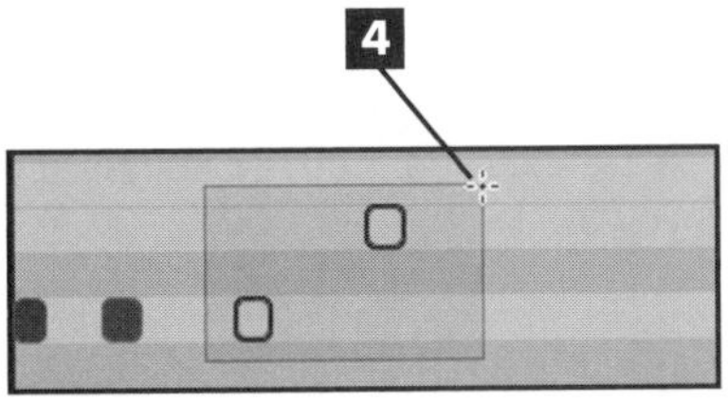

4 If you want to move more than one note at a time, just **click and drag** a box around the **notes** you want to change. The group of notes will be highlighted, indicating that they are selected.

5 **Drag and drop** the **group of notes** in the same manner that you moved a single note.

SELECTIVE SELECTING

There's another way to move a group of notes: Just hold down the Shift key while clicking the notes you want to move. The selected notes will be highlighted.

SELECTING A SINGLE PITCH

Here's a quick way to select *all* the notes of a given pitch on a MIDI or Instrument track: Just click on the desired note on the keyboard at the left of your track's Playlist area. All the notes of that pitch will be selected. This is particularly useful when you are dealing with MIDI drum tracks (which typically use repeated notes of identical pitch)!

The Trimmer Tool

The Trimmer tool enables you to adjust the beginning and/or end of MIDI notes in much the same way you've changed region boundaries when working with Audio tracks.

> **SETTING THINGS UP**
>
> If you're not in the Slip Edit mode, now would be a good time to switch to it so you can change your note lengths freely. Of course, you can use any of the edit modes depending on your work situation, but in this case, Slip will work the best.

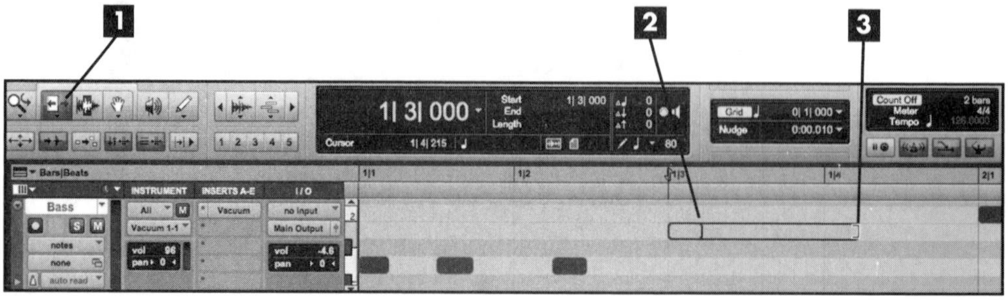

1 If the Trimmer tool isn't already selected, **click** the **Trimmer tool** to activate it.

2 **Click** on **either end** of a note in your track. The note will be highlighted, indicating that it is selected.

3 **Drag** the **end** of the note as desired. The length of a note can be lengthened or shortened using the Trimmer tool.

The Pencil Tool

The Pencil tool might just be the most useful of all the MIDI editing tools. Using the Pencil tool, you can create a MIDI note (or another type of MIDI data) and then modify it after the data is created.

> **SETTING THINGS UP**
>
> In Slip mode, you can create your data anywhere, but in this case, I want to create a quarter note right on beat 4 of the first bar. To make the job easier, let's switch to Grid mode and set a grid value of 1/4 note. (For a review of this process, refer to Chapter 5, "Editing.")

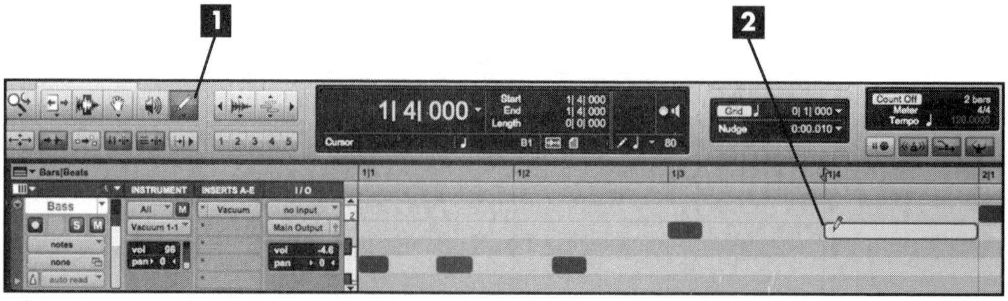

1 If the Pencil tool isn't already selected, **click** the **Pencil tool** to activate it.

2 **Click** on any **open area** of your track. Wherever you click, a MIDI note will be created. Since I've put myself in Grid mode with a grid value of 1/4 note, the note will be placed directly on the beat.

Setting Note Duration and Velocity

In Pro Tools, the Pencil tool defaults to creating notes whose duration follows the current Grid value. However, you have the ability to choose a separate default note duration and MIDI velocity value for notes created with the Pencil tool, making the Pencil tool even easier to use.

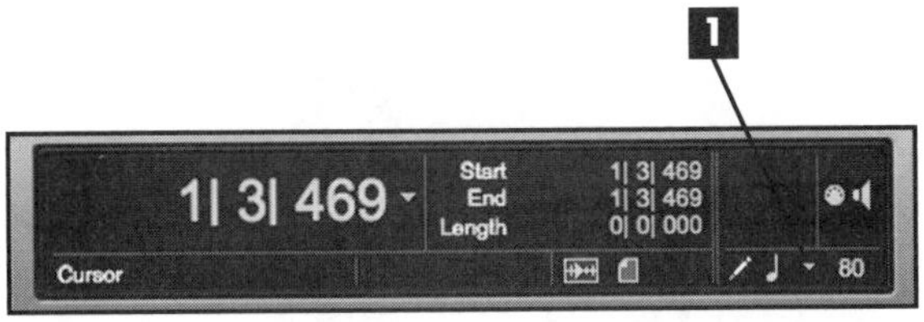

1 **Click** on the **Note Duration pop-up menu**, located in the lower-right area of the Counters and Edit Selections section of the Edit window. The Note Duration menu will appear.

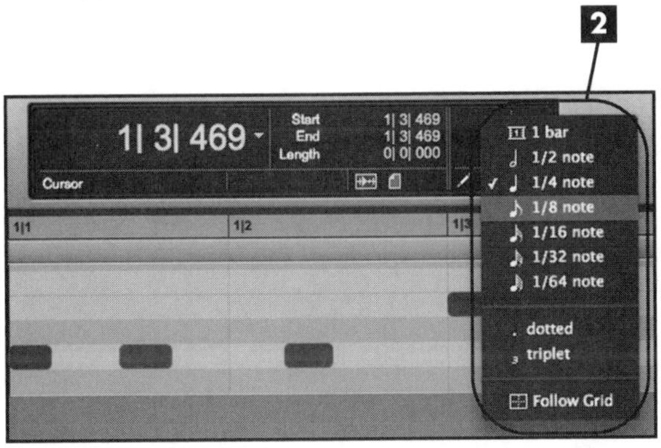

2 **Choose** the desired **note duration** from the list. (The currently selected duration will be indicated by a checkmark.) Choosing the Follow Grid option will change your duration to continually match your grid settings (regardless of whether Grid mode is active).

3 **Click** on the **MIDI Velocity indicator** (the value will be highlighted, as shown here) and **type** the desired default MIDI velocity. To confirm your value, press the Enter key.

Creating a Series of Notes with the Pencil Tool

Creating a string of notes quickly can come in very handy, particularly when you're working with drum tracks. The Pencil tool makes it easy, if you use the Line version of the tool. (The spacing of the string of notes is based on your grid setting.)

1 **Click and hold** on the **Pencil tool**. A list of Pencil tool options will appear.

2 This list of drawing shape variations will come in handy in a variety of situations (particularly when mixing, which we'll explore in the next chapter). In this instance, you'll want to **use** the **Line** variation of the tool, so select it from the list.

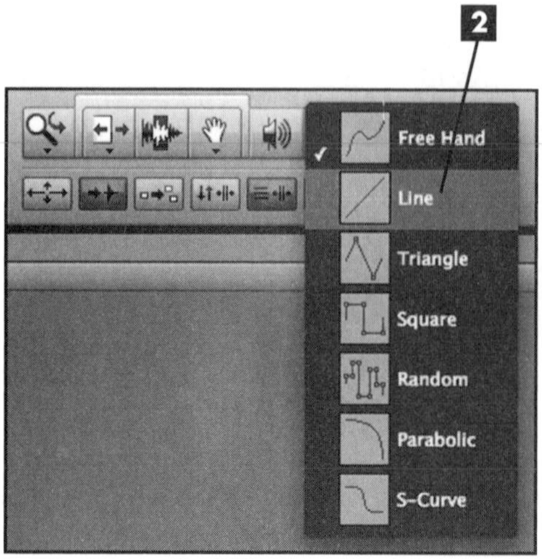

3 **Click and hold** with your Pencil tool at the point where you want to *begin* entering new MIDI note data.

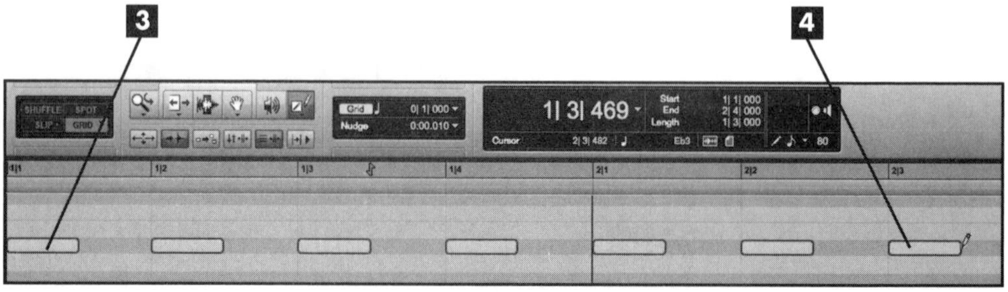

4 **Drag** the **Pencil cursor** left or right to create a string of notes. Note that in this example, the duration of each note is an eighth note (based upon the note duration), and the spacing is every quarter note (based upon the grid value).

MORE POWER WITH THE PENCIL TOOL

The Pencil tool is great for quick MIDI work—not only for its ability to create new notes, but also for its other functions. If you click in the body of an existing note, the Pencil tool will take on the function of a Grabber (enabling you to quickly move the note). If you move the Pencil tool to either end of an existing note, it will become a Trimmer tool (enabling you to adjust the beginning or end of the note).

PLAYING MIDI NOTES WHEN EDITING

Sometimes, it is very convenient to hear notes as you move or tab through them, and sometimes it can be a distraction. Either way, Pro Tools makes it easy to work the way you want.

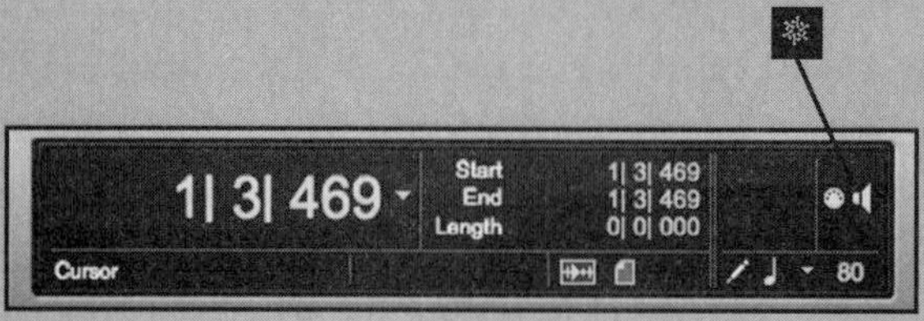

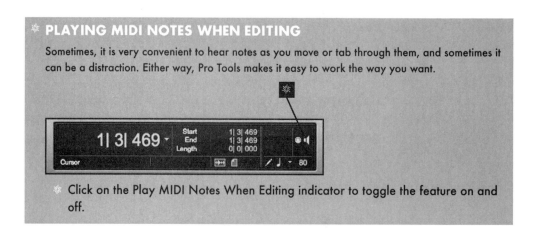

- Click on the Play MIDI Notes When Editing indicator to toggle the feature on and off.

Changing Tempo

As you learned in Chapter 6, "And More Editing," your session's bars|beats time scale and your MIDI tempo settings are interrelated and form the timing basis for your tick-based tracks. You can control tempo quickly and easily from the tempo ruler or even enter values numerically.

- For your session to follow the tempo ruler (as opposed to the static tempo displayed in the MIDI Controls section of the Edit and Transport windows), you'll need to have the Conductor Track button enabled in the MIDI controls section of the Transport or Edit window.

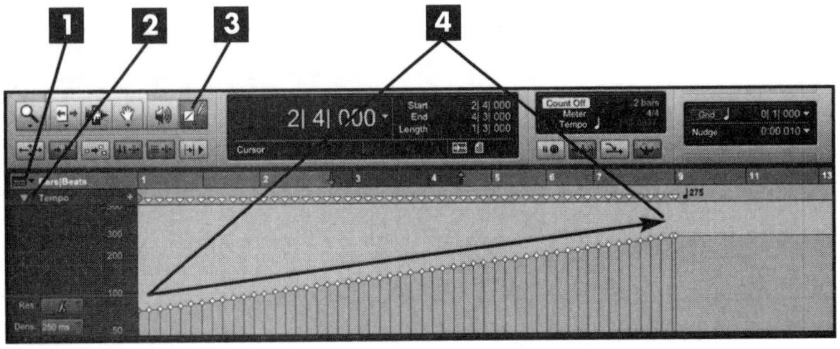

1. If you're not seeing your tempo ruler, you'll need to reveal it in your Edit window now. **Go to** the **View menu**, **select** the **Rulers menu item**, and **choose Tempo**. You can also select it quickly by clicking the Ruler menu icon (indicated here) and choosing Tempo from the menu.
2. **Click** on the **Tempo Editor Expand/Collapse triangle** to reveal the expanded tempo ruler.
3. **Click** the **Pencil tool** (in this example, with the Line option selected).
4. Changing tempo is very simple—just **click and drag** to create tempo change data.

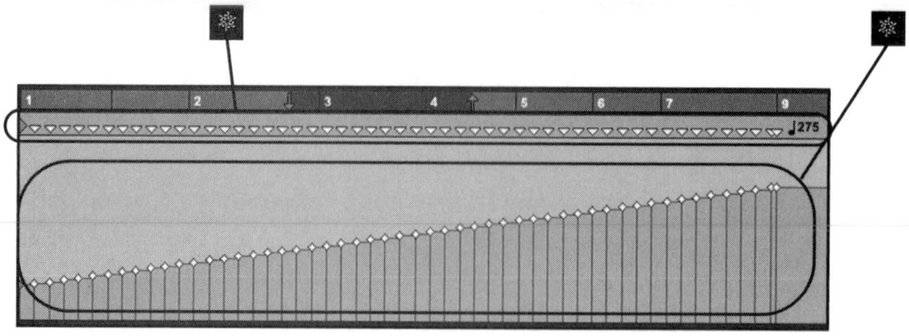

- The tempo change is represented as a straight ramp (because we were using the Pencil tool in Line mode), from 126 beats per minute up to 170 beats per minute. With the Pencil tool, you can write (and overwrite) tempo changes with the Freehand, Line, Parabolic, or S-Curve settings.
- The tempo changes are also shown as a series of triangular value changes. You can also edit these values by clicking and dragging or even double-clicking and typing a specific tempo value, although the more graphic tempo display described earlier is far easier for many Pro Tools users to work with.

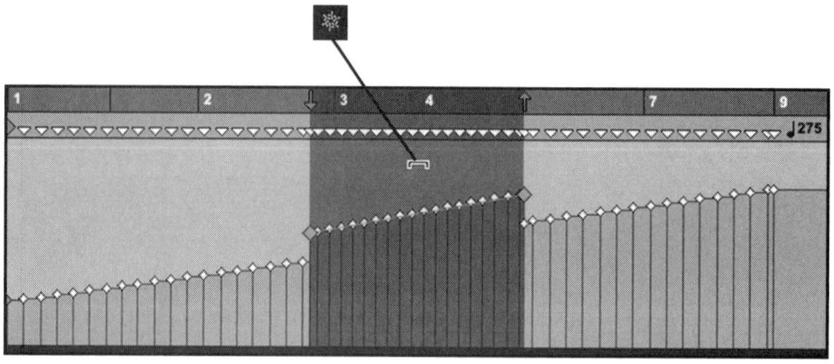

- Although changing tempo with the Pencil tool might be the easiest method, it's not the only way. By using the Trimmer tool (shown here), you can scale tempo up or down as desired. (Note that the Trimmer tool points down when editing tempo, as opposed to the normal horizontal facing of the tool when trimming region boundaries.)

You can also create a tempo change by choosing specific times and values.

1 From the Event menu and then from the Tempo Operations submenu, you can **create a tempo change** in a variety of shapes. The process is similar regardless of the shape you've chosen.

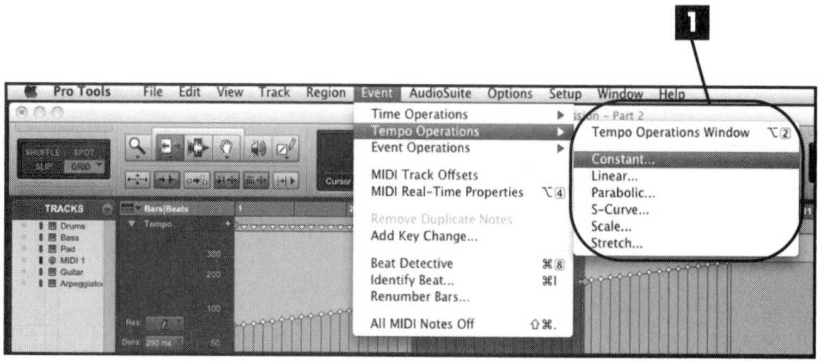

2 **Enter** the **start and end points** for your tempo change.

3 **Select** the **tempo value(s)**.

4 When you're finished, **click** the **Apply button**, and your tempo change will be applied.

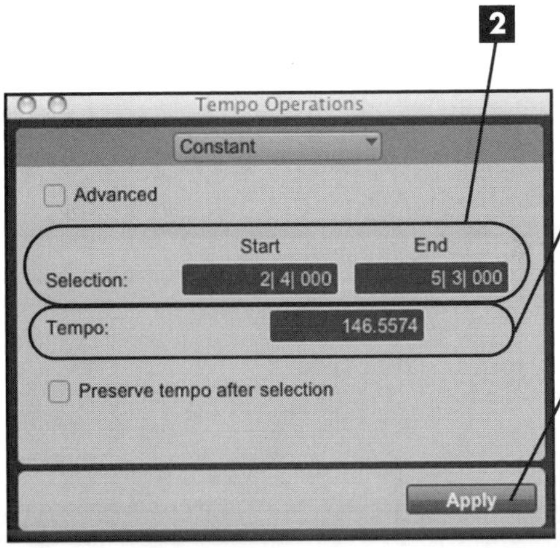

The Event List

Most longtime MIDI users are familiar with the traditional MIDI Event list, a simple yet powerful window in which you can type exact values for your MIDI data. Although it is among the oldest of all MIDI editing environments, it can come in very handy when you want to get specific with your MIDI. Here's how to use it in Pro Tools:

1 **Click** on the **Window menu**.

2 **Click** on **MIDI Event List**. The MIDI Event List window will appear.

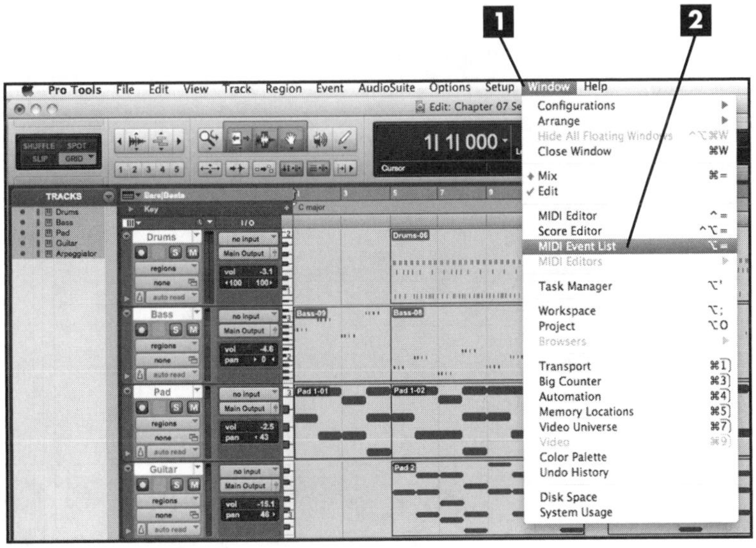

- The button in the upper-left corner of the Event List window indicates the name of the MIDI track being viewed. Clicking this button will reveal a drop-down menu of all MIDI and Instrument tracks, where you can choose different tracks.

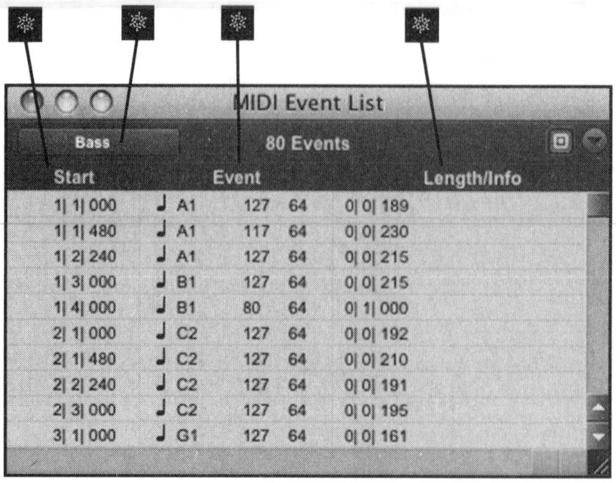

- The Start column shows the beginning time for each event, listed sequentially.
- The Event column indicates the type of individual events (note, pan, and so on), as well as their value.
- The Length/Info column shows more specific information about each event.

- So how do you tweak this data? Easy: Just double-click on the value you want to change, type the new value, and press the Enter key!
- Click the Event List pop-up menu button to reveal more event-related options.

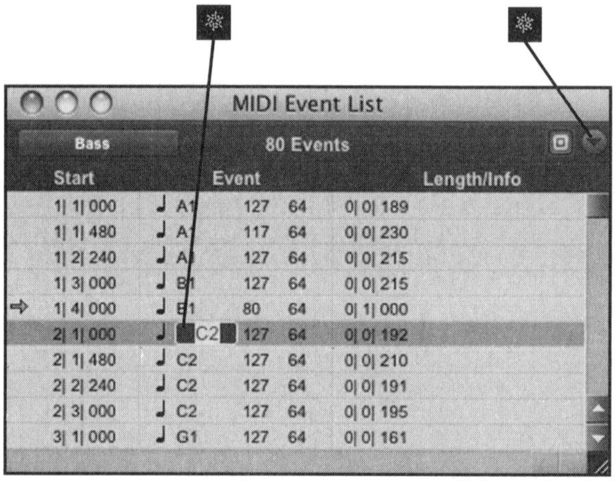

- The Event List pop-up menu will give a variety of viewing options, as well as enable you to create new MIDI events (using the Insert function).

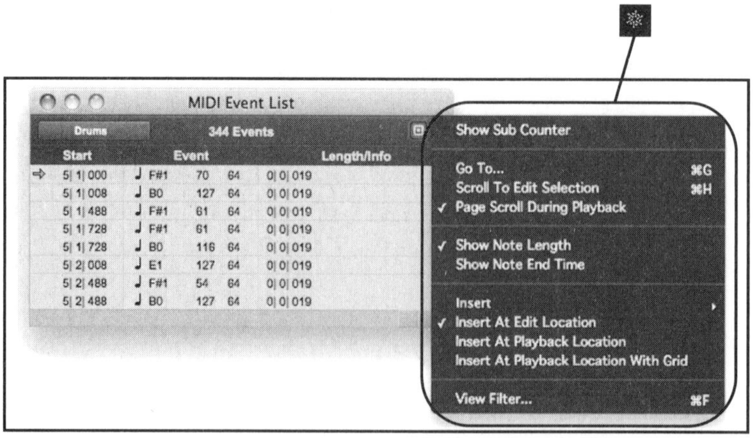

Managing a MIDI Session

Before we move on, here are a few more MIDI operations that will help you work with MIDI. These processes will not only serve you directly if you're a MIDI musician, but will also help non-MIDI users work with MIDI projects that come into their studios.

Importing and Exporting MIDI Data

One of MIDI's greatest advantages is its broad compatibility. Nearly every MIDI application can utilize MIDI's Standard MIDI File (SMF) format, and Pro Tools is no exception. That means you can easily bring in MIDI data from other applications, as well as send MIDI information *to* other applications.

Importing MIDI Data from the File Menu

Just as you can import an Audio file to an Audio track, you can import a standard MIDI file to one or more MIDI tracks in your session.

1. **Click** on **File**.
2. **Select Import**.
3. **Select MIDI**. The Open dialog box will appear.

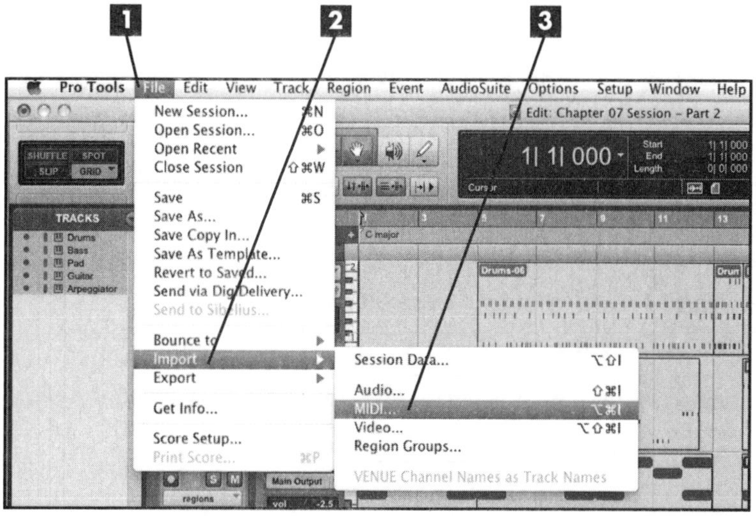

4. In the Open dialog box, **select** the **MIDI file** you want to import.
5. **Click** the **Open button**. The MIDI Import Options dialog box will open.

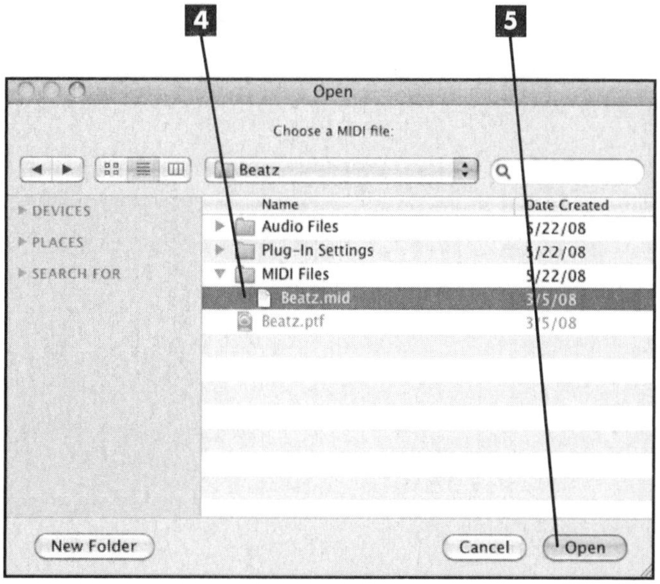

* The Destination section of the MIDI Import Options dialog box will enable you to choose whether the imported MIDI data will go to a new track (or tracks) or simply be added to the Regions list.

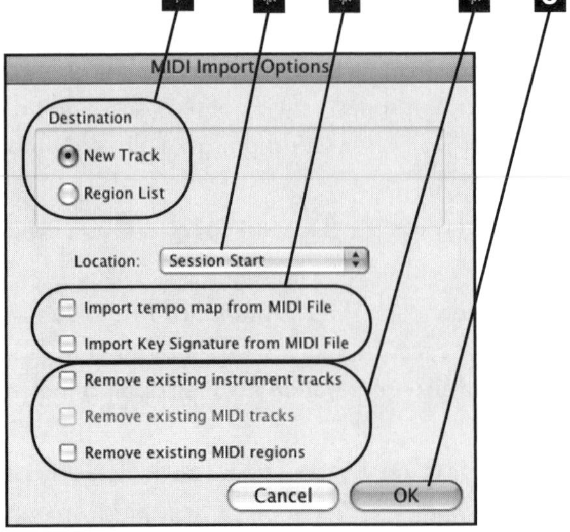

* The Location drop-down menu will let you choose where the region will be deposited on the timeline. In this image, the new MIDI data will begin at the session start, but you also have the option of choosing the song start (if it's different from the session start), the beginning of a selection, or a specific spot in your session. (The same Spot dialog box that you use in Spot mode will appear.)
* You have the option of also importing that MIDI file's tempo map or key signatures. Be careful, though–importing these will overwrite the existing tempo or key signature rulers in your session.
* You have the option of removing any existing Instrument tracks, MIDI tracks, or MIDI regions in your session.

6 When you've chosen the options that work best, **click OK**. The MIDI will be immediately imported into your session according to your settings.

Importing MIDI Data from the Workspace

Just as you can import audio from the Workspace Browser with ease, you can also import MIDI. When it comes to importing MIDI, though, the news gets even better, because you can import an entire song's worth of material with just a click and a drag. Here's how:

1 **Click Window.**

2 **Click** the **Workspace menu item.** The Workspace Browser will appear, as you saw in Chapter 3.

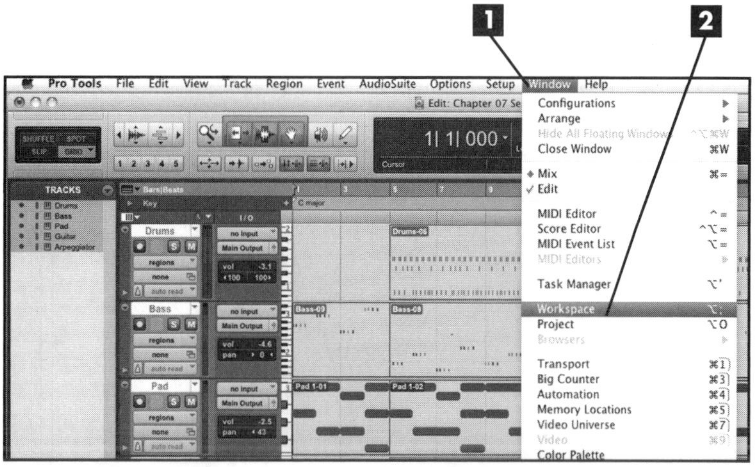

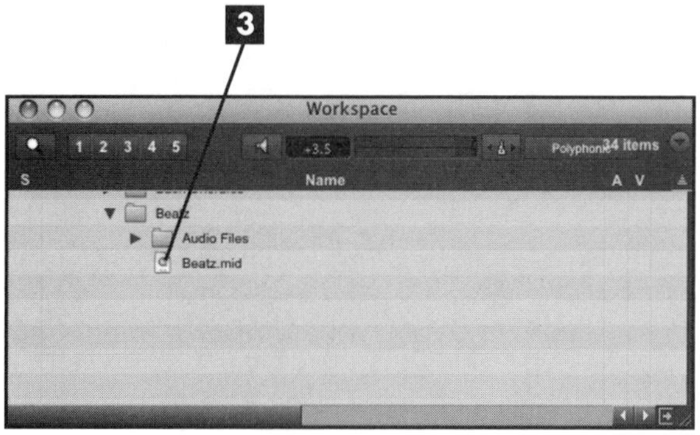

3 **Drag** the desired **MIDI file** into your Edit window's Playlist area, just as you did before with Audio files. (You can also drag to the Regions or Tracks list if you like.) When applicable, the MIDI Import Options dialog box will appear, as you saw earlier in this section. According to your Import Options, the individual MIDI tracks included in the SMF file will be created in your Edit window, and the appropriate regions will be created.

AFTER YOU IMPORT

Keep in mind that even after you import your MIDI data, you'll still have to set your MIDI output and Aux track(s) before you can play and hear your MIDI data through the Pro Tools Mixer.

Exporting MIDI Data

When you save your session, your MIDI data will automatically be saved in that session file. There's usually no need to save your MIDI data as a separate file. However, from time to time, you may need to save the MIDI portion of your session to a Standard MIDI file so that you can open it in a different program.

1 **Click** on **File**.

2 **Click** on **Export**.

3 **Click** on **MIDI**. The Export MIDI Settings dialog box will appear.

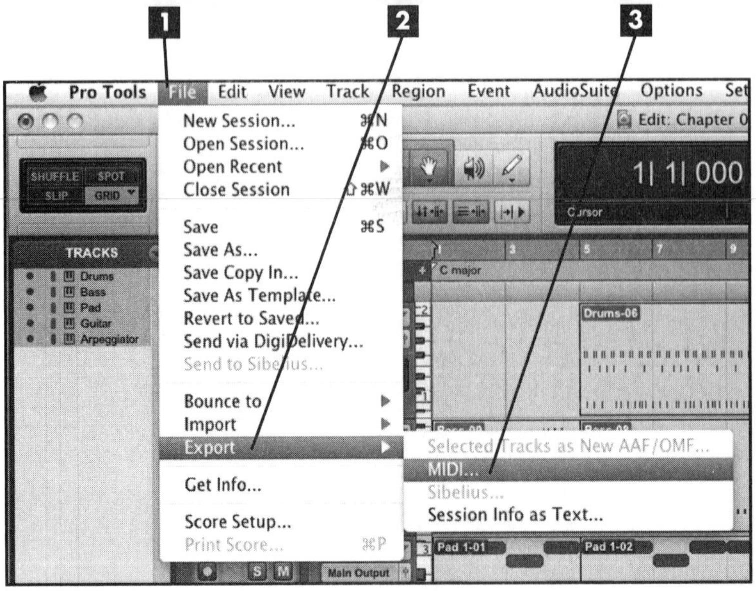

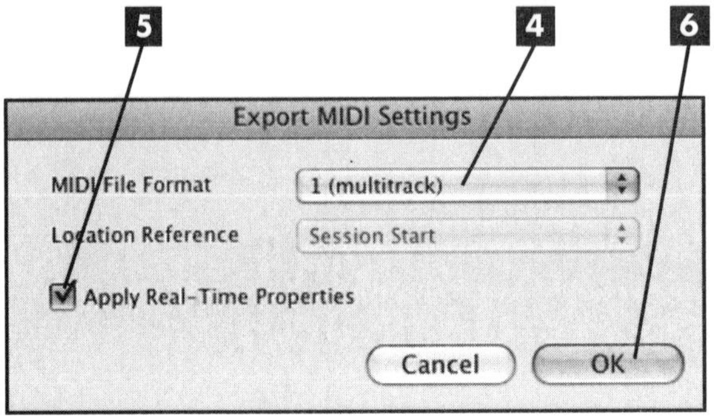

4 Before you can choose where you will save your Standard MIDI file, you'll need to make a few choices in the Export MIDI Settings dialog box. **Click** the **MIDI File Format button** to choose what kind of Standard MIDI File you'll be creating. You have two options:

- Select the 0 (Single-Track) option to save all your data as a single MIDI track, regardless of how many MIDI tracks you may have in your session. (This is commonly used in multimedia applications.)
- Select the 1 (Multitrack) option to preserve the multitrack organization of your MIDI data. This is the type of Standard MIDI file most commonly used in professional circles, enabling your tracks to be recreated in any program that supports Type 1 Standard MIDI files.

5 **Click** the **Apply Real-Time Properties checkbox** to "print" any real-time properties you may have in your session to your new Standard MIDI file. (For more information on MIDI Real-Time Properties, see Appendix A, found on the CD-ROM.)

6 When you're finished, **click** on **OK**. A standard Save dialog box will appear, enabling you to choose the name and location for your new SMF. All tracks that are not muted will be exported.

Here's a way to export MIDI on a track-by-track basis.

1. **Right-click** on the desired **track name** (in either the track itself or the Tracks list). A menu will appear.
2. **Choose** the **Export MIDI menu item**. The Export MIDI Settings dialog box will appear, just as you've seen before.

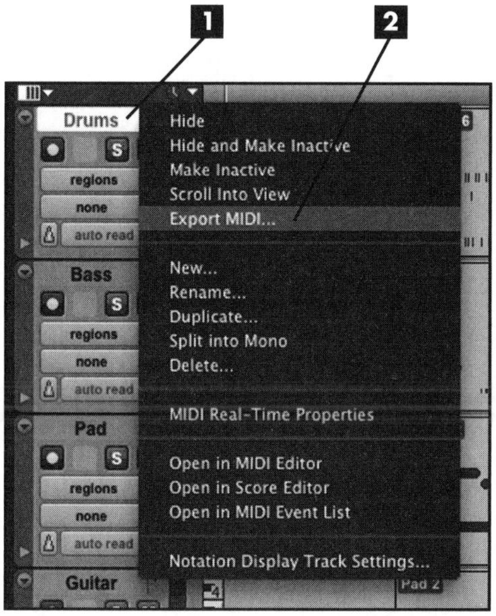

3. **Make** your **choices**, **click** the **OK** button, and **save** your **file**—easy!

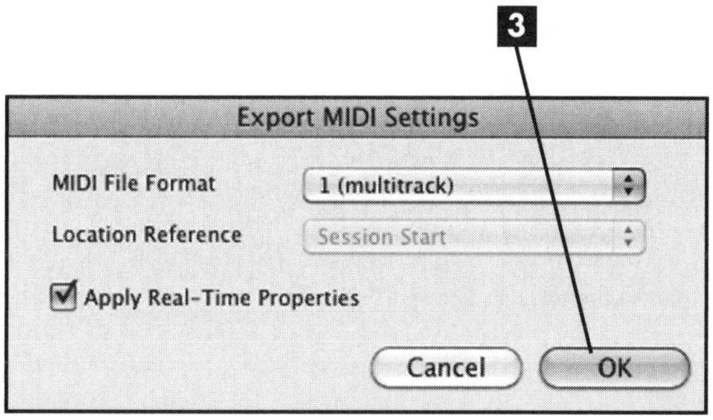

Removing Duplicate MIDI Notes

From time to time, a MIDI note can be doubly triggered during the recording process. (In my personal experience, this has happened mostly with MIDI drum controllers.) Occasionally, these duplicate notes can result in erratic behavior from your MIDI devices—notes being cut off prematurely and so on. To handle this, Pro Tools includes a Remove Duplicate Notes operation.

1. **Select** the **MIDI data** that you want to clean up through the removal of duplicate MIDI notes.
2. **Click** on the **Event menu**.

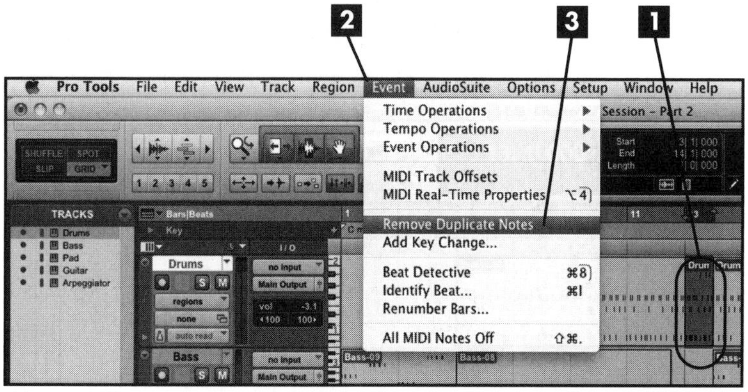

3. **Click** on **Remove Duplicate Notes**. The duplicate MIDI notes will be removed—you're finished!

Panic!

Reality check: Sometimes, things go wrong. Worse yet, sometimes the things that go wrong can be audible, as in the case of a "stuck" MIDI note that never ends. When that happens, the most important thing to do is to stop the data and turn off those notes!

1 **Click** on the **Event menu**.

2 **Click** on the **All MIDI Notes Off menu item** (quickly!). A MIDI note-off command will be sent on all channels, on all ports of your MIDI interface, and through the four virtual MIDI connections.

PANIC SHORTCUT

The fastest way to trigger the All MIDI Notes Off function is to use the shortcut keys: Shift+Command+. (period) will do it on the Mac, and Shift+Ctrl+. (period) will do it on the PC.

MORE ABOUT MIDI

As mentioned at the beginning of this chapter, the discussion here is limited to the sorts of basic MIDI skills that might be expected of any well-rounded Pro Tools user (even if MIDI isn't their thing). The Pro Tools 9 MIDI arsenal includes a whole world of additional—and more powerful—MIDI tools. In fact, over recent versions, Pro Tools has made great strides in the world of MIDI music creation, and has established itself as a serious competitor in the world of MIDI music creation and production. All these new features are beyond the scope of a basic book like this (and would take more than a few extra pages). Does that mean that you're left high and dry? Heck no! Appendix A, on your book's CD-ROM, will deal with these new features, including advanced MIDI editing and timeline operations, production tips, and an introduction to the powerful MIDI and Score Editor windows. Enjoy!

Next stop: mixing!

8 Basic Mixing

When it comes to DAWs, there are two schools of thought on mixing: mixing "inside the box" or mixing "outside the box." Mixing inside the box refers to making use of your DAW's virtual mixer and virtual effects entirely within the Pro Tools environment. At any given time, you will listen to a summed (for example, stereo) output of your mix through your audio interface, and all the required processing is performed by your computer (the "box"). Mixing outside the box refers to the practice of assigning individual tracks to individual outputs of your audio interface, and from there to individual channels on a separate physical mixing board. The mixing and automation are performed by this external mixer, and Pro Tools is reduced to a recording, editing, and playback device (still playing critical roles in any production workflow).

There is lively discussion (and I'm being polite here) within the professional community regarding the virtues of mixing outside the box versus inside the box. There are valid points on both sides of the debate, but for the end-user, the debate boils down to this essential truth: Great work is being done using both methods, and individuals should follow the paths that best allow them to realize their creative vision.

For the purposes of this book, we'll be exploring the world of mixing inside the box—a method that has been used on countless professional projects. In this chapter, you'll learn how to:

- Work with the specific layout and function of the Mix window.
- Use fader groups.
- Use file-based and real-time effects.
- Work with traditional mix routing.
- Use basic automation techniques.

ON MIXING

Those of you who have some experience mixing with older versions of Pro Tools will notice some differences between the way things used to be and how they are now. One of the most obvious differences is that now, you very rarely will have to stop playback to make changes to your Mixer (things such as adding tracks, sends, plug-ins, and so on). In the past, these sorts of things necessitated stopping of playback; now you can go ahead and make these changes as you continue playback. There are two things to keep in mind, though. One, depending upon what you're doing, you might hear a short gap of silence as the mix engine reconfigures itself. Two, if you're recording audio, you *will* have to stop playback to make these sorts of changes so that you don't interrupt the recorded audio.

More Signal Flow

When you're talking about mixing, what you're really talking about is *signal flow*. The more complex your mix gets, the more complex the routing of those signals can be. Even the most complex mixes, however, can be reduced to a few simple elements. The following list will go through the order of audio signal flow through those elements within an Audio or Aux track.

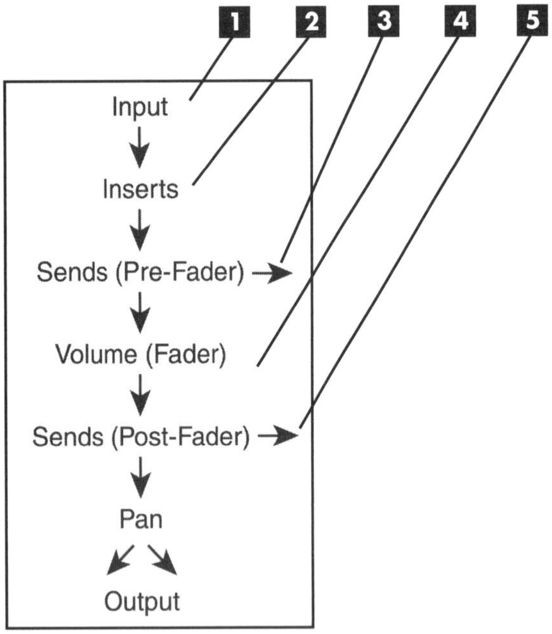

1. **Input.** On an Audio or Aux track, input can be from an interface input, a bus, or in some cases a plug-in.
2. **Inserts.** Inserts are most commonly used as holders for effects. One-hundred percent of your signal passes through your insert.
3. **Sends (Pre-Fader).** A send makes a copy of the signal to be routed to another destination. A *pre-fader* send makes that copy before the signal hits your volume fader. The destination of this send can be an interface output or a bus.
4. **Volume (Fader).** This is where you control the output volume of the track.
5. **Sends (Post-Fader).** This kind of send makes a copy *after* the signal has been altered by the volume fader. As with a pre-fader send, the destination can be an interface output or a bus.

6 Pan. Panning comes next, and allows the level of the signal to be varied between a number of outputs (left and right, in the case of a stereo mix). This is how you can create a stereo mix of several mono or stereo tracks. If, on the other hand, you route your track to a single output, no pan slider will be needed, and you won't see one in the channel strip.

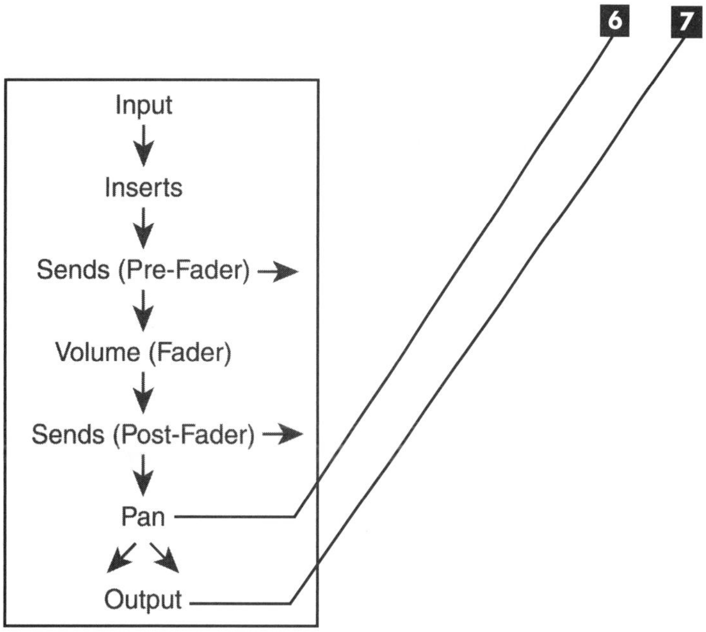

7 Output. After all these stages are passed, the signal goes to the Pro Tools mix engine and out of an interface output or bus.

> **A WORD ABOUT FADERS**
>
> Remember that the volume fader on your track only controls the output of that track. That means the fader has absolutely no effect on the input coming to the track. The net effect is this: If you're recording audio and you see your levels clipping, turn down the output of the instrument or microphone or change the gain on your interface. The fader on an Audio or Aux track cannot prevent clipping.

Exploring the Mix Window

You've visited the Mix window before (way back in Chapter 2, "Getting Around in Pro Tools"), but now it's time to dig deeper. If you're not looking at it already, the first thing to do is to switch over to the Mix window (which you also learned how to do in Chapter 2). Depending on how you left the Mix window last time, the channel strips might appear rather narrow. Although the Narrow Mix view can certainly be useful in some situations, you'll be able to see more information with Narrow Mix view turned off. Here's how to check which view you're in and disable Narrow Mix view if it's currently enabled.

> **SETTING THINGS UP**
>
> For this chapter, please use the tutorial session named Chapter 08 Session, included on the disc that came with your book. Remember, you'll need to copy the session folder to a location on your computer's audio hard drive before working on it.

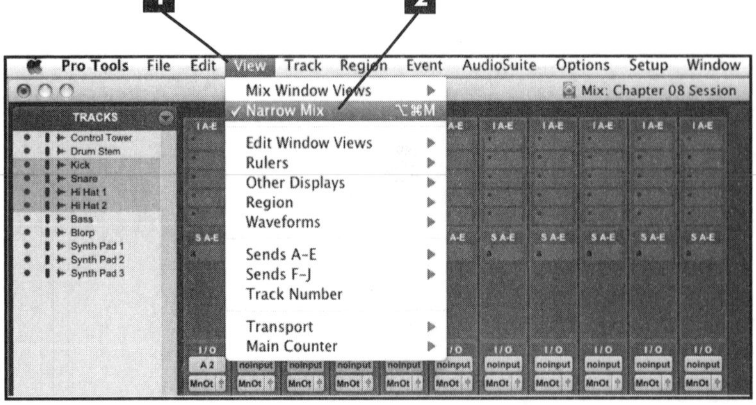

1 **Click** on the **View menu.** In this image, the Narrow Mix option is checked, indicating that Narrow Mix view is active.

2 **Click** on **Narrow Mix** to uncheck it. The channels will be shown in their normal mode.

> **WHEN TO USE NARROW MIX VIEW**
>
> There are certainly times when the Narrow Mix view is desirable. For example, when your session contains too many tracks to be normally displayed at once in the Mix window, switching to Narrow Mix mode will enable you to view more of your mix at once.

Basic Mixer Terminology

Before we progress further, let's review the basic layout of the Mix window:

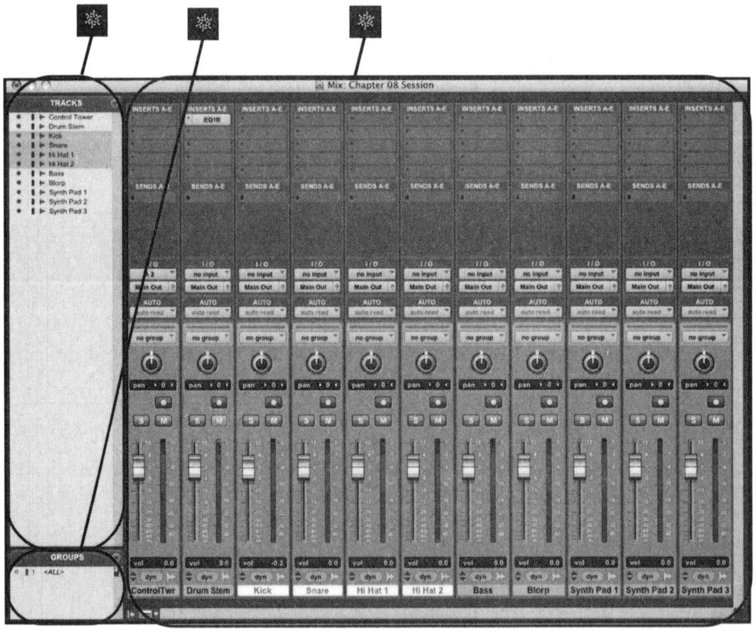

- **Tracks list.** As in the Edit window, a dark dot will appear to the left of shown tracks, and highlighted track names indicate selected tracks.
- **Groups list.** Mix groups will be shown here. (You'll learn how to use them later in this chapter.)
- **Channel strips.** There is a separate vertical channel strip for each shown track.

Now take a look at the different sections of a basic Audio track's channel strip.

- At the top of the channel strip are the Inserts sections. There are 10 inserts for you to use, divided into two sections of five. All audio passing through a channel strip will be routed through the inserts first, in descending order. It is here that you will launch plug-in effects and virtual instruments.
- Next are the sends. Like inserts, you have 10 sends, divided into two sections of five. You'll use sends to route a copy of your track's processed audio to another destination. Sends are commonly used in conjunction with other tracks to create more complex effect situations or to create cue mixes in recording situations. (We'll discuss this further in Chapter 10, "Moving to the Next Level: Tips and Tricks.")

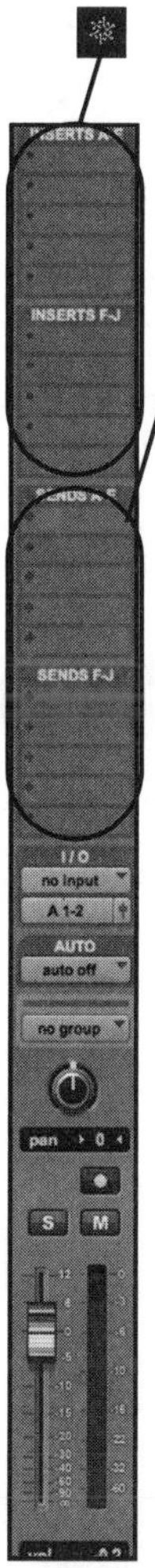

MIDI TRACK SIGNAL FLOW

MIDI tracks have no inserts or sends, as inserts and sends can route only audio data.

Moving down the channel strip, the next section looks and functions just like the I/O column of a track in the Edit window.

- Input Path Selector button
- Output Path Selector button
- Automation Mode Selector button (covered later in this chapter...finally!)
- Group ID indicator
- Pan knob
- Pan indicator

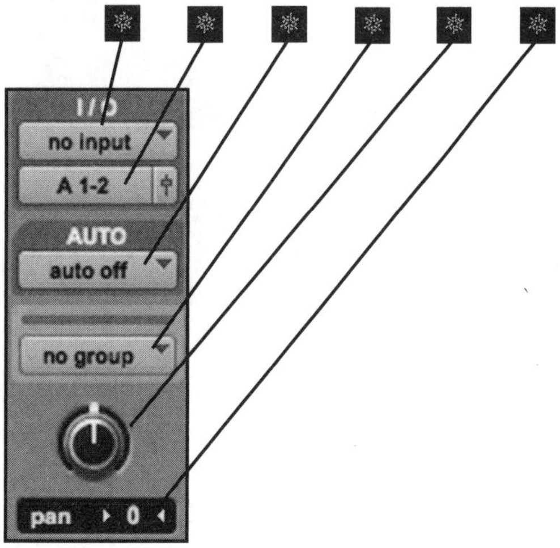

The bottom section of an Audio track's channel strip may look a bit different from what you've seen in the Edit window, but these buttons' functions should be old hat by now.

- Record Enable button
- Solo button
- Mute button
- Volume fader
- Volume Level meter
- Volume indicator
- Track Type icon
- Track name

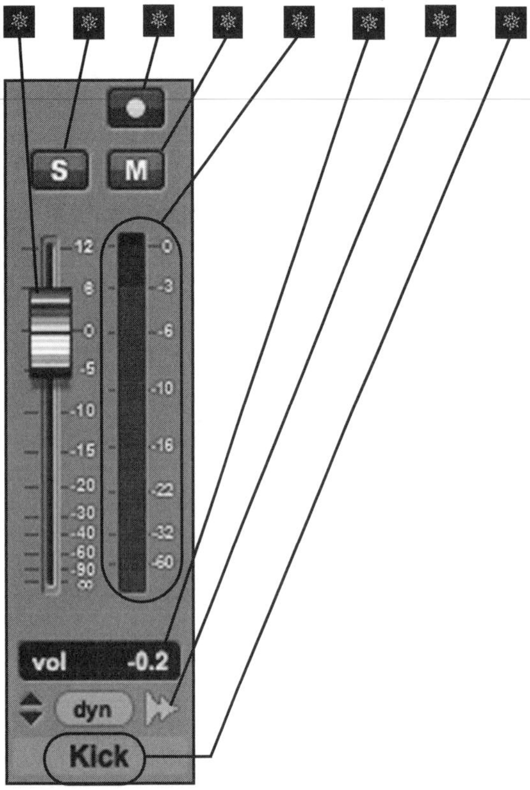

TRACK TYPE ICONS

The Track Type icon at the bottom-right corner of each channel strip will indicate the type of track it is:

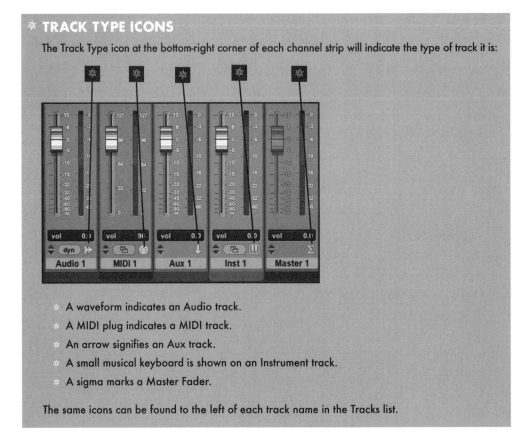

- A waveform indicates an Audio track.
- A MIDI plug indicates a MIDI track.
- An arrow signifies an Aux track.
- A small musical keyboard is shown on an Instrument track.
- A sigma marks a Master Fader.

The same icons can be found to the left of each track name in the Tracks list.

IS IT MONO OR STEREO?

You can easily tell whether the track is stereo or mono by taking a look at the volume meters. One meter indicates a mono track; a stereo track will have two volume meters.

Track Colors

If you take a look at the View menu, and from there the Mix Window Views submenu, you'll see that you have the ability to show track colors—small colored tabs at the top and bottom of each channel strip. Although their function is purely visual, you'll find that using track colors is pretty handy. Let's use track colors to differentiate between the different kinds of tracks:

1. **Select** the **track(s)** you want to color by clicking on the track name(s). If you're following along with the tutorial session, let's start by coloring the drum tracks. All the drum tracks (the Drum Stem, Kick, Snare, Hi Hat 1, and Hi Hat 2 tracks) have been selected for you.
2. **Click** the **Window menu**.
3. **Choose Color Palette**. The Color Palette window will appear.

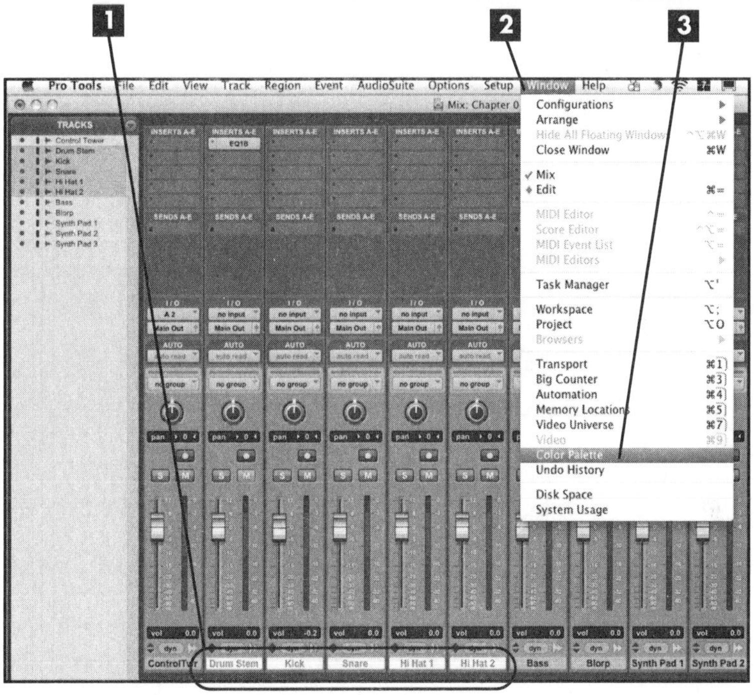

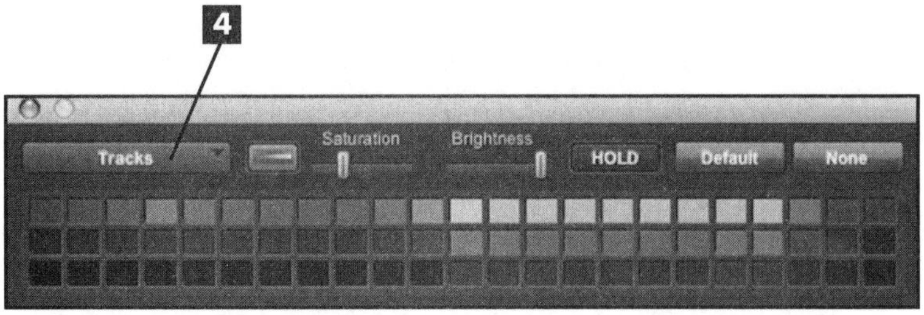

4. The Apply to Selected menu will enable you to change the color of different parts of your session. In this image, the changes you make in this window will be applied to the selected tracks in your session. If the menu button does *not* read "Tracks," **click** the **button**.

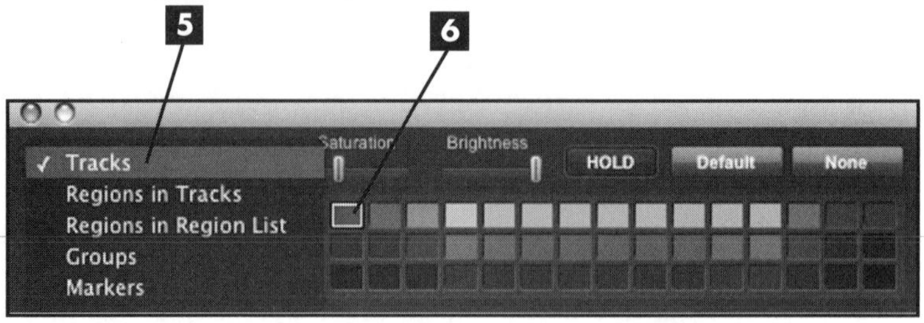

5 In the Apply to Selected menu, the session element targeted for change will be indicated with a checkmark. Since coloring our track is the job at hand, **make sure** that **Tracks** is checked.

6 From this point, it's simple: **Click** the **color tile** that you want to assign to your selected tracks. In this example, I want my drum tracks to be colored red. Once you click the desired color, the tracks' color will change accordingly.

Track coloring isn't limited to the small tabs at the top and bottom of each channel strip. You also have the ability to apply track colors to the entire channel strips, radically changing the look of your Mix window.

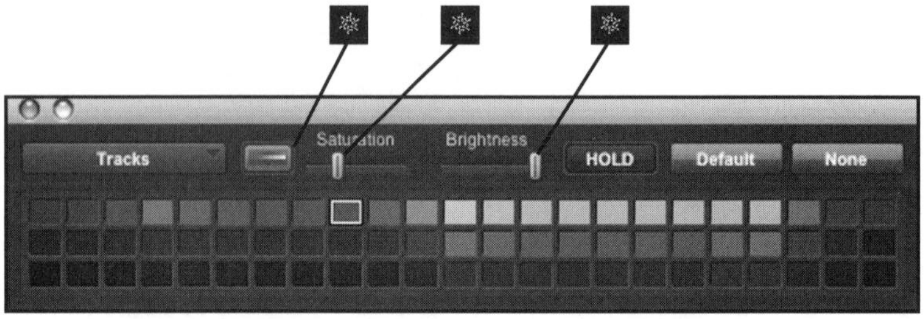

- You can toggle channel strip colors on or off by clicking the Apply to Channel Strip button. When active, the button will be colored blue, and you'll see the track color applied throughout the channel strip.
- Once you've activated your channel strip colors, you then have the ability to adjust the saturation, or intensity of the colors. The farther you move the slider to the right, the stronger your channel-strip colors will become.
- Regardless of whether you're using channel-strip coloring, you have the ability to adjust the brightness of your Mix window. Used in combination with the Saturation slider, you'll be able to tweak your Mix window to suit your taste.

Last but not least, here are some useful options to assist in your track coloring:

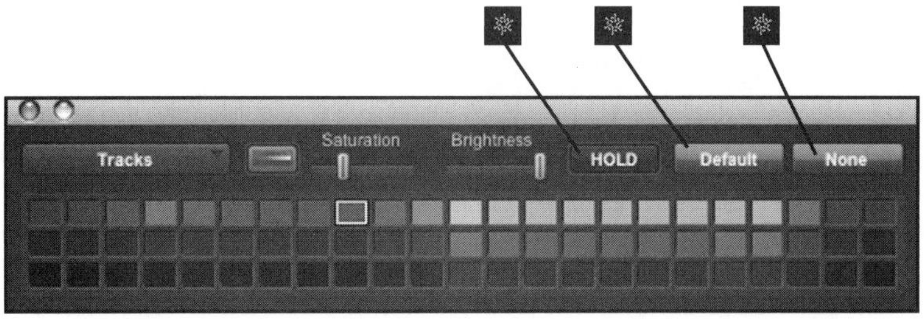

- If you ever want to assign the same color to multiple elements (such as multiple tracks or tracks and regions), the Hold button will come in handy. Just choose the color you want to use and then click the Hold button. The color will remain selected as you navigate different tracks and other session elements, until the Hold button is again clicked.
- Each track type has a default color code. For example, a new Audio track will be colored blue, a new Aux track will be green, and so on. If you want to set a track's color back to its default value, just click the Default button.
- If you want to remove all color labeling from a selected track (or tracks), click the None button.

Mix Groups

One of the neatest things about mixing in Pro Tools is that you can link faders (and more) together. Then, moving one fader will move all the faders in that linked group. This is particularly useful in cases where you have a good relative blend between a number of tracks (for example, a nice balance between all the individual drum tracks), and you want to change the volume of those tracks without changing the blend. By making a mix group, you can do precisely that!

To start off, let's get a feel for what a mix group can do. As luck would have it, Pro Tools automatically creates a group (named All), which always includes all the tracks in your session. Take a look at what it does:

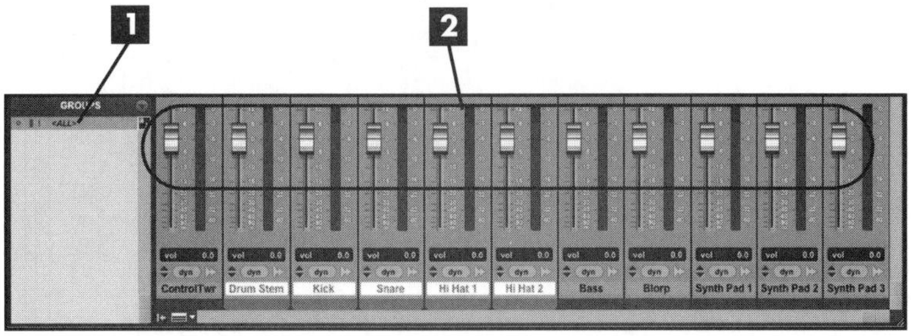

1. Before you can use a mix group, that group must be active (indicated by the group's name being highlighted). If the All group name is not highlighted, **click** on **All**. The group name will be highlighted, and the group (which in this case includes all the tracks in your session) will be active.
2. **Click** on any **volume fader** and **drag it** to change the volume of the track. Because the All group is currently active, the volume controls for all the tracks will move proportionally.

> **GROUP ICONS**
>
> Above each track's Pan knob, the Group ID indicator indicates mix group activity on a track-by-track basis. When a group is activated, the group ID letter and name will be shown on the member tracks.

Creating a Mix Group

Of course, you can also create new mix groups of your own. For this section, I've set up a blend of my drum tracks (the same tracks I colored red in the previous section), and I want to be able to link their volume faders.

Although it's not strictly necessary at this point, selecting the tracks you want to group together will make the process easier. When that's done, you can open the Create Group dialog box in one of two different ways.

1. **Click** the **Track menu**.
2. **Select Group**. The Create Group dialog box will appear.

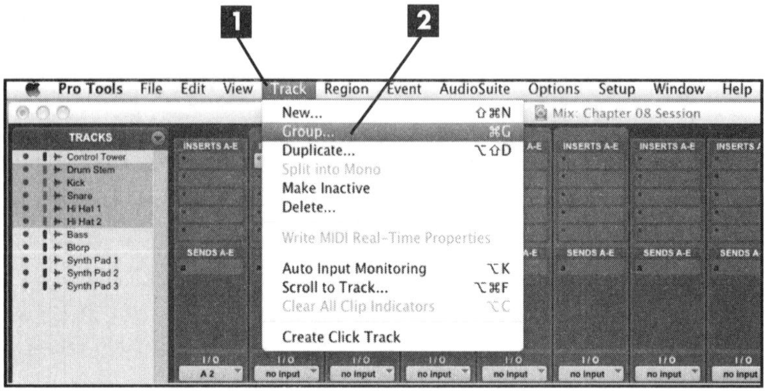

Here's another way to launch the Create Group dialog box:

1. **Click** the **Groups list pop-up button**. A list will appear.
2. **Select New Group**. The Create Group dialog box will appear.

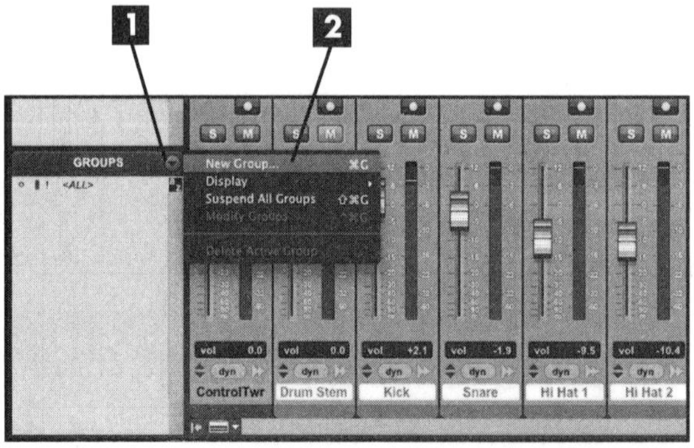

> **NEW GROUP SHORTCUT**
>
> Here's an even quicker way to get to the Create Group dialog box: Press Command+G (Mac) or Ctrl+G (PC).

With the Create Group dialog box open, follow these steps:

1 **Type** a **name** for your new group in the Name field.

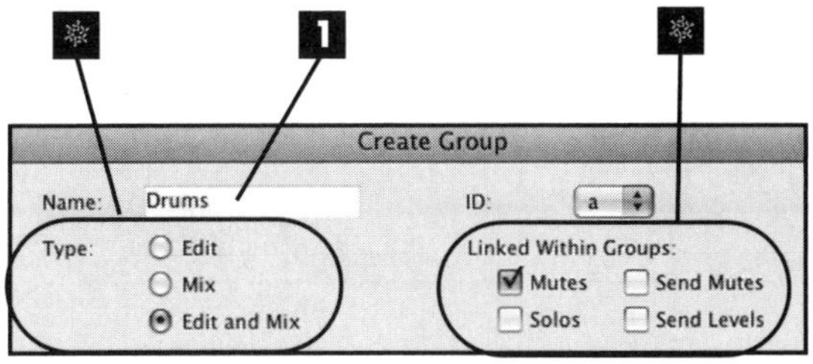

- By default, new groups are created as both edit and mix groups, meaning the group will be accessible from both the Edit and Mix windows. (This default behavior works well in most situations.) If you choose, you can click on either the Edit or the Mix option button to limit the group to a single window.
- Tracks that are grouped together are always grouped together as far as main volume faders are concerned, but you have the ability to group other aspects together as well. I like to have my track mutes grouped together as well, so I've checked the appropriate checkbox. Additionally, you can group solos, send levels, and send mutes.

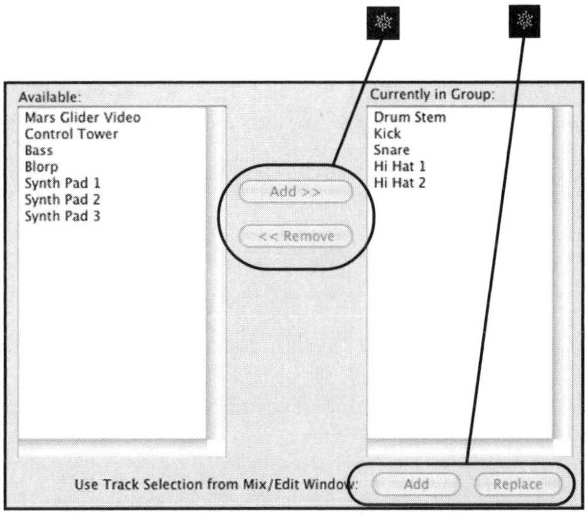

- You can choose the members of your group by populating the Currently in Group area. Initially, your selected tracks will be placed in this area, but if you want to add more tracks to your group, just select the desired tracks in the Available field and then click the Add button. If you want to remove a track from the group, just select the track in the Currently in Group area and then click the Remove button.
- If, after making changes to your group's membership, you want to once again add the selected tracks to the group, you can click either the Add button (to add the selected tracks to any tracks in the Currently in Group field) or the Replace button (which will clear the Currently in Group area and replace it with the selected tracks).

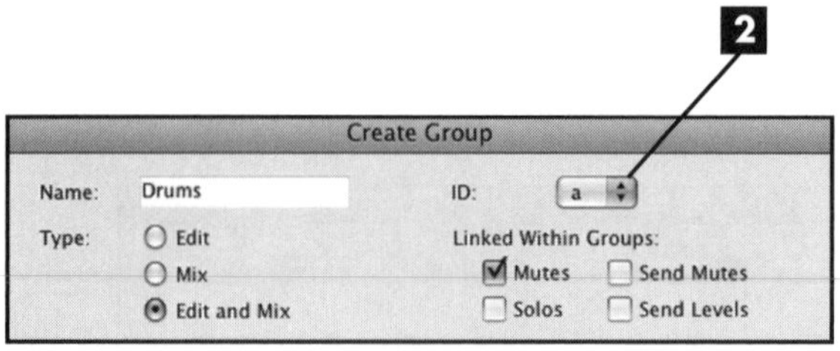

2 Pro Tools will automatically assign a letter to your group for labeling purposes (in this image, it's currently assigned to group a), but let's change that group ID assignment. **Click** on the **ID button**. A list will appear.

3 The ID list is divided into four banks of 26 group letters (for a grand total of 104 user-defined groups). **Choose** the desired **group letter** from this list. Since this is a group named Drums, I've chosen the d group letter from the first bank.

4 **Click** on **OK**, and your group will be created.

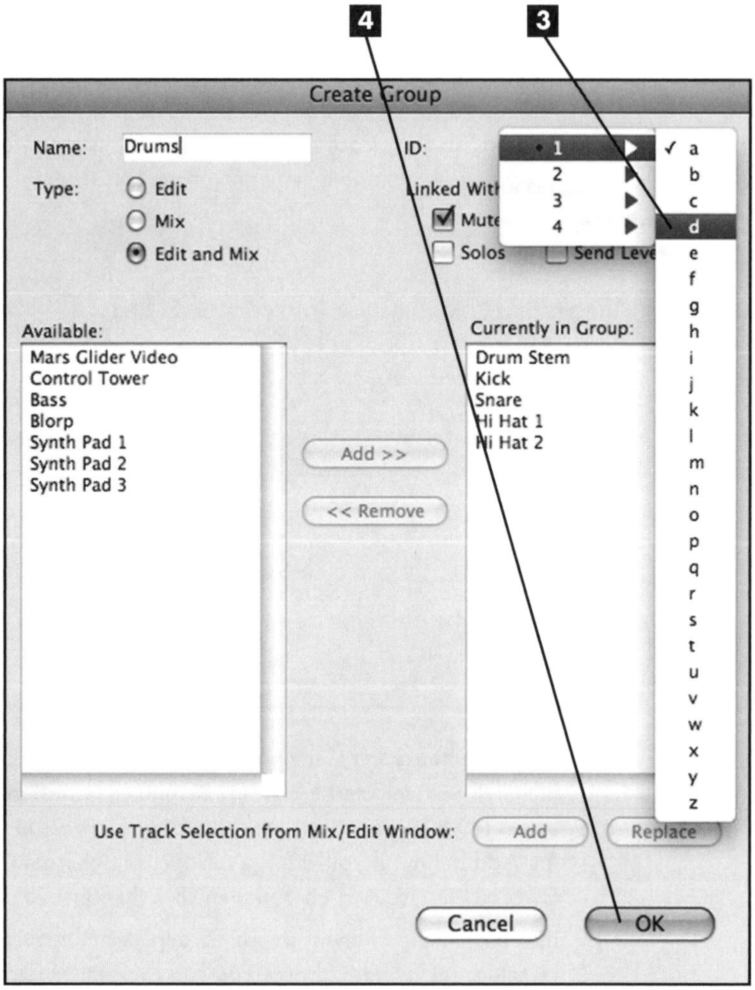

Using the tutorial session, I've created two more groups: a Bass group (which I've assigned to group letter b in the first bank) and a Synths group (assigned to letter s). Here's what I've ended up with:

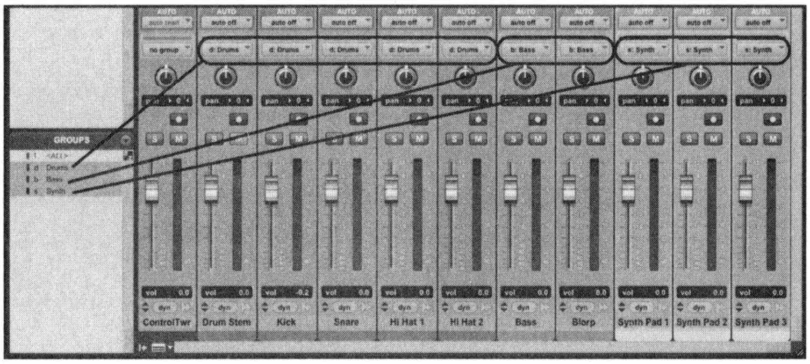

Active mix groups are shown by colored group indicators in member tracks' channel strips (showing the group ID letter and group name). You can activate or deactivate any group by clicking the group name in the Mix Groups list. When a group is deactivated, you will be able to change individual track settings without changing the other members of the group.

ACTIVATING GROUPS

You can highlight more than one group at a time, making multiple groups simultaneously active within your session. Simply click on the name of the group you want to enable, and it will become active.

Here's where the care we took in choosing group ID letters is going to pay off: When you're in the Mix window, you can use your computer's keyboard to activate and deactivate groups by simply pressing the appropriate group ID letter. The way we've set up our session in this example, you can now toggle the Drums group by just pressing the D key on your keyboard. (Pressing B will toggle the Bass group, and pressing S will toggle the Synths group.) I think you'll find that these shortcuts greatly speed up your mixing!

SHORTCUT SHORTCOMING

One limitation of these shortcuts is that they only work for the first bank of group letters. Groups in the other three banks can only be activated or deactivated by clicking the group name in the Mix Groups list.

Using Mix Groups

There's just a little more to learn about mix groups before we continue. For this example, I've created a group of my two hi-hat tracks, which is a subset of the Drums group (referred to as a *nested fader group*). Let's take a look:

- A lowercase ID letter in the Group ID indicator indicates that the track is a member of only one active (highlighted) mix group.

- An uppercase ID letter means that the track is a member of more than one currently active group.
- You can click on a track's Group ID indicator button to reveal a menu of all the active groups of which that track is a member.

- In this example, the Hi Hat 2 track is a member of two active groups: the Drums group and the Hi Hat group. If you move your mouse over either group name, a submenu will be shown, including another submenu that lists all member tracks of that group (shown here).

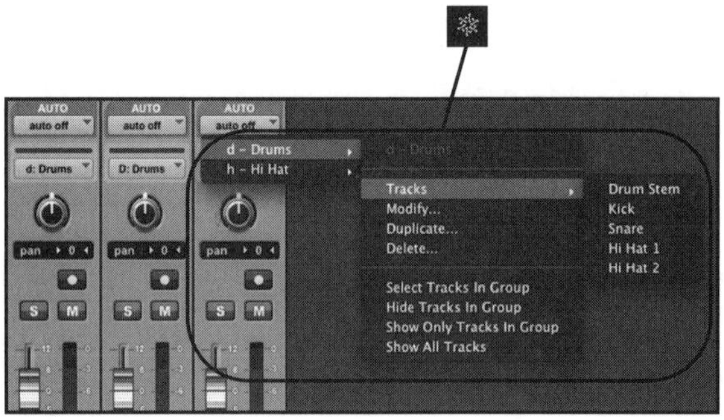

This group options menu deserves a closer look. This list can be shown either by clicking on a track's Group ID indicator or by right-clicking a group's name in the Groups list. (This method works for both mix and edit groups.) Here's how the different options work:

- **Tracks.** Clicking Tracks will display a list of all the member tracks of the group.
- **Attributes.** Clicking Attributes will display a list of the different mix parameters (volume, solo, mute, etc.) that are grouped together in the group.

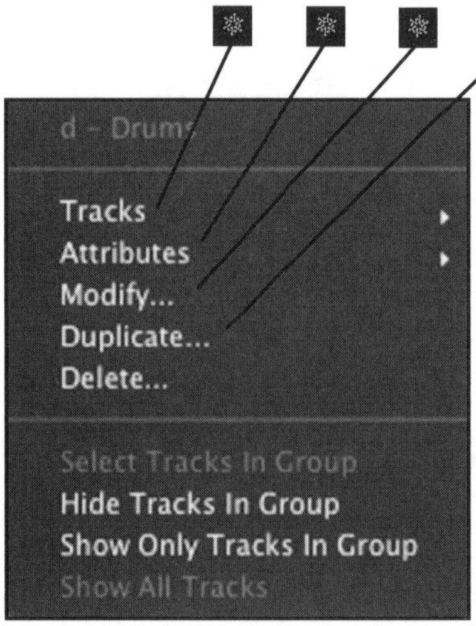

- **Modify.** Clicking Modify will open the Modify Group dialog box (very similar to the Create Group dialog box). Here, you can change group members or any group attribute except the group ID assignment.
- **Duplicate.** The Duplicate menu item will open the Create Group dialog box, with initial settings identical to the selected group.

- **Delete.** The Delete menu item will remove the group (but not the member tracks).
- **Select Tracks in Group.** Clicking Select Tracks in Group instantly selects all the tracks in that group. Only the group's member tracks will be selected.

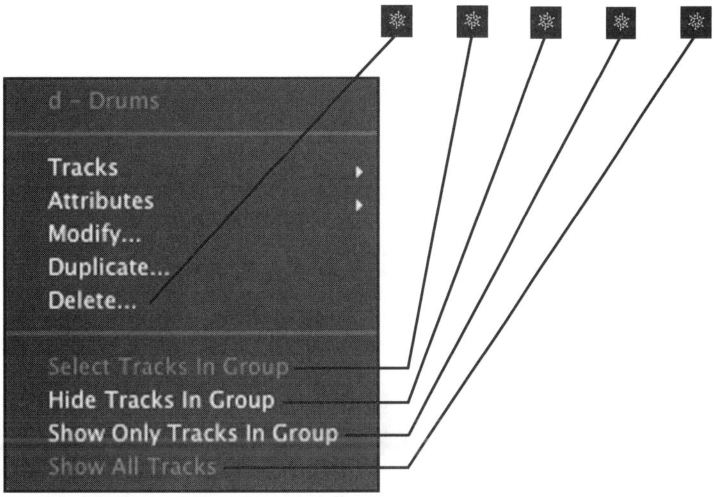

- **Hide/Show Tracks in Group.** Clicking Hide/Show Tracks in Group will hide the group's tracks if they are currently being shown. If the tracks are hidden, this menu item will show them.
- **Show Only Tracks in Group.** Clicking the Show Only Tracks in Group menu item will hide all non-member tracks.
- **Show All Tracks.** The Show All Tracks menu item will show all the tracks in your session.

SELECTING GROUP MEMBERS

Another quick way to select all the members of a group is to click to the left of the group ID in the Groups list.

There's one final list to take a look at before moving on. If you click on the Mix Groups list pop-up button, a menu will be shown, including:

- **New Group.** The New Group option launches the Create Group dialog box.
- **Display.** The Display option shows a submenu (shown here), from which you can choose to see your session's mix groups, edit groups, or all groups in the groups area of your Mix window.

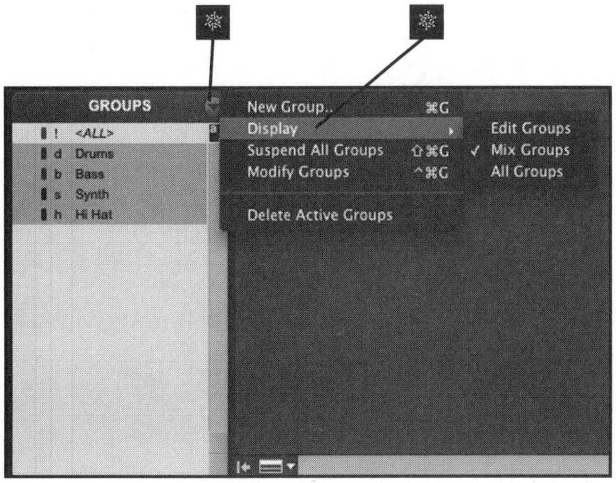

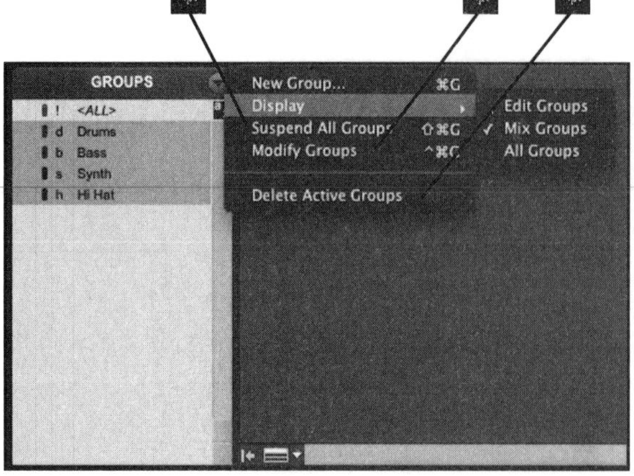

- **Suspend All Groups.** The Suspend All Groups option renders all groups inactive. (The group names will be grayed out.)
- **Modify Groups.** The Modify Groups option opens the Modify Group dialog box.
- **Delete Active Groups.** The Delete Active Groups removes all active groups from your session.

At this point, you have a good sense of the Mix window's layout, and you know how to set up mix groups, which puts you in good shape to start doing a rough mix. Generally speaking, the first draft of a mix consists of simple volume and pan adjustments (which you'll tweak to perfection as your mix evolves). You'll find that the mix groups you've created will serve you well here, especially with larger, more complex sessions.

IF YOU'RE FOLLOWING ALONG...

If you're following along with the tutorial session, you should take some time to get a good rough mix. Once you have a good blend of volume and pan, you'll probably want to add some effects. Read on!

Using Effects

Many software applications use plug-ins—bits of programming designed to operate within a host program. With word processors, plug-ins can be editing tools or macros; graphics applications have visual-effect plug-ins; and so on. Pro Tools is no exception, and Pro Tools plug-ins include all manner of effects processors and virtual instruments. Because they're software (and not hardware), they have great flexibility and can even save you money and rack space in your project studio!

In a Pro Tools 9 system, plug-ins fall into two categories: file-based plug-ins (called *AudioSuite*) and real-time plug-ins (called *Real-Time AudioSuite*, or *RTAS*). First, let's tackle AudioSuite.

AudioSuite

Generally speaking, AudioSuite plug-ins are the most basic of Pro Tools effects. They work directly on files, and this is *not* done in real time as your session plays. That means AudioSuite plug-ins cannot be automated in your Pro Tools session. It also means these plug-ins won't consume your session's valuable real-time resources, making AudioSuite plug-ins well worth exploring. Here's how they work.

1 **Select** the **region** or **area** that you want to process.

2 **Click** on the **AudioSuite menu**. A list of plug-in categories will appear.

3 **Click** on the desired **category** of effect. A submenu will appear, showing all the plug-ins of that type.

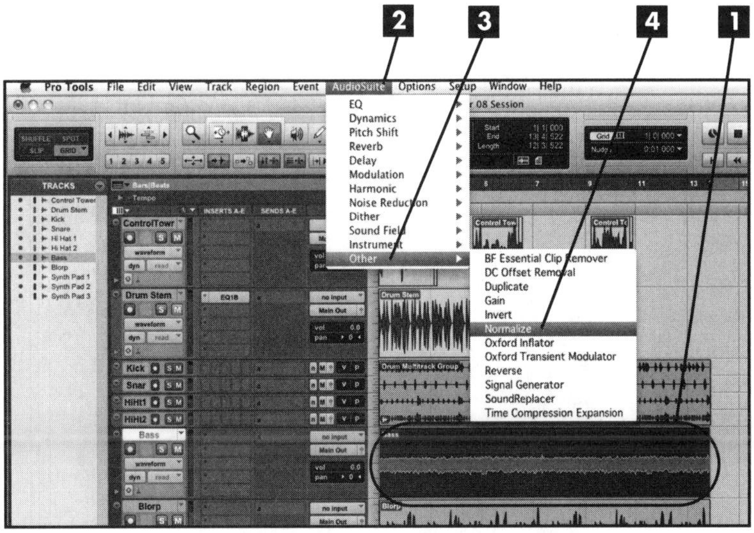

4 **Click** on the desired **plug-in**. The plug-in's window will appear.

NORMALIZE

The effect I've chosen for this section is a handy little process called *Normalize*. This process is a level adjuster that will bring up your entire selection so that the loudest part of the selection matches the value you set. The simplicity of the effect window makes it an obvious choice for tutorial demonstrations.

Normalize can be very useful in some circumstances, but beware of routinely using it to compensate for low recorded levels! Although the volume will be brought up, it will bring up ambient noise levels as well. The bottom line is to record at healthy levels so you won't need to use normalization too often!

GETTING AROUND IN THE AUDIOSUITE PLUG-IN WINDOW

When looking at an AudioSuite plug-in window, it's important to make a distinction between the *function* of some of the buttons and the *labels* they may display at any given time. The buttons at the top of every AudioSuite window show their currently selected settings (as opposed to their function) for quick visual reference.

5 Although different effects will differ in appearance and parameters, they all share some common elements. The Plug-In Selector button (which displays the name of the current plug-in, such as Normalize) will enable you to change effects without closing the window. Just **click** the **Plug-In Selector button**, and a list of AudioSuite plug-ins will appear, identical to the list you saw when you clicked the AudioSuite menu.

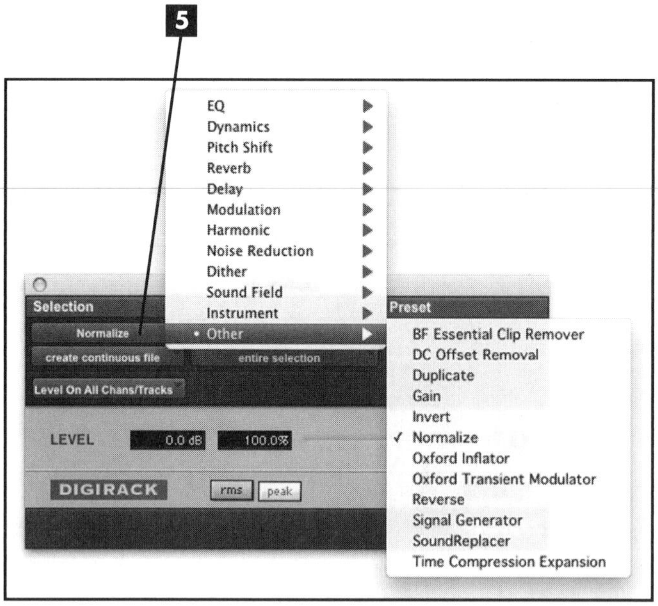

6 **Click** on the **Selection Reference button** (which reads "Playlist" in this image) to determine what will be processed. A menu with two options will appear:

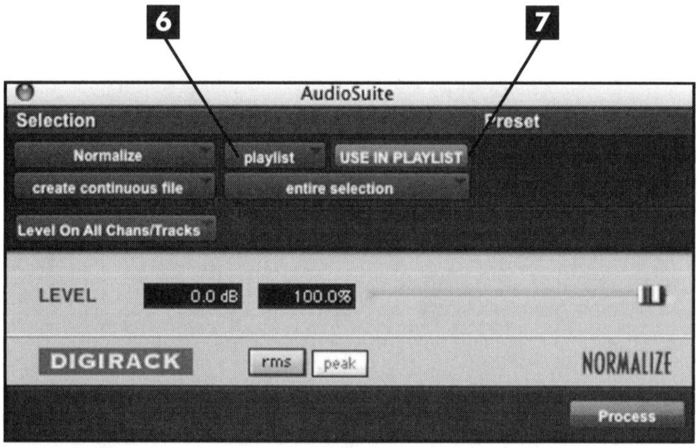

- **Playlist.** When Playlist is selected, the plug-in will process the selected area in your track(s).
- **Region List.** Choosing the Region List option directs the plug-in to process the currently selected regions in the Regions list.

7 **Select Use in Playlist** if you want the processed audio to appear in your tracks (and in the Regions list). When activated, the button will be blue.

USE IN PLAYLIST

If the Use in Playlist button is not active, the processed audio will only appear in the Regions list, and the regions in your track will remain unchanged.

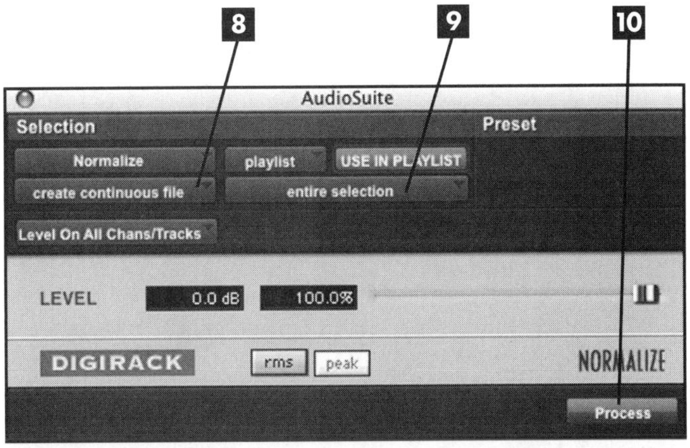

8 **Click** the **File Mode button** (which reads "Create Continuous File" in this image) to determine how audio will be processed. A menu will appear, showing three different processing options:

- **Overwrite Files.** With this option chosen, the selected audio file(s) will be processed directly and *destructively*.
- **Create Individual Files.** This mode is *non*destructive and will create separate audio files for each selected region. If multiple regions are selected, multiple files will be created.
- **Create Continuous File.** This mode is also nondestructive, but in this case it will create a *single* new audio file regardless of the number of regions that are selected.

9 **Click** on the **Process Mode button** (which reads "Entire Selection" in this image) to determine how your regions will be analyzed prior to processing. A menu will appear, showing two options:

- **Region by Region.** With this option chosen, each selected region will be individually analyzed and processed.
- **Entire Selection.** All selected regions will be analyzed prior to being processed.

REGION BY REGION AND NORMALIZE

The Region by Region option is commonly used when normalizing multiple regions of different volumes (different sound effects, for example). With this mode selected, each selected region will be analyzed and processed individually, resulting in multiple regions that all have identical peak volume levels.

10 **Click** the **Process button** to apply your effect.

Here's what you'll end with:

- Since the Use in Playlist button is enabled, a new region has been created to replace the selected region in the track.
- This new region has also been added to the Regions list and has been named "Bass-NORM_01" to indicate that it was created by the Normalize AudioSuite plug-in.

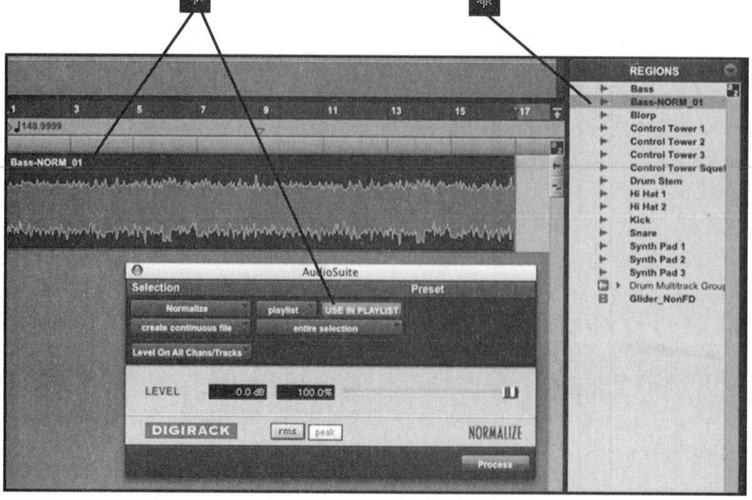

AUDIOSUITE VARIATIONS

The controls discussed here are basic AudioSuite options common to all AudioSuite plug-ins. Different kinds of effects may have additional features relating to their function.

AUDIOSUITE PREVIEW

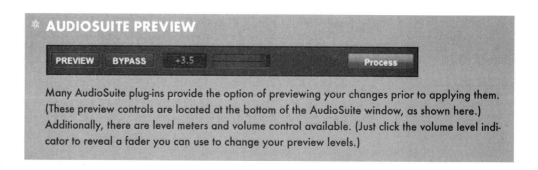

Many AudioSuite plug-ins provide the option of previewing your changes prior to applying them. (These preview controls are located at the bottom of the AudioSuite window, as shown here.) Additionally, there are level meters and volume control available. (Just click the volume level indicator to reveal a fader you can use to change your preview levels.)

RTAS

The next evolutionary step in the world of Pro Tools' plug-in effects is Real-Time AudioSuite (RTAS). Instead of processing audio on a file basis, as is the case with AudioSuite, an RTAS plug-in resides on a track's insert and processes an incoming signal as the session is played (in real time).

Two huge benefits come with using RTAS plug-ins. First, because the audio is being processed in real time, the audio files on your hard drive won't be changed, which enables you to experiment freely with different plug-ins and settings without worrying about filling your hard drive with processed files. Also, as a result of RTAS's real-time operation, you can automate the parameters of your plug-in (something we'll cover later in this chapter), meaning that your effects can change dynamically over time.

IF YOU'RE FOLLOWING ALONG WITH THIS EXAMPLE...

If you've been using the Chapter 08 Session file, you might notice there's a Video track. In this section, we'll be doing a bit of sound design to make the audio work better with the scene. You can view your video by opening the Video window. (Go to the Window menu and choose Video; a Video window will appear.) This short clip shows a space glider zooming over the Valles Marineris (a huge canyon on Mars). Thanks to Dave Oxenreider and Singularity Arts Inc. for creating this and allowing us to use it in this chapter!

Launching RTAS Plug-Ins

Launching (or *instantiating*) an RTAS plug-in is easy once you know the steps. In this example, I'm going to add some equalization (EQ) to the Control Tower track to make it sound like the voice is going over a radio transmission.

1 **Click** on an unused **Insert button** on the track that you want to affect (if you're working with the tutorial session, the Control Tower track). A drop-down menu will appear.

> **ADVICE ON INSERTS**
>
> Because inserts are processed in series from top to bottom, the order in which effects are placed in your tracks is significant. For example, a virtual amplifier placed before a reverb will sound a good deal different from an amplifier placed after a reverb. The good news is, it's easy to change the order (or even the track assignment) of an RTAS plug-in simply by dragging and dropping the insert icon to a new location in your Mixer.

2 **Click** on **Plug-In**. A list of plug-in categories will appear.

3 **Click** on the desired **category** of effect (in this case, let's choose EQ). A sub-menu will appear, showing all the specific plug-ins of that type.

4 **Click** on the desired **plug-in**. The plug-in's window will appear (in this image, I've chosen the EQ 3 7-Band plug-in).

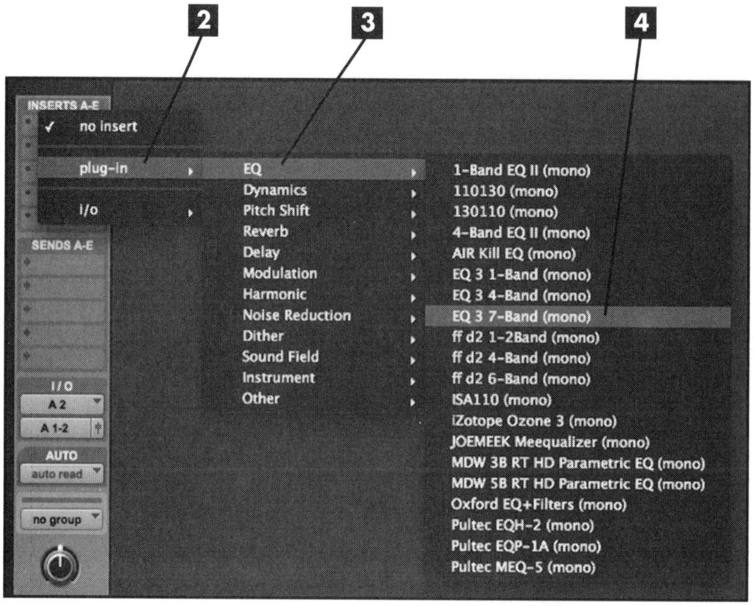

The RTAS plug-in window will vary depending upon the effect, but just as with AudioSuite plug-ins, there are some common buttons at the top of the plug-in window that you should understand.

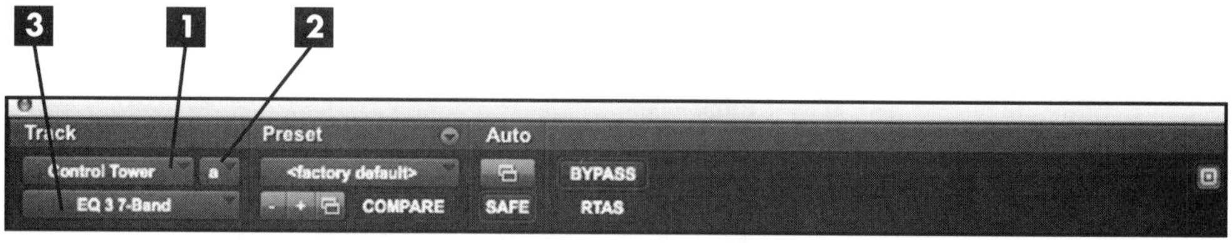

1 **Click** the **Track Selector button** (which shows you the track you're currently working with) to display a list of available tracks in your session. From this list, you can select another track and instantly open an Insert window for that track.

2 **Click** the **Insert Position Selector button** (a small lettered button to the right of the Track Selector button) to indicate the position of the insert on the track. If you click this button, a list of all 10 insert positions will appear. From this list, you can select any position and jump to that insert immediately.

3 Finally, **click** the **Plug-In Selector button** (which shows you the plug-in you're using) to reveal the plug-in menu, from which you can select a different effect without closing the RTAS window.

Recalling Settings

In addition to instantiating plug-ins with ease, you can recall previously created settings (often called *presets*). Here's how we'll recall a good preset for the EQ we just launched. (These steps also work with AudioSuite plug-ins.)

1 **Click** the **Librarian Menu button**. A list of available presets will be displayed.

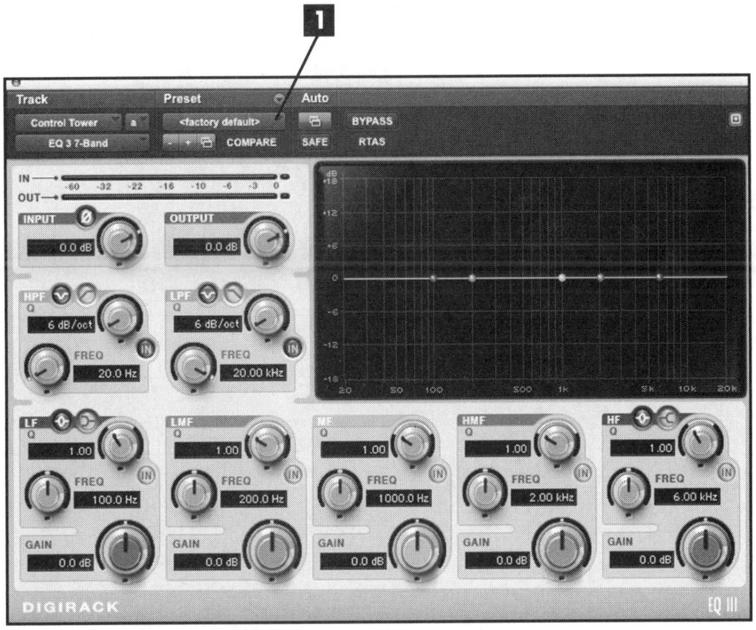

2 Any factory presets for the plug-in will be shown in this menu, plus any presets saved in your session's Plug-In Settings folder (something you'll learn more about in Chapter 9, "Finishing Touches"). If you're using the tutorial session, I've placed a good preset in your session's Plug-In Settings folder, so **click** the **Sessions' Settings Folder menu item**. A list will appear.

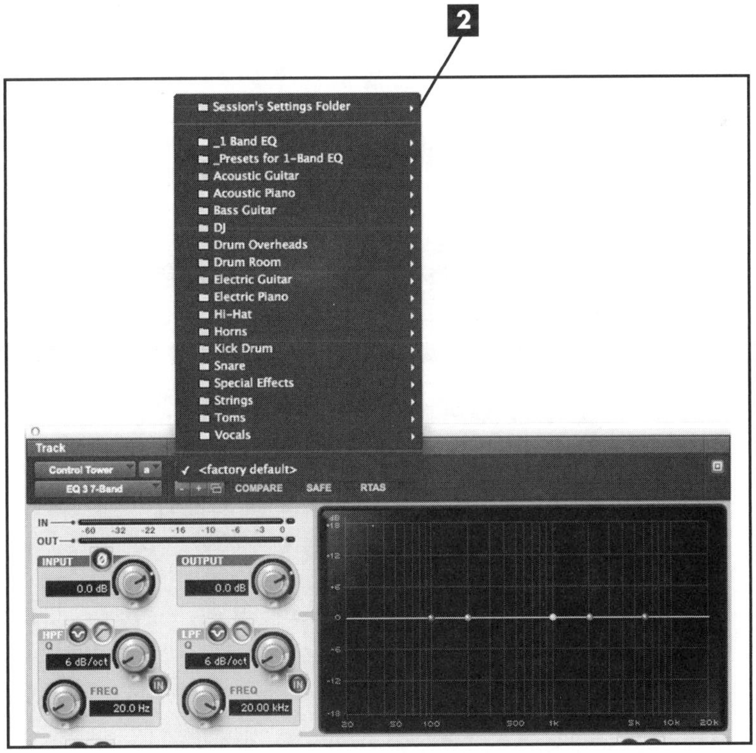

3 If you're using the tutorial session, you'll see that there's only one preset in Session's Settings Folder—appropriately named Control Tower Radio, created by yours truly. **Select** this **preset**, and the parameters will be applied to your plug-in.

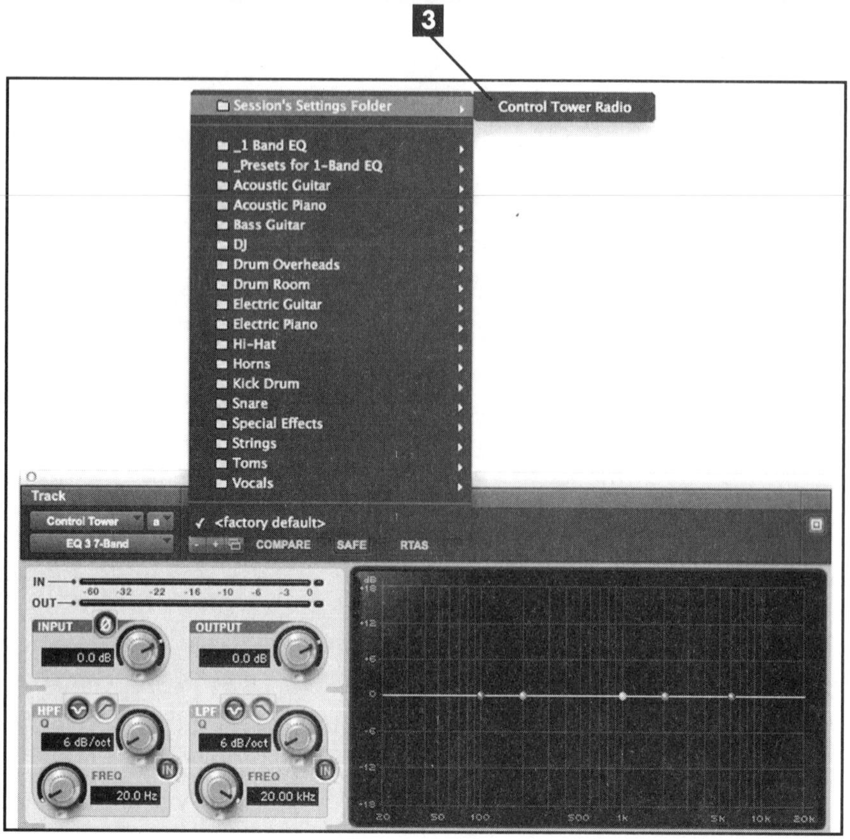

There are a couple other ways that presets can be accessed. (Again, this works for both AudioSuite and RTAS.)

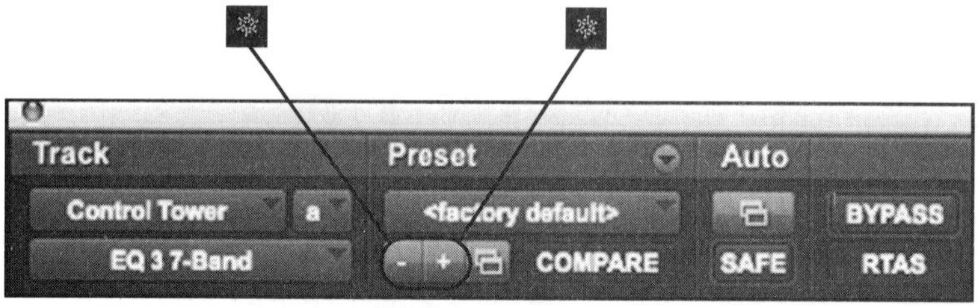

- Use the plus (+) or minus (−) key to increment or decrement through the available presets.
- Click the Plug-In Settings Select button to reveal the plug-in settings dialog box.

- Click the Folder button to reveal a list of all preset folders, and click the desired folder to display the presets in the dialog box's main area.
- Click the desired preset, and your settings will be immediately applied.

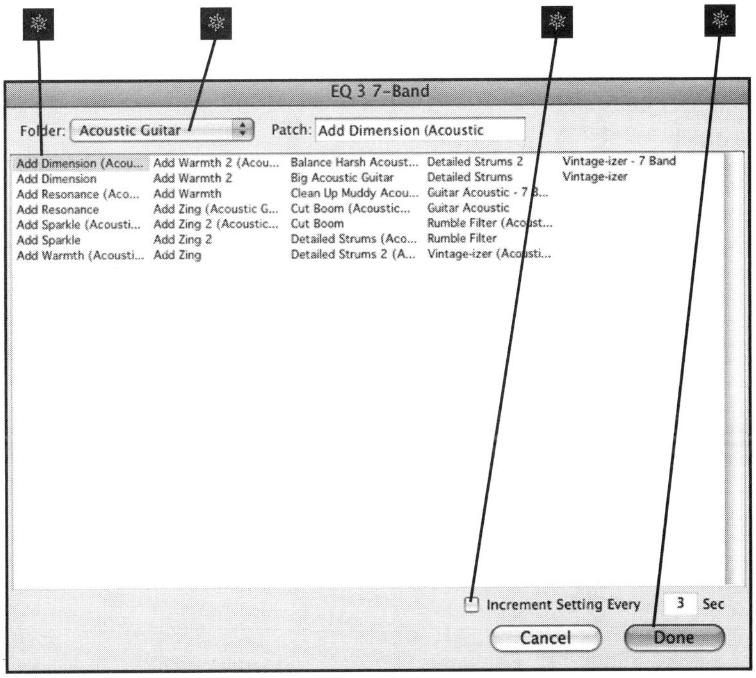

- Click the Increment Setting Every *x* Sec checkbox to automatically cycle through the available presets according to the value entered in the Sec field. (In this image, presets will change every three seconds.) This is a handy way to preview effects settings, especially when there is a large number of presets to choose from.
- When you settle upon the desired setting, click the Done button, and the plug-in setting dialog box will close.

Digging Deeper into RTAS

Okay, so far it's been pretty straightforward, but things will get a little more complicated as we go on. For example, when you open a plug-in on a stereo track, you have the option of choosing between a multichannel and a multi-mono effect. Simply put, a multi*channel* plug-in is a single plug-in that is designed to process more than one audio stream. Choosing to use multi-*mono* will open multiple mono plug-ins in a single plug-in window. Confused? Read on!

For this example, let's set up a multi-mono delay on a stereo Aux track.

SETTING THINGS UP

To follow along with these steps, create a stereo Aux Input track and name it Delay Aux.

1 On a stereo track (in this case, a stereo Aux track named Delay Aux), **click** on an available **Insert button**.

2a **Click** on **Multichannel Plug-In**. In the case of a stereo track (as shown here), a list of stereo plug-ins will appear.

OR

2b **Click** on **Multi-Mono Plug-In**. A list of mono plug-ins will appear.

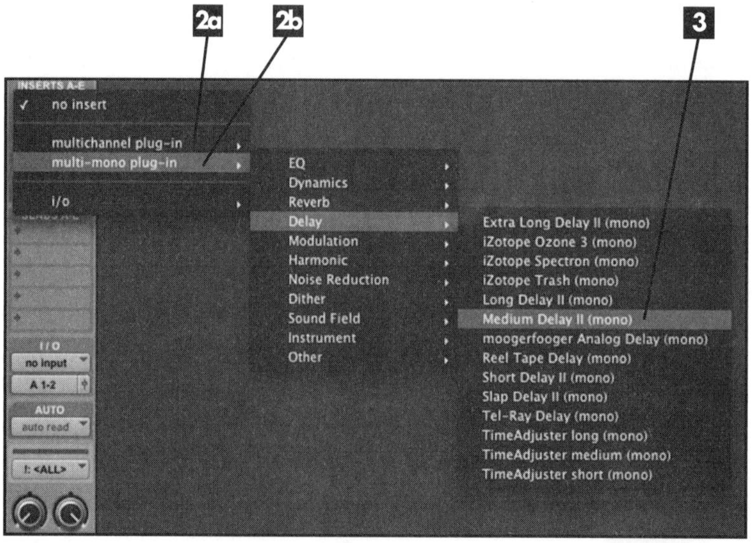

3 For the purposes of this example, **choose Medium Delay II** from the **multi-mono** plug-in family (shown here). The plug-in will be instantiated, and the plug-in window will open.

When you choose multi-mono on a stereo track, the mono plug-in you select will be opened twice, although only one plug-in window will be shown. A multi-mono plug-in window has several unique features:

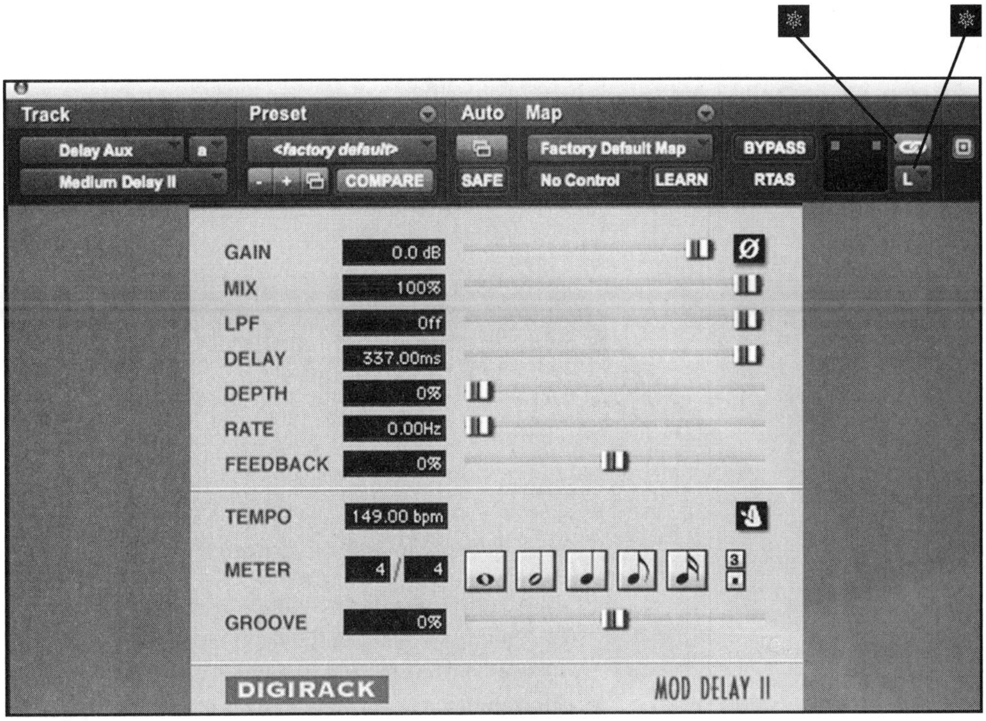

- The Channel Selector button will indicate the channel of the multi-mono plug-in you're presently viewing. Just click this button to reveal a list of available channels, from which you can choose. (In this example, clicking the Channel Selector button will enable you to switch from the Left plug-in to the Right plug-in.)
- The Link button is unique to multi-mono plug-ins. When this button is highlighted, all channels of the multi-mono plug-in will share the same parameter settings. (In the image shown here, changes made to the left side will be mirrored in the right side.) When Link is disabled, both sides are independently configurable, and will enable you to set different delay settings for the left and right sides.

RELINKING MULTI-MONO PLUG-INS

If you unlink a multi-mono effect and later choose to relink, the Relink dialog box will appear. When relinking a multi-mono plug-in, you will need to choose one channel's parameters to be applied to all channels.

Each plug-in that you launch (or instantiate) will appear as a rectangular button next to its corresponding insert. Click on the desired button to open or close the plug-in's window.

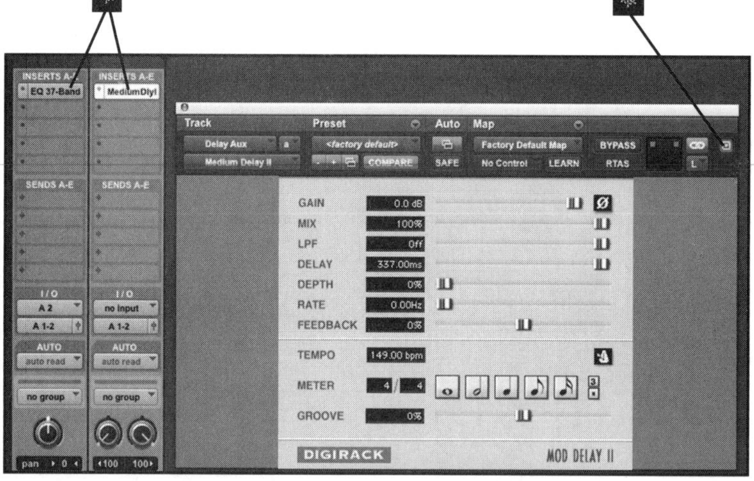

You'll notice that by default, only one plug-in window is shown at a time. Clicking a plug-in button when a plug-in window is already open will change the plug-in displayed in that window. So what if you want to view more than one plug-in window at a time? That's when the Target button comes in handy.

- The rule for the Target button is simple: Only one plug-in window can be "targeted" at a time. If you click on a plug-in window's Target button to deactivate the target (the button will turn gray), you'll be able to open another plug-in window. The next plug-in window that you open will have an active Target button.

OPENING MULTIPLE PLUG-IN WINDOWS SHORTCUT

You can also open more than one plug-in window at a time by holding down the Shift key as you click on a plug-in button on an insert.

Traditional Effects Techniques

The goal of the mixing process is to achieve the perfect blend of audio elements in your session. Over the years, certain conventions have evolved to help mixing engineers reach this goal, and these conventions have become something of a tradition. Before we leave our discussion of effects, let's take a look at some traditional ways to use them—although these are certainly not the only ways they can be used!

Using Dynamic-Based Effects

Effects tend to fall into one of two categories: *dynamic*-based effects or *time*-based effects. Let's begin with dynamic-based effects. Dynamic-based effects change the volume level of the audio (or a portion of the audio) without changing its duration in any way. Some of the most common examples of dynamic effects are equalizers, compressors, and limiters.

Setting up dynamic-based effects is very easy. In fact, you've done it once already with the Control Tower track (if you've been using this chapter's tutorial session). Typically, you'll want dynamic effects to process 100 percent of the track's audio, so you'll simply place the effect on an insert of the track you want to change.

1 **Click** on an **insert** on the desired track and **select** an **effect** (such as the EQ shown here). The plug-in window will appear.

2 **Adjust** the **parameters** of the effect to suit your mix's needs.

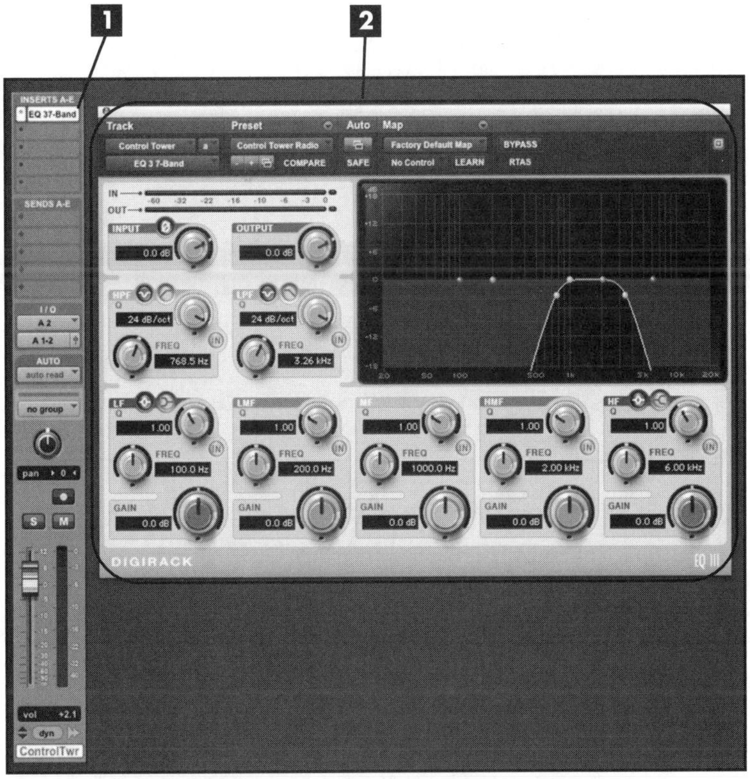

When you're finished tweaking the effect, you're done!

Using Time-Based Effects

Time-based effects *do* affect the duration of the sound beyond that of its original waveform. Effects such as reverb, delay, and echo would fall under this classification. In these cases, you typically will want to have some sort of a wet/dry mixing scenario (wet meaning an effected signal and *dry* referring to an uneffected signal). The generally preferred way to mix these two signals is to use two separate tracks, so that you have the ability to adjust the wet/dry balance with faders in your Mix window. If you've been following along with the tutorial session, let's go through this process and add a little delay to the Control Tower track.

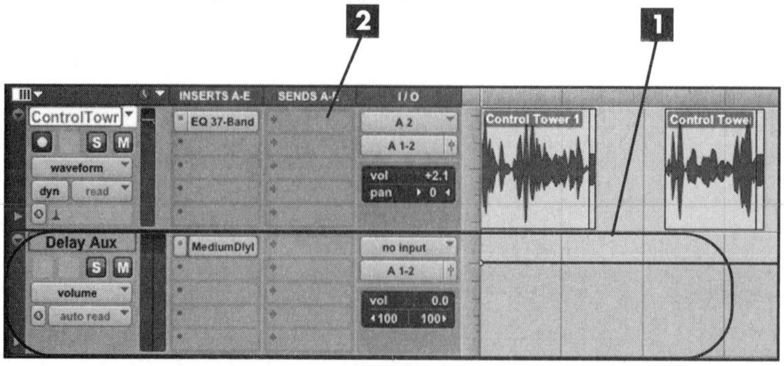

1 **Create** a **stereo Aux track** and **instantiate** the **time-based plug-in** you want to use (in this case, a delay) on an available insert on that track. If you've been following the tutorial session, you can use the stereo Aux track (named Delay Aux) that you created earlier in this chapter.

2 **Click** on any available **Send Selector button** on the dry track (in this case, the Control Tower track). A list will appear.

3 Because you'll be routing audio from one track to another within the Pro Tools environment, you'll want to use a bus. **Click** on **Bus** in the list of output options.

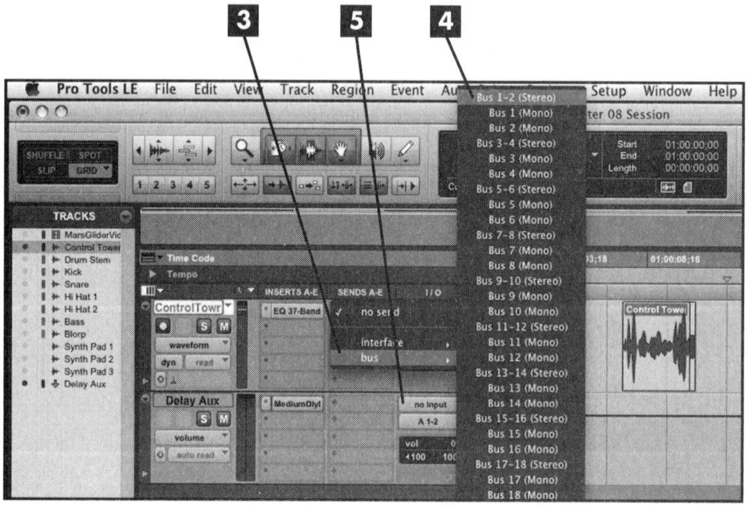

4 **Select** an **unused stereo bus**. (We're using stereo buses because the signal will be sent to a stereo track.) Buses already being used in the session will be shown in a bold amber font.

5 To complete the signal-routing process, you'll need to **set** the **input** of the Aux track to match the same stereo bus you chose for the Audio track's send.

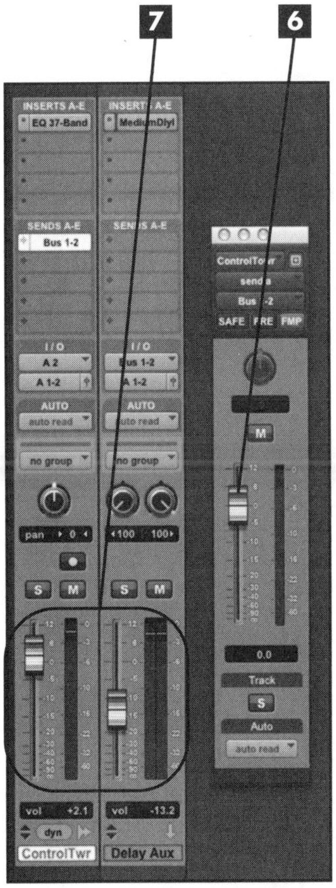

6 **Drag** the **volume fader** on the send's output window (if you're not seeing this window, just click on the send button to reveal it) and increase the volume to an appropriate level. At this point, it's a good idea to play your session to test your setup. If you've routed the audio signal correctly, it will appear in the send output window and the Aux track's main level meter.

7 On the Aux track, **drag** the **volume fader** to achieve the desired blend of wet and dry sound. (The original Audio track is the dry part of the mix, and the Aux track is the wet part.) It's often useful to solo both tracks when adjusting this blend, at least in the initial stage.

LEVEL SHORTCUT

Here's a quick way to move a volume fader (either the main fader or a send fader) to 0 dB (also called *unity*): Just hold the Option key (Mac) or Alt key (PC) and click the fader. The fader will immediately jump to the unity position.

SOLO SAFE

When you solo a track, all other tracks will be muted, including the Aux track with your reverb. Of course, you can always solo that reverb track, but that can be a time-consuming annoyance. Pro Tools allows you to "solo safe" a track, meaning it won't be muted even if other tracks are soloed. To solo safe a track, just hold down the Command (Mac) or Ctrl (PC) key and click on the solo button of the track that you want to solo safe.

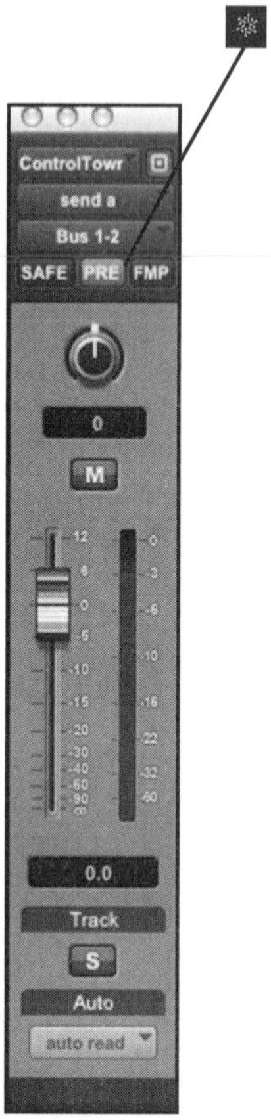

When the PRE button is highlighted on the send's output window (as shown here), the send is known as a *pre-fader send,* meaning the output of the send will not be affected by the track's main volume fader or Mute button. When the PRE button is not highlighted (the default state of sends in Pro Tools), the send is a *post-fader send,* and the volume fader and Mute button of the Audio track will affect the volume going out of the send.

PRE- VERSUS POST-FADER SENDS

Although post-fader sends are generally more commonly used, both pre- and post-fader sends have their uses. It all depends on the results you want: Choose post-fader (the Pro Tools default) if you want your dry track's level to affect the wet track's output. This way, when you raise and lower the volume fader on the dry track, you'll raise and lower the signal being routed to the Aux, maintaining a consistent blend of wet and dry. This is the most common choice when setting up time-based effects (which you just did in the previous section). If, however, you want the wet and dry track levels to be completely independent, use a pre-fader send. Because signal will be routed to the Aux track *before* the dry track's fader, a full signal will be sent to *both* faders, allowing more flexibility with the wet and dry balance. (This is commonly used when setting up cue mixes, which we'll discuss in Chapter 10.) Experiment!

THE MIX PARAMETER AND TRADITIONAL TIME-BASED ROUTING

Most time-based plug-in effects have a Mix parameter in the plug-in window that enables you to blend a dry and a wet signal within the plug-in itself. Usually, this setting defaults to 100-percent wet, but not always. Be sure to check your plug-in's Mix parameter; in the traditional mixing workflow you just learned, you'll want that Mix parameter to be 100-percent wet so you can adjust the wet and dry levels using the tracks' faders.

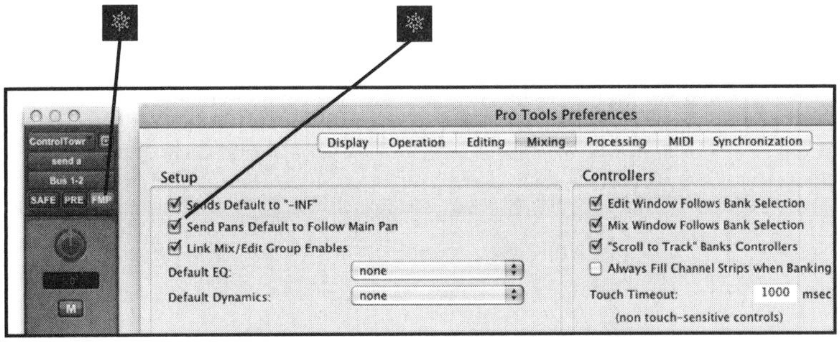

- There's one more send button to talk about: The FMP button (which stands for *Follow Main Pan*) makes panning your sends much easier. Frequently, it's preferable to have the send's pan mirror the panning of the track as a whole. That's just what FMP does. Simply click the FMP button in the send output window, and the send's pan will follow the panning that you choose for your track's output. You can tell whether your send is set to follow the main panner by the lit FMP button and the grayed-out panner in the send output window.
- FMP can be automatically enabled on newly created sends. From the Preferences window, go to the Mixing tab, and from there check the Send Pans Default to Follow Main Pan checkbox.

Here's a variation on the traditional time-based effect workflow—and one that can make production much simpler and boost the performance of your DAW in the bargain!

- A bus can have multiple sources and destinations. That means that you can create sends on a number of tracks and assign them all to the same bus(ses). In this image, I've created sends on all my individual drum tracks and assigned all those sends to buses 3 and 4.
- All these signals can be combined and routed to a single Aux track, as shown here. Remember that you must set the input of the Aux track to match the buses you're using on your source tracks (in this image, buses 3 and 4). The Aux track will contain the effect you want to apply to your tracks (in this example, a reverb).

- It's worth noting that you can independently control the levels and panning of each of your sends, enabling you to individually set the level of each source track going to the effect. In the case of adding reverb to a drum kit, as shown here, I would typically have relatively little of my kick drum going to the reverb Aux track to maintain a crisp low end and send a bit more of my other tracks to the reverb.

That's it! Now you have dry faders (the Audio tracks) and a wet reverb track (the Aux track), and you can adjust the levels to suit your mix.

> **MOVING AND COPYING IN THE MIX WINDOW**
>
> Want to move a plug-in or send from one track to another? No problem. Just click on that plug-in or send button and drag it to any available track. To copy a plug-in or send, just hold down the Option key (Mac) or Alt key (PC) as you click and drag! There's only one limitation to this flexibility: Multichannel plug-ins can only be moved to tracks of the same output format. For example, you can drag a stereo plug-in to another stereo track, but not to a mono track.

Remember, *all* the static parameters you've just set up (send levels, Aux levels, plug-in parameters, and so on) are simply a starting point, setting the stage so you can go on to tweak your mix further. That's where automation comes in...

Automating Your Mix

Automation is one of the coolest things about mixing in a DAW, and in my opinion, nothing beats Pro Tools' automation features. If the term is new to you, *mix automation* refers to the ability to change aspects of your mix (such as volume, for example) over time and to have those changes "written" to your session. Once those changes have been written, they can be adjusted and played back automatically (hence the term *automation*), giving you the ability to control multiple parameters in real time as your session plays.

> **RECORDING VERSUS WRITING**
>
> Before we start dealing with mix automation, we should cover some basic terminology. Audio and MIDI data are *recorded*, but automation is *written*. When your session plays back, the *written* automation can be *read*. This might seem like a matter of semantics at this point, but it'll help keep things clear as we work with automation (and these are the standard industry terms).

The Automation Modes

There are five automation modes, which determine the way your fader, pan, and other parameters will be written. Understanding the distinction between these modes is the best way to start learning about automation.

1 You can set the automation mode for any track, whether you're in the Mix window or the Edit window. **Click** on the **Automation Mode Selector button** on the track that you want to automate (which in this image reads Auto Read or Read). A menu of the five automation modes of Pro Tools will appear.

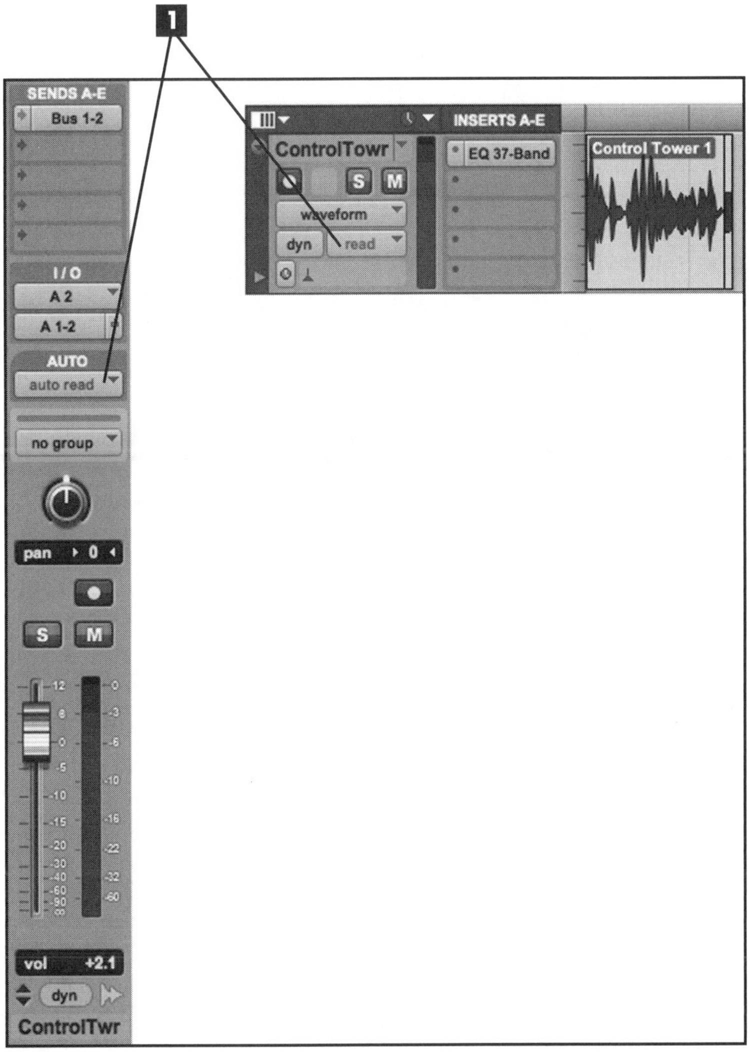

Each automation mode is unique, to fit a wide variety of mixing situations.

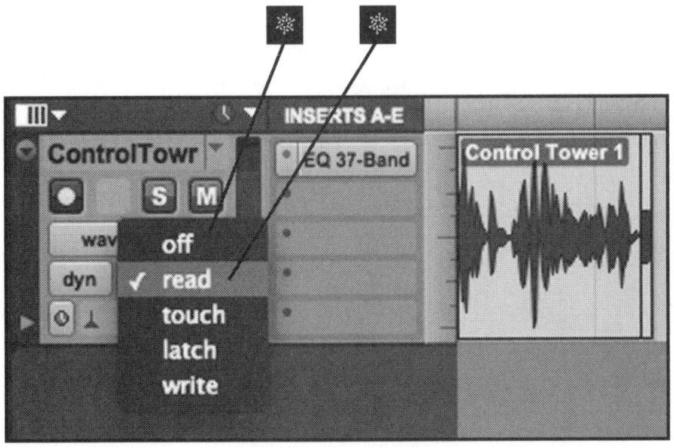

- **Off.** Using this mode, automation will neither be written nor played back. This is a good way to suspend automation on a track that has automation.

- **Read.** Automation cannot be written in this mode, but previously written automation will be played back. Use this mode to play back your automated tracks without running the risk of overwriting that automation.

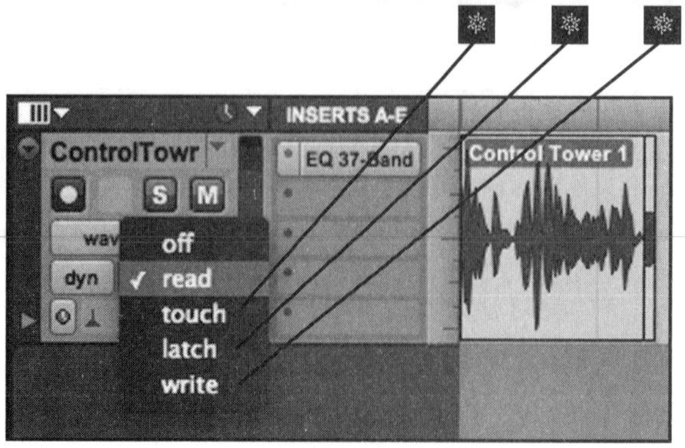

- **Touch.** The track will read previously written automation until a parameter is "touched" (clicked with your mouse or using a control surface), at which time automation will be written for that parameter. When the parameter is released, it will return to its previously written automation.
- **Latch.** This mode is similar to Touch; only when a parameter is "touched" will automation be written. When the parameter is released in Auto Latch mode, however, it will remain at the last value and continue to write automation at that position until you stop playback.
- **Write.** In this mode, automation will be written on all enabled parameters, regardless of whether the parameter is being touched.

AUTOMATION ON A TRACK-BY-TRACK BASIS

You can choose a different automation mode for each track.

A WORD ABOUT AUTOMATION WORKFLOW

With the Touch, Latch, and Write modes, automation will be written during playback, and writing will stop when playback is stopped (or in the case of Touch, when you let go of the parameter that you're automating).

Let's start by using Write mode to change the volume of the Synth Pad 3 track.

SETTING THINGS UP

You can (and often will) do your automation work in the Mix window, but for purposes of visualization, the screenshots in this section will use the Edit window.

1 First, let's set things up so we can see the changes we make. **Click** the **Track View Selector button** to change to a graphical view of the parameter you want to automate.

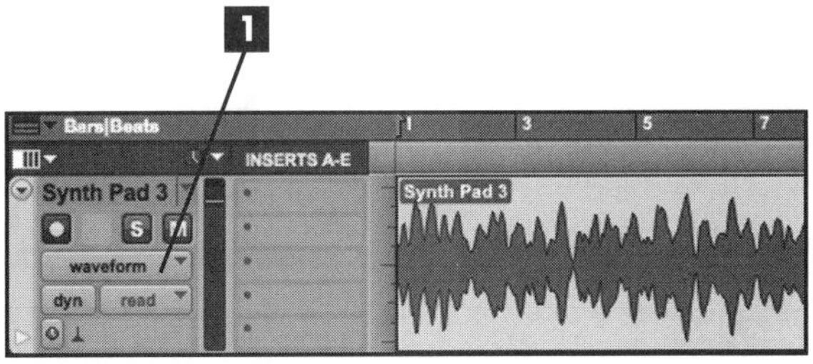

2 **Choose** the **track parameter** you want to view. In this example, I've chosen Volume.

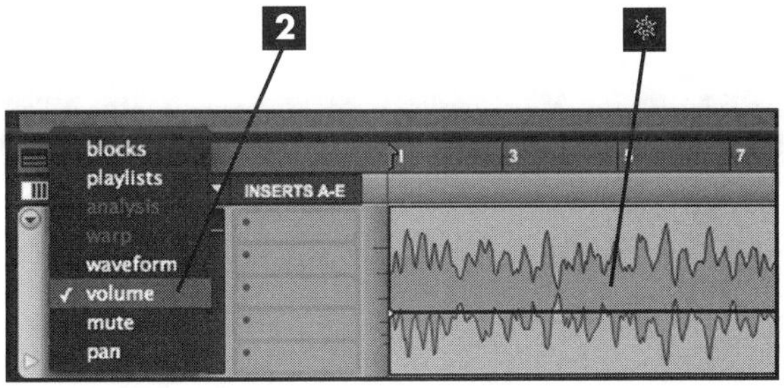

Note that automation parameters are displayed in the track's Playlist area as a (initially) horizontal line.

3 If you're writing volume automation in the Edit window, you'll find that the Output window will help greatly. Just **click** the **Output Window button** to reveal the track's Output window.

4 There is an Automation Mode Selector button on both the Edit window's track strip and the track's Output window. **Click** either **Automation Mode Selector button**.

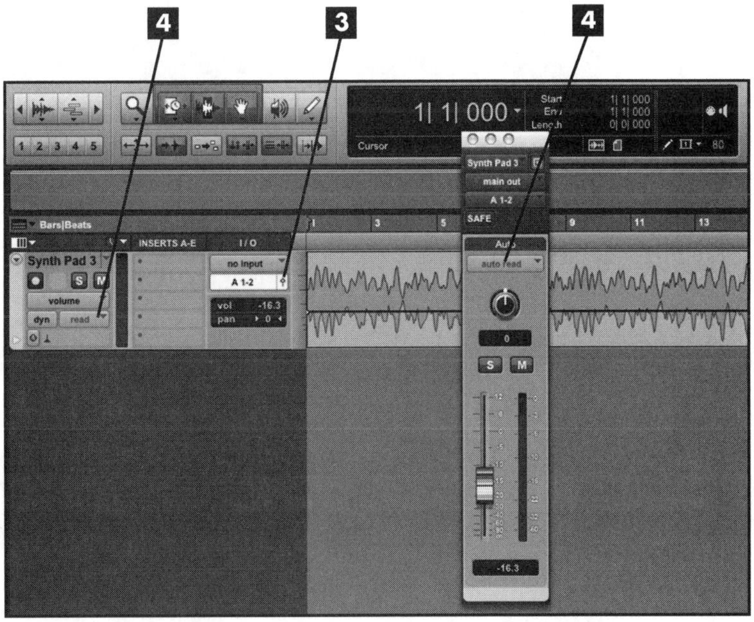

5 For the purposes of this example, let's start by using Write mode, which will create new automation data for all automatable parameters as soon as playback is started. **Choose** the **Write automation mode** from the Automation Mode menu.

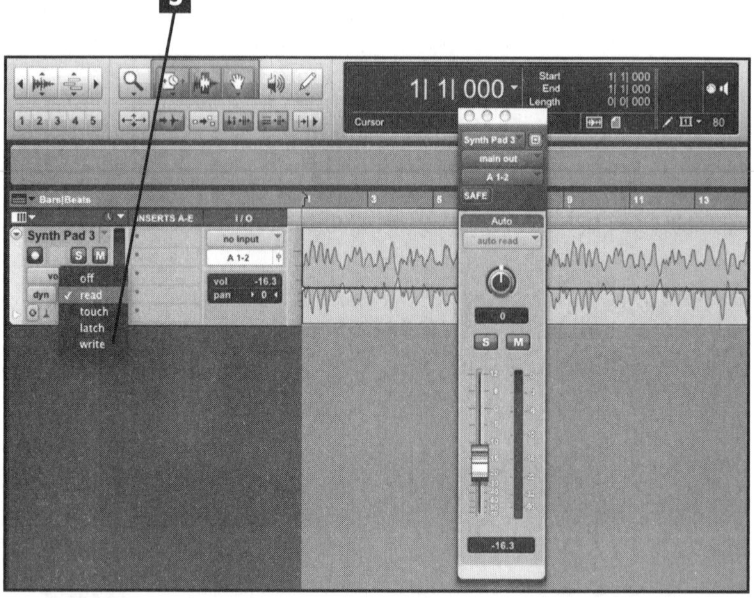

6 Since Write mode will begin writing automation as soon as playback begins, you should **set** your **initial levels**. (In this example, I want to do a fade-in from silence, so I've brought my fader all the way down.) Once you've done that, **move** your **timeline cursor** to the point at which you want to start writing automation (in this case, I've placed my timeline cursor at the beginning of the session) and **begin playback** of your session.

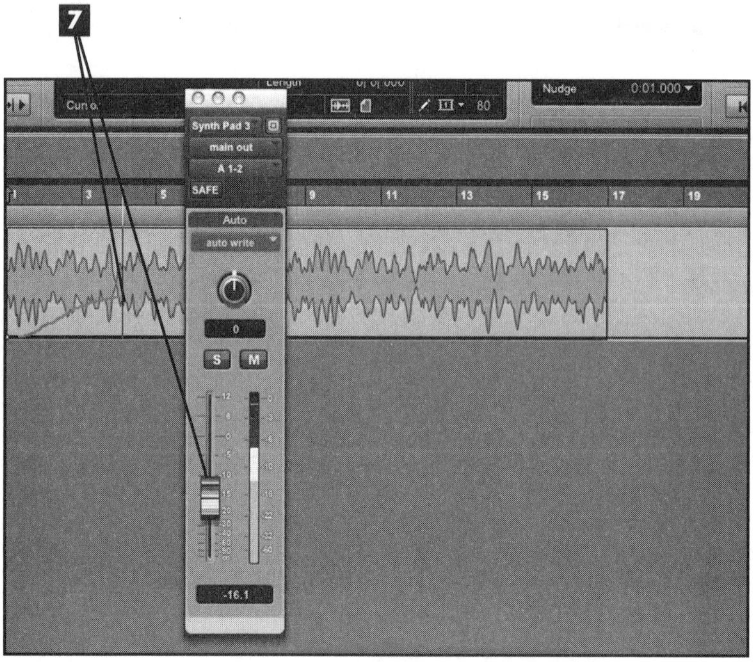

7 **Click** on the desired **mix parameter** (in this case, volume) and **move it** to create automation data. As your automation is being written, you will see the data represented as a red line in the track's automation playlist.

8 When you're finished writing automation, **stop** your session's **playback**.

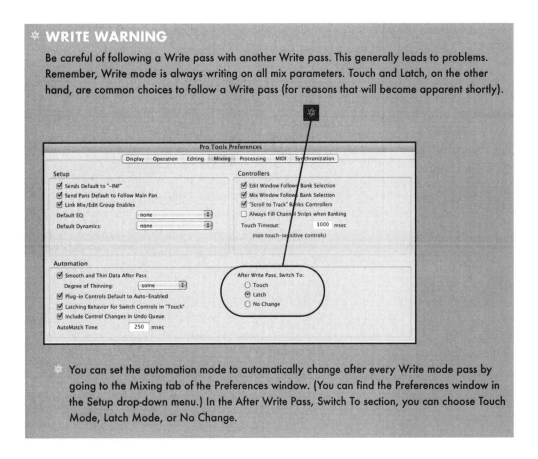

WRITE WARNING

Be careful of following a Write pass with another Write pass. This generally leads to problems. Remember, Write mode is always writing on all mix parameters. Touch and Latch, on the other hand, are common choices to follow a Write pass (for reasons that will become apparent shortly).

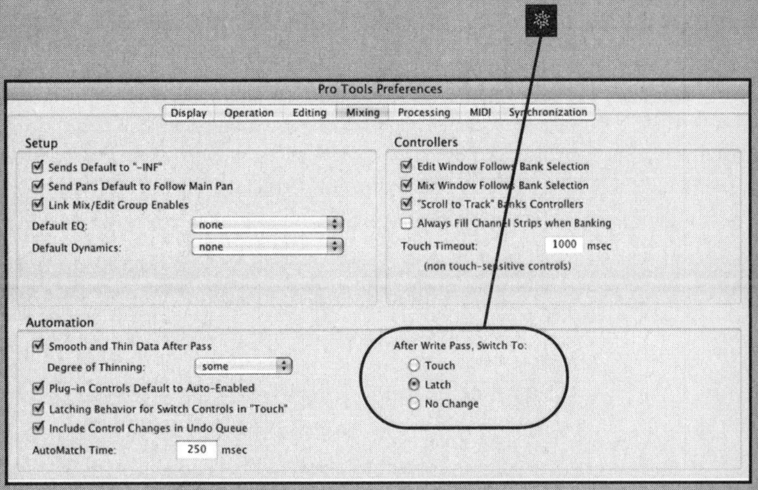

You can set the automation mode to automatically change after every Write mode pass by going to the Mixing tab of the Preferences window. (You can find the Preferences window in the Setup drop-down menu.) In the After Write Pass, Switch To section, you can choose Touch Mode, Latch Mode, or No Change.

You'll see that new automation data has been written, similar to the volume change I created here. So what if you want to change things further, without losing the work you've already done? That's where the "update" modes—Touch and Latch—come into play.

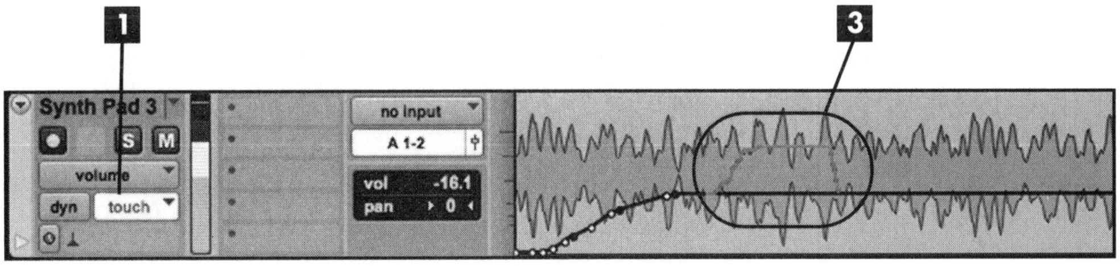

1 **Select** the **Touch automation mode** from the Automation Mode Selector menu.

2 **Play** your **session**. As long as you don't click any parameters, your automation will be read back, and the appropriate controls will move.

3 When you want to make a change in your automation, just **click** on the appropriate **control** and **adjust it**. Let go of the control when you want to stop writing, and you'll see your parameter move back to the previously written automation line (if you're in Touch mode—if you're in Latch mode, the parameter will continue to write the last value until playback is stopped).

In this example, here's what I got:

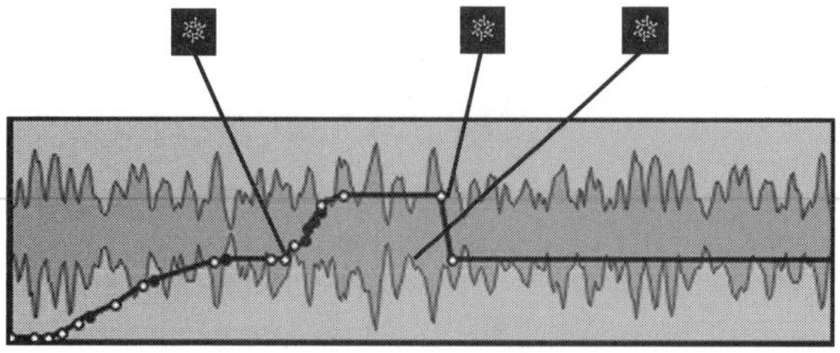

- Automation was played back as originally written until the first point, when I began moving the volume fader.
- At the second point, I released the fader. Because I was in Touch mode, the fader began to move back to the previously written automation playlist.
- Auto Touch mode will take a little time to go back to the previously written automation (a parameter called AutoMatch Time, which you can adjust from the Mixing tab in the Preferences window).

The other update mode, Latch, is written using the same steps you took in writing with Touch mode, but the mode's behavior is a bit different. Here's how a similar update pass would look with Latch mode:

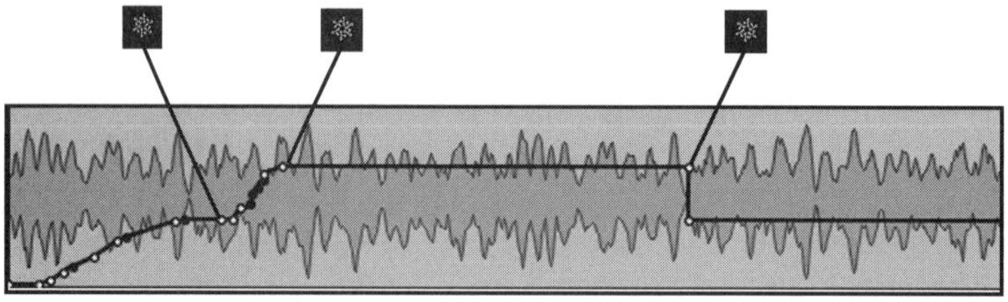

- Automation was played back as originally written until the first point, when I began moving the volume fader. So far, this is the same behavior as you saw with Touch mode.
- At the second point, I released the fader. Since I was in Latch mode, the fader stayed put instead of going back to previously written automation, as you saw in Touch mode.
- When playback stopped, the writing of automation stopped as well.

> **AUTOMATION INDICATORS**
>
> You might have noticed that the track's Automation Mode button turned red as soon as you moved the volume fader. What's up with that? The track's Automation Mode button will turn red when any kind of automation data is being written to it. (When using Write mode, the Automation Mode button will always appear red.)

The Automation Window

The Automation window will enable you to have a different kind of control over mix automation, allowing you to choose what types of data can be automated in your session.

1 **Click** on the **Window menu**.

2 **Click** on **Automation**. The Automation window will appear.

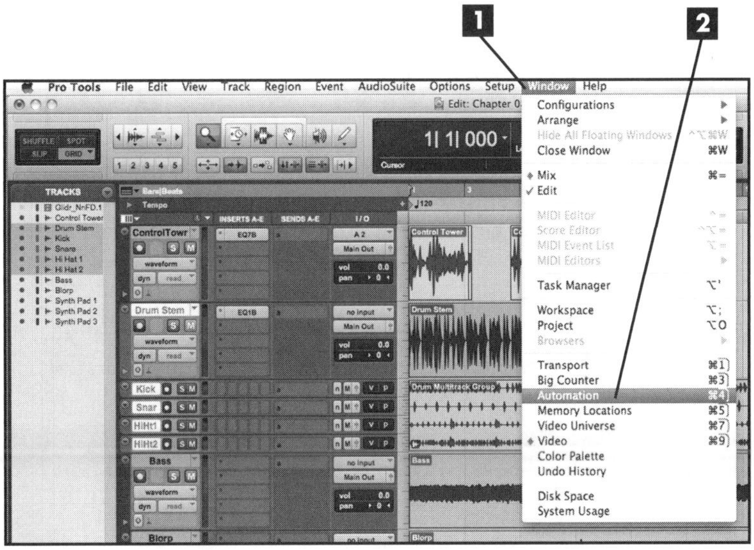

* If you click the Suspend button, all automation (writing and playback) will be disabled.

* The seven Write Enable buttons represent automatable mix parameters: volume, pan, mute, plug-in, send volume, send pan, and send mute. An enabled parameter will be indicated by a red button. If you click on a given button (removing the red highlighting), the parameter will be rendered unwriteable (although written automation will still be read).

Automation Lanes

You've already seen track lanes before (playlist lanes for track comping). Let's take another look and see how track lanes can be used to view multiple mix automation parameters.

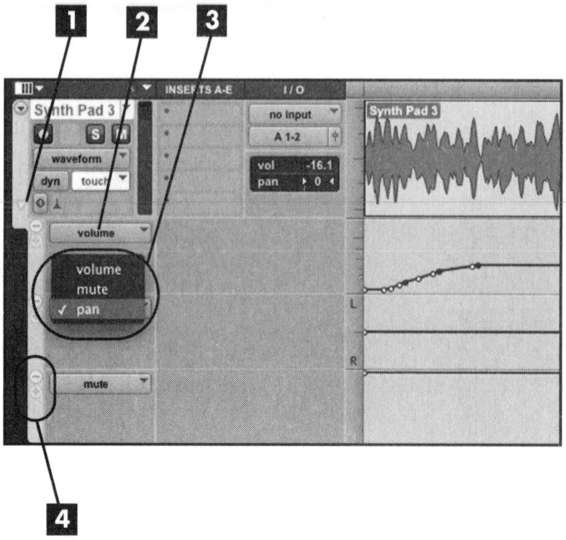

1. **Click** the **Show/Hide Automation Lanes icon** to reveal (or hide) a track's additional lanes.
2. Choosing a lane's view is very similar to what you've done already in the main body of the track—just **click** the **Lane View Selector button**, and a list of available views will appear.
3. **Choose** the desired **automation type** from the list. The currently visible type is indicated by a checkmark.
4. You can add an automation lane by **clicking** the **Add Automation Lane Below This One button** (indicated by a plus [+] icon) or remove one by **clicking** the **Remove This Automation Lane button** (shown as a minus [–] icon).

> **TRACK LANES AND MIDI**
>
> On MIDI tracks, you can use automation lanes to view all kinds of MIDI data, including Continuous Controller (CC) data. On Instrument tracks, you can use lanes to not only view MIDI data, but the same automation data that you'd see on an Audio or Aux track.

Plug-In Automation

Virtually every knob or button of a plug-in can be automated, allowing you to change tonal color, ambience, and more!

> **WORKING WITH THE TUTORIAL SESSION**
>
> If you're following along with this chapter's tutorial session, there's a good example of plug-in automation in store for you—automating a frequency sweep on a drum loop. It's a popular effect these days, and it's very easy to create. Un-mute and solo the Drum Stem track. You'll find that there's a 1-Band EQ 3 already instantiated for you. Once you open the plug-in window, you'll also notice that there is a very strong and very narrow frequency range being emphasized in the plug-in. Your job: Automate that frequency up and down.

Enabling Plug-In Parameters: Method One

Here's one way to enable plug-in parameters:

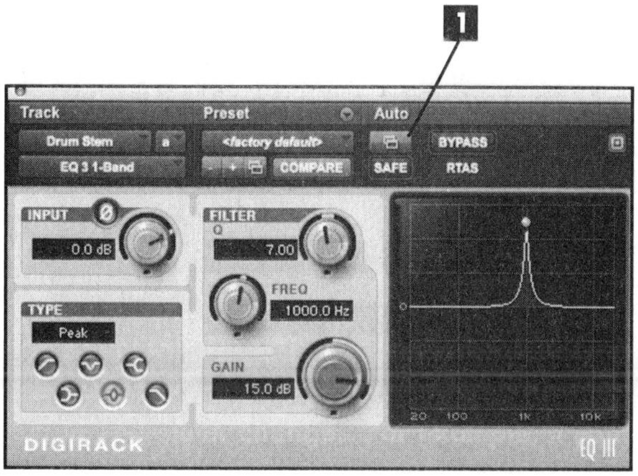

1 **Click** on the **Plug-In Automation Enable button**. The Plug-In Automation dialog box will open. The Plug-In Automation dialog box is structurally similar to the Create Group dialog box that you worked with earlier in this chapter, with a list of available parameters on the left side of the window and a list of enabled parameters on the right.

2 **Click** the **effects parameter(s)** that you wish to automate. (If you're working with the tutorial session, you'll want to automate the plug-in's Frequency parameter.) Selected parameters will be highlighted.

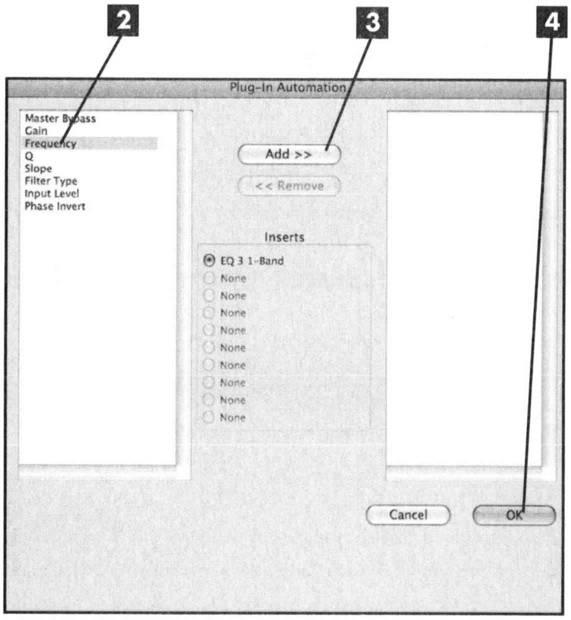

3 **Click** the **Add button**. The selected parameters will move from the left list to the right list.

4 When you're finished, **click OK**.

> **DISABLING A PARAMETER**
>
> You can disable a plug-in parameter using similar steps: Just click the desired parameter(s) in the list on the right and click the Remove button.

Enabling Plug-In Parameters: Method Two

Here's another way to enable plug-in parameters:

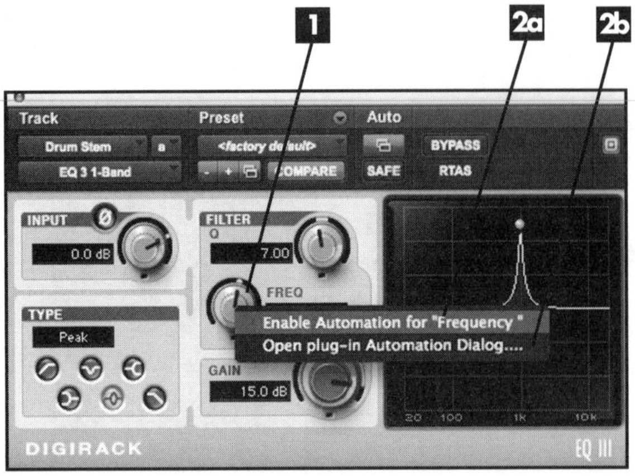

1 **Press and hold** the **Control+Option+Command keys** (Mac) or the **Ctrl+Start+Alt keys** (PC) and **click** on the **parameter** you want to automate (in this case, FREQ). A menu will appear, giving you two options:

2a **Click** on **Enable Automation for [parameter name]** to immediately enable the parameter for automation.

OR

2b **Click** on **Open Plug-In Automation Dialog** to open the Plug-In Automation dialog box that you saw in the previous section. At this point, you can follow steps 2 through 4 from the "Method One" section.

Parameters enabled for automation will be indicated visually. Sometimes it's an outline, a box, or in this image a small light beneath the parameter. This indicator will typically be a "cool" color (blue, green, etc.) when you're in Read mode, indicating that the parameter will play back written automation, or a "warm" color (red, yellow, etc.) when you are in Touch, Latch, or Write mode. When working in Off mode, there will be no indicator.

ENABLING ALL PLUG-IN PARAMETERS

Here's a quick way to enable all the parameters on a specific plug-in: Press and hold the Control+Option+Command keys (Mac) or the Ctrl+Start+Alt keys (PC) and click on the plug-in window's Plug-In Automation Enable button. You can also automatically enable all parameters for automation as soon as a plug-in is instantiated, through the Preferences window. Just go to the Mixing tab and click the Plug-In Controls Default to Auto-Enabled checkbox. Once this checkbox is checked, all plug-ins created from that point on will have all their parameters enabled for automation.

Writing Plug-In Automation

Plug-in automation is largely similar to any other kind of automation, but before we close this chapter, let's take a quick look at how you can view plug-in automation data.

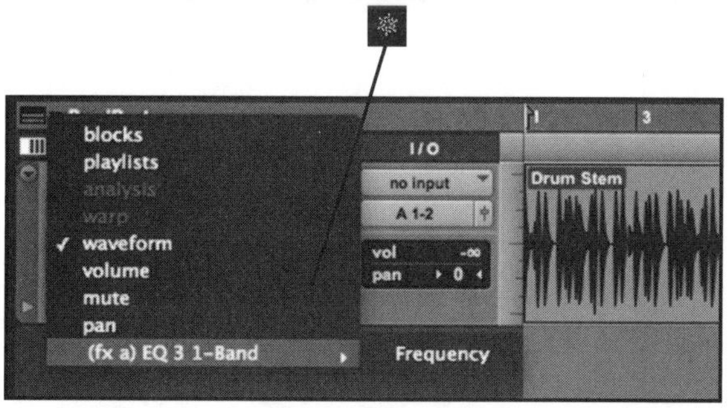

Once a parameter is enabled for automation, the plug-in and parameter will appear as an option when you click the Track View Selector button. Just choose the desired plug-in (which will reveal a submenu) and then choose the specific parameter that you want to view. (This can be shown in track lanes as well.)

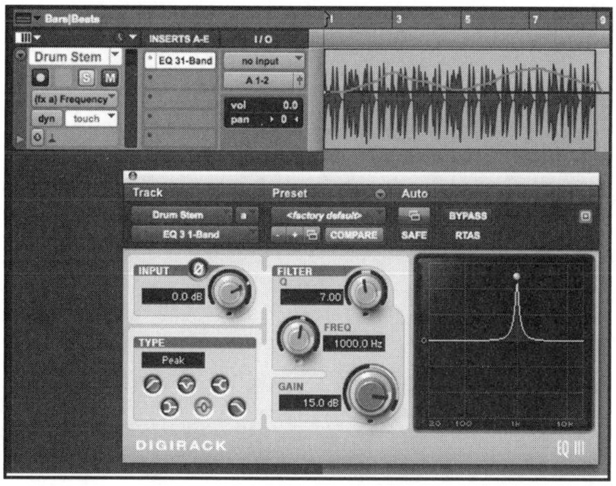

From this point, automation is identical to other kinds of automation: Choose your automation mode, begin playback, and change the parameter to start writing automation!

CHECKING YOUR WORK

To see many of the steps we've gone over in this chapter, open the session file named Chapter 08 Session-Finished, included on your book's disc.

Next stop...the mixdown!

9 Finishing Touches

Now that you're at the threshold of finishing your first project, it's interesting to look back at all you've accomplished to get here, from setting up your system to recording, editing (and more editing), and on to mixing. Now you're moving to the final stages of creating a deliverable product. Good job!

Okay, enough reminiscing—break's over.

Before you can truly consider a project finished, there's usually some tweaking to be done with the mix. Then, when you're satisfied with everything, it's time to do a final mixdown to a file or pair of files that you can listen to on something other than your Pro Tools rig. Last but absolutely not least, there's the business of archiving your session. In this chapter, you'll learn how to:

- Tweak your mix automation in the Edit window.
- Use subgroups and Master Fader tracks.
- Use Pro Tools 9's new track-output features to speed up the mixing process.
- Bounce to disk in a CD-ready format.

USING THE TUTORIAL SESSIONS

If you'd like to follow this chapter's examples, please launch the session named Chapter 09 Session, which is included on the disc that came with your book. (Remember to copy it to your hard drive first.) Alternatively, if you worked with the tutorial session for Chapter 8, "Basic Mixing," and you like your mix, you can continue working with that session as well!

More Fun with Mixing

Although you've certainly gotten a solid start with mixing in the previous chapter, here are a few more techniques that you might find useful.

Plug-In Power

Learning more about managing your plug-in effects will save time and boost creativity!

Creating Presets

Suppose you created the *perfect* slap delay for the Delay Aux track, and you'd like to use the same settings in future projects. No problem—saving a preset is an easy process!

Before we go further, though, there's a setting that you should check—one that will affect where your preset will be stored.

1 **Click** the **Settings menu button** (the small circular button immediately to the right of the word Preset). The Settings menu will appear.

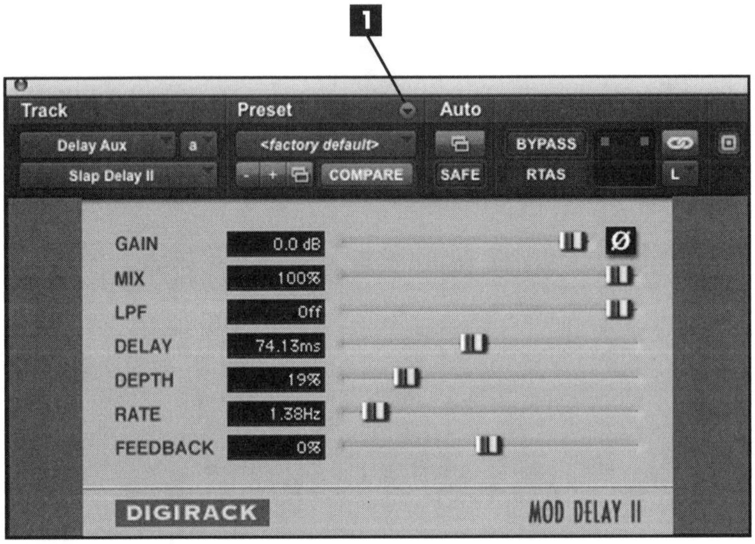

2 **Choose Settings Preferences**. A submenu will appear.

3 **Choose Save Plug-In Settings To**. Another submenu will appear, giving you two options:

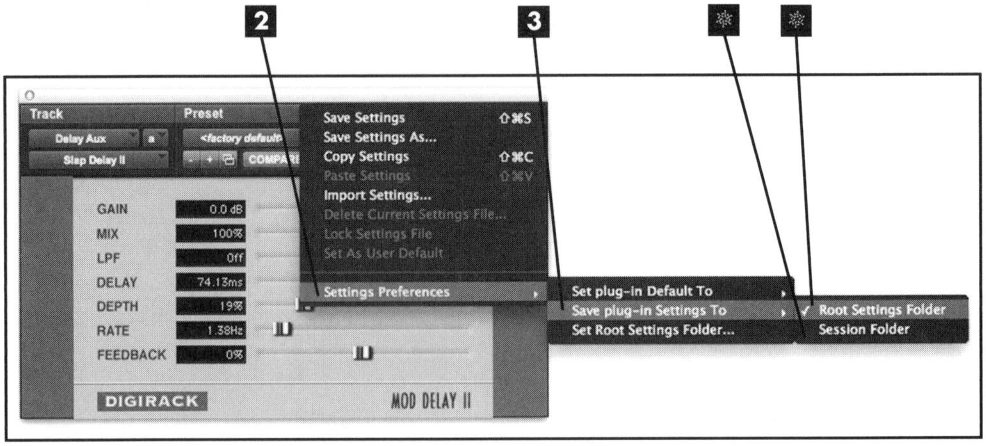

- **Root Settings Folder.** Choose Root Settings Folder to save your preset to your host computer's Plug-In Settings folder (typically on your computer's primary hard drive). With this option selected, you'll be able to recall your saved presets quickly in any sessions you create or open on this computer.
- **Session Folder.** Choose Session Folder to save your preset to the Plug-In Settings subfolder of the session in which you're currently working. Using this option, the plug-in presets will travel with your session folder, and this preset will be recallable on any computer you use to open the session.

> **IF YOU'RE USING THE TUTORIAL SESSION...**
>
> For the purposes of this example, choose Root Settings Folder.

4 **Adjust** the **settings** for your effect until they're just right.

5 **Click** the **Settings menu button** once more and then choose Save Settings As. The Save dialog box will appear.

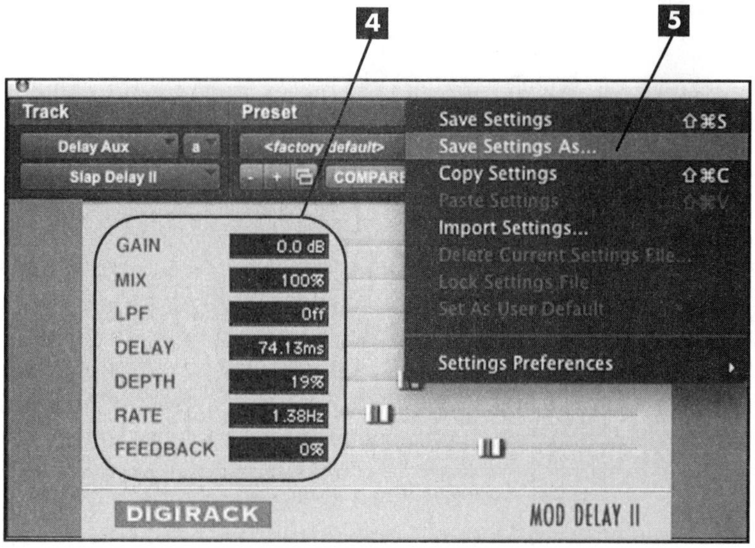

6 **Type** a descriptive **name** for your preset (such as Control Tower Delay, as I've done here).

7 **Click** the **Save button**.

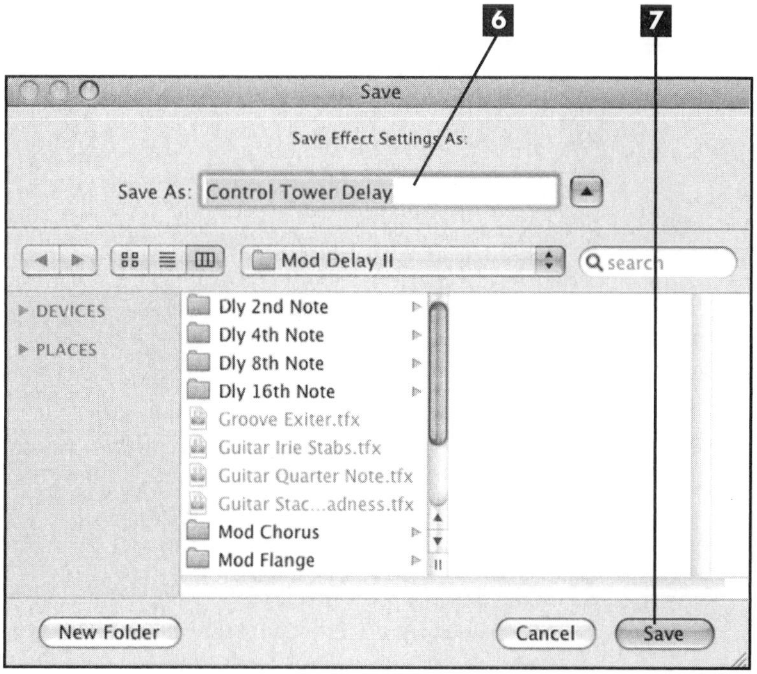

Your saved preset will be added to the list of available presets for that plug-in. The more presets you save, the longer that list will become!

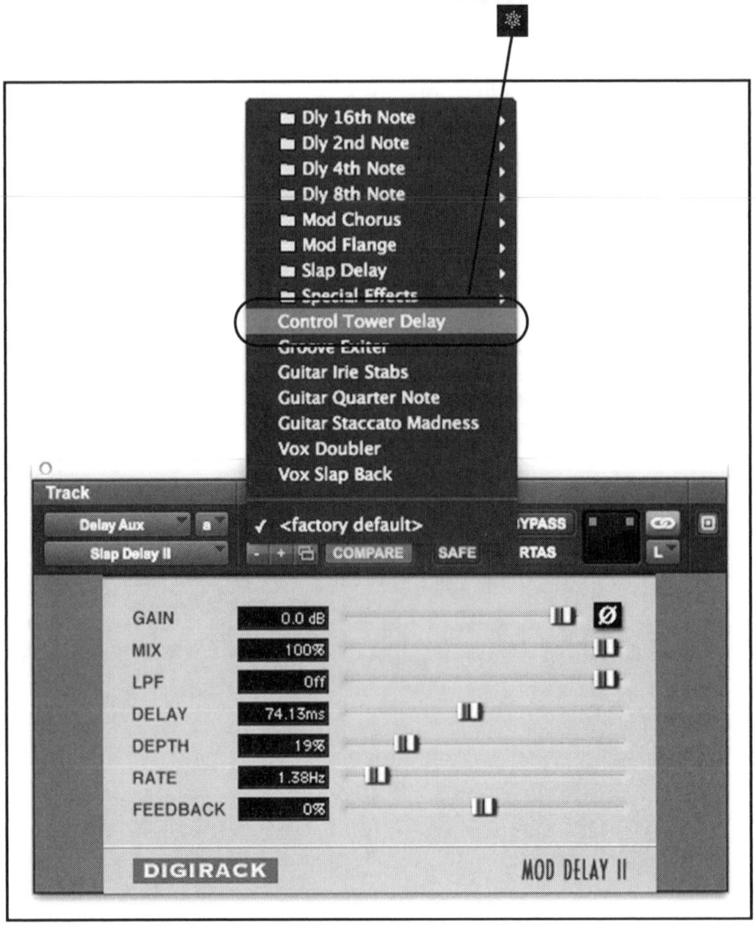

Setting Up Default Plug-Ins

As you gain experience, you might find that you have some favorite EQ and dynamic effects that you use time and time again. Setting them up as *default* plug-ins will help you recall them quickly.

You'll need to go to your old friend, the Preferences window, to set things up:

1. **Click** the **Setup menu**.
2. **Select Preferences**. The Pro Tools Preferences window will appear.

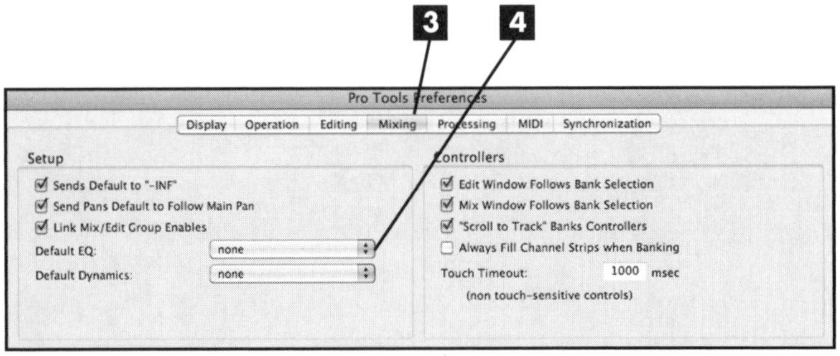

3. **Click** the **Mixing tab** of the Preferences window.

4. In the Setup section, you'll see two menu buttons, enabling you to select a Default EQ and Default Dynamics plug-in. Let's begin by choosing a favorite EQ—**click** the **Default EQ button**. A menu will be displayed.

5 **Click** the **Plug-In menu item**. A submenu will be shown, listing all the EQ plug-ins installed in your system.

6 **Click** your favorite **EQ plug-in** (in this image, I've chosen the EQ 3 7-Band). As soon as you choose your favorite plug-in, the menu will close, and your choice will be set as the default EQ for Pro Tools.

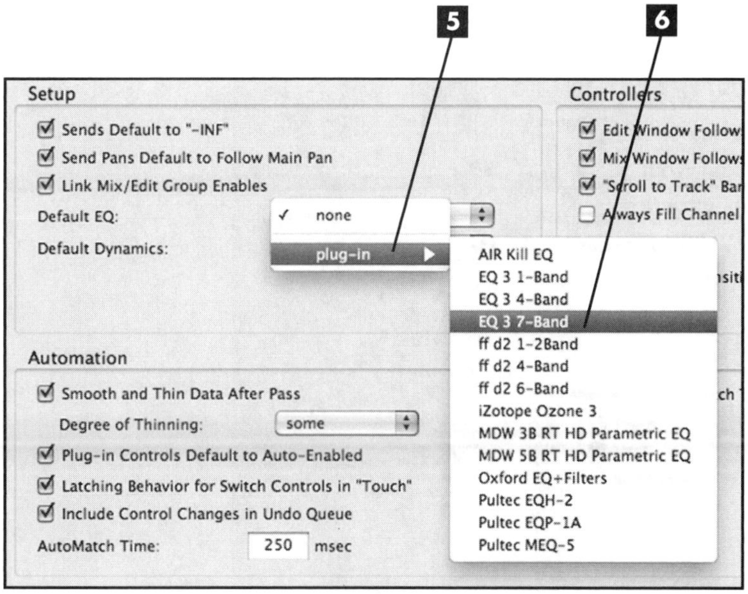

7 Now let's choose a default *dynamic* plug-in. **Click** the **Default Dynamics button**. A menu will be displayed, as shown here.

8 The process for selecting a default dynamics plug-in is identical to the steps you took in choosing a favorite EQ—just **click** the **Plug-In menu item** and **choose** the desired **plug-in** from a list of options. (In this image, I've chosen the Compressor/Limiter Dyn 3.)

9 When you're finished, just **click OK**.

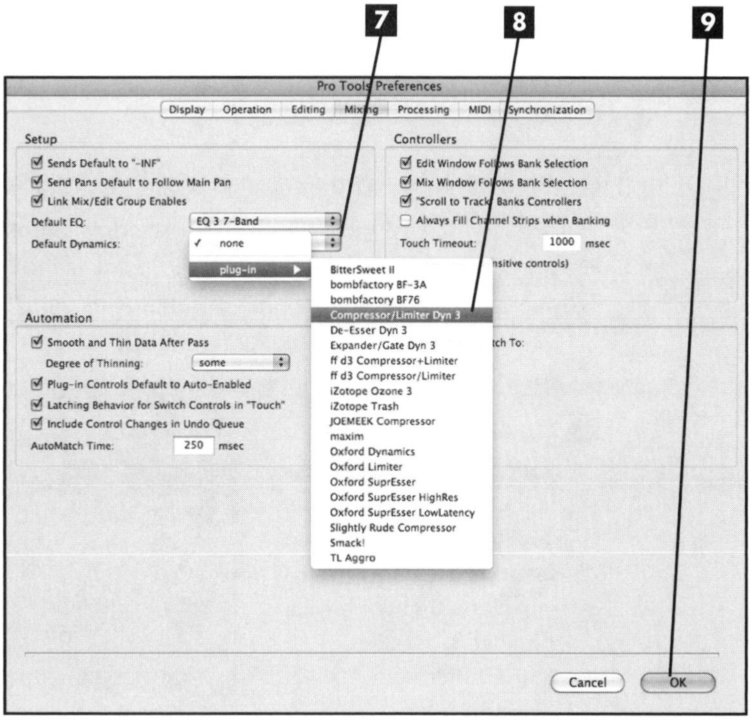

Here's the payoff: Now, when you click on any Insert Selector button, your default plug-ins will appear at the top of the list, easily accessible.

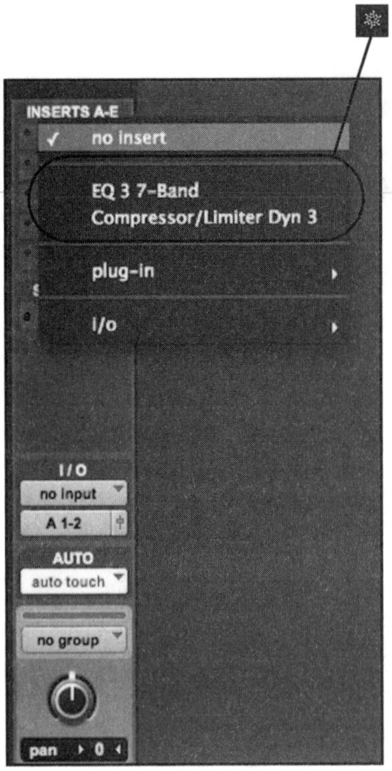

Using the Workspace Browser with Plug-Ins

You've used the Workspace Browser window before and seen how easy it is to import audio files and sessions. Did you know that you can use the Workspace Browser window to import plug-in settings as well?

1 The first step is to locate your desired plug-in preset in the Workspace Browser. You'll find that **using** the **Search function** (which you learned about back in Chapter 3, "Getting Started with Audio") will make the job easier.

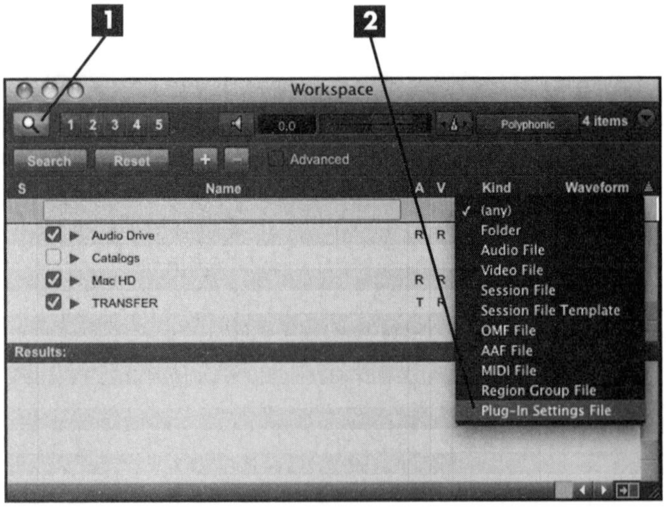

2 Not only can you search by typing in a descriptive name, but you can refine that search by **clicking** the **menu** in the Kind column and **choosing Plug-In Settings File**. This will exclude other kinds of files from your search.

SEARCHING FOR SETTINGS

If you *don't* type in a name, and you only search by plug-in settings file type, Pro Tools will show *all* your plug-in settings files.

PLUG-IN SETTINGS FILES

The default location for your plug-in settings files is <system drive>/Library/Application Support/Digidesign/Plug-In Settings (Mac), or C:\Program Files\Common Files\Digidesign\DAE\Plug-In Settings (PC).

The only thing you need to do is drag your desired plug-in settings file into an Insert position on a track. There are two ways to do it:

- If you drag the plug-in preset onto an insert that contains a plug-in (making sure the plug-in setting matches the plug-in that you're dragging to), the preset will be loaded in the plug-in.
- If you drag the plug-in preset onto an unused insert, Pro Tools will instantiate the plug-in and load the preset automatically. Job done!

Making the Most of Automation

Being able to create mix automation by manipulating knobs, sliders, and faders is a fantastic advantage of using a DAW, but it'll only take you so far. When you need to get really specific with your automation, sometimes the only place to do that is back in the Edit window.

1 If you're not already there, go to the **Edit window**.

2 **Click** on the **track view selector button** of the track you want to work with and **choose** the **data** you want to edit. (In this example, I've chosen to view volume automation on the Synth Pad 3 track.)

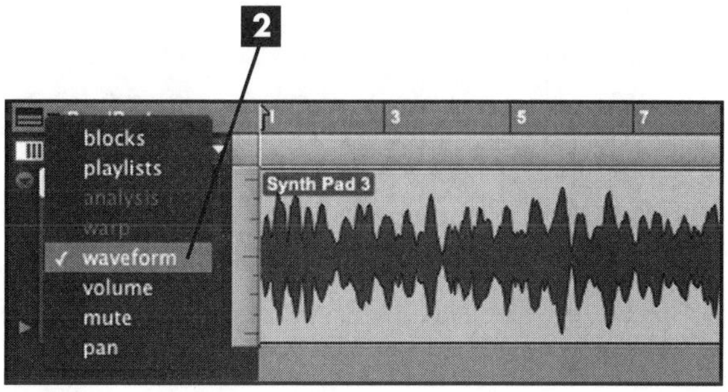

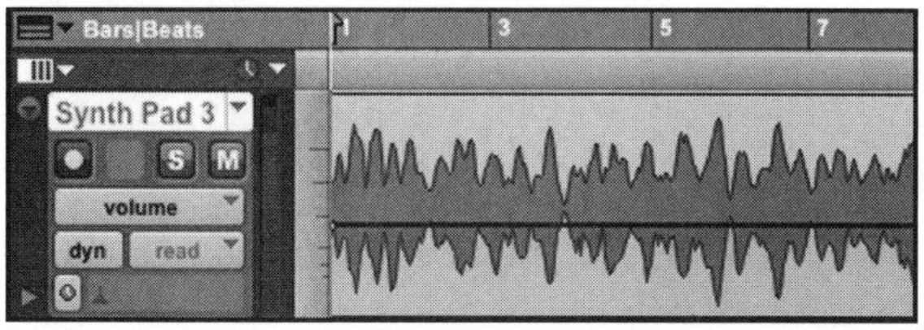

As you learned in the previous chapter, you'll see a line that represents any parameter movements that have been written to the track. If you haven't done any automation passes, the automation playlist will appear as a straight line. Note that you can still see your regions and waveforms in the background.

Automation and the Pencil Tool

Now, let's create some new automation data using the Pencil tool.

1 **Click** on the **Pencil tool**. With the Pencil, you'll be able to write new automation or overwrite previously written automation.

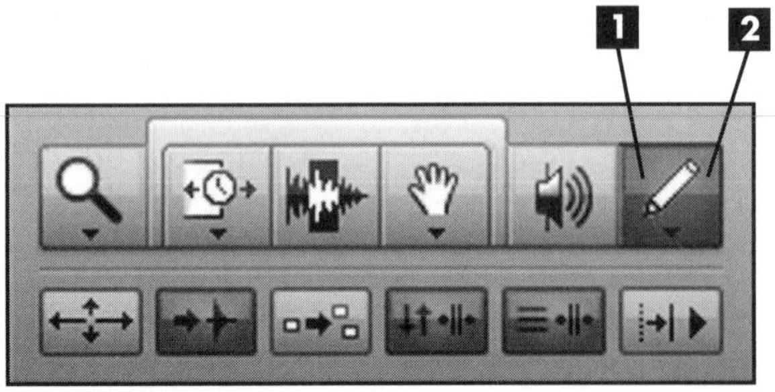

2 To view the different drawing options available to you, **click and hold** the **Pencil Tool button**. A menu will appear.

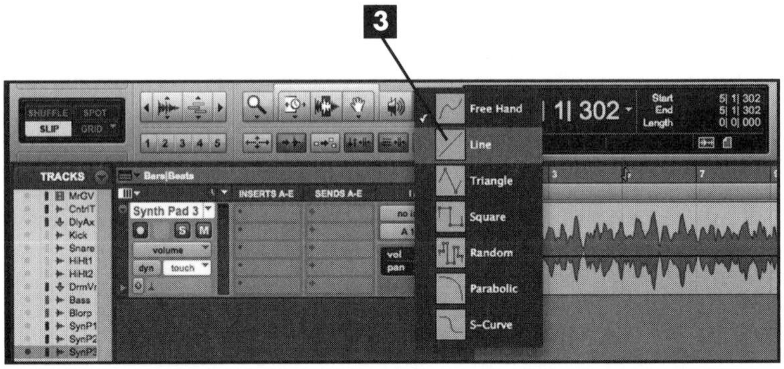

3 Just like the Trim and Grabber tools, the Pencil has some useful variations. For example, you can change the Pencil tool from its default freehand mode into a straight line (which in the case of volume automation would create linear changes in amplitude). **Click** on the **option** you want to use (in this case, the Line variation).

4 **Click and hold** the **Pencil tool** at the point at which you want to begin writing new automation.

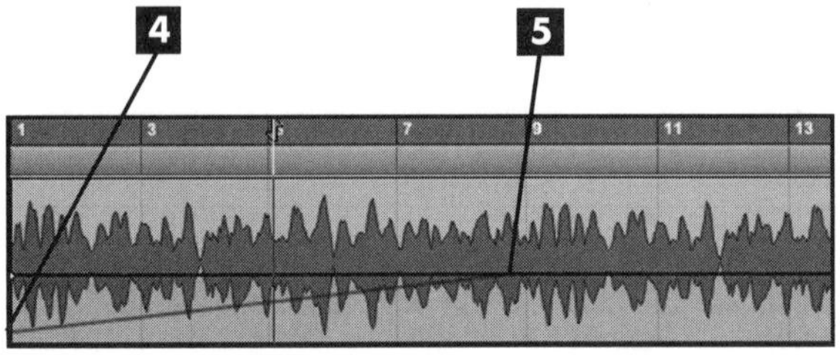

5 **Drag** the **mouse** to the place where you want to stop writing new automation. The Pencil tool will progressively write over pre-existing automation. In this example, a straight line will be drawn because the Line option for the Pencil tool was chosen.

6 **Release** the **mouse button**. Your new automation will be written.

Of course, you can write more than just volume automation with the Pencil tool. Let's try some pan automation on the Blorp track that ping-pongs from left to right. (A pan automation lane has been created in the tutorial session for your convenience.) Although you *could* draw a straight line from left to right over and over again to get a ping-pong effect, there's an easier way to do it.

1 **Click and hold** the **Pencil Tool button**. Again, the Pencil tool options will appear.

2 This time, **click** on the **Triangle menu item**.

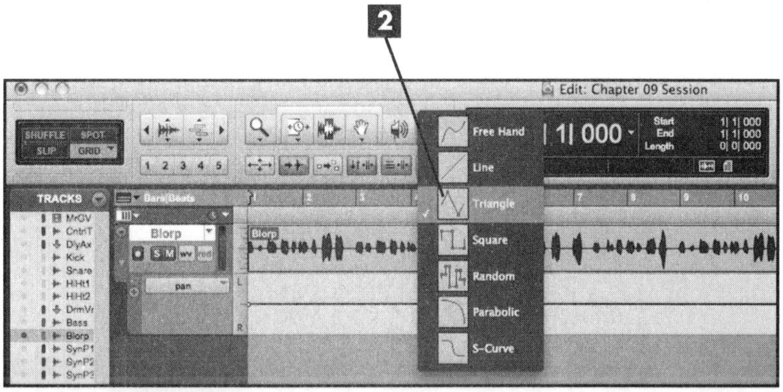

3 When you're dealing with the Triangle, Square, or Random Pencil tool options, the Grid setting will determine the frequency of the automation changes (even if you're not in Grid mode). **Choose** a **grid value**. (In this case, I want to pan from side to side every measure, so I've chosen 1 bar as my grid value in this image.)

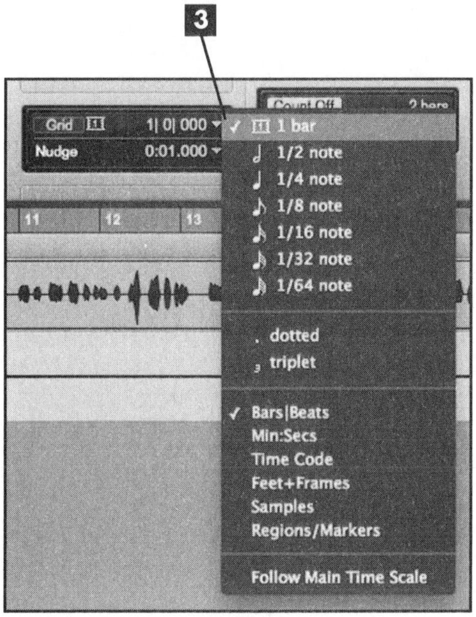

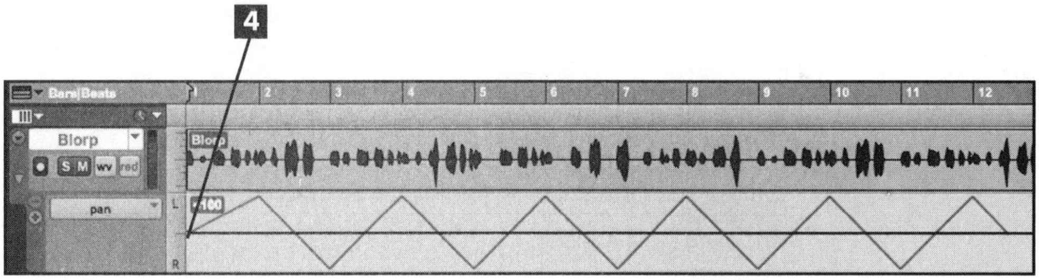

4 **Click and hold** the **Pencil tool** at the point at which you want to begin writing automation. This time, as you drag horizontally, a triangle wave will be drawn across the track. The speed of your panning will be determined by your Grid value. (In my case, it's one measure.) You can change the height of the wave by moving your mouse vertically as you drag. In the case of pan automation, a higher and lower triangle wave will translate into a more extreme pan from left to right.

5 When you're finished, **release** the **mouse button**. The pan automation will be written to your track.

AUTOMATION AND GRIDS

Although a triangle wave can be drawn in any of the edit modes, if you want the apex of the triangle wave to fall on a grid line, you must be in Grid mode.

Copying and Pasting Automation

If you've got a segment of automation that you like, you can cut and paste that automation from one location to another. It's easy!

1. **Click** the **Selector tool.**
2. **Select** the **area of automation** that you want to copy, just as if you were selecting a segment of audio.

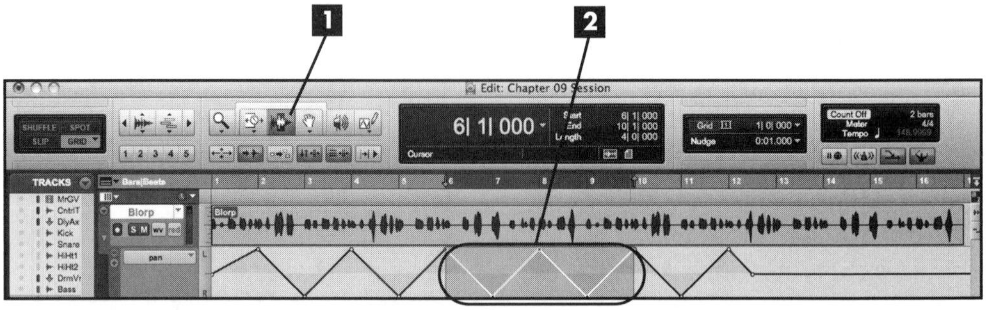

3. **Click** on the **Edit menu** and **choose** any of the basic **editing functions** you've used before (such as Cut, Copy, Paste, or Duplicate). One thing to keep in mind: This will not affect any audio regions or any automation parameters other than the one(s) you have selected.

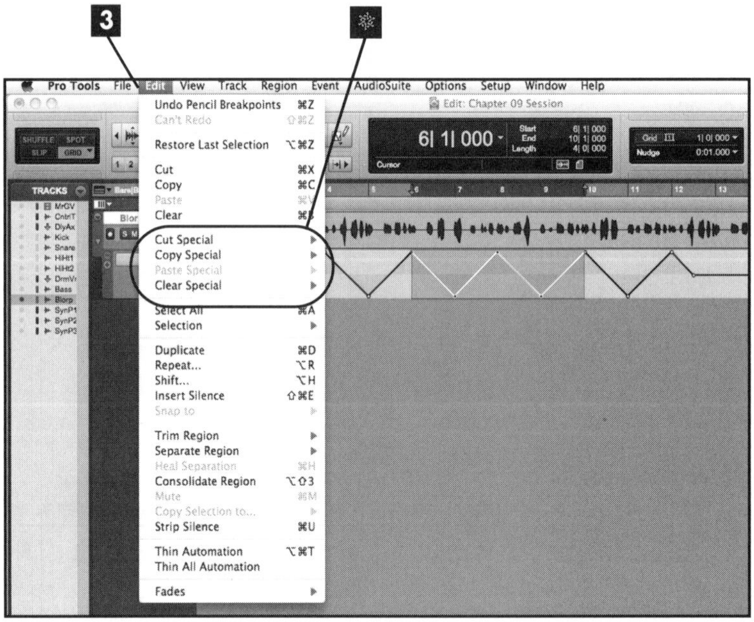

- Clicking the "special" editing items (including Cut Special, Copy Special, Paste Special, and Clear Special) will reveal a submenu that will enable you to edit *all* automation, *only pan* automation, or *all plug-in* automation.

SHORTCUT REMINDER

Remember, you can use the regular Cut, Copy, and Paste editing shortcut keys instead of going to the Edit menu. If you're using a Mac computer, the shortcuts are Command+X, Command+C, and Command+V respectively. If you're on a PC, the shortcuts are Ctrl+X, Ctrl+C, and Ctrl+V.

Trimming Automation

Once you've selected an area of automation, the Trim tool will enable you to scale it proportionally.

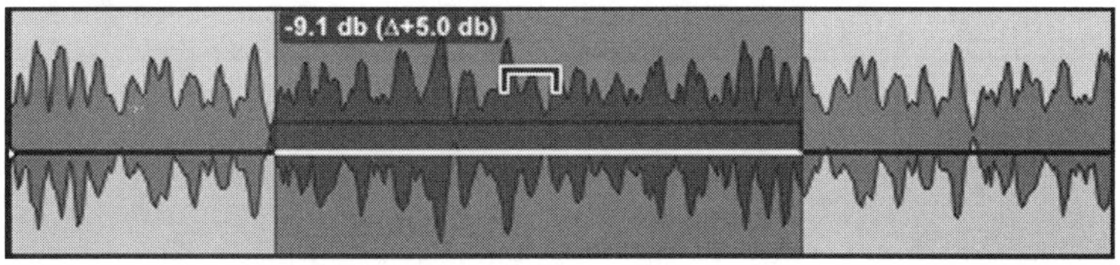

When the Trim tool is moved into a selected area of automation, it will be shown as downward-facing, enabling you to drag your mouse up and down to increase or decrease the level of the automation in that selected area (while maintaining the shape of the automation line).

Note that when you use the Trim tool to change automation, there will be a small box to the left that will not only show you the level of your new automation, but also a delta value (indicated by a triangle) when adjusting volume, which lets you know the amount of change you're applying.

Automation Follows Edit

If you move a region, do you want the automation during that time to follow the region, or do you want it to stay put? Either way, Pro Tools has you covered.

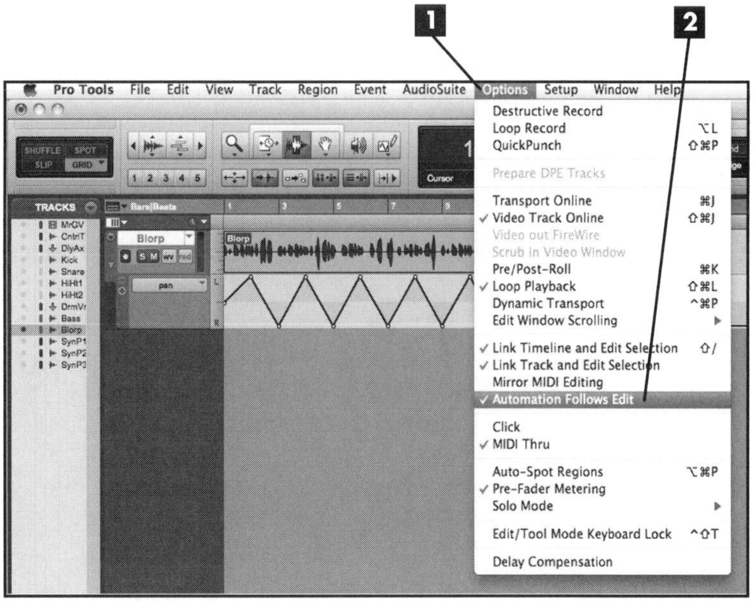

1. **Click** the **Options menu**.
2. The feature we're looking for in this case is called Automation Follows Edit. When active, the menu item will appear with a check-mark, and you can enable or disable this behavior by clicking it in the menu.

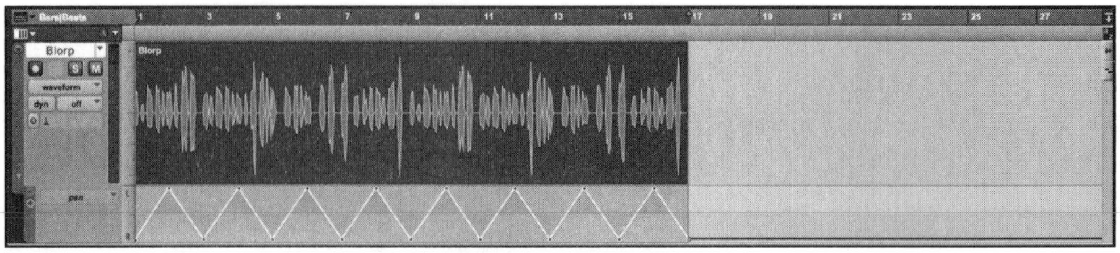

The best way to understand how this feature works is to see it in action. This image shows an example of an unmoved region, showing pan automation in an automation lane below the main playlist. Now, let's say that we move the region. What will happen to the automation?

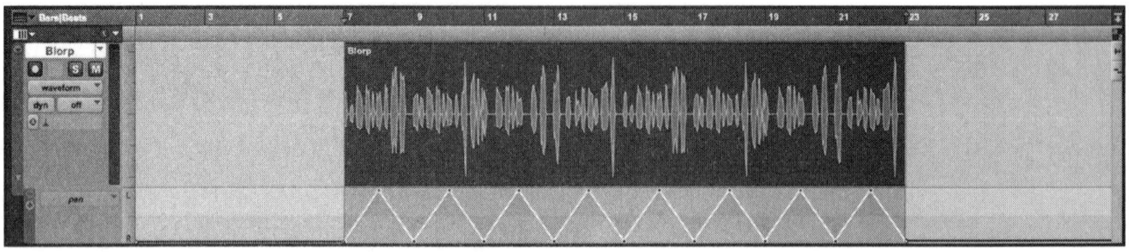

If Automation Follows Edit is enabled, the automation will be moved along with the region.

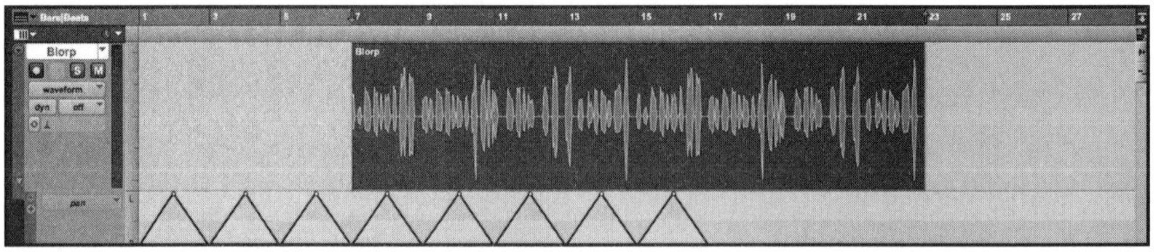

If Automation Follows Edit is disabled, the automation will not be moved along with the region. Instead, it will remain in its original position.

SEPARATING REGIONS WHILE VIEWING AUTOMATION

If you want to separate a region, but you are currently in an automation view on the main playlist, it's no problem. Just use the Selector tool to place your cursor where you want to split the region and separate the region as usual using the processes you learned in Chapter 5, "Editing." Your region will be separated, just as if you were in Waveform view.

SELECTING REGIONS WHILE VIEWING AUTOMATION

Suppose you want to quickly select the area of a region, but you are currently in an automation view on the main playlist. Just double-click the region with the Selector tool (just as if you were in Waveform view). The time corresponding to your region will be selected.

Momentary Switches and How to Use Them

Volume, pan, and plug-ins aren't the only aspects of your mix that can be automated. Switch-style controls (those that have only an on or off state) can be automated as well. In particular, mute and bypass (for plug-in effects) are often automated in order to get even more control over your mix.

Typically, these controls "latch"—that is, if you click the button once, it will change the state of the parameter until the button is clicked again, like a light switch. However, you might find that changing the behavior of these switches so that they don't latch (in other words, the state of the switch will only change while you're pressing the button) opens new creative possibilities. This non-latching kind of switch is called a *momentary* switch and is quite useful for adding delay or reverb to individual words or notes but leaving the rest of the track dry.

Here's a scenario for you: If you take a look at your session, you'll see that you have a Snare track. What we want to do is to add a large amount of reverb to every fourth snare hit. Here's how to do it using momentary (non-latching) switches.

First, let's set things up using the traditional time-based techniques we covered in Chapter 8:

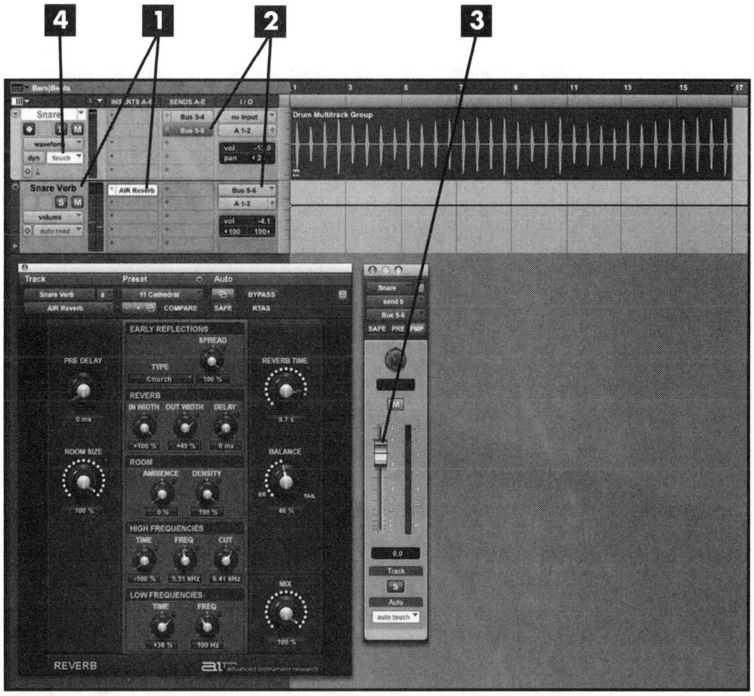

1 **Create** a **stereo Aux track** and **instantiate** a **reverb plug-in** on any available insert.

2 **Create** a **send** on the Audio track that you want to work with (in this image, the Snare track) and **assign** the **output** to an available pair of buses. (I've chosen buses 5–6 in this image.) Set the **input** of the **Aux track** to the same buses.

3 **Click** the **send button** and **set** the send's **volume level**. (Remember, Option-clicking the fader will put it at unity.)

4 Last but not least, **put** your **Audio track** into Touch automation mode and **mute** the **send**, since this is the state that you'll be starting off with.

5 In the Preferences window, **go to** the **Mixing tab**.

6 By default, the Latching Behavior for Switch Controls in "Touch" checkbox is checked. To make the switch momentary, **click** the **checkbox** to remove the checkmark.

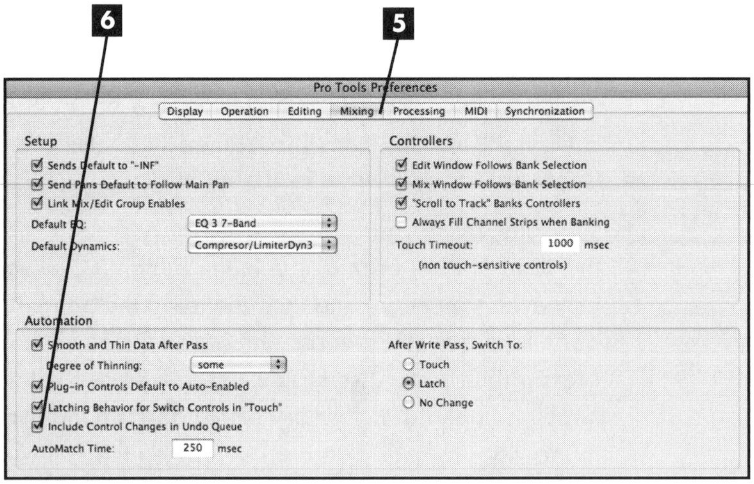

7 Click OK at the bottom of the Preferences window.

Now you're ready to rock. After you start playback, click and hold on the Send Mute button (which you'll see in the Send Output window) during every fourth snare hit. As soon as the snare hit is finished, release the button; this will put the send back into a muted state.

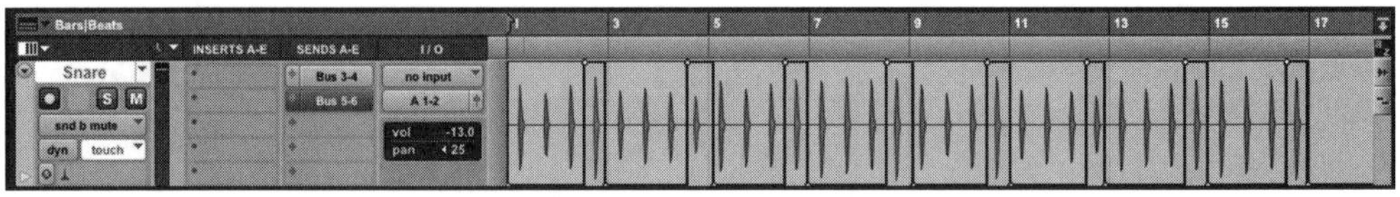

Although it might take a couple of attempts to get it right, here's what you should wind up with. If you look at your send's mute automation playlist, you will see your send alternately mute and unmute. When the send is unmuted, signal will be sent to the Aux track, and you'll hear the reverb.

This technique is known in some circles as a *dub hit*, and it can be used on any kind of track, from beats to vocals. Now that you understand how the effect is achieved, you'll hear it in all sorts of modern music. The most obvious example is a vocal in which some individual words have reverbs (or echo or delay) but others are relatively dry.

BLUE BREAKPOINTS

Before we move on from the world of automation, there's one final detail you should be aware of. From time to time, you might see an automation breakpoint (the small dots that make up an automation playlist) colored blue. This blue color indicates that the automation data has overflowed (think of it as automation "clipping") and exceeds the limit of that parameter.

More Mixing Power with Subgroups

What's a subgroup? Simply put, a *subgroup* is an arrangement whereby the output of a number of tracks is routed to the input of a single track (usually a stereo Aux track). This has the effect of "funneling" the audio through this single track (often referred to as a *subgroup master*), making levels and effects easier to manage. Take a look:

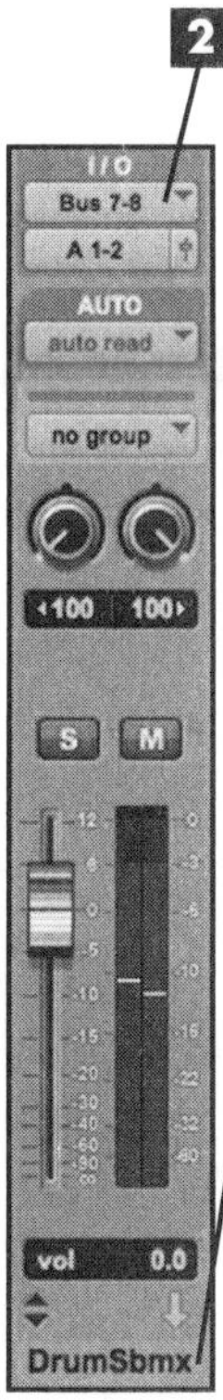

1 **Create** a **track** to be your subgroup master (in this case, I've chosen to create a stereo Aux track) and **name it** appropriately.

2 Because you'll be using internal routing in this sort of situation, **choose** available **buses** for the input of the subgroup master. (In this image, I've chosen buses 7 and 8.)

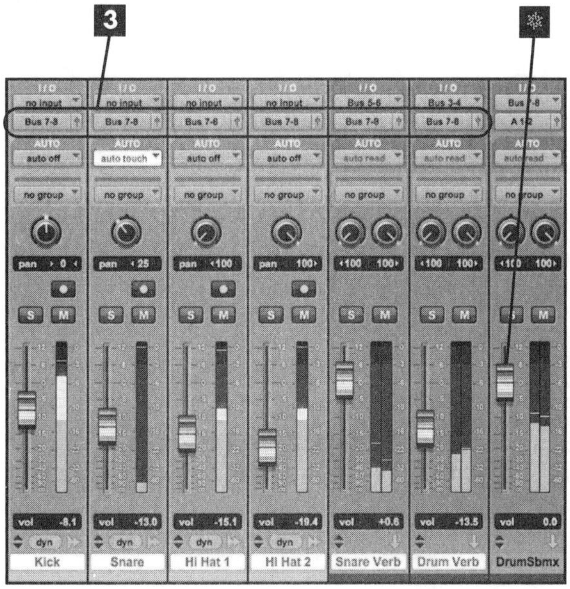

3 **Assign** the **outputs** of the tracks to be grouped (in this example, I've chosen all the drum tracks in this session, including the reverb Aux tracks) to the same buses as you've chosen for the input of your subgroup master.

Your subgroup Master track's fader is now in control of the overall volume of your subgrouped tracks. Note that as you adjust the fader, the relative blend of the drums remains consistent, and the subgroup master controls the overall output.

In addition to making levels more manageable, subgroups can also help you work more efficiently with plug-ins. For example, if you want to apply a compressor to your drums (a very common thing to do), you *could* instantiate a compressor on each of the tracks. That, however, would be unwieldy to work with and wasteful of your limited processing resources. Instead, just launch *one* compressor effect on an insert of the subgroup master. There's only one plug-in to adjust, and it's thrifty use of your CPU!

New in Pro Tools 9: Track-Output Options

In Chapter 8, you routed a send to the input of an existing Aux track as a part of traditional time-based effects routing. In the previous section, you routed the outputs of a number of tracks to the input of an Aux track to create a mix subgroup. Although neither of these operations is particularly difficult, they do take some time (and are common tasks when it comes to mixing). Pro Tools 9 includes a few new output options that can greatly streamline these workflows!

With Pro Tools 9, you have the option to choose a track (new or existing) from the output menu. What this does is automate many of the steps you've had to deal with up to now. Let's start off by looking at how track outputs can speed up time-based effects routing.

Track Output and Time-Based Effects Routing

In this scenario, I have a single vocal track, and I want to add some reverb. Using the new Track Output option, the job gets much quicker!

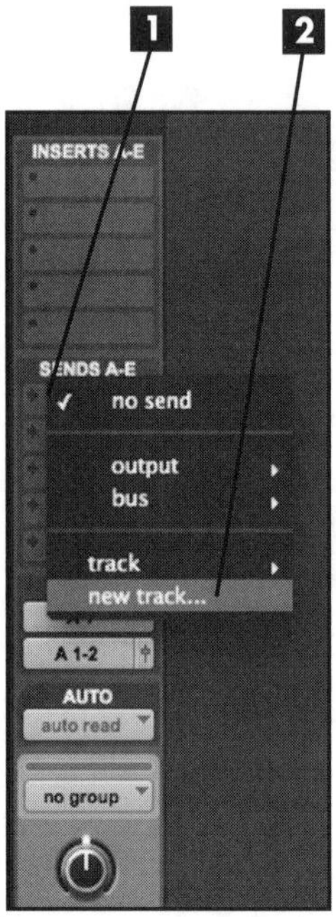

1. **Click** on any available **Send Selector button**. A list of output options will appear.
2. **Choose** the **New Track** menu item. The New Track dialog box will appear.

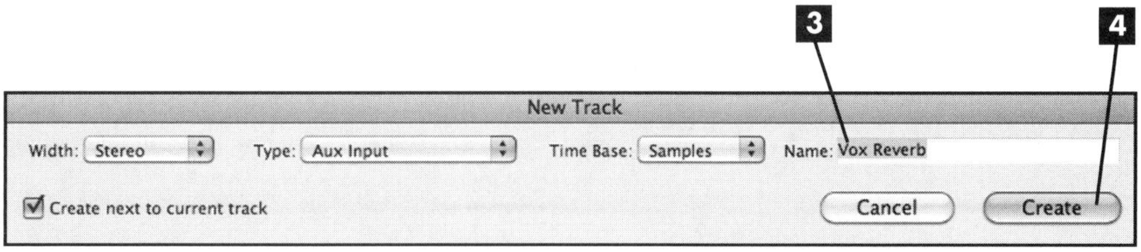

3 Although not identical, this New Track window should look familiar. Here, you can choose the format and name for your new destination track. As it happens, the default format in this window is to create a Stereo Aux Input track, which is perfect for our purposes. All you have to do is **type** a **descriptive name** in the right-most field. This is a fairly important step, so it's best not to skip it.

4 Once you're done, **click** the **Create button**. Here's what you've done, in one easy step:

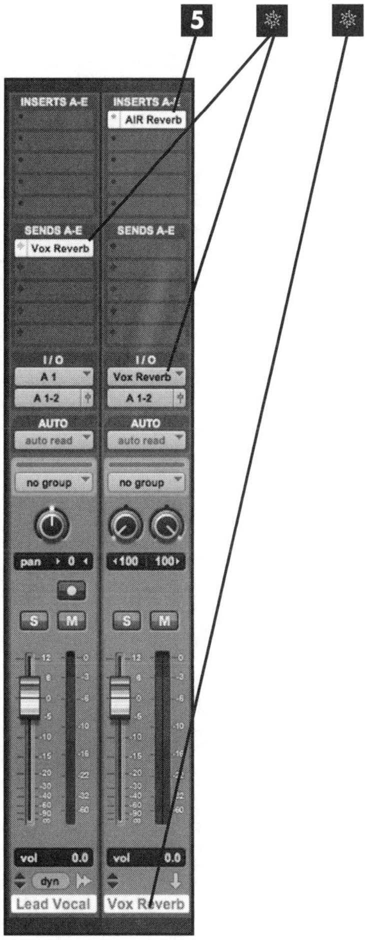

- A new Stereo Aux Input track has been created, named "Vox Reverb."
- The output of the send has been set to a new bus called "Vox Reverb." (Pro Tools created this new bus at the same time the track was created.) You'll note that this same bus is the input of the newly created Aux track. Basically, your routing has been done for you (although you will still need to bring up the level of your send)!

5 Although your track and the routing have all been done for you, you'll still have to **choose a plug-in** for the track. (In this image, I'll choose a reverb.) At this point, you're ready to blend your wet and dry signal, and get back to mixing!

Track Output and Subgroups

Next, let's take a look at how this same feature can be used to quickly create a subgroup. In this situation, I've got a number of drum tracks, and I want to group their outputs for easy level management:

A USEFUL SHORTCUT

Earlier in this book, you learned that holding down the Option (Mac) or Alt (PC) key will apply changes you make to one track to all tracks in the session. Here's a variation on that theme: Holding down Shift+Option (Mac) or Shift+Alt (PC) will apply changes made to one track (things like input, output, etc.) to all *selected* tracks.

1. **Select** all the **tracks** that you want to be a part of the new subgroup.
2. Now it's time to use your new shortcut: Holding down the Shift+Option (Mac) or Shift+Alt (PC) keys, **click** the **track output selector** of one of your selected tracks. A list of output options will appear.
3. Once again, **choose** the **New Track** menu item. The New Track dialog box will appear.

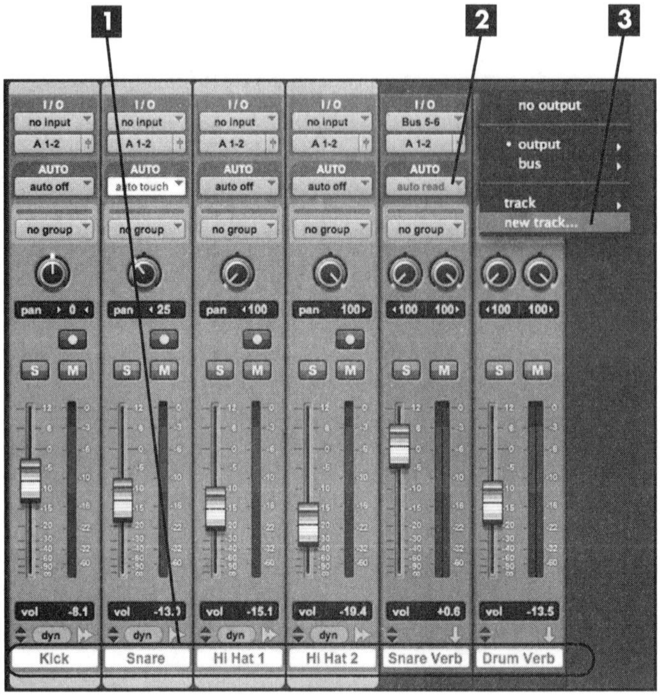

4. In the New Track dialog box, once again **choose** the **default track settings** (the default of a Stereo Aux Input track works best in the majority of cases), and **name** the **track** "Drum Sub."

Here's what you'll wind up with:

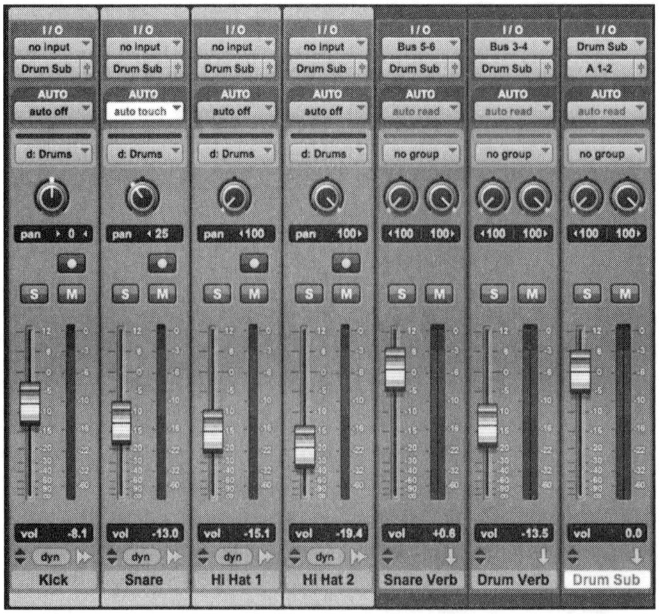

You'll see that, once again, you've created a new Stereo Aux track, except in this case, the outputs of the selected tracks have been routed through a stereo bus to the input of the new track.

OUTPUT TO TRACK

There's more to track outputs than just creating new tracks, though. You can also route the output of a track or a send to an existing Audio or Aux track.

By choosing the Track menu item from the output menu, you'll see a list of all eligible tracks in your session. The tracks shown in this list will either not have an assigned input or have an existing bus input (tracks with interface inputs will not appear on this list).

Using Master Faders

There's one more track type left for us to explore: the Master Fader. Although it looks similar to an Audio or Aux track, its function is substantially different from anything you've seen up to this point. A Master Fader is a way to control output, and it is commonly used to control the output of an interface channel (although it can also be used to control the output of buses in more complex mix situations). With this simple but powerful track, you can control the entire level of your session.

Creating a Master Fader

First things first...you need to *create* a Master Fader before you can use it!

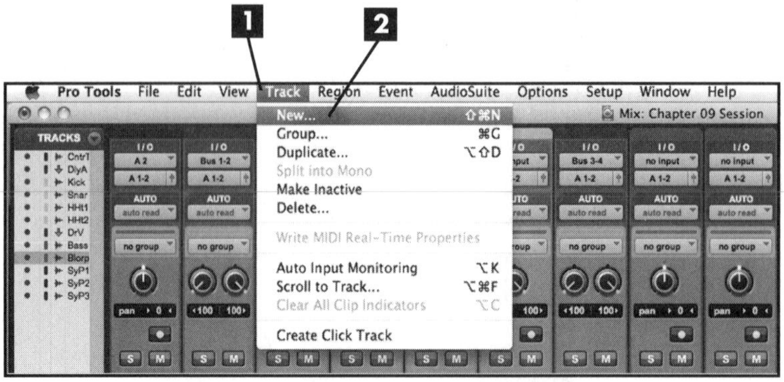

1 **Click** the **Track menu.**

2 **Click** on **New**. The New Tracks dialog box will open.

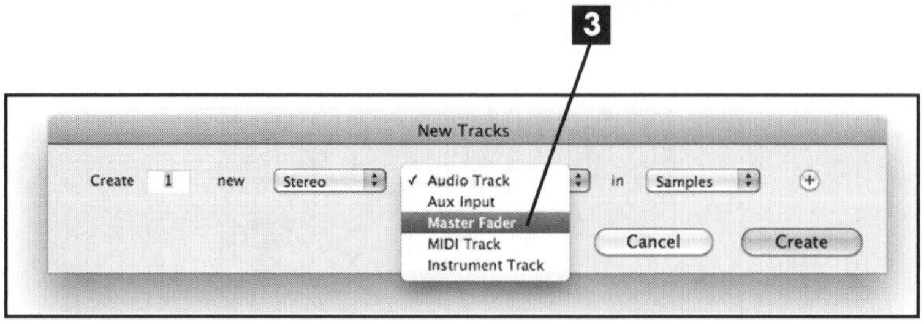

3 Using the techniques you learned back in Chapter 3, **create** a **stereo Master Fader track**. (You'll find Master Fader listed in the track type menu, as shown here.) The new Master Fader track will be created after the last selected track in your session.

The Master Fader looks similar to any other track, but don't be fooled—it's significantly different!

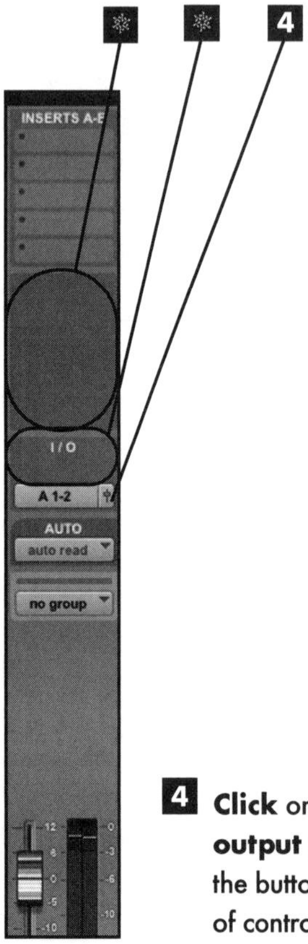

- You'll notice that the area on the channel strip that would normally display an Input button is conspicuously blank. That's because there is no input on a Master Fader; it is only a way to control an output.
- Notice also that there are no sends on a Master Fader.
- If you take a look at a Master Fader track in the Edit window, you'll see that you can't place regions on this track. In this regard, it's similar to an Aux track.

4 **Click** on the **Output Path Selector button** and **select** the **interface output** you're using to listen to your mix (if it's not already being shown in the button). With this output selected, the Master Fader is in its common role of controlling the output of your entire mix.

Controlling Your Mix with a Master Fader

Now let's use your Master Fader to control your entire mix. Let's start by creating a linear fade-out for your entire mix in one easy process.

SETTING THINGS UP

For this section, switch to the Edit window if you're not viewing it already.

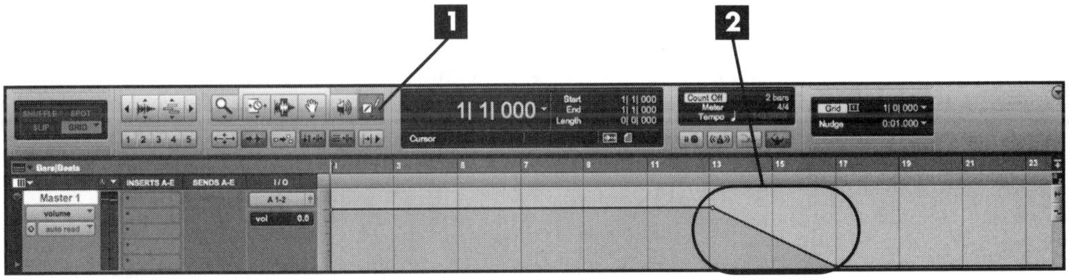

1 **Select** the **Pencil tool** and **choose** the **Line option** to create a straight fade-out.

2 **Write** a **linear decrease** in volume automation on the Master Fader track, just as you would on any other kind of track. Because this Master Fader is controlling the output of your entire mix, you'll hear a linear change in the volume of all of your tracks, starting at the point at which the Master Fader's automation begins.

AUTOMATION AND MASTER FADERS

If you want to write automation onto your Master Fader in the Mix window, it's no problem. Simply write automation just as you would on any other type of track, using any of the automation modes.

Basic Mastering Techniques Using a Master Fader

Mastering is a post-mix process that further refines a piece of work to a professional quality. It's such a detailed and important process that an entire segment of the professional audio community is dedicated to the specific task of mastering others' mixes. These mastering engineers are dedicated to techniques and processes that are quite outside the realm of normal production, and a good mastering engineer can do things with your final mix that border on the miraculous. The bottom line (at least the way *I* see it): The task of professionally mastering a mix is certainly not recommended for the non-specialist.

You might, however, want to try your hand at a little basic mastering to punch up your mix for your own enjoyment or to make an evaluation mix a little more palatable for your client. Here's where Master Faders can really come in handy, due to another interesting difference between a Master Fader and any other track—one that may not be initially apparent. This difference is in the area of signal flow—the inserts are *after* the fader in the signal chain. Read on....

ADVICE ON MASTERING

The discussion in this section relates to the process of mastering a mix *on your own* (as opposed to having your mix professionally mastered by a dedicated mastering engineer). If and when you decide to have your mix professionally mastered, the mastering engineer will want to do the entire job himself (usually with highly specialized and costly gear specific to the process of mastering), so you won't need to go through the steps outlined here. That being said, it's always a good idea to consult with your mastering engineer *before* submitting your mix so you can find out exactly what he or she needs from you.

Using Dither

In overly simplistic terms, dither is a very low-level noise that is added to digital audio to offset some of the negative effects of reducing bit depth. For example, if you're working in a 24-bit session but will be creating a 16-bit file for an audio CD, you can improve the quality of your audio by instantiating a dither plug-in on a Master Fader.

WHEN *NOT* TO USE DITHER

Dither should only be considered when the final product is to be at a lesser bit depth than the original session. For example, if you have a 24-bit session, and will make a 16-bit final mix, you should absolutely add dither. If, however, your final mix is to remain 24 bit, you shouldn't. Sample rates, file formats—all these things have no bearing on dither.

1 On the very last insert on the Master Fader track, **select** a desired **dither plug-in** (in this example, I've chosen POWr Dither) from the Multichannel Plug-In menu. The plug-in's window will appear.

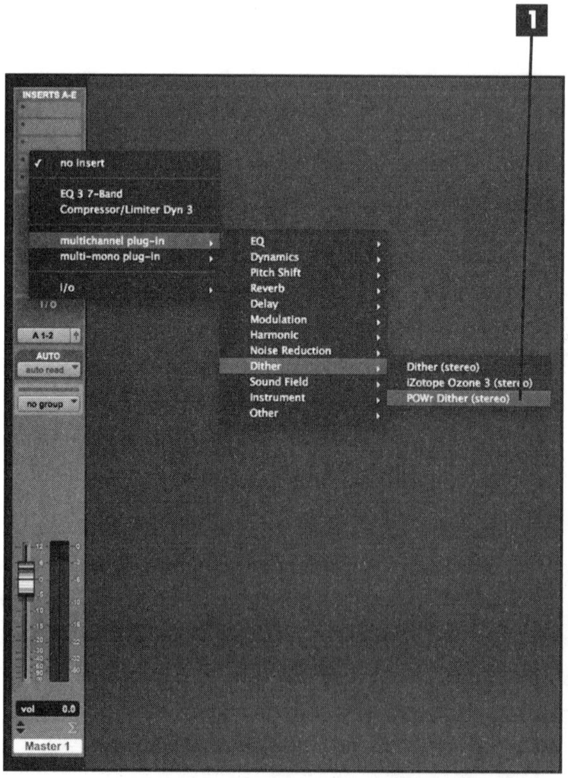

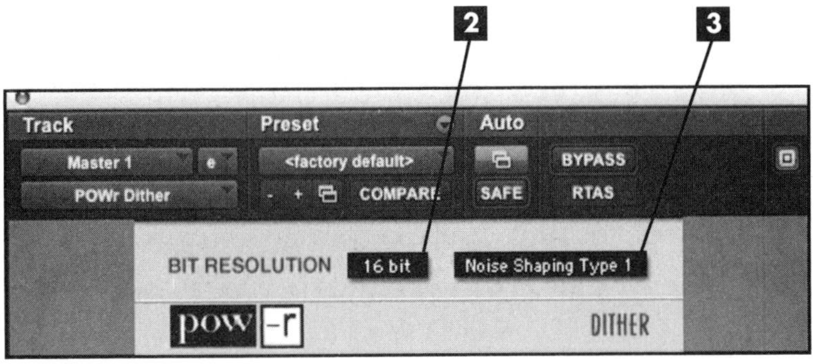

2 **Click** on the **Bit Resolution button** and **choose** the **final resolution** for your mix from a list. For example, if you want to make a Red Book Audio CD of your mix (assuming that your session was at 24 bits), you would choose the 16-bit option (as shown here).

3 Noise shaping can help make dither "noise" even less audible than it normally is. **Click** the **Noise Shaping button** and **select** a **noise-shaping type** from the list. For now, you can safely stick with the default shaping, but be sure to listen to different mixes with different noise shaping later to determine which one is best for you.

Punching Up Your Mix with Compression: Two Ways

Another common step in the mastering process is the application of *compression* to the entire mix. This is a tried-and-true method employed to narrow the dynamic range of your audio, thereby maximizing its overall punch. Here's one easy way to get it done:

1 On your Master Fader, **instantiate** a **compressor plug-in** on an insert before (above) the one you used for dither. The Compressor plug-in window will appear.

2 **Adjust** your compressor's **parameters** to punch up your mix to suit your taste. It'll take some experimentation to find the best settings for any given situation of course, but you can start with a preset configuration, like the one shown in this example.

> ### COMPRESSORS AND DITHER
> If you're using both dither and a compressor on a Master Fader, you'll need to arrange your inserts so that the dither is the last plug-in in the insert signal flow (that is, on the lowest insert). Don't worry if your dither is currently on the top insert; you can just drag it down to a lower insert position (and thus later in the insert's signal path) with your mouse and then launch your compressor in an insert above it.

Those of you with mixing experience might notice a problem with this sort of routing. As you know, a compressor operates by attenuating (or reducing) any level above a certain threshold, which you set up in your plug-in window. Any incoming signal below that threshold will not be affected by the compressor. As long as you don't use your Master Fader for fade-ins or fade-outs, there's no problem with using a compressor on the Master Fader. If you *do* use the Master Fader for any kind of volume automation, however, you might hear your compressor kick in or out, depending on whether you're fading in or out. (The inserts on a Master Fader track are *post*-fader.) How do you get around this problem? I'm glad you asked!

1 **Reassign** the **output** of all tracks previously assigned to your monitors (in this image, A 1–2) to an available pair of buses. (I've chosen buses 9–10.) If you're following the tutorial session, this will include all the tracks *except* your drum tracks. (They're already assigned to a bus, which is routed to a subgroup Aux track. You *will* want to change the outputs on the Drum Subgroup Aux track, though.) Your session should now be completely inaudible—but wait!

2 **Create** a **stereo Aux track** and **assign** the **input** of that track to the same pair of buses that you used as an output for your other tracks. Essentially, you're creating a huge subgroup. Finally, **drag** the **compressor plug-in** from the Master Fader (with its post-fader inserts) to the new Aux track (which has *pre-*fader inserts).

The output to which this Aux track is assigned (in this image, A 1–2) is still ultimately controlled by the Master Fader, making it an ideal place to apply dither. Since the inserts of the Aux track are pre-fader, the signal going to the compressor will be affected by neither the Master Fader *nor* the Aux track's output level, meaning you can apply your global fade automation on either track without losing that punchy sound. That's it!

USING TRACK OUTPUT

As mentioned, what you're essentially doing in this second method is creating a huge subgroup. As you learned earlier in this chapter, you can use the New Track output option to simultaneously create the track and routing you need for this sort of work.

MASTER FADERS AND METERING

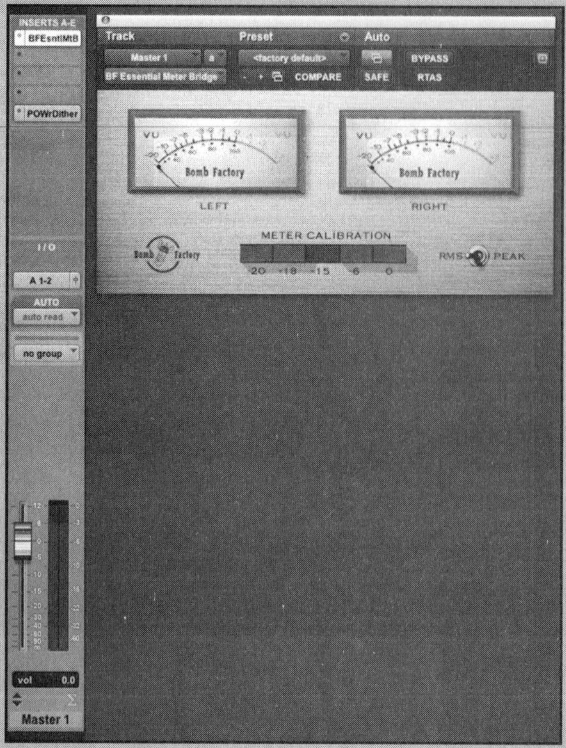

There's one more very important function of a Master Fader track—one for which it is uniquely suited due to its post-fader inserts. Master Faders are great for monitoring the overall levels of your mix. In addition to the track's own level meters, there are a variety of metering plug-ins available to you. A good example of this is the Bomb Factory Essential Meter Bridge shown here. (You'll find it in the Other category of the Multichannel Plug-Ins insert menu.)

A FINISHED TUTORIAL SESSION

A session file that shows many of the topics covered in this chapter in a finished form has been included in your Chapter 09 Session folder. Just open the Chapter 09 Session - Finished session file.

Bouncing to Disk

When you're working with a Pro Tools session, you're in a multitrack environment. (You probably already knew that.) Even though you may be listening through stereo monitor speakers, you're actually hearing many component tracks, artfully combined by Pro Tools' software mix engine. From a production standpoint, it's a very cool way to work, but if you ever want to hear your song *outside* the Pro Tools environment, you'll have to somehow render the mix down to a format that is compatible with the outside world.

The Bounce to Disk function will enable you to mix down your session to a final format—for example, a stereo file that can be played on an MP3 player. It's a simple process, but an important last step that demands some attention to detail, so we'll go over each step carefully. For the purpose of demonstration, here's how to go about bouncing to disk so you can create a file that you could burn onto an audio CD (Red Book format):

1 Using the Selector tool, **select** the **area** of your session you want to bounce to disk in the Ruler area. (In this example, I'll select from the beginning of my session to the end of my Master Fader's fade-out.)

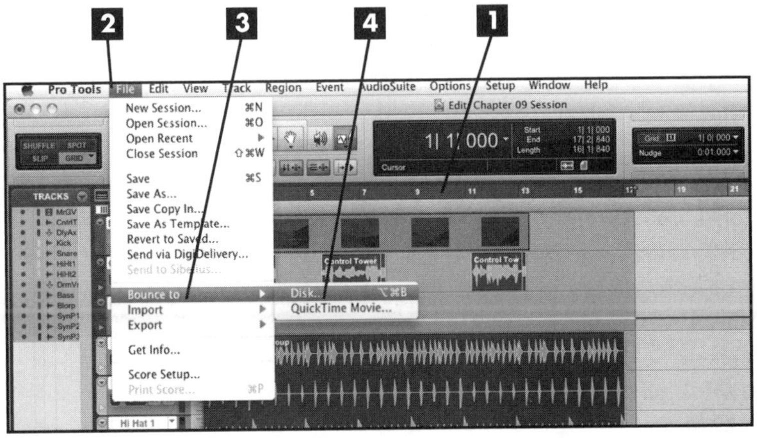

2 **Click** on the **File menu**.

3 **Click** on **Bounce To**. A submenu will be displayed.

4 **Click** on **Disk**. The Bounce dialog box will appear.

5 At the top of the Bounce dialog box, you'll see the Bounce Source menu. (The button will display the currently selected bounce source.) To change the source, just **click** the **Bounce Source menu button** and **select** the **output path** you're using to listen to your mix from a list of options. (In this case, I want to choose A 1–2 as my bounce source bus, which in this case is mapped to a hardware output path also called A 1–2, since that's the path that is connected to my monitor speakers.)

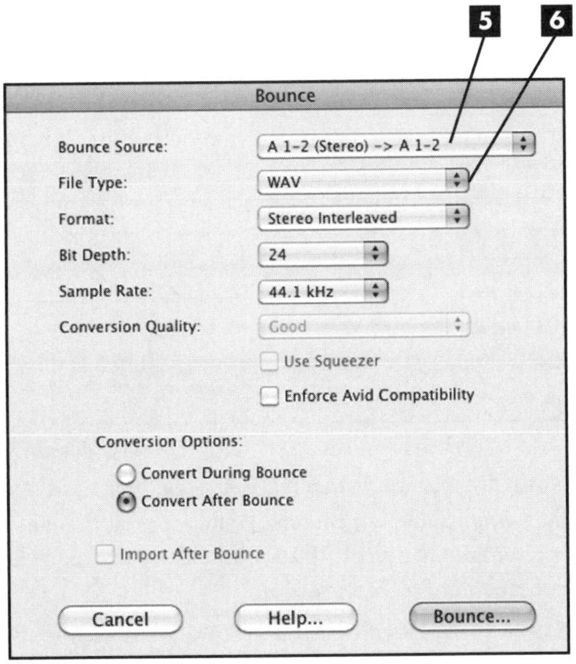

BOUNCE TROUBLESHOOTING

If you do a bounce to disk and then later find that your bounce is a silent audio file, you've probably chosen the wrong bounce source.

6 The File Type menu button will display the type of file you will be creating. (In this example, we'll be creating a WAV file.) If you want to change the file type, just **click** the **File Type menu button** and **choose** the desired **type** from the list of available file types.

NEW IN PRO TOOLS 9: BOUNCE TO MP3 INCLUDED!

MP3 lovers rejoice! In previous versions of Pro Tools, the ability to bounce to an MP3 file was a paid add-on called the MP3 Option. Now, with Pro Tools 9, this functionality is built into all versions of Pro Tools, so you'll be able to bounce to MP3 without any extra purchases, licenses, or installations.

7 The Format menu button will display the channel format of the file(s) you will be creating with your bounce. (In this case, it's Stereo Interleaved.) Let's take a closer look at this. **Click** on the **Format menu button** to reveal a list of bounce options.

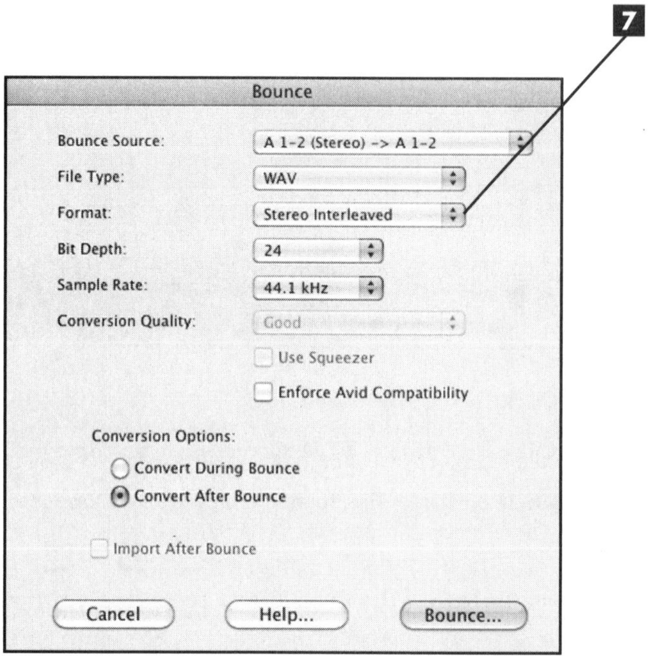

- **Mono (Summed).** With this option selected, your session will be mixed down to a single mono file (even if it's a stereo session).

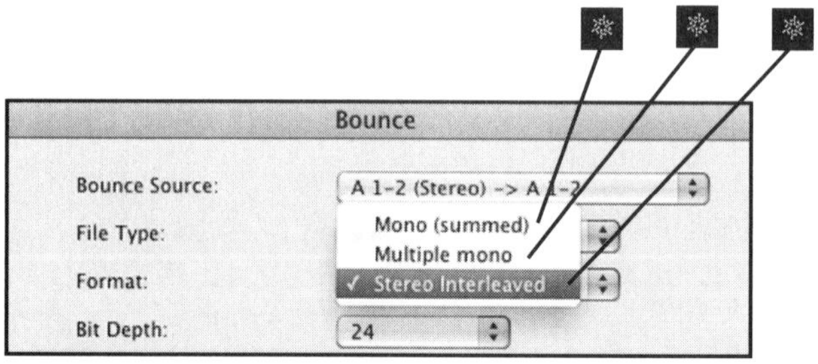

- **Multiple Mono.** When this is chosen, your stereo mix will be output to a pair of mono files–one for the left channel (with a .l after the file name) and one for the right (with a .r after the file name). This is particularly useful for bounces that you intend to import into another Pro Tools session.
- **Stereo Interleaved.** Your mix will be rendered to a single stereo file.

8 The Bit Depth menu button will display the bit depth of the file you will be creating. If you want to change the bit depth, **click** the **Bit Depth menu button** and **choose** the desired **setting** from a list of available resolutions. (In this example, we'll be creating a 16-bit file.)

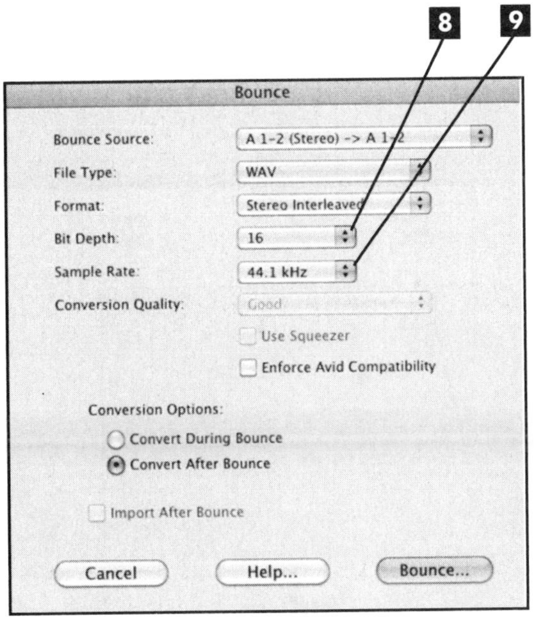

9 The Sample Rate menu button will display the sample rate of the file you will be creating. If you want to change the setting, **click** the **Sample Rate menu button** and **choose** the desired **sample rate**. (In this example, we'll be creating a 44.1 kHz file.)

RED BOOK CD SETTINGS

If your bounced file is going to be put onto a Red Book audio CD, the bit depth should be set to 16, the sample rate should be 44.1 kHz, and the format should be Stereo Interleaved.

- If the sample rate or bit depth you've chosen for your bounced file is different from those of your session (or if you've chosen any format other than Multiple Mono), Pro Tools will need to perform a conversion process. This will be done in one of two ways:

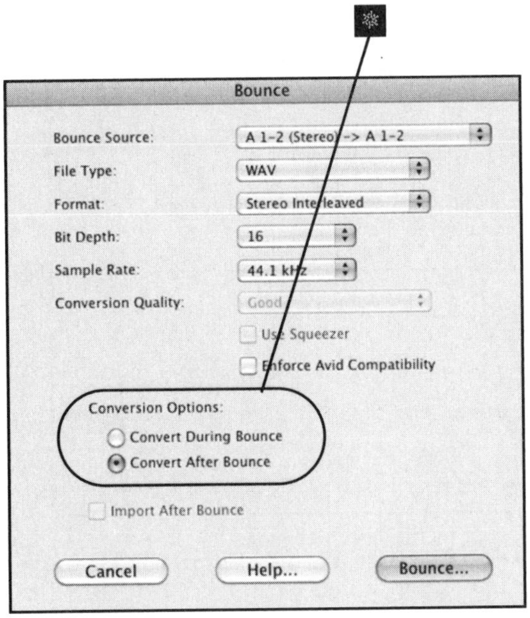

- **Convert During Bounce.** Clicking this option button will direct Pro Tools to convert during the bounce process (as your session plays).
- **Convert After Bounce.** This option will enable Pro Tools to apply its conversion *after* the bounce pass is complete, and it is the recommended setting in most cases.

SOME ADVICE ON BOUNCING

In rare cases, choosing Convert During Bounce can cause Pro Tools *not* to play back some types of automation during the bounce pass because of the extra burden of conversion while bouncing. For consistently accurate results, choose the Convert After Bounce option. It might take a little longer, but the peace of mind is well worth the patience!

- **Import After Bounce.** If the file type, sample rate, and bit depth of your bounced file match your session's setup, and if you've chosen Multiple Mono as a format, clicking the Import After Bounce checkbox will import your bounced file back into your session on an Audio track or to the region list.

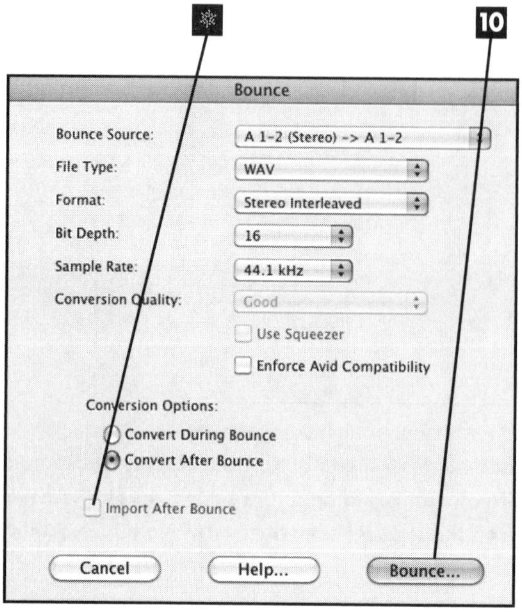

10 Once you have everything set up properly, **click** the **Bounce button**. The Save dialog box will open.

11 By now, you've seen the Save dialog box in a number of different contexts. In this case, you'll **choose** a **name** and **location** for your bounced audio file(s). You can save your file under any name you want, in any recordable drive, and in any folder.

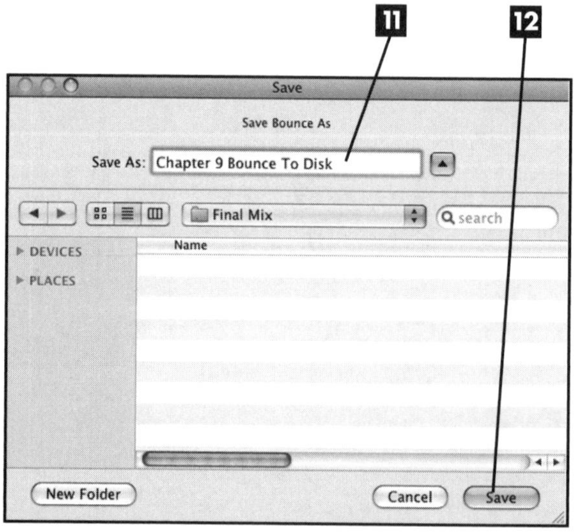

12 Once you've chosen a name and location for your new file, **click** on the **Save button**, and your bounce will begin.

THE IMPORTANCE OF GOOD FILE MANAGEMENT

At this point, I want to emphasize again how important it is to know exactly where and under what name your files are saved. (This goes for session files and other audio files as well.) You can save your bounced file anywhere you choose in your system, but with this great flexibility comes the added responsibility of using this power wisely. Make sure you can find your files when you need them!

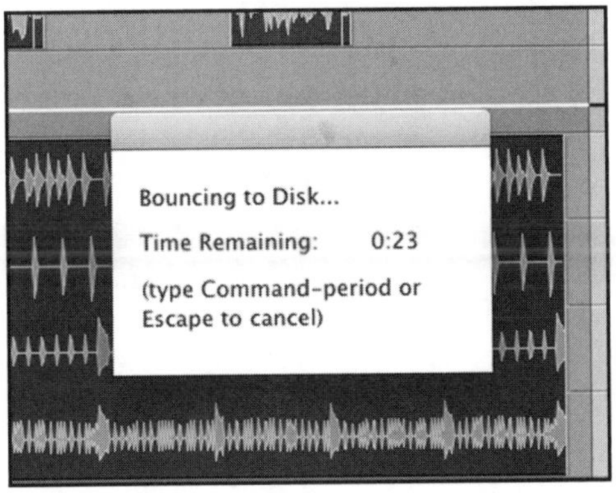

Your session will begin playing, and a small countdown window will indicate that bouncing is occurring in real time.

If conversion is necessary (and assuming you wisely chose to Convert After Bounce), you'll see a quick conversion progress window after your session is done playing. You're finished!

Bouncing to a QuickTime Movie

Because this session happens to have a Video track included in it, you also have the option of bouncing your work to a QuickTime movie file. The process is nearly identical to bouncing to disk.

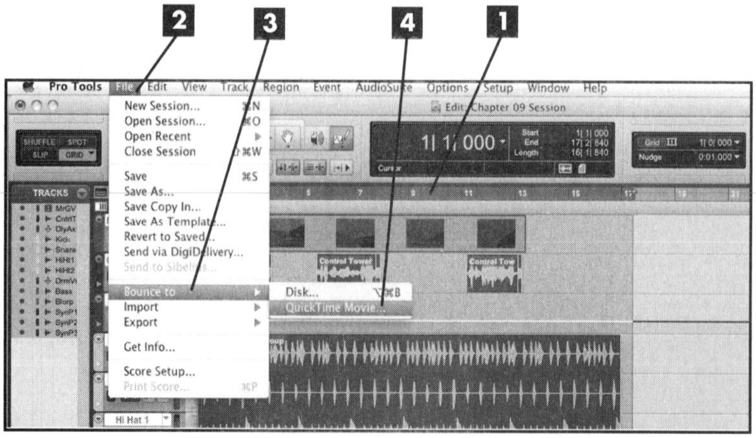

1 Using the Selector tool, **select** the **area** of your session you want to bounce to disk in the Ruler area. (When you're bouncing to a QuickTime movie, a good rule of thumb is to select an area equal to the length of the region on your Video track.)

2 **Click** on the **File menu**.

3 **Click** on **Bounce To**.

4 **Click** on **QuickTime Movie**. The Bounce dialog box will appear.

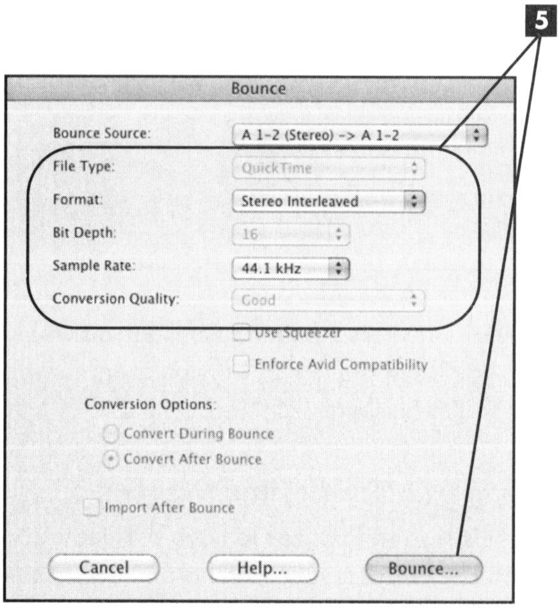

5 The Bounce dialog box that appears here is nearly identical to the one you encountered when you bounced only your audio. You may notice, though, that you have different options with regard to format and sample rate. This is normal, and varies from system to system. When you've made your choices, **click** the **Bounce button**. The bounce process will continue just as it did when you were using the Bounce to Disk feature, except that in this case, you'll be creating a QuickTime movie file.

Whether you're bouncing audio or video, enjoy your final mix—you've earned it!

10 Moving to the Next Level: Tips and Tricks

Pro Tools is a complex, professional application, and mastering it requires dedication, inspiration, and time. This book is meant to provide you with a solid basic understanding of how to use this powerful product—a foundation upon which to build greater knowledge as you gain experience. Through your study and understanding of this book so far, you've attained that basic understanding—good on ya!

This chapter covers a varied list of next-level functions, designed to enable you to be even more productive. In this chapter, you'll learn how to:

- Get the most out of your system.
- Make the most of your recording sessions.
- Edit with more efficiency and flexibility.
- Understand and use Elastic Audio.
- Take your mixing to the next level, and understand how to use Automatic Delay Compensation.
- Import and use movie files.

WORKING WITH THE TUTORIAL SESSION

To follow along with the examples shown in this chapter, launch the session named "Chapter 10 Session." You'll note that in this session, features are demonstrated through a series of memory locations. You'll note also that even though the session is extensive in its tracks and complexity, it's only using a few different audio files, keeping the overall session folder size small!

Boosting Performance with Disk Allocation

When starting out with Pro Tools, many beginners record to their sole system drives. Although this will work for relatively simple sessions, you may eventually find that a single hard drive—especially if it's your system drive—just doesn't cut it. Here are a few things that can place added stress on a hard drive:

- **High Audio track count.** More Audio tracks require more streams of communication to and from your hard drive.
- **High-resolution audio.** Higher-quality audio requires a greater bit rate and more of a hard drive's limited bandwidth.
- **Edit density.** The term *edit density* refers to the frequency with which your session needs to retrieve new audio from your hard drive during playback. Each time you create a region boundary in a track, you require Pro Tools to access a specific location on your hard drive. The more regions you have in a given time, the higher your edit density becomes, and the harder your drive has to work to provide uninterrupted audio playback. There are a few features that tend to increase edit density in a session, including using Beat Detective and Strip Silence—two tools we'll talk about later in this chapter.

One solution to hard-drive-bandwidth problems is to distribute audio playback among *multiple* hard drives, and that's just what the Disk Allocation dialog box lets you do. But first, let's take a quick trip to the Workspace Browser to set up different drives for different jobs:

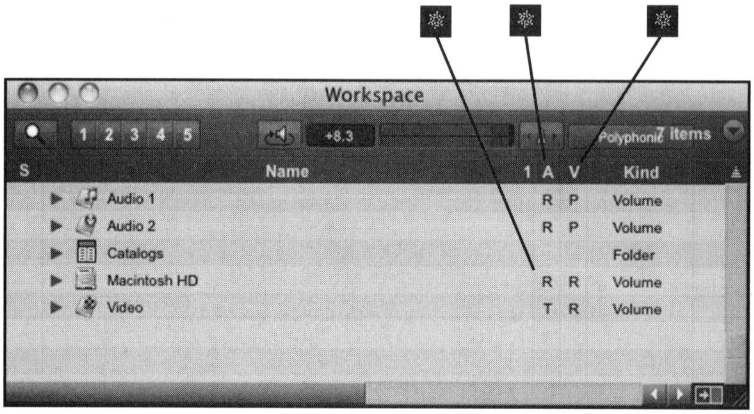

- Immediately to the right of each drive name, you'll see a column headed with an A (for *audio*), which will enable you to set up how each drive deals with audio files with regard to Pro Tools.
- Right next to the A column, you'll see a V (for *video*) column. This does the same thing as the A column, except it's concerned with the way Pro Tools works with video files.
- Just click the letter in the A column that corresponds to the drive you want to set up. (In this case, I want to change the behavior of my system drive.) A menu will appear.

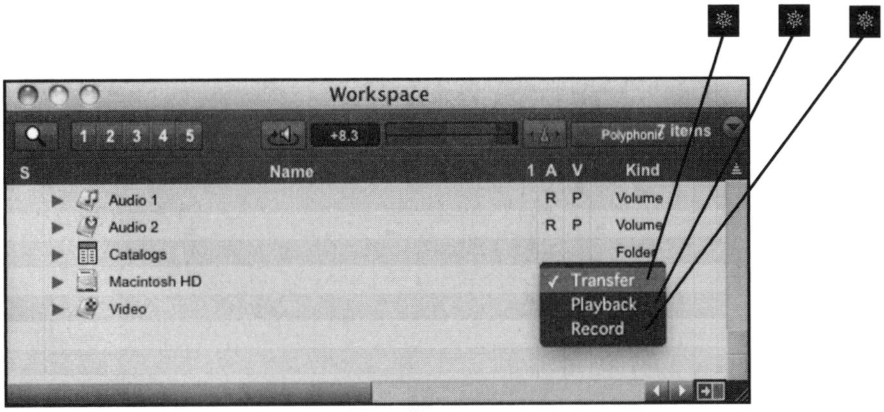

- If you set up a drive to be a Transfer volume (as I have here), your Pro Tools session will not be able to record or play back audio files with that drive. Essentially, the drive is off limits to Pro Tools as far as audio files are concerned (although it is worth noting that you can audition audio files that are stored on Transfer drives). System drives are commonly set up as transfer volumes (assuming there are dedicated hard drives for audio recording and playback).
- A Playback volume will enable Pro Tools to play back audio files, but you may not record new audio to this type of volume. This is a common setting for archive drives, enabling you to listen to your backed-up sessions but not to inadvertently record to that hard drive.
- Finally, a Record volume is fully functional with regard to audio and Pro Tools, which means you can record to it and play back from it. A typical audio drive is set up as a record volume.

The volume designations in the V (video) column work just the same way, only for video files instead of audio files. You can (and should) set up each of your hard drive's accessibility for audio and video files. Here's a common setup for a Pro Tools system with two dedicated audio drives and a dedicated video drive:

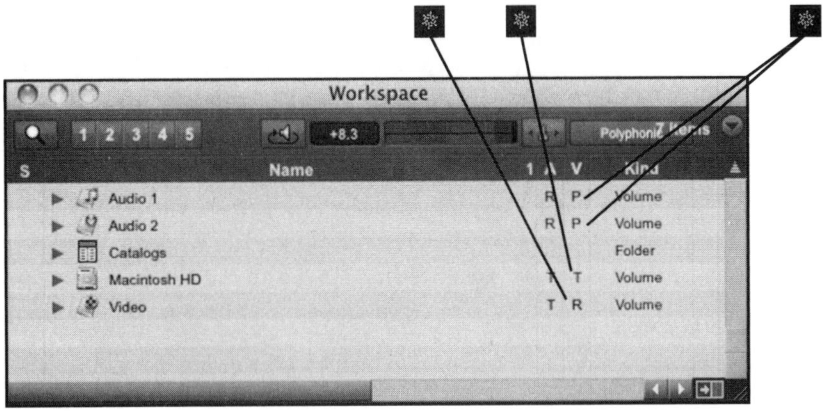

The two audio drives are set up as Record volumes where audio files are concerned, making them fully functional for audio recording and playback. Because I might from time to time have a QuickTime video file in a session folder on those drives, I've set it up as a Playback volume, so that I can play (but not record) video files.

- My system drive has been set as Transfer volume for both audio and video files. I use the system drive for my program files only, so I don't want to be able to record or play back from that drive.
- I use my video drive for the recording and playback of large video files only, so I've set it up to be a Record volume for video files, and a Transfer drive for audio (making it off limits for audio files for Pro Tools).

When the behavior of the drives has been squared away, it's time to do some disk allocation. In this session, I've created 10 pretty generic tracks, and I'm almost ready to do some recording. This is just the time to set up disk allocation—*before* you record any new audio.

1 **Click** the **Setup menu.**

2 **Click Disk Allocation.** The Disk Allocation dialog box will appear.

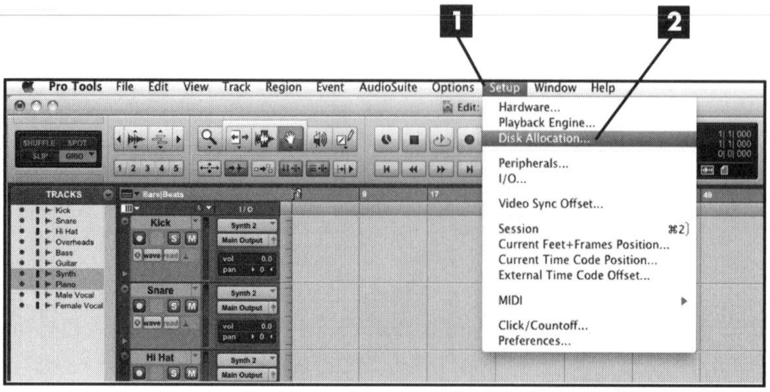

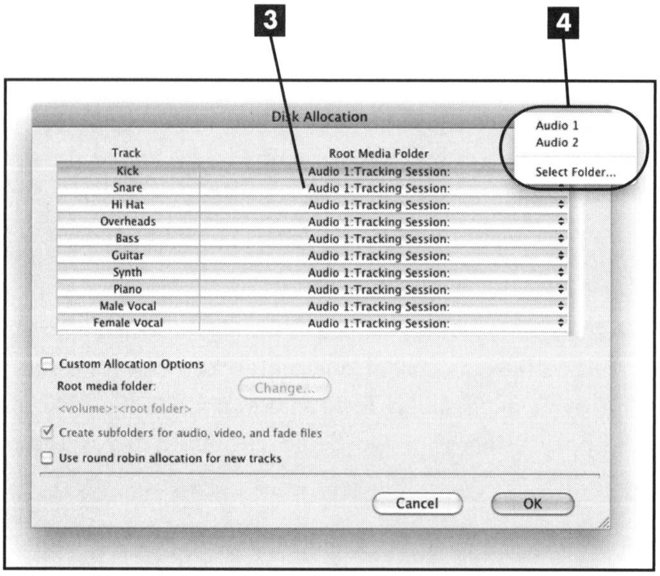

3 In the Disk Allocation dialog box, you'll see a list of all the Audio tracks in your session. The track names will be in the left-most column, and the location to which audio files will be recorded will be shown in the column to the right. From this dialog box, you'll be able to assign individual tracks to available hard drives on a track-by-track basis. Just **click and hold** on the **Root Media Folder column** for a track you want to set up. (In this image, I've chosen the Snare track.) A menu will appear.

4 From this menu, you'll be able to choose which drive will store the audio recorded on that track. You can **choose** one of the **drives** and let Pro Tools create the appropriate folder for you or **click** the **Select Folder option** to choose a specific location.

When dealing with large numbers of tracks, the basic goal when assigning disk allocation is to balance the session's audio workload as evenly as possible between the audio drives that you have in your system to ensure maximum performance. Here's what I've ended up with:

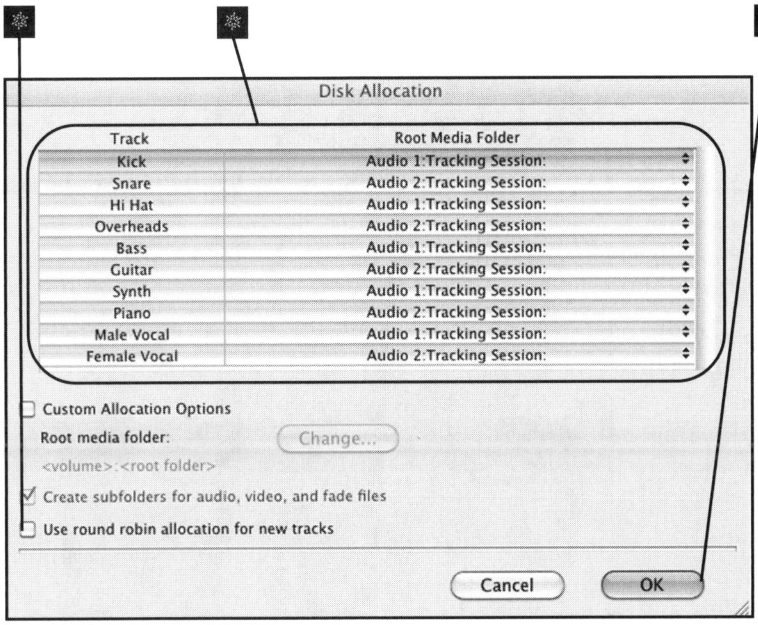

- In this example, I've alternated each track between the two audio hard drives. Basically, each drive is doing about half the work needed to play and record audio for this session.

- Here's a useful feature: If you check the Use Round Robin Allocation for New Tracks checkbox, Pro Tools will automatically cycle through all the record-enabled volumes for your tracks as they are created. The result would be the same as what you're seeing in this image, but would have been done automatically by Pro Tools as you added new tracks.

5 Once you've set things up the way you want them, **click OK**.

DRIVE VOLUMES AND ROUND-ROBIN ALLOCATION

Only the drives that you've designated as Record volumes show up in the drive assignment menu, and they will be the only drives that will be used when the Use Round Robin Allocation for New Tracks checkbox is checked. By setting up your volume designations beforehand, you can make working in the Disk Allocation dialog box quicker, easier, and better.

Now you're ready to record as usual. When you're finished, you'll see regions created in your Regions list. But where have they been recorded to? Let's find out:

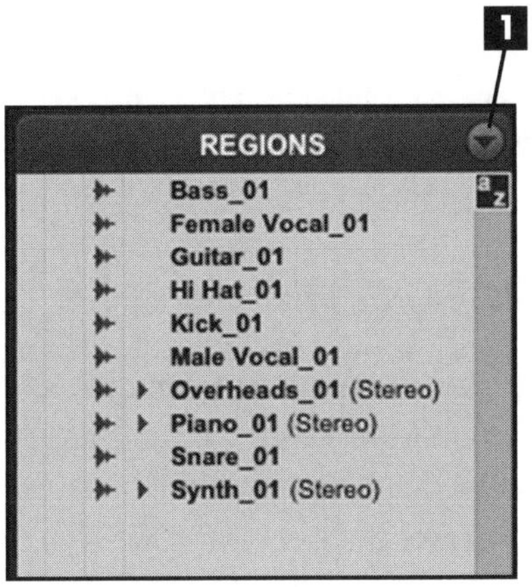

1 **Click** the **Regions List pop-up button**. A menu will appear.

2 **Click** on **Show**. A submenu will appear.

3 This menu will enable you to see different aspects of your regions in the Regions list, with displayed information being indicated by a checkmark. (You may find showing the full path very useful in tracking down individual files!) In this case, we want to see what disk they've been recorded to, so **click Disk Name**.

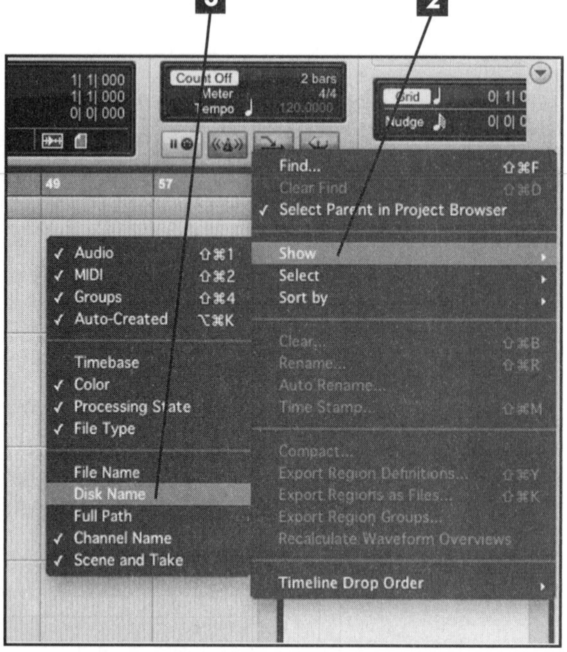

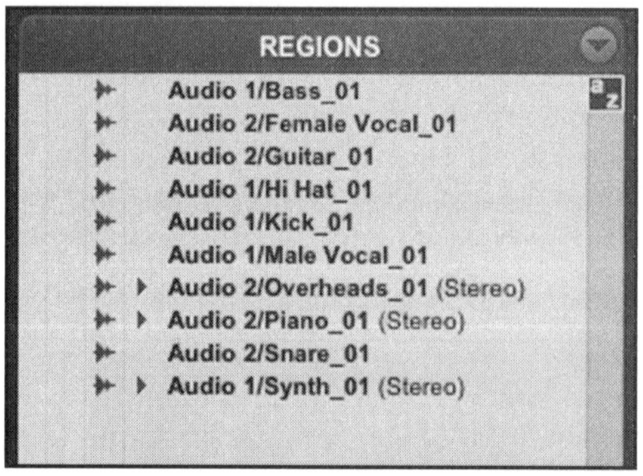

Assuming you've set up your disk allocation correctly, you should see both drives represented in the Regions list. That means you're balancing your hard drives'workload and can get extra performance and higher track counts when you need it.

WHEN TO SET UP DISK ALLOCATION

Remember to set up your disk allocation before you start recording. Changing your disk allocation after your audio has been recorded (and files have been created) will have no effect on the performance of your session.

Recording with Cue Mixes

During the recording process, your artist might want to have a customized mix—something that's different from what the engineer (that's you) in the control room is hearing. In cases where there are multiple musicians, for example, each player will often want their *own* personal mix. Not to worry—creating customized cue mixes is easy to do, using your tracks' sends. Here's a common cue-mix process:

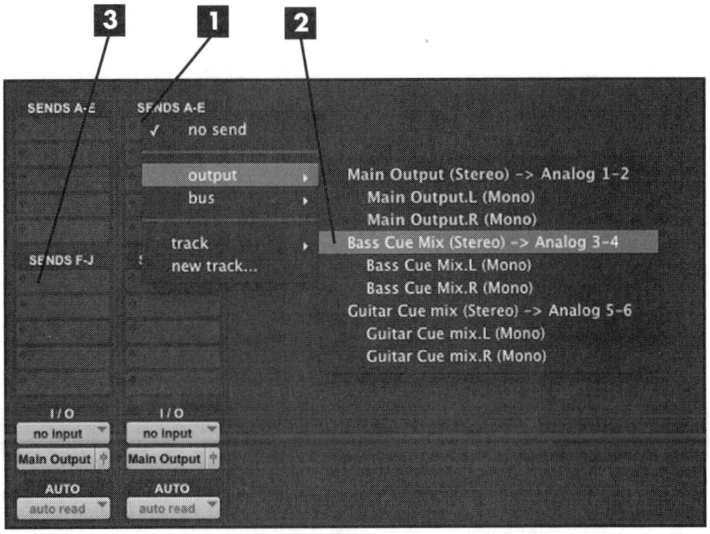

1 While **holding** the **Option key (Mac)** or the **Alt key (PC), click** an available **send selector button**. (In this image, I've chosen Send A.) Because you're holding the Option or Alt key, the send you create on this track will be created on all similar tracks.

CREATING A SEND ON ALL TRACKS TOO MUCH?

If you've already set up submixes in your session, you might not want to create sends on every track. If that's the case, just select the tracks on which you want to create a send and click an available send while holding Shift+Option (Mac) or Shift+Alt (PC). A send will be created on all selected tracks.

2 Because the cue mix will be sent out of a physical output, **assign** the send's **output** to an available interface output path. (In this image, I've created a path named Bass Cue Mix.)

3 If you have additional musicians requiring individual cue mixes, you'll need to **repeat steps 1 and 2** for each cue mix. In this example, I've got a guitarist who wants his own mix, so I'll create my second send at the Send F position (you'll see why in a moment) and assign it to interface output path Guitar Cue Mix.

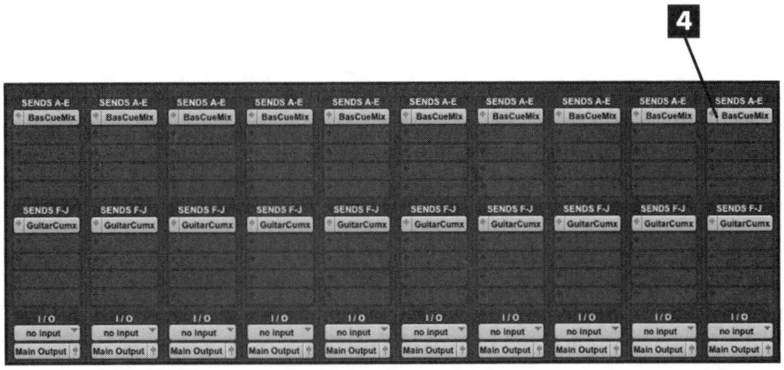

4 If you're following the steps outlined here, when you're finished, you should see one cue-mix send on Send A (for the bass player) and one on Send F (for the guitar). Holding down the Option or Alt key while I was creating the sends made the job easier by creating sends on all the tracks in the session, as opposed to creating sends one at a time. In this example I've created two cue-mix sends, and while I *could* have put them on adjacent sends (Sends A and B, for example), there's an advantage to having them on different banks. While **holding** the **Command key (on a Mac) or the Ctrl key (PC), click** on the **send selector button** for Send A (the one I'm using for my bassist's cue mix).

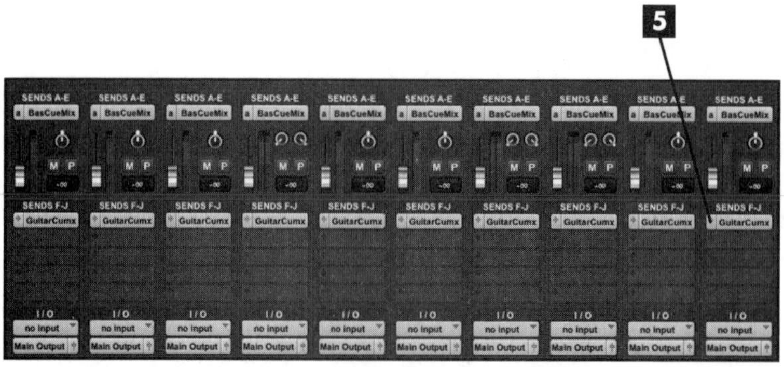

5 You can now see volume, pan, mute and pre/post controls for each track's send, enabling you to view and control the cue mix with ease. To get out of this view, just hold the Command key (Mac) or the Ctrl key (PC) and click the send selector button again. (You'll see a list from which you can choose to view all the send assignments in that bank or to view another send.) Here's where setting up the second cue on a different bank will pay off. **Repeat step 4**, but with the second cue-mix send. (In this example, it's on Send F.)

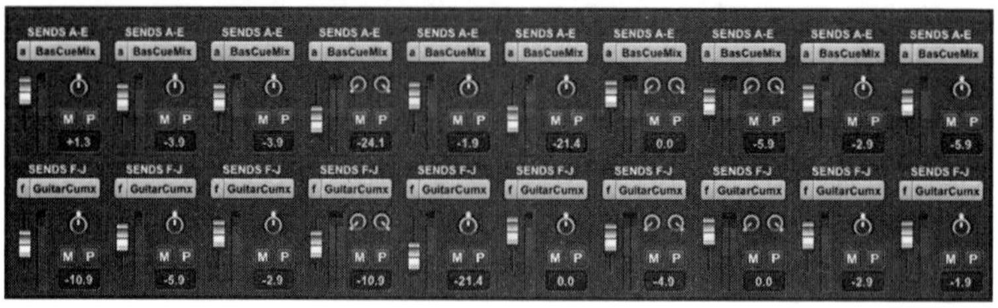

Assuming that the sends' outputs are attached to headphone amplifiers (which are in turn attached to headphones!), you now have the ability to quickly customize a mix for your musicians, as shown here. With Pro Tools' two banks of sends, you can view two cue mixes at once.

Making the Most of Editing

Let's take a look at some techniques that will make editing even more efficient and fun!

> **SETTING THINGS UP**
>
> To follow along with these first steps, go to Memory Location #1—Identify Beat. From the Window menu, open the Memory Locations dialog box, and simply click Location #1—Identify Beat. (For a refresher on how to use memory locations, please refer to Chapter 6, "And More Editing.")

Identify Beat

One of Pro Tools' strengths is its ability to use MIDI and audio in the same environment. To get them to work well together, though, their tempos should agree. That's where the Identify Beat feature comes in. It will let you quickly determine the tempo of a selected area of audio, and once that's set, your tick-based MIDI tracks will naturally follow the tempo of your sample-based Audio tracks.

This memory location (#1—Identify Beat) shows a great example of a very common dilemma. Listen to the region—sounds like eight full measures of drums, right? Now look at the selection length according to the Pro Tools tempo ruler. It says that the region is 6 measures, 1 beat, and 741 ticks! Obviously, *your* judgment is correct. Here's how to get Pro Tools to agree with you!

1 **Make** a **selection** of a specific musical length. (In this example, eight measures have already been selected for you). Use your ears to make a good, loopable selection—*don't* rely on your bars|beats ruler.

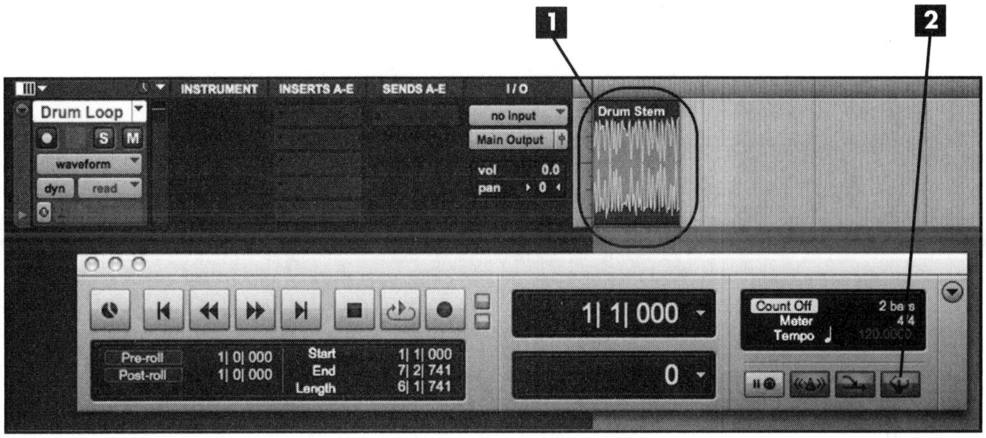

2 **Make sure** the **Conductor track** is enabled if it isn't already. When enabled, the Conductor Track button will be colored blue.

3 **Click** on the **Event menu**.

4 **Click** on **Identify Beat**. The Add Bar|Beat Markers dialog box will appear.

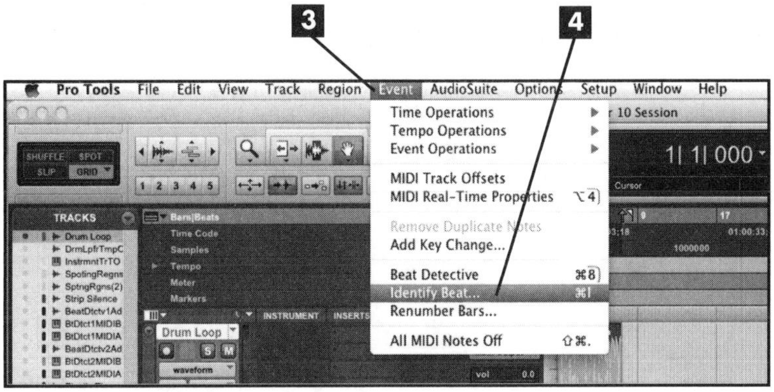

5 **Type** the musical **location** of the beginning of the selection in the Location text box in the Start area. Again, let your ears be your guide. In this example, because the selection begins at the beginning of the timeline, the beginning should be 1|1|000.

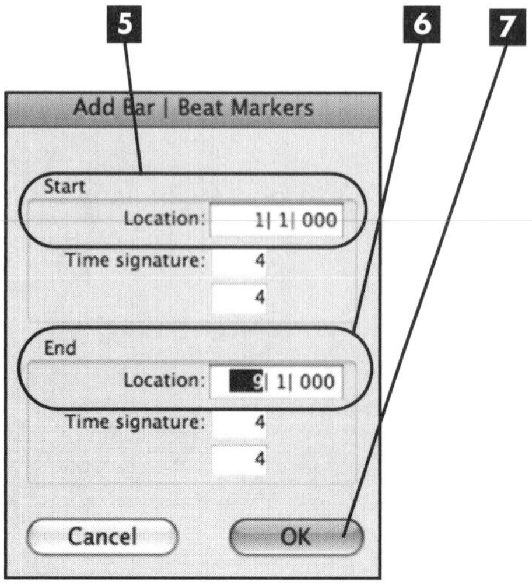

6 **Type** the musical **location** of the end of the selection in the Location text box in the End area. In this example, you are hearing an eight-bar selection, ending at the beginning of bar 9 (9|1|000).

7 **Click OK**. The Add Bar|Beat Markers dialog box will close, and your tempo will change accordingly.

When you're finished, you'll see that your session's bars|beats ruler and your ears are now in agreement as to the tempo of the section of audio, as shown here. Now the grid lines will be aligned with the appropriate musical events (assuming your grid scale is set to Bars|Beats), and the selection you made will be correctly displayed in the Edit Selection display (assuming that your main time scale is Bars|Beats).

IDENTIFY BEAT WORKS ANYWHERE!

You can use the Identify Beat function at any point in a session. For example, if you have a live drummer who goes a little faster during the chorus, just select the chorus and enter the correct musical values in the Add Bar|Beat Markers dialog box.

IDENTIFY BEAT SHORTCUT

If you're like me, you'll use Identify Beat pretty frequently. The shortcut for Identify Beat is Command+I (Mac) or Ctrl+I (PC).

Timeline Versus Edit Selection

Throughout this book, whenever you have made a selection on a track, that selection has been reflected in the Ruler area (also called the timeline) and vice versa. Normally, this is the way to work, but these two selections don't *need* to be linked.

1. **Click** on the **Link Timeline and Edit Selection button** (which is normally blue) to deselect it.
2. **Make** a **selection** on any track.

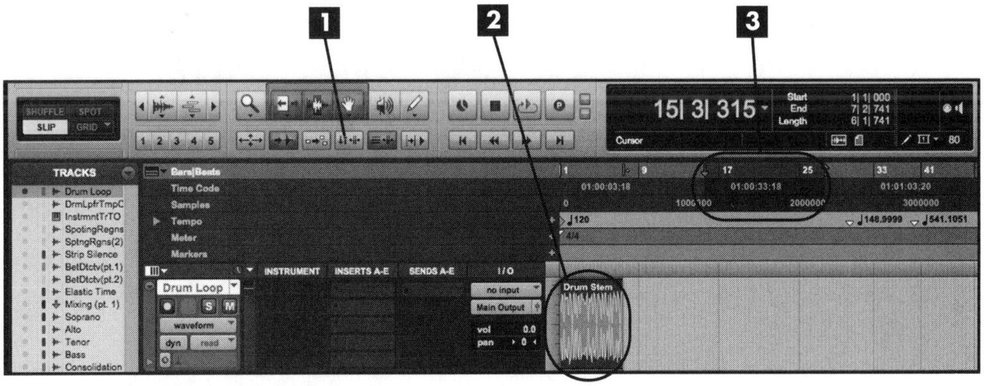

3. Now **make** a **different selection** in the Ruler area. Note that the two selected areas do not reflect each other.

It's important to take a moment to see just how Pro Tools acts in this situation. If you try to play your session, note that what plays back is your timeline selection. In truth, this always has been the case, although many users don't make any distinction between the edit selection and the timeline selection and leave the linking enabled all the time.

Unlinking your timeline and edit selections can be handy when you want to hear a different part of your song than the part that you're editing. For example, if you want to hear a little *before* the region you're working with, *unlink* your timeline and edit selection and make a timeline selection that reflects what you want to hear. Just be careful to relink when you're finished with this unusual mode of operation!

ANOTHER WAY TO LINK OR UNLINK

In addition to being able to link or unlink the timeline and edit selection with the Edit window button as shown previously, you also have a menu-based option: Just click the Options menu and choose the Link Timeline and Edit Selection menu item. When enabled, a checkmark will appear to the left of the menu item.

Dynamic Transport

You have yet another way to treat your selections and playback independently, through a feature called Dynamic Transport. Dynamic Transport gives you the ability to start playback at any point in your session, regardless of the timeline or edit selection. Take a look:

1 **Click** the **Options menu.**

2 **Choose Dynamic Transport.**

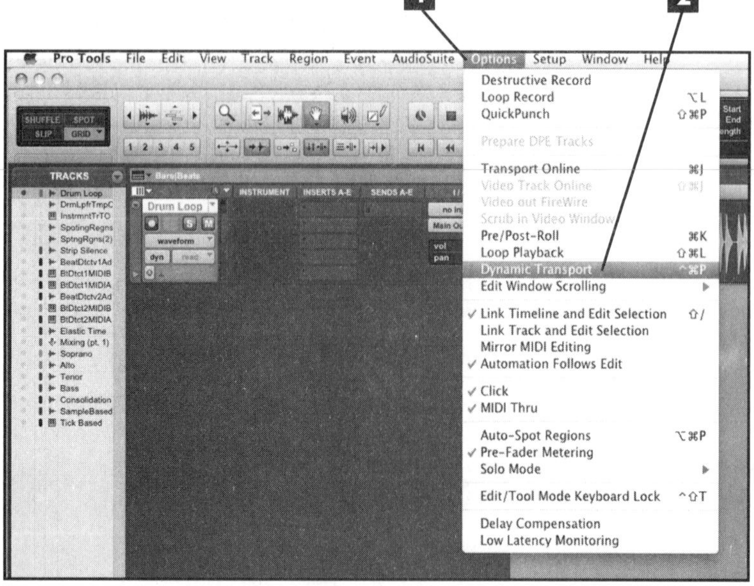

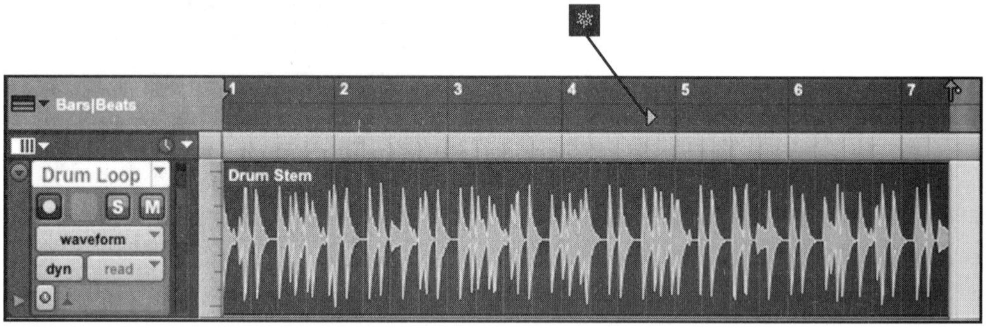

- You'll notice that your main timescale ruler has gotten twice as tall as any other ruler. In the bottom half of the main timescale ruler, you'll now see a right-facing blue triangle (the Play Start Marker), which indicates where your playback will begin. Just click and drag the triangle to any location on the timeline, and your session will play back from that point. This point can be before a selected area, anywhere within a selection (as shown here), or even after a selected area.

By default, your timeline and edit selections are automatically *unlinked* when you turn on Dynamic Transport. (You can relink them at any time). When you turn off Dynamic Transport, your timeline and edit selection will be relinked.

Samples Versus Ticks

You learned back in Chapter 6 about the power of *tick-based* Audio tracks. In this section, we'll talk a little bit more about samples and ticks in a Pro Tools session, and how they interact.

SETTING THINGS UP

If you're using the tutorial session, go to Memory Location #2—Tempo Operations. Make sure you turn off Dynamic Transport!

MIDI Track Timings

Audio tracks, as you know, are created as *sample-based* tracks, meaning that, by default, each region is anchored to a specific sample (or real-time) location. The upshot of this is that tempo, bar|beat, and meter changes will have no effect on the regions of the track.

Instrument tracks and MIDI tracks, on the other hand, are created by default as *tick-based* tracks, which means regions and notes on these tracks *will* respond to tempo and meter changes. For example, if you increase the tempo of your session, your tick-based tracks will speed up accordingly.

Even though these are the *default* states for each kind of track, there are advantages to working unconventionally!

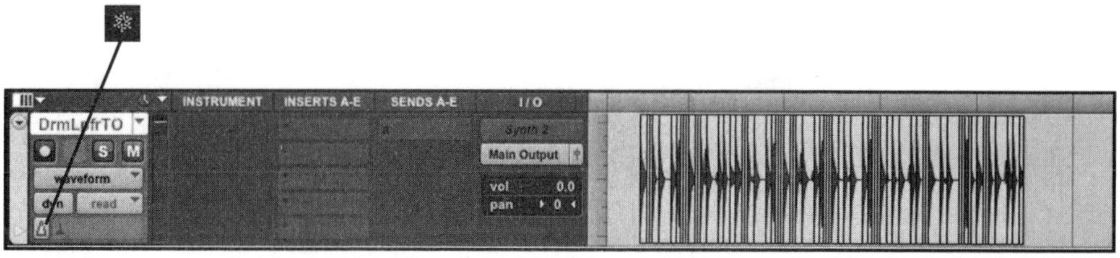

- As you saw in Chapter 6, you can change an Audio track to tick-based timing (indicated by a Metronome icon in the Timebase Selector button), enabling you to put your region timing under the control of your MIDI tempo map. In this example, if you were to change the tempo of your session, your regions would move and change your drum audio's "tempo" as a result.

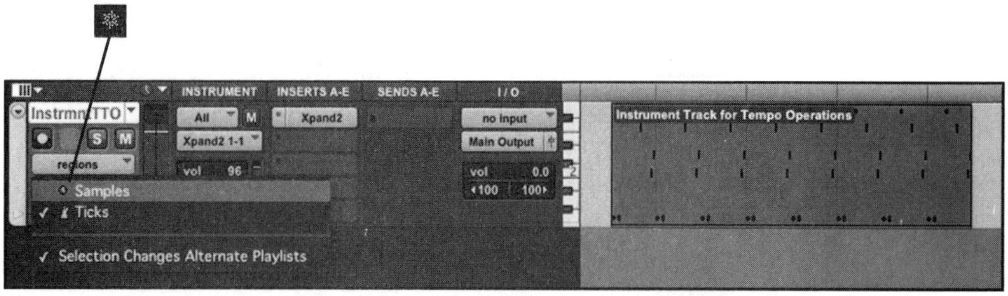

- Less common, but no less possible, is the practice of changing a MIDI (or Instrument) track to sample-based timing. To do it, just click the track's Timebase Selector button and choose Samples from the list of options (as shown here). In this mode, your MIDI track takes on a very interesting behavior, as your MIDI data will not change when you change tempo!

Although sample-based MIDI is somewhat unusual, it opens up interesting opportunities. For example, if you want to use a sampler or other virtual instrument to "play" a sound effect that needs to be synced to video, a sample-based track does the trick nicely. Because MIDI notes on sample-based tracks will ignore tempo changes, you have the freedom to change musical tempo without affecting the timing of these notes, ensuring they remain in sync with the video.

Default Track Timebase

Some users, particularly those primarily doing music production, might want their audio tracks to be tick-based as a general rule.

1. After opening the Preferences window (from the Setup menu), **click** the **Editing tab**.
2. In the lower-left area of the Editing page, you'll see the **New Tracks Default to Tick Timebase** checkbox. Just **click** the **checkbox** to select it, making all your new tracks default to a tick timebase.
3. **Click OK** to exit the Preferences window.

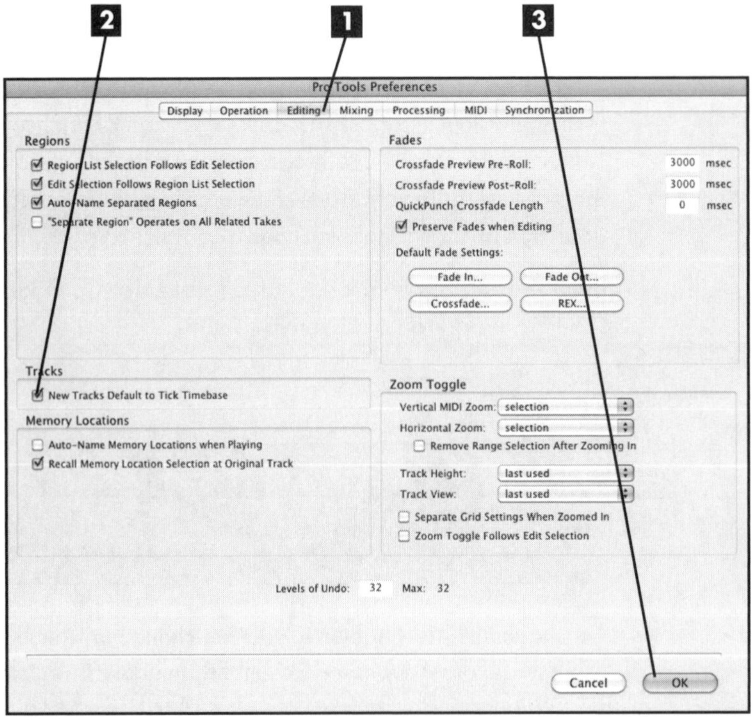

Session Linearity

This next bit can get a little tricky: By default, the rulers of your sessions are evenly spaced (or *linear*) based upon real time, which can be broken down into hours, minutes, seconds, frames (in the case of SMPTE time code), and samples. Another way of saying this is that, by default, Pro Tools uses a Linear Sample Display. This works well in many cases, but from time to time, you might want to look at your timeline in a different way....

> **SETTING THINGS UP**
>
> If you're using the tutorial session, go to Memory Location #3—Session Linearity.

This image shows a Pro Tools session with a linear sample display. Taking a look at your sample-based and tick-based rulers illustrates this mode well.

- Your real-time rulers are evenly spaced.
- Your bar|beats ruler changes its spacing based upon tempo changes in your session. (In this example, the bars and beats get gradually compressed as the tempo increases.)

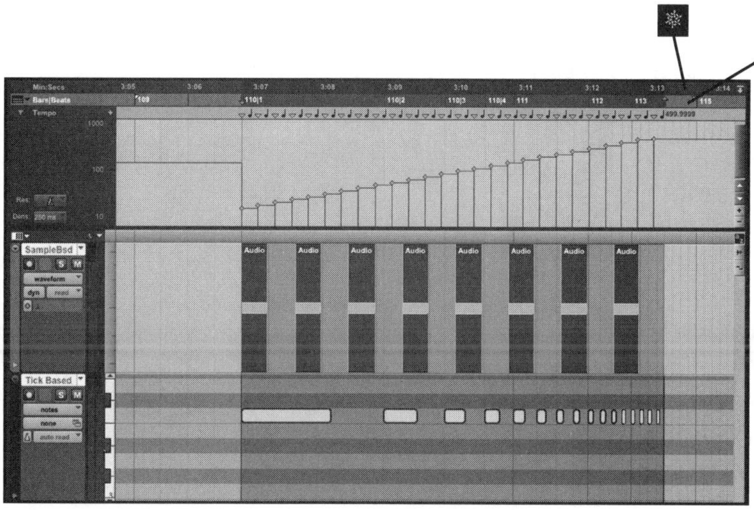

The regions on the Audio track are clearly evenly spaced in real time. The notes on the Instrument track are all eighth notes, but the duration and spacing of these notes changes due to an increasing tempo. Occasionally, it's desirable to be able to see your notes displayed more consistently, regardless of tempo changes (I often do this when I'm composing). It's very easy to do, and it makes quite a difference in your Edit window's view.

1 **Click** the **Linearity Display Mode down arrow** (located in the upper-left area of the tracks column). A menu will appear.

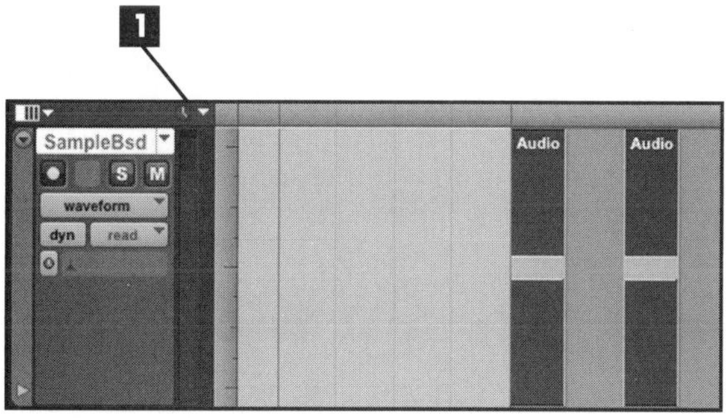

2 **Choose Linear Tick Display**. The Linearity Display Mode icon will change from a blue clock (indicating sample linearity) to a green metronome (indicating tick linearity).

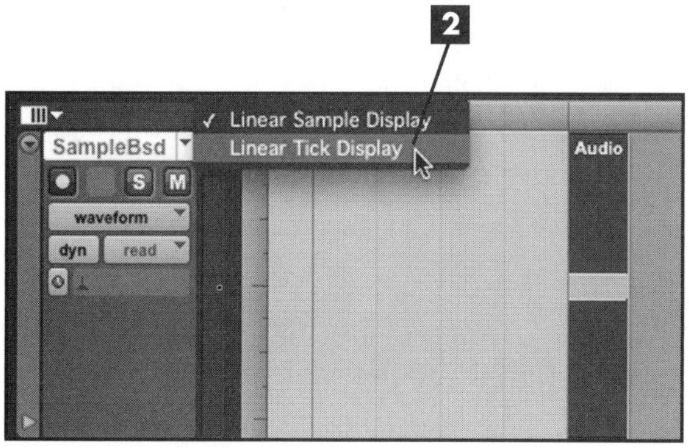

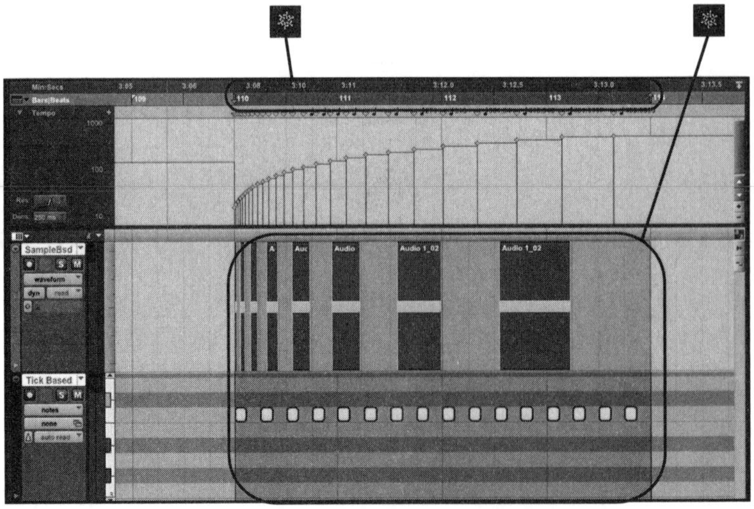

- Your bars|beats ruler (top) is now evenly spaced (despite the tempo change), and the min:secs ruler is now unevenly spaced.
- The spacing of both your Audio and MIDI tracks has changed. Note that regions on the sample-based Audio track are now not as evenly spaced as they once were, whereas each eighth note in the Instrument track (despite the tempo change) appears at regular intervals.

As you listen to and watch the playback of your session, you'll see that the *only* change made to your session has been visual. This change in linearity is simply for ease of use (and can be especially useful when working with MIDI data in sessions with radical tempo changes). Before you go on to the next section, change back to linear sample display.

Cool Editing Tricks

We've already covered a bunch of editing processes. Here are a few more for your bag of tricks!

New Ways to Spot Regions

Back in Chapter 5, "Editing," we talked a little about the Spot edit mode, and how it can make placing regions at specific points in time quick and easy. Spot mode, however, is really only useful if you already know the specific numeric position where you want your region to go. Many times, you'll want your region to go to a specific *selected* place in your session, and Pro Tools makes this easy as well—especially if you have a mouse with a right-click button!

SETTING THINGS UP

For this section, go to Memory Location #4—Spotting Regions.

1 Using the Selector tool, **make** a **selection** or **place** your **timeline insertion cursor** at the place at which you want your region to move.

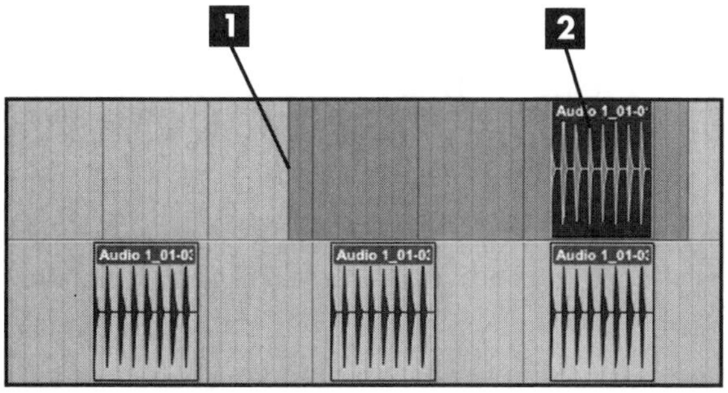

2 **Command+right-click (Mac)** or **Ctrl+right-click (PC)** on the **region** you want to move. A menu will appear.

The third segment of the menu will include three region-moving options:

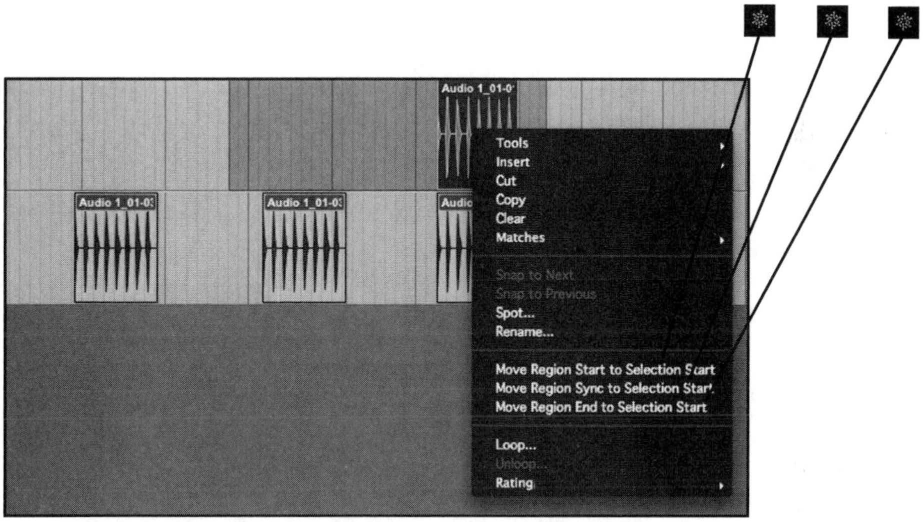

- **Move Region Start to Selection Start** will move the region so the *beginning* of the region aligns with the beginning of the selection or with the timeline insertion cursor.
- **Move Region Sync to Selection Start** will move the region so the region's sync point (if it has one) aligns with the beginning of the selection or with the timeline insertion cursor. (We'll discuss sync points in the next section.)
- **Move Region End to Selection Start** will move region so the *end* of the region aligns with the beginning of your selection or with the timeline insertion cursor.

If you don't have a mouse with a right-click button, all is not lost. Here are some shortcuts to help you get the job done:

- To execute the Move Region Start to Selection Start operation, hold the Control key (Mac) or Start key (PC) and click the region with the Grabber tool.
- To execute the Move Region Sync to Selection Start operation, hold Shift+Control (Mac) or Shift+Start (PC) and click the region with the Grabber tool.
- To execute the Move Region End to Selection Start operation, hold Command+Control (Mac) or Ctrl+Start (PC) and click the region with the Grabber tool.

Sync Points

So far, we've primarily focused on region boundaries (beginning and end) when talking about moving regions. Many times, however, the really interesting part of a region is somewhere *inside* the region. For example, within a drum beat, you might have a specific hit that you want to align with another region, or you might have a specific word in a dialogue region that is particularly easy to spot. *Sync points* will help you mark these places of interest so that you can align them with your timeline insertion using the techniques we discussed in the previous section.

1. Using the Selector tool (or the Smart tool), **place** your **timeline insertion cursor** at the point within your region where you want to create a sync point.
2. **Click** the **Region menu**.
3. **Click Identify Sync Point**. A small green triangle will appear at the bottom of the region to indicate the position of the sync point.

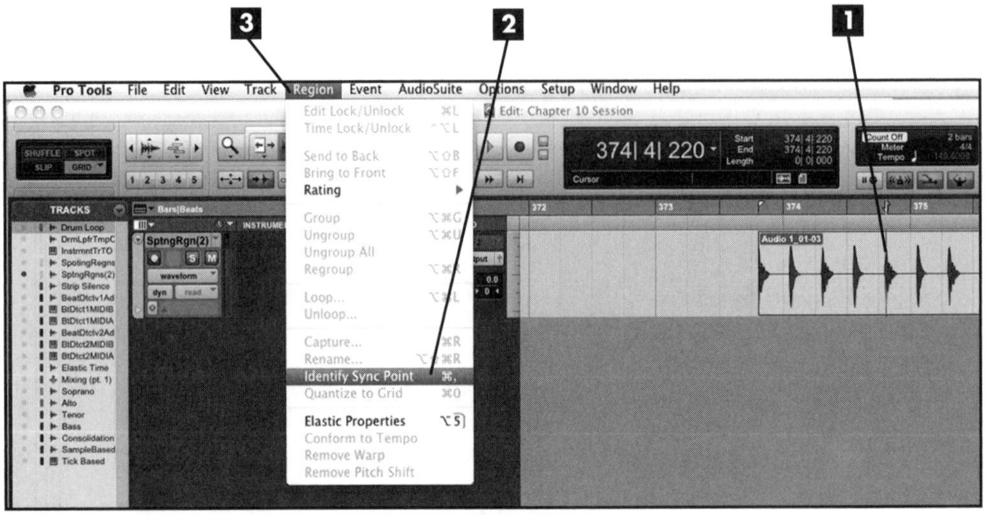

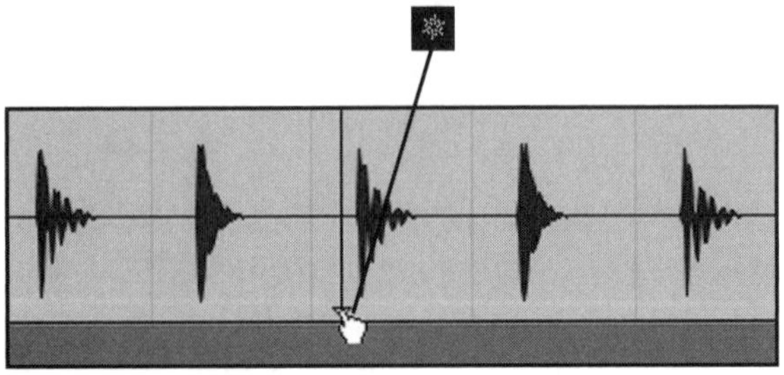

If you need to reposition your sync point after you've created it, the Grabber tool will let you move it. Just move your mouse close to the triangular Sync Point icon. When the Grabber tool turns into the pointing hand shown here, you're ready to move the sync point; just click, drag, and drop the sync point to its new location.

Now that you've created your sync point, you can utilize the right-click and shortcut commands described in the previous section!

SYNC POINT PRACTICE

Using sync points is a skill that can be refined through repetition, so I've included a session to help you do just that. If you open the Chapter 10–Sync Point Practice session, you'll see a number of tracks that aren't lined up properly. (These tracks should look familiar; you worked with them back in Chapter 4, "Recording Audio.") By creating a sync point at the first beep of each track's region and then aligning each sync point to the beginning of the region on the top track, you can fix this problem. I've included a finished version of the session (Session 10–Sync Point Practice–Finished) so you can see how your session should look when you're finished.

Snapping Regions

Sometimes, you'll want a region to move adjacent to the region before or after it. Again, the right-click mouse comes to the rescue!

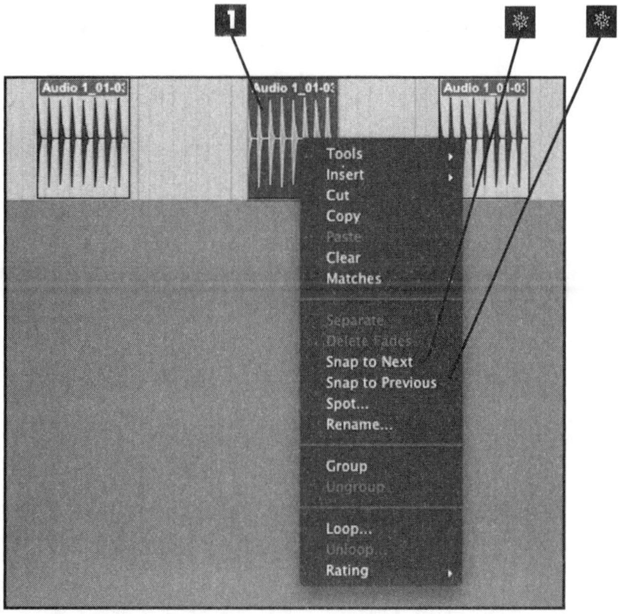

1 **Right-click** the **region** you want to move. A menu will appear, including two region-snapping options:

- Choosing Snap to Next will move the region so that the *end* of the region aligns with the beginning of the region to the *right*.
- Clicking the Snap to Previous menu item will move the region so that the *beginning* of the region aligns with the end of the region to the *left*.

SPOT

Choosing the Spot menu item (just below the Snap to Previous menu item) will open the Spot Dialog dialog box (the same dialog box you would normally encounter in the Spot edit mode).

Using Strip Silence

Strip Silence is a nifty little editing tool that acts upon regions similarly to how a noise gate acts upon audio. When you use Strip Silence, any audio below a specified volume threshold can be removed from your selection, leaving discrete regions that you can move and edit separately. This is a particularly fantastic tool when you work on dialogue tracks!

SETTING THINGS UP

Please go to Memory Location #5—Strip Silence.

1. **Select** an **area** in your session that you would like to strip.
2. **Click** on the **Edit menu**.
3. **Click** on **Strip Silence**. The Strip Silence dialog box will open.

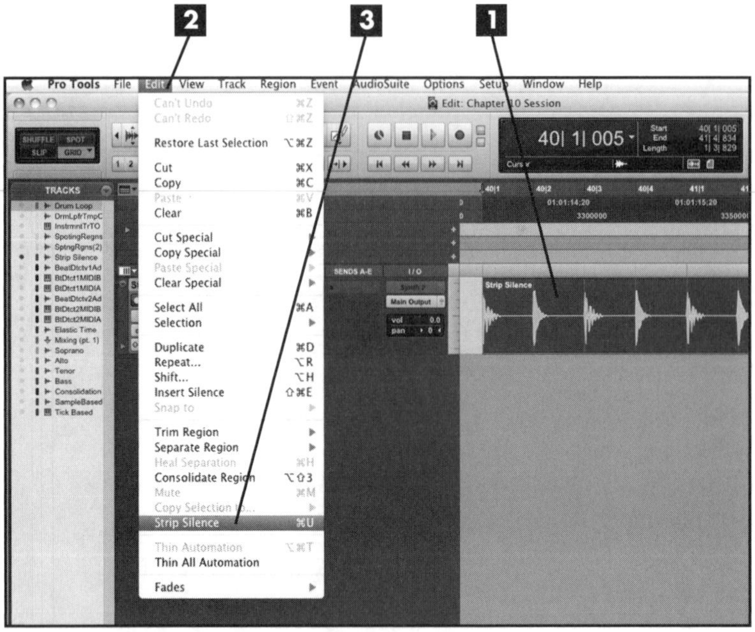

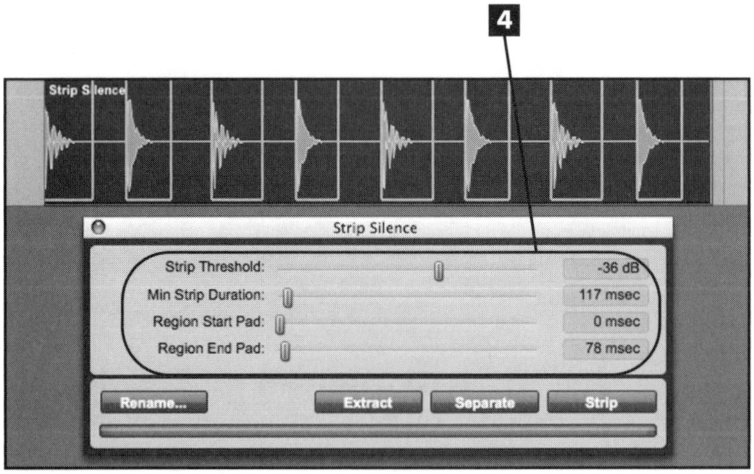

4. At this point, your goal is to **adjust** the **parameters** in the Strip Silence dialog box and separate the useful audio from the audio that you don't want to keep. As you adjust these parameters, you will see boxes indicating where new region boundaries will be created, as shown here. This can take a little time to get just right, as these values are interrelated, so be patient. The four parameters available to you are as follows:

- **Strip Threshold.** This parameter indicates the minimum volume of the audio that you want to keep (with a range from –96 dB to –0 dB). Portions of audio with volume levels *under* the strip threshold can be stripped from your region. As you move the fader from left to right, you'll see that you'll be stripping more and more of the audio.
- **Min Strip Duration.** This value determines the shortest silence Strip Silence can strip out. As you move the fader from left to right, you'll see smaller boxes combine to make larger ones.
- **Region Start Pad.** This slider will move the left boundary of each box earlier in time. If you find that by using Strip Silence, you're cutting off the beginning of words or notes, a small amount of region start padding will fix the problem.

- **Region End Pad.** This slider will move the right boundary of each box later in time. If you find that by using Strip Silence, you're cutting off the end of words or notes, a small amount of region end padding will fix the problem

5 Once you've adjusted these parameters to your liking, **click** on the **Strip button**. Your selection will be chopped into discrete regions, and the unwanted portions of audio will be removed from the track altogether. These newly created regions will be shown in the track and in the Regions list.

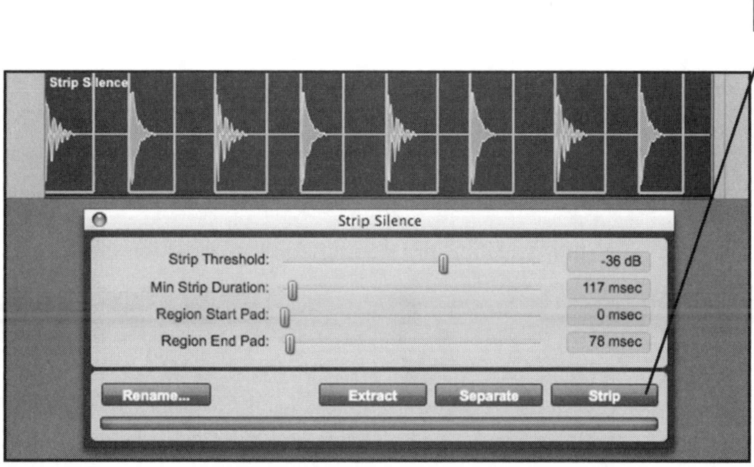

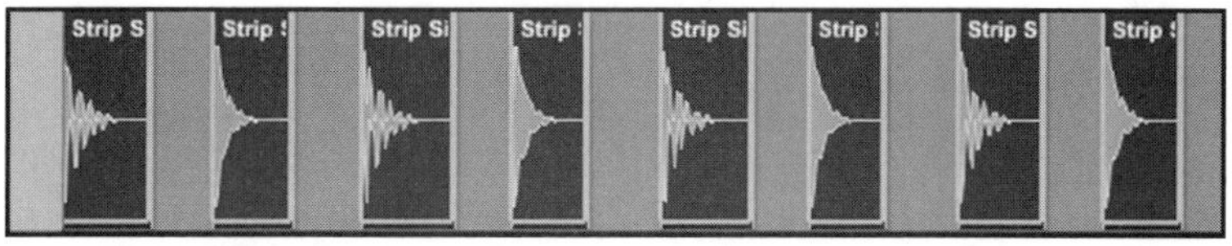

Don't worry; you haven't actually deleted any audio. If you find that you've stripped too much or too little from your track, you can use the Trim tool to adjust individual region boundaries.

- In addition to being able to strip away unwanted audio (by clicking the Strip button), you have a few other options when using Strip Silence:

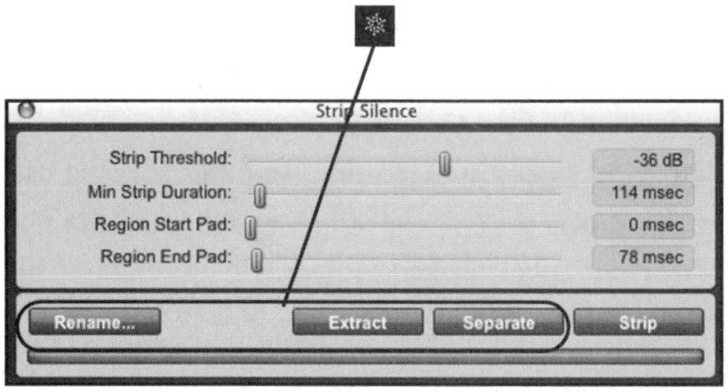

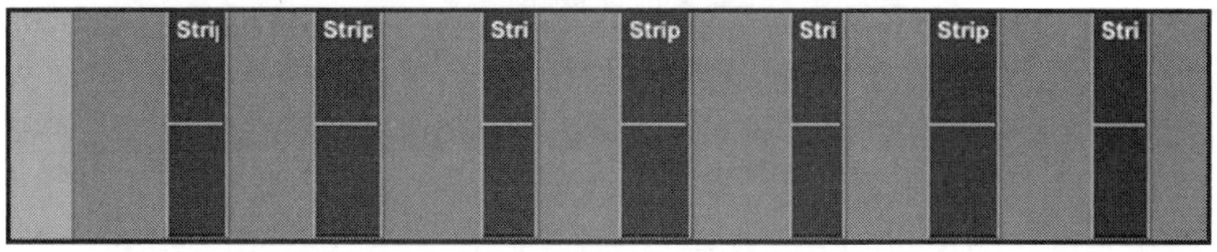

- **Extract.** This does the *opposite* of the Strip button, and will create only regions of audio that are *below* the strip threshold.

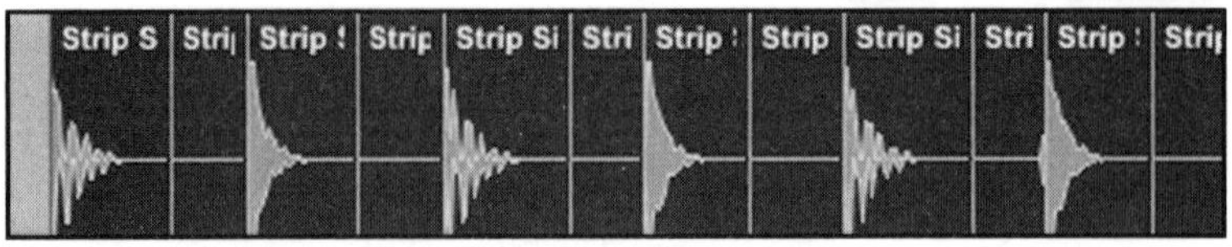

- **Separate.** This mode will not strip any audio, but will only separate your selected area, resulting in alternating regions of sound and silence.
- **Rename.** The Rename option will enable you to automatically rename selected regions.

When you click the Rename button, the Rename Selected Regions dialog box will open.

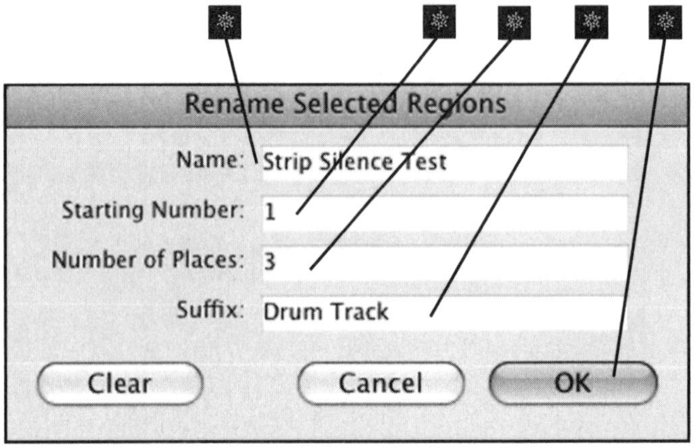

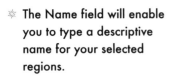

- The Name field will enable you to type a descriptive name for your selected regions.

- You can choose a starting number for your regions as well. For example, in some situations, you might want to have the first region be numbered 0. In other cases, you'll want to start your numbering with the number 1 (as shown here).
- The Number of Places field will enable you to set the number of digits that will be used in your region renumbering. In this example, I've chosen three places, so my files will be numbered 001, 002, 003, and so on.
- Finally, you may want to add a suffix to your file names.
- When you've set up your renaming scheme, click the OK button. Based on the settings shown here, the selected regions will be renamed Strip Silence Test001Drum Track, Strip Silence Test002Drum Track, and so on.

Beat Detective Basics

One of the most interesting music-production tools in Pro Tools' bag of tricks is Beat Detective. Based on the same technology that makes the Tab to Transient feature work so well, Beat Detective can be used in a variety of ways. Essentially, it's used for aligning MIDI and audio. Although it's most commonly used in conjunction with drum tracks, it can be applied to any audio with clearly defined transients (or MIDI). Let's take a look at some basic Beat Detective workflows.

SETTING THINGS UP

If you're following along with the tutorial session, go to Memory Location #6—Beat Detective (pt.1).

TIMELINE AND EDIT SELECTION LINKING

If you've been going through this chapter, you've been linking and unlinking your edit and timeline selection. Going forward, the edit and timeline selections should be *linked*.

The first Beat Detective workflow is based on the idea that, in many cases, a musical groove is *not* mathematically uniform. This "human" element is in opposition to the mathematical precision of a static MIDI tempo. If you're following along with the tutorial session, you'll see just what I mean: Although the Audio track and the Instrument tracks are at the same tempo, they certainly aren't playing well together.

To get your audio and MIDI to groove together, you'll want to create a complex MIDI tempo map (based on the live drum track). Beat Detective will help you do just that!

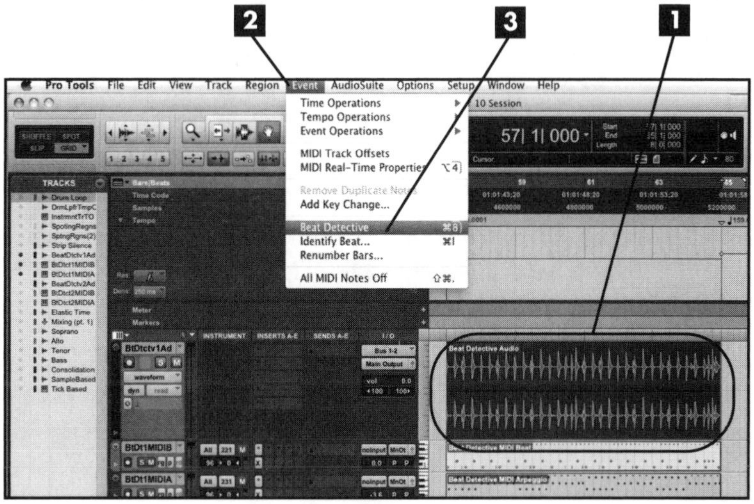

1. **Select** the **segment of drums** that you want to analyze. (If you're following along with the tutorial session, that selection has been made for you.)
2. **Click** on the **Event menu**.
3. **Click** on **Beat Detective**. The Beat Detective window will appear.

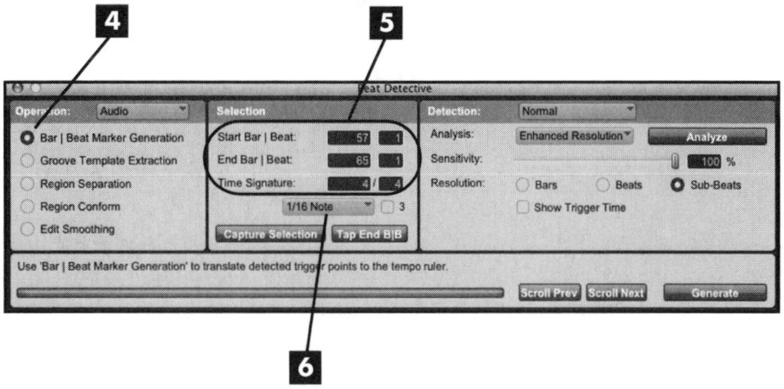

4. The mode you'll use for this sort of work is Bar | Beat Marker Generation. **Click** the **Bar|Beat Marker Generation option button** to enter this mode.
5. This step is *very* important: **Make sure** the **values** in Beat Detective's Selection area correctly reflect the musical start, end, and meter of your selected area. Just as when you used Identify Beat earlier in this chapter, let your ears be your ultimate guide.
6. **Choose** the smallest **musical note value** of your audio. You'll have to use your ears for this. (In this example, it's 1/16 Note.)

USING CAPTURE SELECTION

Assuming your selection is known to be in general agreement with the MIDI tempo, you can click the **Capture Selection** button in the Selection area of Beat Detective. This is an easy way to go with audio in cases where the beat has already been identified.

7 **Click** the **Analyze button**. Beat Detective will search your selected audio for transient events.

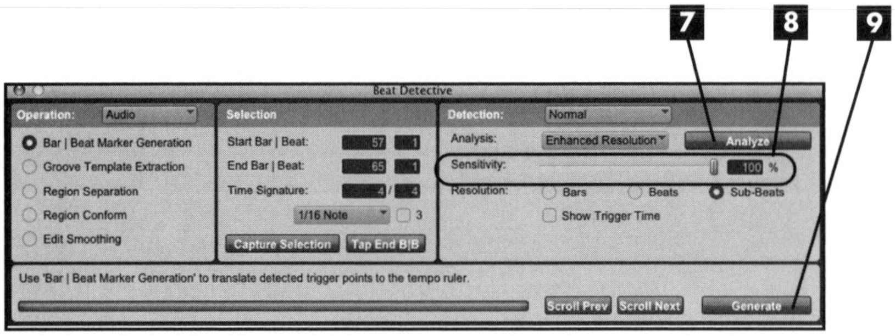

8 Slowly **slide** the **Sensitivity slider** from left to right. Note that as your sensitivity percentage increases, you will begin to see vertical lines intersecting the transients of your audio. (The loudest transients will be marked first.) Once you are satisfied that the important transients have been marked (and no others), stop moving the slider.

9 **Click** the **Generate button**. The Realign Session dialog box will open. The Realign Session dialog box is fairly self-explanatory. The two option buttons will determine how your tick-based tracks will react to the creation of the new bar | beat markers.

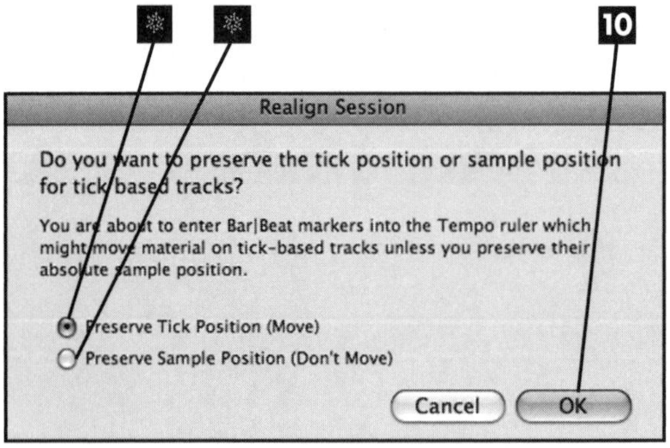

- If you want the timing of your session's tick-based tracks (such as a drum part on a MIDI track) to move to match the timing of the Audio track, choose Preserve Tick Position (Move). This is what we'll choose in this case, and what is most commonly chosen.
- If your tick-based data doesn't need to be matched to your new tempo map, choose Preserve Sample Position (Don't Move). The data on your tick-based tracks will not be changed in any way.

10 When you've made your choice (in this case, **choose Preserve Tick Position**), **click** the **OK button**.

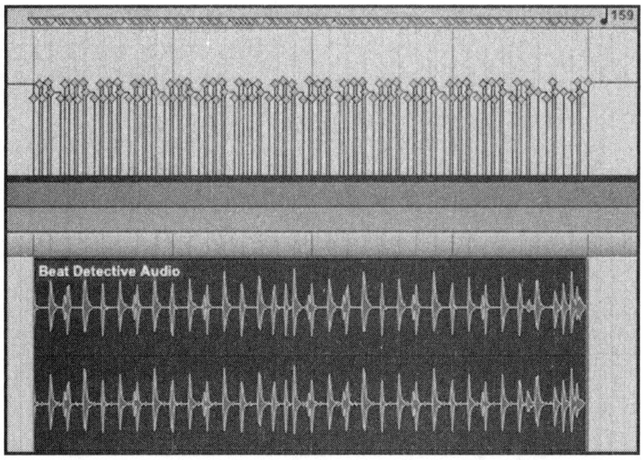

You will see now that a great number of small tempo changes have been added to your tempo ruler, each shown as a blue triangle in the collapsed tempo ruler or as tempo events in the expanded tempo ruler. What you've done is created a tempo map that changes constantly to match the groove of the drum audio, which has effectively created a MIDI grid that also reflects these changes. Because things such as Grid mode and MIDI Quantize rely on this grid for their timing, you can now conform any additional MIDI and audio to this original drum beat, and they will all groove together!

But that's not all that Beat Detective can do—not by a long shot. Let's reverse the process. Suppose that instead of creating a new tempo map based on your Audio track (so that the rest of your session can conform to that audio), you instead want to conform your audio to the *current* tempo of the session. Beat Detective can do that, too. In this example, we'll take the same audio region and conform it to the mathematically static tempo of the session, effectively quantizing it to a 16th-note grid.

SETTING THINGS UP

Please go to Memory Location #7—Beat Detective (pt. 2).

1 **Select** the **segment of drums** that you want to analyze. (If you're following along with the tutorial session, that selection has been made for you.)

OPENING BEAT DETECTIVE

If you're following through this chapter, the Beat Detective window is already open. If it isn't, just go to the Event menu and click on Beat Detective. The Beat Detective window will appear.

2 The first mode you'll use for this sort of work is Region Separation. **Click** the **Region Separation option button** to enter this mode.

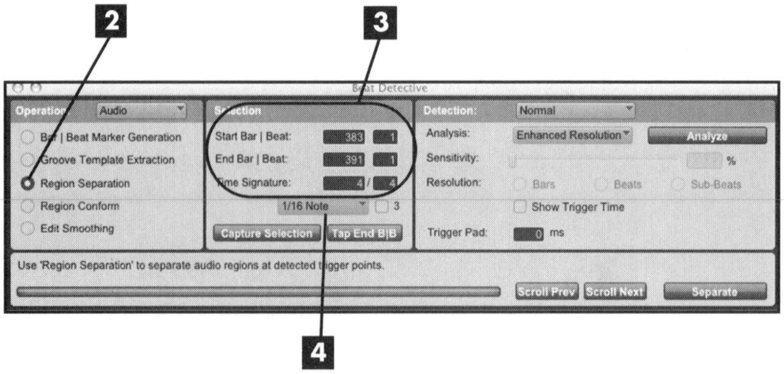

3 Again, **make sure** the **values** in Beat Detective's Selection area correctly reflect the musical start, end, and meter of your selected area. Be careful—Beat Detective does not automatically update its selection values—and if you're using the tutorial session, this memory location is at a different section of your session!

4 **Choose** the smallest **musical note value** of your audio (in this example, 1/16 Note).

5 **Click** the **Analyze** button. Beat Detective will search your selected audio for transient events.

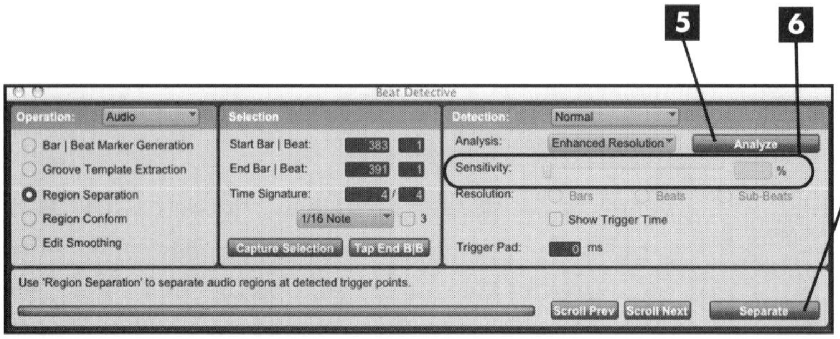

6 Slowly **slide** the **Sensitivity slider** from left to right. Note that as your sensitivity percentage increases, you will begin to see vertical lines intersecting the transients of your audio. (The loudest transients will be marked first.) Once you are satisfied that the important transients have been marked (and no others), stop moving the slider.

7 **Click** the **Separate button**. Your region will be separated into a number of smaller regions. Not only will you see these regions represented on your track, but they will also be shown in the Regions list.

8 Now that you've chopped up your beat, it's time to get those smaller regions in line. **Click** the **Region Conform option button.**

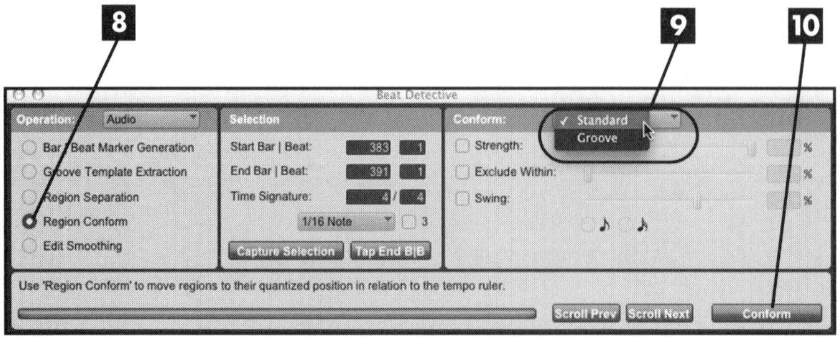

9 If you click on the **Conform** menu button, you'll see that you can move your regions in the standard way (the regions will be quantized to the nearest grid line) or with a groove (using a groove template, similar to MIDI Groove Quantize). For our purposes, **choose** the **Standard mode**.

10 **Click** the **Conform button**. The regions will move subtly to match the existing tempo map. If you listen to the selected area, you'll hear a change in the feel.

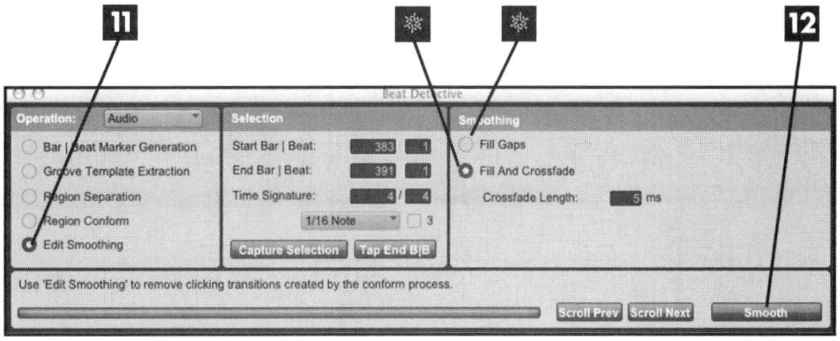

11 As a byproduct of the conforming process, some gaps will be produced between regions, and there may also be a few clicks and pops. Beat Detective's final mode will help us clean things up. **Click** the **Edit Smoothing option button**. The Smoothing section gives you two options:

- If there are no problems with clicks or pops, click the Fill Gaps option button. Region boundaries will be adjusted to minimize gaps between regions.
- If there *are* clicks and pops, a quick crossfade between regions will fix the problem in most cases. Click the Fill and Crossfade option button and then set the Crossfade Length (this will vary from situation to situation; if you're working with the tutorial session, 5ms sounds good).

12 **Click** the **Smooth button**.

Your audio will now have a significantly different feel and no gaps!

There's one more mode included in Beat Detective, called Groove Template Extraction.

1 **Click** the **Groove Template Extraction option button** in the Beat Detective window.

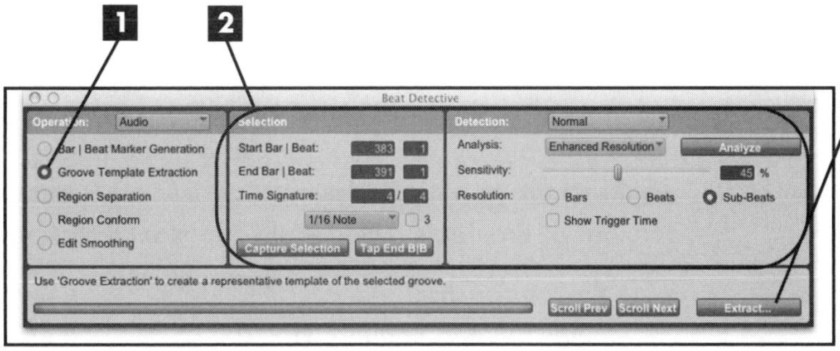

2 Here again, the values you enter in the Selection area of the Beat Detective window are crucial. Once you've done that, **click** the **Analyze button** and **adjust** the **Sensitivity slider**, just as you've done before.

3 **Click** the **Extract button**. The Extract Groove Template dialog box will appear.

- Choose **Save to Groove Clipboard** for immediate use of the extracted groove in your session.
- Choose **Save to Disk** for long-term storage of the groove.

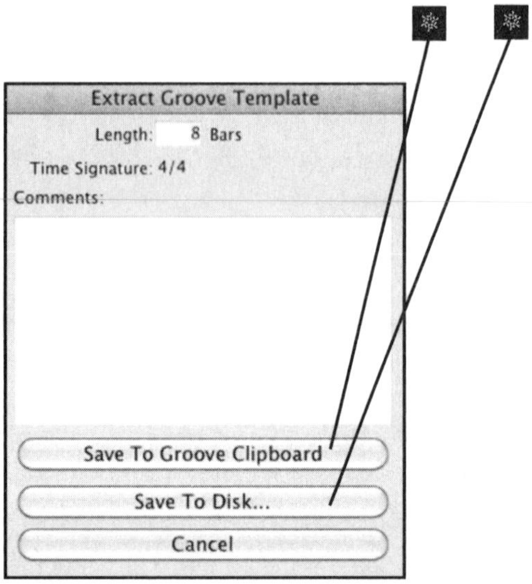

What exactly have you done? Essentially, what you have extracted is the same sort of timing information you used in bar|beat-marker generation, except that in this case you've added this information to your list of available MIDI Groove Quantize options (this is covered in detail in Appendix A, "More MIDI Power," included as a PDF on your book's CD-ROM). More simply put, you've given yourself the option to quantize MIDI data (now or in the future) to have the same feel as these drums you've just analyzed!

New in Pro Tools 9: Multitrack Beat Detective in All Versions

In previous versions of Pro Tools, Beat Detective's functionality was limited in basic Pro Tools LE systems. Specifically, with a basic Pro Tools LE system, Beat Detective could only be used on one track at a time, making it quite challenging to work with multitrack drum setups! Now, with Pro Tools 9, those limitations no longer exist. *All* versions of Pro Tools include fully functional versions of Beat Detective. Woo hoo!

With the introduction of the ability to work with multiple tracks, there are a few new things to keep in mind when using Beat Detective. Let's take a look.

Working with Overhead and Room Tracks

With a fully functional version of Beat Detective, you have the ability to select multiple tracks, and to analyze their transients in a single operation. This works out very well with multitrack drum kits. There's one thing to look out for, however: the overhead and room tracks. Very often, when live drums are recorded, microphones are placed above the drum set (overheads) or elsewhere in the drum room (room) to add ambience to the close microphone tracks.

Because these microphones are farther from the source of the sound than the close mics, their timing is naturally later than that of the closely recorded tracks. This is great for ambience, but can make things just a little more complicated when working with Beat Detective. Here's the risk: If you analyze the overheads and room tracks along with the other drum tracks, you'll be plagued with a horde of double triggers. Worse yet, if you conform all the tracks together, you also run the risk of snapping the individual drum tracks and the ambient tracks, effectively eliminating the natural delay between those tracks and losing your valuable ambience!

The remedy to both these problems is easy. Just follow these steps:

1. **Select** the **desired area** on the close mic tracks *only*. Leave any overhead or room tracks unselected at this point.
2. **Configure Beat Detective's Selection and Detection sections** as normal.
3. Click the **Analyze** button, and **adjust** the **sensitivity slider** as normal.
4. Add the same selected area to your overhead and room tracks, while keeping the selected area of the close-mic tracks. (You learned in a previous chapter how to add selections to additional tracks.) When you're finished, you should have *all* your drum tracks selected, and you'll note that the beat markers extend to all the selected tracks.
5. Here's the only tricky part: As soon as you select the additional tracks, you'll see that the Analyze button will again be available to be clicked (re-analyzing this new selection). Don't click that button! The beat markers will be just a little bit earlier than the transients on the ambient tracks—that's what you want.
6. Proceed to the next step in the process (which is usually to separate the regions), according to the workflow you're involved in.

If you separated those selected regions, you'll notice that the region boundaries on the ambient tracks are a little bit before the transient. Now, when you conform your regions, all the regions will conform uniformly, maintaining the original relative timing differences between the close and the ambient tracks and preserving your sense of ambience while at the same time fixing the timing of the drums!

Collection Mode

In many cases of multitrack drums, musically significant tracks are low in volume in relation to other tracks. A common situation in my experience would be hi-hat cymbals—musically very important, but usually much quieter than kick and snare tracks. When using Beat Detective on multiple tracks, this presents a little bit of a challenge: If you analyze all the regions together, you're likely to create unwanted beat triggers on the louder tracks before you capture the hits you need on the quieter tracks. What you really need here is a way to analyze tracks individually, and that's where Collection mode comes to the rescue!

1 Click on the **Detection** menu button. A list of two options will appear:

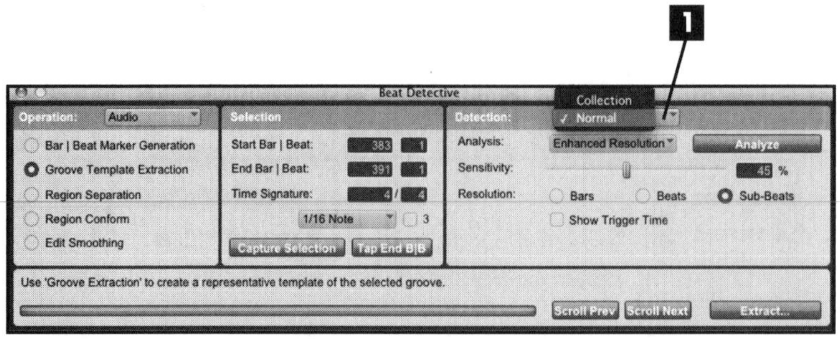

- Normal mode is the one to use if you want to analyze a number of selected tracks in a single operation. In this case, changes to the sensitivity slider will affect beat markers on all tracks simultaneously.
- Collection mode enables you to analyze tracks individually, and progressively add beat markers with each successive analysis.

With these two modes in mind, here are the steps to use Collection mode to its best advantage:

1 With Normal mode chosen, **select** the **desired area** on the first track (let's say the Kick drum track). **Adjust** the **sensitivity slider** so that you are marking all the important transients.

2 **Switch** to **Collection** mode. You'll see that you have three options:

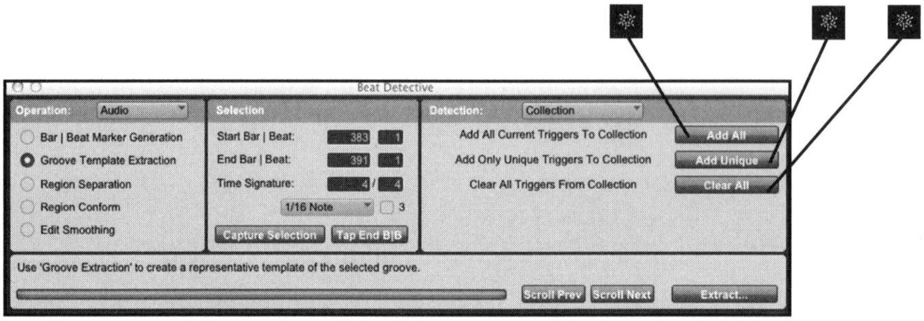

- Add All Current Triggers to Collection (the Add All button) will add all current beat triggers to the collected analysis.
- Add Only Unique Triggers to Collection (the Add Unique button) will add all current beat triggers to the collected analysis, except those that duplicate pre-existing beat triggers.
- Clear All Triggers from Collection (the Clear All button) will remove all beat triggers from the collection.

3 Because you're just starting out, you should **click** the **Add All** button. You'll see the beat triggers appear in the selected area.

4 **Switch back** to **Normal** mode, and **move your selection** to the next track (a snare track, for example). **Re-analyze** the **selection** (this is important), and **adjust** the **sensitivity slider** so that the desired transients are marked.

5 Next, **go back** to **Collection mode**, but this time **click** the **Add Unique button**. You'll see your current beat triggers added to the ones you collected from the first track.

The rest is pretty straightforward: Just repeat steps 4 and 5 until you've analyzed all the desired tracks. Once you're done with that, you can move on to the next step (creating bar|beat markers, extracting groove templates, or separating regions) as normal.

MIDI DETECTIVE

Beat Detective can also analyze MIDI data and perform similar operations. To use Beat Detective with MIDI, just click the Operation Menu button in the upper-left corner (which currently reads Audio) and choose MIDI from the list that's shown. Some subtle changes in the window will appear (and only the first two operation mode option buttons are relevant to MIDI), but the overall workflow is similar to what we've gone through in this chapter.

FOR MORE INFORMATION...

The complex applications of Beat Detective go beyond the scope of an introductory book like this one. If you want to go through every button in Beat Detective, you might want to check out a book called *Working with Beats in Pro Tools: Skill Pack*, written by yours truly and published by Thomson Course Technology PTR (2007).

ONE MORE EDITING SHORTCUT

Before we close this discussion on editing, here's one more useful shortcut (one that can be used in a variety of situations). On either a Mac or a PC, hold the Shift key while starting playback to play back your session at half-speed. This comes in particularly handy when you're setting punch-in or punch-out points for a particularly tight spot. (Be careful when recording that way, though, as your recorded audio will be twice as fast and twice as high in pitch!)

Elastic Audio

Elastic Audio is a relative newcomer to the Pro Tools arsenal of features, and it's already a favorite for Pro Tools users worldwide. On its face, Elastic Audio enables the user to change the timing and pitch of audio in a flexible and nondestructive way and can give you the same kind of control over your audio that you have over MIDI. When you dig deeper, though, you'll see that Elastic Audio can be a tweaker's paradise!

SETTING THINGS UP

Please go to Memory Location #8—Elastic Time.

Basic Operation

You can enable, disable, and customize Elastic Audio on a track-by-track basis. To activate Elastic Audio on an Audio track, follow these steps:

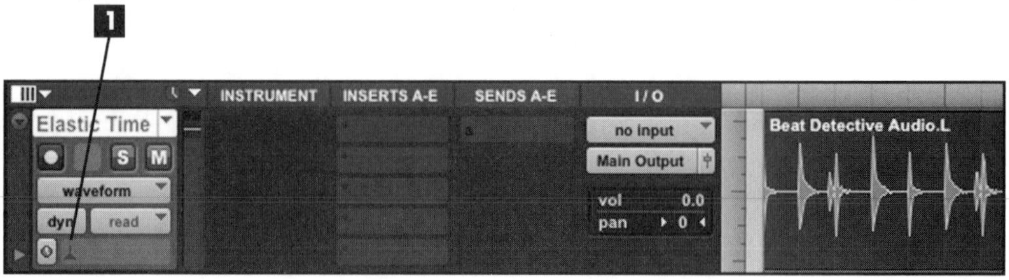

1 **Click** the **Elastic Audio Plug-in Selector button**. A menu will appear.

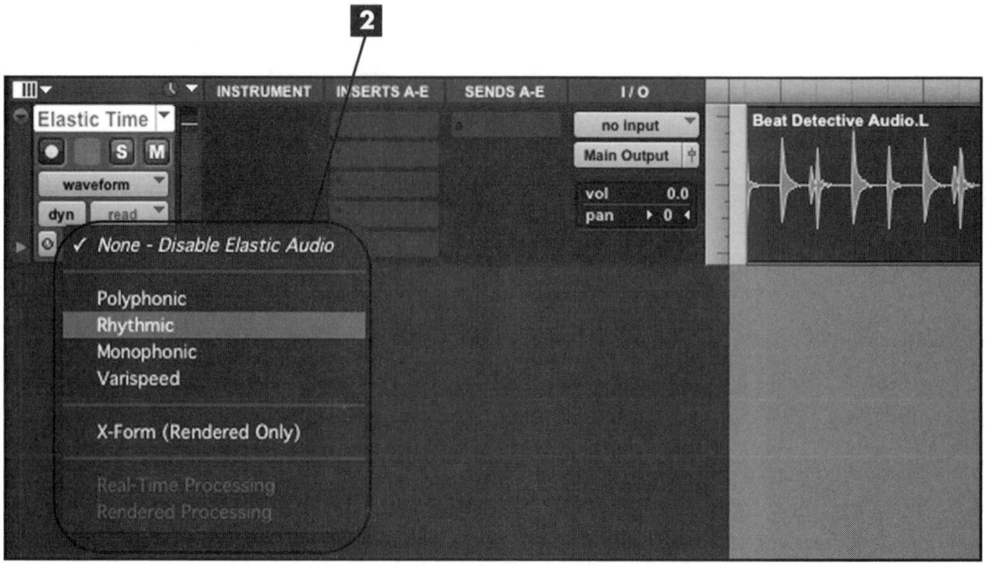

2 **Choose** the appropriate **plug-in** for the job. You have five options:

- **Polyphonic.** This mode is a good general choice and well-suited to audio in which multiple pitches are being played simultaneously.
- **Rhythmic.** This mode is a good choice for drum tracks and other percussive audio.
- **Monophonic.** This mode is great for Audio tracks in which only one note is being played at a time (for example, wind instruments or vocals).
- **Varispeed.** This mode is fundamentally different from the other plug-ins. Elastic Audio's other modes will maintain the original pitches of your audio regardless of whether they're being sped up or slowed down. Varispeed mode, on the other hand, will raise the pitch of your audio when it is being played faster than normal or lower the pitch when it's being played slower. This is particularly handy for turntable or tape-type effects.
- **X-Form (Rendered Only).** This is a high-quality algorithm overall and is often my personal choice, but it is only available as a rendered plug-in, as opposed to being real time. (We will discuss the difference between real time and rendered in a moment.)

IF YOU'RE USING THE TUTORIAL SESSION

If you're following along with the Chapter 10 tutorial session, you'll note that the track shown is a drum loop, so let's choose the Rhythmic plug-in.

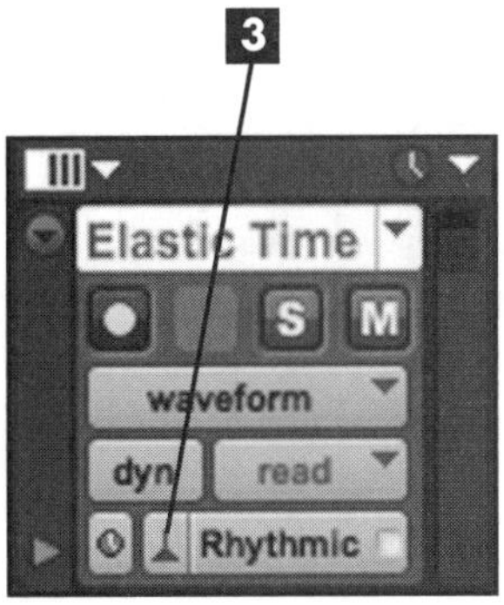

3 You'll notice that once you choose an Elastic Audio plug-in, a button showing your choice will be displayed. Within that button, and next to the name of the algorithm (in this image, Rhythmic), you'll see a small rectangle, which will be either lit with a green color or dark. This will indicate whether Elastic Audio for that track is being processed in real time (green) or in a rendered mode (dark). **Click** the **Elastic Audio Plug-In Selector button** once more, so we can take a second look at the Elastic Audio plug-in list.

4 The bottom segment of the Elastic Audio plug-in list will enable you to choose the processing mode for Elastic Audio on that track. (The currently selected mode will be indicated by a check-mark.) You have two options in most cases:

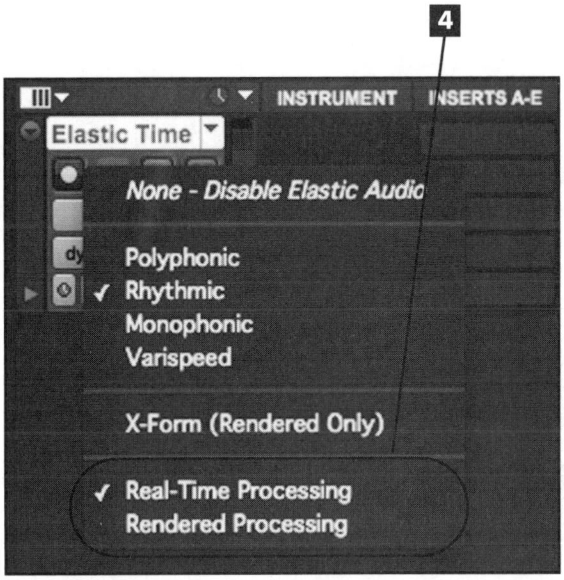

- **Real-Time Processing.** Selecting Real-Time Processing will give you the quickest performance, and any changes you make to your audio will be applied immediately. That being said, processing in real time will place an additional load on your computer's CPU, which can be an issue (particularly with less-powerful computers).
- **Rendered Processing.** When you choose Rendered Processing, your changes will not be immediately applied, but will take some amount of time (depending on the speed of your computer) to apply the change. During that time, the track will not be audible. Your changes will be written (or rendered) to new files that are saved in your session's Rendered Files subfolder.

> **ELASTIC AUDIO AND THE TCE TRIM TOOL**
>
> One of the first things you'll notice when you enable Elastic Audio on a track is that the TCE Trim tool works a bit differently. When Elastic Audio is set up with real-time processing, instead of creating a new file and region each time you use the TCE Trim tool, your audio will simply be time-compressed or expanded immediately. (New files will not be created.) Regardless of the processing mode chosen, you might also notice that as you use the TCE Trim tool repeatedly on the same region, the region's audio quality won't progressively degrade (something that can happen with non-Elastic Audio tracks).

Event and Warp Markers (and How to Use Them)

When Elastic Audio is enabled on a track, you'll notice that there are two new track views that are available to you: Analysis and Warp. Both of these track views have their parts to play. Let's take a look at them one at a time.

1 **Click** the **Track View Selector button** (which in this image currently reads Waveform). The Track View menu will appear.

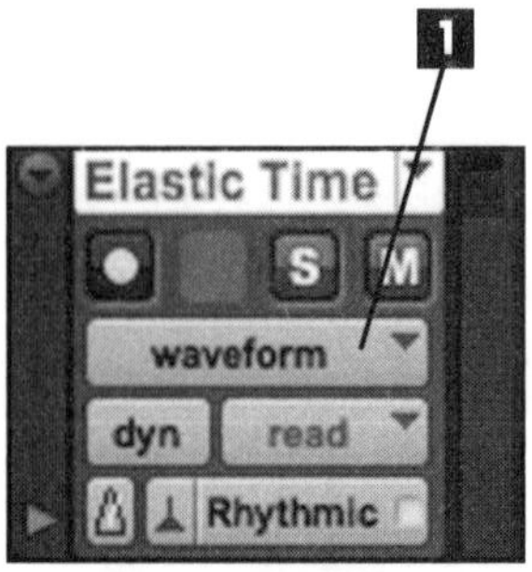

2 **Choose Analysis** from the list of view options.

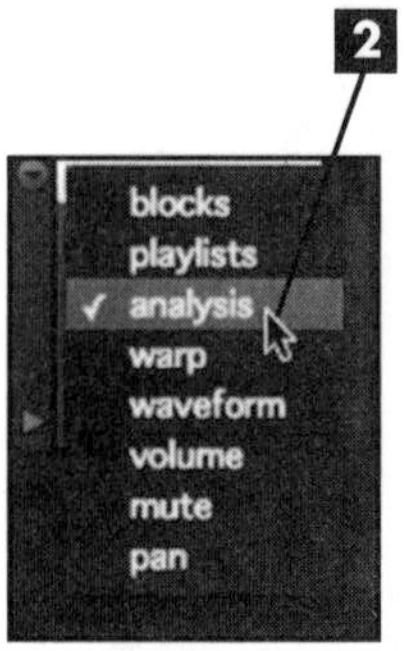

You'll immediately note that there are vertical lines marking transients in your audio, even the very low-level ones. Each of these lines is called an *event marker*.

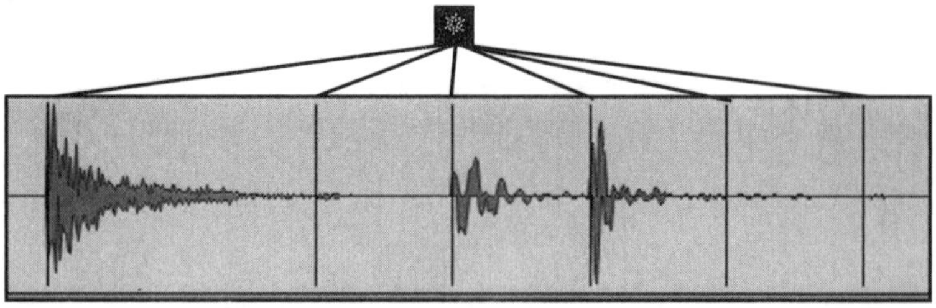

Event markers are loosely analogous to the beat markers you saw earlier in this chapter when you worked with Beat Detective. These markers determine the locations within an audio region that will move as the audio follows tempo changes or when the audio is quantized, which we'll discuss later in this section.

If you need to, you can move, delete, and add event markers. The Grabber tool will help you do this (you can edit Beat Detective's beat markers in the same way).

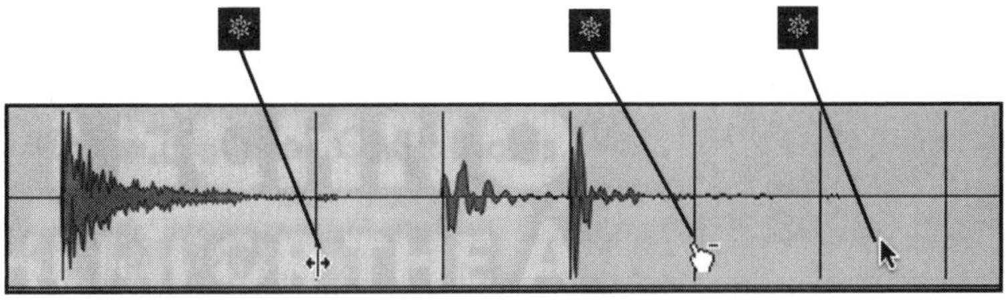

Using the Grabber tool, move your cursor over an existing event marker. Your cursor will change to the double-arrow shown here, and you may click and drag the event marker to a new location.

- You can delete an existing event marker by holding down the Option (Mac) or Alt (PC) key and clicking it using the Grabber tool. The cursor will be shown as a pointing hand with a minus (−) sign next to it.
- If you want to create a new event marker, just double-click where you want to create it!

Now, let's move on to the Warp view:

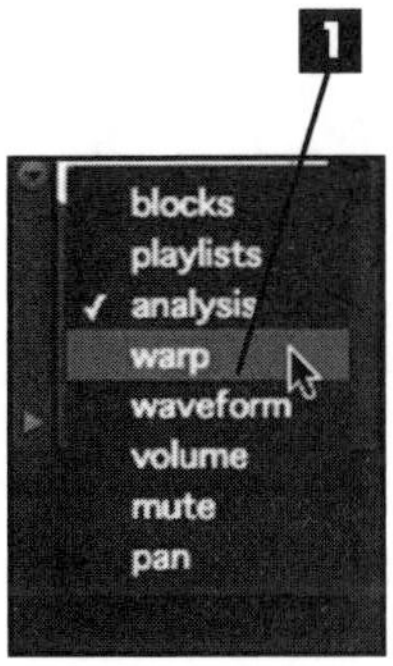

1. **Click** the **Track View Selector button** (again) and **choose Warp** from the list of options.

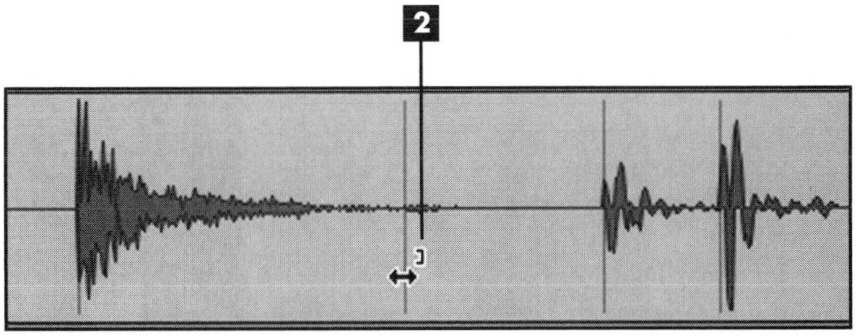

2. Here again, the Grabber tool will be your greatest ally. Move your mouse over any event marker. (Yes, you can still see your event markers, even though you're in Warp view.) The cursor will turn into the icon shown here, indicating that you're ready to use the **Telescoping Warp**. Just **click and drag** to the **left** or the **right** to proportionally compress or expand the entire region. Markers can be dragged smoothly if you're in Slip, Shuffle, or Spot mode. If you're in Grid mode, you'll see that your marker snaps according to your grid resolution.

Although telescoping warp does have its uses, to really make the most of the Warp view, you'll need to create a new kind of marker, called a warp marker. Conceptually, you can think of a warp marker as being a handle that you can grab and move to stretch your audio. Warp markers can be identified by their darker color and the small blue triangle at the base of the marker.

Just as you saw with event markers, you will find that the Grabber tool helps you get started easily:

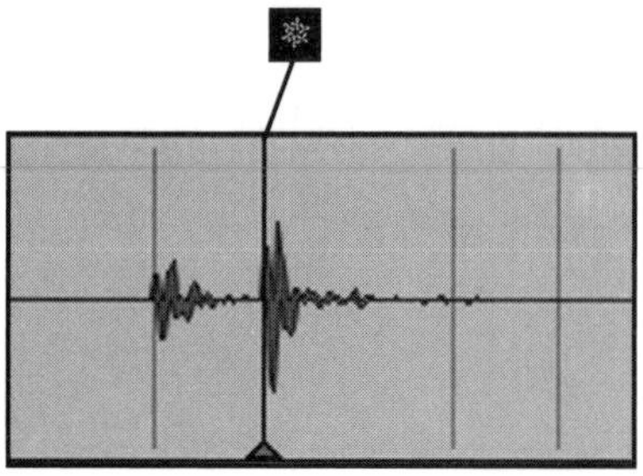

- Here's a common starting point: Double-click an existing event marker to change it into a warp marker (shown here).

Here are a few other ways to create warp markers:

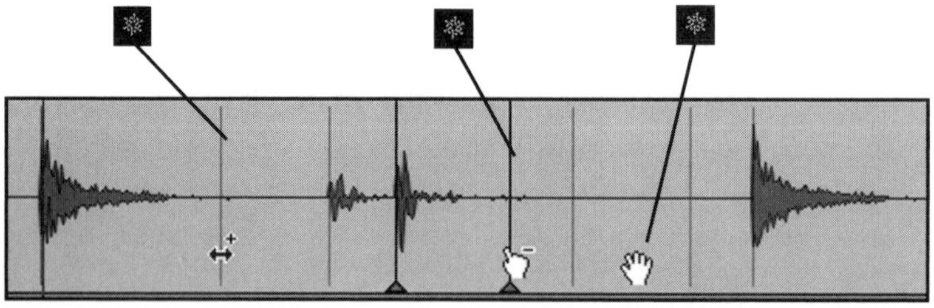

- If you have an existing warp marker to the right of an event marker that you want to promote to being a warp marker, you'll see a small plus (+) sign next to the cursor. In these cases, a single-click will create a warp marker.
- You can remove an existing warp marker by holding down the Option (Mac) or Alt (PC) key and clicking it with the Grabber tool. The cursor will be shown as a pointing hand with a minus (−) sign next to it. Double-clicking an existing warp marker will also remove it.
- If there are no existing event markers at the location where you want to create a new warp marker, no problem—just double-click where you want to create one!

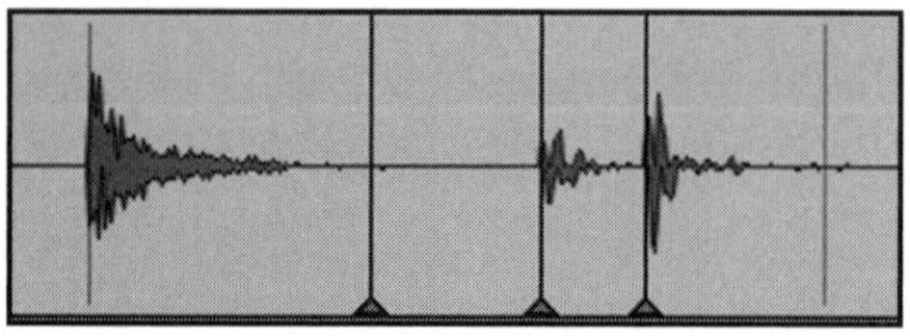

Here's a typical warp-marker setup: The center warp marker in this scenario is the point of audio that I want to move. The warp markers to the left and right of the center warp marker, although they *can* be moved, will act as anchors in this case. Now we're ready to do some serious warping!

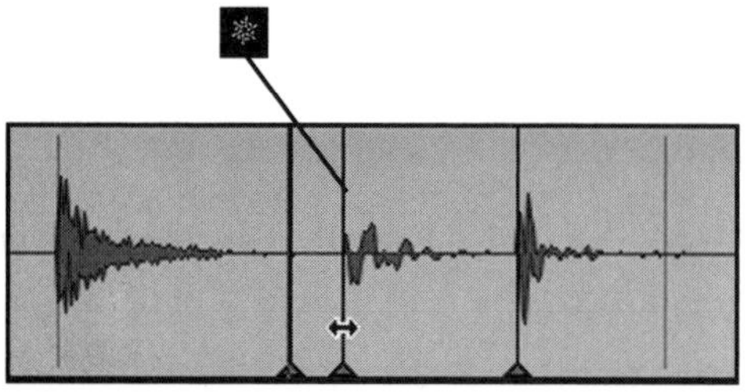

- Click and drag the center warp marker left or right. You'll immediately see that the audio is being pulled like taffy, giving you control over minute aspects of your audio region, with the adjacent warp markers acting as anchors.

Here's an even quicker way to create the warp markers you need for this kind of work:

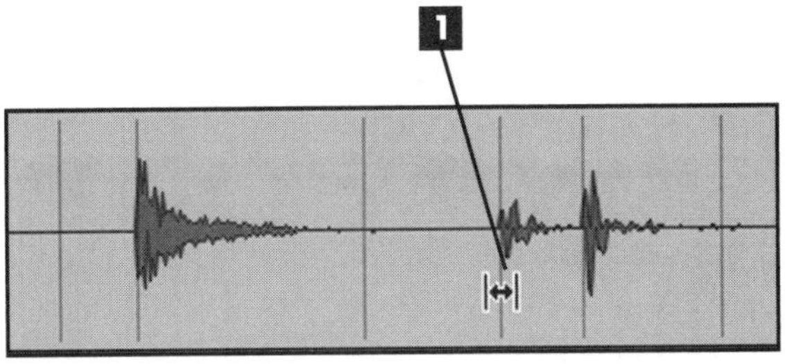

1 **Hold down** the **Shift key** and **move** your **mouse** over an event marker that you want to promote to being a warp marker and then move. The cursor shown here is called an individual warp cursor.

2 **Click** on the **event marker**.

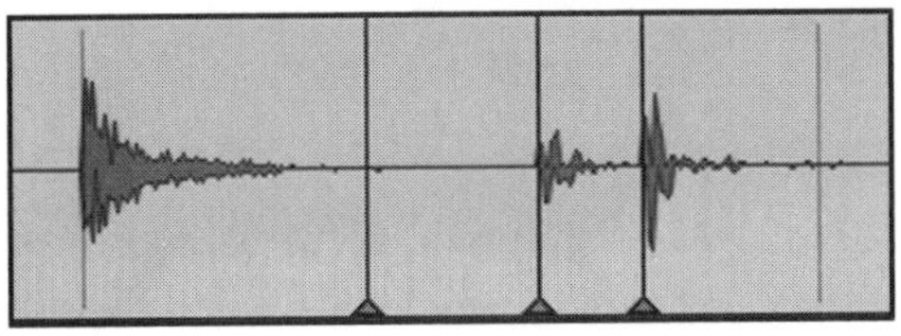

You'll notice that not only has the event marker you clicked changed to a warp marker, so have the markers immediately adjacent to it. This puts you in position to adjust the center warp marker, just as you did earlier in this section.

From time to time, moving a warp marker can case audible side effects. While one possible solution is to eschew the Elastic Audio plug-in for one more suited to the job, you can also tweak the current plug-in a bit to improve its performance.

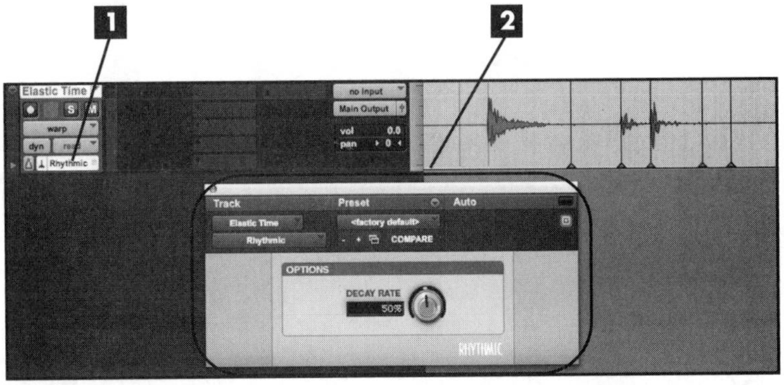

1 **Click** the **Elastic Audio Plug-In button** (which in this image reads Rhythmic, the currently selected Elastic Audio plug-in). The plug-in window will appear.

2 The appearance of the Elastic Audio plug-in window will vary depending on the Elastic Audio plug-in you're using, enabling you to adjust parameters that are most relevant to each one. In the case of the Rhythmic plug-in shown here, you can just **adjust** the **decay rate**, which can remove unwanted artifacts that sometimes accompany this particular plug-in.

You also have the ability to adjust specific Elastic Audio settings on a region-by-region basis.

1 **Select** the **region** you want to work with.

2 **Right-click** the **region**. A menu will appear.

3 **Select Elastic Properties**. The Elastic Properties dialog box will appear.

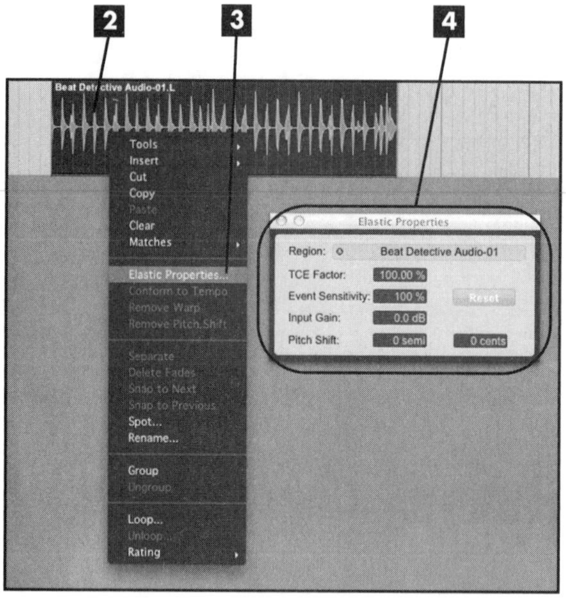

4 The Elastic Properties dialog box will give you overall information about the region (which will vary depending on whether the track is sample-based or tick-based) in the upper part of the dialog box. In the bottom half, you'll see more specific data, including the following:

- **Event Sensitivity.** This is similar in function to the Sensitivity slider you worked with in Beat Detective.
- **Input Gain.** You can adjust this downward if you find that your region clips as a result of warping. A clipping region will be indicated by a small red rectangle in the upper right-hand corner of the region.
- **Pitch.** We'll discuss this later in this section.

You can easily enter new settings here by typing new values into the appropriate fields.

Elastic Audio and Tempo

This party's just getting started! Let's now set up our Audio track to follow tempo changes.

1 **Change** the **Audio track** from being sample-based to being tick-based. (For a refresher on how to do this, take a look at Chapter 6.)

2 Using the Pencil tool, **draw** some **tempo change events** onto the expanded tempo ruler, as shown here.

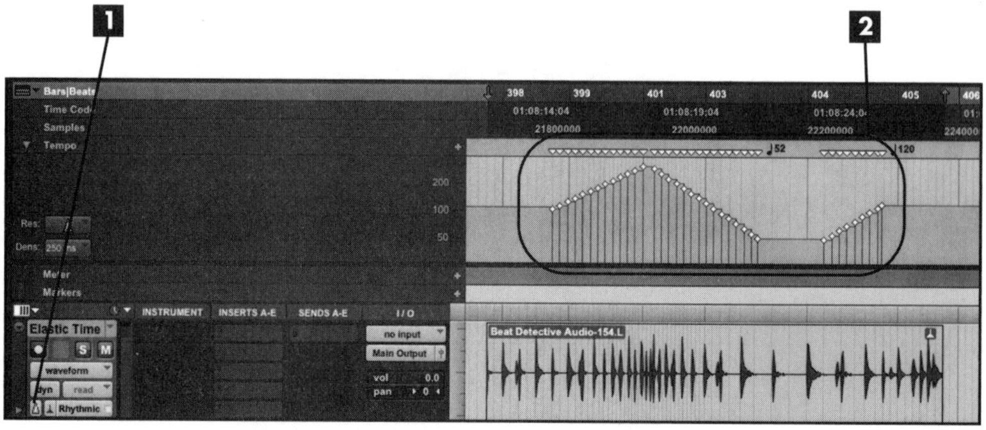

If you play back your session, you'll hear that the region has been compressed or expanded to follow your session's tempo ruler.

IF YOU'RE USING THE TUTORIAL SESSION

If you're following along with the Chapter 10 tutorial session, please undo any tempo changes you've just made, in preparation for the next section.

With Elastic Audio, not only do you have the ability to have your audio follow tempo changes, but you can also quantize it as if it were MIDI!

QUANTIZATION AND TRACK TIMEBASE

The quantization process outlined in the following section can be done on either tick-based or sample-based tracks.

1. **Select** the **area** you want to quantize.
2. **Click** the **Event menu**.
3. **Select Event Operations**. A submenu will appear.
4. **Click Quantize**. The Event Operations/Quantize dialog box will appear.

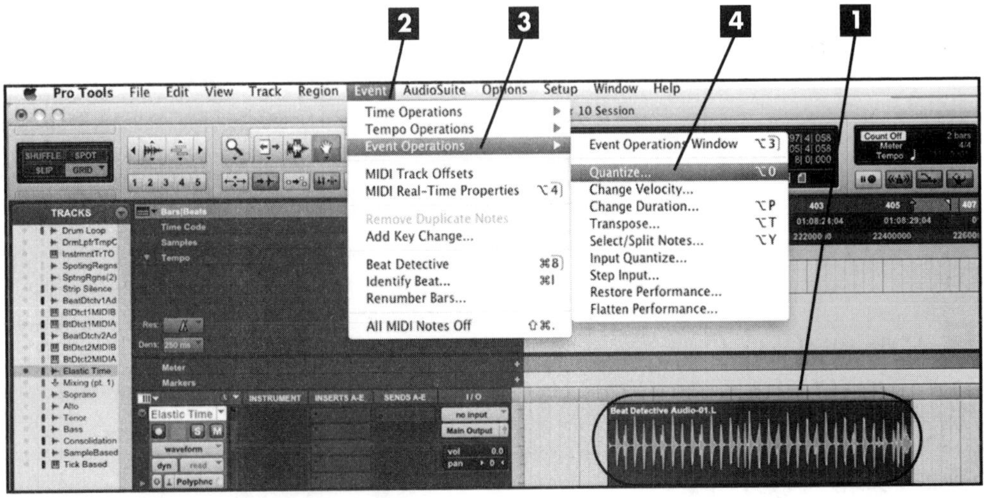

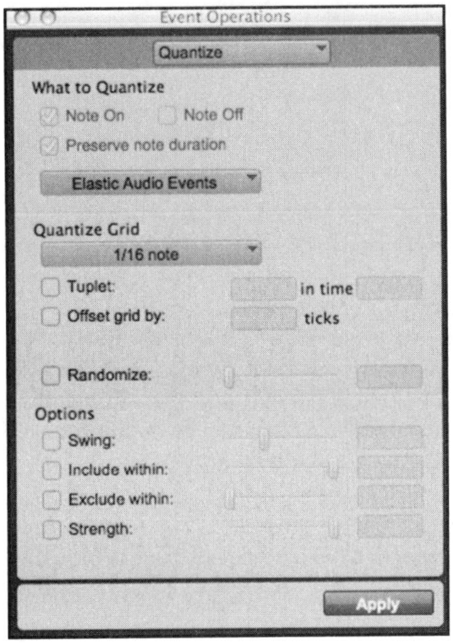

Because you've selected a region on an Elastic Audio–enabled track (which contains Elastic Audio events, which we'll cover next), you have the option of quantizing this drum region, almost as if it were MIDI! Note that when an Elastic Audio region is selected, the What to Quantize menu button reads "Elastic Audio Events." You can quantize to either a grid increment (such as 16th notes, as shown in the previous figure) or a groove template, when quantizing MIDI.

> **COMBINING TOOLS**
>
> Now that you have both Beat Detective and Elastic Audio under your belt, you have many ways to get them to work together. Here's one scenario: Suppose you have two drum regions that you want to have the same feel. Here's one way to go: Choose the drum region whose feel you prefer and use Beat Detective's Bar|Beat Marker Generation mode to change your session's tempo map. Just quantize the other drum region to the new grid (the track needn't be tick-based to do this), and you're all set!

Elastic Audio and the Workspace

Elastic Audio is not only at work in your session, but in the Workspace, Volume, and Project Browsers as well. Within these browsers, audio files that are analyzed by Elastic Audio and are determined to have a musical pattern (such as a drum beat) are listed as being tick-based files (indicated by a green Metronome icon in the Kind column). Files that are analyzed and found not to have this sort of pattern (for example, a single drum hit or a spoken sentence) will be listed as being sample-based (indicated by a blue Clock icon in the Kind column).

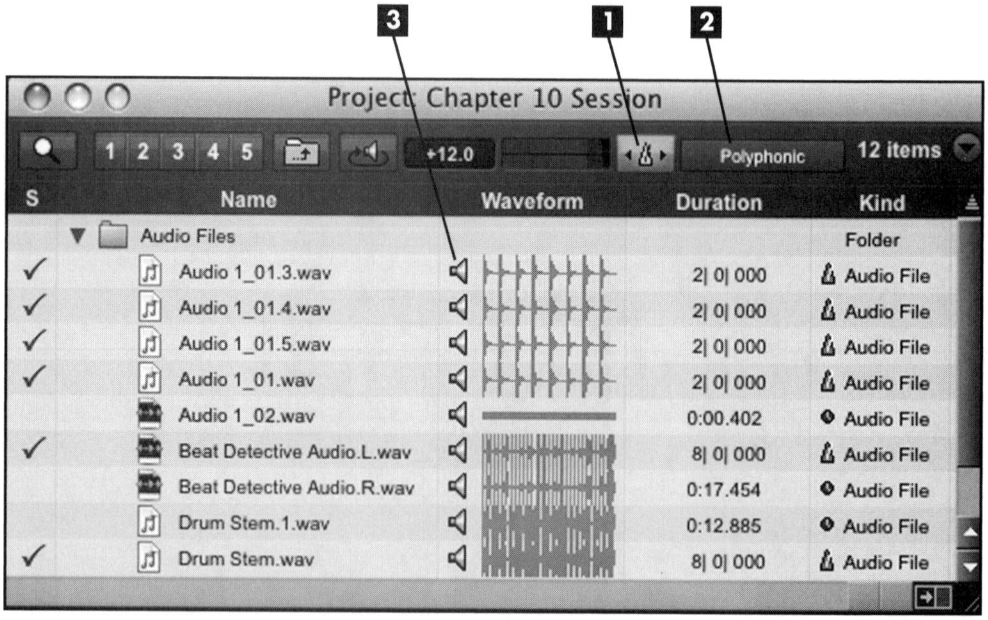

1 At the top of the Workspace Browser, you'll see the green Audio Files Conform to Session Tempo button. When you **click** this **button**, your tick-based audio files will play at your session's tempo (rather than at their original tempo) when previewed.

2 The button to the immediate right of the Audio Files Conform to Session Tempo button will display the currently chosen Elastic Audio plug-in (the one being used for previewing audio files in the browser). **Click** this **button** to reveal a list of all the real-time Elastic Audio plug-in options, from which you can choose the algorithm that sounds best to you.

3 Just **click** the **speaker icon** next to the file waveform that you want to preview. If the file is tick-based, the tempo of the previewed audio will match the tempo of your session.

The Audio Files Conform to Session Tempo feature also has an effect on the process of importing files into your session. When the feature is active, a tick-based file will be imported to a tick-based, Elastic Audio–enabled track, with the same plug-in algorithm that you had in your Workspace Browser being applied to that track.

Making the Most of Elastic Audio

As we discussed earlier, using Elastic Audio in real-time–processing mode will consume some of your computer's limited CPU resources. While switching tracks over to rendered processing whenever possible will give your CPU a break, you can also coax more power out of your computer with the help of the Playback Engine dialog box, which you explored back in Chapter 3, "Getting Started with Audio."

1. **Click** the **Setup menu**.
2. **Click Playback Engine**. The Playback Engine dialog box will open.

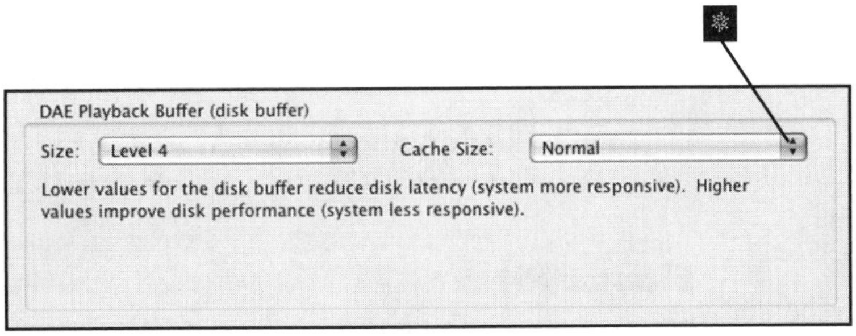

- The Cache Size button, located in the center-right area of the Playback Engine dialog box, will enable you to choose how much memory will be allocated specifically for the playback of Elastic Audio regions. When you click the Cache Size menu button, you'll see that you have three options:
  - Minimum (reduces memory use)
  - Normal
  - Large (improves performance)

You can also tweak the behavior of Elastic Audio through the Preferences window.

1. **Click** the **Setup menu**.
2. **Click Preferences**. The Preferences window will open.

3 In the Preferences window, **click** the **Processing tab**. In the Elastic Audio section of this page, you'll see three useful options:

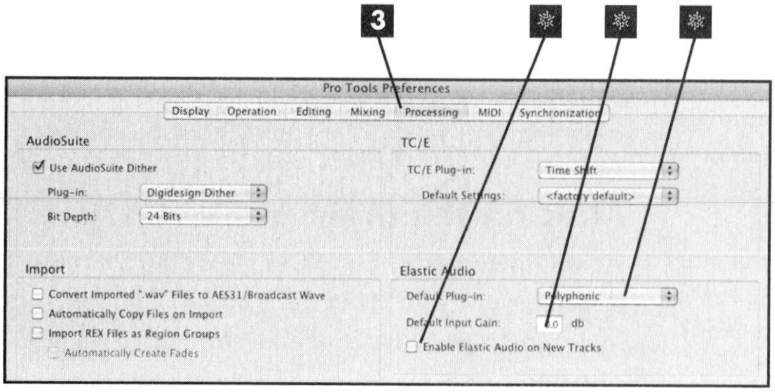

- **Default Plug-in.** Here you can choose the initial plug-in used for auditioning files in the browser windows, as well as the plug-in that is initially used if new tracks are created as Elastic Audio tracks.
- **Default Input Gain.** This will enable you to automatically reduce the volume of Elastic Audio regions, to prevent the clipping that can sometimes occur when a region is warped.
- **Enable Elastic Audio on New Tracks.** When this checkbox is checked, new Audio tracks will be created with Elastic Audio enabled (using the Default Plug-In type).

Elastic Pitch

Elastic Audio can adjust not only the timing of your audio, but its pitch as well. Using Elastic Audio, you can easily change pitch on a region-by-region basis.

> **ELASTIC PITCH LIMITATION**
>
> Adjusting pitch with Elastic Audio can only be done when using the Polyphonic, Rhythmic, or X-Form Elastic Audio plug-ins.

There are two different methods by which you can adjust the pitch of a selected region, each with its own particular advantages. Let's start by looking at a way to transpose a region.

1. **Select** the **region** whose pitch you want to transpose.
2. **Click** the **Event menu**.
3. **Choose Event Operations**. A submenu will appear.
4. **Click Transpose**. The Event Operations/Transpose dialog box will appear.

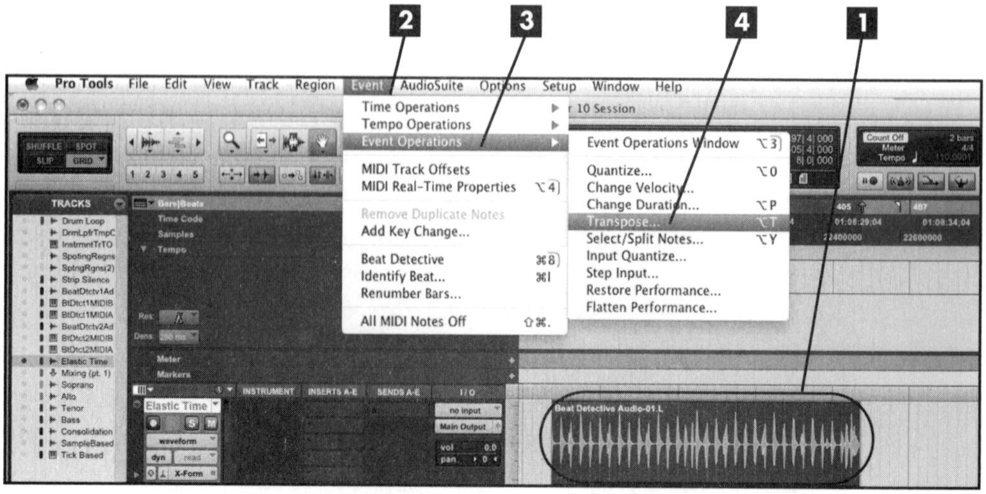

5 **Adjust** the **transposition parameters** just as you would if working with MIDI data. (For more details on the parameters in the Transpose dialog box, see Appendix A, "More MIDI Power," included as a PDF on your book's disc.)

6 **Click** the **Apply button**, and you're finished!

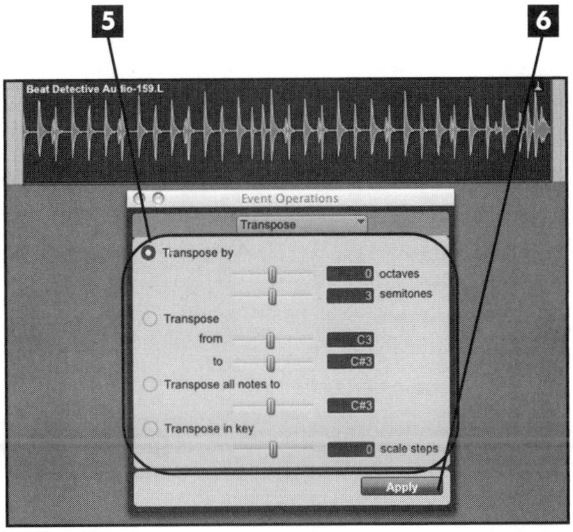

The previous workflow is very handy in situations when you want to make relatively large changes in pitch. But what if you just want to tweak the pitch of a flat note? No problem—you can make those kinds of fine adjustments in the Elastic Properties dialog box.

1 **Right-click** the **region** you want to change. A list of options will appear.

2 **Choose Elastic Properties.** The Elastic Properties dialog box will open.

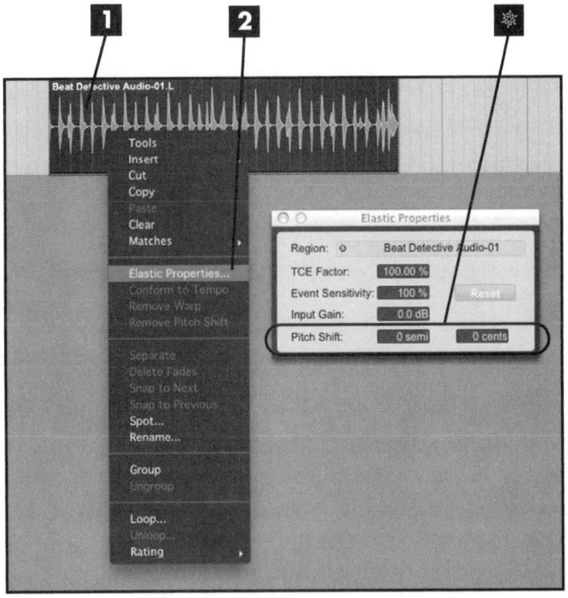

The Pitch Shift controls in the Elastic Properties dialog box will enable you to adjust pitch not only in semitones (something you could also do in the Transpose dialog box), but also in cents, which are very small units of pitch. There are 100 cents in a semitone, or half-step. You will find that by adjusting pitch in terms of cents, you have very fine control over the pitch of the audio.

ARE YOU WARPED?

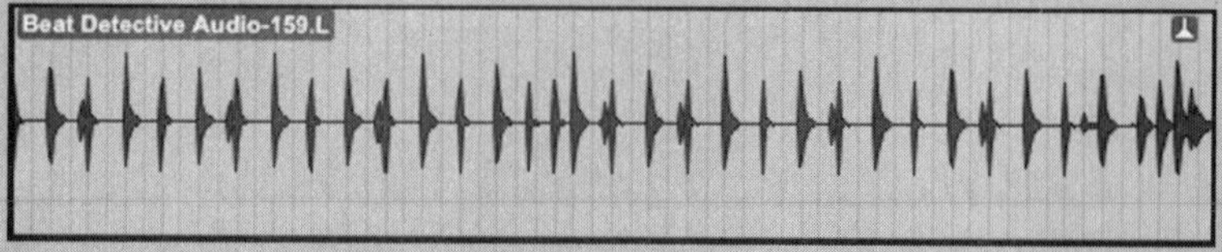

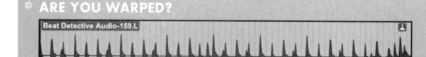

If you're unclear as to whether a given region has been altered through the application of Elastic Audio, the region itself will give you a clue: Regions changed by Elastic Audio (including pitch changes) will be indicated by a small icon in the upper-right corner of the region, as shown here.

ELASTIC WARNINGS

One final point: From time to time, you might see sections of your audio turn red when dragging warp markers. Not to worry—Pro Tools is just letting you know that you've applied a good deal of time compression or expansion. Technically speaking, you've gone beyond Pro Tools' recommended limits, but if it sounds good to your ears, go for it!

Making the Most of Mixing

Here are a few tips to help you make your mixes *rock*!

Using the Edit Tools

So far, you've primarily used the Pencil tool to edit your automation. Let's take a look at how you can use a couple other tools as well.

SETTING THINGS UP

Please go to Memory Location #9—Mixing (pt. 1).

You've seen how useful the Grabber tool can be when working with Beat Detective and Elastic Audio. Here's how you can use it to create, modify, and even delete automation breakpoints.

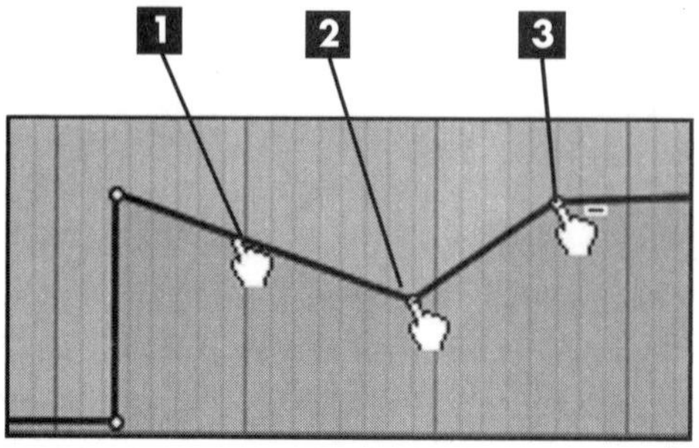

1. To create an automation breakpoint, just **click where you want it to be**.
2. To change the time or value of an existing automation breakpoint, **click and drag** the **breakpoint** to the desired location.
3. You can delete an existing automation breakpoint by **holding down** the **Option (Mac) or Alt (PC) key** and **clicking it**. The cursor will be shown as a pointing hand with a minus (−) sign next to it.

The Trim tool can also come in very useful when you want to proportionally scale your automation—that is, raise or lower the automation line without changing its shape:

1 Using the selector tool, **make a selection** of the area that you want to change.

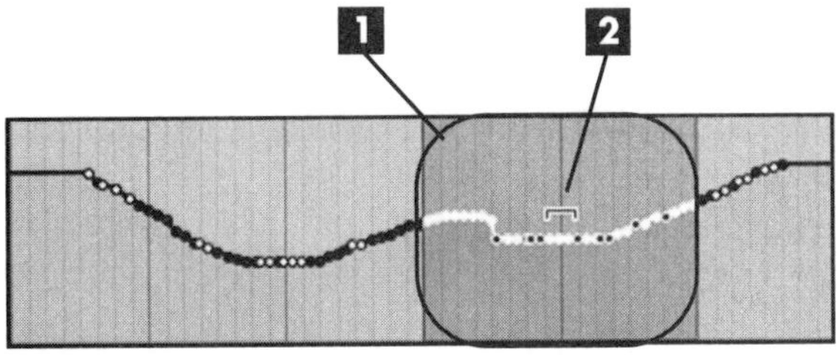

2 **Move** the **Trim tool** into the selected area. The Trim tool will be shown downward-facing, indicating that it's ready to change your automation.

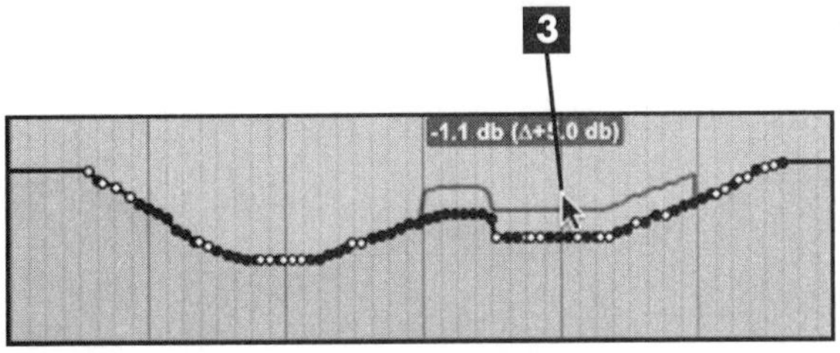

3 **Click and drag** your **mouse** up or down to adjust your automation proportionally. If you're working with volume automation data, you'll see a delta value (the amount of change) shown in parentheses next to a triangle (the Greek letter delta).

4 **Release** the **mouse button**. The automation will be proportionally changed in the selected area.

Scroll Into View

Often, when mixing, you'll run across a track that could use a little editorial tweaking, requiring that you move from the Mix window to the Edit window. That's easy enough, but in cases when you're working with a large number of tracks (more than can be shown in your Mix or Edit window at once), you might find yourself spending a lot of time scrolling through your Edit window to find the track you want! The Scroll Into View function does that work for you!

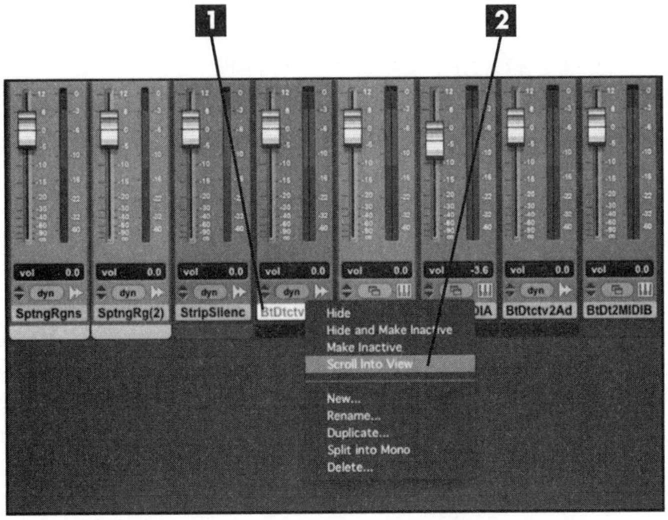

1 **Right-Click** on the desired track name (this works in either the Mix or the Edit window). The track's menu will appear.

2 Choose the **Scroll Into View** menu item. Two things will happen:

- The Mix window will scroll so that the track will appear at the left-most side (or as left-most as possible).
- The Edit window will scroll so that the track will appear at the top of the window (or as high as possible).

There are a couple other ways to scroll a track into view:

- Right-click on the desired track name in the Tracks list (in either the Edit or Mix window), and choose Scroll Into View from the track menu.
- From the Track menu, choose Scroll to Track. You'll be prompted to enter the track number that you want to scroll into view.

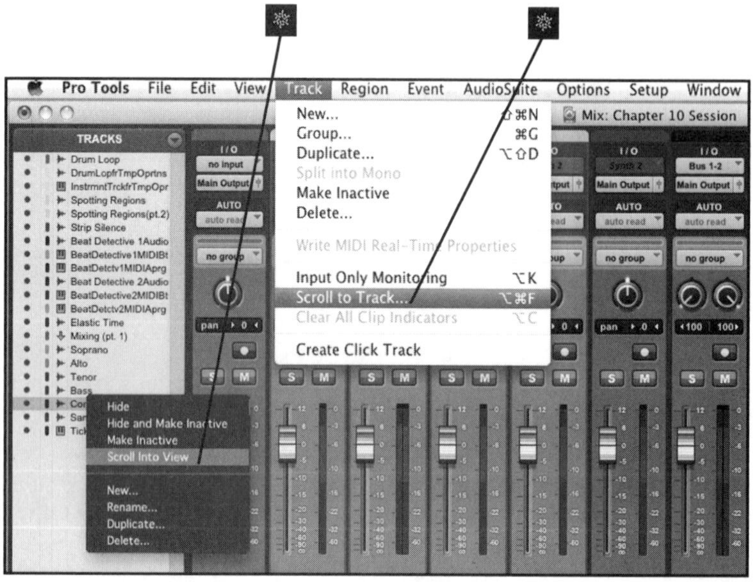

TRACK NUMBERS

The Scroll to Track feature really only works well if you're able to see your track numbers, which can be easily enabled or disabled.

- From the View menu, you can enable and disable track number displays. When this view is enabled, the menu item is indicated with a checkmark.
- Once the track number view is enabled, you'll see numbering to the left of track names in the Tracks list. These are the numbers you'll refer to when using the Scroll to Track feature.

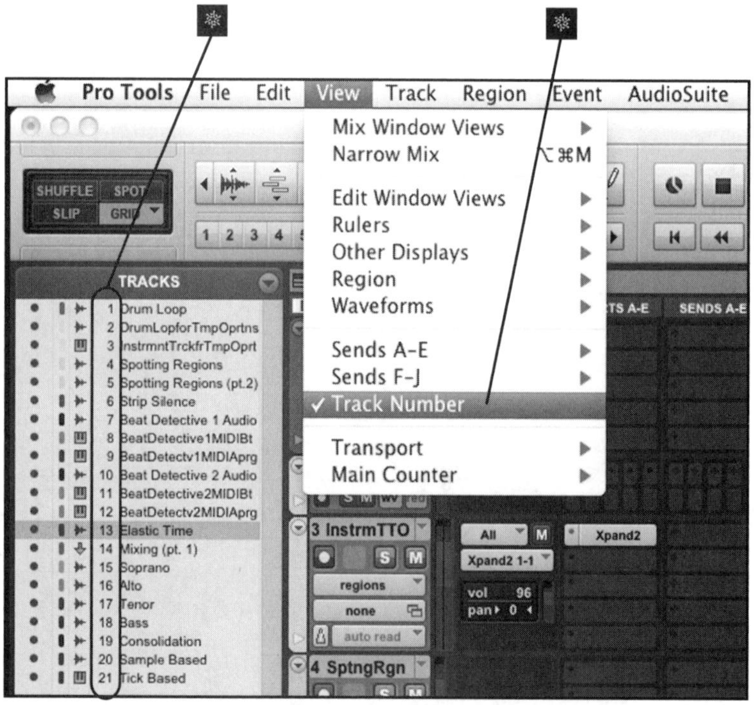

HEY, THIS DOESN'T WORK!

The Scroll Into View (or Scroll to Track) feature only works (and is only really needed) when you're working with sessions where you can't see all of your tracks simultaneously in the Mix and Edit window. Additionally, tracks that are near the bottom of the Edit window or the right of the Mix window will only move to the extent possible.

Toggling Groups

Here's a way to change the balance of a mix (fader) group without the hassle of first having to deactivate the group!

SETTING THINGS UP

For this section, please go to Memory Location #10—Mixing (pt. 2).

In this example, we've got four vocal parts that are grouped together in an active fader group.

1. **Press and hold** the **Control key (Mac)** or the **Start (Windows) key (PC)**, and then **click and drag** the **fader** you want to change. Note that although the group is still being shown as active in the Groups list, you can change individual tracks without affecting the rest of the group.
2. **Release** the **key**. Your group will be re-enabled, and the tracks' faders will move as a group.

MY FAVORITE MIX WINDOW SHORTCUT

While we're on the topic of groups, here's a useful shortcut, especially for those complex sessions with many groups: To quickly show only the tracks in a given group, hold down the Control key (Mac) or the Start key (PC) and click the name of the group that you want to see in the Groups list. (This works in either the Mix or the Edit window.) All tracks that are not members of that group will be hidden.

New Pro Tools 9 Mixing Features

Pro Tools 9 brings new levels of mix quality and compatibility. Let's take a quick look at three significant changes to the world of Pro Tools mixing!

EUCON Support

Recently, Avid purchased a company called Euphonix, adding some truly outstanding control surfaces to their product offerings—from the high-end System 5 to the small but powerful Artist series. These control surfaces communicate with Pro Tools (and other DAWs as well) through a protocol named EUCON (Extended User CONtrol). Here's how to set up your Pro Tools system to communicate via EUCON:

1. Click the **Setup** menu.
2. Choose **Peripherals**. The Peripherals dialog box will appear.

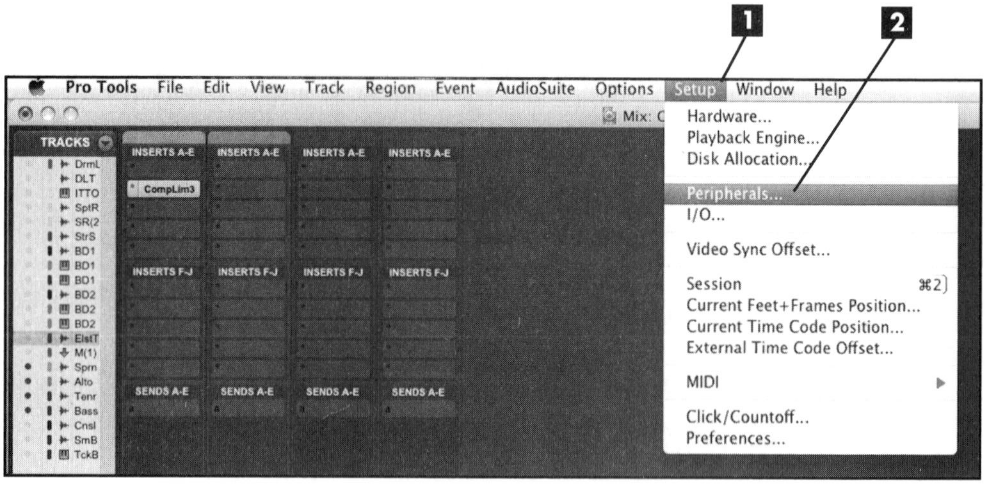

3. Since EUCON is an Ethernet-based protocol, click the **Ethernet Controllers** tab.
4. Click the **Enable EUCON** checkbox. When enabled, a checkmark will be displayed (as shown here).

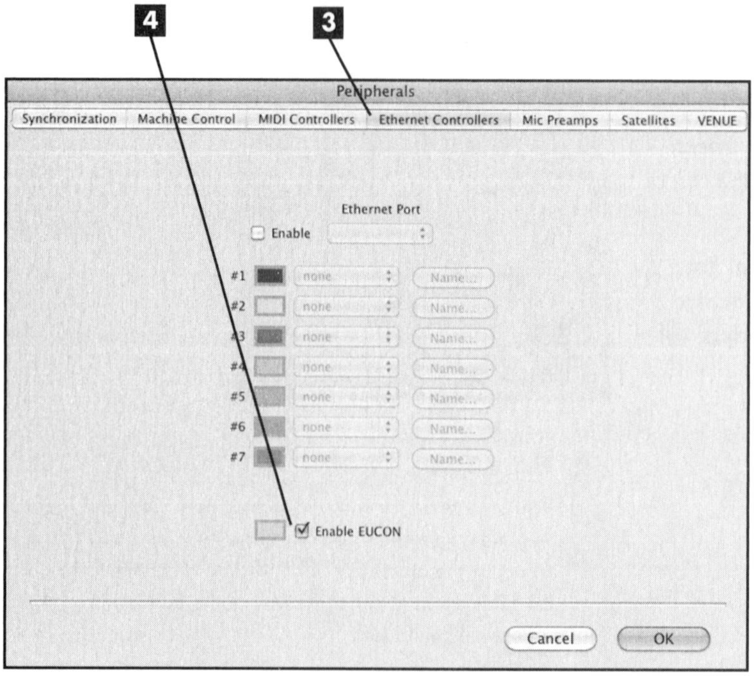

That's it! There are no other Ethernet settings you'll need to worry about in this dialog box (they apply to other kinds of Ethernet controllers). Assuming your control surface is set up (including the installation of the device's EuControl software), you're all set to go!

Pan Depth Options

Okay, this can get a little technical, but hear me out: When identical signals are combined, their levels go up. Makes sense, right? Well, that means when a signal is panned to the center of a stereo pair of speakers, the perceived volume of that signal would be louder than if that signal were panned to the hard left or hard right. Now, if *that* were the case in actual practice, we'd have some pretty serious issues to contend with as we mix, especially when automating things like panning! Clearly, somebody has fixed the problem behind the scene, and that solution is called pan depth.

Basically, what pan depth refers to is an attenuation (reduction in volume) of a signal as it is panned to the center so that the perceived loudness stays the same. The problem is that there's no hard-and-fast rule about which amount of attenuation is the correct one. It depends on a number of factors, including the acoustic quality of the room you're working in. As a result, different mix console and DAW manufacturers use different pan depths. This can really do a number on a mixer's ears, though—particularly when they mix in different systems with different pan laws—so Pro Tools 9 now gives you the ability to choose the pan depth you prefer!

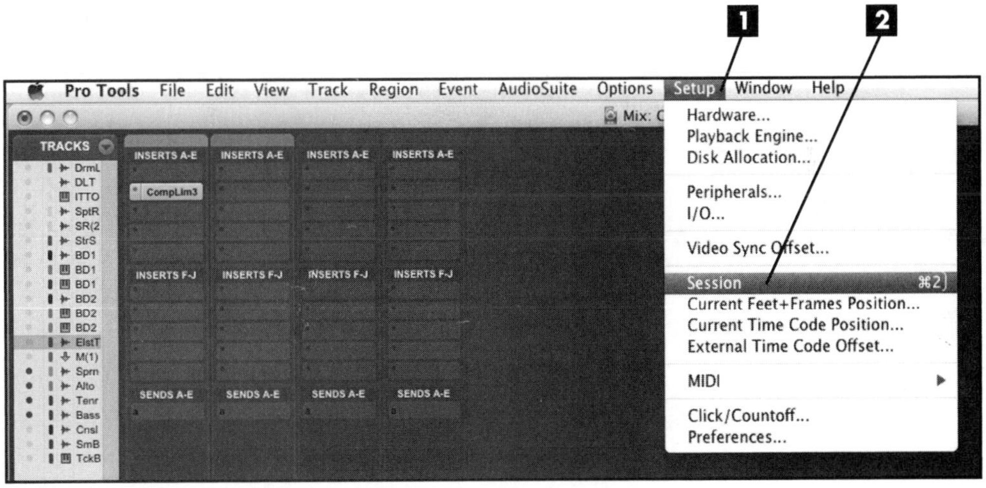

1. Click the **Setup** menu.
2. Choose **Session**. The Session Setup window will appear.

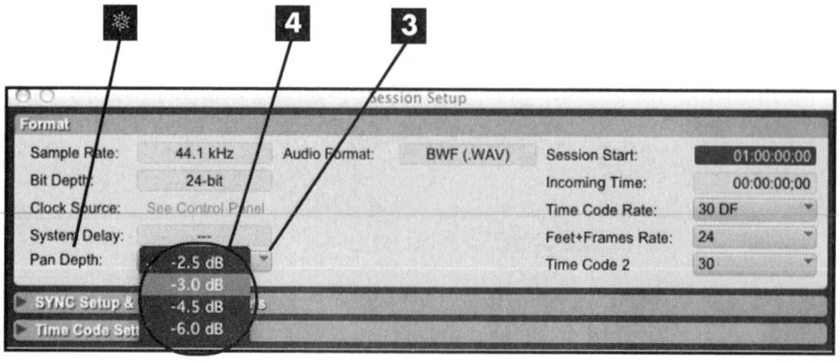

You'll find your session's pan depth displayed in the lower left-hand corner of the Format section of the Session Setup window. The button to the right of the words Pan Depth will display your session's current pan depth setting.

3 **Click** on the **Pan Depth button** to display a list of pan-depth options.

4 You can **choose** a different **Pan Depth setting** for your session from this list (the current setting is indicated by a checkmark). You're sure to find a setting you like—all the standard pan depths are represented here.

Automatic Delay Compensation

Technically speaking, Automatic Delay Compensation isn't new to Pro Tools, but up until now, it's only been available on Pro Tools HD systems. With Pro Tools 9, it's available to every Pro Tools user, so let's talk about it a bit.

When you launch a plug-in, you're effectively adding a mathematical formula to the signal path. Like all math, simple formulae can be processed quickly, whereas more-complex equations take more time. This is as true for computer chips as it is for the human brain, but when we talk about delay caused by plug-in math, we call it latency.

You can probably see where this is going. When you're working with multiple tracks, with different kinds of plug-ins on them (different math, and different amounts of latency), your audio can get out of sync. Although this might not sound like a big deal, these small misalignments can lead to problems of phase alignment, and can quickly muddy up your mix.

Pro Tools' Automatic Delay Compensation (ADC) fixes this problem by adding varying degrees of latency to each track. It uses the most latent track as a guide so that all tracks share the same amount of latency and are thereby perfectly aligned. Let's take a simple example: Say you have three tracks. One has 100 samples of plug-in latency, the second one has 20 samples of latency, and the third one has zero plug-in latency (there aren't any plug-ins on that track). ADC would add 80 samples of latency to the second track and 100 samples of latency to the third track, so that all three tracks have the same amount of latency (100 samples in this case). What's better, ADC is always keeping track of how much latency is on each track and maintains sample accuracy between all the tracks, so all you need to do is to turn ADC on and get to mixing!

There's a little bit of setup involved with using ADC, but it's well worth the effort as you move into the mix stage of production:

1 Click the **Setup** menu.

2 Choose **Playback Engine**. The Playback Engine dialog box will appear.

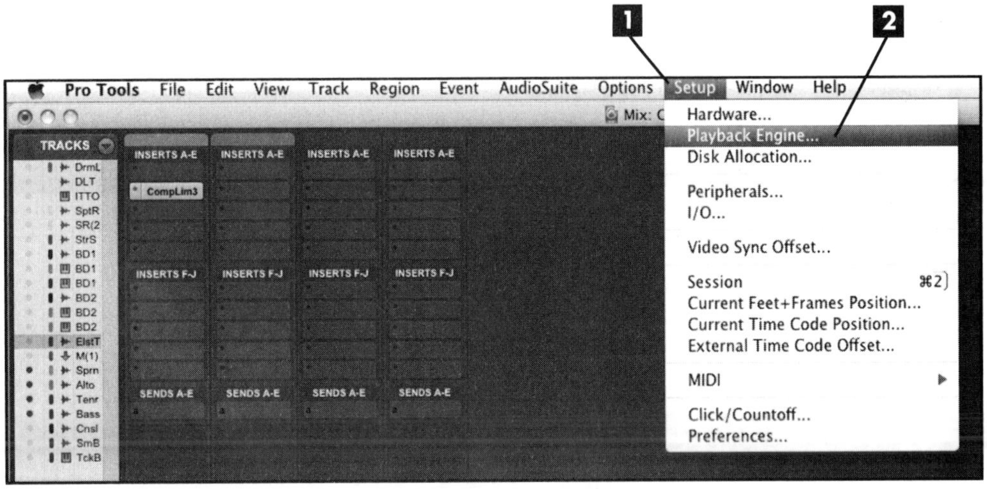

3 The **Delay Compensation Engine** menu button will show the current setting for Automatic Delay Compensation (in this image None, meaning that ADC cannot be enabled for this session as things stand). Click the menu button to view your ADC options:

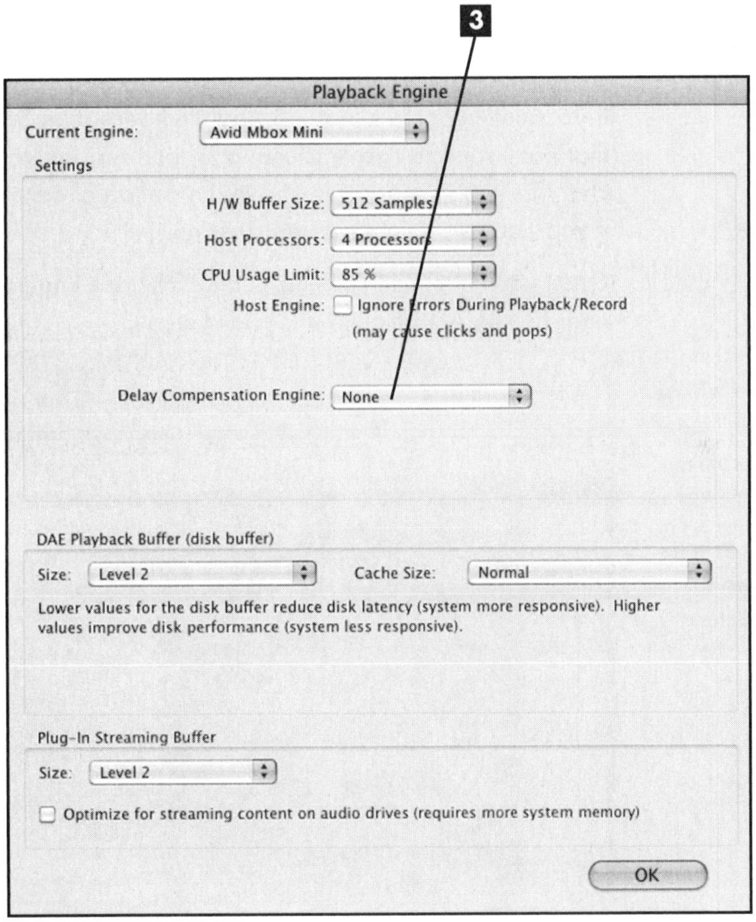

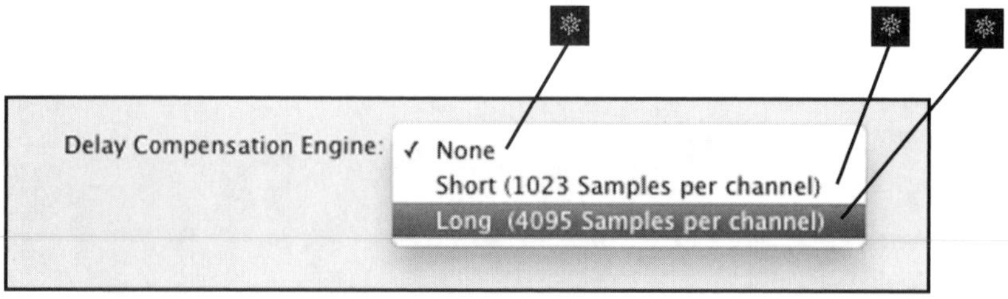

- **None.** This means Automatic Delay Compensation can't be activated. In this image, this is the current mode, as indicated by a checkmark.
- **Short (1023 Samples per Channel).** This will enable ADC to compensate to up to 1,023 samples of plug-in latency per signal path. This is often adequate and has the advantage of keeping the overall system latency low—especially important when syncing Pro Tools with external devices like video decks.
- **Long (4095 Samples per Channel).** This is a good choice if you're going to use a good deal of plug-ins and virtual instruments. It does mean your overall system is a little delayed in its playback, but it doesn't make a real difference if you're not synchronized to external devices.

If you make changes to the Delay Compensation Engine, you'll see a notification that Pro Tools must save, close, and then reopen your session in order to apply the changes you've made. You have the option of canceling your changes at this point if you don't want to save your session.

Once you have set things up in the Playback Engine dialog box, you can enable and disable ADC from the Options menu:

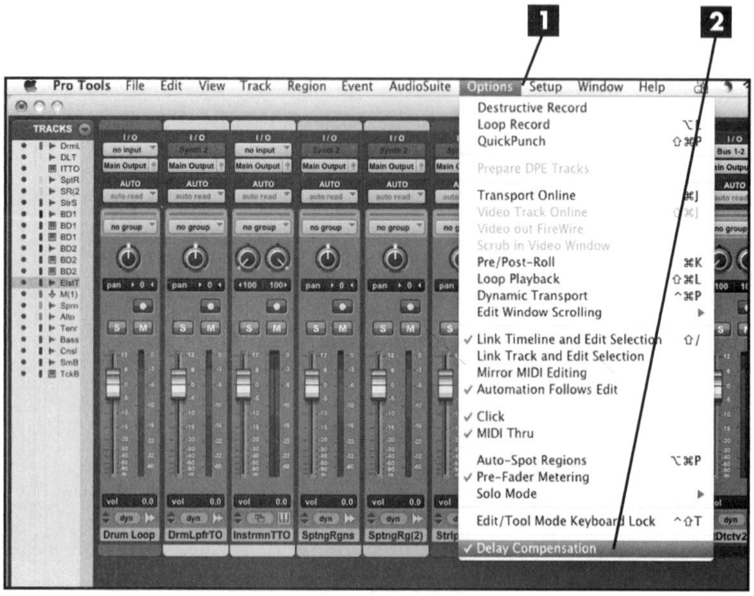

1. Click the **Options** menu.
2. Choose **Delay Compensation.** When it's active, you'll see a checkmark next to the menu item.

You're pretty much done at this point, and can mix secure in the knowledge that your audio is all sample-aligned. There are just a few other tidbits that will come in useful:

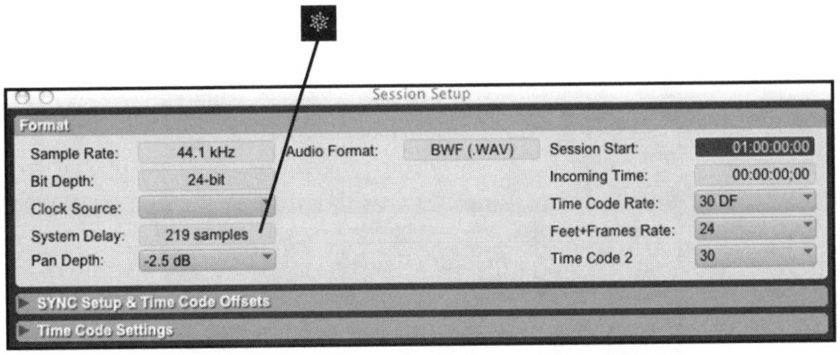

- In the Session Setup window (which you saw in the previous section, when we talked about pan depth), you'll see a System Delay value if ADC is active. This value represents the delay caused by ADC plus the delay of your audio interface. This data is invaluable when synchronizing with an external device. You can compensate for this delay in the Sync Setup & Time Code Offsets section of the Session Setup window.

- By default, your delay values will be shown in Pro Tools in samples, but you have the option of viewing them in milliseconds instead. Just go to the Preferences window (from the Setup menu), and from there to the Operations tab. You'll find the Delay Compensation Time Mode button in the lower-right corner of this page; just click on the button and choose the time scale you want to use (samples or milliseconds).

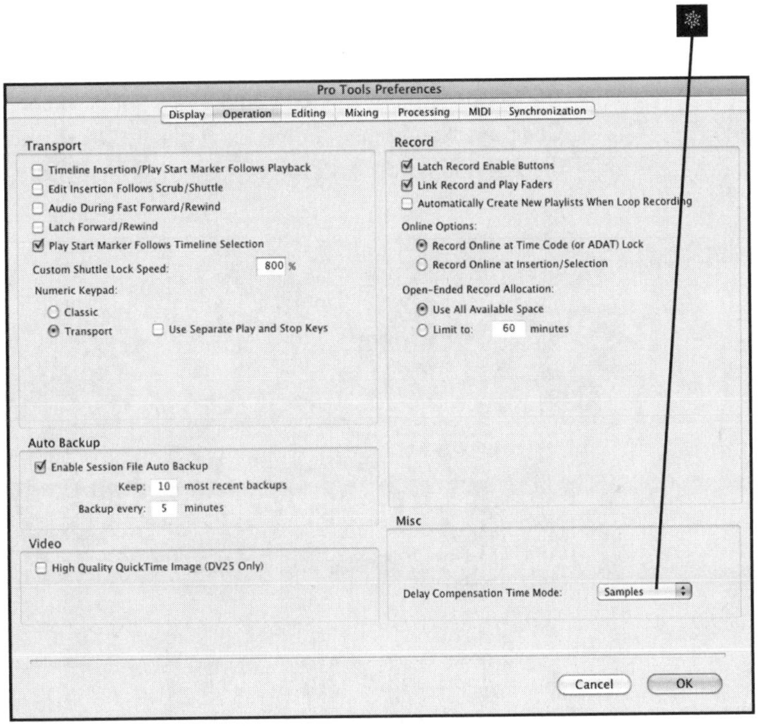

You can easily see what's going on in your session by taking a look at what ADC is doing on a track-by-track basis. There are two ways to show the Delay Compensation view in your Mix window:

- From the View menu, choose Mix Window Views. From there, choose Delay Compensation.
- Click the Mix Window View Selector (in the bottom left-hand corner of the Mix window) and choose Delay Compensation from the menu.

You'll then see a display at the bottom of each track in your Mix window, displaying a variety of useful information:

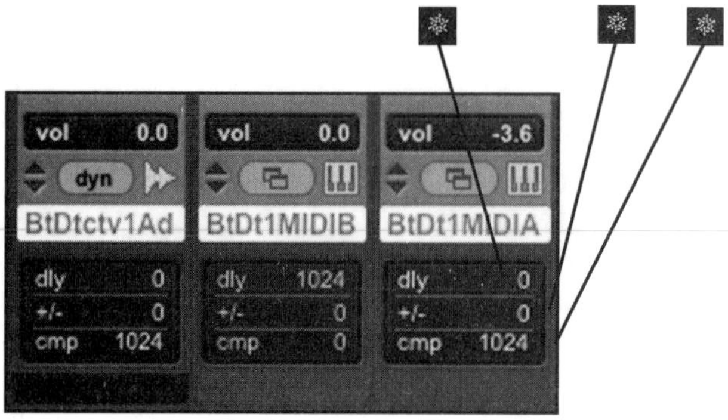

- The top section will show you the original latency of each track. In this image, the first and third tracks have no plug-ins instantiated, and therefore no latency. The second track, however, has some plug-in latency (quite a bit actually—1,024 samples!).
- The middle section enables you to manually add or subtract from this value, effectively nudging the audio forward or backward in time. It's rarely used, but if you need to tweak a particular track's timing, you have the power to do it here.
- The bottom section will tell you the amount of latency that's been added by the Delay Compensation Engine. In this example, 1,024 samples of latency had to be added to the first and third tracks to keep them perfectly lined up with the middle track.

CLIPPING THE ADC

Although it's pretty tough to do, it is possible to accumulate more plug-in latency than the Delay Compensation Engine can compensate for. You can see if you're exceeding the capacity of your ADC in two places:

If a track is clipping the ADC, the displays in its Delay Compensation section will appear red.

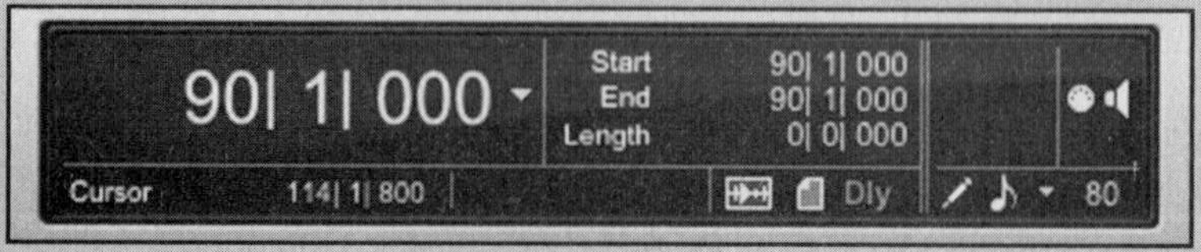

In the counter display section of the Edit window, Dly appears (in the lower-right section) whenever Delay Compensation is activated. If the letters are green, all is well, but if Dly is shown in red type, that means you've clipped at least one track, and the Delay Compensation Engine can no longer keep all your audio in perfect synchronization.

DELAY COMPENSATION AND RECORDING

The Delay Compensation Engine operates by adding delay to your session's tracks. When you're recording, you might think this'll create some issues! Don't worry, though—the Delay Compensation engine is automatically bypassed on recording tracks, and recorded audio and MIDI is time-aligned with the rest of the session once a recording pass is finished.

Advanced Resource Management

Yet more ways to view and manage your data!

The System Usage Window

First, let's take a look at a new window—the System Usage window—which will help you monitor your CPU resources.

1. **Click** on the **Window menu**.
2. **Click** on **System Usage**. The System Usage window will appear.

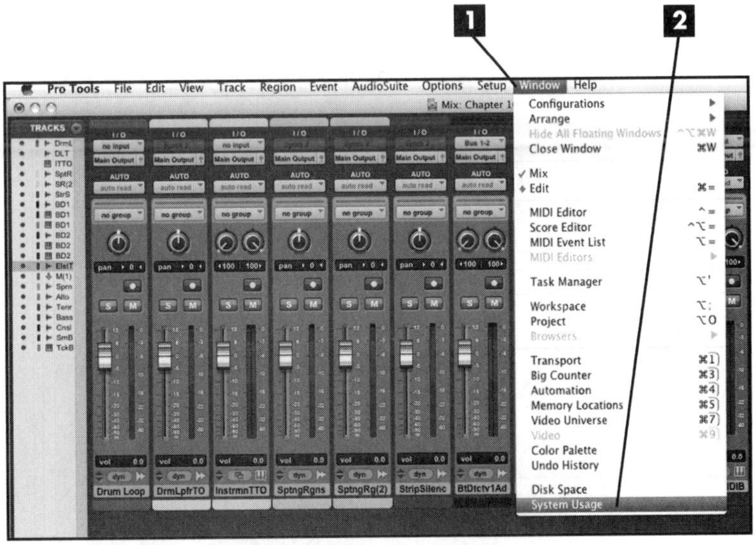

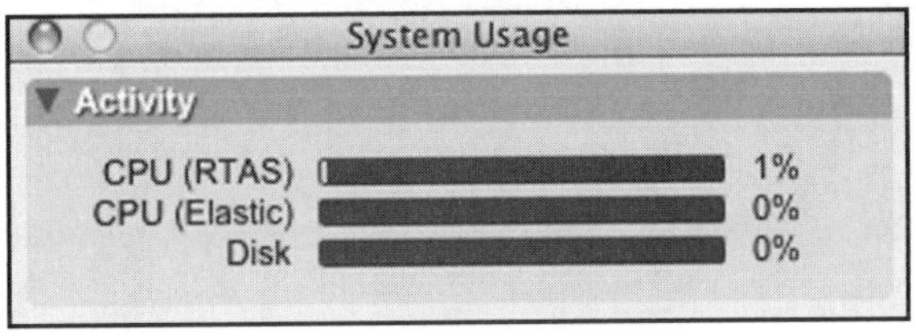

The graphs in this window will help you to view your available hard-drive bandwidth and CPU consumption. Perhaps the most important graphs to watch are the CPU (RTAS) and CPU (Elastic) meters.

Inactive Elements

There's a difference between elements in your session that are offline and those that are inactive. An *offline* region occurs when source media is not found when you open a session. When that happens, a region will appear on a track, but that region will be empty, with the region name in italics. *Inactive* elements, on the other hand, are processes that are somehow disabled (either as a result of not having the appropriate plug-in installed on a system or deliberately by the Pro Tools user).

There are a few good reasons to make a plug-in or track inactive:

- Making a plug-in inactive will free up valuable CPU resources while maintaining automation and preset settings.
- Making tracks inactive can enable you to work with tracks beyond the Audio track limitation of a given Pro Tools system (although an inactive track will not be audible).

There are two easy ways to make a plug-in inactive. Here's one:

1 **Right-click** the **Insert button**. A list will appear.

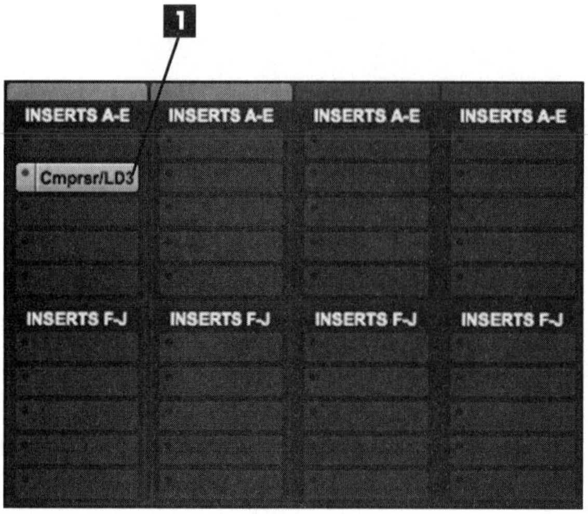

2 **Choose Make Inactive**.

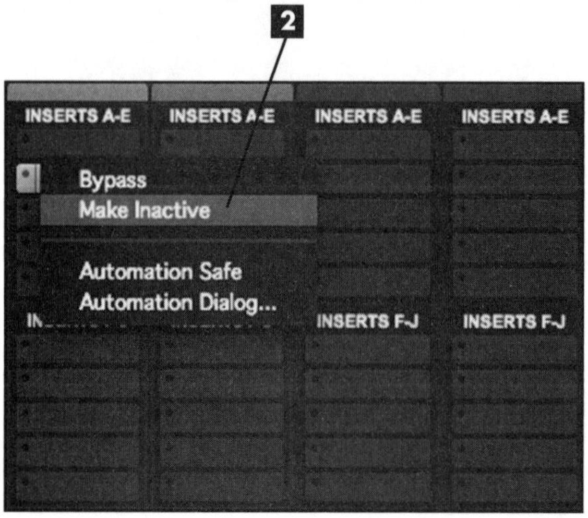

Here's another way to do it:

1 **Press and hold** the **Command+Control keys (Mac)** or the **Ctrl+Start keys (PC)** and **click** on the **Insert button** for the plug-in you want to disable.

Regardless of the method you choose, here's what you'll see:

- The Insert button's text will be italicized, indicating that the plug-in is inactive.
- For every RTAS plug-in you disable, your CPU usage will decrease, leaving more processing room for new effects.

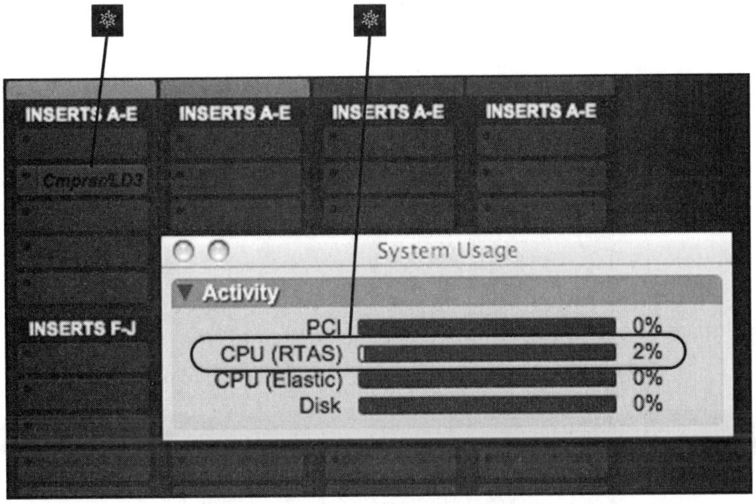

OPENING A SESSION WITH PLUG-INS INACTIVE!

Holding the Shift key while opening a session will cause the session to open with all plug-ins inactive. This can drastically reduce the time it takes to open many sessions (particularly sessions with a high plug-in count).

Similarly, there are multiple ways to deactivate an entire track.

1. **Select** the **track(s)** you want to deactivate.
2. **Click** the **Track menu**.
3. **Choose Make Inactive**.

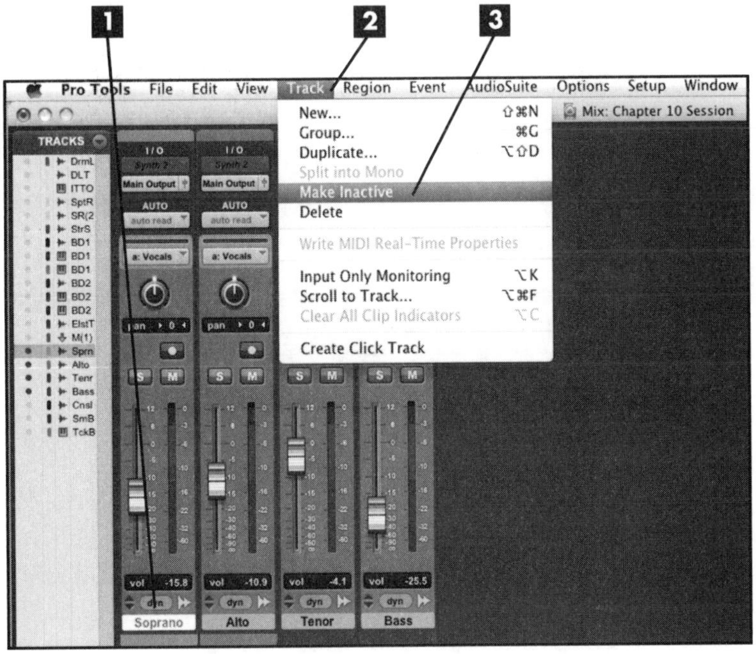

Here's another way to do it:

1. **Right-click** the **name** of the track(s) that you want to deactivate. (You can make this selection in the Mix window, the Edit window, or the Tracks list.) A list will appear.
2. **Choose Make Inactive** (or **Hide and Make Inactive**).

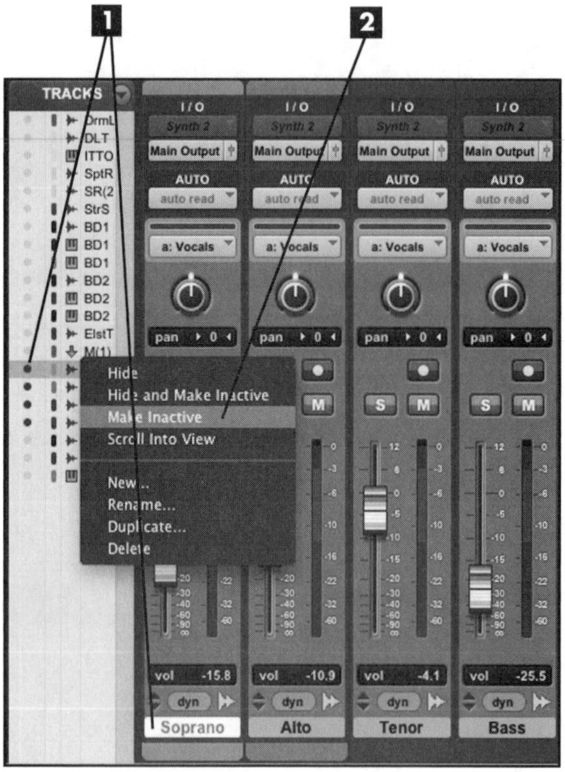

Here's what you'll get:

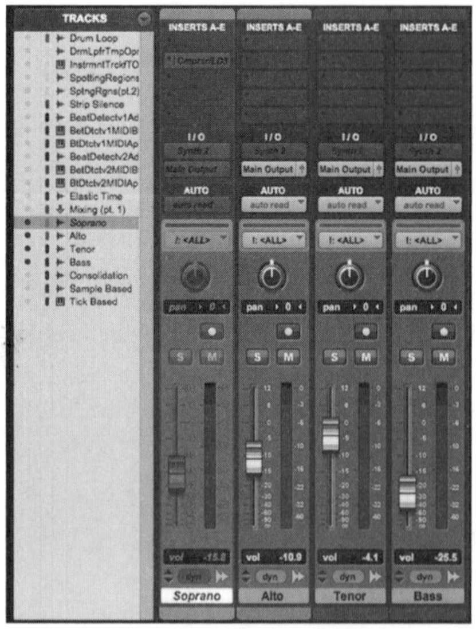

An inactive track's channel strip will be grayed out, and the track name will be italicized.

WORKING WITH HD SESSIONS

When you open a session used on an HD system, you might find that some of your tracks are inactive because HD systems support more active tracks than host-based systems. You can still use them by deactivating any of the currently active tracks and then activating one of the currently inactive tracks.

Edit Density and Consolidation

As I mentioned earlier in this chapter, edit density refers to the number of times your system must acquire audio data from your hard drive during playback. In extreme cases, high edit density can cause playback problems due to high demands placed on the throughput of your hard drive. The trick in those cases is to decrease the number of regions without changing the sound of your session, and the Consolidate function is the key.

SETTING THINGS UP

For this demonstration, go to Memory Location #11—Consolidation. You'll see a section of drums to which Beat Detective's Region Separation feature has been applied, creating lots of regions!

1. **Select** a **section** of your session that is particularly dense with regions. (If you're working with the tutorial session, this has been done for you.)
2. **Click** on the **Edit menu**.
3. **Click** on **Consolidate Region**. A window will display the progress of the consolidate process.

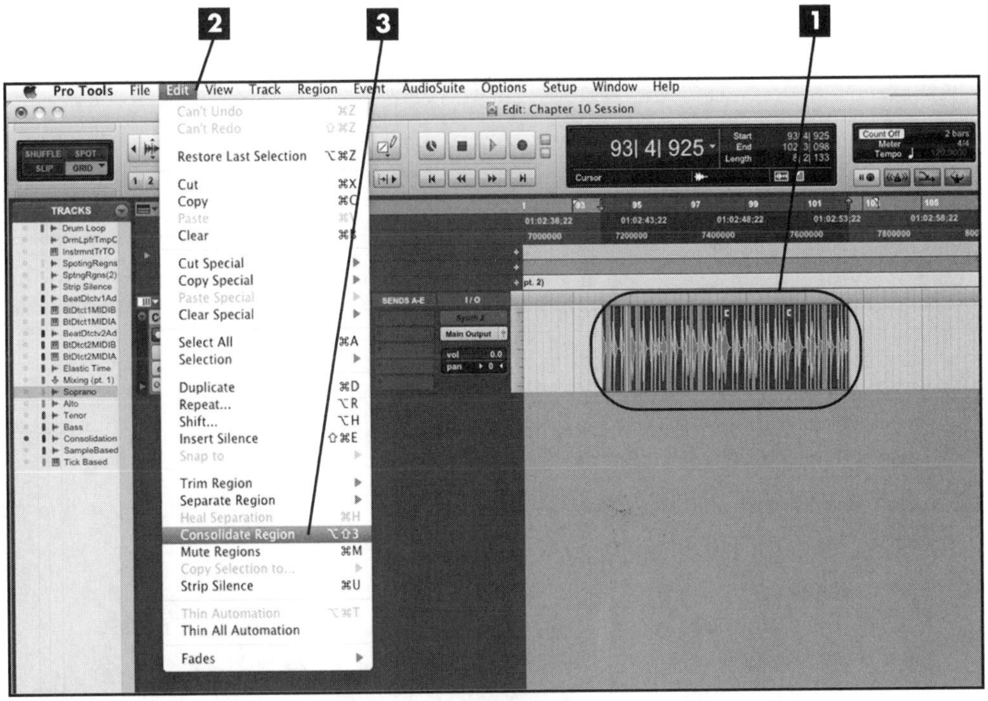

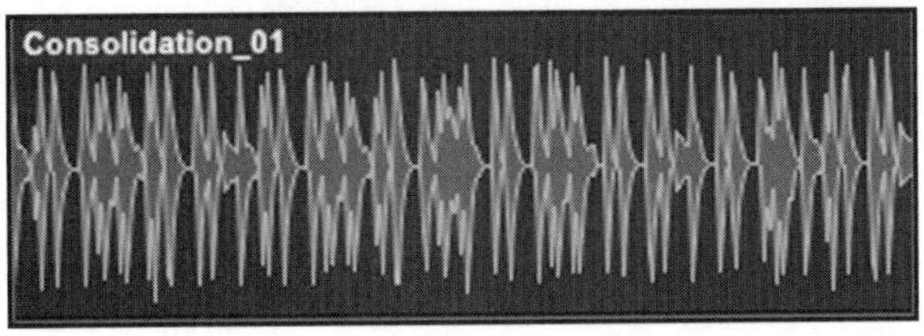

Your selection of multiple regions will be rendered into a *single* region (and a single audio file on your hard drive).

CONSOLIDATING SILENCE?

When you use the Consolidate feature, any selected space that is not occupied by a region will be rendered as silent audio, as will any gaps between regions in your selected area.

CONSOLIDATING MIDI?

MIDI regions can be consolidated as well as audio regions. Note that, although convenient, consolidating MIDI data won't affect your edit density.

Working with Video

Although Pro Tools is certainly an audio-centric program (as are most DAWs), that doesn't mean you can't incorporate video into your sessions. In fact, working with video in your session is a very straightforward process.

COMPLETE PRODUCTION TOOLKIT 2

In a basic Pro Tools 9 system, there are a few limitations with regard to video. For the purposes of this book, we'll limit our discussion on video to basic operations so these limitations won't present a problem. For those of you who need more-advanced video features within Pro Tools, there is a software addition to Pro Tools called the Complete Production Toolkit 2. It adds a number of significant features (many of them video-related) to your system. You can learn more about the Complete Production Toolkit 2 and what it offers by visiting Avid's Web site (http://www.avid.com).

Importing Video

Let's start off with a look at the process of importing a QuickTime movie, which couldn't be easier.

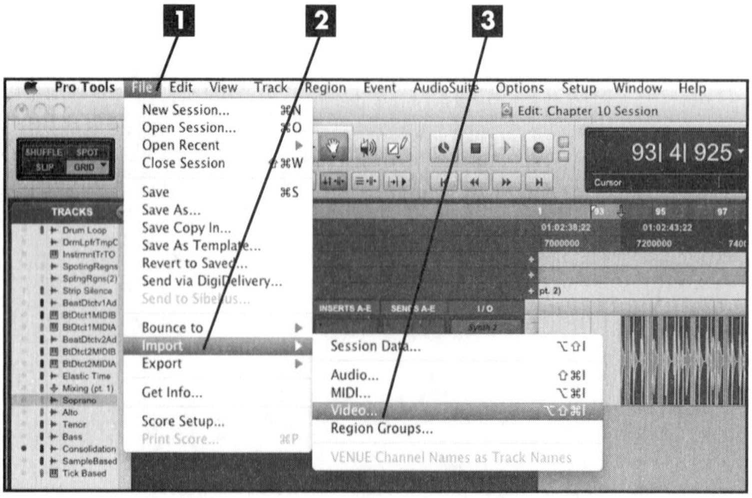

1 **Click** on the **File menu**.

2 **Click** on **Import**, and another menu will appear.

3 In this submenu, **click** on **Video**. The **Open/Select Video File to Import** dialog box will appear.

4 **Navigate to** and **click** on the **file** you want to import and **click** the **Open button**.

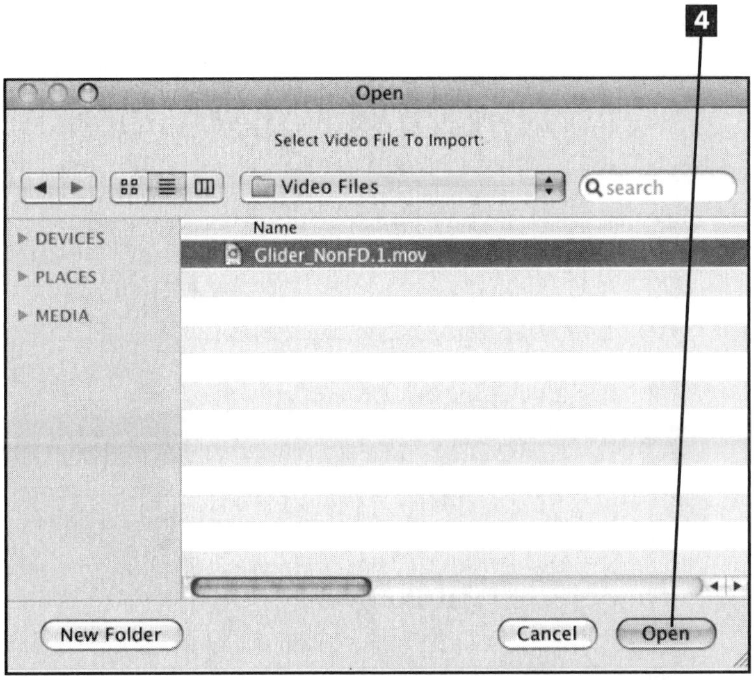

DON'T HAVE ANY QUICKTIME FILES? NO PROBLEM!

If you don't have any other QuickTime files to import, you can just go into the Chapter 10 Session folder and then open the Video Files folder.

You can also import video via any of the Pro Tools browser windows (including the Workspace, Volume, Project, or Catalog Browser windows). This is perhaps the quickest and easiest way to bring video into your session.

1 **Locate** the **file** that you want to import.

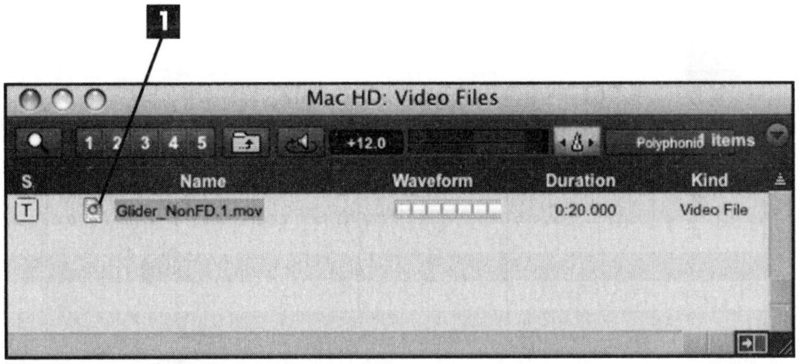

2 **Drag and drop** the **file** into your session. You can drag it to your session's Playlist area, to the Tracks list, or to the Regions list.

Regardless of which import method you choose, the Video Import Options dialog box will appear.

3 If you **click** the **Location menu button**, you'll be presented with a list of options as to *when* to position your Video region:

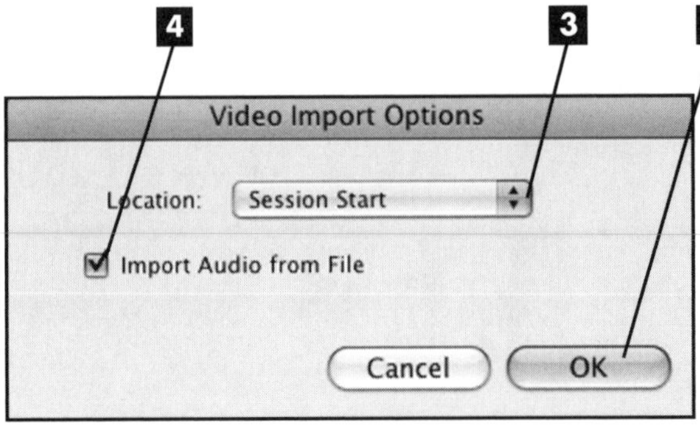

- **Session Start.** This will place the video region at the very beginning of the Video track.
- **Song Start.** You can set your song to start at a place other than the beginning of your session (something we covered back in Chapter 6). If you have done this, you have the option to place your video region at the song start.
- **Selection.** Choosing this option will place your video region at the beginning of the currently selected area.
- **Spot.** Choosing this option will open the Spot dialog box, enabling you to type a specific time location for your video region.

4 If you **click** the **Import Audio from File checkbox**, any audio that is included with the video will be imported to a new Audio track.

5 To import the video into your session, **click** the **OK button**.

Although a Video track isn't an Audio track to be sure, you'll still see it displayed in the Edit window. You can arrange the track in the Edit window just as you would any other track, and you can move the video region just as you would move any audio or MIDI region.

Viewing Video

You can easily show or hide Pro Tools' Video window:

1 **Click** the **Window menu**.

2 **Choose Video** to show the Video window (or to hide it, if it's currently being shown).

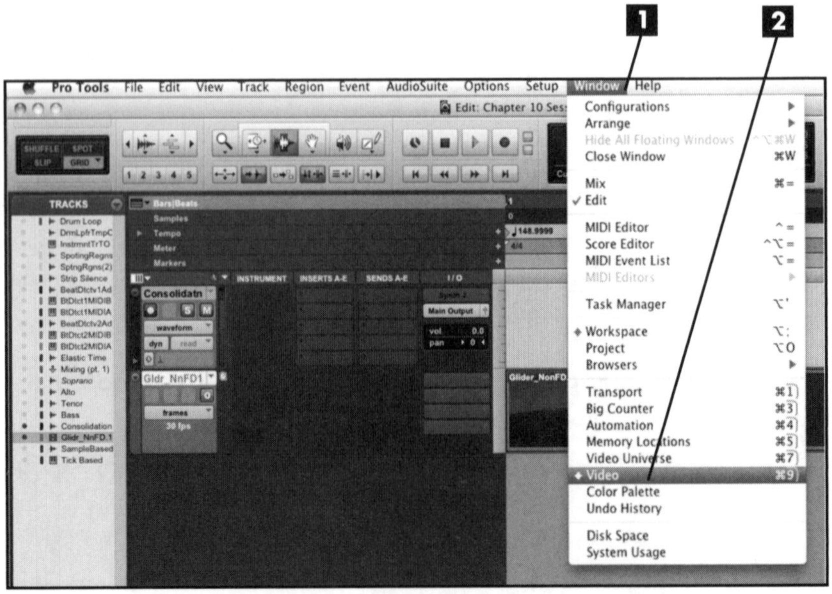

RESIZABLE VIDEO

To resize the Video window, just move your cursor to the lower right-hand corner of the window, click, and drag the window to the desired size. If you want the Video window to fill your entire screen, right-click the Video window and choose Fit Screen from the list of sizing options that will appear.

BOUNCING TO QUICKTIME

For information on how to bounce your session to a QuickTime file, please refer to Chapter 9, "Finishing Touches," in the section titled "Bouncing to a QuickTime Movie."

CHECKING YOUR WORK

To see this chapter's steps in their completed form, check out the Chapter 10 Session-Finished session.

Interoperability: Making Shared Sessions Work

Perhaps the most compelling reason to learn and use Pro Tools is its position as the global standard in the DAW world. From bedroom studios to multimillion-dollar facilities, Pro Tools allows for greater collaboration for amateurs and professionals alike than perhaps any other application. Take your humble author, for example—I wrote a good portion of this book in airports with an Mbox 2 mini system, and I could easily open this book's sessions in any professional studio with a minimum of muss and fuss!

The best way to maximize the interoperability of Pro Tools is to take efforts to ensure that your session can be opened and heard properly on a wide variety of systems and that collaborators can easily understand your work. Here are some recommendations on how to make this happen:

- Name all tracks before recording, and name them in a way that anyone can understand.
- Use the Comments view in both the Edit and Mix windows. The Comments column of every track and the Comment field of memory locations are valuable sources of information to others.
- Use your memory locations. Identify each section of your work and descriptively name it so that anybody can understand the overall layout of your session.
- Internally record (using a bus) all your virtual Instrument tracks to Audio tracks. This ensures that even if your collaborator doesn't have the same virtual instruments installed on his or her system, that person will still be able to hear your session the way it was meant to be heard.
- Use AudioSuite plug-ins when appropriate. Just as with internal recording, this will create a new file that can be played back in any Pro Tools situation, even if the actual plug-ins aren't present on other systems.

- Use a click track. Recording a great beat is all well and good, but if you're not in sync with the MIDI tempo of your session, features such as Quantize, Beat Detective, and Grid mode can do more harm than good!
- Before you archive your session or whenever you're moving it from one system to another, do a Save Copy In of your session and click all appropriate options for saving. This will ensure that all your audio, video, and plug-in settings will be saved in one central location. That's the version you should archive or move to another system for further work. Incidentally, you can also use the Save Copy In feature to save your session as an older version of Pro Tools (if you're collaborating with a user who doesn't have the latest software).

MORE INTEROPERABILITY WITH DIGITRANSLATOR

Pro Tools has long had a paid add-on, called DigiTranslator, used for importing and exporting different file types (AAF and OMF) that are commonly used in professional video production. Although the specific workflows surrounding AAF and OMF files are beyond the scope of this book, it's worth mentioning that DigiTranslator is now included for free in Pro Tools 9.

EXPORTING TEXT

If you want a very detailed record of all the elements of your session, you can create a text log of your entire session (including the files used, and positions of all regions). Just go to the File menu, then to Export, and then to Session Info as Text. You will be prompted to choose what aspects of your session to include in the text log, and the location of your text file.

Good Luck!

Congratulations—you made it! You've gone through a solid introductory tour of Pro Tools' basic operations and features. Although this discussion of Pro Tools is certainly not a comprehensive listing of *everything* Pro Tools can do, you can rest assured that your creative journey has started well. Over time, you'll not only learn more about Pro Tools, but undoubtedly you will find your own working style—a process that will be constantly refined as you gain experience and speed.

STILL WANT MORE SHORTCUTS?

Over the course of this book, we've covered a good number of useful shortcuts, but there are still many more for you to discover. Fortunately, there's a resource for your shortcut-browsing pleasure—the Pro Tools Help menu, which is ready for you to use. From the Help menu, choose the Keyboard Shortcuts menu item to view a comprehensive list of shortcuts. You might also want to take a look at the *Pro Tools Reference Guide*, which you'll also find in the Help menu. You can find updated versions of these documents on the Avid Web site.

As your skills grow, you may crave more in-depth knowledge. Fortunately, Avid has an excellent training program, which they offer through their worldwide network of training partner schools. Avid's Training and Education Program is a constantly evolving curriculum that can take you from where you are now all the way up to an elite Expert Certification, complete with worldwide listing! For more information, visit http://www.avid.com/training.

You've begun a great exploration—and a worthwhile endeavor, in my humble opinion. I personally believe that artistic pursuits nourish the soul not only of the patron, but of the artist as well. It's my fond wish that this book has served to inspire you to push the limits of your creativity and to share your gifts with others.

Good luck!

Index

A

K-L

M

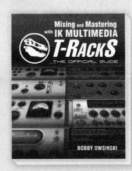

License Agreement/Notice of Limited Warranty

By opening the sealed disc container in this book, you agree to the following terms and conditions. If, upon reading the following license agreement and notice of limited warranty, you cannot agree to the terms and conditions set forth, return the unused book with unopened disc to the place where you purchased it for a refund.

License:
The enclosed software is copyrighted by the copyright holder(s) indicated on the software disc. You are licensed to copy the software onto a single computer for use by a single user and to a backup disc. You may not reproduce, make copies, or distribute copies or rent or lease the software in whole or in part, except with written permission of the copyright holder(s). You may transfer the enclosed disc only together with this license, and only if you destroy all other copies of the software and the transferee agrees to the terms of the license. You may not decompile, reverse assemble, or reverse engineer the software.

Notice of Limited Warranty:
The enclosed disc is warranted by Course Technology to be free of physical defects in materials and workmanship for a period of sixty (60) days from end user's purchase of the book/disc combination. During the sixty-day term of the limited warranty, Course Technology will provide a replacement disc upon the return of a defective disc.

Limited Liability:
THE SOLE REMEDY FOR BREACH OF THIS LIMITED WARRANTY SHALL CONSIST ENTIRELY OF REPLACEMENT OF THE DEFECTIVE DISC. IN NO EVENT SHALL COURSE TECHNOLOGY OR THE AUTHOR BE LIABLE FOR ANY OTHER DAMAGES, INCLUDING LOSS OR CORRUPTION OF DATA, CHANGES IN THE FUNCTIONAL CHARACTERISTICS OF THE HARDWARE OR OPERATING SYSTEM, DELETERIOUS INTERACTION WITH OTHER SOFTWARE, OR ANY OTHER SPECIAL, INCIDENTAL, OR CONSEQUENTIAL DAMAGES THAT MAY ARISE, EVEN IF COURSE TECHNOLOGY AND/OR THE AUTHOR HAS PREVIOUSLY BEEN NOTIFIED THAT THE POSSIBILITY OF SUCH DAMAGES EXISTS.

Disclaimer of Warranties:
COURSE TECHNOLOGY AND THE AUTHOR SPECIFICALLY DISCLAIM ANY AND ALL OTHER WARRANTIES, EITHER EXPRESS OR IMPLIED, INCLUDING WARRANTIES OF MERCHANTABILITY, SUITABILITY TO A PARTICULAR TASK OR PURPOSE, OR FREEDOM FROM ERRORS. SOME STATES DO NOT ALLOW FOR EXCLUSION OF IMPLIED WARRANTIES OR LIMITATION OF INCIDENTAL OR CONSEQUENTIAL DAMAGES, SO THESE LIMITATIONS MIGHT NOT APPLY TO YOU.

Other:
This Agreement is governed by the laws of the State of Massachusetts without regard to choice of law principles. The United Convention of Contracts for the International Sale of Goods is specifically disclaimed. This Agreement constitutes the entire agreement between you and Course Technology regarding use of the software.